The SAGE
Handbook *of*
Dyslexia

The SAGE
Handbook *of*
Dyslexia

Edited by
Gavin Reid,
Angela J. Fawcett,
Frank Manis
and Linda S. Siegel

Los Angeles • London • New Delhi • Singapore • Washington DC

SAGE Publications Ltd
1 Oliver's Yard
55 City Road
London EC1Y 1SP

SAGE Publications India Pvt Ltd
B 1/I 1 Mohan Cooperative Industrial Area
Mathura Road
New Delhi 110 044

SAGE Publications Inc.
2455 Teller Road
Thousand Oaks
California 91320

SAGE Publications Asia-Pacific Pte Ltd
33 Pekin Street #02-01
Far East Square
Singapore 048763

Library of Congress Control Number: 2008921456

British Library Cataloguing in Publication data
A catalogue record for this book is available from the British Library

ISBN 978-1-4129-4513-4

Typeset by Cepha Imaging Pvt. Ltd., Bangalore, India
Printed in India at Replika Press Pvt. Ltd
Printed on paper from sustainable resources

Contents

Notes on Contributors   xi

INTRODUCTION   1
Gavin Reid, Frank Manis, Angela J. Fawcett and Linda S. Siegel

PART I   NEUROLOGICAL/GENETIC PERSPECTIVES   9

1. The Origin of Dyslexia: The Asynchrony Phenomenon   11
   Zvia Breznitz

2. Some Special Issues Concerning the Genetics of Dyslexia:
   Revisiting Multivariate Profiles, Comorbidities and Genetic
   Correlations   30
   Jeffrey W. Gilger

3. The Neurobiological Basis of Dyslexia   53
   John Stein

4. Dyslexia and the Cerebellum   77
   Angela J. Fawcett and Roderick I. Nicolson

5. Familial Predictors of Dyslexia: Evidence From Preschool
   Children With and Without Familial Dyslexia Risk   99
   Dennis L. Molfese, Victoria J. Molfese, Maria E. Barnes,
   Chris G. Warren and Peter J. Molfese

6. Early Identification and Prevention of Dyslexia:
   Results From a Prospective Follow-up Study of Children
   at Familial Risk for Dyslexia   121
   Heikki Lyytinen with Jane Erskine, Timo Ahonen, Mikko Aro,
   Kenneth Eklund, Tomi Guttorm, Sini Hintikka, Jarmo Hämäläinen,
   Ritva Ketonen, Marja-Leena Laakso, Paavo H.T. Leppänen,
   Paula Lyytinen, Anna-Maija Poikkeus, Anne Puolakanaho,
   Ulla Richardson, Paula Salmi, Asko Tolvanen,
   Minna Torppa and Helena Viholainen

PART II   COGNITIVE AND LEARNING PERSPECTIVES   **147**

7. Exploring Heterogeneity in Developmental Dyslexia:
   A Longitudinal Investigation   149
   Frank Manis and Caroline E. Bailey

8. Rediscovering Dyslexia: New Approaches for Identification and
   Classification   174
   Richard K. Wagner

9. Learning, Cognition and Dyslexia   192
   Roderick I. Nicolson and Angela J. Fawcett

10. A Review of the Evidence on Morphological Processing
    in Dyslexics and Poor Readers: A Strength or Weakness?   212
    S. Hélène Deacon, Rauno Parrila and John R. Kirby

PART III   EDUCATIONAL INFLUENCES   **239**

11. Reading Intervention Research: An Integrative Framework   241
    William E. Tunmer and Keith T. Greaney

12. Assessment of Literacy Performance Based on the Componential
    Model of Reading   268
    R. Malatesha Joshi and P.G. Aaron

13. The Definition of Learning Disabilities: Who is the Individual
    with Learning Disabilities?   290
    Linda S. Siegel and Orly Lipka

14. Students with Phonological Dyslexia in School-Based
    Programs: Insights from Tennessee Schools   312
    Diane J. Sawyer and Stuart Bernstein

15. Individual Tutoring for Struggling Readers: Moving Research
    to Scale with Interventions Implemented by Paraeducators   337
    Patricia F. Vadasy and Elizabeth A. Sanders

16. Dyslexia Friendly Primary Schools: What can we
    Learn From Asking the Pupils?   356
    *Mary Coffield, Barbara Riddick, Patrick Barmby,
    and Jenny O'Neill*

17. Dyslexia and Learning Styles: Overcoming the Barriers to Learning 369
    Gavin Reid and Iva Strnadova

18. Dyslexia and Inclusion in the Secondary School – Cross
    Curricular Perspectives   381
    Moira Thomson

19. Dyslexia and Self-Concept: A Review of Past
    Research with Implications for Future Action   395
    Robert Burden

20. Role of Parents   411
    Gavin Reid, Shannon Green and Corey Zylstra

PART IV   DYSLEXIA AND DIFFERENT LANGUAGES   **425**

21. Dyslexia in Different Orthographies: Variability in Transparency   427
    John Everatt and Gad Elbeheri

22. Dyslexia and Foreign Language Learning   439
    Michael Dal

PART V   BEYOND SCHOOL   **455**

23. Adults with Learning Disabilities and Self-Disclosure
    in Higher Education and Beyond   457
    Lynda A. Price and Paul J. Gerber

24. Dyslexia: Workplace Issues   474
    Gavin Reid, Fil Came and Lynda A. Price

    Index   487

BIOGRAPHY OF EDITORS

Gavin Reid

Dr Gavin Reid was formerly senior lecturer in the Department of Educational Studies, Moray House School of Education, University of Edinburgh. He is now consultant to the Centre for Child Evaluation and Teaching (CCET) in Kuwait. He is also consultant psychologist to Reach Learning Center in Vancouver, Canada and a director and consultant to the Red Rose School for children with specific learning difficulties in St. Annes on Sea, Lancashire. He is also a trainer with Learning Works (International).

He is an experienced teacher, educational psychologist, university lecturer, researcher and author. He has written 21 books and lectured to thousands of professionals and parents in 45 countries. He has also had books published in Polish, Italian, Arabic, Hebrew and Slovak. He wrote the first Masters course in Dyslexia in the UK in 1992 and has been external examiner to 15 universities worldwide. He is the author of *Dyslexia: A Practitioners Handbook* (3rd Edition, Wiley 2003), *Dyslexia: A Complete Guide for Parents* (Wiley, 2004), *Dyslexia*, 2nd edition (Continuum Publications, 2007), *Dyslexia and Inclusion* (David Fulton/NASEN, 2005), *Learning Styles and Inclusion* (Paul Chapman/Sage Publications, 2005) and *Motivating Learners in the Classroom* (Sage Publications, 2007). He has also co-authored the *Listening and Literacy Index* (LLI) and the *Special Needs Assessment Profile* – (SNAP), (Hodder and Murray) and '100 Ideas for supporting pupils with dyslexia' and 'Dyslexia: A guide for Teaching Assistants' both with Shannon Green.

Frank Manis

Frank Manis is currently Professor of Psychology at the University of Southern California, where he is serving a 3-year term as a Faculty Fellow in the Center for Teaching Excellence. He has published about 50 articles on reading disabilities, development of literacy and biliteracy, and cognitive neuropsychology. The major focus of his research has been on the identification of sources of heterogeneity among children with developmental dyslexia. He is finishing a 5-year term as editor for *Scientific Studies of Reading* and serves on the editorial board for the *Journal of Experimental Child Psychology*.

Angela J. Fawcett

Angela Fawcett is Professor and Director of the Centre for Child Research at Swansea University. Following experience of dyslexia in her family, Angela was a mature entrant to academia, and has a BA and PhD in Psychology from the University of Sheffield. Her research into dyslexia with Professor Rod Nicolson has influenced both theory (via their Automatisation Deficit and Cerebellar Deficit hypotheses) and practice (via their dyslexia screening tests). She has published 7 normed tests, 4 edited books, over 100 refereed articles and book contributions, together with over 100 conference presentations, including keynote speeches at international conferences on dyslexia. Dr Fawcett is Vice President of the British Dyslexia Association, editor of *Dyslexia: An International Journal of Research and Practice* and chaired the 2004 British Dyslexia Association International Conference.

Linda S. Siegel

Linda Siegel is currently Associate Dean of graduate programs and research and Professor in the Department of Educational Psychology and Special Education at the University of British Columbia in Vancouver, British Columbia, Canada. Professor Siegel holds the Dorothy C. Lam Chair in Special Education. She has conducted research in learning disabilities, language and cognitive development, the role of psychoeducational assessment in the identification of learning disabilities, bilingualism, premature and high-risk infants and the early identification of learning disabilities. She has been the editor of the *International Journal of Behavioural Development* and the associate editor of *Child Development*.

NOTES ON CONTRIBUTORS

P.G. Aaron, PhD. Professor in the Department of Educational and School Psychology at Indiana State University is a recipient of the Albert Harris Award of the International Reading Association for research in reading disabilities. He is the author of the book *Dyslexia and Hyperlexia*. With Malt Joshi, he co-authored *Reading Problems* and co-edited *Handbook of Orthography and Literacy*.

Timo Ahonen, PhD. Professor of Developmental Psychology at University of Jyväskylä, Finland is interested in the neuropsychology of learning disabilities. His special expertise comprises clinical child psychology and child neuropsychology.

Mikko Aro, PhD. is a Researcher with the Niilo Mäki Institute and University of Jyväskylä, Finland. Mikko's core interests are reading acquisition and dyslexia while his specialism comprises interventions for reading difficulties and cross-linguistic study of reading acquisition and dyslexia.

Caroline E. Bailey is Assistant Professor of Human Services at California State University at Fullerton. Her research focuses on developmental dyslexia and neurocognitive disorders such as epilepsy. She is co-author of a book on counseling.

Patrick Barmby is a lecturer and researcher in the education department at Durham University.

Maria E. Barnes is Graduate Research Assistant in the Developmental Neuropsychology Laboratory at the University of Louisville studying the impacts of obstructive sleep apnoea on children's cognitive skills.

Stuart Bernstein is Associate Professor, Department of Psychology and Interim Director, Tennesseee Center for the Study and Treatment of Dyslexia.

Zvia Breznitz is Director of Brain Research Center and Learning Disabilities at Haifa University, Israel. Her research focuses on synchronization in speed and content of the cerebral processes related to reading and reading difficulties.

Robert Burden is currently Emeritus Professor of Applied Educational Psychology at the University of Exeter, where he has been involved for many years in the training of educational psychologists. He is a former President of the International School Psychology Association and the author of several books and many articles on the application of psychology to all aspects of education, including dyslexia. He is the long-standing Chair of the British Dyslexia Association's Accreditation Board and a member of the BDA Management Board.

Fil Came is an independent consultant and Director of Learning Works. He is a respected teacher trainer and uses his extensive experience of teaching mainstream children with special educational needs to help colleagues personalise their teaching and create learning friendly environments for ALL children.

Mary Coffield is County Advisory and Support Teacher for Specific Learning Difficulties working within the Durham County Learning Support Service. She has played a leading role in encouraging both primary and secondary schools in the county to develop dyslexia friendly approaches.

Michael Dal is an assistant professor at School of Education, Iceland University. He has especially specialized in the field of didactics in foreign languages and in the use of new technology in foreign language learning.

S. Hélène Deacon is Assistant Professor in the Department of Psychology at Dalhousie University. Her research examines reading and spelling development across a range of learning contexts.

Kenneth Eklund, MA, works at the University of Jyväskylä as research coordinator with expertise in data collection, research data management, statistical analysis and research methods.

Gad Elbeheri is principal consultant at the CCET in Kuwait. He was the United Nations Development Programme's Expert on Early Childhood Challenges Project in Kuwait. Dr. Elbeheri has been assisting the Kuwaiti Ministry of Education and the Kuwait Dyslexia Association in developing strategies and programmes to cater to students with dyslexia in Kuwait. Dr Elbeheri, an applied linguist who obtained his PhD from the University of Durham, studied the manifestations of developmental dyslexia in Arabic and has a keen interest on crosslinguistic studies of dyslexia and other specific learning difficulties. He has been instrumental in establishing a Dyslexia Higher Educational Committee at the Ministry of Education in Kuwait. He brought the BDA's "Dyslexia Friendly Schools Initiative" to the Middle East.

Jane Erskine, PhD. (Dundee), Researcher and Chartered Psychologist is interested in the cognitive approach to cross-linguistic literacy and numeracy development and disability with co-morbidity. Her special expertise is diagnostics and remediation of dyslexia.

Erskine is employed by the Agora Center, University of Jyväskylä, in the EU's Graphogame Marie Curie Excellence Grants – project for which she has been implementing the English language version in the UK.

John Everatt is a researcher in literacy ability and developmental dyslexia. He lectured in psychology at the Universities of Wales and Surrey, UK, before moving to the College of Education, University of Canterbury, New Zealand.

Angela J. Fawcett is Professor and Director of the Centre for Child Research at Swansea University, in the UK. She is Vice President of the British Dyslexia Association, editor of *Dyslexia: An International Journal of Research and Practice,* She a chaired the 2004 British Dyslexia Association International Conference.

Paul J. Gerber, PhD. is Professor in the School of Education at Virginia Commonwealth University in Richmond , VA., USA. He is the author of four books and numerous book chapters and articles in the area of adults with learning disabilities.

Jeffrey W. Gilger is currently Professor and Associate Dean of Discovery (Research) and Faculty Development in the College of Education at Purdue University. His background includes an MS and certification in Clinical Child/School Psychology, and an MA and PhD in Developmental Psychology, with specialized training in Human Behavioral and Psychiatric Genetics.

Keith T. Greaney is Senior Lecturer in the School of Educational Studies at Massey University, where he teaches courses in literacy education. His current research focuses on reading and spelling difficulties and intervention strategies.

Shannon Green, is Director of REACH Learning Center in BC, Canada and a certified Orton-Gillingham Trainer. She runs workshops for parents and teachers and has presented at international conferences on dyslexia and reading. She is the co-author of *100 Ideas for Supporting Pupils with Dyslexia* and *Dyslexia: A Guide for Teaching Assistants.*

Tomi Guttorm, PhD. Researcher, Agora Center, University of Jyväskylä is interested in the psychophysiology of speech and language-related processing. His area of expertise includes Developmental psychophysiology, especially psychophysiological techniques.

Jarmo Hämäläinen, PhD. is Researcher, University of Cambridge, UK. His research interests comprise dyslexia, ERP-research and auditory cognition. He has special expertise eg. in the analysis of high-density ERP data using modern techniques such as PCA and ICA.

Sini Hintikka is a Doctoral student at University of Jyväskylä and Psychologist and Researcher, Niilo Mäki Institute is interested in dyslexia, dysfluent reading and intervention. Her special expertise involves interventions for reading difficulties and dysfluent reading.

R. Malatesha Joshi is Professor of Reading Education at Texas A&M University.

John R. Kirby is Professor of Education and Psychology at Queen's University (Canada). His research interests include the development of reading and dyslexia.

Ritva Ketonen, Doctoral student, University of Jyväskylä, Speech Therapist, Niilo Mäki Institute, Jyväskylä, Finland. Ketonen specializes in phonological disorders with emphasis on the intervention of dyslexia.

Marja-Leena Laakso, PhD. is professor in Department of Educational Sciences at University of Jyväskylä. Her primary interest and expertise comprises the development of prelinguistic communication and group training for parents of children with ADHD.

Paavo H.T. Leppänen, PhD. Docent, Academy Research Fellow, University of Jyväskylä. Leppänen's special interest areas comprise cognitive neuroscience, learning difficulties, dyslexia and interventions. His areas of expertise include developmental neurocognitive research (event-related potentials), auditory and speech perception.

Orly Lipka is a Michael Smith Foundation postdoctoral Fellow at the University of British Columbia, Child & Family Research Institute, Children's & Women's Health Centre of BC Canada. Her research interests include early identification for children at risk for school failure, language and reading development of at risk children, reading and cognitive development of English as a second language learners, and learning disabilities.

Heikki Lyytinen, PhD. is Professor of Developmental Neuropsychology, University of Jyväskylä, Finland. Lyytinen's primary research interests focus on uncovering core bottlenecks of cognitive development which can compromise a child's opportunity to acquire fluent reading skill. The most immediate research goal is the development and validation of computer-assisted means with which to preventively help such children to minimize the unwanted psychological consequences of dyslexia. His special expertise comprises psychophysiology, developmental neuropsychology and longitudinal research.

Paula Lyytinen, PhD. is Professor of Developmental Psychology at University of Jyväskylä. She is interested in children's language and cognitive development, precursors of dyslexia, symbolic play and parent-child interaction. Her speciality comprises research into the development of language skills.

Frank Manis is Professor of Psychology at the University of Southern California. He has conducted NIH-supported research on reading disabilities and the development of literacy, and serves on the editorial board of several journals.

Dennis L. Molfese is Distinguished University Scholar and Professor in the Birth Defects Center and Editor-in-Chief of *Developmental Neuropsychology*.

Victoria J. Molfese is the Ashland/Nystrand Chair and Professor in Teaching and Learning at the University of Louisville and the Director of the Center for Research in Early Childhood.

Peter J. Molfese is a doctoral student in Developmental Cognitive Neuroscience, the University of Houston. His interests are learning, language, and the use of quantitative methods in Psychological Research.

Roderick I. Nicolson is Professor of Psychology at the University of Sheffield in the UK.

Jenny O'Neill works for Durham Local education Authority as an educational psychologist.

Rauno Parrila is Professor of Educational Psychology at the University of Alberta, Canada. His current research examines the cognitive, linguistic, and socio-cognitive compensation mechanisms of high-functioning adult dyslexics.

Anna-Maija Poikkeus, PhD. Professor of Early Childhood and Primary Education, University of Jyväskylä. Her interest areas are early identification of language and reading problems and supportive early environments (family, day-care and early school grades). Her special expertise includes the development of social skills and group training for parents of children with ADHD

Lynda A. Price, PhD. is Associate Professor in Special Education at Temple University in Philadelphia. She has written many book chapters and articles about the needs of adults with learning disabilities.

Anne Puolakanaho, PhD. is a researcher at the University of Jyväskylä. Puolakanaho's areas of interest are childhood phonological and language development, predictors of dyslexia with special expertise in early phonological sensitivity and language assessment tools.

Gavin Reid was formerly senior lecturer in the Department of Educational Studies, Moray House School of Education at the University of Edinburgh. He is now consultant to the Centre for Child Evaluation and Teaching (CCET) in Kuwait. He is also consultant psychologist to Reach Learning Center in Vancouver, Canada and a director and consultant to the Red Rose School for children with specific learning difficulties in St. Annes on Sea, Lancashire. He is also a trainer with Learning Works (International.)

Ulla Richardson, PhD. is team leader of the Marie Curie Excellence Grant, Agora Center, University of Jyväskylä. Her interest areas are auditory processing, dyslexia, intervention with special expertise in experimental designs for speech and auditory processing as well for interventions for reading difficulties.

Barbara Riddick is a senior lecturer in the school of education at Durham University. She has carried out a number of important research studies on children and students with dyslexia and has published 4 books and numerous articles on dyslexia.

Paula Salmi is a doctoral student at University of Jyväskylä. Paula has interests in dyslexia and naming-related interventions. She has special expertise in interventions for reading and naming difficulties.

Elizabeth A. Sanders, M.Ed. is a doctoral student in measurement, statistics and research design in the College of Education at the University of Washington. Her academic interests are quantitative methods in educational research.

Diane J. Sawyer is an internationally recognized scholar whose work addresses the cognitive-linguistic bases of reading and reading disabilities. She holds the Murfree Chair of Excellence in Dyslexic Studies at Middle Tennessee State University.

Linda S. Siegel is currently Associate Dean of Graduate programs and research and a Professor in the department of Educational Psychology and Special Education at the University of British Columbia in Vancouver, British Columbia, Canada. She holds the Dorothy C. Lam Chair in Special Education.

John Stein is a Fellow and Tutor in Medicine at Magdalen College, University of Oxford in the UK.

Iva Strnadová, PhD. is currently Senior Lecturer at Charles University in Prague, Czech Republic, and Honorary Senior Lecturer in the Faculty of Education and Social Work at the University of Sydney. Dr Strnadová is currently involved in teaching in special education programs at Charles University, and the Erasmus Mundus Special education Needs (EM SEN) program in collaboration with staff from Fontys University, Tilburg, The Netherlands, and Roehampton University, London. She is currently leading a series of projects examining across the life span the experiences of families caring for a child with a disability. She has other research interests in the area of inclusive education and additional learning needs in literacy and numeracy.

Moira Thomson was formerly Principal Teacher of Support for Learning at Broughton High School, Edinburgh. She has also been a Development Officer for City of Edinburgh, Department of Children and Families, an Associate Assessor for HMIe, an Associate Tutor for the Scottish Network for Able Pupils, and a member for Scottish Qualifications Authority focus groups. She is currently an educational consultant, providing Continuing Professional Development for teachers, secretary of the Cross Party Group on Dyslexia in the Scottish Parliament and an independent adjudicator for the Scottish Government's Additional Support for Learning Dispute Resolution. Her 2007 Dyslexia Scotland publication Supporting Dyslexic Pupils in the Secondary Curriculum was distributed free of charge to all secondary schools in Scotland. Her new book, Supporting Students with Dyslexia in Secondary Schools will be published by Routledge in the autumn of 2008.

Asko Tolvanen, PhD. Statistician, University of Jyväskylä is interested in modern multivariate methods. His special expertise comprises the application of such methods to psychological research.

Minna Torppa, PhD. is Researcher at University of Jyväskylä. Her interest areas include dyslexia, the home literacy environment and phonological awareness. She has special expertise in the application of Structural equation modelling and Latent Growth Curve modelling.

William E. Tunmer is Professor of Educational Psychology in the Department of Learning and Teaching, Massey University, New Zealand.

Patricia F. Vadasy, PhD. is senior researcher at Washington Research Institute, Seattle. Her research interests include reading acquisition and reading interventions.

Helena Viholainen, PhD. is Researcher at Niilo Mäki Institute, Jyväskylä is interested in human learning. Her special expertise lies in motor development and its connection to language development and dyslexia.

Richard K. Wagner is Distinguished Research Professor and Binet Professor of Psychology, Associate Director of Florida Center for Reading Research and chairs the Advisory Board of the National Institute for Literacy.

Chris G. Warren is a third-year graduate student working toward his PhD in Experimental Psychology at the University of Louisville. He is primarily interested in perceptual processes and how they relate to cognitive functioning. Chris has also participated in research measuring the effects of minor sleep loss on cognitive and neural processes in children and adults.

Corey Zylstra is an Orton-Gillingham Trainer and is a co-founder and director of the REACH Learning Center in North Vancouver, Canada. She speaks locally and internationally to educators and parents regarding learning difficulties and effective teaching strategies, has authored and co-authored several publications and has developed a wide array of materials to aid literacy teaching.

Introduction

Gavin Reid, Frank Manis, Angela J. Fawcett and Linda S. Siegel

This Handbook provides the most recent and relevant studies, debates and practices in the field of dyslexia. Essentially the Handbook aims to help the reader engage in the dyslexia debate from an informed perspective. For that reason we have included sections on the neurological and genetic areas; from the wider field of cognition and learning and how this impacts on learners with dyslexia; the important aspects relating to the classroom from both research and practical perspectives; including linguistic and cultural diversity and the issues that have an impact in the employment and the education of people with dyslexia beyond the school years. This is also a crucial area and one that has a current focus both from the practical and the legislative perspectives. Additionally there are chapters on classroom practices from both primary and secondary sectors.

We appreciate the field is subject to ongoing studies and revision of ideas and perspectives, but many of the chapters in this book are at the cutting edge of both research and practice and therefore will provide both up to date information as well as pointers for future developments. The book will, therefore, be a useful reference for those undergoing study in dyslexia as well as researchers and practitioners containing many new and innovative ideas and theories.

The key ideas in the first part of the book focus on the neurological/genetic perspectives and include a retrospective and prospective discussion on the genetics of dyslexia. In the first chapter Breznitz presents an innovative concept for our understanding of dyslexia, which refers to Breznitz's recent Asynchrony Theory which proposes that dyslexia is an outcome of the failure to synchronize the various brain entities activated during the reading process.

Jeffrey W. Gilger in chapter 2 acknowledges the advances that have been made in this field but also puts forward new challenges that have to be taken into account in future research. This is followed by the chapter by John Stein who looks at the risk factors of dyslexia. This includes a debate on the role of the Magnocellular and parvocellular visual neurons as well as the role of the auditory m–system and the cerebellum. This chapter also includes a discussion on the reading network in the brain. Fawcett and Nicolson provide an alternative perspective in the following chapter, suggesting that the skills required for reading, writing and spelling all require coordination between different regions of the brain for effective execution. They suggest that the cerebellum is a major player in most cognitive skills associated with speech. They review the status of the cerebellar deficit hypothesis and suggest that it provides a coherent explanation of the developmental antecedents of dyslexia, although they do qualify this by stating that the hypothesis does not claim that only the cerebellum is affected in dyslexia.

Molfese and colleagues in the following chapter discuss the relations between structure and function differences identified from brain-imaging techniques and review familial risk for dyslexia.

The issues of early identification and prevention is taken up by Heikki Lyytinen and colleagues who report on early identification and intervention studies and also comment on the key issues of investigating reading fluency skills of poor readers. This is because developmental dyslexia they assert is not 'a unitary phenomenon but is a common denominator of a number of atypical developmental routes, predominantly characterised by compromised language skills'.

The heterogeneity of developmental dyslexia however needs to be acknowledged and this is considered in the following chapter by Manis and Bailey who look at the individual differences among children with dyslexia. They provide a detailed account of their longitudinal study which includes ground-breaking revelations on the changing nature of phonological deficits over time and suggest a number of possible reasons for this occurrence. The implication of this is that researchers need to consider and characterize the nature and development of phonological deficits further and alternative ways to model individual differences need to be considered. Taking this into account, response to intervention models can offer a promising way forward in the investigation of the heterogeneity of dyslexia. They examine the distinction between phonological and surface dyslexia and review the literature on subtypes of dyslexia.

It is important however to consider the needs of students with dyslexia from a learning perspective. The cognitive dimension is one that is prevalent in the literature incorporating the key aspects of dyslexia – causes, assessment and intervention. For example, the chapter by Deacon and colleagues on the role of morphological processing considers the view that morphology can provide a compensatory avenue for dyslexic readers and may be the means by which some will overcome dyslexia. The authors of this chapter imply that if the phonological route does not respond to training, there may be a need to rely on other routes, such as the morphological pathway, to build up word recognition skills.

Rod Nicolson and Angela Fawcett focus on the cognitive aspects of dyslexia by discussing the skills of reading and learning. They relate their discussion to a number of hypotheses on learning and how learning can go wrong for some and discuss the nature of learning in infancy. They discuss declarative and procedural learning and provide a neural systems framework for developmental disorders. They conclude that it is not only the language-related processes that are affected but also components of motor skills which gives rise to the nature and role of the cerebellum. They conclude by reflecting on how theoretical positions on developmental dyslexia can impact on practice and suggest that the research indicates that learning skills should be practised beyond mastery and refreshed on a daily basis.

The linking of research with practice is noted throughout part three of the book focusing primarily on educational influences. This part looks at conceptualizations of reading models for assessment and intervention as well as practical classroom considerations such as the notion of dyslexia friendly classrooms, the role of learning styles and self-esteem, the specific challenges faced in secondary classrooms and the most effective forms of communication with parents.

Tunmer and Greaney discuss the methodological and conceptual issues relating to reading intervention. They suggest that for children encountering difficulty in developing the ability to perceive patterns and connections between speech and print, explicit instruction in phonemic awareness and alphabetic coding skills is likely to be critical. They engage in the methodological debate around this theme as well as the methodological issues relating to the response to intervention model within the context of reading intervention research. They also consider the role of explicitness and intensity within the design of reading interventions and the part played by phonological awareness, alphabetic coding, vocabulary, fluency and comprehension strategies. In this chapter they emphasise the view that children with more severe reading difficulties appear to require a more highly structured, systematic approach that includes teaching word analysis skills outside the context of reading connected text. The authors engage in a debate which concludes with the positive message that reading disabled students can be taught to activate and utilizse reading skills if remediation is appropriate and will then show similar profiles to normal developing readers.

This theme is also considered by Joshi and Aaron against the context of the componential model of reading. They discuss the problems with discrepancy-based diagnosis and suggest alternative models and practices including the use of listening comprehension as an alternative to IQ and particularly IQ/achievement discrepancy scores. They discuss the computational model and the role of the three components in reading – decoding, comprehension and fluency. They suggest this model offers greater validity and relevance to planning interventions.

This theme is continued in the chapter by Siegel and Orly Lipka who analyze 111 articles from the *Journal of Learning Disabilities* spanning the period from 1968 to 2007. They discuss how the conceptual definition of learning disabilities has been translated into operational definitions. They critically discuss the role of achievement, discrepancy, IQ and exclusionary criteria in the definition of learning disabilities. They suggest that the discrepancy definition is flawed because of the inconsistencies in the use of achievement measures, and against the background of the criticism in the use of IQ measures they suggest that IQ is in fact irrelevant to a definition of learning disabilities.

Regarding the exclusionary criteria they argue that there are too many interwoven variables to distinguish between cause and effect and in fact it may not even be necessary to separate the two. This chapter highlights some important issues to be taken into account for practices in research design and educational assessment and intervention. They propose that the basis for the diagnosis of learning disabilities should be made from an assessment of significant skills deficits based on achievement tests.

Diagnosis and intervention based on an assessment of reading skills and classroom practices is developed further in the following chapter by Sawyer and Bernstein. They discuss the results of a study of 100 children, whose assessment and diagnostic profile was characterized by a core deficit in phonological processing. Their study has implications for teacher education programmes as they suggest that the current pull-out approach to intervention is inadequate and inappropriate. They advocate the widespread infusion of well-crafted instructional programmes in schools but this needs to be supplemented with teacher understanding on the nature of dyslexia and how best to support these children in the classroom situation.

This theme is reiterated in the following chapter by Vadasy and Sanders who suggest that sufficient well-trained teachers are not available to help large numbers of at-risk students who, they argue, are most often enrolled in the lowest quality schools. They maintain that getting research-based reading programmes and trained teachers into all schools is the first priority for translating research on early reading interventions into practice.

An example of this in practice can be seen in the following chapter by Coffied and colleagues on dyslexia-friendly schools. They found that those teachers who were using 'dyslexia-friendly approaches' in their classrooms tended to focus more on making sure that tasks were introduced and explained clearly and provided support materials to help pupils write their own answers rather than looking at ways to assist pupils with the writing process itself. This could have the effect of facilitating learner independence and promoting self-confidence (Reid, 2007). At the same time, they acknowledge that too many students have to face potentially stressful situations in the classroom and this can be avoided through more widespread and more appropriate teacher education. This they suggest should not be vested in one approach but a range of approaches and strategies should be used.

One method of accessing this is through the use of learning styles. Although Coffield et al. emphasize the potential pitfalls in focussing too heavily on learning styles, the clear fact remains that it does facilitate the acknowledgement of individual needs and through establishing the principles of acknowledging learning preferences there will be more opportunity for learners to develop self-confidence in learning and learner autonomy. These points are developed in the following chapter by Reid and Strnadova. They show how the use of learning styles can help to identify and overcome the barriers to learning experienced by students with dyslexia. Importantly it also provides students with insights into their own learning. This is important for developing learner independence. They emphasise that learning styles should be incorporated in the planning processes involving assessment and curriculum development.

Moira Thomson in the following chapter also highlights the role of curriculum development as a vehicle for support for students with dyslexia. She focuses on the secondary school and the subject curriculum. She also looks at learning and teaching preferences, classroom management issues and arrangements for examinations.

The importance of developing self-esteem is the focus of the next chapter. In this chapter Burden reviews previous research findings on the relationship between self-concept and learning disabilities, offers some key issues that need to be addressed and offers some suggestions for future research.

The final chapter in the section on educational influences relates to the role of parents. This is a crucial element in the whole process of identifying and meeting the needs of students with dyslexia. In this chapter Reid, Green and Zylstra discuss the nature of school supports and how parents can be involved in this process. They note the types of strategies that parents can use at home to supplement school intervention. They discuss the tensions that can arise between home and school and the types of anxieties that can be experienced by parents. There may be conflicting priorities between home and school and differences in perception and understanding of the labels and terms used by parents and schools. Effective communication is therefore the key to minimizing these potential conflicts and it is important that this is established and maintained throughout the young persons schooling. This chapter also discusses national and international trends particularly in relation to legislation and rights.

The multinational and multicultural theme is taken further in the chapter by Everett and Elbeheri when they discuss dyslexia in different orthographies. In this chapter they discuss the relationship between orthography and literacy difficulties and highlight this with comparisons between English and Arabic. They suggest that the importance of orthographic transparency can be seen in studies which show that word recognition and non-word decoding processes develop faster in more transparent orthographies. Their discussion has implications for the widespread acceptance of the phonological deficit hypothesis. They suggest that when it comes to distinguishing children with, and without, literacy learning-problems in a relatively transparent orthography, other measures apart from those specifically used to assess phonological awareness, such as rapid naming or short-term/working memory may be better identifiers or certainly compliment the existing test battery. They provide an interesting example in the Arabic language since Arabic goes from a relatively transparent form in early learning (consistent with languages such as German) to a relatively non-transparent form, more akin to English, once initial learning has occurred. This means that an understanding of learning to read and write in Arabic may also require an understanding of learning to read and write across the orthographic transparency dimension. This can make it as challenging as it is to learn an irregular language such as English.

The learning of a foreign language is the theme of the next chapter by Michael Dal from Iceland. He provides an overview of the research and discusses the key features of foreign language learning such as the inter-language, fluency, accuracy, the orthographic mapping system as well as the nature of and suggestions for instruction.

We are all aware of the fact that dyslexia is a lifelong condition. For that reason we have included a number of chapters looking beyond the school context. Price and Gerber provide interesting insights into the perceptions of adults with dyslexia and how dyslexia has had an impact on all aspects of life. They highlight the importance of listening to, and acknowledging the needs of adults with dyslexia. They indicate the importance of this by noting that studies have shown that over half of all American adolescents with learning disabilities will drop-out of high school before graduation. One of the important elements in preventing this they suggest lies in the notion of self-disclosure leading to self-advocacy. It is unfortunate therefore that many of the interviewees in their study emphasized 'the dangers of self-disclosure to the wrong people at the wrong time'. Comments like 'I'm embarrassed to say I have a LD because they'll fire me' indicate the journey that has still to be made to ensure that any stigma stemming from dyslexia is totally removed.

The final chapter of the book is on the challenges and issues relating to the workplace. In this chapter, Gavin Reid and Fil Came and Linda Price discuss the need for employer awareness of dyslexia and the need for employers to obtain a realistic understanding of the skills and needs of adults with dyslexia. It is important that adults feel comfortable disclosing their dyslexia to employers but equally it is crucial that employers play their part and accept that dyslexic people can be a real asset to the workforce, but they will need some consideration and accommodations. Reid, Came and Price discuss the barriers that still exist in the workplace and indicate how with accommodations, adults with dyslexia can access virtually any profession. No restrictions should be placed in their way because they have the potential to add an extra dimension to the workforce in any type of employment (Moody and Bartlett, 2002). It is also interesting to note the comment made by West (2004) that 'people with dyslexia can see the unseen'. This emphasizes the potential of people with dyslexia to enhance the workforce in any profession.

Unfortunately there are still too many examples of discriminatory practices, but by emphasizing the social rather than the medical model of disability these discriminatory practices can vanish. Reid, Came and Price also suggest that the way forward is to ensure that clear and fair career advice is provided as early as possible, to ensure that employers and employees are aware of the legal rights of adults with dyslexia and that every opportunity is provided to develop and encourage self-advocacy in the workplace. As the authors claim 'it will only be when the concept of disability is re-framed in a positive and constructive fashion that people with dyslexia will feel secure to assert their rights in society and in the workplace'. It is hoped therefore that this book will go part of the way in developing this awareness and understanding and help to secure a better future for all people with dyslexia.

REFERENCES

Moody, S. and Bartlett, D. (2002) *Dyslexia in the workplace*. London: Whurr Publications.
Reid, G. (2007) *Motivating learners in the classroom: Ideas and strategies*. London: Sage Publications.
West, T. G. (2004) *In the mind's eye. Visual thinkers, gifted people with learning difficulties, computer images and the ironies of creativity*. Buffalo, NY: Prometheus Books.

PART I
Neurological/Genetic Perspectives

The Origin of Dyslexia: The Asynchrony Phenomenon

Zvia Breznitz

This chapter will

i) discuss synchronization in speed and content as a factor contributing to fluency in the regular and impaired reading process; and
ii) present an innovative concept for our understanding of dyslexia

Reading is a highly composite cognitive task that involves word decoding and comprehending printed or written materials. Effective word decoding is a prerequisite for comprehension. In most cases, the reading process is successful. However, in approximately 10–15 per cent of the population it is not. Reading failures are commonly termed developmental dyslexia. Different theories have been proposed in an attempt to understand the dyslexia phenomenon. Some theories are descriptive and focus on the inaccuracy and slowness/dysfluency of word reading among dyslexics (see British Psychological Society, 1999: 18 for their definition of dyslexia), while others aim to explain dyslexia (Lyon et al., 2003). An abundance of data has pointed to impairments in phonological processing as the cause of poor word reading (e.g., Share, 1995). The lack of orthographic, semantic, syntactic, and morphological skills has also been considered (e.g., see Adams, 1990 for a review). Other evidence has indicated that dyslexia has a neurological basis (Lyon et al., 2003).

This chapter will present an innovative concept for our understanding of dyslexia, which refers to its foundations. Breznitz's recent asynchrony theory proposes that dyslexia is an outcome of the failure to *synchronize* the various brain entities activated during the reading process (see Breznitz, 2002; Breznitz & Misra, 2003; Breznitz, 2006). The asynchrony theory is based on the idea that the word reading process relies on various sources of information with regard to printed materials. This information arrives from different brain entities. These entities have different biological structures. They are activated in separate areas of the brain, and they process information in a different manner and at different speeds. Furthermore, the reading activity requires the flow of relevant information from one brain area (the posterior lobes) to another (the frontal lobe). Whereas the posterior lobes are responsible for perception and physical processing of a stimulus, the frontal lobe provides meaning and motoric pronunciations to the stimulus (Sousa, 2000). In addition, word decoding relies on the transfer of information between brain hemispheres (Sousa, 2000). The left hemisphere processes information in a sequential manner and specializes in linguistic processing. This hemisphere contains Wernicke's area, where the mental lexicon is stored, and Broca's area, which is responsible for language pronunciation. The right hemisphere for most right handed individuals processes information in a holistic way and specializes in the identification of visual patterns (Sousa, 2000). Reading as a linguistic activity requires work in both hemispheres (Marsolek, Kosslyn, & Squire, 1992) and diverse areas of the brain need to communicate in a timely fashion.

Moreover, reading is a cognitive process activated through the various stages of the information processing system, including perception, processing, and output (Atkinson & Shiffrin, 1971). The act of reading must be sufficiently fast to operate within the constraints of limited capacity and rapid decay of the information processing entities (Perfetti, 1985). Above all, word decoding during reading is an inflexible action. In most alphabetic languages each grapheme matches only one phoneme. This grapheme-phoneme correspondence necessitates precision in content and time. This complexity constitutes a major challenge for the human brain as each brain entity activated in this process operates on a different time scale (Breznitz, 2002; Breznitz & Misra, 2003; Breznitz, 2006 for review). As a result, the integration and synchronization in time of the information arriving from the various brain entities, at all levels and stages of activation, is essential for successful word reading to occur.

According to Breznitz (2006), a gap in speed of processing (SOP) between the different brain entities activated in the word decoding process may prevent the precise synchronization of information necessary for an accurate process. This idea lies at the heart of the asynchrony theory, which suggests that the wider the SOP gap between the different brain entities; the more severe the word decoding failure will tend to be (Breznitz, 2002; 2006). There are several preconditions for the asynchrony phenomenon to occur:

1 more than one system, area of brain activation and/or stage of cognitive operation (referred to as entities) are involved in the processing task;
2 there are differences in the speeds at which each entity processes information;
3 the SOP of the various entities is not sufficiently coordinated to allow effective integration.

ASYNCHRONY THEORY OF DYSLEXIA

More than one entity is involved in the word decoding process

Word decoding relies on different brain entities that can be distinguished on the basis of three levels of involvement in the process:

1   the biological brain systems;
2   the cognitive processes;
3   the alphabetic units of various sizes obtained from printed materials.

The three levels of activation

The biological level

The biological level refers to a domain-general notion of processing, of which reading is considered a part. It consists of several entities activated during reading from the entryway to the human brain along the different stages of activation within and between the various neural pathways of the brain. At the end of this process, it is necessary for the brain to provide a solution, which appears in the form of output accompanied, in many cases, by motoric features. The entities at this level are the visual and auditory-acoustic modalities. Each entity is represented by specific brain locations and has a different length and structure to its neural pathway, with the visual pathway being longer than the auditory. The visual system processes information in a holistic manner, while processing in the auditory system is sequential. Each contributes to the reading process at a different point in time and at a different speed. The visual entity is the first to start decoding. It is triggered by printed materials and then works in parallel with the auditory entity. The performance of each entity is subject to its intrinsic capabilities, to the successes and failures of other components, and to the manner in which the entities are synchronized in terms of their speed (rapidity) and content (accuracy).

The cognitive processes

The cognitive processes combine two levels of operation, the domain-general and domain-specific processes. The domain-general processes assembled at the biological level are responsible for distinguishing, selecting, perceiving, categorizing, storing, and retrieving information. The domain-specific processes assembled in the biological modalities activate the orthographic, phonological-recoding, and semantic processes, which are specific to the word decoding process. At the initial stage of activation, attention is first allocated to the printed materials prior to the operation of the biological systems (at the entryway), and then different levels of cognitive operation are assembled along with the activation of the biological processes.

The domain-general processes operate sequentially, while the domain-specific processes function in an interactive manner until word meaning is obtained (Seidenberg and McClelland's PDP model, 1989; Harm & Seidenberg, 2004). There has been considerable debate concerning the mechanisms involved in mapping word meaning from print. Harm & Seidenberg (2004) attempted to resolve this longstanding debate by constructing and testing a computational model based on connectionist principles. According to this model, the meaning of a word is a 'pattern of activation over a set of semantic units that develops over time based on continuous input from both orthography>semantics and orthography>phonology> semantics components' (p. 663). Unlike previous accounts, in which the two pathways operate independently, in this model, both pathways determine meaning simultaneously, and have are mutually dependant on each other. The performance of each component is subject to both its intrinsic capabilities and the successes and failures of other components. An important assumption incorporated in the model is the notion that the reader's task is to compute meanings both accurately and quickly. Although the orthography>phonology>semantics pathway has a clear speed disadvantage, as it involves an extra 'step' compared to the direct pathway (orthography>semantics), the direct pathway actually takes longer to learn.

The asynchrony theory suggests that in an attempt to process information adequately, the system's speed attribute becomes a crucial factor in the further development of activation in the pathways. Moreover, more than one system is activated in each pathway and as such, synchronization is required and can only be achieved if the SOP gap between systems is minimal.

Furthermore, it is not clear whether there are two pathways that are activated during normal reading development. As during most activities, the brain searches for the most economical way to process information. It is conceivable that there is only one pathway used to process information during reading, the indirect pathway (orthography>phonology>semantic) which leads to an effective process. Over the years, the speed at which information is transferred from the orthographic to the semantic system via the phonological system is sped up. In other words, the recoding of printed materials in the phonological system continues to exist throughout, even during advanced word decoding in an inhibitory way, although it becomes very fast, barely manifested and hardly measurable with currently available research measures. Furthermore, the act of recoding the linguistic unit in the phonological system has an advantage, it has been trained over the years by two actions: spoken language and reading. It is possible that the dual training actions of this system assists speed of information processing to the extent that activation of the phonological step becomes barely noticeable during the normal course of word decoding among skilled readers the dual training actions of this system assists speed of information processing to the extent that activation of the phonological step becomes hardly noticeable during the normal course of word decoding among skilled readers.

The alphabetic level
The alphabetic level refers to domain-specific processing, which is an objective process, external to the reader and depends on the level of printed materials.

The printed material units provide content to the biological and cognitive entities. This level includes all of the reading-related subtasks triggered by, and derived from, the printed materials followed by activation in the mental lexicon. It includes all levels of the alphabetic code (letters, sounds, and syllables), the various levels of linguistic units (words and connected text) and their phonological, orthographic, semantic, syntactic, and morphological representations and processes. Activation of the biological systems is triggered by these printed linguistic units, and elevates the various forms of processing to the different cognitive levels.

Successful reading requires a form of 'dialogue' between the different brain entities involved in this process. During the normal course of word decoding, the dialogue takes place at different stages of activation along the neural pathways. This places an additional workload on the decoding activity as it requires different levels of synchronization of the brain entities at different points in time. When the decoding skills are not automatic, are less stable, or have yet to progress through the developmental stages, and when the orthographic representations of words in the mental lexicon have yet to stabilize, the various entities are required to cooperate continuously in order to send whatever information is available (even if inaccurate) regarding the linguistic unit being processed. In an impaired or undeveloped word decoding process, the information in one or more entities may not be completely accurate or available. This may constitute an additional obstacle for precise synchronization between entities. Moreover, partial or incomplete input from one entity might diminish the incoming information arriving in the other entities.

Word decoding complexity is increased further by the fact that from an evolutionary perspective, the human brain has existed for around 60,000 years, and the alphabetic code for only 5000 years. Consequently, the ability to read is not part of our evolutionary heritage. No biological brain system has been developed specifically for the reading process, so the activation of reading must rely on systems that were developed for different tasks. This complexity poses a major challenge for the human brain, and proves too much for some readers.

Speed of processing differences between different brain entities

What are the speeds of processing of the brain entities involved in word decoding? Research indicates that non-linguistic auditory information arrives in the auditory cortex after 30 ms (Heil et al., 1999), whereas visual information arrives in the visual cortex after 70 ms (Schmolesky et al., 1998). In other words, based on the natural operation of these biological entities, auditory stimuli leave the 'entryway' and arrive in the brain faster than visual stimuli. This may be due to the different lengths of the neural pathways, brain sites, and structures of each modality. However, at the linguistic level there is evidence that at least from the word level onwards, linguistic information is processed in the auditory channel in a temporal-serial manner. In other words, the information concerning the phonemes that make up a word arrives sequentially (Rosenzweig and Bennett, 1996). In contrast, word processing in the visual channel is a holistic and simultaneous process (Willows et al., 1993), suggesting that visual processing at this level might be faster than auditory processing.

It is important to note that most existing studies have used behavioural measures of reaction time. This means that the information concerning this entire sequence of cognitive activity has only been provided at the conclusion of processing; in the reader's output. This stage only occurs after the completion of sensory, cognitive and motor processes (Bentin, 1989; Brandeis & Lehmann, 1994; Johnson, 1995). This makes it difficult to determine, on the basis of behavioural measures alone, the extent to which dysfunction or slowness at any particular stage of processing contributes to reading deficits.

In recent years, new methods based on electrophysiological parameters utilizing electroencephalogram (EEG) data have been used in reading research. The EEG method is used to assess on-line processing of cognitive activity. It has been used for the following activities:

1 Measurement of event-related potentials (ERPs). This method permits direct observation of information processing at different levels of analysis, and can provide crucial information by means of real-time imaging of the neural system's responses to sensory stimulation (Bentin, 1989). Thus, it enables us to trace, on-line, the speed at which information is processed during the various cognitive stages of the reading activity. ERPs are extracted from EEG data by averaging brain responses during a number of equivalent trials in a given experiment. ERPs consist of various discrete components, or brain waves, that can be related to different stages of information processing in terms of amplitude and/or latency variations.
2 Estimation of the brain source of ERP's latencies using Low Resolution Electromagnetic Tomography (LORETA) (Pascual-Marqui, Michel, & Lehmann, 1994; Pascual-Marqui, 1999).
3 Estimation of brain connectivity (Malsburg & von der Schneider, 1986; Abarbanel et al., 1996), namely, the manner in which cortical areas act in concert with each other.

By using these methodologies, it is possible to systematically examine the speed of processing (SOP) of the different entities active during word decoding (Breznitz, 2002; 2003; Breznitz & Meyler, 2003; Breznitz & Misra, 2003; Barnea & Breznitz, 1998; Breznitz, 2005; Breznitz, 2006 for review). In these studies, SOP within and between the visual and auditory modalities, and speed of information transfer between different brain areas and at different stages of cognitive activation were measured. In the different experiments, lower level non-linguistic tasks (SOP for tones and flashes) and linguistic tasks (letters and syllables) as well as higher level linguistic (words, pseudowords and sentences) tasks were examined. The stimuli were presented separately as well as simultaneously in the two modalities. The subjects in these experiments consisted of different age groups of dyslexic and regular readers (fourth-grade students, fifth-grade students, and university students) (see Breznitz 2006 for a comprehensive review). These experiments measured SOP using Reaction Time (RT) and ERP latencies. Across the different experiments, the various ERP components were identified. However, two ERP components were systematically recognized across all experiments in both age groups:

1   An early P100-P200 complex, which is thought to index mechanisms of sensory activity elicited by a stimulus (Johnstone, Barry, Anderson, & Coyle, 1996; Tonnquist-Uhlen, 1996) such as feature detection (e.g., Luck & Hillyard, 1994), selective attention (e.g., Hackley, Woldorff, & Hillyard, 1990) and other early sensory stages of item encoding (Dunn, Languis, & Andrews, 1998).
2   P300, which is considered to be a valid index of central information processing during task-related decision-making (Palmer, Nasman, & Wilson, 1994). Processes associated with P300 include the dynamic updating of information held in working memory (Israel, Chesney, Wickens, & Donchin, 1980; Fitzgerald & Picton, 1983), cognitive resource allocation and task involvement (Kramer et al., 1991), as well as mental effort or workload (Humphrey & Kramer, 1994; Wilson, Swain, & Ullsperger, 1998).

Visual and auditory SOP

Figures 1.1–1.6 summarize the results of a wide range of studies (see Breznitz, 2006 for more detail) in which the processing times of visual and auditory stimuli at different levels of complexity were measured in the research population. The results of the experiments carried out among young readers are summarized in Figures 1.1–1.3, and among adults in Figures 1.4–1.6.

Young regular and dyslexic readers

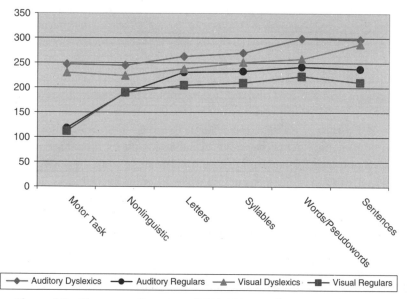

Figure 1.1   The perception stage (P100-200 complex at CZ electrodes)

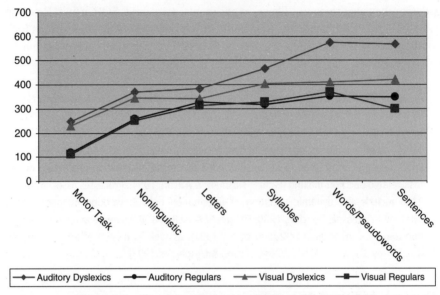

Figure 1.2 The processing stage (P300 at CZ electrode)

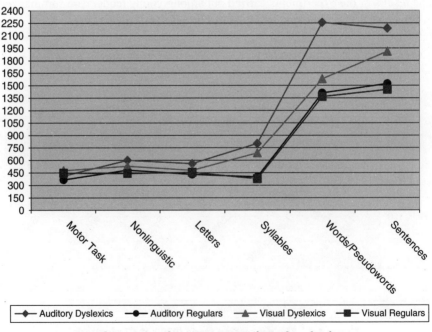

Figure 1.3 The output stage (reaction time)

Adult regular and dyslexic readers

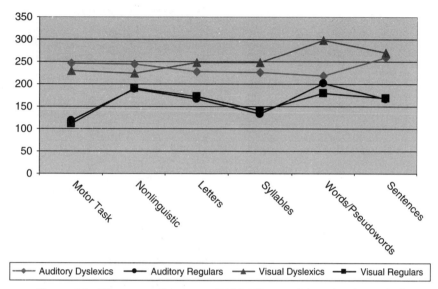

Figure 1.4   The perception stage (P100-200 complex at CZ electrodes)

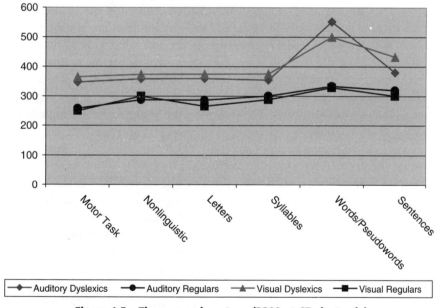

Figure 1.5   The processing stage (P300 at CZ electrode)

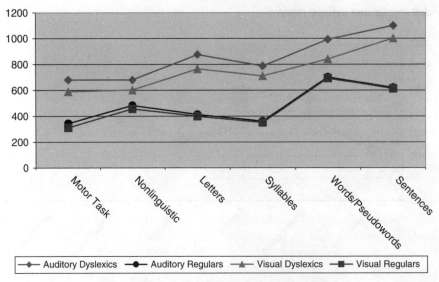

Figure 1.6   The output stage (reaction time)

Examination of speed of processing among the brain entities of young and adult dyslexic and regular readers using behavioural measures and ERP methodology indicated that dyslexics of all ages were significantly slower than the regular readers. This was true at all stages of information processing and at most levels of activation, in processing both visual and auditory information. The differences between both groups of readers in both age groups increased with task complexity. However, close observation of our data shows that during the normal course of processing information there is a natural gap in the speeds at which each modality processes information. Nevertheless, a wider SOP gap was observed among the dyslexics (Breznitz, 2006). Among the young and adult regular and dyslexic readers, auditory processing was slower than visual on most tasks at all levels of activation except for P100-P200 latencies at the linguistic level (letters, syllables, and words/pseudowords decision tasks). At this level, the SOP in the visual modality among adult dyslexics was slower than in the auditory modality. Since decoding any linguistic unit begins with the visual modality it is conceivable that over the years, in order to improve their accuracy, the dyslexics trained their brain to perceive linguistic units from printed materials more slowly, following the logic that slowness implies greater attention and increases accuracy. This suggests that the way in which the linguistic unit enters the gateway to the brain might be a crucial factor in enhancing the decoding process. The idea proposed here is that over the years, any linguistic unit of any size develops not only orthographic patterns but also 'visual speed anagrams'.

What is the visual speed anagram? I would like to suggest that in addition to the orthographic, phonological and semantic aspects of the word there is another separate independent feature that is also decoded, which relates to the speed at which the reader's visual modality receives printed words. At the initial, perceptual stage of processing, the speed at which the linguistic unit is perceived places a marker (imprint) on the way that the word is formed. This speed marker results from the interaction between the characteristics (including SOP) of the reader's visual modality, his/her reading level, and the level of printed materials. At this initial stage of processing, the 'visual speed anagram' is formed and affects the manner in which the linguistic unit enters the brain's entryway, is processed in the different brain entities, and is stored in or retrieved from the mental lexicon.

As 'speed' is a measure of time, it is subject to change. With experience, the speed anagram of each individual orthographic pattern becomes faster until it reaches automaticity and becomes more flexible to accommodate to the readers needs. However, based on the hesitant habits acquired by dyslexic readers in terms of the way they receive linguistic units via the visual modality, this 'visual speed anagram' remains slow and imprints a disrupted marker on the speed at which the various entities process the linguistic unit. The outcome of this impaired process is the creation of an inflexible, non-automatic, and inconsistent word decoding process. Nevertheless, based on the plasticity of the brain to change, our research on the acceleration phenomenon has indicated that even the brains of dyslexic readers can be accelerated to create and retrieve linguistic units at the levels of words and sentence. In other words, the 'visual speed anagram' of the orthographic unit in this population can be improved by training and direct intervention (Breznitz, 2006; Breznitz & Berman, 2003).

Asynchrony between the posterior and anterior brain sites

The word reading process relies on both anterior and posterior brain areas (Sousa, 2000). In the anterior region, there are two crucial centers responsible for linguistic processes. Broca's center is responsible for pronunciation of stimuli and for changing orthographic information into its phonological form (Hagoort et al., 1999; Fiez, Balota, Raichle, & Petersen, 1999). Wernicke's center stores the mental lexicon. In the posterior region, three perceptual lobes are located: the occipital lobe for visual information, the temporal lobe for auditory, and the parietal lobe for motoric processing. These lobes operate separately or in conjunction, depending on the requirements of the task (Petersen, Fox, Posner, Mintun, & Raichle, 1988; Rumsey et al., 1997).

A study examining cerebral activity during reading found that processing began in the visual area of the occipital lobe 100 ms post stimulus presentation and moved toward the occipital and temporal lobes in both hemispheres (around 150–200 ms post stimulus presentation) (Salmelin, Service, Kiesilä, Uutela, & Salonen, 1996). In the next stage of the reading process, the information was transferred to the superior temporal cortex in the left hemisphere only and to the motor cortex in both hemispheres (between 200–400 ms post stimulus presentation).

It can be concluded that a precise reading process involves the transfer of information from the posterior to anterior brain areas, which takes about 300 ms (see Shaul, 2006). Whether the same pathway and the same time framework applies to dyslexic readers is yet another important question. Studies examining differences in cerebral activity between regular and dyslexic readers found significant differences in all activity areas related to reading. There is less activity in the posterior brain sites among dyslexics as compared to regular readers when reading words (Brunswick, McCrory, Price & Frith, 1999; Paulesu et al., 2001; Pugh et al., 2000). This finding was corroborated across various languages (Paulesu et al., 2001; Salmelin et al., 1996). In addition, a strong functional connectivity between the posterior areas and Broca's area (left anterior brain site) was found in regular readers. This suggests accurate integration between the orthographic form of the word and its phonological counterpart received in Broca's area. In contrast, the dyslexic readers exhibited connections between posterior areas and pre-frontal areas in the right hemisphere, which is considered to be related to long-term memory (Fletcher et al., 1994). The impaired transfer from the posterior to anterior brain sites among dyslexics may indicate a further delay in the synchronization of orthographic and phonological information during word decoding.

Shaul and Breznitz (under review) investigated the SOP of information transfer from the posterior to anterior brain sites among adult dyslexics as compared to regular readers during performance of a lexical decision task. The study employed ERP methodology, analysis was performed by comparing pairs of electrodes situated in similar sites in the posterior and anterior regions of the brain (i.e., FP1–O1, F7–P7, F3–P3, FZ–PZ, F4–P4, F8–P8, FP2–O2). Among dyslexics, at the perceptual level (P200) information arrived about 11–12 ms later from the posterior to anterior brain areas. Among regular readers, this delay was limited to 3–4 ms.

Asynchrony between the left and right hemispheres

The human brain is divided into two hemispheres, the right and the left. Even though the two hemispheres appear identical they differ in the number and size of their neurons and in the amount of various neurotransmitters (Banich, 2004). Apart from the structural and chemical differences, each hemisphere specializes in specific abilities. The right hemisphere specializes in pattern recognition, creativity, spatial orientation, face and object recognition as well as emotion and processing of internal information. The left hemisphere is responsible for analysis, language skills (speech, letter recognition, and word recognition), sequence and number recognition, sensitivity to time, and processing of external information (Carter, 1998). Each hemisphere receives information from the opposite perceptual field and controls the opposite side of the body (Carter, 1998). Tasks with a heavy cognitive load, such as reading, require cooperation and synchronization of information from both hemispheres (Markee Warren, Morre, & Theberge, 1996). The transfer time of information between hemispheres among adults ranges from 5–20 ms (Banich, 2004). However, dyslexics exhibit difficulties when transferring information from one hemisphere to another (e.g., Gladstone & Best, 1985; Gladstone, Best, & Davidson, 1989; Gross-Glenn & Rothenberg, 1984; Velay et al., 2002; Markee et al., 1996). The differences in interhemispheric transfer time (IHTT) among dyslexics may stem from information decay in the corpus collosum or a long non-symmetrical delay (Davidson, Leslie, & Saron, 1990; Davidson & Saron, 1992; Markee et al., 1996).

Shaul and Breznitz (under review) measured information transfer between the left and right hemispheres among dyslexics as compared to regular readers when performing various lexical decision tasks. Using the IHTT method, the latencies of electrodes situated in similar sites in left and right brain locations were compared (i.e., FP1–FP2, F7–F8, F3–F4, FC5–FC6, T7–T8, C3–C4, CP5–CP6, P7–P8, P3–P4, O1–O2). Among dyslexics, when stimuli were presented visually to the center of the computer screen, information reflected by the P200 and P300 ERP components arrived in the right hemisphere first, and was transferred to the left hemisphere approximately 9–12 ms later. Among regular readers, the information arrived in the left hemisphere first and was transferred to the right approximately 4–6 ms later. Support for these results was obtained by estimates from source localization of brain activity in these two reading groups during the word decoding process using LORETA (see Figure 1.7). Comparisons between groups revealed greater activation among dyslexic readers between 110 and 140 ms for words, mainly in the right temporal and perisylvian regions, as well as some activation in medial frontal regions. Regular readers exhibited greater activation in left temporal and perisylvian regions between 150 and 200 ms.

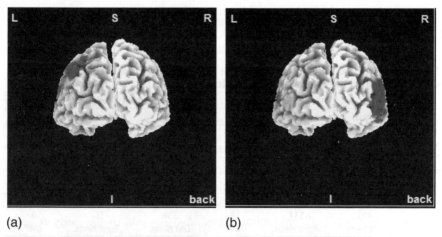

(a)   (b)

Figure 1.7   LORETA resolution for P200 component peak among regular and dyslexic readers during word decoding. a) Regular readers, P200 at 197 ms; b) Dyslexic readers, P200 at 289 ms

As all our subjects were right-handed it seems that the flow of incoming information in the dyslexic group started in right brain sites and moved to the left, and
then again to the right brain sites, moved to the left, and then returned to the
right. We argue that this manner of processing extends the decoding process
among dyslexic readers. Support for this idea can be derived from our reaction
time data. The reaction times of the dyslexic readers during word decoding were
about 121 ms longer than for the regular readers (X = 811.02 s.d = 55.16 among
the dyslexics, and X = 690.13 s.d = 31.12 among the regular readers).

SOP of the various brain entities is not sufficiently coordinated to allow for an effective decoding process

Observation of the results from the different experiments (shown in Figures 1.1–1.6
and Table 1.1) suggests that SOP at all levels of activation is slower among young
and adult dyslexics as compared to regular readers. However, the gap between the
speed of processing (SOP) of the visual and auditory modalities was wider among
dyslexics on most of the experimental tasks and across age groups. The posterior-
anterior SOP gap as well as the SOP gap in information transfer between hemispheres during lexical decision performance was also wider among the dyslexics as
compared to the controls. Moreover, Figure 1.7 shows that the peak of the P200
component among regular readers was observed at 197 ms in the left hemisphere
whereas among dyslexic readers the P200 component peak was observed at 289 ms
in the right hemisphere. Among regular readers, later activation was observed in the
right hemisphere (at about 203 ms), while among dyslexic readers later activation
was observed in the left hemisphere (at about 303 ms). This data indicates not only
that the P200 appears later among dyslexics as compared to regular readers, but
that there is an additional aspect of between hemisphere asynchrony in the brain
activity of dyslexic readers, due to the fact that precise P200 activation occurs in the
left hemisphere as opposed to the right among dyslexics.

**Table 1.1   Reaction time, latencies of the ERP components and Gap scores for the
word decoding process among adult readers**

	Dyslexics (N=60)			Regular Readers (N=60)		
	Visual	*Auditory*	*GAP*	*Visual*	*Auditory*	*GAP*
P2	298	218	−20	180	202	22
P3	501	559	58	320	334	14
RT	841	993	152	690	702	12
P3-P2 Gap	202	334		140	132	
	Posterior	*Anterior*	*GAP*	*Posterior*	*Anterior*	*GAP*
P2	286	299	15	176	180	4
P3	495	511	16	356	362	6
	Left Hems.	*Right Hems.*	*GAP*	*Left Hems.*	*Right Hems.*	*GAP*
P2	303	289	14	197	203	6
P3	509	495	14	361	364	3

However, support for the asynchrony theory was mainly obtained from the analysis performed to clarify whether the direct SOP of the entities or the between-entity SOP gap accounts for most of the variance in the word decoding process. Regression analysis indicated that of all the measures employed in the experiments the gap between visual and auditory processing accounts for most of the variance in the word decoding process (see Breznitz, 2002; Breznitz & Misra, 2003; Breznitz, 2006 for review; and Shaul & Breznitz, under review). Among the young dyslexics, the first predictor was the SOP gap score between grapheme (visual presentation) and phoneme (auditory presentation) at the perceptual stage (P200 latency), and a second predictor was speed of activation during the processing stage (P300) (see Breznitz, 2002). Both variables explained about 72 per cent of the variance in word decoding. Among the adults, the first predictor was the SOP gap score between visual and auditory presentation at the perceptual (P200) level for words, and the second was the processing stage GAP (P300). Both explain 64 per cent of the variance in word decoding (see Breznitz, 2006).

How is the synchronization and asynchrony manifested during word decoding? Ballan (in preparation) measured brain connectivity during the word decoding process using coherence analysis among dyslexic and regular readers. Strong connectivity between most brain areas was found among regular readers for lower level brain wave bands 4–12 Hz. The connectivity was mainly exhibited between the two hemispheres and the posterior and anterior brain sites. Among the dyslexics, moderate connectivity was found within the left hemisphere only at the lower beta band level (13–18 Hz). It is possible that limiting the between entity SOP gap may lead to better brain connectivity and to better brain synchronization. A wider SOP gap may lead to asynchrony between brain entities and therefore to reduced brain connectivity. In other words, effective word decoding may require overall brain activation, but for a short period of time. In such a process, all the entities activated during the process are directed to the tasks, thereby reducing distractibility.

SUMMARY

The complex process of word decoding can be compared to a concert which includes many instruments. The conductor must orchestrate the different musicians, to synchronize the instruments and make the output harmonious. Reading similarly requires one specific 'harmonized' output. This process is also based on the activation of different brain entities (instruments), which are located in different areas of the brain (orchestra), and which process information in a different manner (sounds). However, our data indicates that a crucial initial condition for accurate word decoding regards the speed at which each entity is activated. Different brain entities operate on different time scales, which require synchronization.

A wider between-entity SOP gap occurs among dyslexic readers, which leads to the asynchrony phenomenon.

The asynchrony in the impaired word decoding process begins with the creation of an impaired 'visual speed anagram' for the linguistic unit at the 'entryway' which affects and opens a speed gap between the different brain entities that are activated during word decoding. Moreover, among dyslexic readers this impaired word form continues on into the wrong (right) hemisphere in the brain. With the idea that the slower the reading rate, the more accurate the activation, during the course of their experience with decoding failures, dyslexic readers may attempt to compensate for their inaccuracy by adopting an inflexible, slower speed of visual processing. As a result, an accumulative between-modality gap opens up and continues along all stages of activation. This affects the flow of information from posterior to anterior brain areas and slows down inter-hemisphere transfer. Unfortunately, this adaptation of dyslexic readers to their failures may actually contribute to their reading dysfluency.

The notion that dyslexia is caused by an SOP gap within and between the various entities taking part in the word decoding process, together with the fact that SOP is a time based measure, led us to develop the Reading Acceleration Program (RAP) (Breznitz & Navat, 2004). This program attempted to train the brain to process information at a faster speed and resulted in a substantial improvement among dyslexics in the speed at which information was processed (Breznitz & Itzchak, 2005; Breznitz, 2006, Breznitz & Horowitz, under review). Moreover, this improvement was successfully transferred, as indicated by the enhanced decoding quality and decreased reading times for material not included in the training program. In addition, this progress was also indicated by the early elicitation of the P200 component post-training. We argue that at least for adult dyslexic readers there is a discrepancy between their ability and their performance during word decoding. This discrepancy is an outcome of poor reading habits and an inflexible brain monitor (see Breznitz, 2006 for more details), and appears mainly in the speed at which words are decoded. As a result, we suggest a short-term intervention program that directly targets the SOP of the entities activated in the word decoding process, which may reduce the asynchrony phenomenon.

In conclusion, based on the idea of the plasticity of the brain to change (Sousa, 2000), a properly designed, direct short-term training intervention program instead of an overall remediation program that targets a specific decoding sub-skill, promises to constitute a major contribution to the reduction of dyslexia in the years to come.

REFERENCES

Adams, M. J. (1990) *Beginning to read: Thinking and learning about print.* Cambridge, MA: MIT Press.
Atkinson, R.C. and Shiffrin, R.M. (1971) 'The control of short-term memory', *Scientific American*, 225: 82–90.

Ballan, E. (in preparation) 'Large scale neuronal coordination in reading: A comparison between regular and dyslexic readers'.

Banich, M. T. (2004) *Cognitive neuroscience and neuropsychology.* Boston MA: Houghton Mifflin Company.

Barnea, A. and Breznitz, Z. (1998) 'Phonological and orthographic processing of Hebrew words: Electrophysiological aspects', *Journal of Genetic Psychology*, 159 (4): 492–504.

Bentin, S. (1989) 'Electrophysiological studies of visual word perception, lexical organization, and semantic processing: A tutorial review', *Language and Speech*, 32: 205–220.

Brandeis, D. and Lehmann, D. (1994) 'ERP mapping: a tool for assessing language disorders', in H. J. Heinze, T. F. Mante and G. R. Mangun (eds), *Cognitive electrophysiology.* Boston: Birkhauser. pp. 242–250.

Breznitz, Z. (2002) 'Asynchrony of visual-orthographic and auditory-phonological word recognition processes: An underlying factor in dyslexia', *Reading and Writing*, 15 (1–2): 15–42.

Breznitz, Z. (2003) 'Speed of phonological and orthographic processing as factors in dyslexia: Electrophysiological evidence', *Genetic, Social and General Psychology Monographs*, 129 (2): 183–206.

Breznitz, Z. (2005) 'Brain activity during performance of naming tasks: Comparison between dyslexic and regular readers', *Scientific Studies of Reading*, 9 (1): 17–42.

Breznitz, Z. (2006) *Fluency in reading: Synchronization of processes.* Mahwah, NJ: Lawrence Erlbaum and Associates.

Breznitz, Z. and Berman, L. (2003) 'The underlying factors of word reading rate', *Educational Psychology Review*, 15 (3): 247–265.

Breznitz, Z. and Meyler, A. (2003) 'Speed of lower-level auditory and visual processing as a basic factor in dyslexia: Electrophysiological evidence', *Brain and Language*, 85 (1): 166–184.

Breznitz, Z., and Misra, M. (2003) 'Speed of processing of the visual-orthographic and auditory-phonological systems in adult dyslexics: The contribution of "asynchrony" to word recognition deficits', *Brain and Language*, 85 (3): 486–502.

Breznitz, Z. and Itzhak, Y. (2005) *MA thesis in preparation.* University of Haifa Israel.

Breznitz, Z. and Navat, M. (2004) *Reading acceleration program (RAP).* Unpublished Training Program. University of Haifa.

Breznitz, Z. and Horowitz, T. (under review) 'All the wrong and rights moves: A comparison of cerebral activity during accurate and erroneous reading performance among dyslexics and regular readers, an ERP study'.

British Psychological Society (1999) 'Dyslexia literacy and psychological assessment'. *Report by a working party of the division of educational and child psychology.* Leicester: British Psychological Society.

Brunswick, N., McCrory, E., Price, C. J., Frith, C. D. and Frith, U. (1999) 'Explicit and implicit processing of words and pseudowords by adult developmental dyslexics', *Brain*, 122: 1901–1917.

Carter, R. (1998) *Mapping the mind.* Los Angeles: University of California Press.

Davidson, R. J., Leslie, S. C. and Saron, C. D. (1990) 'Reaction time measures of interhemispheric transfer time in reading disabled and normal children', *Neuropsychologia*, 28: 471–485.

Davidson, R. J. and Saron, C. D. (1992) 'Evoked potential measures of interhemispheric transfer time in reading disabled and normal children', *Developmental Neuropsychology*, 8: 261–277.

Dunn, B.R., Dunn, D.A., Languis, M., and Andrews, D., (1998) 'The relation of ERP components to complex memory processing', *Brain and Cognition*, 36: 355–376.

Fiez, J. A., Balota, D. A., Raichle, M. E. and Petersen, S. E. (1999) 'Effects of lexicality, frequency, and spelling-to-sound consistency on the functional anatomy of reading', *Neuron*, 24: 205–218.

Fitzgerald, P. G. and Picton. T. W. (1983) 'Event-related potentials recorded during the discrimination of improbable stimuli', *Biological Psychology*, 17: 241–276.

Fletcher, J. M., Shaywitz, S. E., Shankweiler, D. P., Katz, L., Liberman, I. Y., Steubing, K. K., Francis, D. J., Fowler, A. E. and Shaywitz, B. A. (1994) 'Cognitive profiles of reading disability: Comparisons of discrepancy and low achievement definitions', *Journal of Educational Psychology*, 86: 6–23.

Gladstone, M. and Best, C. T. (1985) 'Developmental dyslexia: the potential role of interhemispheric collaboration in reading acquisition', in C. T. Best (ed) *Hemispheric Function and Collaboration in the Child*. San Francisco: Academic Press. pp. 87–118.

Gladstone, M., Best, C. T. and Davidson, R. J. (1989) 'Anomalous bimanual coordination among dyslexic boys', *Developmental Psychology*, 25: 236–246.

Gross-Glen, K. and Rothenberg, S. (1984) 'Evidence for deficit in interhemispheric transfer of information in dyslexic boys', *International Journal of Neuroscience*, 24: 23–35.

Hackley, S.A., Woldorff, M. and Hillyard, S.A. (1990) 'Cross-modal selective attention effects on retinal, myogenic, brainstem, and cerebral evoked potentials', *Psychophysiology*, 27: 195–28.

Hagoort, P., Indefrey, P., Brown, C., Herzog, H., Steinmetz, H. and Seitz, R. J. (1999) 'The neural circuitry involved in the reading of German words and pseudowords: APET study', *Journal of Cognitive Neuroscience*, 11: 383–398.

Harm, M. and Seidenberg, M. S. (2004) 'Computing the meanings of words in reading: Cooperative division of labor between visual and phonological processes', *Psychological Review*, 111: 662–720.

Heil, M., Rolke, B., Engelkamp, J., Roesler, F., Oezcan, M. and Hennighausen, E. (1999) 'Event-related brain potentials during recognition of ordinary and bizarre action phrases following verbal and subject-performed encoding conditions', *European Journal of Cognitive Psychology*, 11 (2): 261–280.

Humphrey, D. G. and Kramer, A. F. (1994) 'Toward a psychophysiological assessment of dynamic changes in mental workload', *Human Factors*, 36(1), 3–26.

Israel, J. B., Chesney, G. L., Wickens, C.D. and Donchin, E. (1980) 'P300 and tracking difficulty: Evidence for multiple resources in dual-task performance', *Psychophysiology*, 17 (3): 259–273.

Johnson, R. (1995) 'Effects of color on children's naming of picture', *Perceptual and Motor Skills*, 80: 1091–1101.

Johnstone, S.J., Barry, R.J., Anderson, J.W. and Coyle, S.F. (1996) 'Age-related changes in child and adolescent event-related potential component morphology, amplitude and latency to standard and target stimuli in an auditory oddball task', *International Journal of Psychophysiology*, 24: 223–238.

Kramer, A. F., Strayer, D. L. and Buckley, J. (1991) 'Task versus component consistency in the development of automatic processing: A psychophysiological assessment', *Psychophysiology*, 28 (4): 425–437.

Luck, S. J. and Hillyard, S. A. (1994) 'Electrophysiological correlates of feature analysis during visual search', *Psychophysiology*, 31: 291–308.

Lyon, G. R., Shaywitz, S. E. and Shaywitz, B. A. (2003) 'A definition of dyslexia', *Annals of Dyslexia*, 53: 1–14.

Malsburg, C. and von der, Schneider, W. (1986) 'A neural cocktail party processor', *Biological Cybernetics*, 54: 29–40.

Markee, T., Warren, S. B., Morre, L. H. and Theberge, D.C. (1996) 'Callosal function in dyslexia: Evoked potential interhemispheric transfer time and bilateral field advantage', *Developmental Neuropsychology*, 12: 409–428.

Marsolek, C. J., Kosslyn, S. M. and Squire, L.R. (1992) 'Form-specific visual priming in the right cerebral hemisphere', *Journal of Experimental Psychology: Learning, Memory, and Cognition*, 18: 492–508.

Palmer, B., Nasman, V. T. and Wilson, G. F. (1994) 'Task detection difficulty: Effects on ERPs in a same-different letter classification task', *Biological Psychology*, 38 (2–3), 199–214.

Pascual-Marqui, R.D., Michel C.M. and Lehmann, D. (1994) 'Low resolution electromagnetic tomography: a new method for localizing electrical activity in the brain', *International Journal of Psychophysiology*, 18 (1): 49–65.

Pascual-Marqui, R.D. (1999) 'Review of methods for solving the EEG inverse problem', *International Journal of Bioelectromagnetism*, 1: 75–86.

Paulesu, E., Démonet, J. F., Fazio, F., McCrory, E., Chanoine, V., Brunswick, N., Cappa, S. F., Cossu, G., Habib, M., Frith, C. D. and Frith, U. (2001) Dyslexia: Cultural diversity and biological unity. *Science*, *291*, 2165–2167.

Perfetti, C. (1985) *Reading ability*. NY:Oxford University Press.

Petersen, S.E., Fox, P.T., Posner, M.I., Mintun, M. and Raichle, M.E. (1988) 'Positron emission tomographic studies of the cortical anatomy of single word processing', *Nature*, 331: 585–589.

Pugh, K. R., Mencl, W. E., Jenner, A. R., Katz, L., Frost, S. J., Lee, J. R., Shaywitz, S. E. and Shaywitz, B. A. (2001) 'Neurobiological studies of reading and reading disability', *Journal of Communication Disorders*, 34: 479–492.

Rosenzweig, M. R. and Bennett, E. L. (1996) 'Psychobiology of plasticity: Effects of training and experience on brain and behavior', *Behavioural Brain Research*, 78: 57–65.

Rumsey, J. M., Donohue, B. C., Brady, D. R., Nace, K., Giedd, J. N. and Andreason, P. (1997) 'A magnetic resonance imaging study of planum temporale asymmetry in men with developmental dyslexia', *Archives of Neurology*, 54 (12): 1481–1489.

Salmelin, R., Service, E., Kiesilä, P., Uutela, K. and Salonen, O. (1996) 'Impaired visual word processing in dyslexia revealed with magnetoencephalography', *Annals of Neurology*, 40: 157–162.

Schmolesky, M.T., Wang,Y., Hanes.D.P., Thompson, K.G., Lentgeb, S., Schall, J.P. and Leventhal, A.G. (1998) 'Signal timing across Macaque visual system', *Journal of Neurophysiology*, 79 (6): 3272–3278.

Seidenberg, M. S. and McCleland, J. L. (1989) 'A distributed developmental model of word recognition and naming', *Psychological Review*, 96: 523–568.

Share, D.L. (1995) 'Phonological recoding and self-teaching: Sine qua non of reading acquisition', *Cognition*, 55 (2): 151–218.

Shaul, S. (2006) 'Investigation of processing synchronization between cerebral systems active during word recognition: A Comparison of regular and dyslexic readers', *Unpublished PhD Dissertation*. University of Haifa.

Shaul, S. and Breznitz, Z. (under review) 'Asynchrony of cerebral systems activated during word recognition: A Comparison of regular and dyslexic readers'.

Sousa, A., D. (2000) *How the brain learns*. Thousand Oaks, California: Crowin Press. Inc.

Tonnquist-Uhlen, I. (1996) 'Topography of auditory evoked long-latency potentials in children with severe language impairment: The P2 and N2 components', *Ear and Hearing*, 17 (4): 314–326.

Velay, J. L., Daffaure, V., Giraud, K.M and Habib, M. (2002) 'Interhemispheric sensorimotor integration in pointing movements: A study on dyslexic adults', *Neuropsychologia*, 40: 827–834.

Willows, D. M., Kruk, R. and Corcos, E. (1993) 'Are there differences between disabled and normal readers in their processing of visual information?', in D. M. Willows, R. S. Kruk and E. Corcos (eds), *Visual processes in reading and reading disabilities*. Hillsdale, NJ: Lawrence Erlbaum. pp. 265–285.

Wilson, G. F., Swain, C. R. and Ullsperger, P. (1998) 'ERP components elicited in response to warning stimuli: The influence of task difficulty', *Biological Psychology*, 47: 137–158.

Some Special Issues Concerning the Genetics of Dyslexia: Revisiting Multivariate Profiles, Comorbidities, and Genetic Correlations[1]

Jeffrey W. Gilger

This chapter

i) acknowledges the advances that have been made in the field of genetics; and
ii) puts forward new challenges that have to be taken into account in current practice and future research.

INTRODUCTION

This chapter is both retrospective and prospective. It begins by providing a brief overview of where we have been in the genetic (and neurological) study of dyslexia or developmental reading disability (RD), and then closes with where we might go in the future. Specifically, the first sections of this paper focus on how the biological study of RD was initially considered, and then reflects on where we are at present. The next sections discuss some of the essential problems that have arisen, or have been discovered, in the field as a result of the work so far completed. Finally, in the last sections of this paper, I talk about how the study of RD might be approached in the future given what we now know and what we might do if the field should seek the next levels of understanding of RD and other 'atypical learning skills'.

OVERVIEW OF HOW WE STARTED OUT AND WHERE WE ARE AT TODAY

For many years people have known of the hereditary and likely neurological basis of RD, and the definition of RD has undergone some serious revisions since it was first called 'congenital word blindness' (Hinshelwood, 1895, 1917; Morgan, 1896; Morgan, 1914; Orton, 1928; Clements and Peters, 1962; Kirk and Elkins, 1975; Hallgren, 1950; see also reviews in Smith and Gilger, 2007, Doris, 1998, and Fletcher et al., 2007). Given the current understanding at the time that RD began to draw interest, researchers trained under a medical model considered RD a 'disease' and therefore approached it as they would have many other medical conditions.

For example, some early work on RD considered whether or not it was a condition with a genetic and environmental etiology unique from that for normal reading skills (see reviews in Pennington and Gilger, 1996; Gilger et al., 1996; Miles and Haslam, 1986). Recognizing that the condition was familial, also led many of the early researchers to ponder if it might be a single gene disorder (e.g., Hallgren, 1950; Owen et al., 1971), and later on, when molecular gene searches were first considered, the tools available at that time limited tests to very basic single gene models and a limited number of loci (e.g., Smith et al., 1983). Similarly, the first studies of the neurology of RD tended to focus on unitary and supposedly independent language or visual centers of the brain, with little consideration given to the more complex and realistic neuropsychological models for reading that came later (Mody, 2004; Ramus, 2004a; b; Geschwind, 1982; Geschwind and Galaburda, 1987).

While the original thinking about the etiology of RD may be open to criticism today, it was this early research that inspired the field towards our current understanding of learning disorders. Through the process of the scientific method, where research questions inform study design, and then results guide subsequent research questions, our understanding of the etiology of RD has blossomed in some important ways. For instance, work over the past few decades has provided information on:

- the behavioral and neuropsychological definitions of RD;
- how RD is represented in the population;
- the concept of RD as part of a continuum of reading ability;
- how reading and RD may fit multivariate or cognitive component models, as continuous scales of skills, or as underlying liabilities;

- the development of testable neurocognitive network models;
- how RD relates to other traits or conditions, and how to test for the basis of observed comorbidities or correlated behaviors;
- complex multigene models of RD and neurodevelopment; and
- others.

Based on these advances in RD research, today we can make the nine conclusions listed below.

1   RD is cognitively complex.
2   No single cognitive or neurological model seems to fit all the data.
3   There are significant qualitative and quantitative individual differences in how the disorder is manifest behaviorally and what profile of cognitive abilities may underlie a reading problem.
4   The etiologic factors that put someone at risk for RD are not necessarily distinct from those factors that influence normal variation in reading skill, and RD does not appear to be a 'disease' in classic medical sense.
5   Traits correlated with RD may do so because they, in part or whole, share the same biological etiology.
6   There are some common functional brain patterns, but there is variability and non-specificity in how the brains of RD individuals operate.
7   Similarly, there are some common patterns and atypical brain structures in RD individuals, while there is also significant variability and non-focal differences in morphology.
8   No one single gene seems to be at the basis of RD, and the actual number of genes has yet to be determined.
9   There are other important discoveries not highlighted here (see Fletcher et al., 2007; Schumacher et al., 2007).

There are four well accepted conclusions that apply to RD in general and a closer look shows that our understanding of RD is more complicated than it appears at first glance.

- Primarily a language-based disorder (phonological awareness/processing).
- Neurological in origin (left inferior frontal, inferior temporal-occipital, temporal-parietal).
- In part, neurodevelopmental in origin (disorganized neural pathways, atypical cortical cell connection, gross and fine structural formations different from controls, etc.).
- In part genetic, with specific risk genes (moderate h^2, replicated linkages to specific genes or chromosomal sites).

RD = Developmental reading disability/dyslexia; h^2 = heritability

We have learned that RD is in fact very complex, with variable manifestations that span behaviors related to the language area, but other cognitive and behavioral areas as well. Namely, there are variable reading-related component profiles within the affected people (e.g., skill levels on phoneme awareness, orthographic coding, IQ, non-verbal skills, perceptual speed, namely speed, comprehension, fluency, etc.), the degree of cognitive deficits can vary across people, there are age-related changes in expression within people, there may be gender-related differences in response to risk factors, and more (Fletcher et al., 2007; Smith and Gilger, 2007; Satz et al., 1998).

To further complicate the picture, RD is often associated with other traits, implying that there are common neural, physiologic, and genetic pathways. Among the many traits/conditions reported to correlate with RD are neuro-cognitive abilities not commonly thought of as reading-related (e.g., motor skills, perceptual closure, etc.), immune system function markers, handedness, Attention Deficit Hyperactivity Disorder (ADHD), Developmental Coordination Disorder (DCD), Speech Sound Disorder (SSD), memory performance, Specific Language Impairment (SLI), spelling performance, writing performance, and more (e.g., Fletcher et al.,1999; Bryden et al., 1994; Rhee et al., 2005; Angold et al., 1999).

Thus, as we have come to better understand RD we are now faced with even more questions and problems to solve than when we started back in the early 1900s! This is often the case in science and indicates actual progress. With this in mind, many of the essential problems facing geneticists today are listed below. I will expand on what I see as a key multifaceted issue raised in the list in the next section. I will do so by presenting challenges for current research practices and interpretations in a stepwise fashion and through illustrations of my essential argument in several different, but related ways.

Problems in phenotyping and genotyping reading-related disorders and their neurological basis are:

- the frequency of overlapping disorders (comorbidity);
- consideration of categorical or 'disease' model vs. continuous definitions that are multivariate in approach;
- apparent genetic and environmental etiologic variability;
- unclear or variable neural and cognitive networks resulting in the phenotype;
- variable or diffuse neuroanatomy that is implicitly tied to etiology and expression; and
- application of univariate approaches to an apparently multivariate phenotype.

THE PROBLEM OF OVERLAPPING DISORDERS AND THE CONSIDERATION OF UNITARY OR DISEASE MODELS VS. CONTINUOUS DEFINITIONS AND MULTIVARIATE ANALYSES

Comorbidity and related conditions

One of the more significant questions needing to be addressed today pertains to comorbidity and a great deal of work in this area is ongoing (see below).

Specifically, the field needs to continue its work to find a way to supplement our current thinking towards better including the research that demonstrates the presence of a high degree of RD comorbidity, as well as the related intra-individual and inter-individual variation in cognitive and behavioral profiles (Gilger and Kaplan, 2001; Gilger and Wilkins, in press; Shapiro et al., 2002; Pennington, 1999; Brody and Mills, 1997; Fuchs and Fuchs, 2002; Schumacher et al., 2007; Rhee et al., 2005; Angold et al., 1999). These co-occurrences, or phenotypic correlations, suggest strongly that in some proportion of cases the distinctions between disorders, or approaching these disorders as independent diagnostic categories (e.g., RD, ADHD, DCD, and so on) may, at times, be more artificial than real, and it may also muddle a complete understanding of the individual presenting a complicated symptom profile (Eide and Eide, 2006; Kaplan et al., 2001).

Still, the need for a perspective less limited to RD as a unitary disorder is even more evident when we consider the psychometric research on human abilities (e.g., multivariate factor analytic studies of specific cognitive and/or personality traits). Such factor analytic work, as well as related genetic, and neurological research, supports at least some degree of trait/disorder non-independence, often showing correlated cognitive abilities or cognitive factors, overlapping or multiple neurological substrates, and shared genes for phenotypes, brain morphology and brain function (e.g., Gayán et al., 2005; Ramus, 2004a; b; 2001; Rice and Brooks, 2004; Wood and Flowers, 1999; Voeller, 1999; Willcut et al., 2002; Olson et al., 1994; Sonuga-Barke, 2003; LaBuda et al., 1987; Defries et al., 1979; Thompson et al., 2002; Thompson et al., 2001; Bartley et al., 1997; Simonton, 2005; Butcher et al., 2006; Schumacher et al., 2007; Rhee et al., 2005; Angold et al., 1999). Therefore, when an individual exhibits characteristics of RD and correlated phenotypes it is not clear that the person is displaying co-occurring unitary abilities and/or deficits, or, rather, variable manifestations of one underlying impairment or construct, several underlying impairments or constructs, or etiologic substrates that may or may not be independent (Gilger and Kaplan, 2001; Gilger and Wilkins, in press). The resolution of the question raised here has an important theoretical and practical implications in that it addresses complications in diagnosis, explanatory models, statistical applications and treatment (Gilger and Kaplan, 2001; Gilger and Wilkins, in press; Jeffries and Everatt, 2004; Sonuga-Barke, 2003; Bergman and Magnussen, 1997; Lyytinen et al., 1995; Narhi and Ahonen, 1995; Cloninger, 2002). While the data indicate a genetic basis for much of the comorbidity seen, this finding could be better appreciated in clinical practice and continuing research efforts to identify 'RD genes'. More discussion on the latter issue appears below.

Correlated traits and multivariate phenotypes

To some degree, molecular genetics has begun to consider the issue of comorbidity. Typically this work limits itself to a couple of co-occuring conditions, like studies of the etiology of the RD-ADHD correlation, or perhaps the triad of RD-ADHD and SSD. As the field evolves it will be important to expand research to even better include the work in psychology and psychiatry that suggests that many specific cognitive and personality traits, across the continuum of measurement, are often correlated and this correlation is at least in part genetic in nature (Schumacher et al., 2007; Rhee et al., 2005; Angold et al., 1999). Multivariate models used in behavioral genetics have shown repeatedly that there is often a general genetic (and environmental) factor that along with specialized genetic (and environmental) factors contributes to trait variance and the intercorrelations among traits (e.g., Rutter et al., 1999a; b). Moreover, research suggests that age-to-age changes and/or stability in cognitive and behavioral traits and their interrcorrelations may reflect the operation of certain genes that tend to drive developmental variations and/or moderate developmental change (for studies related to reading see Wadsworth et al., 2006; Butcher et al., 2006). These multivariate models have been reported in a number of publications (see Rutter et al., 1999 a; b; Plomin et al., 2001; Plomin and McClearn, 1993; Silventoinen et al., 2007).

Figures 2.1 and 2.2 summarize how such models work. First, there is assumed to be a common cognitive or behavioral factor that explains some degree of the intercorrelations among several variables. Studies have shown empirically that such a model is reasonable for a number of correlated traits studied (Hewitt, 1993). Figure 2.1 shows such a model with six measured variables and one latent factor. For illustration we might imagine that these six variables are test scores on reading – related skills, memory, spatial and perceptual speed instruments, and so on. Simple expansions of this one factor model are possible to include more variables and factors.

Given such a psychometric model, quantitative genetic analyses have been performed using various familial configurations, including twins, siblings and adopted relatives. These studies provide a way to disentangle genetic and environmental components of within trait and between trait variances and covariances. In such studies it is common to talk about four components of phenotypic variance/covariance (see Rutter et al., 1999 a; b; Plomin et al., 2001; Plomin and McClearn, 1993; Silventoinen et al., 2007; Hewitt, 1993).

- Common genetic influences or the proportion of covariance among traits due to genes that effect multiple traits simultaneously (pleiotropy).
- Common environmental influences or the proportion of covariance among traits due to environmental factors that affect multiple traits simultaneously.
- Non-shared genetic influences or specific genetic effects that contribute to phenotypic variance in a way that is unique to each trait.
- Non-shared environmental influences or specific environmental effects that contribute to phenotypic variance in a way that is unique to each trait.

Figure 2.2 displays the typical findings of these genetic models. Namely, that there is often a common genetic factor and a common environmental factor that

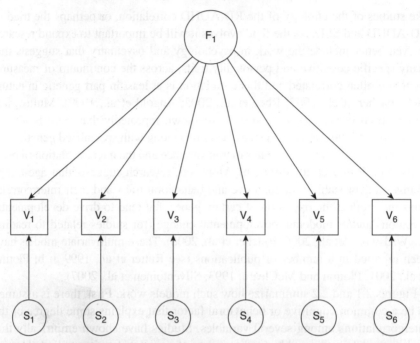

Figure 2.1   The psychometric, phenotypic or latent phenotype general model. Rectangular boxes, V1–V6 are measured variables or phenotypes. Circles are latent or unmeasured explanatory variables. As written, F1 is a common factor that modifies variances and covariances in and among the measured variables (normally covariances or correlations among V1–V6 would be shown by curved arrows connecting the rectangular boxes). S1–S6 represent sources of variation that are unique to each measured variable. The paths are shown by arrows, and they could be quantified in terms of partial correlation coefficients or factor loadings. From Hewitt, 1993.

explains a significant proportion of the shared variance among the six measured variables. Figure 2.2 also shows the existence of specific environmental and genetic effects that independently modify the variance within each of the separate variables tested. In this way, quantitative genetics tells us that there are certain genes that have pleiotropic effects probably because they operate on brain development and/or function in such a way that they have multiple effects at the measured level. Put another way, research supports some degree of biological non-independence among cognitive traits and conditions, and there is evidence that there are shared genes for correlated phenotypes, brain morphology and brain function (e.g., Bartley et al., 1997; Defries et al., 1979; LaBuda et al., 1987; Olson et al., 1994; Ramus, 2004a; b; 2001; Rice and Brooks, 2004; Sonuga-Barke, 2003; Thompson et al., 2001; Thompson et al., 2002; Willcut et al., 2002; Wood and Flowers, 1999; Voeller, 1999; Wadsworth et al., 2006; Butcher et al., 2006; Gayán et al., 2005). In spite of this data, most molecular

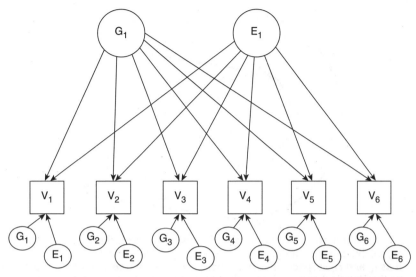

Figure 2.2   The biometric model. This model extends the psychometric model in Figure 2.1 to include the possibility that a general genetic factor (G) and a general environmental factor (E) could contribute to the variation and covariation among the sex measured variables. The circled variables G1–G6 and E1–E6 represent additional genetic and environmental factors that add specifically and uniquely to the V1–V6 variation/covariation. Thus, this model is an example of the commonly identified pleiotropic effects of genes on complex human phenotypes. (As in Figure 2.1 the covariation among the six variables is not shown.) From Hewitt, 2003.

work focuses just on RD, or just on related cognitive subcomponents of reading, and examines genes for RD phenotypes, one phenotype at a time (see more on this below). Of course some studies examine shared genes for specific comorbid disorders such as SSD or ADHD, but again, these are either limited bivariate analyses or univariate comparisons of candidate loci across disorders.

The Importance of the Genetic Correlation (r_G)

The multivariate statistical ability to detect trait correlations and the genetics that may lie behind them, will depend on the assumptions of the underlying model, sample size, strength of the relationships, etc. (Falconer and Mackay, 1996; Neale and Cardon, 1992; Plomin et al., 2001). However, it is important to bear in mind, that even traits with small or zero phenotypic correlations can have high genetic correlations (r_G). That means that apparently unrelated traits at the surface can still have much of their variance explained by the same genes.

Figure 2.3 shows a simple path diagram with two traits that are correlated. As the figure shows, this phenotypic correlation can reflect the operation of correlated genetic or environmental factors (r_G or r_E). If we follow the chains

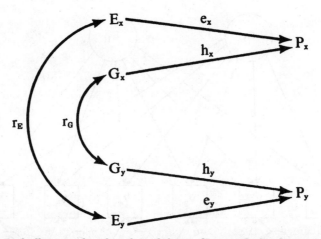

Figure 2.3 Path diagram showing the etiology of a correlation between two phenotypes (P_x and P_y). The genetic correlation and environmental correlation are shown as r_G and r_E, respectively. The other paths designated as h and e represent genetic (heritability) and environmental (environmentality) for each variable. From Plomin et al., 1980.

of paths in Figure 2.3 we can see how the genetic and environmental causes or correlations combine to give the phenotypic correlation:

$$r_{px\text{-}py} = h_x h_y r_G + e_x e_y r_E \qquad\qquad 2.1$$

where $r_{px\text{-}py}$ is the phenotypic correlation between variable x and y; h_x and h_y represent the square roots of the trait heritabilities; e_x and e_y are the square roots of the enviromentalities for traits x and y; r_G is the genetic correlation, and; r_E is the environmental correlation.

Examination of Equation 2.1 reveals that the degree to which shared genes may explain phenotypic correlations depends on the heritabilities for the traits in question: the higher the heritabilities the more important the r_G may be. The interactive effects of genes and environments shown in 2.1 also suggests that we can not determine how important r_G is based on the magnitude and sign of a phenotypic correlation alone. It is even possible for a phenotypic correlation to be negative in sign even though shared genes are extremely important factors in this co-varying relationship (Falconer and Mackay, 1996; Plomin et al. 2001). Therefore, the efficient and resource limited investigator should not always summarily dismiss covariates of small or even negative magnitude as he or she searches for what may be pleiotropic genes effecting multiple traits under study.

In summary then, I would advocate that univariate (limited to RD phenotypes) or even bivariate (comorbidity) approaches to the genetic study of RD are important first steps. But to really advance the field and guide us towards an understanding of how the brain develops and functions in response to genes requires a broader more multivariate approach. Others have offered similar ideas (see Zhou et al., 1989; Andreou and Kuntsi, 2005; Smalley et al., 2004; Thompson et al., 2002). Although quantitative genetics has made the need for this approach explicit, molecular genetics still prefers the unitary or disease oriented approach to RD, even when looking at RD as a continuous measure or comorbid condition.

I want to emphasize here that it is unlikely that there is a simple one-to-one mapping of genes to brain structures or brain areas to cognitive abilities. This is especially true when the concerns are complex cognitive traits, the effects of developmental genes, and the development of cognitive abilities across the lifespan (Changeaux, 1985; Hahn et al., 1978; Johnson et al., 2002; Jones and Murray, 1991; Noctor, et al., 2001; Scerif and Karmiloff-Smith, 2005; Smalley et al., 2004; Thomspon et al., 2001). Perhaps the preference for basic univariate approaches in molecular genetics is due to the statistical complications that exist when analyzing markers or loci using multiple phenotypes simultaneously (e.g., Cherny et al., 2004). But it should not be an insurmountable problem and the practice of reporting on one phenotype at a time in RD research remains standard practice.

The multivariate problem as a problem of discriminate validity

Thus far, this paper has advocated for a more thorough consideration of the multivariate genetic issues in the study of RD. Yet another way to look at this issue pertains to 'discriminate validity'.

At the molecular level, ten or more tentative genes or 'susceptibility alleles' have already been identified as possible contributors to RD risk (reviewed in Schumacher et al., 2007; Pennington, 2002; Smith and Gilger, 2007) and research points out that the genes putting individuals at risk for RD do not necessarily correspond to specific or independent cognitive aspects of reading ability such as memory, orthographic coding or phoneme processing (Fisher et al., 1999; Gayán et al., 1999; Grigorenko et al., 1997; Fisher et al., 2002; Olson et al., 1994; Smith and Gilger, 2006; Gayán and Olson, 2003; Schulte-Körne, 2001; Schumacher et al., 2007). In other words, there are probably multiple heterogeneous effects of the RD risk genes that act alone or together to give rise to multiple profiles of reading-related skills (Ramus, 2001; Frith, 2001; Gilger and Kaplan, 2001; Gilger and Wilkins, in press).

Yet, if you examine the papers published in roughly the last five years, it is clear that researchers are still approaching RD as unitary trait and the genes for RD as 'RD genes', when in fact the authors do not address whether or not the 'RD genes' are related to other phenotypes as well. That is, they will report if genetic markers are associated with RD phenotypes but they do not bother to report if and how these same markers are associated with other phenotypes, save the instances where a specific comorbidity is being discussed.

Some support for my argument, that genetics has typically taken this approach to RD, is shown in Table 2.1 below. The table summarzies over 30 studies that report on 'RD genes' for roughly the past five years. It shows that while the variables going into the diagnosis of RD may be different, in none of these studies do the authors do a good job of addressing if and how these 'RD genes' correlate or link to other cognitive traits. This seems doable in that many of these studies are quite large and include huge psychometric batteries spanning all of the known specific cognitive (and personality) constructs.

One reason why RD genetics has gotten on this track is that focused definitions and limited phenotypes are important in molecular work. The problem is that this limited perspective is best suited to medical diseases and not complex, largely multigene traits, such as cognition and personality. Moreover, while refining RD phenotypes is important work, there is a growing need to expand the conceptualization of learning disability genes, and perhaps better acknowledge that the effects of such genes are not limited to fine grain univariate phenotypes.

In some ways this practice in publication is an issue of a failure to prove 'discriminate validity' for the genes under study. Discriminate validity can be defined as follows (see clinical example in Chung and Martin, 2002): '... A (scientifically necessary) criterion imposed on a measure of a construct requiring that it not correlate too highly with measures from which it is supposed to differ ...' If these genes are related to other traits, can we really consider these 'RD genes' or, rather, should we consider them 'neurodevelopmental genes' or 'neural function genes' that affect the brain to yield variance in a number of abilities/traits simultaneously? For now, I prefer the latter nomenclature.

Special point for consideration: The other end of the continuum of ability

In the prior sections I discussed the issue of comorbidity and correlated phenotypes. I also talked about multivariate approaches which rely on continuous data but are not limited to the low-end of the continuum. I want to briefly highlight that while comorbidity and low-end phenotypic issues are typically the focus of research on RD, there is a less pathological view of a related phenomenon: twice exceptionality or TE, where both learning deficits and higher-order learning abilities are present in the same person. Indeed, many of today's methods of studying the neuroscience of comorbidity and disabilities could, and should, be extended to the study of TE.

There are data indicating that RDs (and other learning disorders or LDs) can be significantly represented in gifted populations (e.g., Brody and Mills, 1997; Ruban and Reis, 2005; Geschwind, 1982; Geschwind and Galaburda, 1987; Karolyi and Winner, 2004). Some estimates, though fraught with definitional

Table 2.1   Genes and Dyslexia Phenotype Linkage

Reference	Dyslexia Phenotype	Region
Grigorenko et al., 2001	Reading and Verbal Ability	1p36
Tzenova et al., 2004	Phonologic Awareness, Coding, Spelling, Rapid Automatized (RAM), and Reading History	1p36
Fagerheim et al., 1999	Orthographic, Phonological, Reading, and Spelling Abilities	2p16-p15
Fisher et al., 2002	Single-Word Reading, Spelling, Phoneme Awareness, Phonological Decoding Orthographic Coding, Orthographic Processing	2p16-p15
Francks et al., 2002	Single-Word Reading, Spelling, Phoneme Awareness, Phonological Decoding Orthographic Coding, Orthographic Processing	2p16-p15
Petryshen et al., 2002	Phonological Coding, Phonological Awareness, Orthographic Coding, Reading History, and Spelling	2p16-p15
Kaminen et al., 2003	Reading, Spelling, Phonological Awareness, Rapid Naming, Verbal Short Term Memory and IQ	2p11
Peyrard-Janvid et al., 2004	Pseudo as well as Non-Word Reading and Writing	2p11
Noploa-Hemmi et al., 2001	Pseudo as well as Non-Word Reading and Writing	3p12-q13
Fisher et al., 2002	Single-Word Reading, Spelling, Phoneme Awareness, Phonological Decoding Orthographic Coding, Orthographic Processing	3p12-q13
Fisher et al., 1999	Word-Recognition, IQ-Reading Discrepancy, Orthographic Coding, and Phonological Decoding	6p22.2
Gayán et al., 1999	IQ, Reading and Language Skills	6p22.2
Grigorenko et al., 2000	Phonemic Awareness, Phonological Decoding, Rapid Automatized Naming, Single-Word Reading, Vocabulary, and Spelling	6p22.2
Fisher et al., 2002	Single-Word Reading, Spelling, Phoneme Awareness, Phonological Decoding Orthographic Coding, Orthographic Processing	6p22.2
Kaplan et al., 2002	Orthographic Choice, Homonym Choice, OC Composite, Oral Reading of Non-Words, Phoneme-Transposition, Phoneme Deletion, Word Recognition, Reading Recognition, Reading Comprehension, and Spelling	6p22.2
Turic et al., 2003	Prose Reading, Word Recognition, Reading Comprehension, Spelling, Reading Accuracy, Phonologic Naming, Orthographic Naming, Automatized Naming, Single-Word Reading, and Single-Word Spelling	6p22.2
Marlow et al., 2003	Single-Word Reading, Spelling, Phonologic Processes, Orthographic Processes, and IQ	6p22.2
Deffenbacher et al., 2004	Reading, Spelling, Cognitive ability, Isolate and Manipulate Phonemes in Speech, Non-Word Reading, Single-Word Reading, and Choose Target Words that were Phonologically Similar	6p22.2
Francks et al., 2004	Single-Word Reading, Spelling, Phonological Decoding, Phonemic Awareness, Orthographic Coding (Spelling Patterns and Irregular Words), Orthographic Choice, Verbal Reasoning, Non-Verbal Reasoning	6p22.2
Petryshen et al., 2001	Qualitative phonological coding, phonological awareness, phonological coding, spelling, and rapid automatized naming speed	6q13-q16.2
Kaminen et al., 2003	Reading, Spelling, Phonological Awareness, Rapid Naming, Verbal Short Term Memory, and IQ	7q32
Hsiung et al., 2004	Phonological Coding, Phonological Awareness, Spelling, Rapid Automatized Naming (RAM), and IQ	11p15.5
Bartlett et al., 2002	Language, Reading, IQ	13q21

Continued

Table 2.1   Genes and Dyslexia Phenotype Linkage—cont'd

Reference	Dyslexia Phenotype	Region
Nöthen et al., 1999	IQ, Spelling, Questionnaire	15q21
Morris et al., 2000	IQ, Reading (Reading age level of 2.5 years behind their age), Prose Reading	15q21
Nopola-Hemmi et al., 2000	Reading, Writing, Phonological Processing, Phonological Retrieval, Verbal Short Term Memory and Reading Comprehension Tasks	15q21
Taipale et al., 2003	Reading, Spelling, Phonological Awareness, Rapid Automatized Naming, and Verbal Short Term Memory	15q21
Chapman et al., 2004	Phonological Decoding, Single-Word Reading, VIQ	15q21
Marino et al., 2004	Assumed an Additive Pattern of Inheritance	15q21
Wigg et al., 2004	Reading, Spelling, Phonological Awareness, Rapid Naming Skills, Language Ability	15q21
Fisher et al., 2002	Single-Word Reading, Phonological processing, Orthographic processing, Phoneme awareness	18p11.2
Fisher et al., 2002	Single-Word Reading, Spelling, Phoneme Awareness, Phonological Decoding Orthographic Coding, Orthographic Processing	Xq27.3
Igo et al., 2006	Real-Word Reading (RWR)	13
Newbury et al., 2005	Review of Phonological Short-Term Memory (STM) and Specific-Language Impairment (SLI)	16
The SLI Consortium, 2002	Expressive and Receptive Language, Phonological Short Term Memory (Non- Word Repetition), IQ	16q and 19q
Raskind et al., 2005	Phonological Decoding (Speed and Accuracy), Non-Word Repetition	2q

and sampling problems, have placed the prevalence rates of TE as low as 1 per cent but with an upper-end of 3, 5 or even 36 per cent (Ruban and Reiss, 2005; Baum and Owen, 1988; McCoach et al., 2004). If severe cases of disabilities are removed from these data (e.g., mental retardation, autism, etc.) and the focus is on developmentally normal but reading disordered children, the rates may be on the low-end, say roughly 1–3 per cent. That is still a relatively high rate of TE in practice or in the classroom.

For discussion purposes, a simple test of the RD-Gifted association, and if the two conditions are independent, can be conducted using the Law of Independent Probabilities and the Multiplicative Rule of Probabilities. If you assume that, say, RD has a base rate of around 7 per cent and is truly independent from giftedness, and if you further, arbitrarily, choose a base rate of gifted IQ to be around 5 per cent, the expected base rate of the co-occurrence of the two conditions can be obtained by multiplying the two rates: 7% x 5% = 0.0035%.[2] This 0.0035 per cent is significantly lower that the observed 3–5 per cent cited above. Thus, this simple model (albeit fraught with methodological problems) suggests some support for the folklore that exists that giftedness is over-represented in RD populations (e.g., West, 1999; Geschwind, 1982; Geschwind and Galaburda, 1987) and more research of better design and control is needed to properly address this belief.

However, recall that even small phenotypic associations can reflect strong underlying genetic correlations or shared genes. Thus, focusing on only the learning deficit (e.g., RD) in TE individuals may limit our understanding of their neurocognitive profile, the etiology of this profile, and what approaches to treatment or educational settings may be best. Current neuroscientific theoretical approaches to the study and treatment of RD do not address twice exceptionality in any explicit or meaningful way. At best, contemporary thinking views RD and giftedness as separate and unrelated conditions that just happen to co-occur. In the majority of cases this may be true, but I suggest that some RD-gifted cases may represent subtypes where the learning problem shares etiology with the learning gift. In other words, the genes that put people at risk for RD operate by modifying brain development and function and these same neural correlates of gene effects may also operate to put people at 'risk' for certain high abilities or gifts (see also Geschwind and Galaburda, 1987; Benbow, 1988; Cassanova et al., 2002). This possibility needs to be examined further. Some preliminary work in our lab in fact supports the hypothesis that in certain cases, unique brain morphologies are related to RD and high spatial skills in family members and that this may be the basis for some of the reports and theories that learning deficits and learning gifts can be associated at the etiologic level (Craggs et al., 2006). Therefore, genetic research that considers comorbidity should also consider giftedness as a potentially correlated phenotype and in this way, perhaps, provide important information on neurogenetics and giftedness as a developmental construct.

CLOSING REMARKS

In this paper I have put forth some challenges to the current practices in molecular genetic and neuroscientific research. I do so with great respect as I recognize how very far the field has come given the hard work of many scientists and clinicians. However, without new challenges and thinking a field can remain overly focused and limited. So, in summary I want to reify what I see as some important considerations for future work.

First, the molecular genetic approaches need to be reconciled better with the volumous literature in quantitative genetics that shows, clearly, that multivariate approaches are valid and reflect the reality of the functioning brain. Although this research does not directly examine genes or the brain per se, it does have strong implications about the underlying genetic, environmental and neuro-logical structure of RD, its related conditions and traits. At least it seems to be a missed opportunity to learn about the brain given that many molecular genetics labs have multivariate phenotypic data available to them but do not examine these data unless they are reading-related.

Second, in published works the authors should be cautious how they talk about genes. Stating that there is a risk gene for RD or a gene for RD on, say, chromosome 3 (Hannula-Jouppi et al., 2005), does not do justice to what the gene may really be. Sure, such a gene may influence reading, but until we know if and how it influences math, naming, attention, IQ, motor skills, or other, we should not call it an 'RD gene'. I propose that we refer to such genes as genes that lead to atypical brain development or brain development/function that in turn effects reading and maybe other traits as well (Gilger and Kaplan, 2001; Gilger and Wise, 2004; Gilger and Wilkins, in press; see example in Dick et al., 2007). The word 'atypical' simply means deviating to some degree on either side of the hypothetical norm of neural development or function or expressed and measured ability.

Consider this point further: even the effects of a single gene variant for traits as complex as human learning may yield multiple typical and atypical behaviors, especially if this gene is influential during the early stages of neural development and brain organization, or if it effects lower levels of neural organization upon which higher levels depend (Luria, 1973; Huttenlocher, 2002; Greenough et al., 2002; Conn, 1992; Gerlai, 1996; Rondi-Reig et al., 1999; Scerif and Karmiloff-Smith, 2005; Johnson et al., 2002; Hahn et al., 1978; Changeaux, 1985; Jones and Murray, 1991; Noctor et al., 2001). Examples relevant to this point include reports finding genes on chromosomes 3 and 6 that are linked to RD risk (Hannula-Jouppi et al., 2005; Meng et al., 2005). These genes are thought to be active in early neurodevelopment, such as neuronal migration. In one case (Meng et al., 2005) variants of the DCDC2 gene on chromosome 6 were shown to cause neuronal migration errors. Although it is not known if these errors show up preferentially in the left hemisphere as would be expected given current preferred theories.

It is very possible that a developmental gene important to cortical cell migration or connection such as DCDC2 for instance, would effect more than one brain area to varying degrees and thus have the potential to influence multiple behavioral areas. Even if the discrimination of primary LD subtypes (RD vs. math disability vs. ADHD, etc.) were a function of several distinct major genes influencing a different primary brain area for each disorder, the enormous co-occurrence of these conditions argues for at least some degree of multifocal action of the pertinent gene(s) and/or multifocal neurodevelopmental effects of single genes that originally operated on only specific brain areas (see also Scerif and Karmiloff-Smith, 2005; Marcus, 2004). Similarly, it is possible that through their broad neurodevelopmental effects, the genes for risk for RD may also yield some unique brains with above average capabilities to process, encode and produce information (Craggs et al., 2006). Interestingly, when other, even non-language areas of the RD brain are examined, they are often found to be structurally atypical as well (e.g., Kibby et al., 2008; Démonet et al., 2004; Mody, 2004; Nicolson and Fawcett, 2001) and as noted above, multivariate behavioral genetic research suggests that many specific cognitive traits have genes in common (Light et al., 1998; Butcher et al., 2006; Mody, 2004).

In closing, Figure 2.4 illustrates a dynamic process between the common and necessary approach to the study of RD and the equally important and broader

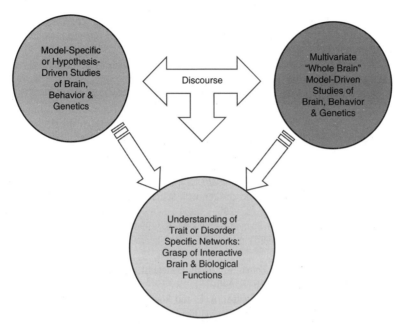

Figure 2.4   Interactive discourse towards the advancement of the genetics of learning disorders. Modified from Gilger & Wilkins (in press).

perspective advocated for herein. Note that both approaches are called for and each can advise the other. It is my hope that as methods advance and our knowledge grows, the field will allow for this scientific discourse.

NOTES

1 Portions of this chapter were presented at the International Workshop On Dyslexia Genetics in Helsinki, Biomedicum, Helsinki, Finland, November, 2006. Funded in part by an APA Foundation Grant, The Esther Katz Rosen Grant for Research and Programs on Giftedness in Children, 2006-2007 (Gilger, PI).

2 Broader definitions of poor reading that do not require a significant discrepancy with non-reading abilities may yield prevalences as high as 20 per cent or more, and in other linguistic populations where written language is more phonetically consistent than English, such as Italian, the frequency of RD can be significantly lower (Paulesu et al., 2001).

REFERENCES

Andreou, P. and Kuntsi, J. (2005) 'Combining quantitative genetic, molecular genetic and cognitive-experimental methods', *Psychiatry*, 4 (12): 27–30.

Angold, A., Costellos, E. J. and Erkanli, A. (1999) 'Comorbidity', *Journal of Child Psychology and Psychiatry and Allied Disciplines*, 40 (1): 57–87.

Bartlett, C. W., Flax, J. F., Logue, M. W., Vieland, V. J., Basset, A. S., Tallal, P. and Brzustowicz, L. M. (2002) 'A major locus for specific language impairments is located on 13q21', *American Journal of Human Genetics*, 71: 45–55.

Bartley, A. J., Jones, D. W. and Weinberger, D. R. (1997) 'Genetic variability of human brain size and cortical gyral patterns', *Brain*, 120: 257–269.

Baum, S., and Owen, S. (1988) 'Learning disabled students: How are they different?' *Gifted Child Quarterly*, 32: 321–326.

Benbow, C. P. (1988) 'Sex differences in mathematical reasoning ability in intellectually talented preadolescents: their nature, effects, and possible causes', *Brain and Behavioral Sciences*, 11: 169–232.

Bergman, L. R. and Magnusson, D. (1997) 'A person-oriented approach in research on developmental psychopathology', *Development and Psychopathology*, 9: 291–319.

Brody, L. E. and Mills, C. J. (1997) 'Gifted children with learning disabilities: A review of the issues', *Journal of Learning Disabilities*, 30: 282–296.

Bryden, M. P., MacManus, I. C. and Bulman-Fleming, M. B. (1994) 'Evaluating the empirical support for the Geschwind-Behan-Galaburda model of cerebral lateralization', *Brain and Cognition*, 26: 103–167.

Butcher, L. M., Kennedy, J. K. and Plomin, R. (2006) 'Generalist genes and cognitive neuroscience', *Current Opinion in Neurobiology*, 16 (2): 145–151.

Casanova, M. F., Buxhoeveden, D. P., Switala, A. E. and Roy, E. (2002) 'Minicolumnar pathology in autism', *Neurology*, 58: 428–432.

Changeaux, J.-P. (1985) *Neuronal Man.* New York: Oxford.

Chapman, N. H., Igo, R. P., Thompson, J. B., Matsushita, M., Brkanac, Z., Holzman, T., Berninger, V. W., Wijsman, E. M. and Raskind, W. H. (2004) 'Linkage analysis of four regions previously implicated in dyslexia: Confirmation of a locus on chromosome 15q', *American Journal of Medical Genetics Part B (Neuropsychiatric Genetics)*, 131B: 67–75.

Cherny, S. S., Sham, P. C. and Cardon, L. R. (2004) 'Introduction to the special issue on variance components methods for mapping quantitative trait loci', *Behavior Genetics*, 34: 125–126.

Chung, T. and Martin, C. S. (2002) 'Concurrent and discriminant validity of DSM–IV symptoms of impaired control over alcohol consumption in adolescents', *Alcoholism: Clinical and Experimental Research*, 26 (4): 485–492

Clements, S.G. and Peters, J. E. (1962)'Minimal brain dysfunctions in the school-age child', *Archives of General Psychiatry*, 6: 185–197.

Cloninger, C. R. (2002) 'Implications of comorbidity for the classification of mental disorders: The need for a psychobiology of coherence', in M. Maj, W. Gaebel, J. J. Lopez-Ibor, and N. Sartorius (eds), *Psychiatric Diagnosis and Classification.* John Wiley and Sons. pp. 79–106.

Conn, M.T. (ed) (1992) *Gene expression in neural tissue.* San Diego, CA: Academic.

Craggs, J., Sanchez, J., Kibby, M., Gilger, J. and Hynd, G. (2006) 'Brain morphological and neuropsychological profiles of a family displaying superior nonverbal intelligence and dyslexia', *Cortex*, 42: 1107–1118.

Deffenbacher, K. E., Kenyon, J. B., Hoover, D. M., Olson, R. K., Pennington, B. F., Defries, J. C. and Smith, S. D. (2004) 'Refinement of the 6p21.3 quantitative trait locus influencing dyslexia: Linkage and association analysis', *Human Genetics*, 115: 128–138.

Defries, J. C., Johnson, R. C., Kuse, A. R., McClearn, G. E., Polovina, J., Vandenberg, S. G. and Wilson, J. R. (1979) 'Familial resemblance for specific cognitive abilities', *Behavioral Genetics*, 9: 23–43.

Démonet, J.-F., Taylor, M. J. and Chaix, Y. (2004) 'Developmental dyslexia', *Lancet*, 363: 1451–1460.

Dick, D. M., Aliev, F., Kramer, J. Wang, J. C., Hinrichs, A., Bertelsen, S., Kuperman, S., Schuckit, M., Nurnberger Jr., J., Edenberg, H. J., Porjesz, B., Begleiter, H., Hesselbrock, V., Goate, A. and Bierut, L. (2007) 'Association of CHRM2 with IQ: converging evidence for a gene influencing intelligence', *Behavioral Genetics*, 37: 265–272.

Doris, J. L. (1998) 'Dyslexia: the evolution of a concept', in B. K. Shapiro, P. J. Accardo, and A. J. Capute (eds), *Specific reading disability: a view of the spectrum.* Timonium, MD: York Press. pp. 3–20.

Eide, B. and Eide, F. (2006) *The mislabeled child: how understanding your child's unique learning style can open the door to success*. New York: Hyperion.

Fagerheim, T., Raeymaekers, P., Tønnessen, F. E., Pedersen, M., Tranebjærg, L. and Lubs, H. A. (1999) 'A new gene (DYX3) for dyslexia is located on chromosome 2', *J. Med. Genet.*, 36: 664–669.

Falconer, D.S. and Mackay, T.F.C. (1996) *Introduction to quantitative genetics* (4th ed.) New York: Longman.

Fisher, S. E. and Defries, J. C. (2002) 'Developmental dyslexia: Genetic dissection of a complex cognitive trait', *Neuroscience (Nature Reviews)*, 3: 767–780.

Fisher, S. E., Francks, C., Marlow, A. J., MacPhie, I. L., Newbury, D. F., Cardon, L. R., et al. (2002) 'Independent genome–wide scans identify a chromosome 18 quantitative–trait locus influencing dyslexia', *Nature Genetics*, 30: 86–91.

Fisher, S. E., Marlow, A. J., Lamb, J., Maestrini, E., Williams, D. F., Richardson, A. J., et al. (1999) 'A quantitative-trait locus on chromosome 6p influences different aspects of developmental dyslexia', *American Journal of Human Genetics*, 64: 146–156.

Fletcher, J. M., Lyon, G. R., Fuchs, L. S. and Barnes, M. A. (2007) *Learning disabilities: From identification to intervention*. New York, NY: Guilford Press.

Fletcher, J. M., Shaywitz, S. E. and Shaywitz, B. A. (1999) 'Comorbidity of learning and attention disorders. Separate but equal', *Pediatric Clinics of North America*, 46 (5): 885–897.

Francks, C., Fisher, S. E., Olson, R. K., Pennington, B. F., Smith, S. D., Defries, J. C. and Monaco, A. P. (2002) 'Fine mapping of the chromosome 2p12–16 dyslexia susceptibility locus: quantitative association analysis and positional candidate genes SEMA4F and OTX1', *Psychiatric Genetics*, 12: 35–41.

Francks, C., Paracchini, S., Smith, S. D., Richardson, A. J., Scerri, T. S., Cardon, L. R., Marlow, A. J. et al. (2004) 'A 77–kilobase region of chromosome 6p22.2 is associated with dyslexia in families from the United Kingdom and from the United States', *American Journal of Human Genetics*, 75: 1046–1058.

Frith, U. (2001) 'What framework should we use for understanding developmental disorders?', *Developmental Neuropsychology*, 20 (2): 555–563.

Fuchs, L. S. and Fuchs, D. (2002) 'Mathematical problem-solving profiles of students with mathematics disabilities with and without comorbid reading disabilities', *Journal of Learning Disabilities*, 35: 564–574.

Gayán, J. and Olson, R. K. (2003) 'Genetic and environmental influences on individual differences in printed word recognition', *J Exp Child Psychol*, 84 (2): 97–123.

Gayán, J., Smith, S. D., Cherny, S. S., Cardon, L. R., Fulker, D. W., Brower, A. M., et al. (1999) 'Quantitative-trait locus for specific language and reading deficits on chromosome 6p', *American Journal of Human Genetics*, 64: 157–164.

Gayán, J., Willcutt, E. G., Fisher, S. E., Francks, C., Cardon, L. R., Olson, R. K., Pennington, B. F., Smith, S. D., Monaco, A. P. and Defries, J. C. (2005) 'Bivariate linkage scan for reading disability and attention deficit–hyperactivity disorder localizes pleiotropic loci', *Journal of Child Psychology and Psychiatry*, 46 (10): 1045–1056.

Gerlai, R. (1996) 'Gene-targeting studies of mammalian behavior: Is it the mutation or the background genotype?', *Trends in Neuroscience*, 19: 177–181.

Geschwind, N. (1982) 'Why Orton was right', The Annals of Dyslexia, 32. The Orton Dyslexia Society Reprint No. 98.

Geschwind, N. and Galaburda, A. M. (1987) *Cerebral lateralization: Biological mechanisms, associations and pathology*. Cambridge, MA: MIT Press.

Gilger, J. W., Borecki, I. B., Smith, S. D., DeFries, J. C. and Pennington, B. F (1996) 'The etiology of extreme scores for complex phenotypes: an illustration using reading performance', in C. H. Chase, G. D. Rosen, and G. F. Sherman (eds) *Developmental dyslexia: neural, cognitive, and genetic mechanisms*. Timonium, MD; York Press. pp. 63–85.

Gilger, J.W. and Kaplan, B.J. (2001) 'The neuropsychology of dyslexia: The concept of atypical brain development', *Developmental Neuropsychology*, 20: 469–486.

Gilger, J. and Wilkins, M. (in press) 'Atypical neurodevelopmental variation as a basis for learning disorders', in M. Mody and E. Silliman (eds), *Language impairment and reading disability: Interactions among brain, behavior, and experience.* (Series on Challenges in Language and Literacy) Guilford Press.

Gilger, J.W. and Wise, S. (2004) 'Genetic correlates of language and literacy', in C. Addison Stone, E.R. Silliman, B.J. Ehren, and K. Apel (eds) *Handbook of language and literacy development and disorders.* New York: Guilford Press.

Greenough, W. T, Black, J. E. and Wallace, C. S. (2002) 'Experience and brain development', in Johnson, M. H., Munakata, Y., and Gilmore, R. O. (eds), *Brain Development and Cognition: A Reader.* Blackwell Publishers. pp. 186–216.

Grigorenko, E. L., Wood, F. B., Meyer, M. S. and Pauls, D. L. (2000) 'Chromosome 6p influences on different dyslexia–related cognitive processes: Further confirmation', *American Journal of Human Genetics,* 66: 715–723.

Grigorenko, E., L., Wood, F. B., Meyer, M. S., Pauls, J. E. D., Hart, L. A. and Pauls, D. L. (2001) 'Linkage studies suggest a possible locus for developmental dyslexia on chromosome 1p', *American Journal of Medical Genetics (Neuropsychiatric Genetics),* 105: 120–129.

Grigorenko, E.L., Wood, F.B., Meyer, M.S., Hart, L.A., Speed, W.C., Shuster, A. and Pauls, D.L. (1997) 'Susceptibility loci for distinct components of developmental dyslexia on chromosomes 6 and 15', *American Journal of Human Genetics,* 60: 27–39.

Hahn, W. E., van Ness, J. and Maxwell, I. H. (1978) 'Complex population of mRNA sequences in large polydenylylated nuclear RNA molecules', *Proceedings of the National Academy of Science,* 75: 5544–5547.

Hallgren, B. (1950) 'Specific dyslexia (congenital word–blindness): A clinical and genetic study', *Acta Psychiatrica et Neurologica Supplement,* 65: 1–287.

Hannula-Jouppi, K., Kaminen-Ahola, N., Taipale, M., Edlund, R., Nopola-Hemmi, J., et al. (2005) 'The axon guidance receptor gene ROBO1 is a candidate gene for developmental dyslexia', *PLoS Genetics,* 1 (4): e50.

Hewitt, J. K. (1993) 'The new quantitative genetic epidemiology of behavior', in R. Plomin and G. McClearn (eds), *Nature, nurture, and psychology.* Washington, D.C.; American Psychological Association. pp. 401–415.

Hinshelwood, J. (1895) 'Word-blindness and visual memory', *Lancet,* 2: 1564–1570.

Hinshelwood, J. (1917) *Congenital word-blindness.* Chicago: Medical Book Co.

Hsiung, G-Y. R., Kaplan, B. J., Petryshen, T. L., Lu, S. and Field, L. L. (2004) 'A dyslexia susceptibility locus (DYX7) linked to dopamine D4 receptor (DRD4) region on chromosome 11p15.5', *American Journal of Medical Genetics Part B (Neuropsychiatric Genetics),* 125B: 112–119.

Huttenlocher, P. R. (2002) *Neural plasticity: The effects of the environment on the development of the cerebral cortex.* Cambridge, MA: Harvard University Press.

Igo Jr., R. P., Chapman, N. H., Berninger, V. W., Matsushita, M., Brkanac, Z., Rothstein, J. H., et al. (2006) Genome wide scan for real–word reading subphenotypes of dyslexia: Novel chromosome 13 locus and genetic complexity. *American Journal of Medical Genetics Part B (Neuropsychiatric Genetics),* 141B: 15–27.

Jeffries, S. and Everatt, J. (2004) 'Working memory: Its role in dyslexia and other specific learning difficulties', *Dyslexia,* 10: 196–214.

Johnson, M. H., Munakata, Y. and Gilmore, R. O. (2002) *Brain Development and Cognition: A Reader.* Blackwell Publishers

Jones, P. and Murray, R. M. (1991) 'The genetics of schizophrenia is the genetics of neurodevelopment', *British Journal of Psychiatry,* 158: 615–623.

Kaminen, N., Hannula-Jouppi, K., Kestilä, M., Lahermo, P., Muller, K., Kaaranen, M., et al. (2003) 'A genome scan for developmental dyslexia confirms linkage to chromosome 2p11 and suggests a new locus on 7q32', *J Med. Genet.,* 40: 340–345.

Kaplan, B. J., Dewey, D. M., Crawford, S. G. and Wilson, B. N. (2001) 'The term comorbidity is of questionable value in reference to developmental disorders: Data and theory', *Journal of Learning Disabilities,* 34, 555–565.

Kaplan, D. E., Gayán, J., Ahn, J., Won, T–W, Pauls, D., Olson, R. K., et al. (2002) Evidence for linkage and association with reading disability on 6p21.3–22. *American Journal of Human Genetics*, 70, 1287–1298.

Kibby, M. Y., Facher, J. B., Markanen, R., Hynd, G. W. (2008) 'A quantitative MRI analysis of the cerebellar deficit hypothesis of dyslexia', *Journal of Child Neurology*.

Kirk, S. A. and Elkins, J. (1975) 'Characteristics of children enrolled in the child service demonstration centers', *Journal of Learning Disabilities*, 8: 630–637.

LaBuda, M., DeFries, J. C. and Fulker, D. W. (1987) 'Genetic and environmental covariance structures among WISC-R subtests: A twin study', *Intelligence*, 11: 233–244.

Light, J. G., DeFries, J. C. and Olson, R. K. (1998) 'Multivariate behavioral genetic analysis of achievement and cognitive measures in reading-disabled and control twin pairs', *Human Biology*, 70 (2): 215–237.

Luria, A. R. (1973) *The working brain*. Baltimore, MD: Penguin.

Lyytinen, H., Leinonen, M., Nikula, M., Aro, M. and Leiwo, M. (1995) 'In search of the core features of dyslexia: Observations concerning dyslexia in the highly orthographic regular Finnish language', in V. W. Beringer (ed.), *The varieties of orthographic knowledge II: Relationships to phonology, reading, and writing*. Dordrecht, The Netherlands: Kluwer.

Marcus, G. (2004) *The Birth of the Mind: How a Tiny Number of Genes Creates the Complexities of Human Thought*. Basic Books.

Marino, C., Giorda, R., Vanzin, L., Nobile, M., Lorusso, M. L., Baschirotto, C., et al. (2004) 'A locus on 15q15–1qter influences dyslexia: Further support from a transmission/disequilibrium study in an Italian speaking population', *J. Med. Genet.*, 41: 42–46.

Marlow, A. J., Fisher, S. E., Francks, C., MacPhie, L., Cherney, S. S. and Richardson, A. J. (2003) 'Use of multivariate linkage analysis for dissection of a complex cognitive trait', *American Journal of Human Genetics*, 72: 561–570.

McCoach, D. B., Kehle, T. J., Bray, M. A. and Siegle, D. (2004) 'The identification of gifted students with learning disabilities: challenges, controversies, and promising practices', in T. Newman, and R. Sternberg (eds), *Students with Both Gifts and Learning Disabilities: Identification, Assessment, and Outcomes*. 25, 31–47.

Meng, H., Smith, S. D., Hager, K., Held, M., Liu, J., Olson, R., K., et al. (2005) 'DCDC2 is associated with reading disability and modulates neuronal development in the brain', *Proceedings of the National Academy of Sciences*, 102 (47): 17053–17058.

Miles, T. R. and Haslam, M. N. (1986) 'Dyslexia: Anomaly or normal variation?', *Annals of Dyslexia*, 36: 103–117.

Mody, M. (2004) 'Neurobiological correlates of language and reading impairments', in C. A. Stone, E. R. Silliman, B. J. Ehren and K. Apel (eds) *Handbook of language and literacy development and disorders*. New York: Guilford Press. pp. 49–72.

Morgan, B. S. (1914) *The backward child*. New York: P. Putnam's Sons.

Morgan, W. P. (1896) 'A case of congenital word blindness', *British Medical Journal*, 2: 1378.

Morris, D. W., Robinson, L., Turic, D., Duke, M., Webb, V., Milham, C., et al. (2000) 'Family-based association mapping provides evidence for a gene for reading disability on chromosome 15q', *Human Molecular Genetics*, 9: 843–848.

Narhi, V. and Ahonen, T. (1995) 'Reading disability with or without attention deficit hyperactivity disorder' Do attentional problems make a difference?', *Developmental Neuropsychology*, 11: 337–350

Neale, M. C. and Cardon, L. R. (1992) *Methodology for genetic studies of twins and families*. Boston: Kluwer Academic Press

Newbury, D. F., Bishop, D. V. M. and Monaco, A. P. (2005) 'Genetic influences on language impairment and phonological short-term memory', *TRENDS in Cognitive Sciences*, 9: 528–534.

Nicolson, R.I. Fawcett, A.J. and Dean, P. (2001) 'Developmental dyslexia: the cerebellar deficit hypothesis', *Trends in Neurosciences*, 24: 508–512.

Noctor, S. C., Flint, A. C, Weissman, T. A., Dammerman, R. S. and Kriegstein, A. R. (2001) 'Neurons derived from radial glial cells establish radial units in neocortex', *Nature*, 409: 714–720.

Nopola-Hemmi, J., Myllyluoma, B., Haltia, T., Taipale, M., Ollikainen, V., Ahonen, T., et al. (2001) 'A dominant gene for developmental dyslexia on chromosome 3', *J. Med. Genet.*, 38: 658–664.

Nopola-Hemmi, J., Taipale, M., Haltia, T., Lehesjoki, A. E., Voutilainen, A. and Kere, J. (2000) 'Two translocations of chromosome 15q associated with dyslexia', *J Med Genet*, 37: 771–775.

Nöthen, M. M., Schulte-Körne, G., Grimm, T., Cichon, S., Vogt, I. R., Müller-Myhsok, B., et al. (1999) 'Gentic linkage analysis with dyslexia: Evidence for linkage of spelling disability to chromosome 15', *European Child and Adolescent Psychiatry*, 8: III/56–III/59.

Olson, R. K., Forsberg, H. and Wise, B. (1994) 'Genes, environment, and the development of orthographic skills', in V.W. Berninger (ed.), *The varieties of orthographic knowledge I: Theoretical and developmental issues*. Dordrecht, The Netherlands: Kluwer Academic Publishers. pp. 27–71.

Orton, S. (1928) 'Specific reading disability – strephosymbolia', *Journal of the American Medical Association*, 90: 1095–1099.

Owen, F., Adams, P., Forrest, T., Stolz, L. and Fisher, S. (1971) 'Learning disorders in children: sibling studies', *Monographs of the Society for Research in Child Development*, 36 (4).

Paulesu, E., Démonet, J.-F. Fazio, F., McCrory, E., Chanolne, V., Brunswick, N., et al. (2001) 'Dyslexia: Cultural diversity and biological unity', *Science*, 291: 2165–2167.

Pennington, B. F. (1999) 'Dyslexia as a neurodevelopmental disorder', in H. Tager-Flusberg (ed.), *Neurodevelopmental disorders*. Cambridge, MA: MIT Press. pp. 307–330.

Pennington, B.F. (2002) 'Genes and brain: Individual differences and human universals', in M. H. Johnson, Y. Munakata, and R. O. Gilmore (eds), *Brain Development and Cognition: A Reader*. Blackwell Publishers. pp. 494–508.

Pennington, B. F. and Gilger, J. W. (1996) 'How is dyslexia transmitted?', in C. H. Chase, G. D. Rosen, and G. F. Sherman (eds) *Developmental dyslexia: neural, cognitive, and genetic mechanisms*. Timonium, MD; York Press. pp. 41–61.

Petryshen, T. L., Kaplan, B. J., Fu Liu, M., de French, N. S., Tobias, R., Hughes, M. L. and Field, L. L. (2001) 'Evidence for a susceptibility locus on chromosome 6q influencing phonological coding dyslexia', *Am J Med Genet*, 105: 507–517.

Petryshen, T. L., Kaplan, B. J., Hughes, M. L., Tzenova, J. and Field, L. L. (2002) 'Supportive evidence for DYX3 dyslexia susceptibility gene in Canadian Families', *J. Med. Genet.*, 39: 125–126.

Peyrard-Janvid, M., Anthoni, H., Onkamo, P., Lahermo, P., Zucchelli, M., Kaminen, M., et al. (2004) 'Fine mapping of the 2p11 dyslexia locus and exclusion of TACR1 as a candidate gene', *Human Genetics*, 114: 510–516.

Plomin, R., DeFries, J. C. and McClearn, G. E. (1980) *Behavioral genetics, a primer*. San Francisco: W. H. Freeman and Company.

Plomin, R., DeFries, C., McClearn, G. E. and McGuffin, P. (2001) *Behavioral genetics*. New York: Worth Publishers.

Plomin, R. and McClearn, G. E. (eds) (1993) *Nature Nurture and Psychology*. Washington, DC: American Psychological Association.

Ramus, F. (2001) 'Dyslexia: Talk of two theories', *Nature*, 412: 393–395.

Ramus, F. (2004a) 'Should neuroconstructivism guide developmental research?', *Trends in Cognitive Sciences*, 8 (3): 100–101.

Ramus, F. (2004b) 'Neurobiology of dyslexia: A reinterpretation of the data', *TINS*, 27: 720–726.

Raskind, W. H., Igo Jr., R. P., Chapman, N. H., Berninger, V. W., Thompson, J. B., Matsushita, M., et al. (2005) 'A genome scan in multigenerational families with dyslexia: Identification of a novel locus on chromosome 2q that contributes to phonological decoding deficiency', *Molecular Psychiatry*, 10: 699–711.

Rhee, S., Hewitt, J., Corley, R., Willcutt, E. and Pennington, B. (2005) 'Testing hypotheses regarding the causes of comorbidity: Examining the underlying deficits of comorbid disorders', *Journal of Abnormal Psychology*, 114: 346–362.

Rice, M. and Brooks, G. (2004) *Developmental dyslexia in adults: a research review.* National Research and Developmental Centre for adult literacy and numeracy. London: UK.

Rondi-Reig, L., Caston, J., Delhaye-Bouchaud, N. and Mariani, J. (1999) 'Cerebellar functions: A behavioral neurogenetics perspective', in B. Jones and P. Mormede (eds), *Neurobehavioral genetics: Methods and applications.* New York: CRC Press. pp. 201–216.

Ruban, L. M. and Reis, S. M. (2005) 'Identification and assessment of gifted students with learning disabilities', *Theory Into Practice*, 44 (2): 115–124.

Rutter, M., Silberg, J., O'Connor, T. and Simenoff, E. (1999a) 'Genetics and child psychiatry: I advances in quantitative and molecular genetics', *Journal of Child Psychology and Psychiatry and Allied Disciplines*, 40 (1), 3–18(16).

Rutter, M., Silberg, J., O'Connor, T. and Simenoff, E. (1999b) 'Genetics and child psychiatry: II empirical research findings', *Journal of Child Psychology and Psychiatry and Allied Disciplines*, 40 (1): 19–55(37).

Satz, P., Buka, S., Lipsitt, L. and Seidman, L. (1998) 'The long-term prognosis of learning disabled children: a review of studies (1954–1993)', in B. K. Shapiro, P. J. Accardo, and A. J. Capute (eds), *Specific reading disability: a view of the spectrum.* Timonium, MD: York Press. pp. 223–250.

Scerif, G., and Karmiloff-Smith, A. (2005) 'The dawn of cognitive genetics? Crucial developmental caveats', *Trends in Cognitive Sciences*, 9 (3): 126–135.

Schulte-Körne, G. (2001) 'Genetics of reading and spelling disorder', *Journal of Child Psychology and Psychiatry*, 42 (8): 985–997.

Schumacher, J., Hoffman, P., Schmäl, C., Schulte-Körne, G. and Nöthen, M. M. (2007) 'Genetics of dyslexia: the evolving landscape', *Journal of Medical Genetics*, 44: 289–297.

Shapiro, B., Church, R. P. and Lewis, M. E. B. (2002) 'Specific learning disabilities', in M. Batshaw (ed.), *Children with disabilities.* Baltimore: Paul Brookes. pp. 417–442.

Silventoinen, K., Posthuma, D., Lahelma, E., Rose, R. J. and Kaprio, J. (2007) 'Genetic and environmental factors affecting self–rated health from age 16–25: a longitudinal study of Finnish twins', *Behavior Genetics*, 37: 326–333.

Simonton, D. K. (2005) *Giftedness and Genetics: The emergenic-epigenetic model and its implications.* Waco, TX: Prufrock Press Inc.

Smalley, S. L., Loo, S. K., Yang, M. H. and Cantor, R. M. (2004) 'Toward localizing genes underlying cerebral asymmetry and mental health', *American Journal of Medical Genetics Part B (Neuropsychiatric Genetics)*, 135B, 79–84.

Smith, S. D. and Gilger, J. W. (2007) 'Dyslexia and related learning disorders', in D. L. Rimoin, J. M. Connor, R. E. Pyeritz, and B. R. Korf (eds), *Principles and practice of medical genetics* (4th ed.). Philadelphia, PA: Churchill Livingstone Elsevier. pp. 2548–2568.

Smith, S. D., Kimberling, W. J., Pennington, B. and Lubs, H. A. (1983) 'Specific reading disability: Identification of an inherited form through linkage analysis', *Science*, 2199: 1345–1347.

Sonuga-Barke, E. J. S. (2003) 'On the intersection between ADHD and DCD: the DAMP Hypothesis', *Child and Adolescent Mental Health*, 8: 114–116.

Taipale, M., Kaminen, N., Nopola-Hemmi, J., Haltia, T., Myllyluoma, B., Lyytinen, H., et al. (2003) 'A candidate gene for developmental dyslexia encodes a nuclear tetratricopeptide repeat domain protein dynamically regulated in brain', *PNAS*, 100: 11553–11558.

The SLI Consortium (2002) 'A genomewide scan identifies two novel loci involved in specific language impairment', *American Journal of Human Genetics*, 70: 384–398.

Thompson, P. M., Cannon, T. D., Narr, K. L., Erp, T. v., Poutanen, V.-P., Huttunen, M., et al. (2001) 'Genetic influences on brain structure', *Nature Neuroscience*, 4 (12): 1253–1258.

Thompson, P., Cannon, T. D. and Toga, A. W. (2002) 'Mapping genetic influences on human brain structure', *Annals of Medicine*, 34: 523–536.

Turic, D., Robinson, L., Duke, M., Morris, D. W., Webb, V., Hamshere, M., et al. (2003) 'Linkage disequilibrium mapping provides further evidence of a gene for reading disability on chromosome 6p21.3–22', *Molecular Psychiatry*, 8: 176–185.

Tzenova, J., Kaplan, B. J., Petryshen, T. L. and Field, L. L. (2004) 'Confirmation of a dyslexia susceptibility locus on chromosome 1p34–p36 in a set of 100 Canadian families', *American Journal of Medical Genetics Part B (Neuropsychiatric Genetics)*, 127B: 117–124.

Voeller, K. (1999) 'Neurological factors underlying the comorbidity of attentional dysfunction and dyslexia', in D. Duane (ed.), *Reading and attention disorders: Neurobiological correlates*. Timonium, MD: York Press. pp. 185–211.

Wadsworth, S. J., Corley, R. P., Plomin, R., Hewitt, J. K. and DeFries, J. C. (2006) 'Genetic and environmental influences on continuity and charge in reading achievement in the Colorado Adoption Project', in A. Huston and M. Ripke (eds) *Developmental contexts of middle childhood: Bridges to adolescence and adulthood*. New York: Cambridge University Press. pp. 87–106.

West, T. G. (1999) 'The abilities of those with reading disabilities: Focusing on the talents of people with dyslexia', in D. D. Duane (ed.), *Reading and attention disorders: Neurobiological correlates*. Baltimore: York Press. pp. 213–241.

Wigg, K. G., Couto, J. M., Feng, Y., Anderson, B., Cate–Carter, T. D., Macciardi, F., et al. (2004) 'Support for EKN1 as the susceptibility locus for dyslexia on 15q21', *Molecular Psychiatry*, 9: 1111–1121.

Willcutt, E. G., Pennington, B. F., Smith, S. D., Cardon, L. R., Gayán, J., Knopik, V. S., et al. (2002) 'Quantitative trait locus for reading disability on chromosome 6p is pleiotropic for attention deficit hyperactivity disorder', *American Journal of Medical Genetics (Neuropsychiatric Genetics)*, 114: 260–268.

Wood, F. and Flowers, L. (1999) 'Functional neuroanatomy of dyslexic subtypes', in D. Duane (ed.), *Reading and attention disorders: Neurobiological correlates*. Timonium, MD: York Press. pp. 129–160.

Zhou, S., Heng, H. G., Zhang, G. Q. and Li, Z. X. (1989) 'A novel method for determining an integrated character in quantitative genetics', *Yi Chuan Xue Bao*, 16 (4): 269–275.

The Neurobiological Basis of Dyslexia

John Stein

This chapter outlines

i) genetic, sensory, motor and psychological evidence that dyslexia is a neurological syndrome affecting the development of the brain;
ii) the important role of visual processing for reading;
iii) the role of magnocellular neurones, timing events, for controlling the focus of visual and auditory attention together with eye and speech movements;
iv) evidence that the development of magnocellular neurones is impaired in dyslexia; and
v) implications as to the remediation of dyslexics' reading problems.

INTRODUCTION

Developmental dyslexia (a reading level far below that expected from a person's general intelligence) is very common, because reading is so difficult. Our large brain seems to endow us genetically with an 'instinct' to learn to speak. So speaking is relatively easy. On a very basic level we do not have to be taught; we simply imitate those around us. But reading does not come so naturally. Because it is a cultural invention made only about 5000 years ago rather than being enshrined in our genome, we have to be taught the letters of the alphabet and how word sounds can be represented as a series of letters. Reading remains the most difficult skill that most of us ever have to learn; few of us are advanced mathematicians or champion chess players. Hence it is not surprising that over a quarter of all children fail to learn to read properly.

The first and most important requirement for skilled reading is rapid visual analysis of the letters in the word being read and of their order on the page. For familiar words we can then translate these visual forms directly into their meanings by referring them to our 'semantic lexicon'. This contains the meaning of all the words we have ever encountered. Skilled readers using this 'lexical' route can therefore translate these tiny visual symbols into meaning at the remarkable rate of about 1800 letters (300 words) a minute (30 letters a second); yet dyslexics struggle to achieve a tenth of this rate.

However for unfamiliar words, and remember that all words are visually unfamiliar to beginner readers, we need to use a much more cumbersome process of translating the letters into the sounds they stand for, then melding them together to reveal the auditory representation of the word, then referring this to our semantic lexicon to discover its meaning. Thus behind this 'sub-lexical' or 'phonological' route we also need to build up a background knowledge of the way in which words can be broken down into their constituent phonemes to match with whatever the letter/sound decoding system presents us with. Early skill at this is in fact the best predictor of how rapidly a child will be able to learn to read, and dyslexics have serious difficulties with this kind of phonological processing.

RISK FACTORS FOR DYSLEXIA

Studying the factors which predict difficulties with learning to read can provide us with powerful insights into how the brain copes with the problems presented by reading, and how these processes go wrong in dyslexics. It is also important that teachers encountering reading problems in the classroom should be aware of these potential indicators of dyslexia, so that they can institute help as early as possible, and thus avoid the downward spiral of failure, loss of self confidence, frustration, misery and depression that dyslexics so often suffer from.

Heredity

The most important influence appears to be heredity. The similarity in reading ability between siblings living in the same family ('familiality') is as high as 80 per cent; Comparing dizygotic with monozygotic (identical) twins has shown that this familiality can be divided into two separate components, namely genetic heritability (h^2) and common environmental (c^2) factors (Olson et al., 1989). Heritability turns out to explain around 60 per cent of familial variance in reading, so that the environment that twins share in common explains only around 20 per cent. Thus more than half of the differences that children show in reading ability can be explained by their genetic inheritance, and this proportion does not change much even after allowing for the effect of non verbal IQ. In other words reading has a very large genetic component that is highly specific.

IQ

The next important influence on reading ability is general intelligence. A quarter of the differences between different children's reading ability is accounted for by their IQ. About half of this effect survives after controlling for the genetic effects that are common to both IQ and reading. But IQ does only explain one quarter of reading variance. For example; some children with Down's syndrome, who may only have an IQ of around 50, can nevertheless be taught to decode words successfully, although they have limited comprehension.

Teaching

Clearly, children must receive enough appropriate teaching to learn to read properly. Those who truant too much – though this is rare in primary school – usually fail to learn to read. By the time they are in secondary school, however, probably the main reason why they truant is because they can't read properly; so they gain very little, apart from humiliation, from attending class. Their teaching has been so unsuccessful that they vote with their feet.

The quality of teaching is therefore clearly important. The fashion for abandoning phonics teaching in favour of real books and flash cards of whole words that took hold in the 1960s may have done children without highly developed visual memories a profound disservice. Many think that the decline in average spelling ability that has occurred in the second half of the 20th century can be attributed to that trend. There is now a welcome return to phonics teaching in primary schools. But let us hope that this development will not be to the exclusion of attention to visual factors in reading as well.

However teaching quality is clearly not the most important factor. Heredity is far more important, independently of general intelligence. The genes involved seem to affect the way the brain develops, in particular the way certain classes of nerve cells migrate to their final positions during development of the cerebral cortex. This will affect how the brain carries out the fundamental visual and auditory processing operations that are required for reading. Thus we find that individuals' visual and auditory temporal processing sensitivity, together with their IQ, can account for over two thirds of their differences in reading ability (Talcott et al., 2000). Hence the quality of their teaching either at school or at home (e.g., how often their mothers read with them or how many books there are in the house), seems to be considerably less important than how well their brains are adapted physiologically for reading.

Developmental speech problems

These include late talking, impaired pronunciation, difficulties learning to identify letter sounds, confusing sound order and failure to identify rhymes. There is now persuasive evidence that these problems are associated with impaired development of the basic temporal processing functions of the auditory system that are required for accurately identifying and discriminating between letter sounds.

In addition developmental speech problems are often associated with clumsiness and generally poor coordination, which are probably caused by deficient operation of the cerebellum. Hence we can conclude that particularly the component of reading ability that depends on acquiring accurate phonological skills, is to a large extent determined by basic auditory temporal processing, whilst the motor side of speech depends on proper maturation of the cerebellum.

Developmental motor problems

Therefore dyslexia is often associated with a variety of other motor symptoms: late crawling, late walking, poor balance, exceptional clumsiness, difficulty learning to ride a bicycle and slow acquisition of consistent handedness. Again these symptoms point to an important role for the cerebellum in developing the sensorimotor skills required for reading.

DOES DYSLEXIA REALLY EXIST?

Nevertheless every ten years or so someone repeats the claim that dyslexia does not really exist at all; that it is only a middle class excuse for laziness or a cover for bad teaching. Stanovich (1988) has argued for the last 20 years that there are no substantial differences between the phonological problems of children with reading difficulties and have a high general (non reading) intelligence compared with those whose reading problems are probably mainly due to their low intelligence. So he thinks that we should call all poor readers dyslexic, whether they have high or low IQ. Elliot in the UK (2006) uses the same argument to go further and suggest that there is no point in diagnosing dyslexia at all: It may as well not exist, he claims, because making the diagnosis does not distinguish any different way of remediating the problems.

What these arguments neglect however is the large amount of genetic and neurobiological evidence that dyslexia is more than just a problem with acquiring phonological skills and reading, but that it is associated with clear brain differences in other areas as well. These amount to a neurological syndrome that is characterized by a very wide variety of symptoms involving impaired temporal processing, which includes, in addition to the phonological difficulties that most dyslexics have, visuomotor, speech, short-term memory, attentional, coordination and general sequencing problems. This neurobiological picture shows very clearly that dyslexia is a real neurological condition, and that it is easily distinguishable from poor reading just associated with low IQ.

It also answers Elliot's argument that there is no point in diagnosing dyslexia, since this does not lead to better treatment. On the contrary, understanding the neurobiological basis of dyslexia has led to and will continue to suggest greatly improved ways of helping these people.

VISUAL INPUT TO READING

The visual system provides the main input to both the lexical and the sublexical routes for reading. Therefore it is natural to assume that the most important sense for reading is vision. But this assumption is strongly disputed by many experts, because they believe that acquisition of phonological skill is in fact much more crucial for successful reading.

However there is now much evidence that children need visual input of letter shapes before they begin to understand the phonemic structure of words. Not until they have learnt that words can be represented as a sequence of visual symbols, do they realize that the syllables which they have learned to speak, can actually be split down further into separate phonemes, and that these can be represented by letters. This is the alphabetic principle; and there is now a lot of evidence that children do not begin to learn it until after they have been exposed to the visual representation of words as a sequence of letters (Morais et al., 1979). Likewise illiterate adults learning to read only begin to grasp the subsyllabic phonemic structure of their language when they are taught how the words can be represented by the letters of the alphabet (Castro-Caldas et al., 1998). Furthermore in ideographic languages, such as Japanese, children's phonological skills never get more detailed than the mora (syllabic) level. Japanese children do not have to learn to subdivide word sounds any further because the writing system does not require it. Indeed the Kanji script does not even require syllabic phonology; they only need to learn mora when they learn Kana, which represents speech at this level.

Therefore in this Chapter we will first deal with the visual requirements of reading. This is not to imply that phonological skills are not important, merely to emphasize how important basic visual processes are for reading. We will even see how learning to analyze the letters in words can actually help children to acquire phonological skills.

Foveal splitting

Because of the way the visual pathways from the retina to the occipital cortex are organized, the left side of each word is first projected to the right primary visual, striate, cortex in area 17, whereas the right side is projected to the left striate cortex, so that the representation of each word is divided in two at the fovea. The left side first three or four letters usually carry more information about a word than subsequent ones do. Furthermore there is mutual inhibition between the primary visual representations in the right and left hemispheres. So this initial foveal splitting means that, unexpectedly, it is the right hemisphere that has the advantage at the very earliest stages of visually processing a word (Shillcock and Monaghan, 2001). But this advantage seems to be missing in very poor readers, who tend to attend less to the left hand side of a word, exhibiting left 'minineglect'(Hari, 2001).

The influence of foveal splitting is probably not restricted to just this initial short time window before the information is projected forwards to extrastriate regions. All these regions also project back to V1 by 'recurrent' connections. Thus an intact V1 appears to be essential for conscious awareness of a visual image, probably because it contains the most detailed and 'authoritative' cortical representation of the retinal image (Stoerig and Cowey, 1997). Hence its division into two halves and the mutual inhibition between them reasserts itself whenever V1 is reinterrogated by recurrent projections from further forward.

Magnocellular and parvocellular visual neurones

One of the main discoveries about the visual system made over the least 25 years is that the different qualities of visual targets are analyzed, not one after the other in series, but by separate, parallel pathways that work simultaneously moving forwards in the visual brain. This separation begins right out in the retina. There are two main kinds of retinal ganglion cell, whose axons project all the visual information back to the brain. Ten per cent are known as magnocellular cells because they are noticeably larger than the others (magno (m-) in Latin), with thicker, more rapidly conducting axons and more extensive dendritic fields that cover an area 50 times greater than those of the much more numerous, but much smaller, parvocells (p-).

In addition to their size m- cells can be distinguished from other retinal ganglion cells by their surface signature molecules which can be detected by specific magnocellular antibodies, such as one termed CAT 301 (Hockfield and Sur, 1990). The precise structure of these surface molecules is controlled by a set of 'major histocompatibility' (MHC) genes situated on the short arm of human chromosome 6 and these same genes also seem to control the development of magnocells (Corriveau et al., 1998). For reasons that may be related to this MHC control, magnocells also seem to be particularly vulnerable not only developmentally but also to drugs and disease; they mature later than p- cells and their development is selectively impaired in prematurity, and in many neurodevelopmental diseases such as dyslexia, dyspraxia and dysphasia.

Magnocellular neurones' extended dendritic trees draw from a very large area of retinal receptors; this means that they are most sensitive to large (low spatial frequency), dim, low contrast stimuli so they can indicate where visual 'blobs' are, but without being able to identify them. Also since magnocells respond only at the onset and offset of a light stimulus (they are 'rapidly adapting'), they are much more strongly excited by visual transients, changing, flickering or moving stimuli which have high temporal frequency content, than by steady, stationary lights.

The main function of visual magnocells is therefore to time visual events and to signal visual motion for visual temporal processing. The large diameter of their axons means that they conduct information about these visual transients very rapidly to the Superior Colliculus for the reflex control of eye movements and to the magnocellular layers of the Lateral Geniculate Nucleus (LGN) in the thalamus, en route to the primary visual cortex. In fact the m- cell signal may arrive in the visual cortex as much as 20 ms ahead of the p- volley.

But m- cells are not as sensitive as the parvocells are to fine detail (high spatial frequencies), nor to color differences. This means that the m- system provides the brain with rapid information about the location and broad outline of letters and words primarily for directing attention and eye movements to each one if necessary, as is required when learning to read a new word. But parallel processing by the p- system is required to identify the fine details of letters, for example to distinguish between 'm' and 'n' or 'c' and 'e'.

Only at the level of the LGN are the m- and p- inputs from the retina completely separated anatomically. In V1 m- axons synapse in cortical input layer $4C\alpha$ whereas p-cells arrive in layer $4C\beta$. Thereafter however, the two kinds of input interact strongly. Nevertheless m- input dominates responses to coarse (low spatial frequency), low contrast, moving or flickering stimuli, whereas p- cells dominate responses to stationary, fine (high spatial frequency), colored stimuli. But m- cell input seems only to be absolutely essential for detecting visual transients and motion. Selective lesions of the m- layers of the LGN only impair these responses, but leave the contrast sensitivity to stationary stimuli, even large ones with low spatial frequencies, relatively unaffected. (Merigan and Maunsell, 1990)

Visual what and where pathways

From the primary visual cortex (striate cortex, V1, in Brodmann's area 17) visual information is projected forwards into extrastriate visual areas, again by two separate pathways. These pass either dorsomedially or ventrolaterally and are often termed the 'where' and 'what' visual streams respectively. The 'where' stream receives mainly visual magnocellular input and projects dorsomedially towards the visual motion area (V5/MT) which is situated in the extension of the superior temporal sulcus into the parietal cortex. After this the where stream projects onwards to the angular and supramarginal gyri in the posterior parietal cortex and from there to the frontal eye fields, dorsolateral prefrontal cortex and, importantly, subcortically to the cerebellum.

The m- neurones supply these areas with information about the timing and movements of targets in the outside world. These signals are then used for the visual guidance of attention and of eye and limb movements. All these areas are known to be important for the visuomotor control functions that are obviously important for reading. Since most of the neurons in this dorsal pathway are large, conduct rapidly and, at least in cats, express the same surface markers that are recognized by antibodies such as CAT 301 as the subcortical visual m- neurons do (Hockfield and Sur, 1990), the dorsal stream can be considered a cortical extension of the subcortical visual magnocellular system.

In contrast the ventrolateral 'what' stream receives equal amounts from the m- and p- cells and it projects ventrolaterally towards the 'visual word form area' (VWFA) on the under surface of the occipital cortex, at the anterior end of the fusiform gyrus. The function of this stream is to identify pattern, form, color and fine detail, to indicate 'what' something is, e.g., to identify letters.

M- system, eye movements and reading

At first sight we might think that this magnocellular dominated where stream would not play any very important role in reading. Its function is to locate targets as blobs, time visual events and to signal visual motion; yet print is small and stationary most of the time, so magnocellular functions might appear not to be needed. But this doesn't take into account the importance of controlling eye movements accurately during reading. The eyes have to flick from one letter or word to the next when reading, and it is now clear that the m-system plays the main role in controlling these 'saccades'. Treating words as blobs because of its low spatial resolution, the m- system guides each saccade to land close to the centre of gravity of the next word, and then it gates the images from that fixation through to the ventral stream visual word form area in order to identify them (Vidyasagar, 2004). Thus high m- sensitivity is required for precisely positioning the eyes onto the next word when reading, and impaired ability to make such accurate saccades to complex targets is one common feature of dyslexics (Crawford and Higham, 2001).

Eye fixation

Perhaps more importantly, the m-system plays a very crucial role for stabilizing the eyes during the fixations on each word between reading saccades. These fixations only last about a quarter of a second, but it is only during them, not during the saccades, that the fine details of the letters in a word can be gated through to the visual word form area for identification (Vidyasagar, 2004). So it is very important to keep the eyes stationary then, and the m- system ensures this.

If the eyes stray off the letter being fixated, a 'retinal slip' motion signal is generated by the m- system, and this is fed back to the oculomotor control system which then brings the eyes back on target. Hence a sensitive m- system is essential to provide these feedback signals. Therefore another important contributory cause of dyslexics' reading problems appears to be poor control of these fixations. This instability can lead to letters appearing to blur and move around, and these problems often occur as the result of impaired development of the visual magnocellular system (Fowler, 1991; Fischer et al., 2000).

Letter order

In addition the motion signals generated by images swishing over the retina during each saccade to the next word are used to help determine how far the eyes have moved during the saccade, even though we are not consciously aware of this. Together with signals about the size of the oculomotor command to move the eyes and probably proprioceptive information provided by the eye muscles about their change of length, magnocellular signals about how far images have moved across the retina during each saccade, help to indicate how far the eyes have moved. This signal can then also be used to locate each letter with respect to the previous one fixated. Thus the m-system not only controls reading saccades and stabilizes fixations, it also seems to be important for determining the positional order of letters and words (Cornelissen et al., 1997), whereas the what stream is left to identify them.

Vergence control

When reading small print at the normal reading distance of about 30 cms the eyes are not parallel, but converged at about 10° towards each other. Control of these vergence movements is also dominated by the m- system, and it is known to be the most vulnerable to drugs and disease. Some of us know this only too well from the double vision that ensues when vergence breaks down after too much alcohol! It has been suggested that delayed maturation leading to mild impairment of the m- system might lead to particularly unstable vergence control (Fowler et al., 1990). This might account for the problems that many beginning readers describe of letters and words appearing to split, reverse themselves and move over each other, so that they find it difficult to decide what order they should be in. This problem is much worse and persists for much longer in many dyslexics; this is another reason why they have such difficulties in building up reliable memorized representations of the visual/orthographic form of words.

M- system and dyslexia

Thus there is now a great deal of evidence that in many, but probably not all, dyslexics, development of their visual magnocellular systems is mildly impaired. This can manifest itself right out in the retina. In many dyslexics their retinal m- ganglion cells exhibit significantly slower responses (Pammer and Wheatley, 2001). Furthermore histological study of the neurones in the selective magnocellular layers of the lateral geniculate nucleus in dyslexic brains post mortem showed that they are smaller and more disorganized (Livingstone et al., 1991). Visual evoked potential studies have demonstrated that the m- volley may arrive in the visual cortex up to 20 ms later in dyslexics than in good readers. The m- system is most sensitive to coarse (low spatial frequency), flickering (high temporal frequency) stimuli; hence contrast sensitivity to these kinds of stimuli tends to be lower in dyslexics (Lovegrove et al., 1980). The visual motion area V5/MT receives most of its input from the m- system; and this, too, has proved to be less activated by visual motion stimuli in dyslexics (Eden et al., 1996); hence their sensitivity to visual motion is lower (Cornelissen et al., 1995).

Indeed sensitivity to visual motion measured either psychophysically (Talcott et al., 2000) or by fMRI (Demb et al., 1997) predicts reading ability in everybody, not just in dyslexics. As might be expected from the role of the m- system in determining the order of letters, this correlation is particularly strong with individuals' visual/orthographic skills.

The m- dominated dorsal visual stream then projects to the angular and supramarginal gyri. Hence the degree of fMRI activation of these areas also correlates with individuals' reading ability; this must derive at least in part from the strength of their dominant magnocellular input.

Over the last few years hundreds of studies of the role of the visual magno-cellular system in dyslexia have been published. The vast majority have supported the idea that they often display m- cell weakness. Nevertheless there is still strong opposition to the idea (Skottun, 1997) mainly because it is wrongly thought to undermine the view that dyslexics' main problems are phonological rather than visual. In fact far from opposing it, the m- theory offers a partial explanation as to why dyslexics show these phonological deficits. M- system visual input enables children to learn how words can be represented as a sequence of letters, after which they can begin to understand how word sounds can be split further down from their syllabic rimes into separate phonemes. Not only this but the magnocellular theory explains why so many children have such problems with letters appearing to blur, move around and reverse themselves.

M- system and attention

The fast track m- inputs to the dorsal stream are not only important for control-ling eye movements, but also for controlling the focus of visual attention. As we have seen, the where stream probably feeds back magnocellular signals to the primary visual cortex that enable us to focus on letters by gating them through one after the other to the ventral stream visual word form area for detailed analysis. This 'attentional spotlight' also helps to determine the spatial location of each letter during fixations, when in about 250 ms, 7 or 8 letters are accessed sequentially without moving the eyes (Vidyasagar, 2004).

Consistent with this, serial visual search has been found to be critically dependent upon activation of magnocellular pathways (Cheng et al., 2004). These gating inputs are presumably also the means by which serial visual search is mediated: the dorsal stream uses its crude spatial resolution and information about the location of targets to select each one sequentially. Each is then analyzed in detail by the ventral stream. Hence there are now numerous studies that have shown that dyslexics are poor at serial visual search (Iles et al., 2000) and unduly affected by distractors (Facoetti et al., 2001).

Thus the main reason why it takes such a long time for children to learn to read fluently is probably because training the visual attentional searchlight is a slow process. Normally visual search is fairly random concentrating on salient features and not systematically or sequentially deployed across the visual field (Horowitz and Wolfe, 1998), but for reading the attentional spot light has to be taught to proceed instead in an unusual linear sequential manner from left to right, accessing each letter in a word in the correct order.

REMEDIATION OF VISUAL PROBLEMS

The recognition that visual weakness can contribute greatly to children's reading problems has led to the development of a wide variety of techniques to attempt to remediate them. These are designed to overcome the children's complaints that letters appear to blur, glare or move around when they try to read, preventing them seeing the words properly. But most of the techniques are commercially driven, and so there has been little incentive to design properly controlled trials to assess their efficacy. Many of the studies that have been published are poorly controlled, few have used standardized reading measures and most do not provide a rationale to explain why the techniques might aid reading. In desperation parents are often persuaded to spend large amounts of money on them. But there are too many anecdotal reports of very great improvements in children's reading to ignore them altogether. It is important therefore that their efficacy should be investigated properly by means of randomized controlled trials, and that research continues to try to explain why they exert their claimed effects.

Since vergence instability is an important cause of letters appearing to move around and cross over each other, we found in 8–10 year-olds with unstable vergence that simply occluding one eye temporarily, only for reading and close work, could markedly improve their binocular control permanently, and when this was successful reading progress accelerated thereafter (Stein and Fowler, 1981). We subsequently confirmed this result in by means of two randomized controlled trials (Stein et al., 1985; Stein et al., 2000).

In 1980 Olive Meares (Meares, 1980) reported that colored filters can markedly reduce children's visual problems. The idea was speedily taken up commercially and the manufacture of colored lenses has turned out to be highly lucrative; now there are several different types of colored filter on the market for the treatment of reading difficulty (Wilkins and Nimmo Smith 1984; Irlen 1991; Harris and MacRow-Hill 1999). But there have been very few properly controlled studies of their effects and the research community remains highly sceptical, particularly as the magnocellular system does not mediate color vision.

Nevertheless m- ganglion cells are differentially sensitive to long and short wavelength light, and they are maximally excited by yellow light. We therefore began experimenting with deep yellow filters to increase magnocellular input and compared them with deep blue that we thought would decrease magno input. We found that these yellow filters sometimes had a dramatic effect improving the vision of children with binocular amblyopia (Fowler et al., 1992) and in about a quarter of all the dyslexics we see they also turned out to improve reading. As expected these yellow filters also improved motion sensitivity, mediated by the m- system. We have recently confirmed these effects in a randomized, controlled trial (Ray et al., 2005).

To our surprise however the deep blue filters that we thought would disadvantage the m- system, seemed to help a different group of dyslexics even more than the yellow filters did; and this effect we have also confirmed by means of a randomized control trial. These filters did not impair motion sensitivity as we had predicted, so we are currently investigating whether they have their effect by a different mechanism.

Although some of these advances in treatment were serendipitous and do not derive directly from our increased understanding of visual factors in dyslexia, nevertheless their efficacy confirms the importance of the visual input to the reading system, which has been undervalued over the last 30 years in favour of the phonological theory.

AUDITORY/PHONOLOGICAL PROCESSING?

There is indeed general agreement that most dyslexics suffer from a phonological deficit; but it is important to try to elucidate what neural processes underlie this deficit. In addition to the role that learning orthography plays in teaching children about the phonemic structure of words, it seems obvious that dyslexics' phonological difficulties might derive from weaknesses in their basic auditory processing capacities. Although logical, this suggestion has proved highly controversial (Talcott et al., 2000). An alternative view is that language is so special that the processing required to comprehend it is exclusively linguistic; hence looking for contributions to dyslexia from lower down in the auditory system is sure to be fruitless.

However it is becoming increasingly clear that language is not so special after all. Chomsky and Lieberman's view was that evolutionarily we developed so far in advance of our closest relatives, the chimpanzees, because a crucial genetic mutation endowed us with a unique 'encapsulated linguistic processor' which provided us with the communication powers of language; and that reading makes use of this. But it has turned out that speech and language are not totally new; they were built on adaptations that evolved for quite different purposes (Stein, 2003). For example hemispheric specialisation probably developed in the right hemisphere for improving an animal's visuospatial skills to find its way to food and back to home. Likewise descent of the larynx may well have been an adaptation for swimming, not speaking. Similarly the mirror cells that are found in Broca's area in the inferior frontal gyrus and enable us to learn our language, probably developed not for speaking at all, but for learning how to imitate other's use of tools. Thus speech and reading probably came to be mediated by the language network of interconnected regions in the left hemisphere, almost by accident, and so they do depend crucially on correctly analysed signals supplied by the peripheral auditory system.

The essential input for this phonological analysis of speech sounds comes from the division of the auditory system that responds to temporal changes in frequency and intensity. Accurate temporal processing of this sort is required to identify the subtle frequency and amplitude changes that distinguish phonemes. Tallal was the first to suggest that the severe problems with language that children with specific language impairment (developmental dysphasics) experience, may be caused by deficient processing of the auditory transients that enable the discrimination of speech sounds (Tallal and Piercy, 1973). In the last few years there have been several hundred studies comparing basic auditory processing capabilities with language and reading skills. Almost all have shown correlations between basic auditory temporal processing and phonological skills, suggesting that the former helps to determine the development of the latter. Indeed auditory sensitivity to frequency and amplitude modulations can account for nearly 50 per cent of individual differences in phonological skill in both good and bad readers (Witton et al., 2002).

However because not all dyslexics with phonological problems can be shown to have these auditory weaknesses, it is sometimes argued that they cannot be significant (Ramus et al., 2003). This is clearly false logic. A cognitive weakness such as poor phonological processing can be caused by a number of different neural abnormalities. The fact that one of these does not explain all instances is no reason for stating that it cannot explain any of them. This would be like saying that because there are many possible causes of lung cancer of which smoking is only one, albeit the most important, smoking is neither necessary nor sufficient to cause lung cancer, so it can never cause it – patently false. The probability is that impaired auditory and visual temporal processing are among a number of possible causes of impaired phonological processing.

Auditory m- system?

The accurate analysis of temporal changes in the frequency and amplitude of speech sounds that is required to distinguish phonemes seems to be mediated mainly by large neurones in the auditory pathways that have rapid temporal processing capacities (Trussell, 1997). These could be called 'auditory magnocells', because they are also recognized by magnocellular specific antibodies, such as CAT 301. However there is no such clear anatomical separation of magno and parvo cells in the auditory system as there is in the visual system; so the existence of discriminable auditory m- and p- streams is not generally accepted.

Nevertheless as in the visual system, development of large auditory cells appears to be impaired in dyslexics; the magnocellular division of the auditory medial geniculate nucleus was found in dyslexic brains post mortem to contain fewer large cells on the left side (Galaburda et al., 1994), like those in the dyslexic LGN. Moreover temporal processing abilities in both auditory and visual domains tend to be similar in individuals, so that most dyslexics, for example, have both lowered visual motion sensitivity and lowered sensitivity to changes in auditory frequency. This suggests that both types of magno cell may have been subjected to the same developmental control in individuals. As in the visual system therefore, individual differences in the development of large (m- type?) cells in the auditory system might also underlie differences in the acquisition of phonological skills.

Cerebellum

The cerebellum is the brain's autopilot responsible for coordinating the precise timing of muscle contractions, but also for planning such movements. Since accurate timing of sensory feedback and motor outflow is an essential requirement for these functions, the cerebellum receives a rich input of visual, auditory, proprioceptive and motor magnocellular timing signals (Stein, 1986). Purely on theoretical grounds therefore, the cerebellum was likely to play an important role in reading. It receives a very large input from the visual m- system, particularly from the parietal supramarginal and angular gyri, and its main function is to mediate the acquisition of automatic skills. It does this by predicting the outcome of upcoming movements in terms of their sensory consequences. If the cerebellum predicts that the outcome of the movement will not be as intended, the motor programme can be modified before emission. Also if the programme once executed, turns out to have failed to achieve its objective, it can be changed to improve the outcome next time. In this way the cerebellum learns motor skills.

Importantly this machinery is probably put to use not only for executing actual movements, such as the eye movements used for reading, the vocal tract movements used for speaking and the hand movements used for writing, but there is now accumulating evidence that cerebellar prediction is also used for planning movements and other movement related cognitive operations such as silent reading and silent speech (Schmahmann, 2004).

Thus the cerebellum probably plays a crucial role in the guidance of eye movements during reading and in visuomotor control for writing. So it is not at all surprising to find that it is highly active during reading. There is now a substantial body of evidence that particularly the right cerebellar hemisphere (linked to the left hemisphere of the cerebral cortex) plays a very important role in reading. Lesions there, particularly in children, are often accompanied by dyslexic type reading problems (Scott et al., 2001). This area is activated in functional imaging studies during reading tasks, even when single words are used and no eye movements are required. In several studies the degree of cerebellar activation has been found to correlate with individuals' facility at the reading tasks employed, so that in dyslexics the right cerebellar hemisphere is significantly less activated than in good readers (Rae et al., 1998), both during reading and during the learning of new motor skills (Nicolson et al., 1999). In anatomical studies, even, it has been shown that the size of the right cerebellar hemisphere predicts the extent of readers' phonological and orthographic skills (Rae et al., 2002). In short there is now very little doubt that cerebellar computations contribute significantly to reading and their lack, to dyslexic problems.

Individual differences in cerebellar function may be assessed using tasks such as balancing, visually guided peg moving from one set of holes to another or implicit learning. There have been numerous studies showing that poor readers are worse at simply balancing on one leg than good readers; moreover children's balancing ability correlates with their reading ability (Stoodley et al., 2005). Nobody claims that balancing is entirely a cerebellar function; clearly the vestibular and other systems are also involved. Nor do we think that the correlation between balance and reading indicates that balancing is directly required for reading. What it suggests is that general cerebellar precision may help to determine both balancing skill and aspects of the motor control required for reading, such as control of attention and eye fixations. Likewise this is the implication of the fact that people's dexterity at visually guided peg moving correlates strongly with their reading ability.

When a complex sequence of finger movements is repeated even when the subject is unaware of the repetition, performance of the sequence improves very significantly, and this is associated with cerebellar activation. The amount of this implicit learning has also been found to correlate with reading ability (Stoodley et al., 2005). Again this suggests that the quality of individuals' cerebellar processing helps to determine their ability to develop the skills necessary for reading.

A pansensory general temporal processing magno system?

Thus large magnocellular neurones specialized for temporal processing are not confined to the visual system. They are also found in the auditory, somatosensory, memory and motor systems, ie throughout the whole brain; and all seem to be recognized by m- cell specific antibodies such as CAT 301 (Hockfield and Sur, 1990). They seem to constitute a specialized subsystem, devoted to temporal processing, probably developing from common precursors. These magnocellular systems throughout the brain are particularly required for reading, which makes use not only of visual but also auditory, cerebellar motor and even hippocampal memory magnocellular neurones as well. Thus dyslexia may at root be due to impaired development of all these magnocellular systems as a result of inheriting genetic alleles that slightly alter the migration of these neurones during early development in utero. The great variety of visual, phonological, kinaesthetic, sequencing, memory and motor symptoms that are seen in different dyslexics may therefore arise from differences in the particular magnocellular systems that are most affected by the particular mix of alleles that each individual dyslexic inherits.

The reading network in the brain

How far has this Chapter taken us towards a greater understanding of the neural basis of dyslexia? It seems that, above all, reading requires the temporal processing skills mediated by magnocellular neurones in the brain, whether visual, auditory or motor. So we will now consider how this translates into the reading network in the left hemisphere, which seems to be specialized for these temporal functions. Modern techniques for imaging cortical areas of increased blood flow by functional magnetic resonance (fMRI) or positron emission (PET) imaging have greatly advanced our understanding of the network of brain areas involved, although actually much of what has been discovered was suspected earlier from the results of lesions.

Dejerine had shown as early as 1891 that 'word blindness' was associated with lesions of the left angular gyrus at the temporoparietal junction, whilst Liepmann had shown that lesions of the fusiform gyrus on the underside of the occipital cortex were associated with visual agnosia of various kinds. Also it was known that lesions of Broca's motor speech area in the left inferior frontal gyrus were often associated with reading problems as well. In severe dyslexics Galaburda and colleagues showed that these areas contained 'ectopias', small outgrowths of neurones, 'brain warts' 1 mm or so in diameter, that disobey stop signals and migrate beyond the outer limiting membrane during development. They are associated with disorganized connectivity both beneath them and extending into the contralateral hemisphere (Galaburda et al., 1985).

But there are many problems with interpreting the results of lesions. Brain damage caused by maldevelopment, strokes, tumors or trauma, seldom removes just one function, partly because the lesions do not neatly dissect out just one anatomical region, but more importantly also because reading, like language in general, is mediated not by one single structure, but by a distributed system of interconnected areas. Hence removing one node alters the performance of the whole network.

Unfortunately this problem applies equally to the activations recorded by functional imaging as well. Observing increased blood flow in an area during a particular task merely shows that the area is more active than under other conditions, but it is silent about how other areas in the network are contributing to the function. Without this knowledge functional imaging reduces to mere 'modern phrenology'; knowing *what* areas are more active does not tell us *how* the network is carrying out the function.

The fact that the reading network is built on that responsible for language makes interpretation of results specifically in terms of reading even more problematical. Nevertheless the results of lesions and functional imaging concur in showing that the reading network is mainly located, though not exclusively, in the left hemisphere. As for language, the reading network consists of the posterior part of Wernicke's area in the temporal lobe together with the supramarginal and angular gyri together with Broca's motor speech area in the inferior frontal gyrus (see Figure 3.1).

Fusiform visual word form area

However there is one completely new region that has developed for the service of reading, the visual word form area (VWFA), which is situated in the anterior part of the left fusiform gyrus on the under surface of the occipital lobe and extending into the back of the middle temporal gyrus (Cohen et al., 2004)). This is the culmination of the ventrolateral visual 'what' processing stream. Access of p- type visual signals to it seems to be under control of the m-dominated visual attentional focusing system.

Further back in the ventral visual stream in the posterior fusiform gyrus, letters seem to be represented by their visual features, not by whether they are orthographic linguistic symbols. But more anteriorly the VWFA comes to represent their visual forms as orthographic symbols at a more abstract level than the lines and curves of which they are constructed. Thus the VWFA is activated equally by upper or lower case versions of a word, but less so by pronounceable nonsense words and not at all by meaningless strings of letter like symbols. Its degree of activation seems to mirror the degree of orthographic skill possessed

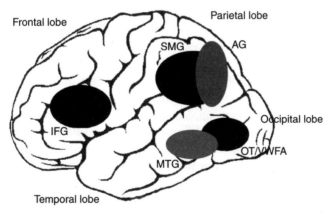

Figure 3.1   Brain areas involved in reading.

by the subject, so that it is underactivated in dyslexics trying to read. Therefore one can consider the VWFA as an important node on the pathway translating visual symbols into their meaning, still representing their visual form but not as the letters themselves, but rather their orthographic meaning. Further forward in the middle temporal gyrus this visual representation then becomes associated with the phonological representation of the word.

Temporoparietal junction

But perhaps the most important region for reading lies at the temporoparietal junction where the posterior part of Wernicke's speech comprehension area meets the angular and supramarginal gyri, Brodmann areas 39 and 40. Here visual/orthographic and auditory/phonological information seems to communicate with the semantic lexicon, the store of word meanings. This crucial conjunction translates the visual forms of letters and words into their sounds, hence their meanings. In skilled readers, this region (particularly the SMG) seems to activate most when dealing with unfamiliar words, e.g., low frequency or pronounceable nonwords rather than familiar words (Simos et al., 2002). In contrast to the VWFA, the degree of activation of these areas seems to correlate with individuals' phonological skills, so that they are underactivated in dyslexics. Hence the fMRI results confirm that the main function of this area is to convert visual symbols into their sounds and thereby discern their meaning. It is not surprising therefore to find that these angular and supramarginal areas are particularly active in children learning to read, and that their degree of activation predicts how successfully children will learn to read.

Inferior frontal gyrus

In addition it is now clear that a number of areas around and including Broca's speech production area in the inferior frontal gyrus (IFG) are activated even during silent reading. The more posterior areas appear to be associated with phonological rehearsal during reading; hence they mediate important metalinguistic functions dependent upon phonological short term memory. Holding the first words in a sentence in your phonological short term memory is crucial for extracting the meaning of the whole sentence, which is often only evident after the order of words and their grammatical relationships (syntax) have become clear.

The more anterior aspects of IFG seem to play a role in semantic retrieval (Poldrack et al., 1999). Like the temporoparietal system, they are more strongly engaged by low-frequency words and pronounceable non-words than by high-frequency words. Like the temporoparietal system also, the anterior IFG is probably particularly important in children learning to read, for helping them to decode new words (Pugh et al., 2005). Later on however, its degree of activation seems to become inversely related to children's reading ability. Unlike in the posterior parietal and occipital regions therefore, the IFG is *more* active in dyslexics. The worse the reader, the more he has to rely on the letter/sound phonological translation route for reading.

Causes of m- cell defect

Recent genetic linkage studies have confirmed what had been widely suspected earlier, namely that several genes are involved in dyslexia. More interestingly all of the genes that have so far been implicated have turned out to be involved in controlling neuronal migration early in the development of the cerebral cortex in utero. The most widely replicated genetic linkage site for reading problems is on the short arm of chromosome 6. We have identified two genes close to each other that seem to help control neuronal migration (Francks et al., 2004). After electro-porating into the developing cerebral cortex of the mouse, complementary RNAi derived from these two genes that inhibits their expression, neuronal migration is completely arrested. In dyslexics it is unlikely that the genes are totally inhibited; rather they are probably down regulated so that neuronal migration would only be slightly affected. In view of their generally greater vulnerability, it seems likely however that magnocell migration would be the disturbed

One of these C6 genes, KIAA 0319, seems to control glycosylation of cell surface molecules. These respond to extracellular control signals and also act as signatures indicating to other cells what lineage they derive from. Thus it may be significant that the magnocells with rapid temporal processing, 'transient' sensitivity important for reading, which are found throughout the nervous system (Hockfield and Sur, 1990), all express the same specific m-cell signature molecules such as CAT 301. As mentioned earlier, visual and auditory transient sensitivity tend to correlate with each other within individuals. Thus all m- cells may be under the same general developmental control regulated by KIAA 0319. It is possible therefore that the development of all the temporal processing (visual, auditory, memory and motor) skills that are required for reading might be under the control of genes like KIAA 0319 (Stein, 2001). Different alleles might affect different individuals more in one system than another, idiosyncratically, so that one dyslexic may be weaker visually, another auditorily, and so on.

Immune control

Another reason why the linkage site on C6 has attracted so much attention is because it is situated within the immune regulatory system of genes, the major histocompatibility control (MHC) system. Many poor readers and their families seem to have a higher incidence of autoimmune problems, such as asthma, eczema and hay fever, and also more serious autoimmune diseases, such as disseminated lupus erythematosis (DLE – Tonnessen et al., 1993). They may also have a greater propensity for inflammatory disorders, but interestingly it appears that this same propensity may protect them from high blood pressure and its deleterious effects on the heart, cerebral blood vessels and kidneys (Taylor and Stein, 2002). Possibly it also protects them from cancer.

As mentioned earlier Corriveau and colleagues (Corriveau et al., 1998) have shown that this same MHC system helps to control the development of magnocells throughout the brain, including memory related neurones in the hippocampus and visual ones in the LGN. Taken in conjunction with the evidence that the KIAA gene controlling surface protein glycosylation may be down regulated in dyslexics, this suggests that their magnocells may be less responsive to MHC signals. This could significantly disrupt their development and partly explain dyslexics' slower acquisition of the visual and auditory temporal processing skills required for reading.

Another possible mechanism for this disruption may be transfer of antimagno-antibodies across the placenta during the rapid development of the foetal brain that occurs during the second trimester of pregnancy. We have injected into pregnant mice serum from mothers who had had two or more dyslexic children. We found that antibodies from this serum could cross both the placenta and the immature foetal blood brain barrier, and bind to magnocellular cells in the developing cerebellum in the pups. After birth therefore, their coordination was significantly impaired and their cerebellar metabolism was found to be abnormal in magnetic resonance spectroscopy studies (Vincent et al. 2002).

Omega-3 fish oils

Polyunsaturated fatty acids (PUFAs) of the omega-3 type, mainly derived from fish oils, constitute 20 per cent of the dry weight of the brain. The rapid responses of magnocells require these PUFAs to preserve the fluidity of their membranes and also to provide the substrates for eicosanoid signaling molecules. So magnocells are known to be particularly vulnerable to PUFA deficiency (Ahmad et al., 2002). But modern diets tend to be severely deficient in oily fish, which is the main source of PUFAs. Many dyslexics show clear signs of PUFA deficiency, such as dry skin, scurfy hair and brittle nails (Taylor et al., 2000). Probably our brains contain so much PUFA because its rapid increase in size that occurred about 100,000 years ago was enabled by an abundant supply of oily fish in our semiaquatic environment. PUFA flexibility endows nerve membranes with high fluidity so that their channels can open and close very rapidly. Also omega 3 PUFAs, in particular, serve as substrates for synthesis of anti inflammatory prostaglandin and thromboxane signalling molecules.

We have recently completed a number of randomized control trials that have confirmed that supplementing the diet of children with reading problems with extra PUFAs can actually improve their attention, behavior and reading (Richardson and Puri, 2002; Richardson and Montgomery, 2005). This adds to the evidence that an adequate supply of PUFAs in the diet is indeed important to the well-being of our magnocells.

CONCLUSION

Thus, it seems that the genes that we inherit from our parents can lead to dyslexic problems, probably by affecting the developmental migration of magnocells in utero and influencing their function later on by a combination of MHC controlled immunological effects and influences on PUFA metabolism, in concert with the availability of PUFAs in the diet. The performance of these magnocellular neurones, in turn, determines how well we can learn to fixate, attend to and perceive the important visual features of print. This therefore is probably how the genetically controlled sensitivity of our magnocellular systems influences how well we can develop and use the orthographic and phonological skills required for reading.

REFERENCES

Ahmad, A., T., N. Moriguchi, and N. Salem (2002) 'Decrease in neuron size in docosahexaenoic acid-deficient brain', *Pediatr Neuro*, 26 (3): 210–218.

Castro-Caldas, A., Petersson, K. M., Reis, A., Stone-Elander, S. and Ingvar, M. (1998) 'The illiterate brain. Learning to read and write during childhood influences the functional organization of the adult brain', *Brain*, 121: 1053–1063.

Cheng, A., Eysel, U. and T. Vidyasagar (2004) 'The role of the magnocellular pathway in serial deployment of visual attention', *Eur J Neurosci*, 20: 2188–2192.

Cohen, L., Henry, C., Dehaene, S., Martinaud, O., Lehericy, S., Lemer, C. and S. Ferrieux (2004) 'The patho-physiology of letter-by-letter reading', *Neuropsychologia*, 42 (13): 1768–1780.

Cornelissen, P.L., Hansen, P.C., Hutton, J.L., Evangelinou, V. and Stein, J.F. (1997) 'Magnocellular visual function and children's single word reading', *Vision Res*, 38: 471–482.

Cornelissen, P., Richardson, A., Mason, A., Fowler, S. and Stein, J.F. (1995) 'Contrast sensitivity and coherent motion detection measured at photopic luminance levels in dyslexics and controls [see comments]', *Vision Res.*, 35 (10): 1483–1494.

Corriveau, R., Huh, G. and Shatz, C. (1998) 'Regulation of class 1 *MHC* gene expression in the developing and mature CNS by neural activity', *Neuron*, 21: 505–520.

Crawford, T. and Higham, M. (2001) 'Dyslexia and centre of gravity effect', *Exp Brain Res*, 137: 122–126.

Demb, J. B., Boynton, G.M. and Heeger, D.J. (1997) 'Brain activity in visual cortex predicts individual differences in reading performance', *Proc Natl Acad Sci U S A*, 94 (24): 13363–13366.

Eden, G. F., VanMeter, J.W., Rumsey, J.M., Maisog, J.M., Woods, R.P. and Zeffiro, T.A. (1996) 'Abnormal processing of visual motion in dyslexia revealed by functional brain imaging', *Nature*, 382 (6586): 66–69.

Elliot, J. (2006) 'Dyslexia: Diagnoses, Debates and Diatribes', *Education Canada*, 46 (2): 14–17.

Facoetti, A., Turatto, M., Lorusso, M.L. and Mascetti, G.G. (2001) 'Orienting visual attention in dyslexia', *Exp Brain Res*, 138: 46–53.

Fischer, B., Hartnegg, K. and Mokler, A. (2000) 'Dynamic visual perception of dyslexic children', *Perception*, 29 (5): 523–530.

Fowler, M. S. (1991) 'Binocular Instability in Dyslexics', in J. F. Stein (ed), *Vision and Visual Dysfunction*, 13, London: Macmillan Press. pp. 25–32.

Fowler, M. S., Mason, A.J.S., Richardson, A.J., Welham, R.A. and Stein, J.F. (1992) 'Yellow glasses improve the vision of children with binocular amblyopia', *Lancet*, 340: 724.

Fowler, M. S., Riddell, P.M. and Stein, J.F. (1990) 'Vergence Eye Movement Control and Spatial Discrimination in Normal and Dyslexic Children', in George Pavlidis (ed) *Perspectives on Dyslexia, Vol. 1*. Chichester: Wiley. pp. 253–274.

Francks, C., Paracchini, S., Smith, S.D., Richardson, A.J., Scerri, T.S., Cardon, L.R., Marlow, A.J., MacPhie, I.L., Walter, J., Pennington, B.F., Fisher, S.E., Olson, R.K., DeFries, J.C., Stein, J.F. and Monaco, A.P. (2004) 'A 77-kilobase region of chromosome 6p22.2 is associated with dyslexia in families from the United Kingdom and from the United States', *Am J Hum Genet*, 75 (6): 1046–1058.

Galaburda, A. M., Menard, M. T. and Rosen, G.D. (1994) 'Evidence for aberrant auditory anatomy in developmental dyslexia', *Proc Natl Acad Sci U S A*, 91 (17): 8010–8013.

Galaburda, A. M., Sherman, G. F., Rosen, G.D., Aboitiz, F. and Geschwind, N. (1985) 'Developmental dyslexia: four consecutive patients with cortical anomalies', *Ann Neurol*, 18 (2): 222–233.

Hari, R. (2001) 'Left minineglect in dyslexic adults', *Brain*, 124: 1373–1380.

Harris, D. and MacRow-Hill, S. J. (1999) 'Application of ChromaGen haploscopic lenses to patients with dyslexia: a double-masked, placebo-controlled trial', *J Am Optom Assoc*, 70 (10): 629–640.

Hockfield, S. and Sur, M. (1990) 'Monoclonal Cat-301 identifies Y cells in cat LGN', *J Comp Neurol*, 300: 320–330.

Horowitz, T. and Wolfe, J. (1998) 'Visual search has no memory', *Nature*, 394: 575–577.

Iles, J., Walsh, V. and Richardson, A. (2000) 'Visual search performance in dyslexia', *Dyslexia*, 6 (3): 163–177.

Irlen, H. (1991) *Reading by colors*. New York, Avery.

Livingstone, M. S., Rosen, G.D., Drislane, F.W. and Galaburda, A.M. (1991) 'Physiological and anatomical evidence for a magnocellular deficit in developmental dyslexia', *Proc Natl Acad Sci U S A*, 88: 7943–7947.

Lovegrove, W. J., Bowling, A., Badcock, D. and Blackwood, M. (1980) 'Specific reading disability: Differences in contrast sensitivity as a function of spatial frequency', *Science*, 210 (4468): 439–440.

Meares, O. (1980) 'Figure/ground brightness contrast and reading disabilities', *Visible Language*, 14: 13–29.

Merigan, W. H. and Maunsell, J. H. (1990) 'Macaque vision after magnocellular lateral geniculate lesions', *Vis Neurosci*, 5 (4): 347–352.

Morais, J., Cary, L., Alegria, J. and Berterlson, P. (1979) 'Does awareness of speech as a sequence of phones arise spontaneously?', *Cognition*, 7: 323–332.

Nicolson, R. I., Fawcett, A. J., Berry, E. L., Jenkins, I. H., Dean, P. and Brooks, D.J. (1999) 'Motor learning difficulties and abnormal cerebellar activation in dyslexic adults', *Lancet*, 353: 43–47.

Olson, R., Wise, B., Conners, F., Rack, J. and Fulker, D. (1989) 'Specific deficits in component reading and language skills: genetic and environmental influences', *J Learn Disabil*, 22 (6): 339–348.

Pammer, K. and Wheatley, C. (2001) 'Isolating the M(y)-cell response in dyslexia using the spatial frequency doubling illusion', *Vision Res*, 41: 2139.

Poldrack, R. A., Wagner, A.D., Prull, M.W., Desmond, J.E., Glover, G.H. and Gabrieli, J.D. (1999) 'Functional specialization for semantic and phonological processing in the left inferior prefrontal cortex', *Neuroimage*, 10: 15–35.

Pugh, K. R., Sandak, R., Frost, S.J., Moore, D. and Mencl, W.E. (2005) 'Examining reading development and reading disability in English language learners: Potential contributions form functional neuroimaging', *Learn Disabil Res Pract*, 20 (1): 24–30.

Rae, C., Harasty, J., Dzendrowskyj, T.E., Talcott, J.B., Simpson, J.M., Blamire, A.M., Dixon, R.M., Lee, M.A., Thompson, C.H, Styles, P., Richardson, A.J. and Stein, J.F (2002) 'Cerebellar Morphology in Developmental Dyslexia', *Neuropsychologia*, 40: 1285–1292.

Rae, C., Lee, M.A., Dixon, R.M., Blamire, A.M., Thompson, C.H., Styles, P., Talcott, J., Richardson, A.J. and Stein, J.F. (1998) 'Metabolic abnormalities in developmental dyslexia detected by (1)H magnetic resonance spectroscopy', *Lancet*, 351 (9119): 1849–1852.

Ramus, F., Rosen, S., Dakin, S.C., Day, B.L., Castellote, J.M., White, S. and Frith, U. (2003) 'Theories of developmental dyslexia: insights from a multiple case study of dyslexic adults', *Brain*, 126: 841–865.

Ray, N., Fowler, S. and Stein, J.F. (2005) 'Yellow filters can improve magnocellular function: motion sensitivity, convergence, accommodation, and reading', *Ann N Y Acad Sci*, 1039 (1): 283–293

Richardson, A. and Montgomery, P. (2005) 'The Oxford-Durham study: a randomized controlled trial of dietary supplementation with fatty acids in children with developmental coordination disorder', *Pediatrics*, 115 (5): 1360–1366.

Richardson, A. and Puri, B. (2002) 'A randomized double blind placebo controlled study of the effects of supplementation with highly unsaturated fatty acids on ADHD related symptoms in children with specific learning difficulties', *Prog Neuropsychology and Beh. Psychiatry*, 26: 233–239.

Schmahmann, J. D. (2004) 'Disorders of the Cerebellum: Ataxia, Dysmetria of Thought, and the Cerebellar Cognitive Affective Syndrome', *J Neuropsychiatry Clin Neurosci*, 16 (3): 367–378.

Scott, R., Stoodley, C. Anslow, P., Stein, J.F., Sugden, M. and Mitchell, C.D. (2001) 'Lateralized cognitive deficits in children following cerebellar lesions', *Dev Med Child Neurol*, 43: 685–691.

Shillcock, R. C. and Monaghan, P. (2001) 'The computational exploration of visual word recognition in a split model', *Neural Comput*, 13: 1171–1198.

Simos, P. G., Breier, J. I., Fletcher, J. M., Foorman, B. R., Castillo, E. M., and Papanicolaou, A.C. (2002) 'Brain mechanisms for reading words and pseudowords: an integrated approach', *Cereb Cortex*, 12: 297–305.

Skottun, B. C. (1997) 'The magnocellular deficit theory of dyslexia', *TINS*, 20: 397–398.

Stanovich, K. E. (1988) 'Explaining the differences between the dyslexic and the garden-variety poor reader: the phonological-core variable-difference model', *J Learn Disabil*, 21 (10): 590–604.

Stein, J. (2001) 'The Magnocellular Theory of Developmental Dyslexia', *Dyslexia*, 7: 12–36.

Stein, J. (2003) 'Why did language develop?' *Int J Pediatr Otorhinolaryngol*, 67: S1–9.

Stein, J. F. (1986) 'Role of the cerebellum in the visual guidance of movement', *Nature*, 323 (6085): 217–221.

Stein, J. F., Richardson, A.J. and Fowler, M.S. (2000) 'Monocular occlusion can improve binocular control and reading in dyslexics', *Brain*, 123: 164–170.

Stein, J. F. and Fowler, S. (1981) 'Visual dyslexia', *Trends Neurosci*, 4: 77–80.

Stein, J. F., P. Riddell and Fowler, S. (1985) 'Dyslexia and monocular occlusion', *Lancet*, 2 (8460): 883–884.

Stoerig, P. and A. Cowey (1997) 'Blindsight in man and monkey', *Brain*, 120 (3): 535–559.

Stoodley, C. J., Fawcett, A.J., Nicolson, R.I. and Stein, J.F. (2005) 'Impaired balancing ability in dyslexic children', *Exp Brain Res*, 167 (3): 370–380.

Stoodley, C. J., Harrison, E. P. and Stein, J.F. (2005) 'Implicit motor learning deficits in dyslexic adults', *Neuropsychologia*, 44 (5): 795–798.

Talcott, J.B., Witton, C., McLean, M.F., Hansen, P.C., Rees, A., Green, G.R. and Stein, J.F. (2000) 'Dynamic sensory sensitivity and children's word decoding skills', *Proc Natl Acad Sci U S A*, 97: 2952–2962.

Tallal, P. and Piercy, M. (1973) 'Defects of non-verbal auditory perception in children with developmental aphasia', *Nature*, 241 (5390): 468–469.

Taylor, K. E., C.M. Calvin, J.A. Hall, T. Easton, A.M. McDaid, and Richardson, A.J. (2000) 'Dyslexia in adults is associated with clinical signs of fatty acid deficiency', *Prostaglandins Leukot Essent Fatty Acids*, 63: 75–78.

Taylor, K. E. and Stein, J.F. (2002) 'Dyslexia and familial high blood pressure: an observational pilot study', *Archi Disease Child*, 86 (1): 30–33.

Tonnessen, F. E., Lokken, A., Hoien, T. and Lundberg, I. (1993) 'Dyslexia, left-handedness, and immune disorders', *Arch Neurol*, 50 (4): 411–416.

Trussell, L. O. (1997) 'Cellular mechanisms for preservation of timing in central auditory pathways', *Curr Opin Neurobiol*, 7 (4): 487–492.

Vidyasagar, T. R. (2004) 'Neural underpinnings of dyslexia as a disorder of visuo-spatial attention', *Clin Exp Optom*, 87 (1): 4–10.

Vincent, A., Deacon, R., Blamire, A.W., Pendlebury, S., Salmond, C., Johansen-Berg, H., Dalton, P., Rajogopalan, Styles, P. and Stein, J.F. (2002) 'Behavioural and cerebellar MRS findings in mice exposed in utero to serum from mothers of children with neurodevelopmental disorders', *J Neuroimmunol*, 130: 87–89.

Wilkins, A. J. and Nimmo Smith, I. (1984) 'On the reduction of eye-strain when reading', *Ophthalmic Physiol Opt*, 4 (1): 53–59.

Witton, C, Stein, J.F., Stoodley, C. J., Rosner, B.S. and Talcott, J.B. (2002) 'Separate influences of acoustic AM and FM sensitivity on the phonological decoding skills of impaired and normal readers', *J Cogn Neurosci*, 14: 866–874.

4

Dyslexia and the Cerebellum

Angela J. Fawcett and
Roderick I. Nicolson

This chapter

i) discusses an alternative perspective for explaining developmental dyslexia; and
ii) reviews the status of the cerebellar deficit hypothesis and suggests that it provides a
coherent explanation of the developmental antecedents of dyslexia.

INTRODUCTION: CO-ORDINATION AND DYSLEXIA

The traditional symptoms of dyslexia in an individual involve weaker attainment
in the literacy skills of reading, writing and spelling than expected on the basis
of the individual's general ability and opportunity (World Federation of
Neurology, 1968).

In an irregular language such as English, the links between reading, spelling and
writing seem apparent. After all, words that are hard to read are hard to spell
and hence hard to write (in that one has to think about spelling while writing).
However, in languages with more transparent orthography (i.e., a more regular
language), these links are by no means obvious. In Spanish the link from writing to
pronunciation is absolutely consistent as is the link from pronunciation to spelling.
In Greek the link from writing to pronunciation is also one-to-one, but the link from
pronunciation to spelling is not, in that many (written) vowels have the same
pronunciation. Consequently one might expect a Greek dyslexic child to have
particular difficulties with spelling and writing, whereas any reading difficulties
would show up as slowness rather than inaccuracy. Interestingly, even in English
there is now solid evidence that there are different genetic influences underlying
phonological and orthographic (spelling) problems in dyslexia (Olson, 2002).

It would appear then that the three criterial difficulties are not as directly linked as one might expect, and it is of interest to consider what characteristics reading, writing and spelling might have in common.

One obvious point (Nicolson and Fawcett, 1990) is that all three are learned skills, requiring hundreds or thousands of hours for expert performance. This perspective leads naturally to an analysis of the sub-processes of learning, and is considered in more detail in chapter 9 of this volume. Another perspective, however, is that these skills all require coordination between different brain regions for effective execution. Reading aloud involves the coordination of vision, eye movements, cognitive processing and speech. Writing involves the coordination of eye movements, hand movements and cognitive processing. Spelling involves the coordination of cognitive processing and speech. Vellutino's seminal studies of learning (Vellutino et al., 1983; Vellutino, 1979) suggest that problems arise in dyslexia when verbal processing has to be combined with processing in some other modality (such as visual). Furthermore, the basis of the traditional approach to helping dyslexic children learn to read is to encourage them to use multisensory processing (Orton, 1966). It may well be that the need for explicit emphasis on multisensory coordination is a method of confronting intrinsic difficulties with the coordination task. Might it be, therefore, that dyslexic children have particular difficulties when tasks require the coordination of different senses, cognitive processes, and different actions? Furthermore, one might expect that the difficulties would become more marked with an increase in the number of coordinations required.

It has been established for many decades that the key brain region for the coordination of actions is the cerebellum (Eccles et al., 1967; Holmes, 1917; 1939; Ito, 1984). However, until relatively recently the cerebellum was not thought to have a role in cognitive processing, and so, despite early proposals by Levinson (Frank and Levinson, 1973; Levinson, 1988) the possibility of cerebellar involvement in dyslexia was discounted by most researchers. A particular concern was Levinson's advocacy of drug-based treatment for dyslexia based on his cerebellar-vestibular hypothesis (see Silver, 1987 for an impassioned critique).

The period from 1990 to the present day has led to a transformation of our knowledge about brain function, and, as we outline in the following section, arguably the most significant change has been in the understanding of the role of the cerebellum, which has moved from a bit-part player to arguably the reclusive star of the entire cognitive operation of the brain. In the following section we outline the evidence that has accumulated relating to the now-established role of the cerebellum in cognition.

THE CEREBELLUM

It is not our intention to provide a detailed description of the cerebellum in this chapter. Readers with the neuroscience knowledge to benefit from such a description probably have a reasonable knowledge, and those who do not may not relish the opportunity! Nonetheless, some information is needed to highlight the quite unique nature of its structure and role.

In humans, the cerebellum accounts for 10–15 per cent of brain weight, 40 per cent of brain surface area, and 50 per cent of the brain's neurons, with 10^{11} granule cells alone (Brodal, 1981). There are two cerebellar hemispheres, each comprising folded cerebellar cortex, which receive massive inputs from all the senses, from the primary motor cortex, and from many other areas of cerebral cortex, either by 'mossy fibres' from the pontine nuclei or via 'climbing fibres' from the inferior olive. Output from the cerebellum is generated by Purkinje cells, goes via the deep cerebellar nuclei and is generally inhibitory. The cerebellar cortex comprises several phylogenetically ancient structures, including the flocculonodular node, which is situated at the caudal end, and receives input from the vestibular system and projects to the vestibular nuclei. The vermis, located on the midline, receives visual, auditory, cutaneous and kinesthetic information from sensory nuclei, and sends output to the fastigial nucleus, which connects to the vestibular nucleus and motor neurons in the reticular formation. On both sides of the vermis, there is the 'intermediate zone' which receives input from the motor areas of cerebral cortex with output via other nuclei to the rubrospinal system for arm and hand movements, and also to the ventrothalamic nucleus.

The lateral zone of the cerebellum is the one that has generated intense interest over its apparent role in cognitive processes. It is phylogenetically more recent, and is much larger in humans (relative to overall brain size) than in other primates (Passingham, 1975) and is referred to as the neocerebellum. It is involved in the control of independent limb movements and especially in rapid, skilled movements, receiving information from frontal association cortex and from primary motor cortex via the pontine nucleus. It also receives somatosensory information about the current position and rate of movement of the limbs. Its role in skilled movement execution is generally thought to be the computation of the appropriate movement parameters for the next movement (possibly the next but one movement), and to communicate these via the dentate nucleus and the ventrolateral thalamic nucleus to the primary motor cortex. The lateral zone also sends outputs to the red nucleus, and thus the rubrospinal tract.

Damage to different parts of the cerebellum can lead to a variety of different symptoms. In humans, damage to the flocculonodular system or vermis may typically lead to disturbances in posture and balance. Damage to the intermediate zone causes problems such as limb rigidity. Damage to the neocerebellum causes weakness (loss of muscle tone) and dyscoordination or decomposition of movement (i.e., previously coordinated sequences of movements, such as picking up a cup, may break down into a series of separate movements). However, one of the features of cerebellar damage is the great plasticity of the system. Typically normal or close to normal performance is attained again within a few months of the initial damage (Holmes, 1922).

plasticity is a key feature.

In terms of its formation, the cerebellum is one of the first brain structures to begin to differentiate, yet it is one of the last to achieve maturity – the cellular organization of the cerebellum continues to change for many months after birth. This protracted developmental process creates a special susceptibility to disruptions during embryogenesis (Wang and Zoghbi, 2001). There is now extensive evidence that the cerebellum is a brain structure particularly susceptible to insult in the case of premature birth, and that such insults can lead to a range of motor, language and cognitive problems subsequently (Limperopoulos et al., 2007; Steinlin, 2007).

One of the fascinating aspects of the cerebellum is that the structure of the cerebellum appears to be quite different from that of the rest of the brain. In particular, the cerebellar cortex comprises a mosaic of relatively independent 'microzones', comprising a Purkinje cell and its associated inputs and output. Several authors (Albus, 1971; Ito, 1984; Marr, 1969) have highlighted the opportunity that these microzones, in combination with the associated pathways to and from the cerebral cortex, may be thought of as a 'cerebellar-cortico-nuclear microcomplex' (CCMC) able to undertake a range of tasks. A key point is that the cerebellum rarely acts alone, but always in conjunction with other brain regions, and it acts to optimize the functioning of the skill that is controlled by that other region.

cerebellum rarely acts alone

The role of the cerebellum in cognition

It has been established for many years that the cerebellum is involved in automaticity. 'The cerebellum is thus a principal agent in the learning of motor skills' (Brindley, 1964). Early studies of the cerebellum focused on its role in skill execution, based on data derived from soldiers with gunshot wounds, examining skills developed before the incident (Holmes, 1939). Major symptoms of damage include hypotonia (low muscle tone), hypermetria (over-shooting of movements) and intention tremor (Dow and Moruzzi, 1958).

However, these established views on the cerebellum needed re-evaluation following recent advances in brain imaging, which have now made it possible for the whole brain to be imaged for the first time, including the cerebellum. This allowed the role of the cerebellum in language processing to be seen for the first time, revealing high levels of activation in skills such as imagining a tennis stroke, speaking, or trying to remember a list of words. This reconceptualization was initially contentious, with several influential researchers arguing for the traditional role of the cerebellum (Eccles et al., 1967; Holmes, 1917; 1939; Stein and Glickstein, 1992), that it is simply limited to motor skills. However, Leiner et al. (1989) noted the evolution of the human cerebellum (the lateral cerebellar hemispheres and ventrolateral cerebellar dentate nucleus in particular) which had become linked with areas in the frontal cortex, including Broca's language area, in addition to the known motor links, thus making the cerebellum central for 'language dexterity'(Leiner et al., 1989; 1991, 1993) and critical in automatization of any skill, whether motor or cognitive.

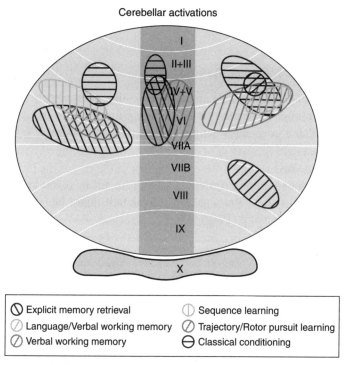

Cerebellar activations

Legend:
- ⊘ Explicit memory retrieval
- ⊘ Language/Verbal working memory
- ⊘ Verbal working memory
- ⊙ Sequence learning
- ⊘ Trajectory/Rotor pursuit learning
- ⊖ Classical conditioning

Figure 4.1 Cerebellar activations in cognitive activities
Schematic diagram of the unfolded cerebellum illustrating the location of activations. Roman numerals appearing in the cerebellar vermis (illustrated by the darker shaded region along the midline) denote the lobule indentification based on Larsells's nomenclature. For the human cerebellar vermis, they correspond to the following lobules: lingula (i), Centrails (II+III), Culmen (IV+V), Declive (VI), Follum vermis (VIIA), Tuber vermis (VIIB), Pyramis (VIII), Uvula (IX), Nodulus (X). Regions of activation were assessed by first transforming a cerebellar volume into the space of the Talairach atlas. All of the locations of significant activation from the reviewed studies were then plotted on this volume. The volume was then inspected slice-by-slice to determine the distribution of foci associated with each type of task. This information was used to depict the areal extent of activation on the unfolded model of the cerebellum. Taken from Desmond and Fiez, 1998.

Since that time evidence has rapidly been built that the cerebellum is indeed a major player in most cognitive skills associated with speech. A valuable summary of the roles of different regions of the cerebellum in different cognitive skills was provided by Desmond and Fiez (1998) – see Figure 4.1. Note in particular that different regions of the cerebellum are associated with different skills, and that the cerebellum is associated with both verbal and motor skills. It is worth highlighting the cerebellum's clear involvement in verbal working memory and in explicit memory retrieval (which reflect operation of the declarative memory system) and the involvement in sequence learning, trajectory learning and classical conditioning (which reflect operation of the procedural learning system).

The role of the cerebellum in dyslexia

Although problems in motor skill and automatization point clearly to the cerebellum, it is important to review the literature on motor skills and dyslexia, to identify any earlier evidence for deficits in these areas in dyslexia.

Motor skills and dyslexia

Clumsiness has been noted in dyslexic children for many years, but it has not been at all clear what the significance of this deficit might be. In a review of Orton's writings, Geschwind (1982) noted

> He pointed out the frequency of clumsiness in dyslexics. Although others have commented on this, it still remains a mysterious and not adequately studied problem. It is all the more mysterious in view of the fact that many of these clumsy children go on to successes in areas in which high degrees of manual dexterity are absolutely necessary.

Impairments in articulation in dyslexia have also frequently been noted, but it has not been clear whether these are related to phonological deficits per se, or to motor skill deficits in the rate or accuracy of articulation. Snowling (1981) initially identified errors in repeating polysyllabic or nonsense words, by contrast with accurate repetition of simple high-frequency words in young dyslexic children. A similar pattern of normal performance on simple articulatory tasks coupled with problems in more complex tasks was identified by other researchers. Brady et al. (1983) reported accurate repetition of monosyllables, whereas Catts (1989) reported problems in repetition of simple and complex phrases. Furthermore, Stanovich (1988a) established that poor readers up to age 10 showed problems with the speed of repetition of even simple couplets, reflecting a developmental lag in motor timing control.

Interestingly enough, for many years there has also been controversy over eye movement abnormalities in dyslexia, based on claims by Pavlidis (1985) for a distinctive pattern of regressive saccades in reading. These results have proved difficult to replicate and may simply reflect attempts to read text that is too difficult for the skills of the reader. Nevertheless, there is consistent evidence of deficits in eye movement control in dyslexia in a range of non reading tasks. (Fischer et al., 1998; 2000), in addition to anomalies in static eye control (Stein and Fowler, 1993; 1982; Stein et al., 2000). It has been suggested that these difficulties would lead to problems in focusing on letters within words, to problems with crowded text, and in keeping track of the correct place on the page in reading, and thus to reading problems. Although Stein (2001) considers that these problems are compatible with the magnocellular deficit, they are even more likely to reflect cerebellar deficits. Nevertheless, it is not clear how common these deficits are within the dyslexic population (Skottun, 2001), and it has been suggested that only a minority of children with dyslexia may show such deficits.

In terms of gross motor coordination, there have been many anecdotal reports of difficulties. Augur (1985) documents several, including swimming and riding a bike. Data from the British Births cohort examined the skills of 12,905 children longitudinally (Haslum, 1989), identifying two motor skills tasks at age 10 which were significantly associated with dyslexia. These were failure to throw a ball up, clap several times and catch the ball and failure to walk backwards in a straight line for six steps. Deficits in fine motor skills have also been identified, in terms of the characteristically poor handwriting (Benton, 1978; Miles, 1983), and copying in young children (Badian, 1984; Rudel, 1985), coupled with difficulty in tying shoelaces (Miles, 1983).

For many years there has been evidence for 'soft neurological signs' in the motor skill deficits noted in dyslexia, including deficits in speed of tapping, rapid successive finger opposition, heel-toe placement and accuracy in copying (Denckla, 1985; Rudel, 1985). This led Denckla to argue for a 'non-specific developmental awkwardness', reflected in poor coordination even in relatively athletic dyslexic children, which is normally outgrown by puberty (Rudel, 1985). Denckla (1985) notes particular impairments in acquiring new skills, followed by normal performance once acquired: 'the part of the "motor analyzer" that is dependent on the left hemisphere and has been found to be important for timed, sequential movements is deficient in the first decade of life in this group of children whom we call dyslexic'. The success of the phonological deficit framework was enhanced by Denckla's later attribution of these soft signs to attention deficit (ADHD), and arguing that these reflect comorbidity with dyslexia (Denckla et al., 1985), rather than dyslexia itself.

Nevertheless, much of the most interesting early work on motor skills in dyslexia could not be attributed to either phonological deficit or ADHD. Wolff and his colleagues (1990) used replication of rhythms beaten out by a metronome to establish motor skill deficits extending into adolescence in 12–13 year old dyslexic boys with language deficits. Despite accurate performance at a slow speed, problems in accuracy arose at a speed threshold in performance with both hands, which Wolff and colleagues ascribe to impaired interlimb coordination, whereby motor patterns are disrupted by attempts to produce speeded movements. They have since established this bimanual coordination deficit in 50 per cent of dyslexics, and linked this to impaired spelling in extended family studies (Wolff et al., 1995) concluding that dysphonetic spelling is linked to impaired temporal resolution, which can be revealed by attempts to coordinate motor actions (Wolff et al., 1996).

THE CEREBELLAR DEFICIT HYPOTHESIS

In the early 1990s we were alerted to the new putative role of the cerebellum in cognition by our colleague Paul Dean, and it seemed clear that if indeed the cerebellum did play such roles in cognition, then cerebellar deficit provided a single coherent explanation of the three criterial difficulties of reading, writing and spelling. Furthermore, it provided a coherent and principled explanation of the three major 'cognitive' explanations of dyslexia, namely a phonological deficit (Stanovich, 1988a; Vellutino, 1979), double deficits (namely, in both phonology and speed) (Wolf and Bowers, 1999), and automatization deficit (Nicolson and Fawcett, 1990). This led to our cerebellar deficit hypothesis (Nicolson et al., 1995), namely that dyslexia was attributable to slightly impaired cerebellar function, probably from birth.

Throughout the 1990s we attempted to test this hypothesis, establishing the following evidence for behavioral, functional and anatomical deficits:

- dyslexic children show significant impairments on clinical tests of cerebellar function such as hypotonia (low muscle tone) and hypermetria (overshooting ballistic movements) and tremor (Fawcett and Nicolson, 1999; Fawcett et al., 1996);
- dyslexic adolescents failed to engage their cerebellum in learning tasks known normally to require cerebellar involvement (Nicolson et al., 1999);

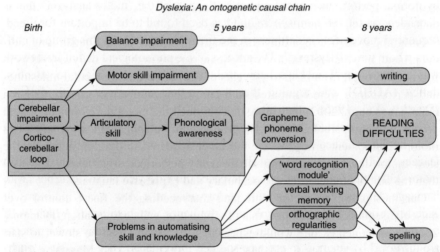

Dyslexia: An ontogenetic causal chain

Figure 4.2   A hypothetical causal chain
The horizontal axis represents both the passage of time (experience) and also the ways that difficulties with skill acquisition cause subsequent problems, leading to the known difficulties in reading, writing and spelling. The text provides a fuller explanation of the processes involved. Of particular interest is the progression highlighted as a central feature. Cerebellar abnormality at birth leads to mild motor and articulatory problems. Lack of articulatory fluency leads in turn to an impoverished representation of the phonological characteristics of speech, and thence to the well-established difficulties in phonological awareness at around 5 years that lead to subsequent problems in learning to read. Other routes outline the likely problems outside the phonological domain, and indicate that the difficulties in learning to read, spell and write may derive from a number of inter-dependent factors.

- analysis of the 'Dyslexia Brain Bank' specimens indicated that the dyslexic brains in the Beth Israel collection showed significantly different neuronal size for the Purkinje cells in the cerebellum and cell size in the inferior olive (Finch et al., 2002).

These data led to an enhancement of the hypothesis (Nicolson et al., 2001) in which we attempted to take a developmental approach to the explanation (Figure 4.2) Regardless of whether this specific explanation is correct, we consider that this 'ontogenetic' analysis is a particularly fruitful way of analyzing developmental disorders because it attempts to explain why problems arise in terms of their antecedents, and therefore provides a route from birth to school, from brain to behavior, explaining problems in our most impressive cognitive skill – reading – in terms of the underlying differences in brain function.

Figure 4.2 traces out the development progression from the very beginning – conception. If a parent has a genetic predisposition to dyslexia it is likely that the infant brain will not develop entirely normally in the womb. Here we consider only the differences in cerebellar development, but it is likely that other regions will also be affected. If an infant has a cerebellar abnormality, this will first show up as a mild motor difficulty – the infant may be slower to sit up and to crawl, and may have greater problems with fine muscular control. We predict that most skills are actually developed somewhat less well than normal, even if they emerge within the normal timescale.

Intriguing evidence regarding this issue is provided by the Finnish longitudinal project, in which 88 children of dyslexic parents in the city of Jyväskylä were followed through from birth to 10 years of age. Their developmental milestones and performance were compared with equivalent numbers of control children (Viholainen et al., 2002) indicating that although the motor development of both groups was comparable, the at risk group could be split into a slow and a fast motor development group. While the latter appeared to develop normally, the slow motor development group subsequently performed significantly less well than the others on measures of vocabulary and expressive language.

Our most complex motor skill, and that needing the finest control over muscular sequencing, is, in fact, that of articulation and coarticulation (Diamond, 2000). Consequently, one would expect that the infant might be slower to start babbling (see e.g., Davis and MacNeilage, 2000; Ejiri and Masataka, 2001; MacNeilage and Davis, 2001), and, later, talking (cf. Bates and Dick, 2002; Green et al., 2000). Indeed, there is long-standing evidence that the early articulatory and manual skills develop in step (Ramsay, 1984). Fowler (1991) found that very young children first perceive words as a loose bundle of articulated gestures, and in time, the coarticulated gestures become grouped into the representations of phonemes. The evidence for this view that speech develops from manual gestures is now growing (Corballis, 2002; Treffner and Peter, 2002). Interestingly, summarizing the Jyväskylä results Lyytinen et al. (2004) conclude that the basic prosodic and phonotactic (permissible sound combination) skills manifested in speech production as well as perception of durational differences in speech predict the development of early reading skills. They go on to propose that early atypicalities of speech processing among at risk children may hinder their linguistic development, leading to cumulative deficits.

Consequently, though the position is far from clear at present, it is certainly justifiable to assume that developmental processes such as those outlined in Figure 4.2 do indeed occur for the pre school years of children who later will be found to be dyslexic.

Let us now turn to the three criterial difficulties for dyslexia – reading, writing and spelling. Interestingly, the ontogenetic analysis suggests that the three arise from different routes. The handwriting difficulties reflect primarily weak motor control (exacerbated by weaknesses in spelling knowledge). The spelling problems arise from multiple routes – automatization problems as well as from the phonological difficulties and weak verbal working memory. The reading problems also arise from multiple routes, including phonological difficulties, weak verbal working memory, and a weak or slow 'word recognition module'.

Finally consider the current theoretical explanations of dyslexia. In terms of phonological deficit, it may be seen that the central route in Figure 4.2 (as discussed above) suggests that a key weakness at age five is in terms of phonological processing. Cerebellar impairment would therefore be predicted to cause, by direct and indirect means, the 'phonological core deficit' that has proved such a fruitful explanatory framework for many aspects of dyslexia. Of course the central role of the cerebellum in skill automatization also provides a principled explanation of automatization deficit, the second major 'cognitive' explanation. It also provides a natural explanation of the more recent 'double deficit' hypothesis (Wolf and Bowers, 1999). This is based on the established difficulties that dyslexic children have on 'rapid automatized naming' tasks (Denckla and Rudel, 1976). Naming speed difficulties are precisely those predicted by the cerebellar deficit hypothesis, given its established role in speech, inner speech and speeded processing. Consequently, all three cognitive level hypotheses appear to be directly consistent with, and indeed, subsumed by, the cerebellar deficit hypothesis.

Subsequent developments of the Cerebellar Deficit Hypothesis

Further findings in the cognitive neuroscience of the cerebellum
The role of the cerebellum in cognitive skills involving language has now been conclusively established. Anatomical studies have confirmed two-way connectivity of the cerebellum with frontal cortex (Kelly and Strick, 2003; Middleton and Strick, 2001; Ramnani, 2006), thereby confirming that there is the appropriate connectivity to the frontal language regions such as Broca's area. Both functional imaging research and research with cerebellar patients strongly supports the role of the cerebellum in language-related tasks (De Smet et al., 2007; Justus and Ivry, 2001; Marien et al., 2001; Marien and Verhoeven, 2007). A particular role is considered to be in support for verbal working memory, though the exact mechanisms

remain unclear. Ackerman and his colleagues (Ackermann et al., 2007) propose that a key role is 'a contribution of the right cerebellar hemisphere, concomitant with language-dominant dorsolateral and medial frontal areas, to the temporal organization of a prearticulatory verbal code ("inner speech"), in terms of the sequencing of syllable strings at a speaker's habitual speech rate' (p. 202). whereas Fiez and her colleagues (Ben-Yehudah et al, 2007) suggest that the role may be in terms of error-driven adjustment and internal timing of internal speech plans.

It is important to note that the above studies are based on skill execution rather than skill learning, but there is also strong evidence of cerebellar involvement in acquisition of a range of complex cognitive/motor skills such as tool use (Imamizu et al., 2003; Miall et al., 2000).

Further findings on the cerebellum and dyslexia
The landmark initial demonstration of brain activity when reading (Petersen et al., 1988) revealed cerebellar activation, but constraints on PET field of view led to omission of the cerebellum from much of the subsequent work and it was another decade before the cerebellar role in reading was clearly confirmed (Fulbright et al., 1999; Turkeltaub et al., 2002). This does of course strengthen the possibility that cerebellar impairment might well affect reading performance.

More directly, several studies have established further evidence of functional and anatomical abnormality of the cerebellum in dyslexia (Eckert et al., 2003; Leonard et al., 2002; Rae et al., 2002; Vicari et al., 2003). Eckert et al. (2003: 482) conclude 'The dyslexics exhibited significantly smaller right anterior lobes of the cerebellum, pars triangularis bilaterally, and brain volume'. For further reviews see Demonet et al. (2004); Habib, (2004) and Lozano et al. (2003).

It is notoriously difficult to isolate cerebellar function, in that the cerebellum appears to be designed to work in conjunction with other brain regions to optimize their performance. Consequently specific evidence of abnormal 'cerebellar' function in dyslexia is difficult to acquire. Our approach to this issue has been to adopt a 'converging operations' approach, in which a range of different tasks is explored, each of which involve the cerebellum plus other structures, but when taken in conjunction, have only the cerebellum as a common structure. It was for this reason that we initially focused on nonlinguistic motor tasks, in that this immediately rules out involvement of language-based processes.[1] We have earlier mentioned the weak performance of dyslexic participants on classical clinical cerebellar tests involving dystonia and dysmetria, together with direct evidence of reduced cerebellar activation in motor sequence learning (Nicolson et al., 1999).

One of the more controversial findings had been the identification of balance difficulties in dyslexia (Fawcett and Nicolson, 1992; Nicolson and Fawcett, 1990). Several groups have only partially replicated these findings (Raberger and Wimmer, 2003; Ramus et al., 2003a; Ramus et al., 2003b; Wimmer et al., 1999). Other groups have found deficits, even in adults (Iversen et al., 2005; Moe-Nilssen et al., 2003; Needle et al., 2006; Stoodley et al., 2006).

Our conclusion would be that at least half of dyslexic individuals do show problems in balance, but that the deficits are relatively subtle and diminish after adolescence, as one might expect for a developmental disorder.

Balance itself is in fact a highly complex task, involving a range of developmental changes in which the cerebellum is a major component but not the only one (Allum et al., 1998; Ioffe et al., 2007; Peterka, 2002). It is therefore valuable to consider other tasks in which the cerebellum is considered to have a major role.

Given the language basis of dyslexia, it is appropriate to establish whether such a basic variable as articulatory speed might be affected. Early research (Fawcett and Nicolson, 1995) identified that dyslexic children did have significantly slower articulation than same age controls, but as Snowling, (1981) and others have argued, articulatory problems could be attributable either to slower motor speed (which might be attributable to slower motor-cerebellar function) or to slower motor planning. The latter would be predicted on the basis of language-based cerebellar impairment as discussed above. In order to distinguish between these possibilities we analyzed sequences of simple phonemic 'gestures' to identify whether it was indeed the gesture time (scored as the time in which the articulators were active) or the planning time (pauses between the gestures). The results (Fawcett and Nicolson, 2002) indicated that the dyslexic children had significant problems in articulation, not only in gesture planning, but also in the speeded production of single articulatory gestures. Consequently the study provided evidence of impairment in both the language-cerebellar circuits and the motor-cerebellar circuits.

Arguably the tasks most closely associated with the cerebellum alone are eye blink conditioning, in which the participant is 'conditioned' to blink the eye on hearing a tone by playing the tone just before a puff of air to the eye (Gerwig et al., 2007; Maschke et al., 2003). In an investigation of conditioning in dyslexia, we established that the dyslexic participants did have significant difficulties, but these were related to the appropriate tuning of the eye blink so that it coincided with the air puff (Nicolson et al., 2002). This response optimization process is the hallmark of cerebellar involvement. A related eye blink conditioning study by Coffin et al. (2005) led to even stronger results, suggesting that both dyslexic children and children who had suffered from fetal alcohol syndrome failed to condition to the tone at all, by contrast with ADHD participants who conditioned normally

A further task thought to be specific to the cerebellum is that of prism adaptation (in which one wears distorting prisms, and rapidly adjusts to the distortion by 'recalibrating' the correspondence between senses and motor system. A study of prism adaptation in dyslexic and dyspraxic children indicated that both groups showed significantly slower adaptation than the control group, suggesting a cerebellar impairment in both dyslexia and dyspraxia (Brookes et al., 2007). This study is discussed further in the context of comorbidities between developmental disorders in chapter 9 of this volume.

CRITICISMS OF THE CEREBELLAR DEFICIT HYPOTHESIS

Despite these successes, the framework remains controversial, and criticisms represent generic challenges for the learning disabilities field.

Criticism 1: Cerebellum too broad [under-specificity]

The cerebellum is a very large structure, containing over half the brain's neurons, and for cerebellar deficit to be a viable framework, it would be crucial to specify which cerebellar region(s) were the key ones affected.

Our response to this point is that this is indeed the next task for investigation – together with analysis of which other brain regions are affected – but that the prior task was to establish whether or not there were indeed cerebellar problems.

Criticism 2: Cerebellum too narrow [over-specificity]

This criticism was put memorably as the 'innocent bystander' hypothesis (Zeffiro and Eden, 2001), namely that the cerebellum receives flawed information from some other brain system, and hence is merely an innocent bystander rather than the true villain – the longstanding issue of distinguishing cause and correlate. This problem is exacerbated by the difficulty in devising techniques that specifically isolate cerebellar function given its extraordinary connectivity and plasticity.

Our response to this point is that it is indeed difficult to distinguish between cause and correlate of problems in complex inter-dependent systems such as the brain. But this does not mean that one should not attempt to do so! We have argued elsewhere that it may indeed be valuable to consider not just the cerebellum but the neural systems involving the cerebellum that may be affected (Nicolson and Fawcett, 2007). Nonetheless, as discussed in this chapter it is possible to design tests that do (when taken in conjunction) provide strong evidence that the cerebellum is indeed one of the key structures involved.

Criticism 3: Cerebellar deficit not a core feature of dyslexia [primacy]

This criticism has three forms: cerebellar deficit is not a necessary criterion for dyslexia (in that at least one third of dyslexic children show no overt motor problems); it is not a sufficient condition (in that many non-dyslexic children show cerebellar deficit); and it is but weakly correlated with the core, literacy-related, symptoms (White et al., 2006).

Our response to this issue was made in Nicolson and Fawcett (2006). In terms of percentages, given the complexity of reading, it is likely that a range of difficulties can give rise to poor reading and with an incidence of at least 5 per cent (hence 3 million dyslexic individuals in the UK) it would be extraordinary if all had the same underlying cause. It is also a major misconception to believe that the cerebellar deficit hypothesis requires dyslexic children to show motor difficulties. As can be seen from Figure 4.1 different regions of the cerebellum are associated with motor skill and language skill. Nonetheless, given that the cerebellar deficit hypothesis presumes that the likely abnormalities in cerebellar organization arise from abnormal cell migration during gestation, or perhaps cerebellar insult perinatally, it is likely that in many cases both motor and language areas of the cerebellum might be affected. In terms of the relatively weak correlation with literacy after the effects of working memory and phonology have been accounted for, it is evident from Figure 4.2 that this is exactly what is predicted by our developmental model. The weak phonology and verbal working memory are (according to the model) caused by the cerebellar deficit. To eliminate them and say that there is then little sign of cerebellar effect on reading is to throw out the baby with the bathwater!

Criticism 4: Cerebellar deficit hypothesis encourages irresponsible treatments

This criticism takes the form that the hypothesis itself may or may not be valid, but that its very existence lends justification to a range of 'alternative' commercial interventions for reading disability that at best waste the money and time of the participants. This was a criticism of Levinson's treatment (Silver, 1987), and, more recently, of the Dore exercise-based 'cerebellar stimulation' treatment (Rack et al., 2007; Reynolds and Nicolson, 2007).

Our response to this criticism is that it is generally considered to be a positive feature of a theory if it leads to a range of potentially fruitful real-world applications. The issue of whether the interventions are indeed valuable is an empirical one. Given that it is established that the current reading interventions for dyslexia (especially after the age of 8) are acknowledged to be less effective than hoped, especially in terms of fluency (NICHD, 2000), it seems to us a major applied imperative to continue to explore methods of improving reading attainment. We must emphasize that it is quite possible for 'cerebellar' treatments to prove ineffective, even though the underlying cause of the problems is cerebellar impairment. It is even possible that 'cerebellar' treatment proves effective even though the underlying cause is not cerebellar impairment.

In summary, the criticisms have some force, but are handled reasonably well by the cerebellar deficit hypothesis. Furthermore, these important issues confront any developmental explanation. Consider phonological deficit – the preferred hypothesis of most of the critics. It too may be considered too broad, in that abnormality in a range of brain structures could lead to phonological problems. It may be considered too narrow, in that phonological deficits are but one of a range of symptoms. It is not a sufficient condition, in that almost all poor readers (whether dyslexic or not) show phonological deficits (Stanovich, 1988a). On the other hand, it does appear to be necessary and it is highly correlated with initial reading problems (though this may reflect teaching strategies). The key issue for the phonological deficit hypothesis, of course, is to specify why there are phonological deficits in terms of underlying brain structures. To our knowledge, the only current explanation that accounts for phonological deficits in terms of developing brain structures is the cerebellar deficit hypothesis. We urge phonological deficit theorists to develop alternative versions of our Figure 4.2, so that appropriate empirical comparisons can be undertaken.

CEREBELLAR DEFICIT AS A CAUSAL EXPLANATION

It is important to note that we put forward the cerebellar deficit hypothesis as a 'causal explanation' of dyslexia. Causal of course refers to the underlying cause of the problems manifested, but this is in fact a slippery concept, in that there are different 'depths' and types of cause. For a beginning reader, the underlying cause of the problem may be lack of sensitivity to rhyme. This may arise from a variety of causes, with the fundamental ones being lack of experience (which is easily addressed) to some deeper problem with hearing or phonology. Phonological awareness problems may arise from causes such as second language issues, otitis media (sometimes known as glue ear) at critical periods, or some deeper problem in terms of the systems that undertake phonological processing. The processing difficulties may be specific to phonological tasks, or may be broader, including for instance the process of automatization of many skills. Underlying these processing problems there may be abnormalities in brain structure or function. Brain structure or function problems may arise from weak sensory processing (perhaps attributable to magnocellular system problems), specific abnormalities in the phonological processing networks, or perhaps wider problems in terms of brain networks or specific brain regions. The deeper one digs, the further removed the proposed cause is from the reading problem, and thus the less direct the link to reading. On the positive side, however, the deeper explanations (referred to as 'distal explanations') are able to handle a wider range of problems than the shallow ('proximal') causal explanations.

Our intention in putting forward the cerebellar deficit hypothesis was therefore to develop a more distal explanation for the automaticity problems we had identified, together with the well-established phonological deficits. As we have seen, the hypothesis provides a principled explanation of the three criterial difficulties for dyslexia – reading, writing and spelling – in terms of the surface level of attainment. It also provides a natural explanation of the three theoretical explanations at one level deeper, the cognitive level, in terms of phonology, speed and automaticity. It also provides a principled explanation of the developmental course of dyslexia over the years before reading. However, there are also suggestions in the specific dyslexia literature of requirements for a causal explanation of dyslexia together with more general suggestions from the science methatheory literature.

For dyslexia the requirements for a causal explanation, proposed by Morrison and Manis (1983) are that any viable theory must address four issues: why does the deficit affect primarily the task of reading – later described by Stanovich (1988b) as the 'specificity principle'; why do dyslexic children perform adequately on other tasks; what is the mechanism by which the deficit results in the reading problems; and what is the direction of causality? Our answers to these points are as follows: the problems appear specific to reading because it is a complex task requiring many years of practice, fluent interplay of eyes, speech and cognition, and for which it is not possible to 'compensate' by greater conscious processing. The problems are clearly described by the 'triple whammy' routes in Figure 4.2. In terms of the apparent 'adequate performance on other tasks' our view is that milder problems will arise in a range of other skills, but these may be less marked (owing to greater opportunities for conscious compensation) or less critical (not a key school attainment). The mechanisms by which the difficulties arise are outlined in Figure 4.2, which also provides a clear indication of the direction of causality in the pre-reading years. Of course, once a child has fallen behind in reading, this factor will also tend to further interfere with the reading progress owing to less practice, less motivation and possible development of literacy avoidance lifestyles – a process termed the 'Matthew Effect' (Stanovich, 1986) in that the rich get richer and the poor get poorer.

In terms of more general theory, Seidenberg (1993: 231) argues that one important requirement for an explanatory theory is that it should 'explain phenomena in terms of independently motivated principles'. This distinguishes explanatory theories, such as the (now established) atomic weights explanation for the atomic table, from *ad hoc* descriptive theories, such as Mendeleev's original theory. A further important criterion introduced by Seidenberg (p. 233) is that 'an explanatory theory shows how phenomena previously thought to be unrelated actually derive from a common underlying source'. The cerebellar deficit hypothesis scores particularly well on both these criteria, in that it does attempt to explain the reading difficulties in terms of the established findings from outside the dyslexia discipline as to the role of the cerebellum in the acquisition and execution of motor and cognitive skills. It also provides not only a principled explanation of the three (rather disparate) literacy-related criteria but also of the otherwise baffling tendency to weakness in skills outside the literacy domain.

SUMMARY AND CONCLUSIONS

In summary we make the following assertions as to the status of the cerebellar deficit hypothesis:

(i) it is consistent with current conceptions of cognitive neuroscience;
(ii) it is consistent with the major cognitive level theories of dyslexia (phonological deficit, double deficit and automaticity deficit);

(iii) it provides a coherent explanation of the developmental antecedents of dyslexia;
(iv) it provides an explanation for why there is considerable comorbidity between dyslexia and the other developmental disorders;
(v)   it provides a theoretical challenge for authors of alternative hypotheses to provide a similar level of detail;
(vi) it provides an applied challenge for theorists to develop methods of detecting abnormalities in cerebellar function;
(vii) a major contribution is to highlight the fact that it is crucial to see dyslexia research within 'mainstream' research on cognitive neuroscience.

However, it is important to highlight what we do NOT claim:

(i)   the hypothesis is not intended to be an explanation for ALL subtypes of dyslexia;
(ii)   the hypothesis does not claim that ONLY the cerebellum is affected in dyslexia;
(iii) the hypothesis remains 'work in progress'. In our view it is only a way station en route to a much fuller understanding of the neural basis of developmental dyslexia and other developmental disorders.

In conclusion, we have outlined some of the reasons for considering that the cerebellum might be one of the key brain structures affected in dyslexia. We consider that the framework is a fruitful one, serving to place dyslexia research within a meaningful context in terms of the cognitive neuroscience of learning while maintaining its position as a key educational issue. We trust that subsequent researchers will be able to develop both these themes further, finally providing the missing link between brain science and educational science, the new discipline of pedagogical neuroscience (Fawcett and Nicolson, 2007; Goswami, 2005).

NOTE

1. This strategy inevitably has drawbacks. As can be seen from Figure 4.1, different regions of the cerebellum have different roles, and it is quite possible that one has impaired function in the motor region of the cerebellum but not the language region, and vice versa. We address this important point subsequently.

REFERENCES

Ackermann, H., Mathiak, K. and Riecker, A. (2007) 'The contribution of the cerebellum to speech production and speech perception: Clinical and functional imaging data', *Cerebellum*, 6 (3): 202–213.

Albus, J. S. (1971) 'A theory of cerebellar function', *Mathematical Biosciences*, 10: 25–61.

Allum, J. H. J., Bloem, B. R., Carpenter, M. G., Hulliger, M. and Hadders-Algra, M. (1998) 'Proprioceptive control of posture: a review of new concepts', *Gait and Posture*, 8 (3): 214–242.

Augur, J. (1985) 'Guidelines for Teachers, Parents and Learners', in M. J. Snowling (ed.), *Childrens' Written Language Difficulties*. London: Routledge. p. 147.

Badian, N. A. (1984) 'Can the WPPSI be of Aid in Identifying Young Children at Risk for Reading Disability', *Journal of Learning Disabilities*, 17 (10): 583–587.

Bates, E. and Dick, F. (2002) 'Language, gesture, and the developing brain', *Developmental Psychobiology*, 40 (3): 293–310.

Ben-Yehudah, G., Guediche, S. and Fiez, J. A. (2007) 'Cerebellar contributions to verbal working memory: beyond cognitive theory', *Cerebellum*, 6 (3): 193–201.

Benton, A. L. (1978) 'Some conclusions about dyslexia', in A. L. Benton and D. Pearl (eds), *Dyslexia: An appraisal of current knowledge*. Oxford: Oxford University Press.

Brady, S., Shankweiler, D. and Mann, V. (1983) 'Speech perception and memory coding in relation to naming ability', *Journal of Experimental Child Psychology*, 35: 345–367.

Brindley, G. S. (1964) 'The use made by the cerebellum of the information that it receives from the sense organs', *International Brain Research Organization Bulletin*, 3: 80.

Brodal, A. (1981) 'The cerebellum', in A. Brodal (ed.), *Neurological Anatomy in Relation to Clinical Medicine*. Oxford: Oxford University Press. pp. 294–393.

Brookes, R. L., Nicolson, R. I. and Fawcett, A. J. (2007) 'Prisms throw light on developmental disorders', *Neuropsychologia*, 45 (8): 1921–1930.

Catts, H. W. (1989) 'Speech production deficits in developmental dyslexia', *Journal of Speech and Hearing Disorders*, 54: 422–428.

Coffin, J. M., Baroody, S., Schneider, K. and O'Neill, J. (2005) 'Impaired cerebellar learning in children with prenatal alcohol exposure: A comparative study of eyeblink conditioning in children with ADHD and dyslexia', *Cortex*, 41 (3): 389–398.

Corballis, M. (2002) *From hand to mouth: The origins of language*. Princeton, NJ: Princeton University Press.

Davis, B. L. and MacNeilage, P. F. (2000) 'An embodiment perspective on the acquisition of speech perception', *Phonetica*, 57 (2–4): 229–241.

De Smet, H. J., Baillieux, H., De Deyn, P. P., Marien, P. and Paquier, P. (2007) 'The cerebellum and language: The story so far', *Folia Phoniatrica Et Logopaedica*, 59 (4): 165–170.

Demonet, J. F., Taylor, M. J. and Chaix, Y. (2004) 'Developmental dyslexia', *Lancet*, 363 (9419): 1451–1460.

Denckla, M. B. (1985) 'Motor coordination in children with dyslexia: Theoretical and clinical implications', in F. H. Duffy and N. Geschwind (eds), *Dyslexia: a neuroscientific approach to clinical evaluation*. Boston, MA: Little Brown.

Denckla, M. B. and Rudel, R. G. (1976) 'Rapid "Automatized" naming (R.A.N.) Dyslexia differentiated from other learning disabilities', *Neuropsychologia*, 14: 471–479.

Denckla, M. B., Rudel, R. G., Chapman, C. and Krieger, J. (1985) 'Motor proficiency in dyslexic children with and without attentional disorders', *Archives of Neurology*, 42: 228–231.

Desmond, J. E. and Fiez, J. A. (1998) 'Neuroimaging studies of the cerebellum: language, learning and memory', *Trends in Cognitive Sciences*, 2 (9): 355–362.

Diamond, A. (2000) 'Close interrelation of motor development and cognitive development and of the cerebellum and prefrontal cortex', *Child Development*, 71 (1): 44–56.

Dow, R. S. and Moruzzi, G. (1958) *The physiology and pathology of the cerebellum*. Minneapolis: University of Minnesota Press.

Eccles, J. C., Ito, M. and Szentagothai, J. (1967) *The cerebellum as a neuronal machine*. New York: Springer-Verlag.

Eckert, M. A., Leonard, C. M., Richards, T. L., Aylward, E. H., Thomson, J. and Berninger, V. W. (2003) 'Anatomical correlates of dyslexia: frontal and cerebellar findings', *Brain*, 126: 482–494.

Ejiri, K. and Masataka, N. (2001) 'Co-occurrence of preverbal vocal behavior and motor action in early infancy', *Developmental Science*, 4 (1): 40–48.

Fawcett, A. J. and Nicolson, R. I. (1992) 'Automatisation deficits in balance for dyslexic children', *Perceptual and Motor Skills*, 75 (2): 507–529.

Fawcett, A. J. and Nicolson, R. I. (1995) 'Persistent deficits in motor skill for children with dyslexia', *Journal of Motor Behavior*, 27: 235–241.

Fawcett, A. J. and Nicolson, R. I. (1999) 'Performance of dyslexic children on cerebellar and cognitive tests', *Journal of Motor Behavior*, 31: 68–78.

Fawcett, A. J. and Nicolson, R. I. (2002) 'Children with dyslexia are slow to articulate a single speech gesture', *Dyslexia: An International Journal of Research and Practice*, 8: 189–203.

Fawcett, A. J. and Nicolson, R. I. (2007) 'Dyslexia, learning, and pedagogical neuroscience', *Developmental Medicine and Child Neurology*, 49 (4): 306–311.

Fawcett, A. J., Nicolson, R. I. and Dean, P. (1996) 'Impaired performance of children with dyslexia on a range of cerebellar tasks', *Annals of Dyslexia*, 46: 259–283.

Finch, A. J., Nicolson, R. I. and Fawcett, A. J. (2002) 'Evidence for a neuroanatomical difference within the olivo-cerebellar pathway of adults with dyslexia', *Cortex*, 38 (4): 529–539.

Fischer, B., Biscaldi, M. and Hartnegg, K. (1998) 'Voluntary saccadic control and fixation in dyslexia', *International Journal of Psychophysiology*, 30: 97.

Fischer, B., Hartnegg, K. and Mokler, A. (2000) 'Dynamic visual perception of dyslexic children', *Perception*, 29 (5): 523–530.

Fowler, A. (1991) 'How early phonological development might set the stage for phoneme awareness', in S. Brady and D. Shankweiler (eds.), *Phonological Processes in Literacy*. Hillsdale: NJ: Lawrence Erlbaum Associates.

Frank, J. and Levinson, H. N. (1973) 'Dysmetric dyslexia and dyspraxia: hypothesis and study', *Journal of American Academy of Child Psychiatry*, 12: 690–701.

Fulbright, R. K., Jenner, A. R., Mencl, W. E., Pugh, K. R., Shaywitz, B. A., Shaywitz, S. E., Frost S.J., Skudlarki, P., Constable, R.T., Lacadie, C.M., Marchione, K.E. and Gore, J.C. (1999) 'The cerebellum's role in reading: A functional MR imaging study', *American Journal of Neuroradiology*, 20: 1925–1930.

Gerwig, M., Kolb, F. P. and Timmann, D. (2007) 'The involvement of the human cerebellum in eyeblink conditioning', *Cerebellum*, 6 (1): 38–57.

Geschwind, N. (1982) 'Why Orton Was Right', *Annals of Dyslexia*, 32: 13–30.

Goswami, U. (2005) 'The brain in the classroom? The state of the art', *Developmental Science*, 8 (6): 467–469.

Green, J. R., Moore, C. A., Higashikawa, M. and Steeve, R. W. (2000) 'The physiologic development of speech motor control: Lip and jaw coordination', *Journal of Speech Language and Hearing Research*, 43 (1): 239–255.

Habib, M. (2004) 'Oral and written language learning disorders: recent contributions of neurobiological research', *Revue De Neuropsychologie*, 14 (1–2): 63–102.

Haslum, M. (1989) 'Predictors of Dyslexia?', *Irish Journal of Psychology*, 10 (4): 622–630.

Holmes, G. (1917) 'The symptoms of acute cerebellar injuries due to gunshot injuries', *Brain*, 40: 461–535.

Holmes, G. (1922) 'Clinical symptoms of cerebellar disease and their interpretation', *Lancet*, 1: 1177–1237.

Holmes, G. (1939) 'The cerebellum of man', *Brain*, 62: 1–30.

Imamizu, H., Kuroda, T., Miyauchi, S., Yoshioka, T. and Kawato, M. (2003) 'Modular organization of internal models of tools in the human cerebellum', *Proceedings of the National Academy of Sciences of the United States of America*, 100 (9): 5461–5466.

Ioffe, M. E., Chernikova, L. A. and Ustinova, K. I. (2007) 'Role of cerebellum in learning postural tasks', *Cerebellum*, 6 (1): 87–94.

Ito, M. (1984) *The cerebellum and neural control*. New York: Raven Press.

Iversen, S., Berg, K., Ellertsen, B. and Tonnessen, F. E. (2005) 'Motor coordination difficulties in a municipality group and in a clinical sample of poor readers', *Dyslexia*, 11 (3): 217–231.

Justus, T. C. and Ivry, R. B. (2001) 'The cognitive neuropsychology of the cerebellum', *International Review of Psychiatry*, 13 (4): 276–282.

Kelly, R. M. and Strick, P. L. (2003) 'Cerebellar loops with motor cortex and prefrontal cortex of a non-human primate', *Journal of Neuroscience*, 23 (23): 8432–8444.

Leiner, H. C., Leiner, A. L. and Dow, R. S. (1989) 'Reappraising the cerebellum: what does the hindbrain contribute to the forebrain', *Behavioural Neuroscience*, 103: 998–1008.

Leiner, H. C., Leiner, A. L. and Dow, R. S. (1991) 'The human cerebro-cerebellar system: Its computing, cognitive, and language skills', *Behavioural. Brain. Research.*, 44: 113–128.

Leiner, H. C., Leiner, A. L. and Dow, R. S. (1993) 'Cognitive and language functions of the human cerebellum', *Trends in Neuroscience*, 16: 444–447.

Leonard, C. M., Lombardino, L. J., Walsh, K., Eckert, M. A., Mockler, J. L., Rowe, L. A., et al. (2002) 'Anatomical risk factors that distinguish dyslexia from SLI predict reading skill in normal children', *Journal of Communication Disorders*, 35 (6): 501–531.

Levinson, H. N. (1988) 'The cerebellar-vestibular basis of learning disabilities in children, adolescents and adults: Hypothesis and study', *Perceptual and Motor Skills*, 67 (3): 983–1006.

Limperopoulos, C., Bassan, H., Gauvreau, K., Robertson, R. L., Sullivan, N. R., Benson, C. B., Avery, L., Stewart, J., Soul, J. S., Ringer, S A., Volpe, J. J. and du Plessis, A J. (2007) 'Does cerebellar injury in premature infants contribute to the high prevalence of long–term cognitive, learning, and behavioral disability in survivors?', *Pediatrics*, 120 (3): 584–593.

Lozano, A., Ramirez, M. and Ostrosky-Solis, F. (2003) 'The neurobiology of developmental dyslexia: A survey', *Revista De Neurologia*, 36 (11): 1077–1082.

Lyytinen, H., Aro, M., Eklund, K., Erskine, J., Guttorm, T., Laakso, M. L., Leppanen, P.H.T., Lyytinen, P., Poikkeus, A.M., Richardson, U. and Torppa, M. (2004) 'The development of children at familial risk for dyslexia: Birth to early school age', *Annals of Dyslexia*, 54 (2): 184–220.

MacNeilage, P. F. and Davis, B. L. (2001) 'Motor mechanisms in speech ontogeny: phylogenetic, neurobiological and linguistic implications', *Current Opinion in Neurobiology*, 11 (6): 696–700.

Marien, P., Engelborghs, S., Fabbro, F. and De Deyn, P. P. (2001) 'The lateralized linguistic cerebellum: A review and a new hypothesis', *Brain and Language*, 79 (3): 580–600.

Marien, P. and Verhoeven, J. (2007) 'Cerebellar involvement in motor speech planning: Some further evidence from foreign accent syndrome', *Folia Phoniatrica Et Logopaedica*, 59 (4): 210–217.

Marr, D. (1969) 'A theory of cerebellar cortex', *Journal of Physiology London*, 202: 437–470.

Maschke, M., Erichsen, M., Drepper, J., Jentzen, W., Muller, S. P., Kolb, F. P., Diener, H.C. and Timmann, D. (2003) 'Cerebellar representation of the eyeblink response as revealed by PET', *Neuroreport*, 14 (10): 1371–1374.

Miall, R. C., Imamizu, H. and Miyauchi, S. (2000) 'Activation of the cerebellum in co-ordinated eye and hand tracking movements: an fMRI study', *Experimental Brain Research*, 135 (1): 22–33.

Middleton, F. A. and Strick, P. L. (2001) 'Cerebellar projections to the prefrontal cortex of the primate', *Journal of Neuroscience*, 21 (2): 700–712.

Miles, T. R. (1983) *Dyslexia: The pattern of difficulties*. Oxford: Blackwell.

Moe-Nilssen, R., Helbostad, J. L., Talcott, J. B. and Toennessen, F. E. (2003) 'Balance and gait in children with dyslexia', *Experimental Brain Research*, 150 (2): 237–244.

Morrison, F. J. and Manis, F. R. (1983) 'Cognitive processes in reading disability: a critique and proposal', in C. J. Brainerd and M. Pressley (eds.), *Progress in Cognitive Development Research*. New York: Springer-Verlag.

Needle, J. L., Fawcett, A. J. and Nicolson, R. I. (2006) 'Balance and dyslexia: An investigation of adults' abilities', *European Journal of Cognitive Psychology*, 18 (6): 909–936.

NICHD (2000) *Report of the National Reading Panel: Teaching children to read*. Washington DC: National Institute for Child Health and Human Development.

Nicolson, R. I., Daum, I., Schugens, M. M., Fawcett, A. J. and Schulz, A. (2002) 'Eyeblink conditioning indicates cerebellar abnormality in dyslexia', *Experimental Brain Research*, 143 (1): 42–50.

Nicolson, R. I. and Fawcett, A. J. (1990) 'Automaticity: A new framework for dyslexia research?', *Cognition*, 35 (2): 159–182.

Nicolson, R. I. and Fawcett, A. J. (2006) 'Do cerebellar deficits underlie phonological problems in dyslexia?', *Developmental Science*, 9 (3): 259–262.

Nicolson, R. I. and Fawcett, A. J. (2007) 'Procedural Learning Difficulties: Re-uniting the developmental disorders?', *Trends in Neurosciences*, 30 (4): 135–141.

Nicolson, R. I., Fawcett, A. J., Berry, E. L., Jenkins, I. H., Dean, P. and Brooks, D. J. (1999) 'Association of abnormal cerebellar activation with motor learning difficulties in dyslexic adults', *Lancet*, 353: 1662–1667.

Nicolson, R. I., Fawcett, A. J. and Dean, P. (1995) 'Time-estimation deficits in developmental dyslexia – evidence of cerebellar involvement', *Proceedings of the Royal Society of London Series B-Biological Sciences*, 259 (1354): 43–47.

Nicolson, R. I., Fawcett, A. J. and Dean, P. (2001) 'Developmental dyslexia: the cerebellar deficit hypothesis', *Trends in Neurosciences*, 24 (9): 508–511.

Olson, R. K. (2002) 'Nature and nurture', *Dyslexia*, 8 (3): 143–159.

Orton, J. L. (1966) 'The Orton-Gillingham approach', in J. Money (ed.), *The disabled reader: Education of the dyslexic child*. Baltimore: Johns Hopkins Press.

Passingham, R. E. (1975) 'Changes in the size and organization of the brain in man and his ancestors', *Brain Behavior and Evolution*, 11: 73–90.

Pavlidis, G. -T. (1985) 'Eye Movements in Dyslexia: Their Diagnostic Significance', *Journal of Learning Disabilities*, 18 (1): 42–50.

Peterka, R. J. (2002) 'Sensorimotor integration in human postural control', *Journal of Neurophysiology*, 88 (3): 1097–1118.

Petersen, S. E., Fox, P. T., Posner, M. I., Mintun, M. and Raichle, M. E. (1988) 'Positron emission tomographic studies of the cortical anatomy of single-word processing', *Nature*, 331 (6157): 585–589.

Raberger, T. and Wimmer, H. (2003) 'On the automaticity/cerebellar deficit hypothesis of dyslexia: balancing and continuous rapid naming in dyslexic and ADHD children', *Neuropsychologia*, 41 (11): 1493–1497.

Rack, J. P., Snowling, M. J., Hulme, C. and Gibbs, S. (2007) 'No evidence that an exercise-based treatment programme (DDAT) has specific benefits for children with reading difficulties', *Dyslexia*, 13 (2): 97–104.

Rae, C., Harasty, J. A., Dzendrowskyj, T. E., Talcott, J. B., Simpson, J. M., Blamire, A. M., Dixon, R.M., Lee, M.A., Thompson, C.H., Styles, P., Richardson, A.J. and Stein, J.F. (2002) 'Cerebellar morphology in developmental dyslexia', *Neuropsychologia*, 40 (8): 1285–1292.

Ramnani, N. (2006) 'The primate cortico-cerebellar system: anatomy and function', *Nature Reviews Neuroscience*, 7 (7): 511–522.

Ramsay, D.S. (1984) 'Onset of duplicated syllable babbling and unimanual handedness in infancy: Evidence for developmental change in hemispheric specialization?', *Developmental Psychology*, 20 (1): 64–71.

Ramus, F., Pidgeon, E. and Frith, U. (2003a) 'The relationship between motor control and phonology in dyslexic children', *Journal of Child Psychology and Psychiatry and Allied Disciplines*, 44 (5): 712–722.

Ramus, F., Rosen, S., Dakin, S. C., Day, B. L., Castellote, J. M., White, S. and Frith, U. (2003b) 'Theories of developmental dyslexia: insights from a multiple case study of dyslexic adults', *Brain*, 126: 841–865.

Reynolds, D. and Nicolson, R. I. (2007) 'Follow-up of an exercise-based treatment for children with reading difficulties', *Dyslexia*, 13 (2): 78–96.

Rudel, R. G. (1985) 'The definition of dyslexia: language and motor deficits', in F. H. Duffy and N. Geschwind (eds), *Dyslexia: a neuroscientific approach to clinical evaluation*. Boston, MA: Little Brown.

Seidenberg, M. S. (1993) 'Connectionist models and cognitive theory', *Psychological Science*, 4: 228–235.

Silver, L. B. (1987) 'The "magic cure": A review of the current controverisal approaches for treating learning disabilities', *Journal of Learning Disabilities*, 20: 498–505.

Skottun, B. C. (2001) 'On the use of the Ternus test to assess magnocellular function', *Perception*, 30 (12): 1449–1457.

Snowling, M. (1981) 'Phonemic deficits in developmental dyslexia', *Psychological Research*, 43: 219–234.

Stanovich, K. E. (1986) 'Matthew effects in reading: Some consequences of individual differences in the acquisition of literacy', *Reading Research Quarterly*, 21: 360–407.

Stanovich, K. E. (1988a) 'Explaining the Differences between the Dyslexic and the Garden-Variety Poor Reader: The Phonological-Core Variable-Difference Model', *Journal of Learning Disabilities*, 21 (10): 590–604.

Stanovich, K. E. (1988b) 'The right and wrong places to look for the cognitive locus of reading disability', *Annals of Dyslexia*, 38: 154–177.

Stein, J. F. (2001) 'The sensory basis of reading problems', *Developmental Neuropsychology*, 20 (2): 509–534.

Stein, J. F. and Fowler, M. S. (1993) 'Unstable binocular control in dyslexic children', *Journal of Research in Reading*, 16 (1): 30–45.

Stein, J. F. and Fowler, S. (1982) 'Diagnosis of dyslexia by means of a new indicator of eye dominance', *British Journal of Ophthalmology*, 66: 332–336.

Stein, J. F. and Glickstein, M. (1992) 'Role of the cerebellum in visual guidance of movement', *Physiological Reviews*, 72: 972–1017.

Stein, J. F., Richardson, A. J. and Fowler, M. S. (2000) 'Monocular occlusion can improve binocular control and reading in dyslexics', *Brain*, 123: 164–170.

Steinlin, M. (2007) 'The cerebellum in cognitive processes: Supporting studies in children', *Cerebellum*, 6 (3): 237–241.

Stoodley, C. J., Fawcett, A. J., Nicolson, R. I. and Stein, J. F. (2006) 'Balancing and pointing tasks in dyslexic and control adults', *Dyslexia*, 12 (4): 276–288.

Treffner, P. and Peter, M. (2002) 'Intentional and attentional dynamics of speech-hand coordination', *Human Movement Science*, 21 (5–6): 641–697.

Turkeltaub, P. E., Eden, G. F., Jones, K. M. and Zeffiro, T. A. (2002) 'Meta-analysis of the functional neuroanatomy of single-word reading: Method and validation', *Neuroimage*, 16 (3): 765–780.

Vellutino, F.R., Scanlon, D.M. and Bentley, W.L. (1983) 'Interhemispheric Learning and Speed of Hemispheric Transmission in Dyslexic and Normal Readers: A Replication of Previous Results and Additional Findings', *Applied Psycholinguistics*, 4 (3): 209–228.

Vellutino, F. R. (1979) *Dyslexia: Theory and research*. Cambridge, MA: MIT Press.

Vicari, S., Marotta, L., Menghini, D., Molinari, M. and Petrosini, L. (2003) 'Implicit learning deficit in children with developmental dyslexia', *Neuropsychologia*, 41 (1): 108–114.

Viholainen, H., Ahonen, T., Cantell, M., Lyytinen, P. and Lyytinen, H. (2002) 'Development of early motor skills and language in children at risk for familial dyslexia', *Developmental Medicine and Child Neurology*, 44 (11): 761–769.

Wang, V. Y. and Zoghbi, H. Y. (2001) 'Genetic regulation of cerebellar development', *Nature Reviews Neuroscience*, 2 (7): 484–491.

White, S., Milne, E., Rosen, S., Hansen, P., Swettenham, J., Frith, U. and Ramus, F. (2006) 'The role of sensorimotor impairments in dyslexia: a multiple case study of dyslexic children', *Developmental Science*, 9 (3): 237–255.

Wimmer, H., Mayringer, H. and Raberger, T. (1999) 'Reading and dual-task balancing: Evidence against the automatization deficit explanation of developmental dyslexia', *Journal of Learning Disabilities*, 32: 473–478.

Wolf, M. and Bowers, P. G. (1999) 'The double-deficit hypothesis for the developmental dyslexias', *Journal of Educational Psychology*, 91: 415–438.

Wolff, P. H., Melngailis, I. and Kotwica, K. (1996) 'Family patterns of developmental dyslexia.3. Spelling errors as behavioral phenotype', *American Journal of Medical Genetics*, 67: 378–386.

Wolff, P. H., Melngailis, I., Obregon, M. and Bedrosian, M. (1995) 'Family patterns of developmental dyslexia.2. Behavioral phenotypes', *American Journal of Medical Genetics*, 60: 494–505.

Wolff, P. H., Michel, G. F., Ovrut, M. and Drake, C. (1990) 'Rate and timing precision of motor coordination in developmental dyslexia', *Developmental Psychology*, 26 (3): 349–359.

World Federation of Neurology (1968) *Report of research group on dyslexia and world illiteracy*. Dallas: WFN.

Zeffiro, T. and Eden, G. (2001) 'The cerebellum and dyslexia: perpetrator or innocent bystander? Comment', *Trends in Neurosciences*, 24 (9): 512–513.

5

Familial Predictors of Dyslexia: Evidence From Preschool Children With and Without Familial Dyslexia Risk

Dennis L. Molfese, Victoria J. Molfese,
Maria E. Barnes, Chris G. Warren, and
Peter J. Molfese

This chapter

i) discusses the relations between structure and function differences identified from brain imaging techniques; and
ii) reviews familial risk for dyslexia.

INTRODUCTION

Attempts to link morphology differences in the early stages of brain development with familial risk for dyslexia are reviewed. While impressive gains have been made over the past two decades, much still waits further investigation. With inconsistencies across reports in identifying specific morphological markers of familial risk, researchers appear to be moving towards a model that multiple brain morphological factors in different combinations may relate to risk for dyslexia either at a general or a more specific level. Investigations into neurofunctional links between brain measures and behavioral assessments in samples of participants at familial risk for dyslexia, on the other hand, seem more advanced. Indeed, there are consistencies noted across a number of labs for event-related potential (ERP) sensitivity to familial risks for dyslexia. Noting the paucity of ERP studies that focus on familial risk beyond the infancy period, a study is included that identifies strong links between ERPs differences in responses to speech sounds and familial risk for dyslexia. ERPs were obtained in response to a series of speech syllables, similar to the work of Guttorm et al. (2005a; b) and Molfese (2000). Results support a strong link between functional measures of neural-based changes and behavioral measures. For early intervention efforts to succeed, understanding both the underlying structure of the brain and its functional components as they relate to behavior are viewed as essential.

BACKGROUND

Much has been learned from studies identifying the cognitive skills of beginning readers that characterize differences in their decoding accuracy (word reading), reading fluency, reading comprehension and spelling skills at school age. This published research has typically focused on broad samples of children and studied the relationship between early cognitive skills, including emergent literacy skills (or those skills evident in the preschool period that are developmental precursors to conventional forms of reading evident at school-age), and subsequent reading skills. However, increasing attention is now paid to identifying the characteristics of young children that place them at-risk for difficulties developing literacy skills even before they show evidence of poor reading. It is hoped that by focusing on the risk characteristics of young children, intervention strategies can be targeted to those children in the early preschool years who are at highest risk and that such early intervention will prevent future reading failure. The purpose of this chapter is to focus on one type of risk characteristic—risk of dyslexia and reading-related skill deficits due to a family history in which one or more close relative has been diagnosed with dyslexia. Literature is reviewed from studies of paediatric populations to understand possible neurobiological bases of dyslexia. However, the main focus of the literature reviewed is on evidence from neuropsychological studies of children who are characterized by familial risk. The results of using different measures of brain functioning are summarized, followed by a review of studies investigating group differences for speech perception and reading skills in groups of children who are and are not at risk for dyslexia.

FAMILIAL RISKS

Risk for poor reading skills in beginning readers can arise from different sources, such as experiential deficits and/or poor reading instruction (Clay, 1987; McGuinness, 2004), genetic or biological sources (Grigorenko, 2001;

Pennington and Lefly, 2001), and from combinations of both experiential and genetic sources (Lyytinen et al., 2003). There is a large body of research on children at risk due to family history of dyslexia, including seven longitudinal studies covering age ranges from preschool/kindergarten through 2nd, 4th or 6th grade (Elbro et al., 1998; Pennington and Lefly, 2001; de Jong and van der Leij, 1999; 2003; Lyytinen et al., 2001; 2004; Scarborough, 1990; Snowling et al., 2003; Wagner et al., 1997). These longitudinal studies include measures of cognitive skills obtained from children as well as measures of later reading skills, and include a comparison or control group. Children participating in these studies are from populations of risk and control families who are English- and non-English-speaking/reading (Dutch, Danish and Finnish). Despite diversity in study design and participants, these studies report early differences in letter knowledge, naming speed, specific phonological skills (e.g., rhyming and short-term memory), and some language skills (e.g., vocabulary and grammar) as markers of group differences at preschool or kindergarten age. For English-speaking/reading children, only phonological processing measures continue to differentiate risk and control children at older ages (Pennington and Lefly, 2001; Snowling et al., 2003). For non-English-speaking/reading children, group differences in phonological skills are seen at early measurement points but not later (depending on task demands); differences on naming measures show persistent group differences at the older ages in Dutch, Finnish and German children (de Jong and van der Leij, 1999; Holopainen et al., 2000; 2001; Wimmer, 1993). The similarities in the types of early cognitive skills that differentiate children at familial risk for dyslexia across different language are striking.

That familial risk is a useful indicator is supported by prevalence rates of dyslexia. The estimated prevalence rate for dyslexia in the general English-speaking population is between 5 and 17 per cent. However, the rate of reading-related skill deficits (e.g., word reading, orthographic coding, phonological decoding and phoneme awareness) based on familial risk studies is between 35 and 40 per cent, and within twin studies the concordance rate ranges from 54 to 72 per cent (Olson and Byrne, 2005; Vogler et al., 1985). In non-English-speaking families, similar rates are reported. For example, in the Jyvaskyla longitudinal study 38 per cent of Finnish children who had family histories of dyslexia developed reading disabilities compared to the 12 per cent of children with no known familial risk. Thus, understanding how familial risk influences the development of reading skills in young children is of great interest to researchers and clinicians interested in the early application of intervention for the prevention and remediation of dyslexia and poor reading skills.

PEDIATRIC STUDIES OF FAMILIAL DYSLEXIA

Given the complex nature of developmental dyslexia and the heritability of the disorder, numerous researchers have sought a neurobiological basis for the disability. Two approaches have focused on morphological and functional abnormalities in the brain in the hope of determining early identifiers for dyslexia. Unfortunately, most published studies focused on adults (Hugdahl et al., 1998). This is problematic because it is unclear whether the abnormalities found in adults are a result of the deficit itself or a product of developmental or compensatory mechanisms. Therefore, studies of young children who are identified as having dyslexia or being at risk due to family history are important. Unfortunately, relatively few such studies exist. The review below will focus on those few studies that have been published.

Morphological studies sought to confirm the anatomical findings established in research on adults with dyslexia by studying samples of children. Hynd et al. (1990) examined MRI scans of 10 children with dyslexia, 10 children with attention deficit/hyperactivity disorders (ADHD), and 10 control children. The children with dyslexia had smaller left planum temporale (PT) resulting in significantly less PT asymmetry than children in ADHD and control groups. The researchers found an expected leftward asymmetry of the PT in 70 per cent of the children with ADHD and control children but only in 10% of children with dyslexia. Larsen et al. (1990) using MRI scans also found a lack of the typical asymmetry in 70 per cent of their sample of adolescents with dyslexia compared to 30 per cent of controls. They concluded that this increased symmetry resulted from a larger right PT. Out of 19 dyslexic subjects, 14 had a history of a phonological deficit, which the researchers concluded was associated with the PT symmetry. Hugdahl et al. (1998) found smaller left PT areas using MRI in children with dyslexia, resulting in a reduced leftward asymmetry relative to controls matched on age, sex, and handedness. Structural differences were also noted in adolescents. Pennington et al. (1999) studied adolescents and young adults from a twin study using quantitative MRI analysis. Participants were 75 individual members of twin pairs (mean age 17.43 years) and 22 controls (mean age 18.69). ADHD was controlled for, but not considered an exclusionary disorder. MRI imaging indicated that subcortical and callosal structures did not vary with reading disability or ADHD. However, individuals with reading disability exhibited a significantly smaller insula, smaller anterior superior neocortex (including Broca's area), and larger retrocallosal cortex in both hemispheres. This pattern of morphological deviation was different from that seen in other developmental disorders.

Not all studies report symmetry of language-supporting brain structures in developmental dyslexia. In one study of 17 children with dyslexia and 14 controls matched for age, sex, handedness, and IQ, Schultz, et al. (1994) noted leftward asymmetries in both groups after controlling for age and overall brain size. Furthermore, they noted significant effects for age (structures increasing in size with age) and sex (structures larger in males than females) for all brain measurements.

In a systematic attempt to develop an analysis method that would utilize consistent anatomical markers for dyslexia, Leonard and colleagues (2002) investigated the use of previously identified anatomical markers in classifying children into groups as dyslexic, good readers, or specific language impairment (SLI). In the first study, they obtained MRI records and behavioral measures of reading skills, verbal ability, and dextrality from 14 children with reading disabilities and 21 children with SLI. They used previously studied (Leonard et al., 2001) anatomical markers of dyslexia—cerebral asymmetry, planum temporale and parietal asymmetry, anterior cerebellar asymmetry, and duplicated left Heschl's gyrus—to distinguish children with reading disabilities from the SLI sample. Children with reading disabilities had significant leftward asymmetry of the PT, increased cerebral volume, and increased size of the left Heschl's gyrus relative to the SLI group. In a second study, all the markers were included in a discriminant function analysis of the combined sample of children from the previous study. The anatomical markers discriminated children with reading disabilities from those with SLI. The researchers developed an 'anatomical risk factor index', and conducted a third study in which they applied a discriminant function analysis to a new sample of 103 children who tested in the 'normal' range for reading skills and who had no neurological or psychiatric diagnoses and no history of learning disability. The results showed that children with an index of 0 had good verbal ability and improved in phonological decoding over time. Children with negative index scores exhibited deficits in verbal ability comparable to those with SLI. Children with positive scores, however, declined in their phonological decoding scores as they aged. This led the authors to conclude that children with reading disabilities and those with SLI exhibited deviations from the norm that were opposite in direction from the population mean. Leonard concluded that it was children with SLI—not dyslexia—who exhibited a lack of asymmetry in the PT. According to Leonard, children with phonological reading deficits exhibited an exaggerated leftward symmetry of the PT and a duplication of Heschl's gyrus. Importantly, she cautioned against looking for a singular deficit as the cause of dyslexia, instead favoring the idea that the different subtypes of dyslexia might have different, complex neurobiological bases (Leonard et al. 2002).

Njiokiktjien et al. (1994) studied a group of 110 children at familial risk for dyslexia using MRI. The study compared mid-sagittal surface area of the corpus callosum from 39 children with dyslexia, 24 children with general learning disabilities, 47 children with severe learning disabilities of a mixed nature (including mental retardation), and 42 control children. The corpus callosum increased in size with age in the control group, but there was no significant difference in relative callosal size between the three subgroups of children of learning disabilities. However, children with familial dyslexia had abnormally larger corpus callosa compared to children without familial dyslexia. Njiokiktjien et al. also noted that children with familial risk and the largest corpus callosa also exhibited a lack of the typical asymmetry in the posterior brain halves.

SUMMARY

Overall, research investigations of anatomical markers for risk of developmental dyslexia has not led to a breakthrough in identifying critical structures that are involved in children at risk. Although this research has primarily focused on structures serving language processing—the perisylvian structures, such as the PT, and central structures, such as the corpus callosum—inconsistencies abound. These discrepancies in findings occur for the symmetry and relative size of such structures. It is possible that such variations may be due to differences in the age, sex, handedness, overall brain size, and IQ of subjects; the parameter measured (length, volume, surface area, convolutional surface area) for a given structure; the thickness of the MRI slice; the definition of anatomical boundaries for the structure of interest; and the visualization technique employed (MRI, CT, or direct examination in post-mortem studies).

Despite the controversies regarding specific anatomical markers for dyslexia, researchers consistently report evidence of *some* anomalies in the brains of dyslexic children. Although no one abnormality is a robust anatomical marker of risk for developmental dyslexia, Grigorenko (2001) argues that the pervasiveness of such anomalies indicates an underlying neuropathological mechanism for dyslexia. Recent studies, such as that of Leonard and colleagues (2002) are consistent with this view and suggest that an anatomical profile involving several anatomical markers yet may prove useful in identifying at-risk children for early intervention. There remains a serious need for more structural research that considers familial risk factors.

EVENT RELATED POTENTIALS (ERPS) AND RISK FOR DYSLEXIA

A second brain-based approach to identifying early risk factors for dyslexia has focused on brain functions, such as the event-related potential or ERP. Numerous studies have used ERP techniques to examine differences in brain processing between groups of dyslexic and non-dyslexic participants ranging in age from infants to adults. ERPs are an ideal method for investigating developmental changes in brain processing in participants of all ages because the procedure is non-invasive, does not require an overt response, and is less impacted by the extensive movement and recording artifacts that occur in other approaches, such as fMRI and PET (Molfese et al., 2001).

The ERP is a portion of the on-going EEG recorded from electrodes placed on the scalp and is time-locked to the onset of a stimulus event. For example, in a speech perception study, the researchers may record ERPs to consonant-vowel (CV) stimuli, such as /ba/and /ga/. These sounds are presented multiple times while the ERPs are recorded to each presentation. Following testing, the ERPs are averaged separately for each stimulus, with these averages used in order to improve signal clarity. The averaged ERPs then become the dependent variable in statistical analyses to determine whether ERP differences exist between groups, participants, and stimuli.

Newborn infant studies

To understand differences in brain processing that reflect early evidence of dyslexia, researchers studied newborn infants at-risk for dyslexia due to family history (e.g., Benasich et al., 2002; Guttorm et al., 2005a; b; 2001; Leppanen et al., 1999; 2002; Molfese, 2000; Pihko et al., 1999. For a more elaborate description of the methods used in these studies see Molfese et al., 2005). In one longitudinal study, Molfese (2000) examined differences in ERPs of newborn infants using ERP markers obtained from an earlier longitudinal study with a different sample of infants (Molfese and Molfese, 1985). Discriminant function analyses of ERP amplitude and latency measures obtained at birth could be used to classify children eight years later with a high degree of accuracy. Indeed, 100 per cent of the poor readers (7 of 7), 76.5 per cent of the children with dyslexia (14 of 17), and 79.2 per cent (20/24) of control children were correctly classified. Subsequently, Andrews Espy et al. (2004) studied whether such changes in brain responses after birth continued to predict later reading development. ERPs to speech and non-speech stimuli were recorded annually when participants were 1 to 8 years of age. The sample included 109 typically developing children. Two measures of word-level reading (one that requires decoding of real words and one of pseudowords) were administered at eight years of age. Growth curve analysis, using the hierarchical linear models, related reading performance (average vs. low) to the longitudinal maturation in the ERP waveform peak and latencies. Maturational changes (e.g., slope, acceleration and cubic growth) in N1 amplitude for speech and non-speech stimuli between ages 1 to 4 were related to proficiency in decoding pseudoword stimuli. Children who were less proficient in decoding pseudowords evidenced steeper declines in negative amplitude with age. In contrast, proficiency in decoding real words was related to developmental changes in N2 amplitudes from ages 4 to 8 at the parietal sites in ERPs to non-speech. These findings were consistent with earlier reports by Molfese and Molfese (1997) that the relationship between early neonatal ERPs to speech and non-speech sounds and later language performance measures at five years of age continues into the elementary school years. Using an equal probability paradigm, they recorded ERPs from 71 full term, newborn infants, in response to consonant-vowel syllables that combined each of the initial consonants, /b, d, g/ with a following vowel, either /a, i, u/. Although there were no differences between groups differing in scores on the Stanford-Binet verbal subtest in prenatal, perinatal, and SES measures, analyses indicated high accuracy ranging from 89 to 97 per cent in classifying children's performance on Stanford-Binet verbal scores at five years of age based on their neonatal ERPs to speech syllables.

Several prospective studies from the Jyväskylä Longitudinal Study of Dyslexia (JLD) also linked early ERPs with later language outcomes in children with and without familial risk for dyslexia (Lyytinen et al., 2004; 2006). These studies, described in more detail below, recorded ERPs to sounds and speech stimuli at birth through age nine years from children at familial risk for dyslexia

($N = 107$) and matched controls ($N = 93$). Global as well as intensive assessments of receptive and expressive language, vocabulary, letter identification, naming skills, phonological, morphological, orthographic skills, IQ, reading, and memory also were measured. The results have helped define ways in which children at familial risk for dyslexia and others who face reading problems at school age can be accurately identified before school entry. Examples of such studies are described in the paragraphs below.

Guttorm et al. (2001) used an equal probability paradigm to study brain processing differences in infants at familial risk for dyslexia. ERPs from 23 at-risk and 22 control newborn infants were collected in response to synthetically produced (/ba/, /da/, and /ga/) speech sounds, the same as those used by Molfese (2000). The main differences that distinguished the at-risk from the control infants were reflected in different magnitudes of ERP responses in the right hemisphere at 50–170 ms period after stimulus onset that reflected discrimination of /ba/ and /da/ from /ga/ and at 540–630 ms that reflected discrimination of /ga/. The role of this right hemisphere ERP component, which the researchers described as an at-risk type response pattern, in impacting later language development was explored by Guttorm et al (2005a; b) in a continuation of the longitudinal study. The researchers reported that the presence of the large and positive ERP component in the right hemisphere at birth was associated with poorer receptive language skills in both at risk and control children at age 2.5 years.

Familial risk effects have been noted across other ERP paradigms. Leppanen et al. (1999) and Pihko et al. (1999) used an oddball paradigm where the frequent CV stimulus had a long vowel /kaa/ (probability of 88 per cent) and the target stimulus /ka/ had a short vowel (probability of 12 per cent). The study compared a slow- to a fast-rate presentation (855 and 425 ms inter-stimulus interval [ISI], respectively) to see how the at-risk and control groups differed in cortical activation. During the slow rate condition, ERPs of the control group to the deviant /ka/ differed from those to the standard /kaa/ over the left hemisphere, while responses of the at-risk group differed at the right hemisphere sites. In the fast-rate condition, ERPs of both groups to the deviant stimulus were seen over left hemisphere sites. Overall, short ISI rates produced more marked differences between groups to deviant stimuli.

Using the same stimulus set, Pihko et al. (1999) studied age effects by testing infants at familial risk for dyslexia and controls at birth and then again at six months of age. In newborns, cortical responses to the deviant /ka/ differed from the standard /kaa/ only at the right frontal site. ERPs to the deviant were more positive than to the frequent stimuli, but these differences were only significant in the at-risk group. At six months, the groups differed during the standard presentation over right central and parietal electrode sites. In both groups, the deviant stimuli showed a larger and longer response in frontal and central regions. This change was apparent over the left parietal area in at-risk six month olds.

Leppanen et al. (2002) studied differences in phonetic discrimination involving time in at-risk (N = 37; 20 male) and control (N = 39, 21 male) newborns.

In this study, the short /ata/ syllable was presented as a frequent stimulus (probability of 80 per cent), and intermediate and long forms of /atta/ (10 per cent probability) were target stimuli. Group differences were found in ERP responses to long and short stimuli. ERPs differences to frequent and target stimuli were less apparent in at-risk compared to control infants. When the long /atta/ was the deviant stimulus, groups showed similar cortical activation over right hemisphere locations. The results were similar when the deviant condition was the short /ata/ with one exception: an additional negative peak occurred in controls at 550 ms, which was absent in the at-risk group in both hemispheres. Together these studies reflect differences in ERP responses by at risk compared to control infants, with some evidence of more increased processing demands at right hemisphere sites in the at-risk compared to control group.

Studies of school-age children

Relatively few studies have been published that investigated brain responses in children who are at risk for dyslexia because of familial factors. The literature that is available on ERP studies of dyslexic and control or other populations focuses for the most part on group comparisons based on current diagnoses (e.g., see Bonte and Blomert, 2004; Rippon and Brunswick, 2000). Fortunately, the JLD continues to provide a rich resource for studying familial risk factors for dyslexia. One such study by Guttorm, et al. (2005a) reported relations between familial risk and developmental outcomes. They evaluated the development of children at familial risk for dyslexia and control children for language and verbal memory skills at 2.5, 3.5, and 5 years of age. ERPs were recorded to consonant-vowel syllables from 26 at risk participants and 23 controls. Subsequent correlation analyses indicated hemispheric differences occurred between 540 and 630 ms, where responses to /ga/ were clearly more positive and prolonged over the right hemisphere electrode sites for the risk group. This right hemisphere response pattern at birth correlated with poorer receptive language skills across both groups by 2.5 years of age. Additionally, ERPs over the left hemisphere were associated with poorer verbal memory skills at 5 years of age.

Conclusions

Our ability to utilize ERPs to identify early functional changes in infants and children at risk for disabilities such as dyslexia appears to be growing. As the review notes, a number of independent laboratories report consistent findings that map across labs to predict a range of later outcomes measures associated with reading skills. On the other hand, our success in linking morphology differences between children with and without familial risk, while showing some impressive findings, still waits for further development. Such advances in the future could perhaps include familial risk as a factor and builds on the notions advanced by Grigorenko (2001) and Leonard et al. (2002) that multiple morphological factors in different combinations may relate to dyslexia risk either at a general level or a more specific one. Whatever the case, for early intervention efforts to succeed, understanding both the underlying structure of the brain and its functional components as they relate to reading development are viewed as essential to future successes.

Parental reports of familial risk and performance of preschoolers

It has been anticipated from two decades of studies that children at-risk for reading disabilities could be identified early and accurately using assessments of cognitive skills and that such early identification could lead to early intervention. While studies provide a wealth of information useful for identifying early cognitive abilities that characterize children and predict later reading outcomes, few studies have reported a high degree of accuracy in identifying children with dyslexia before reading age. More research is needed. The research reported below presents one model of how measures of brain processing of speech sounds by preschool children and their behavioral performance on measures of letter identification provide evidence for the influence of familial risk. Based on our previous research and that of other researchers that speech discrimination skills are important predictors of reading skills, we hypothesized that reliable differences between children at risk for dyslexia due to family history of dyslexia and children not at risk would be identified from ERP measures of discrimination of consonant-vowel speech sounds. We also hypothesized that differential gains in letter identification between fall and spring assessments could be predicted from group differences in ERP measures.

Methods

Participants
The University of Louisville Institutional Review Board approved this study.

Parents of participants provided informed consent for the parent/child dyad to participate in the study and the child provided assent to participate. The children were enrolled in pre-kindergarten programs for economically disadvantaged or developmentally at-risk children in local public schools. District-wide enrollment in these preschool programs is 91% based on family income eligibility. The 20 children included in this study had a mean age of 61.6 months (SD = 7.39 months, range 46.8 to 71.4 months, with 14 males and 6 females. All were typically developing, with English as a first language, and were distributed across classrooms in 3 schools. Children with familial risk of dyslexia were identified using parental responses to a multiple-choice *Parental Learning History Questionnaire* (adapted from Leinonen et al., 2001). Questionnaire items requested information about occurrence of reading and writing difficulties during childhood, adulthood and among close relatives. Ten children of parents who reported a history of reading and writing difficulties in the questionnaire were categorized as 'at-risk' and 10 children whose parents did not report reading and writing difficulties were categorized as 'control'.

The participants' average General Conceptual Ability score on the Differential Ability Scales (DAS: Elliott, 1990) was 93.9 (SD = 13.53, range = 68 to 118). The GCA scores, assessed from block building, verbal comprehension, picture similarities, and naming vocabulary subtests, reflect a range of scores from low to above average. While the low DAS scores may raise concerns about possible developmental delays, children from low-income families often enter preschool with fewer experiences and less developed cognitive skills than children from higher income homes. For decades, research documented the impacts of low income and parental education and less stimulating family environments on children's intelligence (see Bradley and Corwyn, 2002 for a review). For these reasons, federally funded preschool enrichment programs were established (US Department of Health and Human Services, 2001; 2003). To determine if a simpler, 4-stimulus choice, receptive task would reveal different skills, the participants also were administered the Peabody Picture Vocabulary Test Third Edition: (PPVT-III, Dunn and Dunn, 1997). The participants' scores on the PPVT included a mean of 96.45 (SD = 15.14, range = 70 to 129). The population was normally distributed for both the DAS and the PPVT (skewness = −.59, Kurtosis = −.039 and skewness = .3, Kurtosis = −.14, respectively). One-way ANOVAs indicated no difference between at-risk and control children on the DAS General Conceptual Ability Scale, $F(1,18) = .234$, $p<.64$, or on the PPVT, $F(1,18) = .41$, $p<.53$. Taken together, the DAS and PPVT findings indicate that the at-risk group was not characterized by a general developmental delay.

Measures
Letter identification: The WRAT-Reading subscale (Wide Range Achievement Test, WRAT, Wilkinson, 1993) was used to assess letter identification skills. The child is asked to name 15 upper case letters presented in a random order. The WRAT is standardized for use with individuals from age five onwards. Since children in the present study ranged from 46.8 to 71.4 months, raw scores based on the current sample were used since WRAT standard scores could not be used for all children.

Stimuli: ERP responses were elicited in response to series of consonant-vowel syllables. The auditory stimuli included an initial consonant sound (/b, d, g/) followed by a vowel (/a, u/). Each syllable was 300 ms in duration and matched in peak intensity. Twenty-five repetitions of each syllable were presented in a blocked random order via a speaker positioned over the midline of the child's head. Syllables were presented at an intensity level of 75 dB SPL(A).

Screening tests: Children included in the analyses passed several screening tests that included a standard hearing threshold exam, a 10-item neuropsychological assessment was used to screen children for neuropsychological risk factors, and the Edinburgh Handedness Inventory (Oldfield, 1971). All children were right-handed.

Procedures

In the fall of the school year, parents of potential participants were sent information regarding a behavioral study of literacy and mathematics skills. Parents returned signed consent forms and learning history questionnaires. Children were involved in a larger study involving language, emergent literacy and mathematics assessments that were given in two sessions at their preschools: one in the fall and one in the spring. The DAS, PPVT, and WRAT (Tan form) were administered in the fall session, and the WRAT was re-administered (Blue form) in the spring session. Parents were contacted to gain their permission for the child to participate in a third session that took place in the summer. During the summer session, the screening and handedness tests were administered followed by the ERP assessments.

For the ERP assessments, children were tested individually in a sound-attenuated testing room. Each child's head was measured to determine the appropriate electrode net size. After applying the electrode net using standard procedures, the child sat quietly and listened to the 150 speech syllables. Each syllable was presented for 1 S followed by a varied ISI from 4 to 6 s. before the next stimulus was presented. Stimulus presentation was controlled by the Electrophysiological Graphical Imaging System (EGIS), v. 2.2 (EGI, Inc.). During stimulus presentation, the child's EEG, EMG and behavior were continuously monitored in order to track the child's state and determine when stimulus presentation should occur. During periods of motor activity or inattention, stimulus presentation was suspended and resumed when the child's alertness and motor activity returned to an acceptable level.

ERPs were recorded using a 128 Ag/AgCl electrode high-density array (Geodesic Sensor Net, EGI Inc.). During recording, all electrodes were referenced to Cz and then subsequently re-referenced to an average reference during data analysis. All impedances remained at or below 40 kΩ throughout the test. The high pass filter was set to 0.1 Hz and the low pass to 30 Hz. Net Station 2.0 (EGI, Inc.) was used to record the electrophysiological data at 4 ms intervals over a one-second period (250 samples/sec). A 700 ms period immediately following stimulus onset was selected for subsequent analyses based on prior work (Molfese, 2000). The ERP session lasted approximately 60 minutes. The children were rewarded with small gifts after their participation in the sessions.

Results

The children's letter identification scores in the fall and spring ranged from 0 – 15 letters (fall: M = 6.0, SD = 6.36; spring: M = 9.0, SD = 6.03). The focus of the analyses was on change scores from fall to spring. For children in the Risk group, the mean fall to spring change score was 2.1 (SD = 7.67, range –1 to 7) and for the children in the Control group, the mean change score was 3.90 (SD = 4.14, range 1 – 15). The difference between the changes scores of the two groups was not significant (F(1,18) = 1.40, p = .25).

The digitized ERP data from all participants were segmented to include a 100-ms pre-stimulus interval (baseline) and a 700 ms post-stimulus interval. Prior to statistical analyses, data were re-referenced to the average of all electrodes. Next, the segmented data were averaged individually for each participant in that artefacts rejection was carried out on the ERP data for each electrode to eliminate ERPs contaminated by motor movements and eye artifacts from further analysis. Rejection rates were comparable across groups and stimulus conditions. Following the baseline adjustment and averaging procedures, all data from individual electrodes were averaged within each of ten scalp regions (five scalp regions for each hemisphere – frontal, central, parietal, occipital, and temporal) after Key et al. (2006). This approach represented a modification of the clusters proposed by Curran (1999), but altered such that the average of the 10 regions was equal to zero. The purpose of the clustering procedure was to reduce the number of variables in order to increase statistical power. The use of this clustering pattern also provided the opportunity to compare findings from this analysis with prior studies (Molfese, et al., 2006a).

The analyses involved several steps. First, the 1440 averaged ERPs (20 participants x 6 stimulus conditions x 12 scalp regions) were submitted to a Principal Components Analysis (PCA) where a series of orthogonally rotated factors identified regions of variability within the ERP. A Scree test (Cattell, 1966) determined the number of factors for subsequent analyses. Next, the factor scores (weights) from the PCA were submitted to an Analysis of Variance (ANOVA) to identify the source of the variability. Separate repeated measures ANOVAs with Greenhouse-Geisser correction for Group (2: Control, Risk) x Consonant (3: /b, d, g/) x Vowel (2: /a. u/) x Electrode Region (6: frontal, central, temporal, posterior temporal, parietal and occipital) x Hemisphere (2: left, right). The Tukey test was used to assess all interactions. These procedures directly address the question of whether ERP wave shapes at different electrode sites and latencies (characterized by factors) change systematically in response to different group, stimulus features, electrode regions, and hemispheres.

The analytic approach has proven successful both in identifying ERP regions where most of the variability occurred across ERPs and children, and subsequently in determining if the variability characterized by the different PCA extracted factors results from systematic changes in the independent variables under investigation (Rockstroh et al., 1982; Chapman and McCrary, 1995; Beauducel and Debener, 2003).

PCA

Three major peaks were clearly observed in the average ERPs, as depicted in the grand average ERP displayed in Figure 5.1. An initial positive peak that reached its maximum positive value at 40 ms (P40), two subsequent large negative peaks at 128 ms (N232) and 184 ms (N184), a later occurring positive peak at 336 ms (P336), that is then followed by a small negative peak at 400 ms (N400), followed by a positive peak at 496 ms (P496), followed by a large negative going

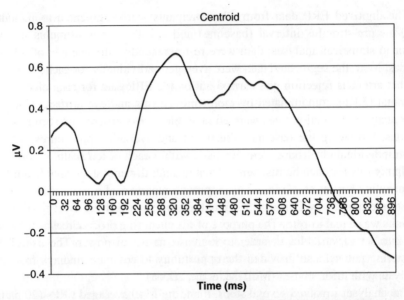

Figure 5.1   The auditory ERP grand average (centroid) for the entire data set. Signal duration includes a 100 ms prestimulus period and a 900 ms post stimulus period. Positive is up.

wave that continues to the end of the epoch. The temporal PCA characterized the entire ERP data set, identifying five factors, whose individual values corresponded to the variability for different specific time regions of the ERP. The analyses reported here focus on Factors 1 and 3 because they were found initially to capture variance associated with group risk differences. These factors are depicted in Figure 5.2. Factor 1 accounted for 23.05 per cent of the total variance

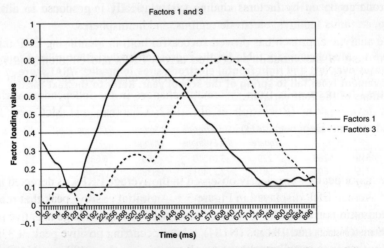

Figure 5.2   The two factors identified through the PCA-ANOVA procedure as sensitive to Familial Risk vs. Control group differences.

and characterized a late slow wave that was maximal at 360 ms, corresponding to the second large positive peak (P336). Factor 3 (20.79 per cent of total variance) captured maximum variability at 600 ms, and appears to capture the variability at the beginning of the late slow negative shift in the ERP.

Factor 1 characterized the variability over the initial portion of the ERP between 184 and 385 ms. A main effect for Group discriminated between the risk and control children, $F(1,18) = 12.313$, $p<.003$, Obs. power = .91. A Group x Consonant interaction, $F(1.96,35.245) = 4.41$, $p<.019$, Obs. power = .723, occurred for Factor 3, the region of variability between 408 and 768 ms. Tests of this interaction indicated that only ERPs recorded from the Control group discriminated between the /b-d/ and /g/ initial syllables.

A regression analysis tested the relationship between the ERP effects related to risk that were identified in Factors 1 and 3, using six ERP variables to predict children's Risk classification based on their parents learning history. The ERP variables were selected based on scalp locations. Since the auditory ERPs from the temporal lobes project initially to the central-frontal region, only the two electrode groups positioned over the left and right hemispheres were used in the analysis. In addition, ERPs elicited in response to front vs. back place of articulation positions (i.e., /d, g/) and high vs. low positioned vowel sounds (i.e., /a, u/). The variables used were the factor scores derived from the PCA for Factor 1 and Factor 3. These included the left and right hemispheres frontal region responses to the /ga/ syllable for Factor 1 and the left and right frontal responses to /du/ for Factor 3. Finally, two additional variables were selected that maximally differed across hemispheres, consonant and vowel sounds: the left frontal response to the /ga/ syllable for Factor 3 and the right frontal response to the syllable, /du/.

This model is depicted in Table 5.1 with four variables to predict the WRAT raw score gains from fall to spring with an adjusted r-square = .839. The right frontal electrode group in Factor 1 responding to /du/ (FRDU1) produced an adjusted

Table 5.1 Model summary table for the regression analysis that utilized four ERP responses over left and right frontal electrode sites to predict WRAT score improvement from fall to spring of the school year. Refer to the text for the definitions of the four variables.

Model	R	R Square	Adjusted R Square	Std. Error of the Estimate	Change Statistics				
					R Square Change	F Change	df1	df2	Sig. F Change
1	.519[a]	.269	.229	3.01519	.269	6.639	1	18	.019
2	.779[b]	.608	.561	2.27401	.338	14.646	1	17	.001
3	.907[c]	.822	.789	1.57805	.215	19.301	1	16	.000
4	.934[d]	.873	.839	1.37941	.050	5.940	1	15	.028

a. Predictors: (Constant), FRDU1

b. Predictors: (Constant), FRDU1, FLGA3

c. Predictors: (Constant), FRDU1, FLGA3, FRDU3

d. Predictors: (Constant), FRDU1, FLGA3, FRDU3, FRGA1

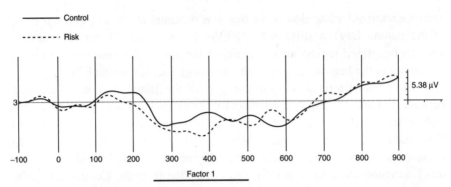

Figure 5.3   ERPs recorded from right hemisphere electrode site 3 to the speech syllable /ga/. The solid line represents the average from Control children while the dashed line indicates the response from the Risk children. The bar labeled 'Factor 1' identifies the major area of difference between the 2 ERPs that was significant in regression analysis. Signal duration includes a 100 ms pre-stimulus period and a 900 ms post stimulus period. Positive is up.

r-square = .269, the left frontal response to /ga/ for Factor 3 (FLGA3) increased the adjusted r-square to .561. The third variable, the right frontal response to /du/ for Factor 3 (FRDU3) increased the overall adjusted r-square to .789, and the fourth variable, the right frontal response to /ga/ for Factor 1 (FRGA1), improved the adjusted r-square to .839. The differences between the two groups are highlighted in Figure 5.3. which depicts the group differences at selected electrode sites within the scalp electrode regions important to the regression analysis for specific speech sounds.

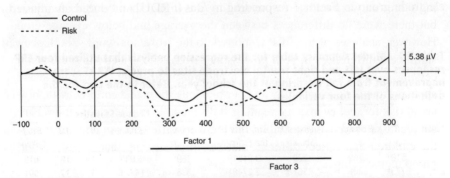

Figure 5.4   ERPs recorded from right hemisphere response at electrode position 3 (same electrode as above) to syllable /du/. The solid line represents the average from the Control children while the dashed line indicates the response from the Risk children. This variability was also caught by Factor 1 but Factor 3 (designated by the later line labeled 'Factor 3' captures the variance between 475–725 ms that was significant in the regression analysis. Signal duration includes a 100 ms pre-stimulus period and a 900 ms post stimulus period. Positive is up.

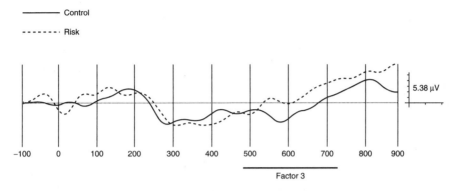

Figure 5.5   ERPs recorded from the left frontal electrode 24 to the syllable /ga/. The solid line represents the average from the Control children while the dashed line indicates the response from the Risk children. This variance is captured by Factor 3. Signal duration includes a 100 ms pre-stimulus period and a 900 ms post stimulus period. Positive is up.

DISCUSSION

The results of this study are interesting in several ways. First, while the children in each group, Risk and Control, did not differ from each other in their perform-ance on the letter identification task as measured by changes between fall and spring assessments, there were significant differences between the groups in their ERP responses to the speech sound stimuli, and significant group differ-ences in ERP responses and gains in letter identification skills. We (Molfese et al., 2006a) reported a similar pattern of results in a study of children 9–12 years of age who were reading above average, average or below average on tests of reading achievement. The performance of children with above average read-ing scores on word and non-word reading was higher than the other two groups, but there were no differences between the average and below average groups. However, analyses of the ERP responses to the word/non-word stimuli showed significant differences in both processing regions (i.e., electrode sites) and pro-cessing speed (i.e., latency) between children with different reading levels. It appears from the current study and our previous study that children with, or who are at risk for, below average reading skills are able to perform on the relatively simple tasks used in these studies, but there are differences in brain responses of the children that reflect different patterns of processing that reliably differ by group membership.

Second, the two portions of the ERP responses that discriminated between pre-school children whose parents reported a history of reading and writing problems and those whose parents reported no such history were similar to those we and others have reported in earlier research. One ERP region at approximately 360 ms discriminated the risk from the control children while a later region found only in the responses of the control children that represented maximum variance at

600 ms discriminated between different speech sounds. When portions of the ERPs for these two regions were included in a regression analysis, nearly 85 per cent of the variance could be accounted for. The two ERP components directly related to gains in letter identification skills for the risk and control children. These data are consistent with previous findings regarding links between variations in ERPs elicited by speech sounds and their relation to subsequent language development (Molfese and Molfese, 1985; 1997) and reading skills (Molfese, 2000) in normal developing children as well as in children at familial risk for learning disabilities (Guttorm et al., 2005a; b). That robust relations that were found between ERPs and letter identification skills reflect the link between letter knowledge and phonological processing skills (i.e., the ability to discriminate phonetic contrasts, to segment and manipulate phonemes, and to detect rhyming) reported in other studies (Burgess and Lonigan, 1998, Johnston et al., 1996; Molfese, et al, 2006b; Wagner et al., 1994). The differential relations found between children at risk for dyslexia and control children adds to what is known about the importance of phonological processing in the acquisition of letter knowledge.

The two ERP components that discriminated between the risk and control groups are similar in latency and amplitude to those reported in previous studies. For example, the latency of the neonatal ERP component noted by Guttorm et al. (2005a) for the /ga/ syllable that occurred between 540 and 630 ms correspond to the second late peak identified by Guttorm, et al. (2001), Molfese and Molfese (1985) and Molfese (2000). Likewise, the amplitude of this peak has been found in previous studies to be correlated with later language skills. Guttorm et al. (2005a) noted that this peak amplitude correlated -.291 (n = 43, p<.029) with receptive language skills at 3.5 years of age. Molfese and Molfese (1985) noted that this same region reliably discriminated between 3 year-old children differing in receptive vocabulary. By 5 years of age, Guttorm noted that this peak amplitude still correlated.374 (n = 42, p<.007) with receptive language skills and −.272 (n = 44, p<.037) with expressive verbal skills. Molfese (2000) used amplitude variations in this same region along with several other variables to correctly classify over 80% of children at 8 years of age who varied in their receptive language skills as indexed by the Wide Range Achievement Test 3 (Wilkinson, 1993). Thus, there appears to be strong convergence in findings across laboratories and developmental periods that note consistent relationships between ERP responses components at these latencies and later language performance measures. We now know that these components are differentially related to letter identification skills in children with and without familial risks for dyslexia.

These findings, when coupled with those reviewed earlier, argue in favor of the use of brain response measures in predicting with high degrees of accuracy differences between children with and without familial risk factors. A number of laboratories are reporting findings converging with those reported here that show a strong link between brain response measures to speech and later outcome measures associated with language and reading. Such findings reinforce the hope that early identification efforts in conjunction with brain and behavior assessments may eventually lead to the early application of interventions that result in a significant reduction in the number of children and families who must deal with the difficulties associated with poor reading development.

The future of advances in neural-functional links is available through several lines of research that perhaps have not been pursued as aggressively as might be warranted. For example, there are a number of advantages to combining neuroimaging techniques (e.g., PET, FMRI, MRI) that provide reasonable spatial resolution with ERP measures that provide temporal information. Such an approach would enable a better understanding of where in the brain and at what time points differences in information processing by at risk and control children occur. The use of two different spatial resolution systems along with temporal information with the same population certainly provides an excellent opportunity for searching for convergence in findings. Coupling these measures during analyses with behavioral performance obtained from different assessments, as illustrated by the work of Guttorm, Lyytinen, and Molfese cited in the present chapter, enriches the data available on different constructs and increases the opportunities for gaining new insights into the complex relationships that surround brain-behavior relationships. Perhaps such steps will provide us with a better understanding of both the underlying structure of the brain and its functional components as they relate to dyslexia.

REFERENCES

Andrews Espy, K., Molfese, D., Molfese, V., Simos, P. and Modglin, A. (2004) 'Development of auditory event-related potentials in young children and relations to word-level reading abilities at age 8 years', *Annals of Dyslexia*, 54: 9–38.

Benasich, A. A., Thomas, J. J., Choudhury, N. and Leppanen, P. H. T. (2002) 'The importance of rapid auditory processing abilities to early language development: Evidence from converging methodologies', *Developmental Psychobiology*, 40: 278–292.

Beauducel, A. and Debener, S. (2003) 'Misallocation of variance in event-related potentials: simulation studies on the effects of test power, topography, and baseline-to-peak versus principal component quantifications', *Journal of Neuroscience Methods*, 124: 103–112.

Bonte, M. L. and Blomert, L. (2004) 'Developmental dyslexia: ERP correlates of anomalous phonological processing during spoken word recognition', *Cognitive Brain Research*, 21: 360–376.

Bradley, R. and Corwyn, R. (2002) 'Socioeconomic status and child development', *Annual Review of Psychology*, 53: 371–399.

Burgess, S.R. and Lonigan, C.J. (1998) 'Bidirectional relations of phonological sensitivity and prereading abilities: Evidence from a preschool sample', *Journal of Experimental Child Psychology*, 70: 117–141.

Cattell, R.B. (1966) 'The scree test for the number of factors', *Multivariate Behavioral Research*, 1: 245–276.

Chapman, R. and McCrary, J. (1995) 'EP component identification and measurement by principal components analysis', *Brain and Cognition*, 27: 288–310.

Clay, M.M. (1987) 'Learning to be learning disabled', *New Zealand Journal of Educational Studies*, 22: 155–173.

Curran, T. (1999) 'The electrophysiology of incidental and intentional retrieval: ERP old/new effect in lexical decision and recognition memory', *Neuropsychologia*, 37: 771–785.

de Jong, P. and van der Leij, A. (1999) 'Specific contributions of phonological abilities to early reading acquisition: Results from a Dutch latent variable longitudinal study', *Journal of Educational Psychology*, 91: 450–476.

de Jong, P. F. and van der Leij, A. (2003) 'Developmental changes in the manifestation of a phonological deficit in dyslexic children learning to read a regular orthography', *Journal of Educational Psychology*, 95: 22–40.

Dunn, L. and Dunn., (1997) *Peabody picture vocabulary test (3rd ed.)*. Circle Pines, MN: American Guidance Service.

Elbro, C., Borstrom, I. and Petersen, D.K. (1998) 'Predicting dyslexia from kindergarten: The importance of distinctness of phonological representations of lexical items', *Reading Research Quarterly*, 33: 36–60.

Elliott, C. (1990) *Differential ability scales: Introductory and technical handbook*. New York: Harcourt Brace Jovanovich.

Grigorenko, E. (2001) 'Developmental dyslexia: an updated on genes, brains and environments', *Journal of Child Psychiatry*, 42: 91–125.

Guttorm, T. K., Leppanen, P. H. T., Poikkeus, A.-M., Eklund, K. M., Lyytinen, P. and Lyytinen, H. (2005a) 'Brain event-related potentials (ERPs) measured at birth predict later language development in children with and without familial risk for dyslexia', *Cortex*, 41: 291–303.

Guttorm, T. K., Leppanen, P. H. T., Richardson, U. and Lyytinen, H. (2001) 'Event-related potentials and consonant differentiation in newborns with familial risk for dyslexia', *Journal of Learning Disabilities*, 34: 534–544.

Guttorm, T., Leppanen, P., Poikkeus, A-M., Eklund, K., Lyytinen, P. and Lyytinen, H. (2005b) 'Brain event-related potentials (ERPs) measured at birth predict later language development in children with and without familial risk for dyslexia', *Cortex*, 41: 291–303.

Holopainen, L., Ahonen, T. and Lyytinen, H. (2001) 'Predicting delay in reading achievement in a highly transparent language', *Journal of Learning Disabilities*, 34: 401–413.

Holopainen, L., Ahonen, T., Tolvanen, A. and Lyytinen, H. (2000) 'Two alternative ways to model the relation between reading accuracy and phonological awareness at preschool age', *Scientific Studies of Reading*, 4: 77–100.

Hugdahl, K., Heiervang, E. Nordby, N., Smievoll, AI., Steinmetz, H., Stevenson, J. and Lund, A. (1998) 'Central auditory processing, MRI morphometry and brain laterality: applications to dyslexia', *Scandinavian Audiology. Supplementum*, 49: 26–34.

Hynd, G. W., M. Semrud-Clikeman, Lorys, A. R. Novey, E. S. and Eliopulo, D. (1990) 'Brain morphology in developmental dyslexia and attention deficit disorder/hyperactivity', *Archives of Neurology*, 47: 919–26.

Johnston, R.S., Anderson, M. and Holligan, C. (1996) 'Knowledge of the alphabet and explicit awareness of phonemes in pre-readers: The nature of the relationship', *Reading and Writing: An Interdisciplinary Journal*, 8: 217–234.

Key, A., Molfese, D.L. and Ratajczak, E. (2006) 'ERP indicators of learning in adults', *Developmental Neuropsychology*, 29: 379–395.

Larsen, J. P., Hoien, T., Lundberg, I. and Odegaard, H. (1990) 'MRI evaluation of the size and symmetry of the planum temporale in adolescents with developmental dyslexia', *Brain and Language*, 39: 289–301.

Leinonen, S., Muller, K., Leppanen, P., Aro, M., Ahonen, T. and Lyytinen, H. (2001) 'Heterogeneity in adult dyslexic readers: Relating processing skills to the speed and accuracy of oral text reading', *Reading and Writing*, 14: 265–296.

Leppanen, P. H. T., Pihko, E., Eklund, K. M. and Lyytinen, H. (1999) 'Cortical responses of infants with and without a genetic risk for dyslexia: II. Group effects', *Neuroreport: For Rapid Communication of Neuroscience Research*, 10: 969–973.

Leppanen, P. H. T., Richardson, U., Pihko, E., Eklund, K. M., Guttorm, T. K., Aro, M. and Lyytinen, H. (2002) 'Brain responses to changes in speech sound durations differ between infants with and without familial risk for dyslexia', *Developmental Neuropsychology*, 22: 407–422.

Leonard, C. M., Eckert, M.A., Lombardino, L.J., Oakland, T., Kranzler, T. and Mohr, C.M., King, W.M. and Freeman, A. (2001) 'Anatomical risk factors for phonological dyslexia', *Cerebral Cortex*, 11: 148–57.

Leonard, C. M., Lombardino, L.J., Walsh, K., Eckert, M.A., Mockler, J.L. Rowe, L., Williams, S. and DeBose, C.B. (2002) 'Anatomical risk factors that distinguish dyslexia from SLI predict reading skill in normal children', *Journal of Communication Disorders*, 35: 501–31.

Lyytinen, H., Aro, M., Eklund, K., Erskine, J., Guttorm, T., Laakso, M. -L., Leppänen, P.H.T., Lyytinen, P., Poikkeus, A. -M., Richardson, U. and Torppa, M. (2004) 'The development of children at familial risk for dyslexia: birth to early school age', *Annals of Dyslexia*, 54: 184–220.

Lyytinen, H., Ahonen, T., Eklund, K., Guttorm, T.K., Laakso, M. -L., Leinonen, S., Leppanen, P.H.T., Lyytinen, P., Poikkeus, A. M., Puolakanaho, A., Richardson, U. and Viholainen, H. (2001) 'Developmental pathways of children with and without familial risk for dyslexia during the first years of life', *Developmental Neuropsychology*, 20: 539–558.

Lyytinen, H., Erskine, J., Arno, M. and Richardson, U. (2006) 'Reading and reading disorders', in E. Hoff and M. Shatz (eds) *Blackwell handbook of language development*. Williston, VT: Blackwell. pp. 454–474.

Lyytinen, H., Leppänen, P. H.T., Richardson, U. and Guttorm, T. (2003) 'Brain functions and speech perception in infants at risk for dyslexia', in V. Csepe (ed.) *Dyslexia: different brain, different behaviour*. Neuropsychology and Cognition Series. Dorthrecht: Kluwer. pp. 113–152.

McGuinness, D. (2004) *Early reading instruction: What science really tells us about how to teaching reading*. Cambridge, MA: A Bradford Book.

Molfese, D. L. (2000) 'Predicting dyslexia at 8 years of age using neonatal brain responses', *Brain and Language*, 72: 238–245.

Molfese, D. L. and Molfese, V. J. (1997) 'Discrimination of language skills at five years of age using event related potentials recorded at birth', *Developmental Neuropsychology*, 13: 135–156.

Molfese, D. L. and Molfese, V. J. (1985) 'Electrophysiological indices of auditory discrimination in newborn infants: The bases for predicting later language development', *Infant Behavior and Development*, 8: 197–211.

Molfese, D.L., Molfese, V.J. and Kelly, S. (2001) 'The use of brain electrophysiology techniques to study language: A basic guide for the beginning consumer of electrophysiology information', *Learning Disabilities Quarterly*, 24: 177–188.

Molfese, D., Key, A.F., Kelly, S., Cunningham, N., Terrell, S., Ferguson, M., Molfese, V. and Bonebright, T. (2006a) 'Below-average, average, and above-average readers engage different and similar brain regions while reading', *Journal of Learning Disabilities*, 39: 352–363.

Molfese, D. L., Fonaryova-Key, A., Maguire, M., Dove, G. and Molfese, V. J. (2005) 'The use of event-related evoked potentials (ERPs) to study the brain's role in speech perception from infancy into adulthood', in D. Pisoni (ed.), *Handbook of speech perception*. London, England: Blackwell Publishers. pp. 99–121.

Molfese, V., Modglin, A., Beswick, J., Neamon, J., Berg, S., Berg, J. and Molnar, A. (2006b) 'Letter knowledge, phonological processing and print awareness: skill development in non-reading preschool children', *Journal of Learning Disabilities*, 39: 296–305.

Njiokiktjien, C., de Sonneville, L. and Vaal, J. (1994) 'Callosal size in children with learning disabilities', *Behavioural Brain Research*, 64: 213–8.

Oldfield, R. C. (1971) 'The assessment and analysis of handedness: the Edinburgh inventory', *Neuropsychologia*, 9: 97–113.

Olson, R. and Byrne, B (2005) 'Genetic and environmental influences on reading and language ability and disability', in H. Catts and A. Kamhi (eds) *The connections between language and reading disabilities*. Mahwah, New Jersey: Erlbaum. pp. 173–200.

Pennington, B.F. and Lefly, D.L. (2001) 'Early reading development in children at family risk for dyslexia', *Child Development*, 72: 816– 833.

Pennington, B. F., Filipek, P.A., Lefly, D.L., Churchwell, J., Kennedy, D.N. and Simon, J.H. (1999) 'Brain morphometry in reading-disabled twins', *Neurology*, 53: 723–9.

Pihko, E., Leppanen, P. H. T., Eklund, K. M., Cheour, M., Guttorm, T. K. and Lyytinen, H. (1999) 'Cortical responses of infants with and without a genetic risk for dyslexia: I. Age effects', N*euroreport: For Rapid Communication of Neuroscience Research*, 10: 901–905.

Rippon, G. and Brunswick, N. (2000) 'Trait and state EEG indices of information processing in developmental dyslexia', *International Journal of Psychophysiology*, 36: 251–265.

Rockstroh, B., Elbert, T., Birbaumer, N. and Lutzenberger, W. (1982) *Slow Brain Potentials and Behavior*. Baltimore: Urban-Schwarzenberg.

Scarborough, H. (1990) 'Very early language deficits in dyslexic children', *Child Development*, 61: 1728–1743.

Snowling, M.J., Gallagher, A. and Frith, U. (2003) 'Family risk of dyslexia is continuous: Individual differences in the precursors of reading skill', *Child Development*, 74: 358–373.

Schultz, R., Cho, N.K., Staib, L.H., Kier, L.E., Fletcher, J.M., Shaywitz, S.E., Shankweiler, D.P., Katz, L., Gore, J.C., Duncan, J. S. and Shaywitz, B. (1994) 'Brain morphology in normal and dyslexic children: the influence of sex and age', *Annals of Neurology*, 35: 732–742.

U.S. Department of Health and Human Services (2003) Performance standards for Head Start education and early childhood development. Available http://www.acf.hhs.gov/programs/hsb/performance/1304b2.htm

Vogler, G. P., DeFries, J. C. and Decker, S. N. (1985) 'Family history as an indicator of risk for reading disability', *Journal of Learning Disabilities*, 18: 419–421.

Wagner, R., Torgesen, J. and Rashotte, C. (1994) 'Development of reading-related phonological processing abilities: New evidence of bidirectional causality from a latent variable longitudinal study', *Developmental Psychology*, 30: 73–87.

Wagner, R., Torgesen, J., Rashotte, C., Hecht, S., Barker, T., Burgess, S., Donahue, J. and Garon, T. (1997) 'Changing relations between phonological processing abilities and word-level reading as children develop from beginning to skilled readers: A 5-year longitudinal study', *Developmental Psychology*, 33: 468–479.

Wilkinson, G. S. (1993) *Wide Range Achievement Test*. Wide Range, Wilmington.

Wimmer, H. (1993) 'Characteristics of developmental dyslexia in a regular writing system', *Applied Psycholinguistics*, 14: 1–33.

6

Early Identification and Prevention of Dyslexia: Results From a Prospective Follow-up Study of Children at Familial Risk for Dyslexia

Heikki Lyytinen with Jane Erskine, Timo Ahonen, Mikko Aro, Kenneth Eklund, Tomi Guttorm, Sini Hintikka, Jarmo Hämäläinen, Ritva Ketonen, Marja-Leena Laakso, Paavo H.T. Leppänen, Paula Lyytinen, Anna-Maija Poikkeus, Anne Puolakanaho, Ulla Richardson, Paula Salmi, Asko Tolvanen, Minna Torppa and Helena Viholainen

This chapter

i) discusses issues of early identification and prevention;
ii) reports on early identification and intervention studies;
iii) comments on the key issues of investigating reading fluency skills of poor readers;
iv) asserts that developmental dyslexia is not 'a unitary phenomenon but is a common denominator of a number of atypical developmental routes, predominantly characterised by compromised language skills'.

INTRODUCTION

The ultimate goal for the majority of dyslexia research is to identify the best way in which to help children for whom reading acquisition poses a significant challenge. The achievement of this goal is contingent on gaining sufficient understanding of dyslexia so that those who are at risk for difficulties can be identified as early as possible. Furthermore, before surmounting the problem, the heterogeneous nature of the 'bottle-necks' that hinder the acquisition of skilled reading must be acknowledged and firmly understood. We now know that developmental dyslexia is not a unitary phenomenon but is a common denominator of a number of atypical developmental routes, predominantly characterised by compromised language skills (Lyytinen et al., 2006b). In the search to unravel the scientific mystery that shrouds dyslexia, the cause(s) of this atypical development should also be accommodated.

It is now almost a decade since we (Lyytinen et al., 1998) acknowledged that there were likely to be issues that affected the phenotype of dyslexia in terms of the types of correlation between genetic and environmental factors (see Plomin, 1994) and subsequently started to consider these correlations in our research. Rutter et al. (1997) outlined three ways in which genetic factors may interact with environmental factors:

1 the passive gene environment (the environment created by the parent for the child);
2 the evocative gene environment (whereby the child's inherited characteristics elicit responses from others); and
3 the active-environment (where experiences and environments are created by the child as a function of the genetic propensity of the child). We know that the precedents of dyslexia comprise an array of factors starting with genetic variation affecting brain development which then, in complex transaction with environmental factors, compromise the potential to acquire reading skill at the expected time. The gene-environment correlations which Plomin (1994) has analysed nicely (see Figure 6.1 for our illustration of Plomin's conceptualization) contribute to reading-related development from birth to reading age (for a more detailed discussion, see Lyytinen et al., 1998). The Jyväskylä Longitudinal study of Dyslexia (JLD) provides empirical data that illustrates attempts to approach the afore-mentioned goals and also uncovers some of the developmental transactions of interest.

For more than ten years, the JLD has followed, since birth, the development of children at risk for dyslexia and their non-risk controls. These children have now passed the third grade of school – a time when diagnosis of dyslexia can be confirmed. From 200 children, half of whom were born to families with confirmed dyslexia in first-degree relatives and report in at least one second-degree relative (see Leinonen et al., 2001 for details of inclusion criteria), we can now document the expected result and confirm that almost 50 per cent of the children born to a parent with dyslexia have ended up facing difficulties in the acquisition of reading skill, as identified in one of the first three school grades.

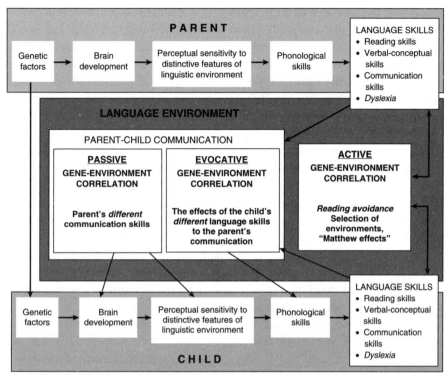

Figure 6.1   Genetic and environmental influences interact in the process leading to dyslexia. Modified from Plomin (1994).

However, as shown below, not all of these children had problems resulting in diagnosis of dyslexia.

This review will chronicle the developmental outcomes of the JLD children from birth to third grade at school. The indices of interest cover many aspects of cognitive and language development with contributions from multiple disciplines, including molecular genetics and psychophysiology. These measures have been deployed from a two-fold perspective: as precursors and predictors. The precursors include those aspects of development that are acknowledged, through decades of research, to be associated with dyslexia. However and importantly, when these precursors also become predictive indices of later difficulty, the onus lies with isolating these measurements as early as possible in development. We aim therefore to convince the reader that early identification of children who will face reading problems is possible, even though the developmental routes vary between individuals.

We begin with the introduction of the description of these developmental routes by using examples from children who showed a heterogeneous range of antecedents to their failure to learn to read over time. An interesting additional feature is the finding that, before becoming skilled readers, children vary also in terms of the time at which the challenges reach their peak. Then, proceeding semi-chronologically, we shall report on the precursors of dyslexia in the context of the JLD children's development with special focus on those precursors which hold special status as a predictive index of later, confirmed, dyslexia. We shall review early indications of the contribution of genetic factors, as seen in the differences between the JLD risk and non-risk as newborns and as very early markers (predictors) of the problems experienced by the at risk children who manifest compromised reading later on. We can also reveal those aspects of language development (during the time-course spanning from birth to school entry age) that hold predictive correlations to later reading acquisition. In addition, we are also in a position to report on those behavioural features outside of the language domain that reveal predictive connections to later reading. Furthermore, we can show how those features of language development which predict difficulties in learning to read are associated with varying degrees of natural environmental support. For this purpose, we can demonstrate how early language development is related to the quality of parent's behaviour known to affect language development and how exposure to written language before reading age is connected to later reading.

The last, but no means least important issue to be discussed is the way in which children at risk for reading problems can be helped. Now that we have sufficiently reliable and valid tools for early identification, a preventive approach is currently underway. The use of this information to facilitate the earliest possible support is important because this helps children to avoid the experience of failure at the beginning of their school career. The detrimental effects to self-esteem and academic motivation of such experiences may make the child vulnerable to wider problems at school.

Morton and Frith (1995) outlined the factors affecting reading as genetic, behavioural and cognitive. We believe that, if the learning environment is optimally effective and motivating, support for learning that is directly related to reading skill at the behavioural level is sufficient to boost reading achievement. The genetic and cognitive factors are beneficial to early identification of children in need of practice, but attempts to affect them at the genetic or cognitive level (e.g., drilling phonological sensitivity out-with the reading-related context, viz. without written stimuli), may not lead to more sustainable results than those obtained by appropriate practice with language and reading itself (i.e., at the behavioural level).

HETEROGENEITY/HOMOGENEITY IN THE DEVELOPMENTAL PATHWAYS LEADING TO DYSLEXIA DIAGNOSIS

We have observed in the JLD-study that children who end up with compromised reading do so via various developmental routes. Although the children can be subcategorised into groups reflecting different developmental routes, there is also a degree of heterogeneity within these routes. Findings of such heterogeneity/ homogeneity have also been observed in dyslexic adults (see Erskine and Seymour's, 2005 'Cognitive Mosaic Model').

Lyytinen et al. (2006b) adopted a novel approach (mixture modelling; Muthén and Muthén, 2004) to the examination of heterogeneity/homogeneity issues among the JLD children with regard to all of the language-literacy measures deployed from birth to school age. In identifying clusters of children with similar trajectories, the modelling facilitated simultaneous examination of the common factor(s) and the individual patterns of development. The language/ literacy measures were composited into seven separate skill domains:

1 receptive skills;
2 expressive language skills;
3 inflectional morphology skills (general language domain);
4 memory;
5 retrieving words efficiently from memory (naming speed);
6 letter knowledge; and
7 phonological awareness skills.

From these composites and as a product of the model, four separate sub groups detailing paths of development (trajectories) were subsequently extracted. We have nominated these groups as declining (phonology), dysfluent, typical and unexpected (see Figure 6.2).

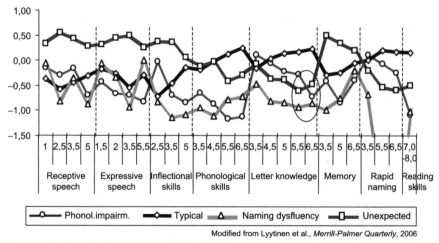

Modified from Lyytinen et al., *Merrill-Palmer Quarterly*, 2006

Figure 6.2   Developmental profiles of subgroup members' average performance in the seven skill domains. Subgroups: Declining (phonological) N = 35; Typical N = 85; Naming dysfluency N = 12; Unexpected N = 67.

Children with a declining phonology trajectory (24 risk, 11 non-risk) showed an increasing lack in the development of phonological skill (i.e., in relation to the average age-related growth of skills) in almost all language skill domains except naming speed. They also had perseverant problems in reading and spelling accuracy and fluency at the end of 1st grade. Thirteen of these children (11 risk and 2 non-risk children) still belonged to the lowest 10th percentile by the end of the 2nd grade, although the group represented otherwise average children (e.g., in terms of IQ and motor skills). Those with a dysfluent trajectory (11 risk and 1 non-risk) were characterised predominantly by slow naming speed. Nine children (8 risk and 1 non-risk) had severe problems in reading acquisition during the first three grades. Their reading and writing was at least 1 SD below the norm on practically any associated measure from grade one to three. IQ was normal. The mean score for motor skills was 1.3 SD below the norm.

Typical trajectory children (38 risk and 47 non-risk) displayed relatively progressive positive development (relative to the other three groups) across all skill domains and the number showing atypical acquisition of reading and spelling was very low.

Those falling into the classification of an unexpected trajectory (33 risk, 34 non-risk) showed strong development with regard to early language skills yet a number of children (14 risk, 8 non-risk) unexpectedly exhibited low and somewhat declining levels of letter knowledge before school entry which was reflected in delayed reading acquisition during the first to third grades. Of the 9 children who showed the most dramatic failure in reading acquisition, 6 (all from the risk group) showed motor problems but average verbal IQ before school age. All had a 'bottleneck' skill (at least 1 SD below the norm) in either the phonological or rapid naming domains or both. In addition, one of the 6 showed attention problems not quite reaching the diagnostic criteria for ADHD.

Although Lyytinen et al. (2006b) have argued from the subgroup-related findings described above that the predictive utility emerges from the trend of the developmental profile itself rather than the level achieved at a specific point in development, a more detailed examination of the unexpected group reveals that this is not necessarily the whole story. One example is the observation that late-emerging (at age five years or more) delay in the development of motor skills can also be associated with compromised reading acquisition.

As mentioned earlier, close to half of the children in the risk group showed some difficulties in reading acquisition. However, the number of children who fulfilled the criterion of dyslexia[1] at the end of the 2nd grade was 43 (35 children, representing 33 per cent of the risk group and 9 per cent of the control group). This outcome nicely complement's Pennington and Lefly's (2001) findings of 34 per cent with respect to the percentage of children with familial risk being later confirmed as dyslexic but is lower than prevalence rates reported by Snowling et al. (2003) – 60 per cent and Scarborough (1990) – 65 per cent.

THE NEUROBIOLOGICAL ROAD TO DYSLEXIA: PRECURSORS AND PREDICTORS FROM BIRTH TO SCHOOL AGE

Advances during the last 20 years in the field of genetics research have brought the search for the underlying genetic basis of dyslexia to the fore (see Fisher and DeFries, 2002 for a review). Recently, the JLD lab was involved in the identification of the first candidate gene for dyslexia (Taipale et al., 2003; see Schumacher et al., 2007 for the most recent review of genetic linkage findings). Innovations in neuro-imaging techniques have also driven the search for a neurobiological basis to dyslexia (for a review, see Lyytinen et al., 2005a and also Demonet et al., 2004; Pugh et al., 2005).

Neurobiological-level results from the JLD have shown that, as early as infancy, children with and without familial risk for dyslexia can be differentiated on the basis of their brain response (event-related potential, ERP) measures using Mismatch Negativity/Oddball paradigms; for reviews, see Lyytinen et al., 2003a; Lyytinen et al., 2005a). In adults, a rarely presented deviant sound embedded within a series of repeated standard sounds in an 'odd-ball' paradigm elicits the Mismatch Negativity (MMN) ERP-response reflecting the detection of auditory change in the brain (for review see Näätänen, 1992). In infants and children, a comparable change detection response has been observed even during sleep (see Cheour et al., 2000; Leppänen et al., 1997; 1999). In the JLD studies, newborns at risk for dyslexia, measured shortly after birth, showed differential hemispheric preference in the processing of vowel duration change embedded in syllabic sound stimuli (Leppänen et al., 1999; Pihko et al., 1999). The risk children differentiated the stimuli more consistently in the right than left hemisphere while the non-risk children's differentiation occurred predominantly in the left hemisphere. The groups also differed in their left hemispheric response to a consonant-duration change embedded in pseudowords at the age of six months (Leppänen et al., 2002). This suggests hemispheric differences in speech development, particularly in processing phoneme durations.

Discrimination of phonetic durations (a crucial skill for quantity distinctions in Finnish) has been observed to be difficult for dyslexic readers (see the next section; Lyytinen et al., 1995). The infant brain responses of the at-risk group to duration changes also predict later language, phonological and reading skills and the group differences also persist in the responses to pseudowords with consonant change at school-age (Leppänen et al., 2003; Leppänen et al., 2004a).

Atypical speech processing in the right hemisphere of the at-risk newborns was also found for another type of speech sound in an ERP paradigm where sounds were presented with equal probability (Guttorm et al., 2001). ERPs to consonant-vowel syllables /ba/, /da/, and /ga/ (with an inter-stimulus interval, ISI, of 4–7 seconds) showed hemispheric group differences at 540–630 ms (latency identified by principal component analysis, PCA; Guttorm et al., 2003).

The responses to /ga/ were clearly more positive and prolonged in the right hemisphere of the at-risk group. This response pattern in the right hemisphere at birth was related to significantly poorer receptive language skills across both groups at the age of 2.5 years. A similar ERP pattern in the left hemisphere was associated with poorer verbal memory skills at the age of 5 years (Guttorm et al., 2005)

In addition to the investigations with speech stimuli, the neurobiological studies in the JLD have explored the processing of non-speech-tones. At infancy, the ERP responses elicited by pitch changes were found to be smaller in newborns at-risk for dyslexia compared to newborns without familial risk (Salminen et al., submitted). Furthermore when ERPs to non-speech-tone pairs were measured at school-age, some children with dyslexia showed atypical processing with respect to the interval between the tones in the pair and the rise time and pitch of the tones (Hämäläinen et al., 2007; 2008).

THE EARLY CHILDHOOD YEARS: PRECURSIVE AND PREDICTIVE ASPECTS OF EARLY LANGUAGE DEVELOPMENT

The JLD results have isolated numerous indices of language development during the early years that predict later development of reading-related skills (Lyytinen et al., 2004; Lyytinen et al., 2005b; Lyytinen, Erskine, Tolvanen, et al., 2006). These include the impact of sound categorisation (Richardson et al., 2003), symbolic play (Lyytinen et al., 2006a) shared reading experience (Torppa et al., 2007a) expressive and receptive language (Lyytinen et al., 2005b), phonological skills (Puolakanaho et al., 2007; in press) and proficiency of inflectional morphology (Lyytinen and Lyytinen, 2004).

A prolific feature of the Finnish language is that of *phonological quantity* which is indicated orthographically by the doubling of letters and manifests phonologically as a longer duration of the sound changing the meaning of the word (e.g., mato 'worm', /matto/(/mat:o/) 'carpet'. Leppänen et al. (2002) and Richardson et al. (2003) showed that, by 6 months of age, Finnish children could successfully differentiate and categorize words according to the duration of a phoneme sound. However, in a behavioural head-turn paradigm (see Kuhl, 1985), Richardson et al. (2003) showed that the JLD risk children required a longer difference in duration of the silent closure stage between short and long /t/ sound-related silence in order to differentiate between the pseudowords 'ata' /ata/ and 'atta' /at:a/. The sound written in Finnish with two t's is associated with at least 60 milliseconds (ms) longer silence (100 ms in the case of risk infants) thus helping the Finnish listener to categorize it as long. Interestingly, the dyslexic parents showed the same subtle differences in categorical discrimination as the at risk infants. The behavioural and neurobiological results thus suggest that the sensory memory for speech sounds and formation of functional long term speech sound representations may not be as adequate among children who later face reading disorder.

Difficulties with *expressive language* have been well documented (see Gallagher et al., 2000; Scarborough, 1990). The JDL-data shows that late talking and poor inflectional skills were significant predictors of risk children's language (Lyytinen et al., 2001) and literacy (Lyytinen et al., 2005b) skills at a later age. Longitudinal monitoring at the ages of 2, 2.5, 3.5, 5.0, 5.5 and 8 years revealed that risk children who displayed a double impediment of poor expressive and receptive language (late talkers, i.e., delayed speech skills at age 2–2.5 years of age), were at a higher risk for later difficulties with reading and spelling than the children without these problems (Lyytinen et al., 2005b).

Table 6.1 summarises the effect sizes (Cohen, 1988) of the most important language-related predictors of failure to acquire reading skill at the appropriate time. In this table, those children who received a diagnosis of dyslexia (DR) are contrasted with children who learned to read normally in the control (NR1) and in the risk (NR2) group. Among the early language markers of dyslexia, essentials findings comprised, for example, smaller vocabulary and fewer morphemes in utterances before 3 years of age.

Phonemic awareness is acknowledged to be the best predictor of reading prowess (Bradley and Bryant, 1983; for a review, see Vellutino et al., 2004). As early as 9 months of age, infants start to become phonologically sensitive by paying attention to the differences in discriminating between meaningful and non-meaningful differences in their native language (Werker and Tees, 1987). Such meaningful differences are fundamental to the course of pronunciation in spoken language development. In terms of becoming phonologically aware in preparation for reading, children must become skilled in the ability to appreciate and manipulate different linguistic components of the language such as phonemes (Snowling, 1980) and rhymes (Goswami and Bryant, 1990).

In the JLD data, from 3 years of age, *phonological skill* joins language skills in terms of predicting risk for later difficulties (Puolakanaho et al., 2004). These authors showed that, even by the tender age of 3.5 years, group differences emerged whereby risk children scored poorer on tests of phonological awareness than non-risk children. In a recent analyses (Puolakanaho et al., in press) involving 200 of the JLD children, Structural Equation Modelling was used to model a battery of closely correlated predictors (phonological awareness, verbal short-term memory, rapid serial naming, expressive vocabulary, pseudoword repetition, as well as performance IQ and familial risk status), their developmental stability, and their associations to reading at second grade. The modelling confirmed that a common core factor behind the early phonological and language measures could be identified in the results of developmental data collected at ages 3.5, 4.5 and 5.5 years. This was termed the Early Phonological and Language Processing (EPLP) factor. The EPLP factor predicted grade 2 reading achievement when measured as early as the age of

Table 6.1 Effect sizes for comparisons between the groups (labelled in the first and second row)

	Normal readers (NR1) from control families		Normal readers (NR2) from dyslexic families
Measures	Disabled readers (DR) d	Normal readers (NR2) from dyslexic families d	Disabled readers (DR) d
1.5 years			
Vocabulary Production (CDI)	0.42	0.03	0.39
Maximum Sentence Length (CDI)	0.39	−0.01	0.42
Reynell Receptive	0.22	−0.04	0.28
Reynell Expressive	0.41	−0.06	0.48
2 years			
Vocabulary Production (CDI)	0.54	−0.07	0.61
Maximum Sentence Length (CDI)	0.50	0.19	0.38
2.5 years			
Vocabulary Production (CDI)	0.55	0.17	0.29
Maximum Sentence Length (CDI)	0.60	0.01	0.50
Reynell Receptive	0.64	0.21	0.36
Reynell Expressive	0.31	−0.01	0.31
3.5 years			
Comprehension of Instruction	0.53	0.06	0.44
Inflectional Morphology Test	0.66	0.28	0.35
Boston Naming Test	0.74	0.41	0.32
Phonological Processing	0.73	0.31	0.41
Rapid Naming (time)	−0.52	−0.05	−0.52
Letter Naming	0.56	0.06	0.56
5 years			
Peabody Picture Vocabulary Test	0.66	0.37	0.23
Inflectional Morphology Test	0.85	0.38	0.45
5.5 years			
Comprehension of Instruction	0.72	0.35	0.32
Boston Naming Test	0.79	0.40	0.31
Phonological Processing	0.71	0.30	0.35
Rapid Naming (time)	−1.49	−0.35	−0.65
Letter Naming	1.37	0.38	0.76

Note a. Effect sizes which are .5 or more have been underlined.
Note b. Measures: Vocabulary Production, Maximum Sentence Length, CDI (MacArthur Communicative Development Inventories, Fenson, et al., 1994; Finnish version; Lyytinen and Lyytinen, 2004). The Reynell Developmental Language Scales (Reynell and Huntley, 1987), Comprehension of Instruction, the subtest of Developmental Neuropsychological Assessment, NEPSY (Korkman et al., 1998), the Peabody Picture Vocabulary Test-Revised, PPVT-R (Dunn and Dunn, 1981), Berko-type Inflectional Morphology Test (Lyytinen and Lyytinen, 2004), Boston Naming Test, BNT (Kaplan et al., 1983), Phonological Processing, the subtest of NEPSY (Korkman et al., 1998), Rapid Naming of Objects (Denckla and Rudel, 1976), Letter Naming (Lyytinen, H. et al., 2006).

3.5 years. Closer analyses indicated that individual differences in second grade reading and spelling accuracy were well predicted (up to 55 per cent of the variance) by the early EPLP factors with no additional contribution from letter naming skills. The EPLP factors predicted second grade reading fluency only to a minor extent but, together with early letter naming skills, accounted for a moderate amount of the variance (at the highest 33 per cent). Thus, the early skills, especially phonological awareness, predicted reading accuracy effectively. However, the early abilities were poor at predicting variation in fluency and, only together with the developing letter naming skills, was a moderate prediction achieved. The findings support the view that reading accuracy is built on very early core phonological skills whereas reading fluency is only partly derived from the same origins.

Figure 6.3 illustrates our attempt to summarize the most central language-related results predicting reading acquisition (composite of accuracy and fluency) in a statistical model (using Mplus 4.0; Muthén and Muthén, 2004) computed with all the JLD-children as the data. The model tested revealed four direct language paths leading into age-appropriate reading skill at the end of the second grade. The paths of letter naming, rapid naming and inflectional morphology started as early as 3.5 years, with letter naming yielding the highest standardized coefficients. The fourth path, representing phonological processing, started 2 years later at 5.5 years of age. Although expressive language had no direct path to reading, it was indirectly connected to reading through inflectional morphology, phonological processing and letter naming. This finding is compatible with that of Silvén et al. (2007) who also observed the contribution of morphological skills following the development of early vocabulary in the prediction of phonological skills and reading. As shown in the figure, the extensive involvement of the development of general language skills was comparative to the role of phonological skills. In the highly agglutinative Finnish language,

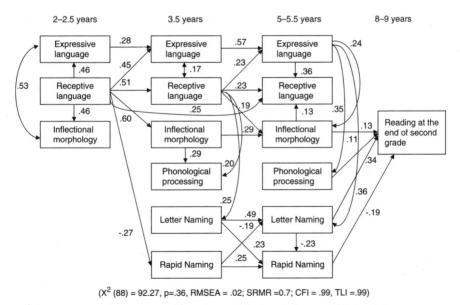

$(X^2 (88) = 92.27, p=.36, RMSEA = .02; SRMR =0.7; CFI = .99, TLI =.99)$

Figure 6.3 Predictive paths of language skills to reading at the end the second grade

learning to inflect words is a good predictor, not only of later language development in general (Lyytinen and Lyytinen, 2004) but also of reading acquisition as well (see Figure 6.3). Phonemic awareness maps closely knowledge of phonemic sounds, each of which is exclusively represented by its own letter in Finnish. The fact that children who are highly interested in letters from an early age become early readers[2], explains why letter name learning has the highest predictive association with reading acquisition.

THE EARLY GROWTH OF FINE AND GROSS MOTOR SKILLS: THEIR RELATIONSHIP TO LANGUAGE AND READING DEVELOPMENT

Prevalence rates for the co-morbidity of motor difficulties and dyslexia are estimated at 60 per cent (Kaplan et al. 1998; Johansson et al. 1995) yet the connections between motor development, early language, and reading development, are little understood (but see Nicolson and Fawcett, 2000; Fawcett and Nicolson, 2007).

Examination of the predictive relationship between the emergence of early motor milestones in infancy and later development of fundamental motor skills in toddlers (Viholainen et al., 2006) confirmed that the early appearance of body control skills predicts good gross motor skills at 3.5 years of age. Predictive exploration of early motor milestones and language and reading skills (Viholainen et al., 2002) suggested that compromised growth rate (slower in both gross and fine motor development) was found only among children belonging to the risk group. This concurs with findings relating to early motor milestones (Trauner et al., 2000) and language development (Robinson, 1987). Risk children who showed motor delays had smaller vocabulary and produced shorter sentences than non-risk children at 18 and 24 months of age (Viholainen et al., 2002) and also had smaller vocabulary and poorer morphology at the ages of 3.5 and 5 to 5.5 years of age (Viholainen et al., 2006). By the end of first grade (age 7–8 years in Finland), delay in attaining motor milestones linked to slowed word, pseudo-word and text reading. Based on these and the other finding (Campos et al., 2000), there is a strong possibility that motor and language development are intertwined and hence, early delay in motor development may be associated with a delay in language development.

NURTURE VS. NATURE: THE IMPACT OF THE ENVIRONMENT ON PRECURSIVE AND PREDICTIVE INDICES OF DYSLEXIA

Environmental factors (see e.g., Castles et al., 1999; Harlaar et al., 2005; Petrill et al., 2005) have long been recognised as making a significant contribution to the development of literacy. Furthermore, it is known that there are strong biological influences on the development of both language and literacy abilities. Parents with high verbal abilities are likely to be more interested in literacy activities and tend also to provide more stimulating linguistic environments for their children. This reveals one of the routes of the gene-environment correlations where both the passive and also evocative effects are observed (see Figure 6.1). It is also most likely that active choice of environments varies according to the biologically founded readiness and consequent interest in stimulating activities, such as use of language and reading. Both endogenous and exogenous (Scarborough and Dobrich, 1994) explanations have their merits and the child's developing language and reading interest and home experiences reciprocally foster each other during early childhood.

Play is an integral part of any child's development. McCathren et al. (1996) demonstrated that symbolic play is representative of the prelinguistic skills necessary for subsequent language development. Our longitudinal assessments (Lyytinen et al., 2003b) at 14, 18 and 30 months of age showed that maternal supportive behaviour in play situations contributed on their children's later language development. Mothers of the non-risk group engaged significantly more in symbolic play and play-related language with their children than children of the mothers with dyslexia. As a predictive index, the mothers' child-directed symbolic language was associated significantly with their children's language comprehension. Interestingly this prediction was especially strong between dyslexic mothers and their children at 14 and 18 months of age. Mother's poor reading skill did not compromise her opportunity to support language development, but poorly-reading mothers may not necessarily use this opportunity as often as typically-reading mothers.

Our analysis of *shared reading* between the JLD parents and their children raised two interesting observations (see Scarborough et al., 1991 with regard to the importance of shared reading for risk children). The first relates to the child's own active role in interactions with environmental stimuli and the second, to the important role of a supportive interactional context for developing language skills. We found that, as early as 14 months of age, children who displayed a high interest and engagement in shared reading had more advanced language skills later on (see Laakso et al., 1999b). Another finding supporting children's own active role came from longitudinal follow-up of shared reading at 14 and 24 months and later language and letter knowledge at 3.5 years. Interestingly, only children in the non-risk group appeared to benefit from shared reading interactions in their later language and letter knowledge. (Laakso et al., 2004). Analyses of shared reading also showed (Laakso et al., 1999a) that maternal activating strategy was more beneficial for children's later language skills than mere description of the elements in the relevant book. Correspondingly, in another study, we found that maternal strategies that expanded the infant's level of functioning were the most effective in stimulating children's later language development (Laakso et al., 1999a).

Furthermore, in line with the earlier results by Scarborough and Dobrich (1994), Lyytinen et al. (1998) found that children who displayed greater interest in reading were likely to be read to more frequently than other children and these children exhibited good language skills at ages 14 and 24 months. The toddlers who had larger vocabularies also attended to books earlier, made more initiations for reading and engaged for longer periods in shared reading with the parents than children who were less linguistically advanced. It may be assumed that, from early on, the larger vocabulary helped these children to follow their parents' story reading. Thus, children's interest in reading is likely as much a prerequisite as a consequence of shared reading.

Applying new advanced statistical methods to the JLD data, Torppa et al. (2007a), have shown that *environmental and interaction-based factors* can make a significant contribution in terms of explaining some of the variability in risk children's language and literacy skills. They applied Latent Growth Curve Analysis to a longitudinal examination of the influence of the home literacy environment and children's own interest in literacy and how this relates to the development of phonological awareness. The findings showed that the more the child engaged in shared reading with their parents and the higher their interest in reading, the faster was their vocabulary development, which in turn promoted their phonological awareness. Similarly, teaching the names of letters in the home environment was shown by Torppa, Poikkeus, Laakso, Eklund, & Lyytinen (2006) to be a significant predictor of children's later letter knowledge.

MINIMISING THE CONSEQUENCES: PRACTICE MAKES PERFECT

The JLD data have shown that the earliest language measures collected at the age of 3.5 are solid predictors of future difficulty (albeit the primacy of these indices has yet to be established). However, in terms of the most practical to implement, early identification of potential difficulty with literacy can be made on the basis of *letter-sound learning* between 3 and 5 years of age. This is not surprising if we consider that the impact of including letters in phonological training programmes are additive (Bus and van Ijzendoorn, 1999; Ehri et al., 2001; Hatcher et al., 2004). Blaiklockb (2004) also highlighted that initial significant correlations between phonological awareness and later reading ability were reduced to non-significant when letter knowledge was controlled for (see also Johnston et al., 1996).

In keeping with these observations and, based on the JLD data, the single most reliable and practical to implement predictor (with fewest false negatives) of reading difficulty in later schooling is the child's proficiency in letter knowledge at the age of 3–5 years (Lyytinen et al., 2007). Letter knowledge is also most predictive in terms of avoiding false positives, when combined with rapid naming measures (RAN; Denckla and Rudel, 1976) at the age of 5 (Lyytinen et al., 2006b; Lyytinen et al., 2007).

If the goal is to identify all children who will face difficulties in learning to read, then observing the development of letter name knowledge years before school is an easily implemented and accurate measure. However, this can be accomplished, only at the expense of identifying a number of children who will be able to overcome the risk (i.e., false positives). Many of them will be lucky enough to have sufficient opportunities to learn the beginnings of reading (letter-sounds) at the appropriate time. What seems to be the case is, however, that children with severe difficulties in learning to read fail to store letter names comparably with others.[3]

Difficulty with the learning of letter-sound relations manifests as a 'bottleneck' to learning, irrespective of the many heterogeneous influences that may have been exerted during the course of the child's preceding development (Lyytinen et al., 2006b). In transparent writing systems, the number of connections between letters and sounds required for accurate decoding of any written item is low (23 in Finnish plus 2 rare additional connections). Despite this, learning letter-sound correspondences manifests as a 'bottleneck' to literacy acquisition. This difficulty could reflect underlying problems in forming associations between phonological and orthographic representations or in the use of rapid and efficient conversion of visual symbols to phonological codes.

Having now identified the children most in need of learning support, the current undertaking of the JLD lab is to implement a programme of support in an attempt to level the school playing field with respect to literacy acquisition. The recent development of the computer game 'Literate' or 'Graphogame' (EC Marie Curie Excellence Grant) provides such a platform for support of basic literacy.

To the extent that, in Finnish, grapheme-phoneme-grapheme correspondences are consistent at the level of single letters, teaching phonemic awareness using a synthetic phonics approach containing letters is an effective way in which to support reading acquisition. For this reason, transparent orthographies have the advantage – reading instruction at school is highly effective and systematic phonics teaching leads to success in a short time among typically learning children (Lyytinen et al., 2006a; see Lyytinen et al., 2004 for an elaboration of the structure of the Finnish language). In English, the situation is quite different, albeit that instruction in systematic phonics is generally acknowledged to be the most effective way in which to initiate reading instruction (Ehri et al., 2001; Johnston and Watson, 1997). Nonetheless, UK children learning English have been shown to require more than two more years of instruction to attain similar levels to their counterpart readers of more consistent languages such as Finnish (Seymour et al., 2003). The number of connections to be learned in English is estimated to be close to 2000, although a substantially lower number is sufficient for accurate learning of most familiar words (through some generalisation of basic rules, through analogy with known words, see for more details, from Goswami, 1995, or perhaps even guessing via semantic-phonological feedback with less consistent pronunciations).

This heavy learning burden is a real challenge to children whose phonological sensitivity is poor or who are otherwise impaired at learning the connections between spoken and written language. For successful acquisition of reading skill in orthographically complex languages, the optimal solution is to provide a learning environment that operates as naturally as it does in transparent orthographies.

The Literate/Graphogame computer game is based on a simple concept of a 'catching game' that drills children in the translating of sounds to letters in both directions as for spelling and reading. In relating phonemes to graphemes, the child is presented via headphones with a sound (phoneme/syllable/word) with the task requirement to catch with the mouse the corresponding falling ball target (containing grapheme/letter string/word). The target item is simultaneously presented with up to 8 alternative written items presented as falling balls (distracters), the content of which prevents selection on the basis of the target's first-letter or other 'easy' routes to identification. The child's task is to catch the correct item before it reaches the bottom of the screen. In the converse direction, when relating graphemes to phonemes, the child is presented with a visual array of letter combinations with the requirement to click on the correct combinations in the correct order to effectively 'build' the target. (e.g., for the auditory target /GREEN/, the child is required to 'build' the correct word by clicking on the visually presented but jumbled components 'gr', 'ee' and 'n' in the correct order). Incorrect attempts at assembly are prompted by the computer's pronunciation of the wrongly spelled item (e.g., if a child clicks on the visual order 'ee', 'n' and 'gr', they are auditorily prompted that they have spelled the pronunciation /EENGR/).

An important dynamic element is incorporated into the game which facilitates adaptation to the level of each child's ability and therefore sustains motivation and thwarts frustration in that the optimum level of playing is adapted to their performance based on the previous trials. In short, if a child progresses with the learning quickly, then the rate at which the balls fall increases and the number of distracter items also increases. Conversely, if the child starts to experience difficulty, the rate of ball falling will slow down and the number of distracter items will reduce. Motivation is further sustained with the facility for the child to collect a series of virtual stickers with which to populate their own virtual sticker scenario as a prize for level completion. Progression to subsequent levels is based on attainment of correct identification of 85 per cent of targets with intermediate provision of extra practice for targets that prove problematic. The most recent versions of the game will be adapted on-line using computational tools (Bayesian statistics; Vilenius et al., 2007; Kujala et al., in press). In its Graphogame form, the computer game is also implemented in other languages including English, German and Dutch.

Results from preliminary short training programmes in Finnish schools are promising, at least in terms of learning letter-sound correspondences. Hintikka et al. (2005) and Lyytinen et al. (2007), have demonstrated that short intervention programmes have produced accelerated growth in letter-sound knowledge in children with initially poor prereading skills. In reading skill outcomes, the results have varied. Hintikka et al. (2005) found no differential outcomes in reading acquisition between children in an intervention group and control group children when they were in receipt of regular reading instruction. When the factors mediating responsiveness to training were analysed more carefully, it was observed that the intervention was more effective than ordinary instruction in reading acquisition for children with low phoneme awareness skills and attention difficulties, as defined by teacher ratings. In Lyytinen et al. (2007) study, the positive results of the game intervention were achieved after only a very short period (1–3 hours) of playing the game whereby risk children playing the game advanced from behind to eventually match the performance of non-game-playing non-risk peers. This exact same pattern has recently emerged from implementation of the game in UK schools whereby risk children playing the game advanced to the level of their non-risk peers while the non-playing risk children unfortunately still continued to lag behind.

The important factor here is that the playing field was levelled between the two groups and perhaps the impending development of children's negative perceptions of their own failure relative to their peers was thwarted – factors which are so crucial to children's self-esteem and optimum receptiveness to further learning. These early findings have subsequently prompted the Ministry of Education in Finland to finance a nation-wide implementation of the game on a general basis in every school and home connected to the Internet in Finland.

CONCLUDING REMARKS

In the Jyväskylä Longitudinal study of dyslexia we have observed – quite in line with earlier comparable results reported from other written language environments (Elbro et al., 1998; Pennington and Lefly, 2001; Scarborough, 1990; Schulte-Körne et al., 1996) – that parent's dyslexia multiplies the likelihood of problems in reading acquisition among their children. Almost half of children with familial risk faced problems in learning to read and almost one-third of them ended up getting diagnosis of dyslexia. At this stage most of the children with familial background were clearly less fluent decoders. It is likely that the highly consistent symmetric connection between letters and phonemes. Their reading rate developed, however, less successfully. Later on the relative difference between groups tended to change in such way that by the end of the third grade, the children with lower accuracy, and those with low accuracy and low reading rate (14/29) characterized the reading of the at risk children reducing the multiplier of at risk children (in relation to controls) with diagnosis of dyslexia reduced to 3.9.

Almost all children who faced severe reading difficulty failed to store letter names during the 1–3 years before Finnish school entry at 7 years at the same rate as their age-mates, despite being given adequate opportunity to learn them in kindergarten environment (1–2 years before school entry). It is important to note that supportive family environment had a clear positive effect on language development including phonological skills during these years. The relative effect of the reading related activities and interests in reading skill was stronger among at risk children (Torppa et al., 2007a). Interestingly, the supportive language behaviour of mothers with dyslexia had as good or better contribution to their children language comprehension as that of typically-reading mothers (Lyytinen et al., 2003, 2003b). These observations show that the development of language skills of children with familial risk for dyslexia can be supported by the parents (independent on their possible dyslexia). This makes it important that people are made aware with regard to the familial nature of the reading difficulties.

Practically all the children with dyslexia who ended up with the most persistent reading problems in the JLD sample, belonged, to the 100 children with familial risk. This provides us with clues to the genetic influences more than about the efficiency of the support available in natural family and school environments. In a clear majority of the cases of the half of the at risk children who were apparently affected by genes in the JLD sample these latter environments (members of which were sensitive to the risk in the JLD-study) clearly failed to minimize the reading-related challenges—although this may be less difficult in the highly transparent orthography we have been observing here. More intensive interventions are required.

Reliable predictive indicators of later language and reading development were observable already from the first year of life among children at risk. Delayed expressive and especially receptive language skills tended to compromise language development among many of the children to whom reading acquisition become a challenge. The association between receptive skills and reading skill was so high that, even at the age when they were instructed to read at school, the speech perception measure (of phonemic duration which were also the earliest predictors) was an as or more reliable correlate of reading skill than the measures of phonological awareness (Lyytinen et al., 2006a).

Delayed development of expressive language was the earliest (2 years) and easily observable difference between children facing reading problems and those who did not face such reading problems among the group of children at familial risk for dyslexia. Although the observations of these early delays could be useful in helping children's language development early on, the information of later predictive measures is more easily used for this purpose. The parental behaviour during the first 2 years of life which supports language development among non-risk children failed to be as effective among at risk children (Laakso et al., 1999b). This is in contrast to the mentioned observation that from age 3 wards, many aspects of parental behaviours were shown to support language development and relatively more efficiently among at risk children.

As expected more than one developmental route characterized difficulties in reading acquisition. Atypical routes identified in language development tended to be much more likely among at risk children. The two most explicit routes were characterised by 1) delayed development of phonological skills and 2) highly compromised fluency of naming visual objects – both of which are also well known from earlier literature. Our data reveal that these two routes can co-occur or appear independently.

Additionally a substantial number of children who faced reading problems showed difficulties in motor development which was usually associated with comparable delay in language development. Independent of which of these predictive characteristics was most pronounced before school the development of letter knowledge tended to be compromised and work as a single most indicative cue.

This easy to observe early step towards literacy – acquisition of letter knowledge – was increasingly predictive from age 4. This is early enough to start assisting these children. Our observations of thousands of children (defined by their teachers to be at risk of facing difficulties in learning to read) using a simple game designed to teach connection building between written and spoken units as a preventive training (Lyytinen et al., 2007) are very encouraging. When implemented only a few months before school entry, outcomes showed that Finnish children can be helped to avoid the experience of failure that a very easily noticeable difference from classmates in reading acquisition would otherwise produce. The observations of Lyytinen et al. (2007) may be generalized to children learning to read a highly transparent writing system such as Finnish as indicated by the observation that only a very small number of the children have required to continue the training during the first grade and/or play for more than six hours. At the same time, the reports from hundreds of teachers have, without exception, been very positive.

The consistency of the Finnish language makes it well-suited to the observation of more serious difficulties invoked when learning to read. Children who are very slow to learn the very basics of reading skill – the 23 letter-sound connections – as is the case among children with dyslexia in Finland, may provide useful data for observing the 'core' problems of dyslexia. Of those JLD children who faced the most serious difficulties in reading acquisition, only two had no reported familial background of dyslexia. Non-specific language-related problems were not present in 10 of the 37 diagnosed dyslexics from the familial risk group, but most had several low scores in reading-related language skills.

By concentrating on practising the core skill of reading: the connections between spoken and written units emphasising the consistent connections, we are optimistic of helping most children who are at risk of failing to learn to read normally. Such explicit connection-building seems to become interesting to children at 6 years of age. Practice of letter-sound connections before this age – even if it occurs in a playful game environment, seems not to help efficiently. We believe also that, independent of the bottleneck which hinders reading acquisition, this type of training is in place as the starting point of reading instruction. This is because there seems to be one common denominator between all different developmental routes preceding difficulties in the acquisition of reading skill, viz. letter name and letter sound learning. Letter naming works very well in terms of prediction but only sounds associated directly with written language (not letter names) are worthy of intensive training for reading acquisition.

We wish to caution that the above-described type of training is a good way in which to complement the ordinary reading instruction or special education that children with learning difficulties may require. The benefit of the programme is that it provides for the easy implementation of individually targeted training. In addition, teacher time does not need to be allocated for tasks that require drilling. However, it is not intended to be used as a sole support for the poor reader.

In regular orthographies, many children learn to overcome the difficulties associated with accurate decoding but — possibly as a consequence of their early experiences associated with slower learning rate of the basic skills – are unmotivated towards reading and do not engage in reading activities to the extent that the skill becomes sufficiently automatised or fluent. Relatively little is known about the course of development and predictors of reading fluency. As mentioned earlier, in the JLD study the early phonological and language abilities predicted well second grade reading and spelling accuracy. However, these early abilities were poor at predicting variation in fluency and, only together with the developing letter naming skills, was a moderate prediction achieved (Puolakanaho et al., in press).

In longitudinal studies, high stability in the development of reading fluency skills has been observed (de Jong and van der Leij, 2002; Klicpera and Schabmann, 1993; Landerl and Wimmer, 2008). In the JLD-data it was found that the risk children were over-represented in the reading subtype with difficulties in fluent word recognition, particularly in the slow decoders subtype (Torppa et al., 2007b). In a recent study Torppa et al. (2007a) showed that the reading comprehension of slow decoders seemed to begin to develop rapidly only after their word recognition skills had reached the necessary level for text comprehension. Thus, slow word recognition affects attainment of the purpose of reading – mediation of the meaning from the written language.

Earlier intervention studies (Thaler et al., 2004; Torgesen et al., 2001) have indicated that low reading fluency shows high stability, whereas accuracy scores can be significantly enhanced (Torgesen et al., 2001). The few intervention studies targeted at fluency (e.g., Hintikka et al., in press; under revision) show that it is possible to enhance the reading fluency skills of poor readers with reading-related practices, for example, with tutored reading interventions or using a computer-mediated learning environment described here. However, the on-going challenge concerns motivational factors in terms of sustaining poorly reading children's interest in the process of reading for reading's sake. Furthermore, the long-term transfer of these trained skills to every-day reading situations still requires exploration and documentation. The investigation of the development of reading fluency in typical readers and the enhancement of reading fluency in children with dyslexia is a challenge – a goal worthy of much more attention than it has received thus far.

ACKNOWLEDGEMENTS

The Jyväskylä Longitudinal study of Dyslexia (JLD) has been supported by the Finnish Centre of Excellence Programs No. 44858 and No. 213486 (2000–2005 and 2006) of the Academy of Finland, Niilo Mäki Institute and University of Jyväskylä.

NOTES

1 The criteria for dyslexia diagnosis entailed a WISC-III Performance quotient > 80 on 4 subtests (Picture Completion, Block Design, Object Assembly and Coding; Wechsler (1991) Intelligence Scale for Children-Third Edition (WISC-III) and scores below the 10th percentile of the members of the JLD control group (N = 93) performance on at least 3 out of 4 measures in reading/spelling accuracy (oral text reading, oral pseudoword text reading, single word and pseudoword list reading, word and pseudoword spelling) or 3 out of 4 measures in reading speed (oral text reading, oral pseudoword text reading, single word and pseudoword list reading, word list reading with a time limit (Häyrinen, Serenius-Sirve & Korkman, 1999). In addition, those children who fulfilled the discrepancy criteria on any combination of two accuracy plus two speed indices were also included as dyslexic (see Hämäläinen et al., 2008, for detailed description of the diagnostic procedures).

2 35 per cent of children read before school entry in Finland.

3 They may have difficulties with the storing of letter names as these, effectively, are pseudowords which are devoid of semantic support at this stage.

REFERENCES

Blaiklock, K. (2004) 'The importance of letter knowledge in the relationship between phonological awareness and reading', *Journal of Research in Reading*, 27: 36–57.

Bradley, L. and Bryant, P. E. (1983) 'Categorising sounds and learning to read: A connection', *Nature*, 301: 419–421.

Bus, A. G. and van Ijzendoorn, M. H. (1999) 'Phonological awareness and early reading: A meta-analysis of experimental training studies', *Journal of Educational Psychology*, 91: 403–414.

Campos, J. J., Anderson, D. I., Barbu–Roth, M. A., Hubbard, E. M., Hertenstein, M. J. and Witherington, D. (2000) 'Travel broadens the mind', *Infancy*, 1: 149–219.

Castles, A., Datta, H., Gayan, J. and Olson, R. K. (1999) 'Varieties of developmental reading disorder: genetic and environmental influences', *Journal of Experimental Child Psychology*, 72: 73–94.

Cheour, M., Leppänen, P. H. T. and Kraus, N. (2000) 'Mismatch negativity (MMN) as a tool for investigating auditory discrimination and sensory memory in infants and children', *Clinical Neurophysiology*, 111: 4–16.

Cohen, J. (1988) *Statistical power analysis for the behavioral sciences* (2nd ed.) New York: Academic Press.

De Jong, P. F. and van der Leij, A. (2002) 'Effects of phonological abilities and linguistic comprehension on the development of reading', *Scientific Studies of Reading*, 6: 51–77.

Demonet, J. F., Taylor, M. and Chaix, Y. (2004) 'Developmental dyslexia', *The Lancet*, 363: 1451–1460.

Denckla, M.B. and Rudel, R.G. (1976) 'Rapid "automatized" naming (R.A.N.): Dyslexia differentiated from other learning disabilities', *Neuropsychologia*, 14: 471–479.

Ehri, L.C., Nunes, S.R., Willows, D.M., Schuster, B.V., Yaghoub-Zadeh, Z. and Shanahan, T. (2001) 'Phonemic awareness instruction helps children learn to read: Evidence from the National Reading Panel's meta-analysis', *Reading Research Quarterly*, 36: 250–287.

Elbro, C., Bornstrøm I. and Petersen, D. (1998) 'Predicting dyslexia from kindergarten: The importance of distinctness of phonological representations of lexical items', *Reading Research Quarterly*, 33: 36–60.

Erskine, J.M. and Seymour, P.H.K. (2005) 'Proximal analysis of developmental dyslexia in adulthood: the cognitive mosaic model', *Journal of Educational Psychology*, 97: 406–424.

Fawcett, A. J. and Nicolson, R. I. (2007) 'Dyslexia, learning, and pedagogical neuroscience', *Developmental Medicine and Child Neurology*, 49: 306–311.

Fisher, S. E. and DeFries, J. C. (2002) 'Developmental dyslexia: genetic dissection of a complex cognitive trait', *Nature Reviews, Neuroscience*, 3: 767–780.

Gallagher, A., Frith, U. and Snowling, M. J. (2000) 'Precursors of literacy delay among children at genetic risk of dyslexia', *Journal of Child Psychology and Psychiatry and Allied Disciplines*, 41: 202–213.

Goswami, U. (1995) 'Phonological development and reading by analogy: What is analogy, and what is not?', *Journal of Research in Reading*, 18: 139–145.

Goswami, U. and Bryant, P. B. (1990) *Phonological skills and learning to read*. London: Erlbaum.

Guttorm, T. K., Leppänen, P. H. T., Poikkeus, A.-M., Eklund, K. M., Lyytinen, P. and Lyytinen, H. (2005) 'Brain event-related potentials (ERPs) measured at birth predict later language development in children with and without familial risk for dyslexia', *Cortex*, 41: 291–303.

Guttorm, T. K., Leppänen, P. H. T., Richardson, U. and Lyytinen, H. (2001) 'Event-related potentials and consonant differentiation in newborns with familial risk for dyslexia', *Journal of Learning Disabilities*, 34: 534–544.

Guttorm, T. K., Leppänen, P. H. T., Tolvanen, A. and Lyytinen, H. (2003) 'Event-related potential in newborns with and without familial risk for dyslexia: Principal component analysis reveals differences between the groups', *Journal of Neural Transmission*, 110: 1059–1074.

Harlaar, N., Spinath, F.M., Dale, P.S. and Plomin, R. (2005) 'Genetic influences on early word recognition abilities and disabilities: A study of 7-year-old twins', *Journal of Child Psychology and Psychiatry*, 46: 373–384.

Hatcher, P.J., Hulme, C. and Snowling, M.J. (2004) 'Explicit phoneme training combined with phonic reading instruction helps young children at risk of reading failure', *Journal of Child Psychology and Psychiatry*, 45: 338–358.

Hintikka, S., Aro, M. and Lyytinen, H. (2005) 'Computerized training of the correspondences between phonological and orthographic units', *Written Language and Literacy*, 8: 155–178.

Hintikka, S., Landerl, K., Aro, M. and Lyytinen, H. (under revision) 'Training reading fluency: Many ways to the goal?' Annals of Dyslexia.

Hintikka, S., Landerl, K., Aro, M. and Lyytinen, H. (in press) 'Training reading fluency: Is it important to practice oral articulation and is generalization possible?'. Annals of Dyslexia.

Hämäläinen, J.A., Leppänen, P.H.T., Guttorm, T.K. and Lyytinen, H. (2007) 'N1 and P2 components of auditory event-related potentials in children with and without reading disabilities', *Clinical Neurophysiology*, 118: 2263–2275.

Hämäläinen, J. A., Leppänen, P. H. T., Guttorm, T. K. and Lyytinen, H. (2008) 'Event-related potentials to pitch and rise time change in children with reading disabilities and typically reading children', *Clinical Neurophysiology*, 119(1): 100–115.

Häyrinen T., Serenius-Sirve, S. and Korkman, M. (1999) *Lukilasse*. Helsinki: Psykologien Kustannus Oy.

Johansson, A. E., Forssberg, H. and Edvardsson, M. (1995) 'Har läs- och skrivsvaga dålig motorik?' [Do children with reading and writing difficulties have poor motor skills?], in C. Jacobson and I. Lundberg (eds), *Läsutveckling och dyslexi. Frågor, erferenheter och resultat*. Falköping: Liber Utbildning. pp. 108–113.

Johnston, R., Anderson, M. and Holligan, C. (1996) 'Knowledge of the Alphabet and Explicit Awareness of Phonemes in Pre–readers: the nature of the relationship', *Reading and Writing: An Inter-Disciplinary Journal*, 8: 217–234.

Johnston, R.S. and Watson, J. (1997) 'Developing reading, spelling, and phonemic awareness skills in primary school children', *Reading*, 31: 37–40.

Kaplan, B. J., Wilson, B. N., Dewey, D. and Crawford, S. G. (1998) 'DCD may not be a discrete disorder', *Human Movement Science*, 17: 471–490.

Klicpera, C. and Schabmann, A. (1993) 'Do German-speaking children have a chance to overcome reading and spelling difficulties? A longitudinal survey from the second until the eighth grade', *European Journal of Psychology of Education*, 8: 307–334.

Korkman, M., Kirk, U., and Kemp, S. L. (1998). *NEPSY – A Developmental Neuropsychological Assessment*. San Antonio, TX: Psychological Corporation.

Kuhl, P. K. (1985) 'Methods in the study of the infant speech perception', in G. Gottlieb and N.A. Krasnegor (eds), *Measurement of audition and vision in the first year of postnatal life: A methodological overview*. Norwood, NJ: Ablex. pp. 223–251.

Kujala, J., Richardson, U. and Lyytinen, H. (in press) 'Estimation and visualization of confusability of matrices from adaptive measurement data', *Journal of Mathematical Psychology*.

Laakso, M. L., Poikkeus, A. M., Eklund, K. and Lyytinen, P. (1999a) 'Social interactional behaviors and symbolic play as predictors of language development and their associations with maternal attention-directing strategies', *Infant Behavior and Development*, 22: 541–556.

Laakso, M. L., Poikkeus, A. M. and Lyytinen, P. (1999b) 'Shared reading in families with and without genetic risk for dyslexia: Implications for toddlers language development', *Infant and Child Development*, 8: 179–195.

Laakso, M. L., Poikkeus, A. M., Eklund, K. and Lyytinen, P. (2004) 'Children's interest in early shared reading and it's relation to later language and letter knowledge in children with and without genetic risk for dyslexia', *First Language*, 24: 323–345.

Landerl, K.: and Wimmer, H. (2008) 'Development of word reading fluency and spelling in a consistent orthography: An eight-year follow-up', *Journal of Educational Psychology*, 100(1): 150–161.

Leinonen, S., Muller, K., Leppänen, P., Aro, M., Ahonen, T. and Lyytinen, H. (2001) 'Heterogeneity in adult dyslexic readers: Relating processing skills to the speed and accuracy of oral text reading', *Reading and Writing: An Interdisciplinary Journal*, 14: 265–296.

Leppänen, P. H. T., Eklund, K. M. and Lyytinen, H. (1997) 'Event-related brain potentials to change in rapidly presented acoustic stimuli in newborns', *Developmental Neuropsychology*, 13: 175–204.

Leppänen, P. H. T., Guttorm, T. K., Eklund, K. M., Poikkeus, A. M., Lyytinen, P. and Lyytinen, H. (2003) 'Infant brain activation measures for temporal speech cues are associated with later language skills in children with and without risk for familial dyslexia', *Journal of Cognitive Neuroscience, Suppl., Abstracts of Cognitive Neuroscience Society Annual Meeting 2003*, 92.

Leppänen, P. H. T., Guttorm, T. K., Pihko, E., Takkinen, S., Eklund, K. M. and Lyytinen, H. (2004b) 'Maturational effects on newborn ERPs measured in the mismatch negativity paradigm', *Experimental Neurology*, 190: 91–101.

Leppänen, P. H. T., Pihko, E., Eklund, K. M. and Lyytinen, H. (1999) 'Cortical responses of infants with and without a genetic risk for dyslexia: II. Group effects', *NeuroReport*, 10: 901–905.

Leppänen, P.H.T., Richardson, U., Pihko, E., Eklund, K.M., Guttorm, T.K., Aro, M. and Lyytinen, H. (2002) 'Brain responses to changes in speech sound durations differ between infants with and without familial risk for dyslexia', *Developmental Neuropsychology*, 22: 407–422.

Lyytinen, H., Ahonen, T., Aro, M., Aro, T., Närhi, V. and Räsänen, P. (1998) 'Learning disabilities: A view of developmental neuropsychology', in R. Licht, A. Bouma, W. Slot and W. Koops (eds), *Child neuropsychology. Reading disability and more ...*. Delft: Eburon. pp. 29–54.

Lyytinen, H., Aro, M., Eklund, K., Erskine, J., Guttorm, T.K., Laakso, M. L., Leppänen, P.H.T., Lyytinen, P., Poikkeus, A. M., Richardson, U. and Torppa, M. (2004) 'The development of children at familial risk for dyslexia: birth to school age', *Annals of Dyslexia*, 54: 185–220.

Lyytinen, H., Aro, M. and Holopainen, L. (2004) 'Dyslexia in highly orthographically regular Finnish', in I. Smythe, J. Everatt and R. Salter, (eds), *International book of dyslexia, Part I: Languages*. West Sussex: John Wiley pp. 81–91.

Lyytinen, H., Aro, M., Holopainen, L., Leiwo, M., Lyytinen, P. and Tolvanen, A. (2006a) 'Children's language development and reading acquisition in a highly transparent orthography', in R. M. Joshi and P. G. Aaron (edss), *Handbook of orthography and literacy*. Mahwah, NJ: Lawrence Erlbaum. pp. 47–62.

Lyytinen, H., Erskine, J., Tolvanen, A., Torppa, M., Poikkeus, A. M. and Lyytinen, P. (2006b) 'Trajectories of reading development: A follow-up from birth to school age of children with and without risk for dyslexia', *Merrill-Palmer Quarterly*, 52: 514–546.

Lyytinen, H., Guttorm, T.K., Huttunen, T., Hämäläinen, J., Leppänen, P.H.T. and Vesterinen, M. (2005a) 'Psychophysiology of developmental dyslexia: A review of findings including studies of children at risk for dyslexia', *Journal of Neurolinguistics*, 18: 167–195.

Lyytinen, H., Leinonen, S., Nikula, M., Aro, M. and Leiwo, M. (1995) 'In search of the core features of dyslexia: Observations concerning dyslexia in the highly orthographically regular Finnish language', in V. Berninger (ed.), *The varieties of orthographic knowledge II: Relationships to phonology, reading, and writing*. Dordrecht, Netherlands: Kluwer. pp. 177–204.

Lyytinen, H., Leppänen, P.H.T., Richardson, U. and Guttorm, T.K. (2003a) 'Brain functions and speech perception in infants at risk for dyslexia', in V. Csepe (ed.), *Dyslexia: Different Brain, Different Behavior*. Neuropsychology and Cognition Series. Dorthrecht: Kluwer Academic Publishers. pp. 113–152.

Lyytinen, H., Ronimus, M., Alanko, A., Poikkeus, A. M. and Taanila, M. (2007) 'Early identification of dyslexia and the use of computer game-based practice to support reading acquisition', *Nordic Psychology*, 59: 109–126.

Lyytinen, P., Eklund, K. and Lyytinen, H. (2003b) 'The play and language behaviour of mothers with and without dyslexia and its association to their toddler's language development', *Journal of Learning Disabilities*, 36: 74–86.

Lyytinen, P., Eklund, K. and Lyytinen, H. (2005b) 'Language development and literacy skills in late-talking toddlers with and without familial risk for dyslexia', *Annals of Dyslexia*, 55: 166–192.

Lyytinen, P., Laakso, M. L. and Poikkeus, A. M. (1998) 'Parental contribution to childs early language and interest in books', *European Journal of Psychology of Education*, 13: 297–308.

Lyytinen, P. and Lyytinen, H. (2004) 'Growth and predictive relations of vocabulary and inflectional morphology in children with and without familial risk for dyslexia', *Applied Psycholinguistics*, 25: 397–411.

Lyytinen, P., Poikkeus, A. M., Laakso, M. L., Eklund, K. and Lyytinen, H. (2001) 'Language development and symbolic play in children with and without familial risk for dyslexia', *Journal of Speech, Language and Hearing Research*, 44: 873–885.

McCathren, R. B., Warren, S. F. and Yoder, P. (1996) 'Prelinguistic predictors of later language development', in K. N. Cole, P. S. Dale and D. J. Thal (eds), *Assessment of communication and language*. Baltimore: Paul H. Brookes. pp. 57–75.

Morton, J. and Frith, U. (1995) 'Causal modeling: A structural approach to developmental psychopathology', in D. Cicchetti and D. J. Cohen (eds), *Developmental Psychopathology*. New York: Wiley. pp. 357–390.

Muthén, L. K. and Muthén, B. O. (2004) *Mplus User's Guide*. Los Angeles, CA: Muthén and Muthén.

Näätänen, R. (1992) *Attention and brain function*. Hillsdale, NJ: Lawrence Erlbaum.

Nicolson, R. I. and Fawcett, A. J. (2000) 'Long-term learning in dyslexic children', *European Journal of Cognitive Psychology*, 12: 357–393.

Pennington, B. F. and Lefly, D. L. (2001) 'Early reading development in children at family risk for dyslexia', *Child Development*, 72: 816–833.

Petrill, S.A., Deater-Deckard, K., Schatschneider, C. and Davis, C. (2005) 'Measured environmental influences on early reading: Evidence from an adoption study', *Scientific Studies of Reading*, 9 (3): 237–259.

Pihko, E., Leppänen, P. H. T., Eklund, K. M., Cheour, M., Guttorm, T. K. and Lyytinen, H. (1999) 'Cortical responses of infants with and without a genetic risk for dyslexia: I. Age effects', *NeuroReport*, 10: 901–905.

Plomin, R. (1994) *Genetics and experience. The interplay between nature and nurture*. Thousand Oaks: Sage.

Pugh, K. R., Sandak, R., Frost, S. J., Moore, D. and Mencl, W. E. (2005) 'Examining reading development and reading disability in English language learners: Potential contributions from functional neuroimaging', *Learning Disabilities Research and Practice*, 20: 24–30.

Puolakanaho, A., Ahonen, T., Aro, M., Eklund, K., Leppänen, P.H.T., Poikkeus, A., Tolvanen, A., Torppa, M. and Lyytinen, H. (2007) 'Very early phonological and language skills: Estimating individual risk of reading disability', *Journal of Child Psychology and Psychiatry*, 48: 923–931.

Puolakanaho, A., Ahonen, T., Aro, M., Eklund, K., Leppänen, P.H.T., Poikkeus, A. M., Tolvanen, A., Torppa, A., and Lyytinen., H. (in press) 'Developmental links of very early phonological and language skills to the 2nd grade reading outcomes: strong to accuracy but only minor to fluency', *Journal of Learning Disabilities.*

Puolakanaho, A., Poikkeus, A. M., Ahonen, T., Tolvanen, A. and Lyytinen, H. (2004) 'Emerging phonological awareness as a precursor of risk in children with and without familial risk for dyslexia', *Annals of Dyslexia*, 54: 221–243.

Reynell, J., & Huntley, M. (1987). *Reynell Developmental Language Scales Manual (2. ed.)* Windsor, Great Britain: NSFER-Nelson.

Richardson, U., Leppänen, P.H.T., Leiwo, M. and Lyytinen, H. (2003) 'Speech perception of infants with high familial risk for dyslexia differ at the age of 6 months', *Developmental Neuropsychology*, 3: 385–397.

Robinson, R. J. (1987) 'The causes of language disorder: introduction and overview', in *Proceedings of the first international symposium on specific speech and language disorders in children.* pp. 1–19.

Rutter, M. L., Dunn, J., Plomin, R., Simonoff, E., Pickes, A., Maughan, P., Ormel, J., Meyer, J. and Eaves, R. (1997) 'Integrating nature and nurture: Implications of person–environment correlations and interactions for developmental psychopathology', *Development and Psychopathology*, 9: 335–364.

Salminen, H. K., Hämäläinen, J. A., Guttorm, T. K., Eklund, K., Lyytinen, H. and Leppänen, P. H. T. (submitted) 'ERPs reveal atypical pitch–change processing in newborns at–risk for dyslexia who later become dyslexic'.

Scarborough, H. S. (1990) 'Very early language deficits in dyslexic children', *Child Development*, 61: 1728–1734.

Scarborough, H. S. and Dobrich, W. (1994) 'On the efficacy of reading to preschoolers', *Developmental Review*, 14: 245–302.

Scarborough, H. S., Dobrich, W. and Hager, M. (1991) 'Pre-school literacy experience and later reading achievement', *Journal of Reading Disabilities*, 24: 508–511.

Schulte-Körne, G., Deimel, W., Müller, K., Gutenbrunner C. and Remschmidt, H. (1996) 'Familial aggregation of Spelling Disability', *Journal of Child Psychology and Psychiatry*, 37: 817–822.

Schumacher, J., Hoffman, P., Schmäl, C., Schulte-Körne, G. and Nöthen, M. (2007) 'Genetics of dyslexia: the evolving landscape', *Journal of Medical Genetics*, 44: 289–297.

Seymour, P. H. K., Aro, M. and Erskine, J. M. (2003) 'Foundation literacy acquisition in European orthographies', *British Journal of Psychology*, 94: 143–174.

Silvén, M., Poskiparta, E., Niemi, P. and Voeten, M. (2007) 'Precursors of reading skill from infancy to first grade in Finnish: Continuity and change in highly inflected language', *Journal of Educational Psychology*, 99: 516–531.

Snowling, M. J. (1980) 'The development of grapheme–phoneme correspondences in normal and dyslexic readers', *Journal of Experimental Child Psychology*, 29: 294–305.

Snowling, M. J., Gallagher, A. and Frith, U. (2003) 'Family risk of dyslexia is continuous: Individual differences in the precursors of reading skill', *Child Development*, 74: 358–373.

Taipale, M., Kaminen, N., Nopola–Hemmi, J., Haltia, T., Myllyluoma, B., Lyytinen, H., Müller, K., Kaaranen, M., Lindsberg, P. J., Hannula-Jouppi, K. and Kere, J. (2003) 'A candidate gene for developmental dyslexia encodes a nuclear tetratricopeptide repeat domain protein dynamically regulated in brain', *Proceedings of the National Academy of Sciences*, 100 (20): 11553–11558.

Thaler, V., Ebner, E. M., Wimmer, H. and Landerl, K. (2004) 'Training reading fluency in dysfluent readers with high reading accuracy: Word specific effects but low transfer to untrained words', *Annals of Dyslexia*, 54: 89–113.

Torgesen, J. K., Alexander, A. W., Wagner, R. K., Rashotte, C. A., Voeller, K. K. and Conway, T. (2001) 'Intensive remedial instruction for children with severe reading disabilities: Immediate and long-term outcomes from two instructional approaches', *Journal of Learning Disabilities*, 34: 33–58.

Torgesen, J., Rashotte, C. and Alexander, A. W. (2001) 'Principles of fluency instruction in reading: Relationships with established empirical outcomes', in M. Wolf (ed.), *Dyslexia, fluency, and the brain.* Timonium, MD: York Press. pp. 333–355.

Torppa, M., Poikkeus, A. M., Laakso, M. L., Eklund, K. and Lyytinen, H. (2006) 'Predicting delayed letter name knowledge and its relation to grade 1 reading achievement in children with and without familial risk for dyslexia', Developmental Psychology, 42: 1128–1142.

Torppa, M., Poikkeus, A. M., Laakso, M. L., Leskinen, E., Tolvanen, A., Leppänen, P. H. T., Puolakanaho, A. and Lyytinen, H. (2007a) 'Modelling the early paths of phonological awareness and factors supporting its development in children with and without familial risk for dyslexia', *Scientific Studies of Reading*, 11: 73–103.

Torppa, M., Tolvanen, A., Poikkeus, A. M., Eklund, K., Lerkkanen, M. K., Leskinen, E. and Lyytinen, H. (2007b) 'Reading development subtypes and their early characteristics', *Annals of Dyslexia*, 57: 3–32.

Trauner, D., Wulfeck, B., Tallal, P. and Hesselink, J. (2000) 'Neurological and MRI profiles of children with developmental language impairment', *Developmental Medicine and Child Neurology*, 42: 470–475.

Vellutino, F. V., Fletcher, J. M., Snowling, M. J. and Scanlon, D. M. (2004) 'Specific reading disability (dyslexia): what we have learned in the past four decades', *Journal of Child Psychology and Psychiatry*, 45: 2–40.

Viholainen, H., Ahonen, T., Cantell, M., Lyytinen, P. and Lyytinen, H. (2002) 'Development of early motor skills and language in children at risk for familial dyslexia', *Developmental Medicine and Child Neurology*, 44: 761–769.

Viholainen, H., Ahonen, T., Cantell, M., Tolvanen, A. and Lyytinen, H. (2006) 'The early motor milestones in infancy and later motor skills in toddlers: a structural equation model of motor development', *Physical and Occupational Therapy in Pediatrics*, 26: 91–113.

Viholainen, H., Ahonen, T., Lyytinen, P., Cantell, M., Tolvanen, A. and Lyytinen, H. (2006) 'Early motor development and later language and reading skills in children at risk of familial dyslexia', *Developmental Medicine and Child Neurology*, 48: 367–373.

Vilenius, M., Kujala, J., Richardson, U., Lyytinen, H. and Okamoto, T. (2007) 'Bayesian modelling of confusability of phoneme-grapheme connections', *Proceedings of the 7th IEEE International Conference on Advanced Learning Technologies (ICALT 2007)*. pp. 285–287.

Wechsler, D. (1991) 'Wechsler Intelligence Scales for Children – Third Edition', The Psychological Corporation, Sidcup. Finnish translation (1999): Helsinki: Psykologien Kustannus Oy.

Werker, J. F. and Tees, R. C. (1987) 'Speech perception in severely disabled and average reading children', *Canadian Journal of Psychology*, 41: 48–61.

PART II

Cognitive and Learning Perspectives

Exploring Heterogeneity in Developmental Dyslexia: A Longitudinal Investigation

Frank Manis and Caroline E. Bailey

This chapter is about:

 i) individual differences among dyslexic children;
 ii) the nature of phonological and surface dyslexia; and
 iii) the longitudinal stability of subtypes.

BACKGROUND

Children and adults with developmental dyslexia are characterized by moderate to severe difficulties learning to read and spell printed words (Fletcher et al., 2007). Dyslexic children are often viewed in research studies, review papers and theoretical papers as a homogeneous group of individuals suffering from a fairly circumscribed set of deficits, usually phonologically based. Although this perspective captures much of the truth about dyslexic children as a group (i.e., they usually fare poorly on tests of phonological decoding, such as the ability to pronounce orthographically correct non-words, such as *trone* and *fippert*), there are multiple sources of heterogeneity among typical cases of developmental dyslexia. Heterogeneity exists at the level of cognitive subskills correlated with reading (e.g., Morris et al., 1998), genes (e.g., Grigorenko, 2001), and response to intervention (e.g., Vellutino et al., 2000).

The purpose of this chapter is to describe a longitudinal study focusing on heterogeneity at still another level, the level of word identification and phonological processing skills. We will examine the distinction between *phonological* and *surface dyslexia*. Put simply, children with phonological dyslexia (PD) are relatively more impaired than other dyslexic children in phonological decoding and related processes, such as phonological awareness, whereas children with surface dyslexia (SD) are relatively more impaired than other dyslexic children in reading exception words (e.g., words such as *island, beauty*, and *yacht* that violate common spelling-sound correspondences) (Castles and Coltheart, 1993).

BRIEF REVIEW OF THE LITERATURE ON SUBTYPES OF DYSLEXIA

Interest in developmental dyslexia subtypes stems from considerable prior work establishing that subtypes of acquired adult dyslexia could be characterized at least in part by dual-route theory, or variants thereof (see Marshall and Newcombe, 1973; Coltheart, 1978; Saffran, 1985). According to the dual-route model, skilled readers use both a lexical and a sublexical procedure in identifying printed words. The lexical procedure involves using the orthographic representation (i.e., the spelling) of a printed word to retrieve a phonological representation of the word from the mental lexicon. The sublexical procedure involves using knowledge of the correspondences between spelling patterns and phonemes to generate a pronunciation for a printed letter string. Fundamentally, the dual-route model proposes that skilled readers use the lexical procedure to pronounce familiar words, including words that violate typical spelling-sound correspondence 'rules', so-called irregular or *exception words* (e.g., *have, island, colonel*), as well as so-called *regular* words that follow those rules (e.g., *wave, illegal, collect*). Conversely, the sub-lexical procedure is used to pronounce familiar and unfamiliar regular words, and to pronounce nonsense words. Part of the original rationale for the dual-route model was the existence of adult cases who had selectively lost the ability to pronounce unfamiliar regular words and nonsense words (phonological dyslexics) (e.g., Beauvois and Derousne, 1979) or the ability to pronounce exception words (surface dyslexia) (e.g., Coltheart et al., 1983).

Child and adolescent cases of PD and SD have been reported, and these have been termed 'developmental' phonological and surface dyslexia because they appeared to stem from developmental factors rather than brain injury (e.g., Coltheart et al., 1983; Temple and Marshall, 1983). Castles and Coltheart (1993) galvanized the recent upsurge in studies of subtypes of reading processes with their attempt to categorize a large sample (n = 53) of clinic-referred developmentally dyslexic boys (aged 7–14 years) in terms of the PD/SD dichotomy, using a comparison group of normally achieving same-aged readers. They reported that a small number of 'pure' SD and PD cases (8 and 10, respectively) scored normally on one stimulus type (exceptions or non-words) and low on the other. The majority of cases (32/53) were low on both exception and non-word reading. Castles and Coltheart reclassified all of the dyslexic cases, using a regression methodology, into groups that were relatively more impaired in reading non-words (29/53) or exception words (16/32). The authors concluded that a substantial number of clinic-referred dyslexic children have individual profiles of reading failure, echoing earlier work by Boder (1973).

This study was controversial. Murphy and Pollatsek (1994) used a similar methodology, but concluded that although children varied in the degree to which words and non-words were impaired, they did not fall into distinct subgroups. Snowling et al. (1996) criticized Castles and Coltheart (1993) for basing the subgroup classifications on normally achieving readers of the same chronological age (CA comparison group), rather than of the same reading level (RL comparison group), as this does not distinguish between developmental lag vs. deviance. Snowling et al. (1996) also criticized the adaptation of the dual-route model to children, as it is not a developmental model.

Using the same regression methodology with a different set of stimuli, Manis et al. (1996) compared 9–15 year-old dyslexic children (14 females, 37 males) to both a CA and RL comparison group. Twelve of the 17 children classified as PD in relation to the CA comparison were also classified as PD in relation to the RL comparison group. The study also showed that the PD group performed below both CAs and RLs on a phonological awareness task, and had a different pattern of pronunciation errors on the exception word reading task than either of these groups. On an orthographic choice task (judge which of two homophonic spellings was the correct spelling of a word, e.g., *rain* vs. *rane*), the PD group performed more poorly than the CA group, but better than the RL group. PD children were also deviant in the pattern of reading errors on exception words. PD cases made proportionately more lexicalization errors (reading 'sad' for *said*) than either SDs or RLs, and proportionately fewer regularization errors (pronouncing *have* to rhyme with *gave*) than SDs. In contrast, only 1 of the 15 children classified as SD in relation to CAs was SD in relation to RLs. The SD group also did not differ from the CAs or RLs on the phonological awareness task and did not differ from RLs on exception word reading, nonword reading, orthographic knowledge, or the pattern of exception word pronunciation errors.

Manis et al. (1996) concluded that the PD profile in most cases could be described as developmentally deviant, whereas the SD group appeared to have a developmental delay – i.e., the SD children performed very similarly to the RL group on all measures. There were only a few pure cases of PD or SD in their community-based sample of dyslexic children, and even the pure cases of SD appeared to fall within normal limits of variation in reading skill, once their overall level of reading skill was taken into account. They utilized the framework of connectionist models of word reading (see Plaut et al., 1996; Seidenberg and McClelland, 1989) to argue that severe phonological deficits would tend to produce a mixed pattern of poor reading (poor on both exceptions and non-words), whereas mild to moderate, or partially remediated phonological deficits might produce the purer pattern.

Harm and Seidenberg (1999) found evidence supporting this hypothesis in their demonstration that a connectionist system of learning to read with faulty phonological representations simulated the PD performance pattern very closely. Severe phonological impairment tended to produce poor performance on both exceptions and non-words, with discrepancies favoring exception words, whereas milder phonological impairments tended to impair only nonword reading. They argued that the SD profile could arise from many factors, such as lack of practice in reading, limits in general computational resources dedicated to reading, and extensive remediation of a phonological deficit.

Testing a younger group of dyslexic children (all third graders) Stanovich et al. (1997) found the same pattern of developmental deviance and delay in children classified as PD or SD, respectively. In a reanalysis of the data from Castles and Coltheart (1993) and Stanovich and Siegel (1994), they showed that PD cases were much more likely (15–28 per cent) to deviate from the profile of exception word and nonword reading in RL-matched normal readers than SD cases (0–4 per cent). Stanovich et al. (1997) proposed that PD originated primarily from biologically based deficits in phonological processing, whereas SD was a byproduct of milder phonological deficits, combined with inadequate reading experience. An interesting finding was that their sample had a very high incidence of mixed deficits.

Castles et al. (1999) utilized discrepancies between z-scores calculated for a large, representative sample of twins with reading disability (i.e., low word reading and normal verbal and nonverbal ability) to identify 322 cases with the PD profile (the 33 per cent of the sample showing the largest discrepancy favoring exception words) and 322 cases with the SD profile (the 33 per cent of their sample showing the largest discrepancy favoring non-words). Using the MZ vs. DZ regression to the mean to separate genetic and environmental influences, they found that the genetic contribution to the group word reading deficit (measured with the Peabody Word Recognition subtest) was larger for the PD group (67 per cent of the variance) than for the SD group (31 per cent of the variance). In contrast, the shared environmental contribution to the group word reading deficit was 63 per cent for the SD group, and 27 per cent for the PD group. The subgroups differed in the directions predicted by the findings of Manis et al. (1996) and Stanovich et al. (1997) on measures of orthographic knowledge and phonological awareness, regularization errors (reading *have* to rhyme with *save*) and lexicalization errors (reading *said* as *sad*) in pronunciation and print exposure (book and magazine title recognition). They concluded genetic factors were more involved in PD and environmental factors were more involved in SD.

A final study of note was conducted by Bowey and Rutherford (2007). They pointed out that existing methods do not converge on an estimate of the relative incidence of PD and SD. One problem may be insufficient attention to the composition of the normal reader comparison groups. They utilized a CA 'benchmark' group (children performing very close to their age level in both word reading and verbal ability) coupled with reliability scores on the exception word reading and non-word reading tasks to calculate the difference in sample-based standard scores for exception word and non-word reading that was statistically significant (at $p < .01$). The difference turned about to be about one standard deviation. An interesting finding was that statistically significant word-reading imbalances favoring exception words were about as common (17 per cent) as imbalances favoring non-words (19 per cent) in a large sample of normally achieving readers. In contrast, children scoring below the 25th percentile (scaled score of 90) in word identification were more likely to have imbalances favoring exception words (the PD pattern) (38.6 per cent) compared to imbalances favoring non-words (the SD pattern) (13.6 per cent). Moving to more severely disabled readers (word identification standard scores of 80 or lower), the imbalances were much more likely to be of the PD pattern (31.3 per cent) than the SD pattern (6.3 per cent). When the sample was limited to poor readers who were in the bottom quartile for word reading and above the bottom quartile for verbal ability, the incidence of PD was estimated at 60 per cent, whereas the incidence of SD was 0 per cent. A related finding was that SD poor readers had significantly lower verbal ability (on the Peabody Picture Vocabulary Test-Revised) than PD poor readers. Finally, Bowey and Rutherford (2007) replicated previous findings that the incidence of PD was much higher than that of SD when defined in relation to younger readers matched in word reading ability. In fact, they found only one pure case of SD defined in relation to the RL comparison group (out of 44 cases).

To summarize, there is clear evidence that the PD and SD profiles occur in typical samples of dyslexic children, whether identified from clinic samples (e.g., Castles and Coltheart, 1993) or community-based samples (Bowey and Rutherford, 2007; Castles et al., 1999; Manis et al., 1996; Stanovich et al., 1997). The characteristics of these subtypes appear consistently across studies, and indicate that the PD profile is more likely a developmentally deviant pattern with strong biological influences, whereas the SD profile is more likely a developmentally delayed pattern with diverse and largely unspecified origins.

The broad purpose of our study was to examine the consensus view of subtypes by means of longitudinal data (grades 3 to 5). One direct implication of the consensus view of PD and SD is that the PD profile should show developmental delay and deviance (i.e., from both RL and CA comparison groups), it should be relatively stable over time, and perhaps should increase in frequency over time. In contrast, SD cases should fit the developmental delay profile over time (i.e., consistently below the CA comparison group, but equivalent to an RL comparison group), it should be less stable over time, and it should perhaps decrease in frequency over time (due to the cumulative beneficial effects of reading remediation and exposure to print in general).

In one previous study using this data set, we analyzed stability over a one-year period (Manis et al., 1999). The findings were that the PD profile was more stable than the SD profile. The PD group differed from both the CA and the RL comparison group specifically on phonological decoding and awareness. In contrast, the SD group showed a broader range of deficits in relation to the CA group, and no deficits in relation to the RL group. However, the method of identifying the subgroups differed in the present study and the period under study was two instead of one year.

METHOD

Participants

The participants were selected from public school classrooms in a medium-sized city. To identify dyslexic readers, we asked teachers in several third-grade classrooms to nominate all children who were performing in the bottom 25 per cent of reading ability, and who did not have low English language fluency, or any obvious emotional, sensory or cognitive impairment. After obtaining parental consent, we screened children with the Word Identification subtest of the Woodcock Reading Mastery Tests. Ninety of the 103 nominated children met our criterion of a Word Identification score at the 25th percentile or less. Of the original 90 children, 67 remained in the study at the 5th grade testing. We applied further screening criteria at this point. Children had to achieve a standard score of 85 or higher on one of two tests, the Peabody Picture Vocabulary Test-Revised (PPVT-R) (Dunn and Dunn, 1981), or the Visual Closure subtest of the Woodcock-Johnson-Revised Cognitive Abilities test (Woodcock and Johnson, 1989) and not have a standard score below 70 on either of these tests. This reduced the dyslexic sample to 63 cases.

Teachers also nominated average to above average readers in the third grade and they were included in the study in the chronological age (CA) comparison group if parental consent was given and if they scored at or above the 40th percentile on Word Identification in both the 3rd grade and 5th grade. The PPVT-R and Visual Closure criteria were applied to this group as well. Out of the original 55 children nominated, 44 remained in the study in 5th grade, and 30 qualified based on the Word Identification and cognitive test criteria.

A group of reading-level (RL) matched normal readers was selected for each grade level of the dyslexic group (3rd–5th). These three groups were selected in the following way. In every year of the study, teachers nominated average to above average first and second graders (approximately 37 per grade). We screened them using the same criteria as the CA comparison group. Generally 30–35 met the criteria. We included the children in the RL group for a given year if their Word Identification scores fell within .25 grade levels of a given dyslexic child during that year. This process resulted in groups varying in size from 24 to 31 (total n = 70).

Table 7.1 presents the mean Woodcock Word Identification grade-equivalent and standard scores for each group, at each grade level, including the RL group that was selected to match the dyslexic group at each grade.

Measures

Standardized tests

Standardized tests included the Woodcock Reading Mastery Test-Revised subtests of Word Identification (Woodcock, 1987), given in each year of the study, the Wechsler Intelligence Scale for Children-III (Wechsler, 1992) Vocabulary test, given in years 1 and 2, the Peabody Picture Vocabulary Test-Revised

Table 7.1   Mean scores for the dyslexic, normative comparison, CA comparison and RL comparison groups at each grade level (note: the normative comparison group overlapped partially with the dyslexic and CA groups)

Measure	Dyslexic Group (n = 63)	Normative Group (n = 50)	CA Group (n = 30)	RL Group (n = 24)
3rd Grade				
Word Ident. G.E.	2.2 (.4)	3.5 (1.0)	4.3 (.5)	2.3 (.3)
Word Ident. S.S.	79.6 (6.7)	99.3 (15.5)	111.9 (6.5)	116.1 (10.0)
Exc. No. Correct	21.6 (8.6)	37.9 (12.9)	46.6 (5.8)	23.3 (7.9)
Pseudoword No. Correct	12.7 (9.6)	29.6 (13.9)	39.6 (11.8)	16.5 (11.3)
4th Grade				
Word Ident. G.E..	2.9 (.5)	4.3 (1.3)	5.1 (1.2)	2.9 (.6)
Word Ident. S.S.	81.1 (9.2)	97.9 (14.1)	108.4 (6.6)	122.0 (9.9)
Exc. No. Correct	34.2 (9.0)	46.5 (11.3)	53.4 (4.8)	31.3 (9.9)
Pseudoword No. Correct	21.2 (10.3)	37.4 (12.6)	46.5 (10.7)	27.2 (14.9)
5th Grade				
Word Ident. G.E.	3.5 (.6)	5.0 (1.8)	6.3 (1.9)	3.5 (.7)
Word Ident. S.S.	78.7 (9.4)	94.4 (13.7)	104.9 (7.6)	110.9 (8.6)
Exc. No. Correct	43.1 (9.3)	53.6 (10.2)	59.9 (3.2)	41.9 (10.5)
Pseudoword No. Correct	28.2 (11.2)	45.3 (11.2)	54.0 (11.6)	36.5 (15.6)

(Dunn and Dunn, 1981), and Visual Closure, from the Woodcock-Johnson Revised Cognitive Battery (Woodcock and Johnson, 1989).

Experimental tests

The experimental tests were given in each year of the study, with exceptions noted. In *Exception Word Reading* children read upto 70 words that violated common spelling-sound correspondences in English (e.g., *have, people, island, yacht, silhouette*). The words were arranged in approximate order of difficulty, based on their length, orthographic complexity, and printed frequency value in *The Word Frequency Book* sample of five million words (Carroll et al., 1971). Children stopped reading when they missed six items in a row. Reading had them pronounce upto 70 orthographically legal pseudowords. Many of the items were created by changing one letter of a common English word (e.g., *nug, chome, stining*). Others were composed of orthographically legal graphemes that had no matching rimes in the English lexicon (e.g., *cleesh, troaze*). Again, the stop rule was six in a row incorrect. *Phoneme Deletion* (Keating and Manis, 1998) consisted of 40 items, 25 involving real words (e.g., say 'snow' without the /s/), and 15 involving non-words, with a non-word response (e.g., say 'kimp' without the /m/). All items were administered. *Orthographic Choice* required children to view two letter strings on a screen (e.g., *sheep* and *sheap*) and decide which one, the left or right, was a correctly spelled word. They pressed a button and were timed, but due to a procedural error reaction time (RT) data were missing on many participants in the first year of the study, and hence were not used in analyses. *Rapid Automatic Naming-Letters (RAN-L)* required children to name 5 rows of 10 letters that consisted of the letters a, d, s, o, and p, repeating in random order. An overall time was obtained for two separate runs and the mean of the two was calculated for each participant. At 5th grade only, we gave a measure of print exposure, the Title Recognition Test (TRT). This test follows the same format as the original measure designed by Cunningham and Stanovich (1990). Children read and heard the experimenter pronounce the names of 30 books that should be known to literate children in grades 3–7 (based on pilot tests we conducted in the school district using different classrooms), only 20 of which are real books. The children checked off titles they thought were real. They were told that some of the books were not real, and there was a penalty score for guessing. We avoided using any titles that were highlighted in the children's classrooms, or that had been made into well-known movies (such as *Charlotte's Web*). The actual score is expressed as a percentage of target items correctly checked, minus the percentage of foils incorrectly checked.

At 5th grade only, we gave Semantic Categorization. Children were shown a category name (e.g., 'fruit' or 'part of the body') which was read aloud by the experimenter, and 500 ms later, they were shown a single word in the center of a computer screen and pushed a button to indicate whether the word belonged to the category or not. Three types of items were used: targets (fruit: *pear*), visual foils which differed from the target word's spelling by one or two letters (fruit: *pore*) and homonym foils (fruit: *pair*). A child who saw one member of this set of three words did not see another member, to avoid guessing strategies based on the child's previous response to that item. Three counterbalanced lists were created, such that across children, the target, visual foil and homonym foil for a given set of three words were seen equally often. The task is sensitive not only to semantic processes in reading, but also phonological processes – children who cannot easily reject the homonym foil can be thought of as being highly reliant on phonological decoding strategies in the processing of word meanings. Visual foils were included as a control for the possibility that children fail to reject homonym foils because of visual-orthographic similarity to the target item; across the 24 stimuli in each condition, visual foils shared as many letters with the target words as homonym foils. The design, and the interpretation of the differences among conditions is based on earlier work by Van Orden (1987).

RESULTS

Defining the subgroups

As a first step in defining the subgroups, we selected 50 third graders whose Word Identification standard scores approximated the distribution of scores in the norming population for the test. The numbers of subjects and the standard score ranges (mean of 100, standard deviation of 15) were: 9 (51–84), 14, (85–99), 18 (100–114) and 9 (115–130). Some of the children were in the dyslexic group (n = 12), some in the group of children nominated for the CA group, but excluded due to low reading scores (n = 13) and the remainder in the CA comparison group (n = 25). Using this sample as a norming group, we converted every participant's exception word and pseudoword raw scores into z-scores. Obviously the normative comparison group cannot be assumed to have the properties of a true norming group, so caution should be exercised in interpreting the z-scores we calculated. The normative group's mean scores are shown in Table 7.1 at each grade level (the same 50 participants were used at each grade level). To identify the subgroups, we subtracted the exception word z-score from the pseudoword z-score. Using the value of 2/3 of a standard deviation as a cut-off (z score of 0.67), we defined the following groups: surface dyslexics (SDs) (exception word score a minimum of 0.67 below the pseudoword score), phonological dyslexics (PDs) (pseudoword score a minimum of 0.67 below the exception word score), mixed dyslexics (difference score between –0.66 and 0.66 and both exception and pseudoword z-scores –0.67 or less), and *balanced readers* (difference score between –0.66 and 0.66 and one or both exception and pseudoword z-scores greater than –0.67). The cut-off value of 2/3 of a standard deviation was chosen because on the average (assuming a normal distribution), it should identify about 15 per cent of the sample as falling into one subgroup or another 25% of the sample as falling below the cut-off on one of the two measures[1].

Characteristics of the subgroups at time 1

We identified 9 PDs and 12 SDs at the third grade test point. The z-scores for Exception Word and Pseudoword Reading for each case are shown in Table 7.2, with the mean z-scores of the CA and RL comparison groups shown for convenience. The manner in which the four dyslexic subtypes were distributed can be most easily seen in Figure 7.1, top panel. We found that 7 of the 9 PDs qualified as 'pure' cases in that their Exception word reading scores fell within 2/3 of a standard deviation of the normative group, but their Pseudoword Reading scores fell below this range. Using the same criteria, 10 of the 12 SD cases qualified as 'pure' cases. Comparing their scores to the RL group mean, four of the seven pure PD cases continued to appear deviant (Pseudoword scores 2/3 standard deviation or more below the RL group), and two additional cases now qualified as pure because the Exception Word scores, which were low compared to the CAs, were comparable to those of the RLs. However, only two of the 10 pure SD cases fell below the RL group's range on Exception Words and within the RL group's range on Pseudowords.

The proportion of PD cases (pure plus mixed) is smaller than previous reports and the proportion of SD cases a bit larger (e.g., Bowey and Rutherford, 2007; Castles and Coltheart, 1993; Manis et al., 1996). However the proportion of pure cases based on the normative group (11 per cent of the sample for the PDs and 16 per cent for the SDs) was comparable to rates reported in past studies

Table 7.2 Exception and Pseudoword z-scores for the children classified as surface or phonological dyslexic

	Exception Words	Pseudowords
CA mean z-scores:	0.67 (.44)	.71 (.84)
RL mean z-scores:	−1.14 (.61)	−0.94 (.81)

Case	Exception Word z-score	Nonsense Word z-score
SD # 1 (pure – CA only)	−1.78	−0.12
SD # 2 (pure – CA only)	−1.78	−0.41
SD # 3 (pure – CA only)	−1.55	−0.19
SD # 4 (pure – CA only)	−1.16	0.17
SD # 5 (pure – CA only)	−1.55	−0.41
SD # 6 (pure – CA only)	−0.93	0.17
SD # 7 (pure – CA only)	−1.47	−0.41
SD # 8 (pure – CA only)	−1.24	−0.19
SD # 9 (pure – RL only)	−1.86	−0.84
SD # 10 (pure – RL only)	−2.01	−1.12
SD # 11 (pure)	−0.77	0.10
SD # 12 (pure)	−0.93	−0.12
PD # 1 (pure – RL only)	−1.16	−1.98
PD # 2 (pure – RL only)	−0.93	−1.77
PD # 3 (pure – CA only)	−0.31	−1.19
PD #4 (pure – CA + RL)	−0.85	−1.77
PD #5 (pure – CA + RL)	−0.85	−1.84
PD #6 (pure – CA only)	−0.07	−1.19
PD # 7 (pure – CA +RL)	−0.31	−1.77
PD # 8 (pure – CA + RL)	−0.31	−1.84
PD # 9 (pure – CA only)	0.08	−1.48

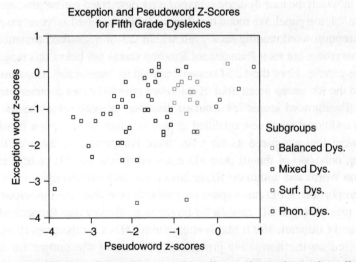

Exception and Pseudoword Z-Scores
for Fifth Grade Dyslexics

Figure 7.1 Distribution of Exception word reading and Pseudoword reading z–scores for the dyslexic sample

(Bowey and Rutherford, 2007; Castles and Coltheart, 1993; Manis et al., 1996). The preservation of pure PDs (6 out of 9) and the reduction in the number of pure SDs (to 2 out of 12) when comparisons were made to the RL group confirms past findings (e.g., Bowey and Rutherford, 2007; Manis et al., 1996). For example, Bowey and Rutherford (2007) found that 12 of 17 poor readers defined as PDs using a CA-matched comparison group remained when they used an RL-based comparison group, but only 1 of the 6 SD cases remained.

The key variables we used to evaluate the validity of the subgroups were the defining variables, Exception Word and Pseudoword Reading, and what we labeled as the validating variables, Orthographic Choice and Phoneme Deletion. Table 7.3 presents the mean scores of the subgroups on all variables. We conducted ANOVAS for each variable comparing all groups except the Balanced Dyslexics, with post hoc comparisons set at alpha = .05 (Duncan Multiple Range Test). The first question we addressed with these analyses was whether the PD and SD groups showed a double dissociation on the definitional measures. We found that they indeed differed in the expected ways on Exception Words (PD > SD) and Pseudowords (SD > PD). Based on past studies (e.g., Bowey and Rutherford, 2007; Castles et al., 1999; Manis et al., 1996; Stanovich et al., 1997) we expected the SD and PD groups to differ on measures of orthographic knowledge and phonological awareness. PDs were more accurate than SDs on Orthographic Choice, but no differences were observed on Phoneme Deletion.

The next question concerned whether the pattern of performance in the subgroups fit a delayed profile (lower than CAs) or a deficit profile (lower than both CAs and RLs). Post hoc tests revealed that the PD subgroup was more accurate than the RL group on Orthographic Choice and Exception Word Reading, and had a higher grade equivalent score on Woodcock Word Identification but performed more poorly than the CA group on each of these measures. In contrast, the PD subgroup was less accurate than the RL group (as well as the CA group) on Pseudoword Reading and Phoneme Deletion. The PD subgroup fits the classic definition of phonological dyslexia, in that they were comparable to or better than the RL group on word recognition tasks, yet lower on phonological processing tasks. They showed a delayed profile on the RAN-L task (lower than CAs but no different from RLs), indicating they did not have broad-based phonological processing deficits, but specific phonological awareness/decoding deficits.

The SD subgroup did not differ from the RL group on Exception Words, Orthographic Choice, Phoneme Deletion, and Woodcock Word Identification grade equivalent, but they performed better than the RL group on Pseudoword Reading. The SD subgroup performed more poorly than the CA group on all four tasks. Their profile fits the developmentally delayed pattern obtained repeatedly in the literature (e.g., Bowey et al., 2007; Castles et al., 1999; Manis et al., 1996; Stanovich et al., 1997), although the relatively good performance on pseudowords is atypical. Because we collected longitudinal data, we are able (in analyses reported later in this paper) to determine whether the SD group catches

Table 7.3 Mean scores (standard deviation in parentheses) for the subgroups identified in Third Grade and the CA and RL comparison groups

Measure	Time 1 Group/Subgroup					
	Phon. Dys. (n = 9)	Surface Dys. (n = 12)	Mixed Dys. (n = 33)	Balanced Dys. (n = 9)	CA Group (n = 30)	RL Group (n = 24)
Word Ident. G.E.	2.6 (.4)	2.2 (.3)	2.0 (.4)	2.7 (.3)	4.3 (.5)	2.3 (.3)
Word Ident. S.S.	85.6 (6.7)	81.2 (6.1)	74.5 (11.0)	89.9 (3.2)	111.8 (6.5)	116.1 (10.0)
Exc. Pct. Corr.	44.6 (7.9)	28.1 (7.5)	24.4 (9.5)	44.8 (6.7)	66.6 (8.2)	33.3 (11.3)
Pseudoword Pct. Corr.	9.5 (5.8)	36.8 (7.8)	10.0 (7.5)	31.4 (7.3)	56.5 (16.8)	23.6 (16.2)
Orth. Choice Pct. Corr.	73.7 (8.8)	66.5 (13.2)	62.6 (8.5)	69.7 (10.5)	77.8 (6.5)	62.0 (14.1)
Phon. Del. Pct. Corr.	35.0 (28.6)	44.2 (10.5)	35.4 (15.9)	56.4 (20.1)	72.8 (17.9)	50.2 (20.5)
RAN–L Time (sec)	26.2 (4.3)	23.8 (5.1)	24.5 (4.1)	21.5 (5.2)	20.9 (4.1)	24.7 (4.1)
WISC–R Vocabulary S.S.	7.8 (1.5)	8.6 (1.8)	8.4 (2.6)	8.4 (2.4)	11.0 (2.5)	11.1 (3.1)

up to the normal readers, or whether their delay is best regarded as a relatively permanent across-the-board reading deficit.

A third question concerned the performance of the less 'pure' subgroups, the mixed and balanced dyslexics on the defining and validating tasks. We have already pointed out that the PD and SD groups were in a sense both mixed, as their group mean scores on all reading variables were below the CA group. It is clear from Table 7.2 that the mixed dyslexic subgroup, aside from being the largest, was the poorest performing group across the board. Their scores on the two defining tasks (Exception Words and Pseudowords) and the two validating tasks (Orthographic Choice and Phoneme Deletion) measures were on a par with the lower performing group (either PD or SD) on each measure, in keeping with their status as a mixed dyslexic subgroup. They also had the lowest Word Identification scores of the four dyslexic subgroups.

The high prevalence of mixed cases is consistent with Stanovich et al.'s (1997) data, and as their sample also was in the third grade, it may be characteristic of younger dyslexic children. Griffiths and Snowling (2002) point out that most cases of developmental dyslexia are mixed, given that both exception word and nonsense word reading are impaired to some degree. According to connectionist models of reading acquisition (e.g., Harm and Seidenberg, 1999) and other models, including the self-teaching model of phonological decoding (Share, 1995), phonological deficits would tend to affect the learning of all types of words, including exception words. Over time, children with phonological deficits might achieve 'work arounds', using semantic context, lexical retrieval and orthographic memorization strategies, among other techniques, to learn exception words. However, in the early phases of learning to read, phonological decoding and awareness deficits might tend to create a mixed profile, particularly if they are severe (Harm and Seidenberg, 1999).

To reduce the tendency to make Type I errors, thus requiring a more severe post hoc correction, and a reduction of statistical power, we did not include the balanced subgroup of dyslexics in the analyses. However, it can be seen in Table 7.3 that they were a mildly reading impaired group, as their Word Identification scores averaged close to the 25th percentile and their performance on the other tasks fell generally in between those of the CA and RL groups.

The final question we addressed with the third grade sample concerned Bowey and Rutherford's (2007) hypothesis that poor vocabulary scores are associated with the SD profile. Both SDs and PDs performed more poorly than the CA and RL groups on WISC-III Vocabulary scaled scores (means of 8.6 and 7.8, respectively), but did not differ from one another. A further test of Bowey and Rutherford's (2007) hypothesis will be made at the 4th and 5th grade.

Taken together, the results indicate we were able to identify relatively pure cases of SD and PD in the third grade. SDs fit the delayed profile observed in past studies, whereas PDs had deficits in phonological decoding and awareness based on the RL comparisons. Dyslexics as a group showed poor performance on the Vocabulary subtest. Additional comparisons on verbal and nonverbal ability tests are reported for 4th and 5th grade.

Characteristics of the subgroups at time 2 (4th grade)

The subgroups were defined using the same criteria at time 2 (by means of current scores of the 50 normative group children). The key questions concerned the stability of the subgroups over one year, whether PDs would become more common than SDs, and whether the subgroups would become more distinct and well-defined than was the case at 3rd grade, when the dominant pattern was a mixed profile, deficient on both exception words and pseudowords.

It is apparent from Table 7.4 that the proportion of PDs more than doubled (rising from 9 to 20), and the proportion of SDs remained about the same (changing from 12 to 11). However, the most interesting finding concerns the stability of the subgroups. PDs were much more stable than SDs. Eight of the 9 PDs identified at time 1 were reclassified as PDs one year later, in contrast to only three of the 12 SDs. Of the 20 PDs at time 2, eight additional cases came from the mixed subgroup at time 1, supporting the hypothesis that mixed dyslexics with phonological deficits are eventually able to work around their word recognition difficulties, and eke out a larger sight word vocabulary. The high stability of the PD group fits the notion of a core deficit in phonological processing as several authors have hypothesized (Fletcher et al., 2007; Shaywitz et al., 2002; Wagner and Torgesen, 1987).

Using the same method that we used at time 1, we identified pure cases in each subgroup. Of the 20 PDs at time 2, 11 fit the criteria for a pure case in relation to the normative group (low on pseudowords, but within the normal range on exception words). Of these, six cases remained pure in relation to the RL group. Eight additional cases had a pure profile in relation to the RL group only. For the SDs, 3 of 11 cases fit the criteria for a pure case based on the normative group, none of whom also fit the RL group criteria for a pure case. However, three additional cases fit the criteria for a pure case in relation to the RL criteria. The results are consistent with time 1 and with the literature – PDs are more distinct in their profile of cognitive strengths and weaknesses in relation to comparison groups. A new finding presented here is that PDs are also more stable than SDs.

The instability of the SDs is interesting. We explored this phenomenon by asking what happened to former SDs. Are they only temporarily delayed in reading? If this were the case, many SDs might end up in the balanced group. However, the movement of SDs into other subgroups seemed fairly evenly distributed (3 remained SD, 4 became mixed, 2 became PD, and 3 became balanced dyslexic readers). This creates further questions as to what the source of the SD profile might be at each age level.

To determine whether the subgroup profiles fit the deviant vs. delayed pattern obtained at grade 3, we compared the two dyslexic subgroups with each other and with the CA and RL comparison groups. It is important to point out that the

Table 7.4   Mean scores (standard deviation in parentheses) for the subgroups identified in Fourth Grade and the CA and RL comparison groups

Measure	Time 2 Group/Subgroup					
	Phon. Dys. (n = 20)	Surface Dys. (n = 11)	Mixed Dys. (n = 21)	Balanced Dys. (n = 11)	CA Group (n = 30)	RL Group (n = 31)
Word Ident. G.E.	3.0 (.5)	2.6 (.6)	2.8 (.4)	3.5 (.4)	5.1 (1.2)	2.9 (.6)
Word Ident. S.S.	81.1 (8.7)	75.4 (12.2)	79.0 (5.6)	90.6 (4.7)	108.4 (6.6)	122.0 (9.9)
Exc. Pct. Corr.	55.4 (9.7)	35.4 (13.4)	43.5 (7.6)	60.3 (7.3)	76.3 (6.9)	44.7 (14.2)
Pseudoword Pct. Corr.	19.2 (10.0)	40.4 (15.2)	26.1 (8.3)	48.2 (5.5)	66.4 (15.3)	38.8 (17.3)
Orth. Choice Pct. Corr.	78.8 (7.9)	71.8 (9.7)	71.8 (9.0)	76.2 (11.7)	82.0 (7.9)	71.6 (9.0)
Orth. Choice RT (ms)	1842 (487)	4115 (2741)	3238 (3003)	2647 (626)	1938 (504)	2969 (1758)
Phon. Del. Pct. Corr.	33.9 (16.0)	56.9 (13.1)	47.2 (15.1)	61.8 (17.6)	75.8 (15.8)	54.9 (20.1)
RAN–L Time (sec)	28.3 (4.6)	30.9 (3.7)	31.5 (5.6)	29.1 (4.1)	25.5 (3.8)	32.6 (4.6)
WISC–R Vocabulary S.S.	8.6 (2.8)	9.3 (3.7)	10.6 (1.9)	8.7 (1.9)	11.0 (2.9)	12.1 (3.2)

analytic method was the same as time 1, but the analyses were done on substantially new groups of children (almost all of the SDs were new to the category, and half of the PDs). An additional measure this time was Orthographic Choice RT (calculated on correct trials only). Mean scores for all variables are shown in Table 7.4. Similar to time 1, we found a double dissociation of PD and SD subgroups on Exception Word and Pseudoword Reading. In addition, there was a double dissociation in the predicted direction on both validating tasks, Orthographic Choice and Phoneme Deletion. Comparing the subgroups to the CA and RL groups, we found that both groups were inferior to the CA group on all measures, with the exception of Orthographic Choice, where the PD mean did not differ from the CA mean. PDs performed more poorly than the RLs on both Pseudoword Reading and Phoneme Deletion, and higher than the RLs on Exception Words and Orthographic Choice accuracy. SDs were considerably slower than the PD and CA group on Orthographic Choice; they took nearly twice as long as the PDs to decide which of two words was a correctly spelled word. The SDs did not differ from the RLs. Their slow RTs on this task were not due to a speed-accuracy trade-off, as they were 7% less accurate than the PDs. SDs were not generally slow in response time, as they did not differ from the PD group on RAN-L, and both groups were slower than the CA group, and did not differ from the RL group on RAN-L naming times.

We looked again at WISC-III Vocabulary performance. Both PD and SD groups had higher scores on this task than at time 1. The range of scaled scores was 5 to 16 for PDs, 5 to 18 for SDs, and 6 to 14 for Mixed Dyslexics, compared to ranges of 5 to 17 and 8 to 19 for CAs and RLs, respectively. This indicates that none of the dyslexic cases had severe delays in vocabulary development. The SD group did not differ from the PDs or the CAs on this task, but scored lower than the RLs. PDs were lower than both CAs and RLs.

To summarize, the PD subgroup from time 1 was remarkably stable, but the SD subgroup was not. In addition, many PDs seemed to be pure cases, in the sense that they had a selective impairment on phonological decoding and awareness, relative to their other reading and cognitive skills. In contrast, SDs for the most part continued to fit the delayed-across-the-board pattern. The data revealed a very interesting pattern of development. PD appears to become more common between the 3rd and 4th grade, and most children had earlier phonological deficits (i.e., 16 out of 20 cases were either PD or Mixed at time 1). The PD pattern appeared to be stable and predictable, and fit the hypothesis that a significant group of dyslexic children have a selective deficit in phonological processing.

In contrast, the SD subgroup fluctuated from year to year. There was almost complete turn-over in the cases from the 3rd to the 4th grade. However, apparently when SD cases 'emerge', they have a characteristic profile of poor orthographic knowledge of printed words, and very slow processing of orthographic information. There were even a few cases at time 2 that showed as distinct a profile as has been cited in the case study literature (e.g., Hanley et al., 1992), i.e., completely normal phonological decoding and awareness, with very poor exception word and orthographic choice performance. The SD profile is 'real', even if it is only temporary. We tentatively hypothesize that environmental factors that can change over the course of a year's time (such as opportunities to practice reading, tutoring of reading, or the child's motivation to read) might be the primary origin of the SD profile. In addition, it seems to be the case that SDs (in agreement with Stanovich et al., 1997) have mild delays in phonological decoding and awareness (i.e., they are behind the CA group, but equivalent to or ahead of the RL group), but have more extreme difficulties identifying the orthographic form of a printed word and retrieving its pronunciation from memory.

Characteristics of the subgroups at time 3 (5th grade)

The subgroups were defined using the same criteria as those for times 1 and 2. The key questions concerned the stability of the subgroups over an additional year, whether PDs would continue to become more common than SDs, and whether the subgroups would become more distinct and well-defined than was the case at 3rd and 4th grade.

It is apparent from Table 7.5 (and the bottom panel of Figure 7.1) that the number of PDs continued to rise (from 20 to 26), and the proportion of SDs began to fall (from 11 to 8). Once again, PDs were much more stable than SDs. Of the 26 PDs, 21 had been identified as PDs at time 1 or 2. All 9 children who were classified as PD at time 1 were still classified as PD at time 3 (one case had been classified as Balanced at time 2 and changed back to PD at time 3). In contrast, only four of the eight SDs had been identified as SDs at either time 1 or 2. The high stability of the PD group shown at time 2 was confirmed by the results at time 3.

Using a method identical to the methods at times 1 and 2, we identified pure cases in each subgroup. Of the 26 PDs at time 3, 15 fit the criteria for a pure case in relation to the normative group (low on pseudowords, but within the normal range on exception words). Of these, 12 cases remained pure in relation to the RL group. Ten additional cases had a pure profile in relation to the RL group only. Thus, 22 out of 26 PD cases fit the criteria for a pure PD profile in relation to the RL group. For the SDs, 6 of 8 cases fit the criteria for a pure case based on the normative group, but none of them fit the RL group criteria for a pure case and neither of the 2 remaining cases fit the RL criteria. Thus, none of the 8 cases fit the criteria for a pure SD profile in relation to the RL group.

The results are striking. By the 5th grade, a large percentage of the PD group fit the criteria for a specific deficit in phonological aspects of reading, but all of the SD cases fit the criteria for a reading delay profile.

At time 3 we continued to explore the characteristics that defined the PD and SD subgroups. Some additional measures were added to the regular test battery, and are discussed below. The data are shown in Table 7.5. Once again, we found a clear double dissociation between the PD and SD subgroups on Exception and Pseudoword Reading, but this time the Phoneme Deletion measure did not

Table 7.5 Mean scores (standard deviation in parentheses) for the subgroups identified in Fifth Grade and the CA and RL comparison groups

Measure	Phon. Dys. (n = 26)	Surface Dys. (n = 8)	Mixed Dys. (n = 17)	Balanced Dys. (n = 12)	CA Group (n = 30)	RL Group (n = 27)
			Time 3 Group/Subgroup			
Word Ident. G.E.	3.7 (.5)	3.2 (.9)	3.2 (.6)	3.7 (.4)	6.3 (1.9)	3.5 (.7)
Word Ident. S.S.	81.6 (7.1)	73.4 (15.5)	74.8 (9.2)	81.6 (6.2)	104.9 (7.6)	111.0 (8.6)
Exc. Pct. Corr.	67.8 (8.3)	54.1 (19.9)	50.0 (10.0)	69.4 (5.4)	85.6 (4.5)	59.8 (15.0)
Pseudoword Pct. Corr.	32.7 (11.1)	60.2 (13.6)	32.4 (13.9)	54.4 (5.4)	77.1 (16.6)	52.1 (17.1)
Orth. Choice Pct. Corr.	82.1 (8.2)	72.0 (6.9)	77.0 (6.4)	79.2 (5.7)	86.5 (5.5)	77.0 (10.3)
Orth. Choice RT (ms)	2083 (562)	2848 (1235)	2292 (631)	2216 (733)	1624 (391)	2274 (944)
Phon. Del. Pct. Corr.	48.8 (18.7)	58.1 (21.2)	50.6 (12.3)	70.2 (12.7)	76.8 (14.7)	63.2 (23.2)
RAN–L Time (sec)	26.0 (3.2)	26.1 (3.2)	26.2 (3.2)	27.1 (4.7)	22.8 (3.7)	27.5 (3.7)
PPVT–R Vocabulary S.S.	96.9 (13.1)	90.8 (11.0)	98.5 (10.5)	95.9 (11.0)	108.6 (14.1)	103.6 (15.4)
Visual Closure S.S.	101.5 (15.3)	100.2 (12.0)	102.2 (16.7)	99.0 (12.6)	101.4 (10.2)	104.0 (12.3)
Title Recognition Test	37.2 (13.2)	30.9 (21.3)	34.4 (15.3)	31.4 (17.1)	37.1 (16.5)	21.6 (17.9)
Sem. Dec. – Target Pct Corr.	89.7 (7.5)	82.8 (9.3)	87.9 (13.0)	85.8 (6.3)	94.0 (7.6)	89.3 (7.6)
Sem. Dec. – Vis Foil Pct Corr.	90.4 (12.8)	86.5 (15.4)	88.2 (9.4)	90.9 (10.8)	96.6 (5.7)	95.3 (96.4)
Sem. Dec. – Hom Foil Pct Corr.	61.8 (17.5)	50.0 (14.4)	46.1 (11.1)	50.8 (17.7)	75.3 (16.7)	58.7 (17.6)

differ between subgroups. The SDs were significantly slower than the PDs on Orthographic Choice, as well as significantly less accurate, according to post hoc comparisons. As before, the PDs were significantly higher than the RLs on Exception Word Reading, and lower on Pseudoword Reading and Phoneme Deletion. PDs were lower than the CAs on all three tasks.

The PD group had relatively strong performance on Orthographic Choice; they did not differ from either the RL or the CA group on either accuracy or RT. The SD group showed a more mixed pattern of results than in the past. They were lower than the CAs on Exception Words, Pseudowords, Phoneme Deletion and both Orthographic Choice accuracy and RT. The SDs did not differ from the RLs on Exception Words, Pseudowords, Phoneme Deletion, and Orthographic Choice accuracy, but they were lower than the RLs on Orthographic Choice RT. This is the first departure from the generally delayed profile that SDs showed on every other reading-related measure at times 1, 2 and 3, so perhaps not much should be made of it. However, it is striking that SDs were nearly 600 ms slower at deciding on the correct spelling of printed words, compared to children two to three years younger than them. Once again, the PD and SD groups were both slower than the CA group, but not the RL group on RAN-L, but did not differ from one another, indicating that the difference between SDs and RLs, in this case, was not due to overall slow responding to alphabetic stimuli.

A new measure of receptive vocabulary, the Peabody Picture Vocabulary Test-Revised (PPVT-R) (Dunn and Dunn, 1981) was given (the same task as Bowey and Rutherford, 2007), and there was a non-significant trend for SDs to be lower than PDs on the PPVT-R. SDs were significantly lower than RLs and CAs on this task, and PDs were lower than CAs. This indicates that receptive vocabulary, as Bowey and Rutherford (2007) hypothesized, might be lower in SD children. However, caution must be exercised, as the SD group was unstable, and only half of the time 3 subgroup of SD children was classified as SD in either of the two earlier years.

Stanovich et al. (1997) hypothesized that SDs have a mild phonological decoding deficit, accompanied by low print exposure, and that this profile creates the pattern of performance (low general reading ability, with exception words lower than nonsense words). Thus, it was of interest how the subgroups performed on our version of the Title Recognition Test (TRT) (see Method section). Castles et al. (1999) found that SDs had poorer TRT scores than PDs, and their sample was defined in a similar fashion to the current study (deviation from a local normative group). Griffiths and Snowling (2002) found that exception word reading analyzed as a continuous variable within a sample of 59 dyslexic children, was related primarily to age and to a measure of print exposure. We found a non-significant trend for SDs to have lower print exposure than PDs. There were no group differences in print exposure between any of the dyslexic groups, or between the dyslexic groups and the CA group. However, the RL group scored significantly lower by post hoc test than the PD, mixed and CA groups (balanced dyslexics were not included in the analyses). This indicates that the test had some sensitivity to group differences in print exposure, as younger children would be expected to know fewer book titles than older children. We must be cautious also because of the small sample sizes involved in our study. Castles et al. (1999) had over 300 cases in each subgroup, and found that the TRT difference accounted for only a small portion of the variance. There is clearly room for improvement in the assessment of the Stanovich et al. (1997) hypothesis about print exposure. Our results were equivocal.

Semantic Categorization scores allowed us to examine phonological processing in the context of reading a word for meaning (see Method section). First, we expected that SDs would have greater difficulty rejecting homonym foils (e.g., a fruit? – *pair)* than PDs owing to their higher reliance on phonological decoding in reading. Second, we anticipated SDs would make fewer correct responses to target items (e.g., a fruit? – *pear)* because of their difficulty in accessing the visual-orthographic representation of printed words, associating this representation with word meaning, or both processes. Results (shown in Table 7.5) were that SDs were poorer than CAs, but not PDs or RLs on all three stimulus types, and less accurate than RLs on visual foils and targets. PDs did not differ from RLs on any of the three stimulus types, but were poorer than the CAs on the homonym foils. The results don't support the first hypothesis regarding greater reliance by SDs on phonological decoding. In fact, SDs and PDs both had difficulty rejecting homonym foils, relative to target words, indicating both subgroups relied on phonological decoding, however challenging it might be. A similar conclusion about weaker phonological decoding, but paradoxically stronger reliance on it by dyslexic children was reached in a review of the literature by Metsala et al. (1998).

The second hypothesis was partially supported, as SDs, but not PDs, were poorer than RLs at recognizing target items, and yet SDs did not differ from RLs in general Word Identification or phonological processing skills. Although other explanations are possible, we hypothesize that the difficulty SDs showed on the Orthographic Choice task extends to the semantic processing of printed words.

In sum, the time 3 results reveal that the PD subgroup was again remarkably stable, even over a two-year period. In addition, nearly all PDs seemed to be pure cases, as we saw at time 2, based on the comparison of their Exception Word and Pseudoword Reading scores to the normative comparison group as well as the RL comparison group. Furthermore, as was the case at time 2, the PD subgroup had a selective impairment on phonological decoding and awareness, relative to their other reading and cognitive skills, and showed relatively strong performance on a measure of word-specific orthographic knowledge. It thus seems reasonable to conclude that the PD subgroup had a stable and specific deficit in phonological awareness and decoding. However, the PD subgroup somewhat paradoxically relied on phonological decoding in a semantic judgment task involving printed word recognition. We cannot further explicate the phonological deficit, as we did not include additional measures of component phonological skills. In contrast, the SD subgroup was not stable, and none of the SD subjects had a pure profile in comparison to the RL group. The SDs for the most apart continued to have the delayed-across-the-board pattern for phonological and orthographic skills.

GENERAL SUMMARY AND CONCLUSIONS

Taking all three test years into account, the data revealed an interesting pattern of development. PD cases appeared to become increasingly more common between the 3rd and 5th grades, and most children in the final PD group had earlier phonological deficits (i.e., they were either in the PD subgroup or the mixed subgroup at earlier ages). The following is a complete list of the 'pathways' (in terms of subgroup membership) that the 26 PDs at time 3 took from time 1 to time 3: 9 were PD at time 1, 2 were SD at time 1, 12 were Mixed at time 1, and 3 were Balanced at time 1. From time 2 to time 3, there was more consistency: 15 were PD, 5 were Mixed, 5 were Balanced, and 1 was SD. Thus, 21 of the 26 cases at time 3 had a history of phonological decoding difficulties, either with or without accompanying exception word reading problems. It makes sense that there would be changes in subgroup membership between 3rd and 5th grade as this is a very active period of growth in reading, and the subgroup boundaries used here were arbitrary. The PD pattern was reasonably stable and predictable, and fit the hypothesis that a significant group of dyslexic children have a selective deficit in phonological processing.

The most interesting finding is that the incidence of selective phonological deficits in our sample increased dramatically over time. To our knowledge, this is the first longitudinal data on changes in subgroup membership over time using the phonological/surface dyslexic distinction. Taking theoretical perspectives on reading into account, how can we explain this pattern? Dual route theory (Coltheart et al., 2001) is not an explicitly developmental theory, and hence it is difficult to construct an explanation for the developmental pattern. However, based on connectionist models of reading acquisition (Harm and Seidenberg, 1999) and other models, such as Ehri's four step model of reading acquisition (Ehri, 1992) and Share's self-teaching model of orthographic development (Share, 1995), two explanations for the increase in the incidence of PDs seem reasonable.

First, children with phonological awareness and decoding problems can be expected to have difficulty with all types of words (regular and exception words found on the Woodcock Word Identification Test and in our Exception Word Reading task) and pseudowords, based on these models. Until children acquire (or are taught) a modicum of phonological decoding skill, it is difficult for them to read printed words successfully and build-up orthographic knowledge (Ehri, 1992; Share, 1995). In Harm and Seidenberg's (1999) connectionist simulation of reading acquisition, models with the most severe phonological deficits were impaired in reading exceptions, regular words and pseudowords. Most printed words do not occur very often in text, and hence it is critical for orthographic learning that children decode them successfully when they encounter them. Poor decoders would suffer delays in the build-up of orthographic knowledge (Ehri, 1992; Share, 1995).

A second, related explanation is that apart from phonological decoding skill, and its role in the build-up of orthographic knowledge, the sheer amount of exposure to print children get over a two-year period of time is huge even for dyslexic children. Children with phonological or mixed profiles at time 1 or time 2 can be expected to make progress in exception word reading, owing to a year of exposure and instruction, and grow out of the Mixed Subgroup or Mixed-PD profile. In both cases, a discrepancy exists favoring exception words, but both exception and non-sense words are below the normative group. Faster growth of exception word reading than pseudoword reading over a two-year period was previously demonstrated by Manis et al. (1993). They followed 21 dyslexic children over a two-year period. They found greater growth in exception word and general word reading measures than in pseudoword reading and phonological awareness measures.

The developmental pattern for the SD subgroup is harder to characterize. Membership in the group fluctuated from year to year. There was almost complete turn-over in the cases from the 3rd to the 5th grade (only 2 cases remained consistently SD over the three test periods). However, apparently when SD cases 'emerge', they have a characteristic profile of poor orthographic knowledge of printed words, and very slow processing of orthographic information. The majority of cases at time 2 and time 3 were pure cases, and several cases showed as distinct a profile as has been cited in the case study literature (e.g., Castles and Coltheart, 1996; Goulandris and Snowling, 1991; Hanley et al., 1992), i.e., completely normal phonological decoding and awareness, with very poor exception word and orthographic choice performance. The SD profile is 'real', even if it is only temporary.

However, it is very clear from our study, as well as past studies (Bowey and Rutherford, 2007; Castles et al., 1999; Manis et al., 1996; Stanovich et al., 1997) that SD cases do not have deficits when they are compared to RL-matched younger readers. We tentatively hypothesize that environmental factors that can change over the course of a year's time (such as opportunities to practice reading, tutoring of reading, or the child's motivation to read) might be one important source of the SD profile. In addition, it seems to be the case that SDs (in agreement with Stanovich et al., 1997) have mild delays in phonological decoding and awareness (i.e., they are behind the CA group, but equivalent to or ahead of the RL group). By the 5th grade, most of the SD cases were within the normal range for Pseudoword Reading, but the profile was becoming rarer. This would be expected because environmental factors, such as availability of a good tutor, an improvement in the child's reading services at the school, and greater parental encouragement of reading can have a large effect at an individual child level, as clinical experience attests. The bottom line on surface dyslexia may be that there are a fairly large number of factors at work, but the outcome for a child who happens to experience one of the critical combinations of factors at a given age is relatively similar across children. Here we have characterized that pattern as slightly delayed phonological decoding and awareness (more so in the 3rd grade than was the case in 5th grade), poor exception word reading accuracy, and a combination of low accuracy and slow performance of orthographic judgment tasks.

Is it valuable to continue to study phonological and surface dyslexic profiles? Griffiths and Snowling (2002) also raise the question of whether it is more useful to study subgroups, or the sources of the continuous variation in cognitive skills that underlie dyslexia. It is our opinion that this enterprise has served its purpose (highlighting individual differences among dyslexic children), and that the clearest conclusion we can make at this point is that there is a core subgroup with selective phonological deficits that is relatively stable and easy to identify. The remainder of dyslexic children appear to have delays in phonological decoding and a varying set of difficulties that are difficult to characterize (such as inadequate intervention, low motivation and low print exposure). There doesn't seem to be a selective deficit underlying any cases of surface dyslexia. Even extreme cases reported in the literature have not had a consistent set of problems, such as visual memory deficits, slow rates of learning, or severe orthographic processing deficits (Bailey et al., 2004; Castles and Coltheart 1996; Goulandris and Snowling, 1991; Hanley et al., 1992).

At this point, researchers need to characterize the nature and development of phonological deficits further. Intervention work targeting phonological deficits, and providing general boosts to print exposure is very important as well. Alternative ways to model individual differences, such as the use of at-risk designs, molecular genetic studies of families, brain imaging work that focuses on individual differences, and response to intervention models are promising future avenues of investigation (Fletcher et al., 2007).

NOTES

1 A word should be said about the variety of methods used in the literature to identify subgroups. Our method was not the same as the regression method used in some studies (Castles and Coltheart, 1993; Manis et al., 1996; Stanovich et al., 1997), or the benchmark method used to assess reading imbalances by Bowey and Rutherford (2007). Our method is similar to the technique used by Castles et al. (1999). In preliminary analyses, we attempted to use a benchmark group of average readers to define the subgroups as in Bowey and Rutherford (2007). However, we discovered that the standard deviation for Exception Word Reading was much smaller than that for Pseudoword Reading. This would result in the identification of many more SDs than PDs. In contrast, for the normative group, the standard deviations for Exception Word and Pseudoword Reading were of about the same magnitude (see Table 7.1). Thus, the measurement properties of our stimulus lists did not lend themselves to Bowey and Rutherford's (2007) method.

REFERENCES

Bailey, C. E., Manis F. R., Seidenberg, M. S. and Pedersen, W. C. (2004) 'Variation among developmental dyslexics: Evidence from a printed word-learning task', *Journal of Experimental Child Psychology*, 87(2): 125–154.

Beauvois, M. F. and Derousne, J. (1979) 'Phonological alexia: Three dissociations', *Journal of Neurology, Neurosurgery, and Psychiatry*, 42: 1115–1124.

Boder, E. (1973) 'Developmental dyslexia: a diagnostic approach based on three typical reading–spelling patterns', *Developmental Medicine and Child Neurology*, 15: 663–687.

Bowey, J. A. and Rutherford, J. (2007) 'Imbalanced word reading profiles in eighth-graders', *Journal of Experimental Child Psychology*, 96 (3): 169–196.

Carroll, J. B., Davies, P., and Richman, B. (1971) *Word Frequency Book*. American Heritage, New York.

Castles, A. and Coltheart, M. (1993) 'Varieties of developmental dyslexia', *Cognition*, 47(1): 149–180.

Castles A. and Coltheart, M. (1996) 'Cognitive correlates of developmental surface dyslexia: A single case study', *Cognitive Neuropsychology*, 13(1): 25–50.

Castles, A., Datta, H., Gayan, J. and Olson, R. K. (1999) 'Varieties of developmental reading disorder. Genetic and environmental influences', *Journal of Experimental Child Psychology*, 72 (2): 73–94.

Coltheart, M. (1978) 'Lexical access in simple reading tasks', in G. Underwood (ed.), *Strategies of information processing*. London, United Kingdom: Academic Press. pp. 151–216.

Coltheart, M., Masterson, J., Byng, S., Prior, M. and Riddoch, J. (1983) 'Surface dyslexia', *Quarterly Journal of Experimental Psychology*, 35A, 469–495.

Coltheart, M., Rastle, K., Perry, C., Langdon, R. and Ziegler, J. (2001) 'DRC: A dual route cascaded model of visual word recognition and reading aloud', *Psychological Review*, 108 (1): 204–256.

Cunningham, A.E. and Stanovich, K.E. (1990) 'Assessing print exposure and orthographic processing skill in children; a quick measure of reading experience', *Journal of Educational Psychology*, 28(4): 733–740.

Dunn, L.M. and Dunn, L.M. (1981) *Peabody Picture Vocabulary Test-Revised*. Circle Pines, MN: American Guidance Service.

Ehri, L.C. (1992) 'Reconceptualizing the development of sight word reading and its relationship to recoding', in P.B. Gough, L.C. Ehri, and R.Treiman, (eds), *Reading Acquisition*, Hillsdale, New Jersey: Lawrence Erlbaum Associates.

Fletcher, J. M., Lyon, G. R., Fuchs, L. S. and Barnes, M. A. (2007) *Learning disabilities: From identification to intervention*. New York: Guilford Press.

Goulandris, N.K. and Snowling, M. (1991) 'Visual memory deficits: a plausible cause of developmental dyslexia? Evidence from a single case study', *Cognitive Neuropsychology*, 8(2): 127–154.

Griffiths, Y. M. and Snowling, M. J. (2002) 'Predictors of exception word and nonword reading in dyslexic children: The severity hypothesis', *Journal of Educational Psychology*, 94: 34–43.

Grigorenko, E. L. (2001) Developmental dyslexia: An update on genes, brains, and environments', *Journal of Child Psychology and Psychiatry*, 42(1): 91–125.

Hanley, R., Hastie, K. and Kay, J. (1992) 'Developmental surface dyslexia and dysgraphia: An orthographic processing impairment', *Quarterly Journal of Experimental Psychology*, 44: 285–319.

Harm, M.W. and Seidenberg, M.S. (1999) 'Phonology, reading and dyslexia. Insights from connectionist models', *Psychological Review*, 106 (3): 491–528.

Keating, P. and Manis, F. R. (1998) 'The Keating-Manis phoneme deletion test', in *UCLA Working Papers in Phonetics*. Los Angeles: UCLA Phonetics Laboratory. Vol. 96: pp. 162–165.

Manis, F.R., Custudio, R. and Szeszulski, P.A. (1993) 'Development of phonological and orthographic skill: A 2 year longitudinal study of dyslexic children', *Journal of Experimental Child Psychology*, 56(1): 64–86.

Manis, F.R., Seidenberg, M.S., Doi, L.M., McBride-Chang, C. and Petersen, A. (1996) 'On the basis of two subtypes of developmental dyslexia', *Cognition*, 58(2): 157–195.

Manis, F.R., Seidenberg, M.S., Stallings, L., Joanisse, M.F., Bailey, C.E., Freedman, L.B., Curtin, S. and Keating, P. (1999) 'Development of dyslexic subgroups: A one year follow up', *Annals of Dyslexia*, 49: 105–136.

Marshall, J. and Newcombe, F. (1973) 'Patterns of paralexia: A psycholinguistic approach', *Journal of Psycholinguistic Research*, 2: 175–199.

Metsala, J., Stanovich, K and Brown, G. (1998) 'Regularity effects and the phonological deficit model of reading disabilities: A meta-analytic review', *Journal of Educational Psychology*, 90 (2): 279–293.

Morris, R.D., Stuebing, K.K., Fletcher, J.M., Shaywitz, S.E., Lyon, G.R., Shankweiler, D.P., Katz, L., Fracis, D. and Shaywitz, B.A. (1998) 'Subtypes of reading disability: Variability around a phonolocial core', *Journal of Educational Psychology*, 90: 347–373.

Murphy, L. and Pollatsek, A. (1994) 'Developmental dyslexia: Heterogeneity without discrete subgroups', *Annals of Dyslexia*, 44: 120–146.

Plaut, D., McClelland, J.L., Seidenberg, M.S. and Patterson, K. (1996) 'Understanding normal and impaired word reading: Computational principles in quasi-regular domains', *Psychological Review*, 103(1): 56–115.

Saffran, E. M. (1985) 'Acquired dyslexia: Implications for models of reading', in G. E. Mackinnon and T. B. Waller (eds), *Reading research: Advances in theory and practice*. New York: Academic Press. Vol. 4, pp. 231–258.

Seidenberg M.S. and McClelland, J.L. (1989) 'A distributed, developmental model of word recognition and naming', *Psychological Review*, 96(4): 523–568.

Share, D.L. (1995) 'Phonological recoding and self-teaching: The sine qua non of reading acquisition', *Cognition*, 55(1): 151–218.

Shaywitz, B., Shaywitz, S., Pugh, K.R., Mencl, W.E., Fulbright, R.K., Skudlarksi, P, Constable, R.T., Marchione, L.E., Fletcher, J.M., Lyon, G.R. and Gore, J.C. (2002) 'Disruption of posterior brain systems for reading in children with developmental dyslexia', *Biological Psychiatry*, 52 (2): 101–110.

Snowling, M. J., Bryant, P. E. and Hulme, C. (1996) 'Theoretical and methodological pitfalls in making comparisons between developmental and acquired dyslexia: Some comments on Castles and Coltheart (1993)', *Reading and Writing*, 8: 443–451.

Stanovich, K.E., Siegel, L.S. and Gottardo, A. (1997) 'Converging evidence for phonological and surface subtypes of reading disability', *Journal of Educational Psychology*, 89(1): 114–128.

Stanovich, K.E. and Siegel, L. S. (1994) 'The phenotypic performance profile of reading-disabled children: A regression-based test of the phonological core variable-difference model', *Journal of Educational Psychology*, 86(1): 24–53.

Temple, C.M. and Marshall, J.C. (1983) 'A case study of developmental phonological dyslexia', *British Journal of Psychology*, 74 (4): 517–533.

Van Orden, G.C. (1987) 'A ROWS is a ROSE: Spelling, sound and reading', *Memory and Cognition*, 15(3): 181–189.

Vellutino, F.R., Scanlon, D.M. and Lyon, G.R. (2000) 'Differentiating between difficult-to-remediate and readily remediated poor readers: More evidence against the IQ-achievement discrepancy definition of reading disability', *Journal of Learning Disabilities*, 33 (3): 223–238.

Wagner, R.K. and Torgesen, J.K. (1987) 'The nature of phonological processing and its causal role in the acquisition of reading skills', *Psychological Bulletin*, 101(2): 192–212.

Weschler, D.A. (1992) *Weschler Intelligence Scale for Children-III*. San Antonio, TX. Psychological Corporation.

Woodcock, R.W. and Johnson, M.B. (1989) *Woodcock-Johnson tests of cognitive ability-revised*. Allen, TX: DLM Teaching Resources.

Woodcock, R.W. (1987) *Woodcock reading mastery test-revised*. Circle Pines, MN: American Guidance Service.

8

Rediscovering Dyslexia: New Approaches for Identification and Classification

Richard K. Wagner

'The greatest enemy of the truth is not the lie – deliberate, contrived, and dishonest, but the myth – persistent, pervasive, and unrealistic.' John F. Kennedy

This chapter:

i) compares traditional and new approaches to identification of individuals with reading disabilities.

Developmental dyslexia or reading disability refers to unexpected poor performance in reading. Poor performance in reading typically is defined as performance markedly below that of one's peers or expectations based on some form of standards. What constitutes an unexpected level of poor performance in reading has been more difficult to define. Traditionally, the definition of unexpected poor performance in reading has been based on normative data comparing an individual's reading performance to his or her performance in reading-related areas such as oral language or general cognitive ability. An additional consideration has been that the observed poor reading performance cannot be explained either by lack of an opportunity to learn (i.e., ineffective instruction) or by other potential causes including severe, generalized intellectual deficits or impaired sensory capacities in areas required for reading such as vision.

One of the most remarkable aspects of dyslexia, compared to other disorders such as mental retardation or autism, is the prevalence of persistent myths about its key features or causes (Piasta and Wagner, 2007; Wagner and Muse, 2006). By far the most widespread myth about dyslexia is that it is caused by seeing mirror images of words or letters. Thus, individuals with dyslexia are reported to read 'WAS' as 'SAW,' or to confuse the letters 'b' and 'd.'

A likely explanation for this popular myth about the cause of dyslexia comes from observations of typical errors made by children with dyslexia. In the US, children with developmental dyslexia are not typically noticed or identified until second or even third grade (i.e., aged 7–8). When second-grade children with dyslexia attempt to read English print, they indeed can be observed to confuse 'WAS' for 'SAW' and 'b' for 'd.' But these kinds of reversal errors are among the easiest kinds of errors to make, and they can be observed any day in normally-developing beginning readers who are in kindergarten or first grade. The convention in English that words are read from left to right as opposed to from right to left – that 'WAS' should be decoded as 'WAS' rather than 'SAW' – is indeed a convention that must be learned by beginning readers. Other systems of print are read from right to left or even from top to bottom. Confusing 'b' for 'd' can be explained by the fact that these letters are similar visually as well as in sound. Very young children sometimes see them as a 'stick and a ball' or a 'ball and a stick' respectively, and whether the 'ball' or 'stick' comes first again depends on whether one moves from left to right or from right to left. Both of these letters also are voiced stop consonants that are produced by first blocking and then releasing air in the vocal tract. Whether one pronounces a 'b' or 'd' depends upon subtle differences in the position of the teeth, tongue, and lips.

In fact, second-grade readers with dyslexia make no more reversal errors than do reading-level matched younger normal readers (Crowder and Wagner, 1991; Werker et al., 1989). What probably explains the popular misconception that dyslexia involves perceptual reversals is that by second grade, the only children still making these errors are well behind in reading and are distinct from their peers on that basis. Adding fuel to the fire in the US was the popular scientific explanation of dyslexia provided by Orton's theory of mixed cerebral dominance (Hallahan and Mock, 2003). According to this theory, dyslexia was caused by a failure in the normal localization of language functioning to a single, typically left hemisphere of the brain. Someone with dyslexia therefore was believed to have both hemispheres remaining heavily involved in reading, and reversals would result when the opposite hemisphere happened to take the lead in processing.

Another popular myth about dyslexia that enjoyed support in both scientific and lay circles was the idea that dyslexia results from problems in eye-movements. Without a doubt, reading requires remarkably sophisticated and coordinated eye-movements (Rayner, 1998). As you read this, your intuition is that your eyes are gliding smoothly across the page. In fact, they jump across the page a little bit at a time in a series of tiny ballistic movements called saccades. When the eyes are moving during a saccade, the movement prevents clear viewing of print. Consequently, nearly all information is acquired during the fixations or brief pauses between saccades.

You can observe this for yourself by asking a friend to read directly across from you, having them hold the reading material below eye level so you can watch their eyes move. If you look carefully, you will observe their eyes moving in rapid, small jerky movements. If you make the same observation with an individual who has dyslexia, you will notice that the eyes move more erratically, even moving in the wrong direction with considerable frequency. These observations suggest the possibility that faulty eye-movements are a cause of dyslexia. However, it turned out that this view has it backwards. When normal readers are given material to read that is as difficult as grade-level reading material is for individuals with dyslexia, the eye-movements of normal readers deteriorate and resemble the eye-movements of individuals with dyslexia. Conversely, when individuals with dyslexia are given very easy reading material that they can read well, their eye-movements become indistinguishable from those of normal readers (Crowder and Wagner, 1992; Rayner, 1985). Further evidence of the fact that the faulty eye-movements of individuals with dyslexia are a by-product rather than a cause of their reading problems comes from the results of attempting to improve reading by training eye-movements. Although eye-movement training can improve performance on various eye-movement tasks such as smooth pursuit in which the eyes are trained to follow a moving target, reading performance does not improve (Crowder and Wagner, 1992; Kavale and Mattson, 1983).

New and as yet unproven theories about the nature of dyslexia continue to be propagated by well-meaning researchers. It is important that they be regarded as likely myths until proven otherwise. The focus of the present chapter is on what may turn out to be the next highly pervasive and persistent myth about dyslexia, namely, that response-to intervention (RTI) represents a key advancement in the identification and treatment of individuals with dyslexia.

TRADITIONAL APPROACHES TO IDENTIFICATION

Because developmental dyslexia refers to unexpectedly poor performance in reading, traditional approaches to identification use exclusionary criteria in order to operationalize unexpectedness. The goal is to exclude poor readers whose impairments are primarily due to sensory or motor impairments, pervasive cognitive deficiencies, or emotional disturbance. Also to be excluded are poor readers who have not had adequate instruction in reading (Lyon et al., 2003). Typically, eligibility for special education services in the US due to the presence of a specific learning disability in reading has required evidence of a discrepancy between IQ and reading performance. This IQ-achievement discrepancy approach has come under attack for three major reasons: the approach is viewed as a 'wait to fail' model; questions have been raised about the reliability of IQ-achievement discrepancy scores; and questions have been raised about the validity and educational relevance of the distinction between poor readers who are IQ discrepant and poor readers who are not (Fletcher et al., 2006; 1992; 2003; Francis et al., 1996; Lyon et al. 2003; President's Commission on Excellence in Special Education, 2002; Siegel, 1992; Spear-Swerling and Sternberg, 1996; Stanovich, 1991; Stanovich and Siegel, 1994; Stuebing et al., 2002.).

A 'wait to fail' model

Largely because of floor effects on common reading achievement tests, and the fact that formal reading instruction does not begin in earnest in the US until first grade, it is virtually impossible to demonstrate a discrepancy between aptitude and achievement much before the end of first grade or early second grade. For the case of reading disability, a problem with failing to identify children until second or third grade is that it appears that reading problems become more difficult to overcome the longer they exist. Longitudinal correlational studies of the development of reading skills suggest that a child's proficiency compared to his or her peers is relatively stable by second grade (Francis et al., 1996; Wagner et al., 1997). For example, in Wagner et al.'s (1997) five-year longitudinal study of over 200 children from kindergarten through fourth grade, year-to-year correlations for word-level decoding were .84, .96, and .96, for the time periods first to second grade, second to third grade, and third to fourth grade respectively. The longitudinal design of this study allowed the magnitudes of the causal influences of various constructs on subsequent decoding to be estimated via analysis of associations among latent variables. The key result for present purposes was the growing magnitude of the estimated causal influence of prior decoding on subsequent decoding across the three time periods examined. This accumulating effect reflects the increasing stability of individual differences in reading and the increasingly intractable nature of reading problems as children develop. A related concern of a 'wait to fail' approach is that struggling with early reading may generate undesirable concomitants such as a negative academic self-concept or an aversion to schooling.

There is no question that the traditional approach to identification does not identify poor readers in the US until second grade on average, and this is less than ideal. However, new developments in our understanding of early literacy may eliminate or reduce the 'wait to fail' nature of approaches that compare reading achievement to expectations based on performance in other areas. Reading does not appear out of nothing when children are first taught to read, but rather reading ability is better conceptualized as a developmental phenomenon that builds on emergent print awareness. Print awareness can be assessed reliably in children as young as 3, and is highly predictive of later decoding (Burgess and Lonigan, 1998). Reliable and valid measures of print awareness are becoming available and could be used to identify preschool-age children whose early literacy development is lagging behind that of their peers (Lonigan et al., 2007).

Reliability issue

The second concern with the IQ-achievement discrepancy approach is that the reliability of a difference score that represents a discrepancy between aptitude and achievement (e.g., a difference of 15 standard score points) is likely to be less reliable than the reliabilities of either test used to calculate the discrepancy. This is especially true when the two scores that are used to generate the difference score are correlated. The formula for calculating the reliability of a difference score is the following:

$$r_{diff} = \frac{[(r_{aa} + r_{bb})/2] - r_{ab}}{1 - r_{ab}}$$

In this formula, r_{diff} is the reliability of the difference score, r_{aa} and r_{bb} are the reliabilities of the two scores used to create the difference score, and r_{ab} is the correlation between these two scores. Consider what happens as the correlation between the two scores begins to approach their reliabilities. Referring to the numerator of the formula, because the correlation between the two scores is subtracted from their average reliability, the numerator becomes smaller. In the extreme case, when the correlation between the two scores is equal to their average reliability, the reliability of the difference score is zero! For typical real-world situations, the reliability of difference scores is substantially greater than zero but less than that of the variables used to create them.

Fletcher et al. (2006) identified two additional problems that impact the reliability of IQ-achievement difference scores. The first is the imposition of an arbitrary cut-point on a continuous distribution. IQ and scores on reading achievement tests are continuously distributed variables. A difference score created by subtracting an achievement score from an IQ also will be continuously distributed. When categorization is based on an arbitrary cut-point such as a 15-point difference in standard scores on an IQ and an achievement test, reliability is reduced because individuals who score close to the cut-point are likely to vary in the side of the cut point on which their score lies on successive testing. Francis et al. (2005) examined the effects of imposing arbitrary cut-points on continuous distributions for the Connecticut Longitudinal Study and for simulated data. The results were that classification was not highly stable longitudinally, in part because of the effect of imposing an arbitrary cut-point on a continuous variable.

The second problem identified by Fletcher et al. (2006) that has a detrimental effect on the reliability of classification decisions based on IQ-achievement discrepancy scores is that of regression to the mean. When individuals are selected on the basis of an extreme score, repeated testing with either the same test or a different test that is correlated with the first test will produce scores closer to the mean of the tests. The reason this happens is that an individual's observed scores on any assessment contain measurement error and will vary about the individual's 'true' score. If low scorers are selected, they will contain a greater proportion of individuals whose observed scores were lower than their 'true' score for the specific test used for selection. Conversely, if high scorers are selected, they will contain a greater proportion of individuals whose observed scores were higher than their 'true' scores for the specific test used for selection. When tested again, the scores will regress to the 'true' scores, which means that low scorers will tend to score higher and high scorers will tend to score lower. Fletcher et al. (2006) concluded that this will result in overidentification of individuals as having a learning disability in the higher IQ range and underidentification of individuals as having a learning disability in the lower IQ range. They do not provide a rationale for this conclusion. One potential rationale is that individuals who score above average in IQ are likely to score lower if tested again, and individuals who score below average in IQ are likely to score higher if tested again. This would tend to reduce the number of high IQ individuals whose difference between IQ and achievement exceeded the cut score, and increase the number of low IQ individuals whose difference between IQ and achievement exceeded the cut score. Whether this actually happens is unclear, because it would depend on whether individuals are actually selected on the basis of an extreme score, and on which score. If both high- and low-IQ individuals are initially identified on the basis of a low extreme score on achievement, it is not obvious how regression to the mean will work differently for the two groups.

Another way of thinking about the problem is to recognize that initial identification depends on obtaining a difference score between IQ and achievement that exceeds the cut point. Extreme 'discrepancy' scorers would be overselected, which refers to individuals who happened to have observed achievement scores that are lower than their true achievement scores and observed IQ scores that are higher than their true IQ scores. Regression to the mean would work at both ends of the discrepancy by resulting in a higher achievement score and a lower IQ score upon repeated testing. This would result in formerly identified individuals no longer being identified upon subsequent testing. Individuals who showed the opposite pattern by having an observed achievement score that exceeds their true score and an observed IQ score that is less than their true score will not be identified upon initial testing but will be identified upon repeated testing. The existence of both kinds of individuals will reduce the reliability of identification.

There is no question that the reliability of a discrepancy score will not match that of the scores it is based upon. However, if this were the only concern about the traditional approach, reliability could be improved by obtaining multiple measures of ability and achievement. The multiple measures could be used to create multiple discrepancy scores, and reliability could be enhanced by using the mean or median discrepancy score.

Validity issue

Even if it is possible to identify IQ-discrepant poor readers reliably, do they differ in meaningful ways from poor readers whose reading is not discrepant from their IQs? Fletcher et al. (2006) summarized the literature comparing IQ-discrepant and non IQ-discrepant groups of poor readers. For common measures of decoding and constructs thought to predict decoding such as phonological awareness, phonological memory, and rapid naming, differences tend to be small albeit statistically significant. As expected, group differences were larger for IQ-related variables such as vocabulary and syntax. One meta-analysis of studies comparing IQ-discrepant and non-discrepant poor readers included reading comprehension and surprisingly (given the expected association of vocabulary and syntax scores with comprehension), there was no difference between the groups (Stuebing et al., 2002). This may have been due to the fact that the studies were primarily of early readers and poor decoding limits comprehension substantially on measures of reading comprehension for early readers.

The other argument made about the validity of differentiating poor readers on the basis of their IQ-discrepancy status is that such a distinction does not have implications for the kind of intervention that is recommended (Fletcher et al., 1992; 2006; 2003; Francis et al., 1996; Lyon et al., 2001; 2003; Shaywitz et al., 1992; Shaywitz and Shaywitz, 2003; Siegel, 2003; Stanovich, 1991; Stanovich and Siegel, 1994). Common interventions for poor decoders often include some phonological awareness training, some explicit instruction in decoding, and practice to develop sight word reading and fluency. At the present time, there is no reason to believe that these interventions are more or less appropriate for poor readers depending on the IQ-discrepancy status. Most of the research that questions the validity of the distinction between IQ-discrepant and non-discrepant poor readers is focused on decoding and decoding-related variables for children who score at beginning levels of reading. Whether the conclusion of minimal differences associated with IQ-discrepancy poor reading generalizes from decoding to comprehension, and from beginning reading to more skilled reading remains an open question. One of the best predictors of reading comprehension once children have mastered basic decoding is vocabulary, which also turns out to be the best single measure of verbal aptitude. This seems to conflict with the assertion that IQ is immaterial in reading, when the context goes beyond beginning reading with a focus on decoding to more skilled reading with a focus on comprehension.

Poor readers, regardless of their IQ-discrepancy status, show weaknesses in measures of phonological processing and decoding. But some children have weaknesses that are confined largely to phonological processing and decoding, whereas others have weaknesses that extend to broader oral language areas including vocabulary and comprehension. Even if children with broader oral language deficiencies can acquire adequate decoding skills, their ability to comprehend what they read will be limited by weaknesses in vocabulary and comprehension (Torgesen, 2000).

Although the report of the National Reading Panel provided some support for improving reading comprehension through training of comprehension strategies, interventions for reading comprehension that are comparable in effectiveness to those that exist for decoding accuracy may not exist yet. Nevertheless, knowing whether a poor reader has adequate vocabulary and listening comprehension skills or also shows impaired performance in these areas can have implications for teaching outside the context of interventions designed to improve basic skill deficiencies. For example, a preview discussion that provides information about key vocabulary, concepts, or background knowledge relevant to comprehending a passage about to be read is likely to be more useful for a poor reader who is weak in these areas compared to a poor reader who is not.

RESPONSE TO INTERVENTION (RTI) APPROACHES TO IDENTIFICATION

A major conclusion of the President's Commission on Excellence in Special Education (2002) is that traditional approaches for identifying individuals with learning disabilities and providing required intervention have not succeeded in helping individuals meet the ever-increasing literacy-related demands of modern society. A proposed solution to the problem is to base identification on limited response to effective instruction or intervention (RTI) (Fuchs and Fuchs, 1998; Lyon et al., 2003). An RTI approach seeks to avoid the possibility that the observed poor reading results from inadequate instruction by first ensuring that students receive effective reading instruction in their general education classrooms. Response to effective reading instruction is measured, and only students who don't respond are considered as possible candidates for more focused intervention, and if warranted, eventual identification as an individual with a learning disability.

Provision of effective reading instruction is generally the first of several increasingly focused efforts to improve reading performance (McMaster et al. 2005; Simmons et al., 2003; Vaughn and Fuchs, 2003). This commonly is referred to as the first tier of a multi-tier RTI approach. Some form of progress monitoring is implemented and individuals who do not respond to the provision of effective reading instruction in their general education classrooms are then given more intensive instruction or intervention, typically in small groups rather than classroom-wide settings (Fuchs et al., 2003b). This is commonly referred to as the second tier of a multi-tier RTI approach. Progress monitoring continues and individuals who still do not respond are then candidates for either more intensive intervention or identification as an individual who is eligible for special education services on the basis of having a reading disability. This is referred to as the third tier of a multi-tier RTI approach.

Although the RTI approach is relatively new and only a handful of studies have been carried out to investigate its effectiveness (Case et al., 2003; Fuchs et al., 2004; 2003a; 2003b; Fuchs and Fuchs, 1998), it has been included as a possible means of identification in legislation that governs provision of special education services in public education in the US. This legislation, which became

law in 2004, is the Individuals with Disabilities Education Improvement
Act (IDEA) (Public Law 108-466). It includes the following language:

SPECIFIC LEARNING DISABILITIES

(A) IN GENERAL. — Notwithstanding section 607(b), when determining whether a child
has a specific learning disability as defined in section 602, a local educational agency
shall not be required to take into consideration whether a child has a severe discrepancy between achievement and intellectual ability in oral expression, listening comprehension, written expression, basic reading skill, reading comprehension, mathematical
calculation, or mathematical reasoning.

(B) ADDITIONAL AUTHORITY. — In determining whether a child has a specific learning
disability, a local educational agency may use a process that determines if the child
responds to scientific, research-based intervention as a part of the evaluation procedures described in paragraphs (2) and (3).

A cure for the 'wait to fail' problem?

An RTI approach has been implemented in law despite the fact that little evidence
exists that it solves the problems that have been identified with traditional
approaches based on IQ-achievement discrepancy. Perhaps the most widely cited
criticism of the traditional IQ-achievement discrepancy approach is that of it being
a 'wait to fail' model. Ironically, it is not clear how RTI approaches as currently
implemented are anything but wait to fail models themselves. The RTI approach
begins with the provision of effective reading instruction in a regular classroom. In
the US, this presumably happens in first grade. Progress monitoring is carried out
and additional help only is provided after documenting a failure to respond to effective instruction in the regular classroom. This presumably requires a period of
months. The next step typically is to add small-group based tutoring and resume
progress monitoring for an additional period of several months. Only at this point
is a determination made that a child has a specific learning disability and needs even
more help. If this process doesn't begin until formal reading instruction is underway in earnest in first grade, it is unlikely that children with learning disabilities will
be identified much earlier than they have been using the traditional approach.

If the RTI approach implemented in first grade will not lead to early identification,
what might? As mentioned previously, efforts to identify children with learning
disabilities no longer need to be hampered by floor effects on common measures
of word decoding for beginning readers. Decoding grows out of more rudimentary forms of print awareness, and these more rudimentary forms of print awareness can be assessed reliably and in children as young as age 3 (Lonigan et al.,
2007). This should make it possible to identify children who are showing
unexpected performance in early reading. An alternative approach would be to
investigate the possibility of implementing an RTI approach for preschool-age
children, using progress monitoring of print awareness.

Addressing reliability issues

Turning to the concerns about the reliability of discrepancy scores used to identify
unexpected underachievement using the traditional approach, it is disconcerting

that there appear to be no published studies that assess the reliability of an RTI approach. Fletcher et al. (2006) suggest several possible reasons why the reliability of an RTI approach might be enhanced over that of a traditional approach based on a single assessment. First, the approach is based on multiple measures collected over an extensive time period as opposed to measures obtained during a single time point, and performance across multiple measures is assumed to be more reliable than performance assessed once. Second, multiple measures improve the precision with which change in performance can be detected compared to having just a pretest and posttest. When more than two measures are obtained, it is possible to estimate the reliability with which change is assessed. However, there also are reasons to be skeptical about the reliability of identification based on an RTI approach until empirical evidence is forthcoming. Although it is true that the reliability with which change is measured increases as a function of the number of measurements obtained, measures of change tend to be noticeably less reliable than are measures of status. For example, Schatschneider (2007) compared measures of change and measures of status as predictors of subsequent performance in reading for a large scale sample of elementary age readers. Measures of growth did not add to prediction compared to measures of status, and in general, measures of status were considerably more reliable than were measures of change. It makes sense that measures of status are more reliable than are measures of change when you consider that measures of status represent the long-term acquisition of a skill that reflects not only rates of change but also initial status.

Another reason to be skeptical about the reliability of identification based on an RTI approach is uncontrolled variability associated with teacher quality and differential effectiveness in both the primary reading instruction and the secondary intervention. For the RTI approach, teacher quality and effectiveness will vary within and between schools. The same will be true of the small-group interventions that are provided to children who do not make adequate progress in their regular reading program.

The reliability concerns raised against the traditional approach of applying a cut-point to a continuous distribution also applies to the RTI approach. Measures of change in response to intervention are as likely to be continuously distributed as are measures of status. Yet, as Fletcher et al. (2006) acknowledge, a cut-point will need to be used to determine which children go where and receive what in an RTI-based approach to identification and intervention.

Progress-monitoring measures have not been as carefully developed as traditional measures of aptitude and achievement, and progress monitoring poses additional measurement challenges compared to development of traditional measures of achievement because it requires creation of multiple, equivalent forms.

An additional problem is that there is not yet a consensus on criteria for deciding whether a given student is a non-responder and thus requires additional assistance. Fuchs and Deshler (2007) identified five alternative methods that have been used in research studies or in practice to identify nonresponders. Vellutino et al. (1996) derived slope estimates from hierarchical linear modeling and used a *median-split of the slope estimates* to differentiate responders and nonresponders. Torgesen et al. (2001) used a *normalization criterion* of achieving standard scores at the 25th percentile on nationally standardized tests of reading. A related approach by Good et al. (2001) relies on a *final benchmark criterion* of scoring at a specified level on an oral reading fluency criterion-related benchmark. Fuchs and Fuchs (1998) proposed a *dual discrepancy criterion* of scoring one or more standard deviations below classroom peers on both slope of improvement and final status on a curriculum-based measurement test of reading fluency. Finally, Fuchs et al. (2004) proposed a *slope discrepancy criterion* in which non-responders are identified using a cut-point on slope that can be referenced to classroom peers or to norms derived from district, state, or national performance levels.

Fuchs et al. (in press) reported results from a longitudinal comparison study of several traditional and RTI approaches for identifying children with reading disabilities that addresses the issue of whether alternative criteria identify the same or different children. A sample of 253 children at risk for reading disability was identified by selecting the six lowest performing first-grade children from each of 42 first-grade classrooms. Selection was based on a combination of word identification, rapid letter naming, and teacher judgment. The criterion to be predicted was end of second-grade reading disability status. Traditional approaches that were examined included initial low achievement and IQ-achievement discrepancy at the end of first grade. RTI criteria that were examined included final normalization, final benchmark, median split of slopes, slope discrepancy, and dual-discrepancy. Two key performance measures for comparing the alternative criteria were sensitivity and specificity. Sensitivity refers to the proportion of children determined to have a reading disability at the end of second grade who were identified as such by the identification procedure. It is the probability that the identification criterion will predict a reading disability for children who turn out to have a reading disability. Specificity refers to the proportion of children determined to be not reading disabled at the end of second grade who were identified as such by the identification procedure. It is the probability that the identification criterion will predict the absence of a reading disability for children who turn out not to have one. Sensitivity and specificity tend to trade off against one another. A conservative identification procedure that requires overwhelming evidence before predicting a reading disability will have poor sensitivity but good specificity. A liberal identification procedure that requires little evidence before predicting a reading disability will have poor specificity but good sensitivity.

For the traditional identification procedures, initial low achievement in word identification was characterized by reasonable prevalence estimates, acceptable specificity, and poor sensitivity. The IQ-achievement discrepancy was characterized by unreasonably low prevalence estimates, strong specificity, and poor sensitivity. Turning to RTI methods, final normalization was characterized by reasonable prevalence estimates, marginal specificity, and marginal sensitivity. Slope discrepancy and dual-discrepancy criteria were characterized by unreasonably high-prevalence estimates, adequate sensitivity, and adequate specificity. Benchmark and median-split methods also were characterized by unreasonably high-prevalence estimates. Perhaps the most important result was that the use of the different identification criteria resulted in different students being identified.

Addressing validity issues

Turning to validity issues, a criticism of the traditional aptitude-achievement discrepancy approach to identification has been that differences between IQ-discrepant and non-discrepant children tend to be minimal on reading and reading-related variables. Differences between the groups in decoding and decoding-related constructs such as phonological awareness, phonological memory, and rapid naming, tend to be small although significant statistically (Hoskyn and Swanson, 2000; Fletcher et al., 2006; Stuebing et al., 2002). What do we know about differences between responders and nonresponders to effective instruction and intervention?

Al Otaiba and Fuchs (2002) reviewed 23 studies of child characteristics that were related to differential response to instruction and intervention. Based on their review, they identified seven characteristics that were associated with being non responsive to instruction or intervention:

(a) phonological awareness;
(b) verbal memory;
(c) rapid naming;
(d) vocabulary, verbal ability, and intelligence;
(e) attention or behavior problems;
(f) orthographic awareness; and
(g) home background (including SES).

For these studies, deficiencies in phonological awareness received the strongest support as an indicator of nonresponsivess to instruction and intervention. A follow up meta-analysis by Nelson et al. (2003) reported effective sizes for a number of predictors of responsiveness to instruction and intervention: rapid naming ($Z_r = 0.51$), problem behavior ($Z_r = 0.46$), phonological awareness ($Z_r = 0.42$), phonological memory ($Z_r = .31$), IQ ($Z_r = 0.28$), and demographic variables ($Z_r = -0.01$).

Fuchs and Young (2006) reviewed 13 studies involving over 1,500 students who were at risk for, or had reading disability to examine the extent to which IQ predicted response to intervention. They reported that IQ reliably predicted response to intervention, especially under the following circumstances:

(a) the intervention was comprehensive;
(b) the outcome measure was reading comprehension;

(c)   when fidelity-of-treatment was assessed; and

(d)   when IQ was assessed with a valid measure.

IQ accounted for 15 per cent of the variance in response to intervention when the reading instruction was comprehensive. This level of prediction corresponds to a correlation of .4, which is comparable to effect sizes reported for reading-related variables by Nelson et al. (2003). IQ accounted for 12 per cent of the variance in response to intervention when the intervention was primarily phonological awareness training alone. This level of prediction corresponds to a correlation of .35, also comparable to effect sizes reported by Nelson et al. (2003).

The contrast is remarkable. Although variables such as phonological aware-ness, phonological memory, and rapid naming are not strong predictors for differentiating IQ-discrepant and nondiscrepant poor readers, they do predict differential response to effective instruction and intervention.

The problem of treatment resisters

A pernicious problem that is likely not to be addressed with the move to an RTI model for identification and intervention is the problem of treatment resisters (Torgesen, 2000). The problem of treatment resisters refers to the fact that between 2 and 6 percent of all children are essentially non-responsive to even the best, most intensive known interventions for reading problems. This percentage range corresponds roughly with the estimate that the incidence of severe or classic learning disability is about 5 per cent for all children. It should be noted that the estimate of 2 to 6 per cent of children that resist even the most effective treatments comes from intervention studies with a focus on word-level decoding. This is the domain for which the most is known about effective intervention. These figures are likely to be conservative estimates of the percentage of children who would be considered to be treatment resisters if we expand the scope of reading to include reading connected text fluently for meaning.

More recently, and independently of Torgesen (2000), McMaster et al. (2005), and Mathes et al. (2005) both estimated that between 2 and 5 per cent of students are nonresponsive to high-quality, secondary interventions that supplement enhanced classroom instruction. A study of the effectiveness of an intervention for severely impaired readers was reported by Denton et al. (2006), who evalu-ated the effects of an intensive, tier 3 reading intervention for 27 students with severe reading difficulties. Half of the students had been in a prior RTI study and had been determined to be inadequate responders to tiers one and two of reading instruction. The other half of the students consisted of poor readers who had not participated in the prior RTI study. Intervention was provided for four months. For the first two months, a two-hour intervention was provided daily that focused on decoding accuracy. For the next two months, one hour of intervention was provided daily that included tasks designed to promote decoding fluency. Of the 27 students with severe reading difficulties, 15 of them did not show a significant response to the interventions. Using a score at the 30th percentile as a liberal criterion for adequate performance, 74 per cent of the sample failed to meet the criterion for Woodcock Johnson Test of Achievement-III Word Attack and Letter and Word Identification; 81 per cent failed to meet the criterion for word-level fluency on the Test of Word Reading Efficiency, and 100% failed to meet the criterion on fluency for reading connected text on the Gilmore Oral Reading Test-4.

A limitation, then of the RTI approach to identification and remediation of learning disabilities, and of the traditional approach it seeks to replace as well, is the absence of an effective treatment for the very children nearly everyone would agree fit the description of having a learning disability.

A HYBRID MODEL

Although much of the discussion of the RTI approach has necessarily involved pitting it against the traditional approach, it may be more useful to consider ways in which a hybrid model of identification that combines elements of the traditional and RTI approaches might make the most sense given the existing state of the literature. The part of the traditional model that has the most empirical support is not the relevance of the IQ-achievement discrepancy distinction but rather that poor readers commonly show impairments in phonological processing and rapid naming. Coincidently, measures of phonological processing and rapid naming are among the best predictors of which children are likely to be non responders in an RTI model.

Rather than simply implementing an RTI model that arguably is as much a wait to fail model as is the traditional model based on an IQ-achievement discrepancy, a hybrid model would seem to make more sense. In this model, children are identified as candidates for possible reading failure on the basis of poor performance on an initial evaluation that consists of measures of phonological processing, rapid naming, and print awareness, constructs that are known to be predictive of reading performance (Manis et al., 2000) as well as response to intervention. Then, an RTI model is implemented in which students are initially assigned to levels or tiers of support on the basis of the initial evaluation. Students would be free to move up or down levels of support based on progress monitoring. This hybrid approach would also address logistic complications for staffing that will be faced when attempting to scale-up RTI approaches for widespread implementation. A non hybrid version of an RTI approach requires increasing numbers of support personnel across the school year as new waves of children pass from tier 1 to tier 2 and ultimately tier 3. Varying numbers of support personnel across the school year creates problems because of the need to hire staff for year-long contracts.

Support for a hybrid model is provided by Compton et al. (2006). They first identified potential poor readers at the beginning of first grade by giving two screening measures – word identification fluency and Rapid Letter Naming from the Comprehensive Test of Phonological Processing (CTOPP) (Wagner et al., 1999). Word identification fluency involved presenting lists of 50 high-frequency words and seeing how many could be named accurately in one minute. The lowest six students in first-grade classrooms were identified to their teachers, who concurred that the children were the lowest readers 90 per cent of the time. When the teachers did not concur, a replacement was made from a list of alternate low-scoring children. An initial prediction battery was given consisting of measures of phonological awareness (Sound Matching from the CTOPP), rapid naming (Rapid Digit Naming from the CTOPP), oral vocabulary, and word identification fluency. Progress monitoring measures were obtained by administering alternate forms of word identification fluency weekly for five weeks. Word identification fluency slope was the predicted increase in number of words correctly read per week using ordinary least squares regression. Word identification level was the estimated level of week five word identification fluency. The criterion to be predicted was end of second-grade reading disability status defined by a composite made up of timed and untimed word level decoding and reading comprehension measures.

For the initial prediction battery, sensitivity was 85.0 and specificity was 80.6. These are acceptable values of sensitivity and specificity. When the progress-monitoring measures of word identification fluency slope and level were added, sensitivity increased to 90.0 and specificity increased to 82.7. When the prediction algorithm was switched from one based on logistic regression to one based on classification tree analysis, sensitivity increased to 100.0 and specificity to 93.5 using the identical prediction and progress-monitoring variables. The results need to be cross-validated on another sample, but clearly show the promise of a hybrid model that combines assessment information from an initial battery with assessment data made available from an RTI model.

Although identification models based on response to instruction (RTI) appear potentially promising, the notion that they represent real progress for identification and intervention for children with dyslexia should be considered to be a popular myth until evidence from rigorous evaluation is available. The basic idea of monitoring performance data to inform instruction makes a lot of sense for general and special education. Even the criticized traditional aptitude-achievement discrepancy approach represents an implicit response to instruction model. You teach children to read, and those who do not learn eventually show up with achievement that lags behind expected levels. In the context of identifying children with learning disabilities, it is important to evaluate the fundamental assumption of the current crop of explicit RTI models, namely, that it is essential to observe response to effective instruction to make intelligent choices about who needs extra help. It also important to compare RTI models to non-RTI alternatives, including those that feature new assessments of emergent literacy, and to hybrid combinations of traditional and RTI models. Finally, it is essential to evaluate the psychometric properties of all new models with the same rigor that has been applied to more traditional forms of assessment.

ACKNOWLEDGEMENT

Support for this research has been provided by Grant P50 HD052120 from NICHD.

REFERENCES

Al Otaiba, S. and Fuchs, D. (2002) 'Characteristics of children who are unresponsive to early literacy intervention: A review of the literature', *Remedial and Special Education*, 23 (5): 300–316.

Burgess, S. R. and Lonigan, C. J. (1998) 'Bidirectional relations of phonological sensitivity and prereading abilities: Evidence from a preschool sample', *Journal of Experimental Child Psychology*, 70: 117–141.

Case, L. P., Speece, D. L. and Molloy, D. E. (2003) 'The validity of a response-to-instruction paradigm to identify reading disabilities: A longitudinal analysis of individual difference and contextual factors', *School Psychology Review*, 32: 557–582.

Compton, D. L., Fuchs, D., Fuchs, L. S. and Bryant, J. D. (2006) 'Selecting at-risk readers in first grade for early intervention: A two-year longitudinal study of decision rules and procedures', *Journal of Educational Psychology*, 98: 394–409.

Crowder, R. G. and Wagner, R. K. (1991) *The psychology of reading*. New York: Oxford University Press.

Denton, C. A., Fletcher, J. M., Anthony, J. L., and Francis, D. J. (2006). *Journal of Learning Disabilities*, 39, 447-466.

Fletcher, J. M., Coulter, W. A., Reschly, D. J. and Vaugh, S. (2004) 'Alternative approaches to the definition and identification of learning disabilities: Some questions and answers', *Annals of Dyslexia*, 54: 304–331.

Fletcher, J. M., Francis, D. J., Rourke, B. P., Shaywitz, S. E. and Shaywitz, B. A. (1992) 'The validity of discrepancy-based definitions of reading disabilities', *Journal of Learning Disabilities*, 25: 573–331.

Fletcher, J. M., Lyon, G. R., Fuchs, L. S. and Barnes, M. A. (2006) *Learning disabilities*. New York, NY: Guilford.

Fletcher, J. M., Morris, R. D. and Lyon, G. R. (2003) 'Classification and definition of learning disabilities: An integrative perspective', in H. L. Swanson and K. R. Harris (eds), *Handbook of learning disabilities*. New York: Guilford Press. pp. 30–56.

Francis, D. J., Fletcher, J. M., Stuebing, K. K., Lyon, G. R., Shaywitz, B. A. and Shaywitz, S. E. (2005) 'Psychometric approaches to the identification of learning disabilities: IQ and achievement scores are not sufficient', *Journal of Learning Disabilities*, 38: 98–110.

Francis, D.J., Shaywitz, S.E., Stuebing, K.K., Shaywitz, B.A. and Fletcher, J.M. (1996) 'Developmental lag versus deficit models of reading disability: A longitudinal individual growth curves analysis', *Journal of Educational Psychology*, 1: 3–17.

Fuchs, D., Compton, D. L., Fuchs, L. S., Bryant, J. and Davis, N. G. (in press) 'Making "secondary intervention" work in a three-tier responsiveness-to-intervention model: Findings from the first-grade longitudinal study of the National Research Center on Learning Disabilities', *Reading and Writing Quarterly: An Interdisciplinary Journal*.

Fuchs, D. and Deshler, D. D. (2007) 'What we need to know about responsiveness to intervention (and shouldn't be afraid to ask)', *Learning Disabilities Research and Practice*, 22: 129–136.

Fuchs, D., Deshler, D. D. and Reschly, D. J. (2004) 'National Research Center on Learning Disabilities: Multimethod studies of identification and classification issues', *Learning Disability Quarterly*, 27: 189–195.

Fuchs, L. S. and Fuchs, D. (1998) 'Treatment validity: A unifying concept for reconceptualizing the identification of learning disabilities', *Learning Disabilities Research and Practice*, 13: 204–219.

Fuchs, D., Fuchs, L. S. and Compton, D. L. (2004) 'Identifying reading disability by responsiveness-to-instruction: Specifying measures and criteria', *Learning Disabilities Quarterly*, 27: 216–227.

Fuchs, D., Fuchs, L. S., McMaster, K. N. and Al Otaiba, S. (2003a) 'Identifying children at risk for reading failure: Curriculum-based measurement and the dual-discrepancy approach', in H. L. Swanson and K. R. Harris (eds), *Handbook of learning disabilities*. New York, NY: Guilford Press. pp. 431–449.

Fuchs, D., Mock, D., Morgan, P. L. and Young, C. L. (2003b) 'Responsiveness-to-intervention: Definitions, evidence, and implications for the learning disabilities construct', *Learning Disabilities Research and Practice*, 18: 157–171.

Fuchs, D., and Young, C. L. 'On the irrelevance of intelligence in predicting responsiveness to reading instruction'. *Exceptional Children*, 73, 8-30.

Good, R. H., Simmons, D. C. and Kame'enui, E. J. (2001) 'The importance and decision–making utility of a continuum of fluency-based indicators of foundational reading skills for third-grade high-stakes outcomes', *Scientific Studies of Reading*, 5: 257–288.

Hallahan, D. P. and Mock, D. R. (2003) 'A brief history of the field of learning disabilities', in H. L. Swanson and K. R. Harris (eds), *Handbook of learning disabilities*. New York: Guilford Press. pp. 16–29.

Hoskyn, M. and Swanson, H. L. (2000) 'Cognitive processing of low achievers and children with reading disabilities: A selective meta-analytic review of the published literature', *School Psychology Review*, 29: 102–119.

Kavale, K. and Mattson, P. D. (1983) 'One jumped off the balance beam: Motor training', *Journal of Learning Disabilities*, 16: 165–173.

Lonigan, C. J., Wagner, R., Torgesen, J. and Rashotte, C. (2007.) *Test of Preschool Early Literacy*. Austin, TX: Pro-Ed.

Lyon, G. R., Fletcher, J. M., Shaywitz, S. E., Shaywitz, B. A., Torgesen, J. K., Wood, F. B., et al. (2001) 'Rethinking learning disabilities', in C. E. Finn, A. J. Rotherham and C. R. Hokanson, Jr. (eds), *Rethinking special education for a new century*. pp. 259–287.

Lyon, G. R., Shaywitz, S. E. and Shaywitz, B. A. (2003) 'A definition of dyslexia', *Annals of Dyslexia*, 53: 1–14.

Manis, F. R., Doi, L. M. and Bhadha, B. (2000) 'Naming speed, phonological awareness, and orthographic knowledge in second graders', *Journal of Learning Disabilities*, 33: 325–333.

Mathes, P. G., Denton, C. A., Fletcher, J. M., Anthony, J. L., Francis, D. J. and Schatschneider, C. (2005) 'An evaluation of two reading interventions derived from diverse models', *Reading Research Quarterly*, 40: 148–183.

McMaster, K. L, Fuchs, D., Fuchs, L. S. and Compton, D. L. (2005) 'Responding to nonresponders: An experimental field trial of identification and intervention methods', *Exceptional Children*, 71: 445–463.

Nelson, J. R., Benner, G. J. and Gonzalez, J. (2003) 'Learner characteristics that influence the treatment effectiveness of early literacy interventions: A meta-analytic review', *Learning Disabilities Research and Practice*, 18 (4): 255–267.

Piasta, S. B. and Wagner, R. K. (2007) 'Dyslexia: identification and classification', in E. Grigorenko and A. Napes (eds) *Single word reading: Behavioral and biological perspectives*. Mahwah, NJ: Erlbaum. pp. 309–326.

President's Commission on Excellence in Special Education (2002) *A new era: Revitalizing special education for children and their families*. Washington, DC: U.S. Department of Education.

Rayner, K. (1985) 'The role of eye movements in learning to read and in reading disability', *Remedial and Special Education*, 6: 53–60.

Rayner, K. (1998) 'Eye movements in reading and information processing: 20 years of research', *Psychological Bulletin*, 124: 372–422.

Schatschneider, C. (2007). *RTI and classification*. Paper presented at the 58th Annual Conference of the International Dyslexia Association, Dallas, TX, November.

Shaywitz, B. A., Fletcher, J. M., Holahan, J. M. and Shaywitz, S. E. (1992) 'Discrepancy compared to low achievement definitions of reading disability: Results from the Connecticut longitudinal study', *Journal of Learning Disabilities*, 25: 639–648.

Shaywitz, S. E. and Shaywitz, B. A. (2003) 'Neurobiological indices of dyslexia', in H. L. Swanson and K. R. Harris (eds), *Handbook of learning disabilities*. New York: Guilford Press. pp. 514–531.

Siegel, L. S. (1992) 'An evaluation of the discrepancy definition of dyslexia', *Journal of Learning Disabilities*, 25: 618–629.

Siegel, L. S. (2003) 'Basic cognitive processes and reading disabilities', in H. L. Swanson and K. R. Harris (eds), *Handbook of learning disabilities*. New York: Guilford Press. pp. 158–181.

Simmons, D. C., Kame'ennui, E. J., Stoolmiller, M., Coyne, M. D. and Harn, B. (2003) 'Accelerating growth and maintaining proficiency: A two-year intervention study of kindergarten and first-grade children at-risk for reading difficulties', in B. R. Foorman (ed), *Preventing and remediating reading difficulties*. Baltimore: York Press. pp. 197–228.

Spear-Swerling, L. and Sternberg, R. (1996) *Off track: When poor readers become learning disabled*. Boulder, Colorado: Westview Press.

Stanovich, K. E. (1991) 'Discrepancy definitions of reading disability: Has intelligence led us astray?', *Reading Research Quarterly*, 26: 7–29.

Stanovich, K. E. and Siegel, L. S. (1994) 'Phenotypic performance profile of children with reading disabilities: A regression-based test of the phonological-core variable-difference model', *Journal of Educational Psychology*, 86: 24–53.

Stuebing, K. K., Fletcher, J. M., LeDoux, J. M., Lyon, G. R., Shaywitz, S. E. and Shaywitz, B. A. (2002) 'Validity of IQ-discrepancy classifications of reading disabilities: A meta-analysis', *American Educational Research Journal*, 39: 469–518.

Torgesen, J. K. (2000) 'Individual responses in response to early intervention in reading: The lingering problem of treatment resisters', *Learning Disabilities Research and Practice*, 15: 55–64.

Torgesen, J. K., Alexander, A. W., Wagner, R. K., Rashotte, C. A., Voeller, K., Conway, T. and Rose, E. (2001) 'Intensive remedial instruction for children with severe reading disabilities: Immediate and long-term outcomes from two instructional approaches', *Journal of Learning Disabilities*, 34: 33–58.

Vaughn, S. and Fuchs, L. S. (2003) 'Redefining learning disabilities as inadequate response to instruction: The promise and potential problems', *Learning Disabilities Research and Practice*, 28: 137–146.

Vellutino, F. R., Scanlon, D. M., Sipay, E. R., Small, S., Chen, R., Pratt, A. and Denckla, M. B. (1996) 'Cognitive profiles of difficult-to-remediate and readily remediated poor readers: Early intervention as a vehicle for distinguishing between cognitive and experiential deficits as basic causes of specific reading disability', *Journal of Educational Psychology*, 88: 601–638.

Wagner, R. K. and Muse, A. (2006) 'Phonological memory and reading disability', in T. Alloway and S. Gathercole (eds), *Working memory in neurodevelopmental conditions*. East Sussex, England: Psychology Press. pp. 41–57.

Wagner, R. K., Torgesen, J. K. and Rashotte, C. A. (1999) *Comprehensive test of phonological processing*. Austin, TX: PRO-Ed.

Wagner, R. K., Torgesen, J. K., Rashotte, C. A., Hecht, S., Barker, T., Burgess, S. and Garon, T. (1997) 'Causal relations between the development of phonological processing and reading: A five-year longitudinal study', *Developmental Psychology*, 33: 468–479.

Werker, J. F., Bryson, S. E. and Wassenberg, K. (1989) 'Toward understanding the problem in severely disabled readers: Ii. Consonant errors', *Applied Psycholinguistics*, 10: 13–30.

9

Learning, Cognition and Dyslexia

Roderick I. Nicolson
and Angela J. Fawcett

This chapter:

i) discusses a number of hypothesis on learning and how learning can go wrong for some;
ii) refers to the nature of learning in infancy;
iii) discusses declarative and procedural learning;
iv) provides a neural systems framework for developmental disorders;
v) suggests that it is not only the language related processes that are important but also components of motor skills;
vi) discusses how this gives rise to investigating the nature and role of the cerebellum; and
vii) reflects on how theoretical positions on developmental dyslexia can impact on practice.

INTRODUCTION

What a wonderful skill it is to be able to read! This is the centenary of Huey's seminal book (Huey, 1908) that provided the first scientific analysis of the skill. Huey's studies revealed that many processes combine seamlessly and without conscious monitoring. When reading aloud, the articulatory tract is speaking each word in sequence; the eyes are fixating from word to word several words ahead of the voice (the eye-voice span) and the 'mind' is somehow identifying the word fixated, accessing its meaning, combining the meaning with those already read, looking up the appropriate pronunciation (a complex pattern of tightly coordinated muscular movements), determining the appropriate prosody (pitch, emphasis etc) and planning the next fixation. Silent reading is harder to investigate, but is no longer limited to the articulation speed, typically occurring 50 per cent faster than speech, with the capability of much greater speeds for skills such as skimming. At the very least, skilled reading involves automatic word recognition, eye movement control and speech internalization, seamlessly combined in some process that requires minimal attentional monitoring. Of course these skills are not achieved overnight, and involve the cumulative effort of several years and thousands of hours of practice. In some ways, therefore, it is more remarkable that anyone is able to learn to read fluently than that some, otherwise highly competent, individuals do not.

When attempting to investigate the underlying causes of reading difficulties, it is evident that a problem in almost any component of the cumulative skill acquisition process might lead to dysfluency. Two analogies may prove helpful. When investigating complex skills, the estuary analogy is helpful. The Thames estuary is the confluence of many rivers. If there is pollution in the estuary, one has to navigate upstream, tracing back the pollution to its source. Sampling the estuary (cf. skilled reading) provides a quick screen for problems but not the underlying cause. For the underlying cause more specific tests are needed, aimed at sampling the contributory streams. The second analogy is the medical one of cause and symptom. The primary symptom of malaria is high fever, caused by plasmodia protozoal parasitic infection arising from a bite by an infected anopheles mosquito. The high fever symptom could alternatively be caused by influenza or meningitis, but of course the appropriate treatments are completely different and faulty diagnosis might lead to death. In the case of malaria, secondary behavioural symptoms such as paroxysms are a clear indication, but the key test is the physiological one for plasmodia in the blood. A mature science of learning ability and disability would be able to provide a similar set of diagnostic and treatment tools for dyslexia, both at behavioural and physiological levels. In this chapter we outline the faltering progress that has been made toward this goal.

Following an outline of early contributions on learning and dyslexia, we note that at behavioural level many difficulties can be described as lack of automaticity – not just within literacy-related skills, but often in other skills as well – and this led to our fruitful automaticity deficit hypothesis (Nicolson and Fawcett, 1990). The 1990s were the 'decade of the brain' and more was discovered about the physiological bases of learning than had been discovered in the previous two millennia, with discoveries continuing apace. These developments promise to transform the understanding of learning, and we attempt to characterise the new insights arising, together with studies attempting to apply these new techniques to the analysis of dyslexia. These analyses lead to the hypothesis that dyslexic individuals may suffer from a specific difficulty in some component of 'procedural learning'. We conclude with a brief outline of the implications of this research and directions for further investigations.

EARLY STUDIES IN DYSLEXIA AND LEARNING

In the early days of dyslexia research, it was taken for granted that there was some learning problem underlying the disability. The revered Orton-Gillingham multi-sensory method for teaching of reading (Gillingham and Stillman, 1956) stresses the need for simultaneous use of all three 'learning channels', namely visual, auditory and kinesthetic-tactile. June Orton made the interdependency clear, citing the two basic principles as:

1. Training for simultaneous association of visual, auditory and kinesthetic language stimuli – in reading cases, tracing and sounding the visually presented word and maintaining consistent direction by following the letter with the fingers during the sound synthesis of syllables and words.
2. Finding such units as the child can use without difficulty in the field of his particular difficulty and directing the training toward developing the process of fusing these smaller units into larger and more complex wholes (Orton, 1966, p. 131) cited by Henry (1998, p. 11).

This approach reflects the belief of Orton and her colleagues that dyslexic children have specific difficulties in automatically combining information from two or more modalities (or combining sensing, thinking and doing), difficulties that they addressed by means of forcing the children to do all three.

Vellutino's seminal work on the language basis of dyslexia (Vellutino, 1979) also started from a learning perspective. In particular, he investigated the belief that dyslexic children have particular difficulties in cross-modal transfer (Birch and Belmont, 1964). In order to avoid possible confounds with verbal working memory and verbal coding ability, Vellutino and his associates (Vellutino, 1979; 1987; Vellutino and Scanlon, 1982) compared poor and normal readers on both intra-modal (visual–visual, auditory–auditory) and cross-modal (visual–auditory) non-verbal learning tasks that minimised the influence of verbal coding ability. They established that the poor readers had no deficits on these tasks, and yet they had a selective impairment on a visual–verbal learning tasks (i.e., the problems arose for cross-modal tasks but only when the auditory dimension required verbal processing). They interpreted the data in terms of verbal deficit although a more general explanation in terms of cross-modal transfer that involves speech is also tenable.

THE AUTOMATISATION DEFICIT HYPOTHESIS

Following the emergence of the phonological deficit hypothesis as a key explanatory construct for dyslexia (Bradley and Bryant, 1983; Snowling, 1987; Stanovich, 1988; Vellutino, 1979) interest in learning and dyslexia was diverted to the applied issue of how to help dyslexic children acquire phonological skills.

Arguably the major alternative hypothesis that considered learning as a central explanatory construct was our own automatisation deficit hypothesis (Nicolson and Fawcett, 1990). This proposed that dyslexic children have difficulties making skills automatic (so that one no longer needs to think how to do the skill). Automaticity develops from long practice under consistent conditions, and underpins almost all of our highly practised skills from speech to walking to arithmetic. Acquisition of automaticity is a long and painful process, and most of us will remember only the travails of late adolescence in terms of learning to drive, where the absence of automaticity is only too obvious!

In our original research (Nicolson and Fawcett, 1990), we noted that, unlike language, reading is not a 'special' skill for humans. Humans are not evolutionarily adapted to read – few people could read at all until the last two or three hundred years. Consequently, in investigating why dyslexic children fail to learn to read, we felt an analysis of the learning processes involved must be of value. One of the critical aspects of learning a skill is to make it automatic, so that one can do it fluently without thinking about it. By adulthood, most skills –·walking, talking reading – are so deeply overlearned that we no longer have any insight into how we acquired them and consequently, to illustrate the processes involved, cognitive psychologists use two skills that are acquired relatively late in life. The skills involved are driving (which most adults eventually master pretty comprehensively) and typing (which most adults comprehensively fail to master). In learning to drive, the beginner can either steer, or change gear, but not both at the same time, because of the need to consciously attend to each procedure. An expert driver changes gear and steers 'automatically', thus leaving more 'capacity' for watching the traffic, planning a manoeuvre, or holding a conversation. Most of us when typing still have to look at the keyboard (even if using several fingers), and, compared with a touch-typist, our typing is slower, more error-prone and requires much more effort.

There is no theoretical reason to expect that automatisation of the processes in reading is qualitatively different from the general processes of automatising any other complex skill. Of course, automatisation is a key requirement for reading, and as noted above, there is extensive evidence that dyslexic children, even when reading well, are less fluent, requiring more time and effort to read than would a non-dyslexic child of the same reading age. Consequently we proposed the hypothesis that dyslexic children would have difficulty in automatising any skill (cognitive or motor). All dyslexia hypotheses predict poor reading and therefore critical tests of the hypothesis needed to be undertaken outside the reading domain. The automatisation deficit hypothesis was clearly supported by a set of experiments in which we asked dyslexic children to do two things at once. If a skill is automatic, then one ought to be able to do something else at the same time (assuming it does not directly interfere with the first skill) with little or no loss of performance. A theoretically significant finding was for balance – a highly automatic skill with no language component. We found (Nicolson and Fawcett, 1990) that although a group of dyslexic adolescents were normally able to balance as well as 'controls' (non-dyslexic children matched for age and IQ), their balance deteriorated very significantly when they had to do something else at the same time, whereas the controls' balance was not affected at all. The deficit obtained for a range of secondary tasks, including concurrent counting, concurrent reaction time tasks, and blindfold balance (Fawcett and Nicolson, 1992). These findings strongly suggested that dyslexic children were not automatic even at the fundamental skill of balance. For some reason, dyslexic children had difficulty automatising skills, and had therefore to concentrate harder to achieve normal levels of performance. We have used the analogy of driving in a foreign country – one can do it, but it requires continual effort and is stressful and tiring over long periods. On our account, life for a dyslexic child is like always living in a foreign country. Alternatively, from the viewpoint of a dyslexic child, it may be as though the rest of the world touch types, whereas he or she has to look at the keyboard!

It may be valuable to report briefly two further extended studies that clarified the breadth of deficit and the locus of the deficit within the learning process.

SKILL TESTS

In an attempt to minimise confounding factors arising from differences in experience together with use of compensatory strategies, we decided to test 'primitive' skills in the major modalities – skills that are not normally trained explicitly, and are not easily subject to compensatory strategies. In addition to psychometric tests, four types of test were used, namely tests of phonological skill, working memory, information processing speed and motor skill (Fawcett and Nicolson, 1994; 1995a; b). In almost all tests of naming speed, phonological skill, motor skill and also non-word repetition and articulation rate, the dyslexic children performed significantly worse than their chronological age controls. In general, the performance of the dyslexic children was somewhat below that of their reading age controls, but significant differences compared with reading age controls were obtained only for simple reaction (better performance than the reading age controls) and phonological skills, picture naming speed, bead threading and balance under dual task conditions or when blindfolded (worse than reading age controls).

LEARNING AND DYSLEXIA

One of the most severe limitations of the above work (and, indeed, of almost all dyslexia research) is that the investigations involve a 'snapshot' of the abilities of various groups of children at one point in time. For a sensitive analysis it is crucial to follow a child's performance over a period of time, while he or she acquires a skill. In the above skills tests we had established that the dyslexic children had normal speed of simple reaction (SRT). However, when a choice needed to be made, the dyslexic children were differentially affected by the increase in task complexity (Nicolson and Fawcett, 1994). We therefore undertook (Nicolson and Fawcett, 2000) a study investigating the time course of the blending of two separate simple reactions into a choice reaction (CRT).

In order to avoid any problems of left–right confusions or of stimulus discriminability, we used two stimuli of different modalities (tone and flash) and different effectors (hand and foot) for the two stimuli. Twenty-two subjects participated, 11 dyslexic and 11 control matched for age and IQ. In brief, following baseline performance monitoring on simple reaction time (SRT) to each stimulus separately, the two simple reaction tasks were combined into a choice reaction task (CRT) in which half the stimuli were tones and half flashes, and the subject had to press the corresponding button, using the mapping established in the simple reactions. Each session comprised three runs, each of 100 stimuli, and participants kept returning every fortnight or so until their performance stopped improving (in terms of speed and accuracy). The results are shown in Figure 9.1.

Analysis of the SRT performance indicated that there were no significant differences between the groups either for foot or hand, tone or flash. By contrast, initial performance on the CRT was significantly slower, and final performance was both significantly slower and less accurate for the dyslexic children. The group data were then fitted using the appropriate 'power law' parametric

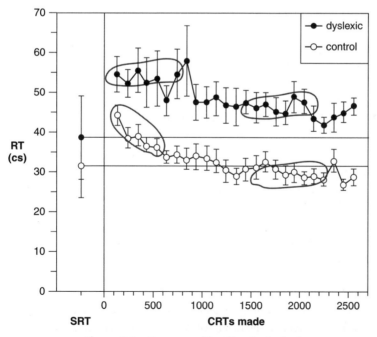

Figure 9.1   Response blending in dyslexia

technique (Newell and Rosenbloom, 1981). In brief, the curve fitted is $P(n) = A \pm Bn^{-\alpha}$ where $P(n)$ refers to performance on trial n, A is the asymptotic performance as n tends to infinity (taken as 0 here), B is a scaling parameter linked directly to initial performance, and α is the learning rate. The learning rate, α was about 1.5 times faster for the controls than the dyslexic children (0.141 vs. 0.073; 0.116 vs. 0.086 for the hand and foot responses respectively). This is a huge difference. Bearing in mind that the learning varies as a function of the time to the power α, if a skill takes a normal child 100 repetitions to master, it would take a dyslexic child $100^{1.5}$ i.e., 1,000 repetitions (10 times as long) to learn the skill to the same criterion, That is, their deficit increases with the square root of the time needed to learn the skill – our 'square root law'.

In summary, the dyslexic children appeared to have greater difficulty in blending existing skills into a new skill, and their performance after extensive practice (such that the skill was no longer improving noticeably) was slower and more error-prone. In other words, they were simply less skilled; their 'quality' of automatised performance was lower. It seems reasonable, therefore, to argue that this group of dyslexic children have difficulties both with the initial proceduralisation of skill, and with the 'quality' of skill post-training.

Taking these findings together, it is clear that automatisation deficit gives a good approximation to the range of difficulties suffered on a range of tasks, and captures reasonably well the general performance characteristics (lack of fluency, greater effort more errors) established by 'snapshot' studies. Perhaps most satisfying, the hypothesis had ecological validity in that many dyslexic people and dyslexia practitioners came to us to say that our account seemed exactly right to them – they did have to concentrate on even the simplest skills.

Before addressing the possible causes of these differences, it is valuable to step back and to attempt to characterise the different types of learning that occur. We start at the beginning, learning in infancy.

LEARNING IN INFANCY: ACQUISITION OF LANGUAGE

One of the major debates of the late twentieth century related to the acquisition of language. Chomsky (1965) had thrown down the gauntlet to learning theorists, suggesting that the way humans learn language is qualitatively different from other types of learning, and that humans have an innate 'language acquisition device' that somehow incorporates universal features of human language, but gets tuned to the requirements of one's mother tongue via experience (Chomsky, 1995). Over the years, it became clear that the hypothesis had strengths and weaknesses, but evidence steadily built up to suggest that the universal features were perhaps more general than just language.

By the 1990s it was established that at the age of six months most children have the ability to detect all the basic sounds in all the human languages, but over the next three months or so they actually lose these abilities, such that they

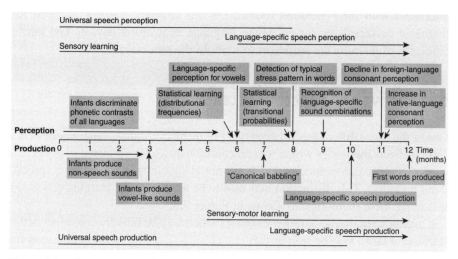

Figure 9.2 The processes of early language acquisition. Taken from Kuhl (2004:832.).

become specialists in their mother tongue, developing 'categories' specific to their own phonemes. A classic example of this is the difficulty Japanese people have in distinguishing /l/ versus /r/ in that there is no such distinction in spoken Japanese. The issue of how these processes happen has been systematically investigated by Kuhl and her colleagues (Kuhl, 2000; 2004), to the extent that there is now converging evidence from a range of studies that suggests the following broad processes.

Figure 9.2 summarises the findings of a range of studies and suggests that the initial processes of language acquisition involve sensory analysis of the environmental input, a task made easier by the inbuilt ability of the mammalian auditory system to analyse speech sounds. At the age of six months or so, something magical occurs. The infant has been automatically analysing the statistical properties of the speech it hears, and it is in position to adjust the way it hears to better match the sound regularities it is encountering. In particular, it decides to lump some similar-sounding inputs into the same category (phoneme) whereas other similar-sounding inputs will be allocated to different categories. These categories are not 'hard-wired' into the human cortex but are derived via a 'statistical learning' process (which is hard-wired into the mammalian cortex). Once this learning process has occurred, the brain then changes itself to incorporate these generalizations (a process Kuhl calls 'neural commitment'), perhaps by eliminating some of the neural connections that previously allowed all sounds to be accurately analysed. The advantage of this neural commitment process is that it allows the sounds heard to be better mapped on to the sounds produced, since it is during this period that the infant also starts to produce its first language-based 'utterances'. Following these irreversible changes, the language and speech abilities continue to develop at an amazing rate for the next few years. Nonetheless, the key processes are statistical learning and comparison of the sounds of one's utterances with their intended sounds. On this analysis, there is no need for linguistic universals or for an innate language acquisition device. The innate processes of learning are sufficient to scaffold the processes.

DECLARATIVE AND PROCEDURAL LEARNING

One of the major differences between types of memory (Squire, 1987; Squire et al., 1993) reflects memories which we can consciously access (referred to as declarative memory) and memories which are not available to consciousness (procedural memory). This distinction may also to be applied to the learning processes that make these memories, as shown in Figure 9.3.

It may be seen that declarative learning (which may be broadly construed as the learning of facts) may be split further into episodic learning (where one learns via experiencing situations) and semantic learning (where one learns more general information, relating to meanings). We have split procedural learning into three sub-types: statistical learning, skill learning and conditioning. It is perfectly possible from the outset that dyslexic children might have difficulties in any of these five types of learning. On the other hand, given that dyslexia is associated with normal levels of intelligence, and intelligence is generally measured via declarative tasks, it would seem more likely a priori that learning problems in dyslexia would be associated with one or more of the three types of procedural learning.

Learning and cognitive neuroscience

The 1990s were the 'decade of the brain' and it is not just the understanding of language acquisition that was transformed.

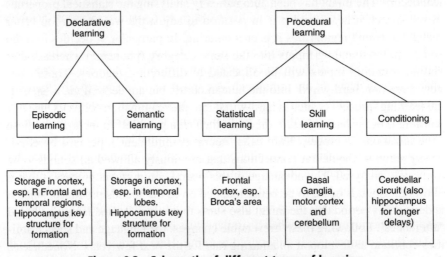

Figure 9.3   Schematic of different types of learning

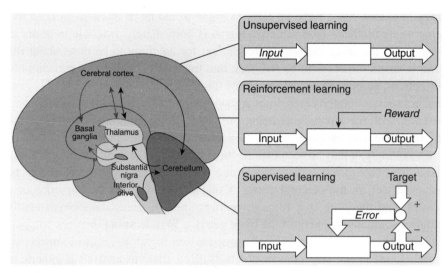

Figure 9.4   Learning competences and the brain. Taken from Doya (1999).

One of the aspects of brain learning processes that is not fully enough recognised is the fact that different brain structures have different competences. This point is well illustrated in Figure 9.4 which is taken from Doya (1999).

Doya makes the point that the cerebral cortex has the ability for 'unsupervised' learning. This may be considered a form of pattern recognition, an alternative term for statistical learning (see Figure 9.2), in which the brain automatically learns to detect and classify patterns in incoming sensory information via well established connectionist principles. The learning is termed unsupervised because it is driven primarily via environmental input rather than any goal-directed process. One relevant example of unsupervised learning is the 'connectionist' learning capability that underpins much of our early sensory learning, such as the effortless ability to learn to recognise visual or auditory (language) patterns.

To survive in a competitive environment, however, it is crucial for the organism to be able to mark some processes as more important than others. Processes that result in changes in primary drives (positive or negative) are therefore granted special status, and this occurs via the dopaminergic systems of the basal ganglia. These are referred to as 'reinforcement learning' by analogy with the concept of reinforcement that is so influential in animal learning. Reinforcement is built on the unsupervised learning processes but has the major difference that (after the actions have occurred, and the reinforcement or secondary reinforcement obtained) the reward signal primes the circuitry essentially to undertake a post-action review and, in an optimal case, to adjust the likelihood of the key responses occurring again when a similar situation occurs.

The third competence is supervised learning. Here there is a 'training signal' that in some way reflects the difference between the desired output and the planned output. For a baby, an early example would be its attempts to keep fixating on its mother's face. An error signal is immediately available in terms of slippage of the image across the retina, but for anything to be done about the error it needs somehow to be fed back into the controller that was carrying out the actions, so that the processes can be tuned to reduce the error. There is general consensus that the cerebellum is the only brain structure that has this competence, with the error signal being provided via the climbing fibers from the inferior olive, and the patterned sensory information coming in via the thalamus.

Interestingly, it may be seen that the three types of procedural learning fall into these three categories: statistical learning is unsupervised and therefore can be achieved well in the cerebral cortex. Conditioning requires the presence of a reward, and therefore is a form of reinforcement learning, and consequently requires some involvement of the basal ganglia. Skill learning involves comparison of the actual with the desired outcome, and therefore requires supervised learning, and hence cerebellar involvement. Note that this analysis is generic to any mammalian brain. For humans at least we need to add the capability of declarative learning, in which the supervisor can be provided by language input. Consequently, the language capability does allow humans to transcend the processing constraints implicit in the above analysis. Nonetheless, these procedural learning capabilities form the bedrock of much human learning, and, as we have seen, they seem to be the main focus of the problems experienced by dyslexic individuals.

If one was designing a system that was able to learn adaptively from its own environment, one would design it such that it exploited to the hilt the competences available to it. In particular one would ensure that the basal ganglia's reinforcement learning capabilities and the cerebellum's supervised learning capabilities were made available to the cortical learning processes. That is, one would design a complex, highly interactive system, involving interplay between all of these structures. It would appear that this is indeed how the brain does these procedural computations, as we see below.

Timescales of procedural learning

The inspiration for our automatisation deficit framework was the Fitts and Posner (1967) three-stage model of motor skill learning that Anderson (1982) generalised to cognitive learning also. The three stages in this model were declarative learning, then proceduralisation then essentially automatization. More recently, cognitive neuroscientists have provided an expanded and more brain-based set of stages. The following representative analysis is a combination of the analyses from Doyon and Benali (2005) and Doyon and Ungerleider (2002).

• Stage 1: fast (early) learning stage – minutes: considerable improvement performance occurs within a single training session; brain regions involved include motor cortex, parietal cortex, medial temporal cortex, basal ganglia cerebellum.

- Stage 2: slow (later) learning stage – hours: further gains can be seen across several sessions of practice; motor cortex, parietal cortex, basal ganglia, cerebellum.
- Stage 3: Consolidation stage – typically overnight: spontaneous increases in performance can be experienced: motor cortex, parietal cortex plus either basal ganglia or cerebellum depending on skill type.
- Stage 4: Automatic stage during which the skilled behaviour is thought to require minimal cognitive resources and to be resistant to interference and the effects of time: motor cortex, parietal cortex plus either basal ganglia or cerebellum depending on skill type.
- Stage 5: Retention stage in which the motor skill can be readily executed after long delays without further practice on the task: motor cortex, parietal cortex plus either basal ganglia or cerebellum depending on skill type.

The reference to skill type reflects the view that there are two distinct motor learning circuits, a cortico-striatal (with striatal meaning basal ganglia) system and a cortico-cerebellar system (Doyon et al., 2003; Doyon and Ungerleider, 2002). They propose that the cortico-striatal system is particularly involved in learning sequences of movements, whereas the cortico-cerebellar system is particularly involved in adapting to environmental perturbations.

We find on this model, therefore, that impairment in any one brain region – cerebellum, motor cortex or basal ganglia – would lead to an impaired ability to acquire the skills initially (fast learning stage). Relating this back to our declarative/procedural circuits hypothesis, an impairment in any component of the procedural learning system would lead to some impairment in the initial acquisition of motor skill. While this deficit might be overcome subsequently, there would be a developmental delay in its acquisition. For those with impairment in the cortico-striatal circuit there would be long-term problems in motor-sequence activities (corresponding to a slight clumsiness). For those with abnormality in the cortico-cerebellar circuit there would be long-term problems in skills such as balance and adaptive timing.

In short, the Doyon/Ungerleider model proposes that motor cortex, basal ganglia and cerebellar structures are involved in the fast and slow learning processes, but that the cortico-striatal systems contribute primarily to motor sequence learning, whereas cortico-cerebellar systems contribute primarily to motor adaptation (especially to variable temporal requirements), with the dissociation between the two systems occurring at the automatization phase. Given that most tests of attainment conflate these types, stages and structures, it is not surprising that there remains confusion in the developmental disabilities literature.

STUDIES ON DYSLEXIA AND LEARNING

It is interesting to interpret six recent dyslexia studies within this framework. A motor sequence learning study (Nicolson et al., 1999) established that the dyslexic participants failed to activate their cerebellum either when first learning a task (fast learning stage) or after they had practised the task to automaticity. By contrast, striatal activation was within the normal range for both tasks. These results indicate that the dyslexic participants were not using their cortico-cerebellar system at any stage in the learning. Interestingly, this task was a declarative and procedural task, in that participants had to learn a sequence of four finger presses by trial and error.

The 'response blending' task (Nicolson and Fawcett, 2000) discussed above also indicates problems at the fast learning stage, the automaticity stage and all intervening stages. This suggests problems within either the cortico-striatal system or the cortico-cerebellar system or both. It is clearly a skill learning task, and would therefore be expected to require supervised learning, and hence cerebellar involvement. It is also worth noting that dyslexic children showed deficits on a mirror drawing (Vicari et al., 2005) – also considered to be mediated via the skill learning circuits.

Moving to the third type of procedural learning, eye blink conditioning provides a relatively primitive learning form, with a cerebellar and/or striatal substrate (Christian and Thompson, 2003; Maschke et al., 2003). In this the participant experiences an air puff to the eye (causing an involuntary blink) that occurs soon after an auditory tone. Over the space of tens of pairings, the tone acquires the status of 'conditioned stimulus', such that the participant blinks after the tone and before the air puff. Significant problems for dyslexic participants have been established (Coffin et al., 2005; Nicolson et al., 2002), with the latter study suggesting that problems were particularly marked for the response adaptation to the onset of the air puff.

In a fourth study (Brookes et al., 2007) a group of dyslexic participants and a group with Developmental Coordination Disorder (DCD) were compared with controls on their ability to adapt to the visual field displacement caused by prisms – a cerebellar task (Baizer et al., 1999). The dyslexic group showed significantly slower adaptation than the controls, with 10 out of 14 showing an individual impairment. Even stronger deficits obtained for the DCD group, with all 14 participants showing individual impairments.

Moving on to the first category of procedural learning, statistical learning, we cannot trace any dyslexia studies. However, studies of implicit learning in dyslexia have found clear deficits on the serial reaction time task, with specific activation differences in the supplementary motor area, parietal regions and cerebellum (Menghini et al., 2006). Interestingly, good performance on the serial reaction time task (in which participants respond faster to stimuli that are more likely in the current situation) can be considered as a simple case of statistical learning. By contrast, superior performance was obtained on an implicit spatial learning task considered to be mediated via medial temporal lobe structures (Howard et al., 2006).

A sixth study (Needle et al., under review) explicitly analysed overnight changes in performance, so as to investigate the effect of consolidation. The task was a motor sequence learning task studied extensively by Karni and her colleagues (Karni et al., 1998; Korman et al., 2003). Thirteen dyslexic adults and

12 control adults matched for age and intelligence were asked to repeat a sequence of finger movements as many times as possible in 30s. They were then trained on the sequence for 160 slow-paced trials and then re-tested for maximum speed. A third testing session was carried out 24 hrs after the initial tests (without any further practice). Performance of the two groups did not differ immediately after training, but the dyslexic group showed significant performance deficits initially and immediately after the 24-hr break. The latter strongly suggests an impairment in consolidation of learning (a prerequisite for normal automatisation), together with normal ability to learn during explicit practice.

The above studies were all designed using non-linguistic tasks, because use of language would significantly hinder the interpretation of any underlying problems, since it is expected that phonological problems and verbal working memory problems will be associated with dyslexia. Nonetheless, a major limitation of the learning framework discussed so far is that we have not addressed the issue of language, and in particular the question of whether there are declarative and procedural language systems corresponding to those for motor skills. Here we turn to the recent analyses of Michael Ullman (Ullman, 2004).

THE DECLARATIVE AND PROCEDURAL LANGUAGE SYSTEMS

Given that dyslexia has been seen as primarily a language-based disorder, many theorists have discounted insights from motor skill learning. However, Ullman (2004) applied the procedural/declarative categorisation to language skills, proposing that the 'Declarative Memory System' underlies the 'mental lexicon', subserving the acquisition, representation and use not only of knowledge about facts and events, but also about words. It depends centrally on medial temporal lobe structures involved in the encoding, consolidation and retrieval of new memories: the hippocampal region, entorhinal cortex, perirhinal cortex, parahippocampal cortex and ventro-lateral prefrontal cortex.

The 'Procedural Memory System' underpins the 'mental grammar' – the learning of new rule-based procedures that govern the regularities of language – together with the learning of new skills and the control of established sensori-motor and cognitive habits. It comprises the basal ganglia; frontal cortex, in particular Broca's area and pre-motor regions; parietal cortex; superior temporal cortex and the cerebellum. The system has clear commonalities with the cortico-striatal and cortico-cerebellar motor learning systems, the difference being that the language-based system interacts with the language-based regions of the frontal lobe, whereas the motor-skill system interacts with primary motor cortex. Both systems include pre-motor regions.

The neural systems framework for developmental disorders

We refer to the combined framework as the 'procedural learning system', highlighting the role in language and in motor skill, and also the role in skill acquisition as well as skill execution. The system is assumed to include cortico-striatal and cortico-cerebellar loops for both motor-related and language-related cortical regions. Interestingly, in his model, Ullman proposes that the declarative memory (DM) and procedural memory (PM) systems form a dynamically inter-acting network which yields both cooperative and competitive learning and processing, leading to a *see-saw effect*, such that a dysfunction of one system leads to enhanced learning in the other, or that learning in one system depresses functionality of the other. This would appear to be analogous to the 'conscious compensation' mechanism introduced in the automaticity deficit account (Nicolson and Fawcett, 1990) to explain that dyslexic individuals had to make relatively fuller use of their declarative system to compensate for weaknesses in their procedural system.

Turning to developmental disorders, Ullman argues that SLI may best be viewed as an impairment of procedural memory, resulting from the dysfunction of the brain structures underlying this system (Ullman and Gopnik, 1999). He notes that SLI is strongly associated with grammatical impairments, morphology, and phonology, whereas lexical knowledge is relatively spared. More critically, he argues that SLI is associated with deficits in motor skill and to abnormalities of the brain structures underlying procedural memory, especially Broca's area, the basal ganglia (particularly the caudate nucleus), SMA and the cerebellum. He also discusses dyslexia, ADHD and autism from this perspective.

In recent work (Nicolson and Fawcett, 2007) we have considerably extended this framework, suggesting that the developmental disorders can be considered fruitfully as affected by one or more of the possible neural systems for learning (see Figure 9.5). We distinguish between the declarative systems and the proce-dural systems, splitting the procedural system into a language-based component and a motor-based component, and then into the cortico-striatal and cortico-cerebellar components of each. It may be seen that the distinctions provide an outline typography for the major developmental disorders. It is evident, however, that this typography is still at best schematic, and much work is needed before such a classification can be fully justified.

REFLECTIONS

We have moved at considerable speed through a range of approaches to learning and dyslexia. Readers requiring a fuller treatment are referred to (Nicolson and Fawcett, 2008). It is time to take stock and reflect.

Initially we highlighted the complexity of the reading process, and suggested that one way of identifying the underlying problems was to attempt to 'trace the stream back' from the estuary, to identify which of the tributaries were affected. It must be said that the waters have turned out to be rather muddy, and that many tributaries flowing into the estuary!

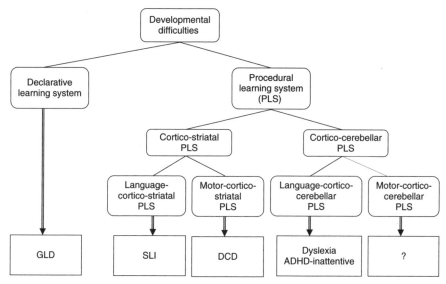

Figure 9.5   A neural systems typography for learning difficulties. Taken from Nicolson and Fawcett (2007).

In terms of the learning processes, we have demonstrated clearly that it is not just the language-related processes that are affected, but that many of the procedural learning processes – for motor skills as well as language skills – function at a relatively low level. The reasons for this are beyond the scope of this chapter. In a sister chapter we have outlined the reasons for thinking that impaired cerebellar circuitry is a prime candidate for this range of problems. This is made particularly plausible by the now-established roles of the cerebellum in language skills and in reading, as discussed in that chapter.

Nonetheless, it is also important to acknowledge that in many ways it is not important quite which parts of the brain are in fact the underlying cause. First, as discussed above, a wide variety of brain regions is involved in the neural circuitry for learning procedural and declarative skills, and consequently a problem in one or several regions is likely to lead to a similar difficulty say in automatisation of procedural language skills. Second, if an eight-year-old child is referred for difficulties in reading, the key requirement is to help the child rather than undertake brain scans (especially as the brain analyses are unlikely to lead to clearly different teaching and learning procedures).

We therefore conclude with two key questions.

How can we identify the specific brain regions affected?

Consider Figure 9.5. It provides an outline of which brain regions are likely to be affected in different developmental disorders. What it does not provide is some means of determining from which problems a particular individual suffers.

The problem of determining the underlying brain regions is aggravated by two major factors: first, the brain is 'plastic', changing itself to better exploit the regularities of its environment – see the 'neural commitment' component of the section on language acquisition. Different individuals will have made different adaptations to their brains by the age of six, thereby providing unique differences in the underlying circuitry as well as stored knowledge and skill. Studies of attainments in reading are therefore of only limited use in identifying the antecedent conditions. Second, neural circuits are designed to work cooperatively, and it is therefore very difficult to isolate the function of a single component. Even in situations such as eye blink conditioning or prism adaptation, which are thought to be relatively specific to the cerebellum, it is critical to note that different cerebellar sub-regions may well work independently, and so knowledge about prism adaptation does not in itself provide clear information about language automatisation.

Faced with these difficulties, one might conclude that it is not worthwhile to attempt to establish, for an individual, which brain regions are affected. Our view is to the contrary. The task is difficult but not impossible. We have a range of tools – brain imaging, genetic analyses fine-grain analyses of learning at different timescales – well suited to the task. The techniques have not yet proved effective because we have not yet determined a broad enough framework for analysis. For example, genetic analyses find specific loci, but cannot tie them well enough to the underlying causes because the phenotype (reading measures) is not specific enough (Fisher and Francks, 2006; Grigorenko, 2005; Ramus, 2006). Brain imaging studies of reading (Price and Mechelli, 2005; Shaywitz and Shaywitz, 2005; Turkeltaub et al., 2003) establish differences in the activation and development of brain regions associated with skilled reading, but do not indicate why this might be.

In our view, what is needed is a 'toolbox' of techniques for identifying problems in the various forms and stages of learning, and (ideally) for tying the problems down to some specific brain regions and (as discussed in the following section) for matching the problem to an appropriate remediation strategy. We have outlined several tools that are of clear utility. The response blending study (Nicolson and Fawcett, 2000) provides in the first 10 minutes a useful prediction of the motor skill learning component. Possibly analyses of the serial reaction time task will pin down effectiveness of statistical learning. Prism adaptation and eye blink conditioning provide reasonably specific evidence on other procedural learning parameters. Brain imaging studies such as (Nicolson et al., 1999) provide further valuable evidence. Of particular interest is the motor sequence learning study (Needle et al., under review) that suggests that the dyslexic participants had specific difficulties in overnight skill consolidation.

At present, however, we have simply not developed and validated enough tools to be able to dissect out the many components of the learning process. This must surely be a key objective for the next few years.

How can we best help dyslexic children with their reading problems?

Consider the response blending study (Nicolson and Fawcett, 2000). The 'square root rule' suggested that for a complex skill such as reading that may require say 10,000 stimulus presentations a dyslexic child might take 100 times longer (that is, one million presentations). It is evident that no intervention, however powerful, will be able to deliver this amount of support. This will lead to disillusion and even despair.

Interestingly, the traditional approaches to dyslexia support (Hickey, 1992; Miles, 1989; Orton, 1966) have recognised these difficulties, advocating a 'step at a time' approach, so that complex skills are split into sub-skills, such that the effective number of trials to mastery for each sub-skill is effectively reduced to achievable levels. A key requirement is of course that the sub-skills are truly mastered before being used as building blocks for the next skill.

The consolidation study (Needle et al., under review) is also particularly interesting. It seems to show that there is a danger that dyslexic children will lose much of their learning overnight. If so, this is a novel finding with considerable applied importance. It also provides a theoretical rationale for good practice in teaching which suggests that skills should be practised past mastery, and then refreshed on a daily basis.

Clearly we will be encroaching on the applied chapters in this handbook if we develop these themes further. See Nicolson and Fawcett (2004) for further analyses. In our view, however, a key goal for the next decade is to develop the toolbox of 'learning microtests' outlined in the preceding section, and then, for each learning type to develop methods of intervention that are tuned specifically to the characteristics of learners impaired in that dimension. If we were to achieve this we would have married the fields of cognitive neuroscience and of pedagogy, providing a new discipline of pedagogical neuroscience (Fawcett and Nicolson, 2007) that would transform the opportunities for dyslexic children, and for children with other developmental disorders.

REFERENCES

Anderson, J. R., (1982) 'Acquisition of cognitive skill', *Psychological Review*, 89: 369–406.

Baizer, J. S., Kralj-Hans, I. and Glickstein, M. (1999) 'Cerebellar lesions and prism adaptation in Macaque monkeys', *Journal of Neurophysiology*, 81: 1960–1965.

Birch, H. G. and Belmont, L. (1964) 'Auditory–visual integration in normal and retarded readers', *American Journal of Orthopsychiatry*, 34: 852–861.

Bradley, L. and Bryant, P. E. (1983) 'Categorising sounds and learning to read: A causal connection', *Nature*, 301: 419–421.

Brookes, R. L., Nicolson, R. I. and Fawcett, A. J. (2007) 'Prisms throw light on developmental disorders', *Neuropsychologia*, 45: 1921–1930.

Chomsky, N. (1965) *Aspects of the Theory of Syntax*. Dordrecht, Netherlands: Foris.

Chomsky, N. (1995) *The Minimalist Program*. Cambridge, MA: MIT Press.

Christian, K. M. and Thompson, R. F. (2003) 'Neural substrates of eyeblink conditioning: Acquisition and retention', *Learning and Memory*, 10: 427–455.

Coffin, J. M., Baroody, S., Schneider, K. and O'Neill, J. (2005) 'Impaired cerebellar learning in children with prenatal alcohol exposure: A comparative study of eyeblink conditioning in children with ADHD and dyslexia', *Cortex*, 41: 389–398.

Doya, K. (1999) 'What are the computations of the cerebellum, the basal ganglia and the cerebral cortex?', *Neural Networks*, 12: 961–974.

Doyon, J. and Benali, H. (2005) 'Reorganization and plasticity in the adult brain during learning of motor skills', *Current Opinion in Neurobiology*, 15: 1–7.

Doyon, J., Penhune, V. and Ungerleider, L. G. (2003) 'Distinct contribution of the cortico-striatal and cortico-cerebellar systems to motor skill learning', *Neuropsychologia*, 41: 252–262.

Doyon, J. and Ungerleider, L. G. (2002) 'Functional anatomy of motor skill learning', in L. R. Squire and D. L. Schacter, (eds), *Neuropsychology of Memory*. New York: Guilford Press, pp. 225–238.

Fawcett, A. J. and Nicolson, R. I. (1992) 'Automatisation deficits in balance for dyslexic children', *Perceptual and Motor Skills*, 75: 507–529.

Fawcett, A. J. and Nicolson, R. I. (1994) 'Naming speed in children with dyslexia', *Journal of Learning Disabilities*, 27: 641–646.

Fawcett, A. J. and Nicolson, R. I. (1995a) 'Persistence of phonological awareness deficits in older children with dyslexia', *Reading and Writing*, 7: 361–376.

Fawcett, A. J. and Nicolson, R. I. (1995b) 'Persistent deficits in motor skill for children with dyslexia', *Journal of Motor Behavior*, 27: 235–241.

Fawcett, A. J. and Nicolson, R. I. (2007) 'Dyslexia, learning, and pedagogical neuroscience', *Developmental Medicine and Child Neurology*, 49: 306–311.

Fisher, S. E. and Francks, C. (2006) 'Genes, cognition and dyslexia: Learning to read the genome', *Trends in Cognitive Sciences*, 10: 250–257.

Fitts, P. M. and Posner, M. I. (1967) *Human Performance*. Belmont, CA: Brooks Cole.

Gillingham, A. and Stillman, B. W. (1956) *Remedial Training*. Cambridge, MA: Education Publishing Service.

Grigorenko, E. L. (2005) 'A conservative meta-analysis of linkage and linkage-association studies of developmental dyslexia', *Scientific Studies of Reading*, 9: 285–316.

Henry, M. K. (1998) 'Structured, sequential, multisensory teaching: The Orton legacy', *Annals of Dyslexia*, 48: 3–26.

Hickey, K. (1992) The Hickey Multisensory Language Course. 2nd edition. J. Augur and S. Briggs, (eds.) London: Whurr.

Howard, J. H., Howard, D. V., Japikse, K. C. and Eden, G. F. (2006) 'Dyslexics are impaired on implicit higher-order sequence learning, but not on implicit spatial context learning', *Neuropsychologia*, 44: 1131–1144.

Huey, E. B. (1908) *The Psychology and Pedagogy of Reading*. New York: Macmillan.

Karni, A., Meyer, G., Rey-Hipolito, C., Jezzard, P., Adams, M. M., Turner, R. and Ungerleider, L. G. (1998) 'The acquisition of skilled motor performance: Fast and slow experience-driven changes in primary motor cortex', *Proceedings of the National Academy of Sciences of the United States of America*, 95: 861–868.

Korman, M., Raz, N., Flash, T. and Karni, A. (2003) 'Multiple shifts in the representation of a motor sequence during the acquisition of skilled performance', *Proceedings of the National Academy of Sciences of the United States of America*, 100: 12492–12497.

Kuhl, P. K. (2000) 'A new view of language acquisition', *Proceedings of the National Academy of Sciences of the United States of America*, 97: 11850–11857.

Kuhl, P. K. (2004) 'Early language acquisition: Cracking the speech code', *Nature Reviews Neuroscience*, 5: 831–843.

Maschke, M., Erichsen, M., Drepper, J., Jentzen, W., Muller, S. P., Kolb, F. P., Diener, H. C. and Timmann, D. (2003) 'Cerebellar representation of the eyeblink response as revealed by PET', *Neuroreport*, 14: 1371–1374.

Menghini, D., Hagberg, G. E., Caltagirone, C., Petrosini, L. and Vicari, S. (2006) 'Implicit learning deficits in dyslexic adults: An fMRI study', *NeuroImage*, 33: 1218–1226.

Miles, E. (1989) *The Bangor Dyslexia Teaching System*. London: Whurr.

Needle, J. L., Nicolson, R. I. and Fawcett, A. J. (under review) 'Motor sequence learning and dyslexia: Is consolidation the key?'.

Newell, A. and Rosenbloom, P. S. (1981) 'Mechanisms of skill acquisition and the law of practice', in J. R. Anderson, (ed.), *Cognitive Skills and their Acquisition*. Hillsdale, NJ: Lawrence Erlbaum.

Nicolson, R. I., Daum, I., Schugens, M. M., Fawcett, A. J. and Schulz, A. (2002) 'Eyeblink conditioning indicates cerebellar abnormality in dyslexia', *Experimental Brain Research*, 143: 42–50.

Nicolson, R. I. and Fawcett, A. J. (1990) 'Automaticity: A new framework for dyslexia research?', *Cognition*, 35: 159–182.

Nicolson, R. I. and Fawcett, A. J. (1994) 'Reaction times and dyslexia', *Quarterly Journal of Experimental Psychology*, 47A: 29–48.

Nicolson, R. I. and Fawcett, A. J. (2000) 'Long-term learning in dyslexic children', *European Journal of Cognitive Psychology*, 12: 357–393.

Nicolson, R. I. and Fawcett, A. J. (2004) 'Climbing the reading mountain:
Learning from the science of learning', in G. Reid and A. J. Fawcett, (eds.) *Dyslexia in Context: Research, Policy and Practice*. London: Whurr.

Nicolson, R. I. and Fawcett, A. J. (2007) 'Procedural learning difficulties: Re-uniting the developmental disorders?', *Trends in Neurosciences*, 30: 135–141.

Nicolson, R. I. and Fawcett, A. J. (2008) *Dyslexia, Learning and the Brain*. Boston, MA: MIT Press.

Nicolson, R. I., Fawcett, A. J., Berry, E. L., Jenkins, I. H., Dean, P. and Brooks, D. J. (1999) 'Association of abnormal cerebellar activation with motor learning difficulties in dyslexic adults', *Lancet*, 353: 1662–1667.

Orton, J. L. (1966) 'The Orton-Gillingham approach', in J. Money, (ed.), *The disabled reader: Education of the dyslexic child*. Baltimore, MD: Johns Hopkins Press.

Price, C. J. and Mechelli, A. (2005) 'Reading and reading disturbance', *Current Opinion in Neurobiology*, 15: 231–238.

Ramus, F. (2006) 'Genes, brain and cognition: A roadmap for the cognitive scientist', *Cognition*, 101: 247–269.

Shaywitz, S. E. and Shaywitz, B. A. (2005) 'Dyslexia (specific reading disability)', *Biological Psychiatry*, 57: 1301–1309.

Snowling, M. (1987) *Dyslexia: A Cognitive Developmental Perspective*. Oxford: Blackwell.

Squire, L. R. (1987) *Memory and Brain*. Oxford: Oxford University Press.

Squire, L. R., Knowlton, B. and Musen, G. (1993) 'The structure and organisation of memory', *Annual Review of Psychology*, 44: 453–495.

Stanovich, K. E. (1988) 'The right and wrong places to look for the cognitive locus of reading disability', *Annals of Dyslexia*, 38: 154–177.

Turkeltaub, P. E., Gareau, L., Flowers, D. L., Zeffiro, T. A. and Eden, G. F. (2003) 'Development of neural mechanisms for reading', *Nature Neuroscience*, 6: 767–773.

Ullman, M. T. (2004) 'Contributions of memory circuits to language: The declarative/procedural model', *Cognition*, 92: 231–270.

Ullman, M. T. and Gopnik, M. (1999) 'Inflectional morphology in a family with specific language impairment', *Applied Psycholinguistics*, 20: 51–117.

Vellutino, F. R. (1979) *Dyslexia: Theory and Research*. Cambridge, MA: MIT Press.

Vellutino, F. R. (1987). 'Dyslexia'. *Scientific-American*, 256(3): 34–41.

Vellutino, F. R., Scanlon, D. M. (1982). Verbal processing in poor and normal readers. In C. J. Brainerd M. Pressley (eds.), Verbal processes in children (pp. 189–264). New York: Springer-Verlag.

Vicari, S., Finzi, A., Menghini, D., Marotta, L., Baldi, S. and Petrosini, L. (2005) 'Do children with developmental dyslexia have an implicit learning deficit?', *Journal of Neurology Neurosurgery and Psychiatry*, 76: 1392–1397.

10

A Review of the Evidence on Morphological Processing in Dyslexics and Poor Readers: A Strength or Weakness?

S. Hélène Deacon, Rauno Parrila
and John R. Kirby

This chapter

i) reviews current conceptualizations of morphological processing in dyslexics and poor readers;
ii) considers the impacts of participant and task characteristics on empirical investigations;
iii) examines the evidence on morphological strengths and weaknesses in dyslexics and poor readers; and
iv) concludes with suggestions for next steps in research.

INTRODUCTION

This chapter describes the current conceptualizations and studies of morphological processing in dyslexics and poor readers. These findings support the existence of both morphological strengths and weaknesses in these individuals. Accordingly, we investigated the conditions within which findings of strengths and weaknesses emerge, specifically targeting the types of tasks and the participant characteristics. Our review suggests that reciprocal relationships among reading related variables may explain findings of strengths and weaknesses.

Morphology may provide a compensatory avenue of instruction for dyslexics and poor readers, and may be the means by which some individuals have overcome dyslexia. In this chapter we will provide suggestions for a framework for the evaluation of the evidence to date and for the design of new research.

A REVIEW OF THE EVIDENCE

Children and adults with reading difficulties, as a group, have difficulties with tasks involving the manipulation of sounds, or phonemes (for reviews see National Reading Panel, 2000; Snowling, 2000). Accordingly, phonological processing is a central concept in most theoretical models (see e.g., Vellutino and Fletcher, 2005, for a review) and in some definitions (for example, IDA, 2006) of dyslexia. In striking contrast to this near empirical and theoretical unanimity, morphological processing, another key component of language, is depicted both as a strength and as a weakness in empirical research with dyslexics. Morphemes are the smallest units of meaning in language, for example, *magician = magic + ian*, and they affect pronunciation and spelling of a range of words in English and in many other orthographies. For example, the pronunciation of the letters *ea* in *reading* and *react* is determined by the placement of the morpheme boundary in the two words (*read + ing* and *re + act*), and reference to the morphemes could help in understanding the meaning of these words. Processing of these units of meaning generally plays a minimal, or no role in theoretical models of reading and reading disabilities, in which morphological processing is typically characterized as a late emerging ability that builds on the core foundation of phonological knowledge (e.g., Seymour, 1999; Ehri, 2005). The question that we address in this chapter, through a review of the empirical evidence to date, is whether morphological processing is a relative linguistic strength or weakness for readers who experience difficulty in learning to read their native language.

This is an important question to address for several reasons. First of all, we need to ask whether morphological ability is as fundamentally affected in these individuals as are other language abilities such as phonological awareness. Answering this question would tell us about the origins and the pervasiveness of the effects on morphology. Secondly, we need to establish boundaries around the reading difficulty to define the conditions in which morphology is an area of strength or of weakness. Finally, if morphology is an area of relative strength, it may serve as a medium for instruction, especially in dyslexics who are known to have fundamental weaknesses in other areas (e.g., phonology).

For simplicity of expression in this chapter, we use the term dyslexics to refer to individuals with more clearly diagnosed reading disabilities and poor readers for those with well below average reading abilities without specified cause. As will become clear, few studies have used a strict definition of dyslexia, so our conclusions may be more about poor readers than dyslexics per se. In using the term dyslexia, we do not make any assumptions about the root causes of the reading difficulties or about their malleability. Certainly, both the choice of participants and the measure of morphological abilities can affect results.

CURRENT CONCEPTUALIZATIONS OF MORPHOLOGICAL PROCESSING IN DYSLEXICS: EXPLANATIONS OF MORPHOLOGICAL PROCESSING WEAKNESSES

There is extensive evidence of morphological difficulties in dyslexics and poor readers, at least in comparison to same age peers. It is possible that this deficit is due to a fundamental difficulty in the area of morphology that is also responsible, at least in part, for their reading problems. Leikin and Zur Hagit (2006) argued that this interpretation is implicit in the research demonstrating two findings: a deficit in morphological awareness in dyslexics (e.g., Abu-Rabia et al., 2003) and a contribution of morphological awareness to reading that is independent of phonological awareness (e.g., Nagy et al., 2003). Yet, as we will see in the review that follows, few, if any, researchers would explicitly argue that poor morphological awareness is a causal factor in the development of dyslexia.

Perhaps the most common explanation of morphological difficulties is based on the long-standing research documenting the important role of phonological abilities in typical reading development (e.g., Bradley and Bryant, 1983; National Reading Panel, 2000). This approach advocates that phonological difficulties are the primary deficit and that these in turn cause both morphological and reading problems (e.g., Shankweiler et al., 1995). According to this proposition, the phonological quality of morphemes makes them more difficult to access and manipulate in oral language tasks.

Central deficits other than phonology have been nominated as causes of both morphological and some forms of reading difficulties. One possibility is that dyslexics have deficits in morphological awareness due to general language delays (see Joanisse et al., 2000), especially given that morphology is considered to be a sensitive indicator of language ability (see e.g., Leonard et al., 1997). Similarly, there has been some suggestion that dyslexics differ from normal readers in metalinguistic processing in general. Leikin and Zur Hagit (2006) suggested that dyslexics might be *more* likely to use morphological decomposition as a means of lexical access than typically developing readers, due to a relative weakness in grapheme-to-phoneme decoding skills (due to phonological processing difficulties) and to more widely based difficulties with metalinguistic processing. Findings of differences in lexical access also suggest that quantitative differences in the size of the lexicon are likely less important than qualitative differences in its morphological organization or in the specificity of these morphologically based representations.

More complex views are emerging in recent research, particularly in advocating for reciprocal relationships between several variables. Tsesmeli and Seymour (2006) suggested that reading ability may limit the development of explicit morphological knowledge, resulting in similarity to reading-level matches in some morphological tasks. Morphemic representations can only be made explicit in the orthographic lexicon once literacy development is relatively advanced, a stage that some poor readers and dyslexics do not necessarily reach. Difficulties with reading acquisition are also likely to lead to less developed orthographic representations, and, according to Egan and Pring (2004), this in turn may affect the ability to represent morphological information in print, resulting in poorer performance on spelling based tasks. Views of the reciprocal relationships among phonological and morphological awareness and reading often still place the greatest emphasis on difficulties with phonology.

To summarize, the vast majority of current positions see any morphological processing weaknesses as secondary to primary deficits in some other domain (e.g., general language skills or phonological processing).

EXPLANATIONS OF RELATIVE MORPHOLOGICAL PROCESSING STRENGTHS

Some researchers have advocated that morphological processing could be a domain of strength for dyslexics, at least at certain stages of reading development. Bryant et al. posited that children who develop reading difficulties initially have a relative 'linguistic strength [in morphology] as well as linguistic weakness [in phonology]' (1998: 509). Despite beginning the learning trajectory with strong morphological skills, children's initially low phonological abilities hold back their reading and spelling skills. Given the reciprocal relationships between phonological abilities and learning to read (Goswami and Bryant, 1990; Perfetti et al., 1987), development of dyslexics' phonological awareness and decoding skills may be held back even further due to reliance on morphological strategies. Poor initial decoding in turn leads to a lack of exposure to print which then constrains further development of morphological abilities. In contrast to the phonological deficit approach, this hypothesis specifies that early morphological strengths can co-occur with phonological difficulties, and that this early reliance on morphological awareness can be detrimental to reading development.

Elbro and Arnbak (1996) suggested that the use of morphology can support reading, at least amongst older dyslexics who are actively compensating for reading difficulties. This view is based on the assumption that dyslexics' primary difficulties lie elsewhere (e.g., in phonology). While Elbro and Arnbak do not specify how such a strength may emerge, it is worthwhile to consider the possibility that any morphological 'strengths' may in fact be only relative to weaknesses in phonological processing (Bryant et al., 1998).

Regardless of its origins, we need to specify how such an alternative route through morphology to reading may work. Written morphemes are essentially orthographic units that can be recognized quickly, just as lexical units are recognized quickly within either dual-route (Coltheart et al., 2001) or connectionist

(Plaut, 2005) models. Morphological processing could help to bypass or minimize dependence upon phonological processing, which is known to be weak in dyslexics. The use of morphological information may help to speed lexical access, and this hypothesis is clearly dependent on the widespread evidence of lexical organization that depends at least in part on morphology (e.g., Marslen-Wilson et al., 1994). This has not, to our knowledge, been specified in Coltheart et al.'s model, though it could manifest through the hypothesized third (semantic) route. Alternatively, it is possible that morphemes become decoding units that are generalizable across words. There are at least two (possible) benefits to morphemes in this regard: many are visually the same across words (providing repetitions in processing if processed as a unit), and, given their status as meaning-units, they should be easier to activate than meaningless bigrams and trigrams. These are all potential explanations of how morphology could support effective reading.

CRITICAL ISSUES TO CONSIDER

It is necessary to consider the nature of the tasks and participant samples employed. This informs the analysis of studies utilizing a wide range of tasks with groups of poor readers that vary greatly in their composition.

Participants and design

There are two main issues to consider regarding the possible effects of participants on the observed results: (a) how the poor reader or dyslexic group was defined, and (b) how the dyslexic or poor reader and control groups(s) are matched. The optimal design depends upon the theoretical framework selected and questions posed. We illustrate the complexities with a few examples below.

When researchers identify participants as dyslexics or poor readers there is potential for large variability between studies in oral (e.g., phonological and vocabulary) or written (orthographic) skills that may be relevant to performance in morphological processing tasks. To give an example, two widely publicized definitions of dyslexia by ICD-10 (World Health Organization, 2006) and DSM-IV (American Psychiatric Association, 1994) both conceptualize reading broadly ('reading achievement' in DSM-IV, and 'reading skill' in ICD-10). In contrast, many researchers and organizations have advocated for more limited definitions that focus on word reading (e.g., Berninger, 2001; Lyon et al., 2003). The latest definition adopted by the International Dyslexia Association (2006; Lyon et al., 2003) focuses on word reading, and it includes an additional causal assumption of phonological processing deficit as the 'typical' cause of word reading problems, with potential reading comprehension, reduced reading experience, vocabulary, and background knowledge problems as secondary.

The variability in the definitions should make the danger for research consumers obvious: Studies on individuals with dyslexia (or specific reading disability) may examine quite different samples of individuals depending on the definitional framework researchers adopted and assumptions made. This has been demonstrated by several researchers. For example, Share and Leikin (2004) showed that using decontextualized word reading accuracy rather than reading comprehension as the criterion can change which children are classified as reading disabled: in their sample, only 35 per cent of the children showing a deficit in one measure also showed a deficit in the other measure. Perhaps more importantly, the two groups showed only partially overlapping profiles on other language skills. Children classified as reading disabled on the basis of decontextualized word reading accuracy were inferior to a same age and IQ control group on phoneme segmentation, whereas differences in syntactic and semantic abilities were not statistically significant. In contrast, children classified as reading disabled on the basis of reading comprehension were poorer than a control group on all language measures (see also Bishop and Adams, 1990). These results suggest that if word reading (or decoding) performance is used to identify the participants as poor readers, as advocated by many researchers, the resulting sample will likely have more limited general language deficiencies than when a broader selection of reading tasks is used as advocated by ICD-10 and DSM-IV.

In the choice of control groups, the critical issues are whether and how reading level (RL) and general abilities (GA) are matched. The procedure traditionally advocated in reading research (see e.g., Goswami and Bryant, 1989) is to use two control groups, one consisting of normally achieving participants matched on chronological age (CA) and GA, and the other consisting of normally achieving (usually younger) participants matched on RL and GA. The logic behind this design is that if the poor readers perform poorer than RL+GA matched controls, then reading ability (or experience with print) cannot explain the difference. As a result, the assessed skills can be treated as potential causal factors in poor reading (e.g., Goswami and Bryant, 1989), or possibly as secondary deficits related to the primary deficit that also causes poor reading, as in the phonological deficit hypothesis (see above). On the other hand, if the poor readers perform equally to the CA+GA matched, but better reading, controls on some tasks, it is unlikely that the skills measured by these tasks are associated with poor reading. No differences in RL+GA match comparisons or differences in CA+GA matched comparisons are more difficult to interpret; many argue that these cannot be interpreted in any clear manner (e.g., Goswami and Bryant, 1989), while others suggest that such findings can identify important variables in reading development if replicated across a number of studies with a variety of measures and if they fit a coherent theory of reading acquisition (Vellutino and Scanlon, 1989).

A critical issue for RL+GA matching is that the use of different reading and general cognitive ability tests as criteria for matching can lead both to identifying very different kinds of children as poor readers (see Share and Leikin [2004] example above) and to differently composed control groups. RL matching can be even more challenging when poor readers are older. For example, Deacon et al. (2006) presented data on dyslexic university students (mean age 30 years) whose mean performance levels in word decoding, word identification, and reading comprehension were comparable to those of grade 7, grade 11, and second-year university students, respectively (see also Bruck, 1990). In this particular study, RL matching on the basis of any one reading measure would have resulted in groups that would have differed not only on other reading measures but possibly also on many additional relevant characteristics, such as general language skills, background knowledge, and reading experience, which is the key feature of RL matching.

Similarly, the criterion for general ability matters. The choice of verbal or performance IQ can have a large impact on how many children are identified with a discrepancy between reading and general ability and to whom their performance is compared. Bishop and Snowling (2004, Figure 3) showed that far fewer children show the discrepancy between reading and general ability when verbal IQ is used as the criterion in comparison to performance IQ. Verbal IQ (usually measured with a vocabulary test) is also correlated highly with other language deficits, such as specific language impairment (SLI), that result in syntactic and semantic problems and frequently in poor reading (Bishop and Snowling, 2004; Catts et al., 1994), whereas performance IQ is less correlated with language deficits. As a result, using performance IQ as a criterion is more likely to result in a poor reading or dyslexic group that includes children who have both reading and other language-based problems, such as SLI (Bishop and Snowling, 2004), that are likely to be linked to morphological processing (e.g., Leonard et al., 1997). On the other hand, poor reading progress has been associated with significant declines in verbal IQ over time (e.g., Bishop and Butterworth, 1980; Share, et al. 1989), making verbal IQ a problematic criterion of general ability (Share and Silva, 2003), particularly with older children and adults with dyslexia.

A related issue is the scores used to match students. As GA matching is frequently done on the basis of standard scores, this means that very different raw scores are needed for the standard scores to be equivalent between individuals that differ greatly in age (e.g., comparing adults with grade 7 students). The general language knowledge (such as vocabulary) and experiences of an adult with a standard score of 100 are not the same as those of a grade 7 student with the same verbal IQ standard score and word reading level. To the extent that general language knowledge is dissociated from word reading (a common modularity assumption) but not from morphological processing, we would expect the older poor readers in studies with this kind of comparisons to show relative strengths in morphology (see below for evidence of this).

In sum, if dyslexia, or poor reading ability, is defined as a word recognition problem whose primary cause is deficient phonological processing abilities (but not a general language deficit), then more credible evidence of the relationship between morphological ability and dyslexia or poor reading ability would come from the use of verbal IQ as the general ability criterion for matching, or ensuring that the sample does not exhibit more generalized language processing problems. In addition, matching samples on the basis of phonological processing, vocabulary (raw scores), orthographic processing, or general language ability may be necessary before we can isolate morphological processing as a primary cause of poor reading or as a secondary deficit.

A taxonomy of morphological tasks

It is important to consider the measures that are used to assess morphological processing. Because of the known cognitive weaknesses of less able readers (e.g., phonological awareness, and naming and word reading speed), these individuals' performance on morphological tasks could be seriously compromised under certain task constraints. Morphological processing has not been studied from a construct validity or latent trait perspective; what follows is therefore an 'armchair' task analysis of the domain, and the likely implications for research with poor or disabled readers. The construct of morphological processing concerns the mental representations of morphemes and the manipulation/use of those representations. Morphemes are either bases or affixes; a stem is a base plus one or more affixes, to which a further affix can be added. For example, *sign* is a base, and the affixes *re-*, or *–al* make new words; each could be a stem for further derivations: *re + sign + ing* or *sign + al + ing*. Someone with greater morphological processing ability would have a greater number of morphological representations, and/or have more efficient access to those representations, and/or be able to manipulate those representations more efficiently. Morphological awareness involves the 'conscious awareness of the morphemic structure of words and (the) ... ability to reflect on and manipulate that structure' (Carlisle, 1995: 194). Morphological awareness could be seen as a subset of morphological processing tasks in which explicit awareness of morphemes is required (see process section below), but this may be difficult to determine, and in many cases, researchers have used it to refer to performance on almost any morphological processing task. Typically, the term morphological awareness has been used to describe tasks administered to children, and these often require productive generation of correct morphological forms, while the term morphological processing is generally used to describe performance on more implicit tasks such as lexical decision often used with adults. Broadly speaking, there are three task dimensions that are relevant: modality of input/output, content, and process. Each of these, in different ways, may affect the performance of poor readers in general and of dyslexics in particular.

Input and output modality

Morphological tasks may be presented orally or in writing, and accordingly, responses can be gathered in either of these formats. At first glance it would seem that oral presentation would put less stress upon the weakness of the poor reader or dyslexic, and, as a result, run less risk of confounding the morphological skill with other abilities (especially reading). And yet, one must be concerned about possible verbal short-term memory difficulties (e.g., Avons and Hanna, 1995).

In terms of written presentation, it would of course be invalid to infer that individuals who could not read the morphological task had a morphological weakness, unless findings were confirmed with oral tasks. This concern is particularly relevant to beginning readers. Written presentation may allow greater application of morphological skill for adult readers, and perhaps even for children, because English orthography preserves morphology so consistently. Some poor readers and dyslexics, especially older ones, may have enough reading ability to process the task content, and a written presentation may avoid their well-established phonological weaknesses (Bowers and Kirby, 2006). Further, it is important to remember that in written presentation, every morpheme is also an orthographic unit. Dyslexics and poor readers are likely to have reduced orthographic knowledge (through lack of reading experience and lack of successful phonological decoding experiences), and so it is necessary to determine whether poor performance on a morphological task can be explained by deficits in orthographic knowledge.

Responses in morphological tasks may be oral or written. A written response may stress working memory and thus on other aspects of processing, especially given that phonological working memory is a well-known area of weakness in dyslexics and yet spoken responses can stress the articulatory system (Catts, 1989). A further question lies in whether speed or accuracy is the dependent measure. A task can be speeded either by measuring response time or by providing a limited amount of time for the task. This may be critical for dyslexics, in that many have reading speed problems.

Task content

A number of important content variations have been employed. One distinction can be made between inflectional and derivational morphology. English inflections are relatively few in number and straightforward, so many of these may be mastered early, especially orally (e.g., Berko, 1958). However, some inflections can be more difficult to recognize orally because of inconsistent phonology (e.g., the various sounds of past tense verb inflections). Derivations are more numerous and more likely to involve phonological and orthographic changes, and some are relatively unfamiliar. Thus derivational tasks may discriminate better among older or more able readers, because older readers should know all of the inflections and therefore show little variability. However, the risk is that rarer derivations will be unknown to dyslexics or poor readers because of their reduced reading experience – thus poor performance may be due to a lack of vocabulary, not morphological skill.

A second content factor concerns whether phonological or orthographic shifts take place when morphemes are added to a base or stem. For example, the morphological link between related words can be made more difficult by pronunciation shift (e.g., *sign* and *signal*) or orthographic changes (e.g, *cosy* and *cosiness*). Both types of shift may affect poor readers more than better readers. Coping with multiple phonological representations for the same morpheme may place more stress on phonological ability. Orthographic shifts may cause problems (at least in visual presentation) for those with less reading experience, such as poor or dyslexic readers, who may have had fewer opportunities to see particular morphemes or derivations.

Poor or dyslexic readers may be more affected by low frequency of words due to reduced reading experience. This may be especially true for written stimulus presentations, but, because many advanced words are learned through print, this may also be true for orally presented words. Word length may also differentially affect dyslexics. Longer words are often less frequent and require sublexical processing, which could increase task demands that may affect less able readers more (e.g., van der Leij and van Daal, 1999; Zoccolotti et al., 2005). Such concerns highlight the importance of control words. If a particular difficulty in morphology is being investigated, performance needs to be contrasted with words of equal frequency, and phonological and orthographic complexity (such as 'pseudo-derived' words like *corn* and *corner*, e.g., Deacon et al., 2006).

Task or process

There are a number of critical variations in tasks and of cognitive processes underlying these tasks. One concerns whether the task requires explicit or only implicit knowledge. For example, in a sentence completion task, participants could perform well just by judging what 'sounds best'; this is a type of implicit knowledge, whereas a task that requires specific identification of morphemes would draw on more explicit knowledge. This explicit awareness of morphology may be a key feature in the application of oral language to written language (see e.g., Casalis et al., 2004). A related question is whether the task requires choice between provided alternatives (judgement) or production of a response. Production tasks are generally more difficult, and guessing rates are much lower in them; they may distinguish among poor readers better than among better readers.

EXAMINING THE EVIDENCE TO DATE

Evidence for morphological problems in poor readers

The comparison of elementary school age poor readers to same age peers has been a common approach in the research literature to date. As discussed above, observed differences in CA designs are difficult to interpret as they cannot be attributed unambiguously to any single source of individual differences. As such, these studies could identify potentially important relationships between dyslexia and morphological processing for further examination if the dyslexic sample meets stringent constraints, such as selection within a strict definition of dyslexia (decoding and word reading problems), the elimination of a more general language deficit, and the matching of the CA comparison group on the basis of verbal IQ. As we will see below, these conditions were not really met by any of the studies. Nevertheless, CA differences, or the lack thereof, can be informative about students' strengths and weaknesses, which would be important for instructional planning.

A number of researchers have demonstrated poorer morphological performance by children who are poor readers in comparison to same age peers.[1] Leong (1989b) showed that poor readers (selected on the basis of an aggregate reading comprehension and vocabulary score) in grades 4 to 6 were slower than their better-reading peers in reading words when these were divided according to morphological rather than phonological divisions (e.g., *ACTor* versus *ACtor*, respectively; Taft, 1979). They were also slower in generating correct base and derived forms to complete sentences (based on Carlisle, 1988; see Leong and Parkinson, 1995, for similar results in repetition priming tasks). Out of a large battery of tasks, reaction times in the morphological production task, especially those items involving orthographic changes (e.g., *funny - funnier*), were most clearly related to reading and spelling ability within the poor reader group (Leong, 1989a). Further, the poor readers did not have disproportionate difficulty with any one type of morphological transformation (e.g., comparing phonological change to no change). This pattern conflicts with that from two later studies. Fowler and Liberman (1995) examined children aged 7 to 9 years old whose word reading skills were average but decoding skills were slightly below average. Like Leong (1989b), Fowler and Liberman reported that compared to peers of similar age and verbal IQ, poor readers experienced greater difficulties with Carlisle's production task, even in an untimed format. And yet the poor readers in this study experienced particular difficulty with the derived forms involving phonological changes between the base and the derived word (e.g., *heal - health*). Shankweiler et al. (1995) examined 7- to 9-year-old dyslexics selected on the basis of (a) showing a clear discrepancy between word reading or decoding performance and full-scale IQ scores, or (b) exhibiting poor performance in one or both of the reading tests in spite of normal IQ. They found a similar pattern of heightened difficulties on the morphological tasks involving phonological changes, in addition to generally poorer performance on morphological awareness and phonological tasks in comparison to chronological age controls (who had much higher full-scale IQ). Further, for the group of children as a whole, morphological awareness contributed 5 per cent of the single word reading variance, after controlling phoneme awareness and IQ. Poor readers' greater difficulty with the production of morphologically complex words to complete sentences in comparison to same age peers has emerged across several studies, but special difficulties with items involving a phonological change in the stem (taken to support a phonological deficit as the core difficulty) are not found consistently.

Poorer performance on morphological tasks than same age peers has also emerged in studies with adolescent poor readers. Carlisle et al. (2001) compared 10- to 15-year-old poor readers (defined on the basis of depressed word reading and normal verbal IQ scores) and CA match controls (who had significantly higher word reading and vocabulary scores). While all of the readers were less accurate and slower in their responses to naming and lexical decision tasks with multi-morphemic words with phonological changes in the stem (e.g., comparing *natural* and *cultural*), the phonological changes were particularly problematic for the poor readers. Shankweiler et al. (1996) tested morphological skills, with oral production and written tasks, of 16-year-old learning disabled adolescents (many of whom did not meet the criteria for reading disability but as a group showed depressed reading performance) and 14-year-old typically developing readers who were not matched on the basis of IQ, reading, or any other perform-ance. Their results showed that the learning-disabled adolescents had greater difficulties with morphological and phonological tasks in comparison to normal readers. Difficulties with spelling included poorer performance with morpholog-ically complex words, as well as with orthographically complex words. Findings of greater difficulties than same age peers across a range of tasks do not allow us to disentangle the different explanations of morphological difficulties.

The few studies of the morphological abilities of adults with reading difficulties have also uncovered poorer performance than same age peers. Fischer et al. (1985) compared two groups of undergraduate students: poor spellers (spelling skills on average 4 years below grade level) and good spellers (grade level spelling skills). Their analyses suggested that poor adult spellers were relatively insensitive to the morphemic composition of words and non words in spelling tasks in comparison to their same age peers with good spelling abilities. Fischer et al. concluded that difficulties with spelling are partly accounted for by differences in the appreciation of morphological consistencies in spelling. Leikin and Zur Hagit (2006) made a similar comparison in their examination of college students with a childhood diagnosis of dyslexia and same-age performance-IQ-matched peers, but emerged with a more complex picture. The dyslexics were poorer than their peers on more traditional morphological awareness tasks involving manipulation of morphemes, but they were similar on a masked priming task. Notably, dyslexic participants had greater benefit from morphological priming than regular readers. The authors concluded that dyslexics' lexical representations were relatively intact, and that the greater priming may reflect heightened reliance on a slower morphological decomposition route (see e.g., Chialant and Caramazza, 1995) by the 'greatly compensated' dyslexics, rather than faster whole word recognition through orthographic or phonological codes. One problem in interpreting these results lies in the selection of comparison groups, as with all studies with same age peers, and yet it is not clear what the perfect control group might be in a study of adult dyslexics. We will return to this issue.

Within the studies comparing performance to same age peers, one study stands out in its advocacy for morphological awareness as a core deficit. This comes from work by Shu et al. (2006) on the acquisition of a morphosyllabic orthography by Chinese developmental dyslexics in grades 5 and 6 (selected on the basis of depressed character recognition scores). Path analyses revealed that morphological awareness, assessed with a production task, made a much greater contribution to reading outcomes than did phonological awareness. Shu et al. suggested that morphological awareness may be 'a core theoretical construct necessary for explaining variability in reading Chinese' (p. 122), usurping the traditional authority of phonological awareness. It is highly likely, as they suggest, that this is due to the primacy of the morpheme in Chinese orthography. Alternatively, it is also possible that the dyslexic group experienced more general language problems rather than phonological problems usually associated with dyslexia as the two groups were similar on nonverbal IQ, but significantly different on verbal IQ (measured with vocabulary). These results highlight the need to consider both the comparison group and the orthography under acquisition.

In sum, several studies have utilized CA comparison design and reported that poor readers exhibit morphological processing problems. Findings of accentuated difficulty with phonological change items have been taken to implicate phono-logical processing as the core difficulty (e.g., Fowler and Liberman, 1995), but this pattern has not emerged in all cases (see e.g., Leong, 1989b). However, the observed differences in these studies may not tell us much about morphological processing in dyslexics as participants have seldom fit a strict definition of dyslexia, a more general language deficit was not controlled, and, with the exception of Fowler and Liberman, verbal IQ was not used as the matching criterion for the CA comparison group.

COMPARISONS TO YOUNGER NORMALLY READING PARTICIPANTS

More clear evidence on the possibility that morphological difficulties are a causal factor in dyslexia can come from studies using reading level matched control groups (e.g., Goswami and Bryant, 1989). As we noted earlier, the key assumption here is that if dyslexics perform more poorly than reading level matched controls, then reading ability (or experience with print) itself cannot explain any differences in morphological processing. Further, to distinguish whether morphological processing problems are primary or secondary to more fundamental deficits, we need to consider the basis for matching of reading level (decoding, word reading, or comprehension) and general ability (verbal or performance IQ), or to otherwise control for alternative explanations, such as general language or phonological processing skills.

Findings of dyslexics' insensitivity to morphological information come from Giraudo (2001) who reported on a comparison between 10-year-old English dyslexic children and 8-year-old typically developing children. She employed a priming task in which either derived or pseudo-derived words (e.g., *pottery* and *potato*, respectively) were presented prior to target words (e.g., *pot*). Eight-year-old normally developing children were significantly faster at recognizing words primed by morphological relatives, but there was no such difference for the 10-year-old dyslexic children. It is not clear from this report whether the two groups were balanced for reading abilities, nor is it clear what definition of dyslexia was employed to identify participants. Nevertheless, these results can be taken to indicate that morphological processing is not a strength in young dyslexics, in contrast with Leikin and Zur Hagit's (2006) study with adults, suggesting that morphologically driven lexical access may come only with greater reading experience.

Similar findings of poorer performance on morphological tasks come from Abu-Rabia et al.'s (2003) examination of the acquisition of Arabic orthography, a writing system in which the pronunciation of words is based on the addition of vowel patterns (infixes) to written root forms (or more extensive word forms) that are consonantal patterns. Abu-Rabia et al. targeted ten-year-old dyslexic children (selected on the basis of severely depressed word reading and spelling performance) and two groups of control children: CA matched and younger children who had significantly better word reading, spelling, and performance IQ standard scores than the dyslexics; as a result of these differences, ANCOVAs were used to adjust for differences in word reading and IQ.[2] The extensive battery of tasks included two morphological tasks, in which participants were asked to decide if words presented in a written format were from the same morphological family and to orally generate as many morphological relatives as possible for a base form. The dyslexic children performed less well than both comparison groups in performance on these two tasks (see Abu-Rabia, 2006, for similar results in a chronological age match design). The fact that dyslexic children performed worse than younger participants (after statistically controlling for higher reading abilities and IQ) provides indication of a morphological deficit.

Abu-Rabia et al.'s (2003) also found that, following phonological awareness, morphological awareness was the most powerful predictor of reading ability. Similar results come from a study of second-grade English poor readers, for whom morphological awareness predicted reading comprehension beyond phonological and orthographic knowledge (Nagy et al., 2003; recall also Shankweiler et al., 1995). Findings of the unique prediction from morphological awareness (beyond phonological awareness) provide some cause to consider the possibility that morphological awareness could be a second source of poor readers' difficulties in reading acquisition (e.g., Deacon and Kirby, 2004). If phonological awareness were the source of both morphological awareness and reading difficulties for young poor readers, then it would be unlikely for morphological awareness to account for distinctive variance in reading.

Carlisle's (1987) work supports morphological deficits in adolescent poor readers. She compared 13-year-old learning-disabled children (identified with specific learning disabilities in reading and written language skills despite normal full-scale IQ) with younger typically developing children with similar general spelling abilities. The learning-disabled children outperformed their younger spelling ability matched peers on the oral generation of appropriate base or derived forms to complete sentences, but they demonstrated some notable difficulties in spelling. They were more likely than their spelling-age-matched peers to spell only one member of base-derived pairs correctly (e.g., either *warm* or *warmth* for the pair). Carlisle interpreted this result to suggest that poor readers do not appreciate the consistent spellings of words sharing morphemes, though it is difficult to exclude the possibility of orthographic difficulties. Further, the learning disabled children in her study did not commit proportionately more errors with phonological change items (such as *heal - health*) and their misspellings were often phonologically accurate; her results do not support the phonologically based explanation put forward by researchers such as Fowler and Liberman (1995). Given that these are older children than those studied by Fowler and Liberman, differences in findings could reflect a developmental trend in dyslexics' spelling abilities and/or strategies.

Tsesmeli and Seymour's (2006) recent study of adolescent dyslexics' (all diagnosed as dyslexic) spelling of morphologically complex words in comparison to reading and chronological age match controls is particularly informative. They found that dyslexics did not perform as well in spelling of stem or morphologically complex words as either of the comparison groups, and yet differences between spelling of stem and derived forms were of the same magnitude for all of the groups. Poorer overall spelling cannot be explained by vocabulary problems, as dyslexics had similar vocabulary knowledge of the dictation words as their chronological age mates and more than reading level matches. Further, dyslexics were below age-matched individuals in both their implicit and explicit morphological awareness, and similar to the reading-level-matched group. Accordingly, Tsesmeli and Seymour suggested that knowledge of morphological status of the derived words or of the meanings of these words is not the problem, but rather dyslexics that have more 'fundamental structural problems well below the level of morphology' (p. 597). They concluded that dyslexics had not developed lexicalised spelling systems, due to both phonological and morphographic difficulties.

We now move to work with adult dyslexics in which comparisons were made to reading-ability-matched groups. The selection of such groups is a far thornier issue than with younger dyslexics. The performance level of adult dyslexics can vary substantially across different reading measures (see e.g., Deacon et al., 2006), and matching on the basis of one will likely result in significant differences in other reading measures – as well as many other skills that can affect performance on morphology tasks, such as general language skills (e.g., vocabulary and syntactic knowledge), educational experiences, and reading experience (both quantitatively and qualitatively). As we noted earlier, controlling for general ability does not typically solve this problem as the matching on the basis of standard scores in GA often requires very different raw scores. To the extent that general language knowledge (such as vocabulary) is more associated with morphology than phonology, we would expect older poor readers to demonstrate morphological strengths when compared to word (and even more so with nonword) reading-level matched younger participants. Such a pattern could emerge simply on the basis of the method of matching groups.

Deacon et al. (2006) compared two groups of university-educated adults with similar levels of untimed reading comprehension (but different word reading and decoding skills): those with a history of reading difficulties and those without. Response times in a lexical decision task with derived and pseudo-derived words indicated that normal readers were sensitive to morphology, but the adults with a history of reading difficulties were not. Further, for the sample as a whole the degree of sensitivity to morphology (measured in the difference between the response time to derived and pseudo-derived words) was related to timed reading comprehension, but not to untimed reading comprehension or single word identification. More fine-grained analyses revealed that this relationship held primarily for the normal readers and for the items involving an orthographic change (see also Leong, 1989a). Findings of insensitivity to morphological structure in time-sensitive tasks (see also Giraudo, 2001) do not disambiguate between the different explanations of morphological difficulties.

In sum, comparisons to reading-level matches have revealed a complex pattern of findings. Dyslexics are generally poorer than reading-level matches in spelling of morphologically complex words, but this does not appear to be a result of deficits in morphological awareness (Carlisle, 1987) or vocabulary knowledge (Tsesmeli and Seymour, 2006). There is a clear need to study patterns of performance in morphological processing tasks with different demands, given findings of poorer performance on some, but not all tasks, such as difficulties with judgment (Abu-Rabia et al., 2003), but not production tasks (Carlisle, 1987), and a lack of sensitivity in lexical decision and priming tasks examining morphological organisation of the lexicon (e.g., Deacon et al., 2006). This would allow examination of the possibility that reciprocal relationships between different reading and language skills may permit the development of some, but not all aspects of morphological abilities.

EVIDENCE FOR (AT LEAST RELATIVELY) INTACT MORPHOLOGICAL SKILLS IN POOR READERS

Findings of morphological 'strengths' have typically emerged as a lack of differences between performance of poor readers and their reading-age matched peers. As introduced above, the interpretation of such null results, or even of better performance by dyslexic or poor reader participants, in RL-matched designs is problematic. We suggest that null results in RL match designs can identify morphological skills as relatively intact (and unlikely to be affected by poor reading) if the RL matching permits the exclusion of alternative explanations, such as better general language skills or vocabulary (absolute, not age-adjusted).

Stronger evidence for this argument would then result from comparing less able readers' performance to CA-matched sample with similar general language skills (excluding phonology). A similar logic would apply to situations where dyslexics or poor readers exhibit better performance than the comparison groups and arguments are made about morphological strengths.

To begin, we consider findings of no differences between dyslexic or poor readers and control groups matched on some aspect of reading (or spelling). Bourassa et al. (2006) found that dyslexic children (all diagnosed as such and with normal full-scale IQ) were as likely as their younger, normally developing peers (matched on word reading and spelling accuracy) to represent morphological information in their spelling. Carlisle and Stone (2003) found that poor readers, along with chronological and reading-level (word reading accuracy and speed) matches, were more accurate in reading derived than pseudo-derived words (e.g., *hilly* and *silly*, respectively). The size of the difference between conditions was similar for all groups; the lack of developmental effect may reflect a lack of sensitivity in the measure. Equivalence to reading-level matches is supported by the findings that dyslexics and reading-level matched group were similar in overall accuracy (both were poorer than chronological age-matched group). Leong (1999) compared adult discrepancy-defined dyslexics' performance to a reading-level (but not IQ or education) matched control group of Japanese exchange students for whom English was a second language. The morphological task measured the time to generate correct derived forms of words to complete sentences (based on Carlisle, 1988). Leong reported that dyslexics were similar in performance on timed phonological and morphological tasks to reading level matched exchange students, though they were slower than chronological age matched peers. Finally, in Bruck's (1993) study, adult dyslexics (all with childhood diagnosis of dyslexia) were similar in their use of morphology in spelling than a group of younger readers matched on spelling and word recognition.

As noted earlier, null results in comparison to reading level matches can be ambiguous, particularly when other factors that can affect morphological processing are not controlled and if the sensitivity of the tasks are not established in other comparisons. At the most, these studies suggest that adolescent and adult dyslexics are similar to individuals with comparable levels of reading skills in their use of morphology across several different tasks, but show no evidence of morphological processing being a strength.

More compelling evidence of a morphological strength in dyslexics comes from Elbro and Arnbak (1996). These researchers found that dyslexic 15-year-old Danish students were faster at reading words with semantically transparent morphological structure (e.g., *sunburn*) than matched words (e.g., *window*). This pattern did not emerge for the 9-year-old RL-matched children. Intriguingly, the quantity of decrease in response time to the compound words was correlated with better reading comprehension, suggesting that morphological processing could offer a compensatory mechanism for dyslexics to overcome their phonological difficulties. This conclusion, however, is challenged by the fact that the

RL matching in this study was done on the basis of reading comprehension whereas the target task depended on word reading skills.[3] A second experiment by Elbro and Arnbak (1996) addressed these concerns, at least in part, by matching the older dyslexic group to younger normally reading group on word and passage reading accuracy and speed. Dyslexic adolescents were significantly better in reading text parsed into morphemes than text parsed into syllables, with the RL-matched group showing a trend in the opposite direction. These researchers also report briefly on other data demonstrating that the dyslexics in this sample had poorer performance on several more explicit measures of morphological awareness, such as the reversal of morphemes in a compound word (see Elbro, 1990). These findings help to reduce the likelihood that results in the reading tasks reflect the much older dyslexics' better general language skills. Overall, these findings implicate the use of morphology in reading as a possible area of relative strength that dyslexics use to compensate for poor phonological skills (see also Bryant et al., 1998). Controlling for general language skills, however, is necessary to verify these conclusions.

Joanisse et al.'s (2000) work went some steps further towards defining appropriate control groups. Their initial analyses revealed morphological deficits among 'dyslexic' children when this group included all poor readers in their sample: these children were poorer on tasks of productive inflectional morphology than younger control participants with similar word identification skills. Joanisse et al. took this to indicate that the poor readers had general language delays, including those in morphology. They subsequently divided the 'dyslexic' group into three more homogeneous subgroups: phonological dyslexics (PD), children with more general language impairments (LI), and globally delayed children. Comparisons to RL-matched children showed that the LI group was significantly poorer in inflectional morphology whereas the trend towards differences between the PD and RL groups did not achieve significance. Given that the phonological dyslexics in this study had similar word-reading accuracy and vocabulary raw scores than the RL group (the RL group had significantly higher standard scores), these results could be taken to support the notion that phonological awareness is the core deficit, because when groups have similar reading and vocabulary (general language) skills, they also have similar morphological awareness. As such, this study supports the notion of relatively intact morphological abilities, and yet, given the near significant results with a very small sample (n = 8 in the PD group), these findings clearly need to be explored further with larger groups.

Another approach to uncovering the origins of reading difficulties lies in retrospective analyses. Bryant et al. (1998; see also 1997) presented analyses of a large dataset, comparing children who went on to become poor readers to those who did not. The two groups were equated on their initial word reading ability, and full-scale IQ differences were controlled statistically. Interestingly, the group that developed reading difficulties began their reading and writing careers with better morphological awareness, as well as stronger morphologically based and weaker phonetically based spelling than the comparison group. By later testing points, the groups were virtually indistinguishable in their morphological awareness and the poor readers were much worse than age-matched peers in morphologically based spelling (though similar to a RL-matched group). Bryant et al. argued that, despite an initial strength in morphological approach, the lack of the core foundation of phonological knowledge led to reading difficulties, and, in turn, to a lack of further growth in morphological awareness.

Such an interpretation bears similarities to the findings of Casalis et al's. (2004) study of 8- to 12-year-old French dyslexic children (none of whom suffered from language impairment). While the dyslexic children lagged behind their age-matched peers on measures of phonological, syntactic, and morphological abilities, the comparisons with younger RL-matched (matched on the basis of oral text reading accuracy and speed) children showed a more complex pattern. Results suggested that French dyslexic children had difficulties with segmenting words into morphemes in an oral task, but their abilities were intact in an oral sentence completion task and more advanced with an oral production task (in comparison to RL-matched peers). Casalis et al. concluded that the development of phonological and morphological abilities is interdependent, especially under certain task constraints. Further support for this view comes from a comparison between two groups of dyslexic children, those with and without severe phonological difficulties. Phonological dyslexics were relatively impaired in their morphemic segmentation when this required phonological analysis (breaking the syllable boundary) and in the production of morphologically complex pseudo-words after being provided with their definition. And yet they were equivalent to delayed dyslexics in sentence completion, even when there were phonological changes involved (in contrast to Shankweiler et al., 1995, among others). Productive morphological knowledge may develop in tandem with reading abilities, in a way that it is at least partly separable from phonological abilities. Such findings conflict with the phonologically based explanations of morphological deficits, and suggest that some, if not all, morphological abilities are intact, relative to the level of reading ability.

A similar pattern of specific areas of deficits and strengths in morphological knowledge emerges from Egan and Pring's (2004). They compared 12-year-old children with IQ-reading ability discrepancy-defined dyslexia with poor readers of the same age and reading level without an IQ discrepancy (PR), chronological age-matched children, and a group of reading and spelling level matched children (RL-SL). The researchers found that children with dyslexia made disproportionately more errors in spelling regular past tense verbs in comparison to all other groups. In contrast, dyslexic children performed similarly to the two reading-level matched groups on an inflectional sentence analogy task and on an oral and written tense judgment task. Further investigations demonstrated impairments in phonological and/or orthographic processing; dyslexics were less affected by disruption in the boundaries of both morphologically complex and simple words (e.g., *walKEd* or *walkED* in comparison to *clOCk* and *cloCK*) than the PR or the RL-SL groups. The authors took this to reflect phonological difficulties. They advocated that difficulties with written morphology are likely a consequence of phonological difficulties, given the relatively weak phonetic information available in past tense forms. Dyslexics may lag behind their chronological age peers due to lesser exposure to print, as the dyslexics are similar in oral morphological awareness to their peers of the same reading and spelling level.

To summarize, equivalence to reading-level matches has been uncovered in several tasks, including those tapping production of morphologically complex words in sentences and the use of morphology in reading. Similarities to reading-level matches are difficult to interpret, though they do imply that morphological processing is unlikely to be a cause of reading difficulties. They also suggest that phonological and/or reading abilities could limit the development of at least some aspects of morphological awareness. Certainly, this is the suggestion made by Casalis et al., who proposed that phonological knowledge may limit explicit segmentation of affixes, but not productive morphological knowledge, especially when there is a sentence context provided (recall poor performance in a productive task without a sentence context in Abu-Rabia et al., 2003). Further evidence of 'strengths' came from two studies: one by Bryant et al. (1998) demonstrating that poor readers begin with at least a relative strength in morphology, and another by Elbro and Arnbak suggesting that older dyslexics have developed a relative strength in employing morphological strategies in reading (see also Leikin and Zur Hagit, 2006).

CONCLUSIONS

It is clear from the above review that dyslexics and poor readers typically perform more poorly on morphological tasks than their same age peers with much better reading abilities. This is the case across all studies that we have been able to locate.[4] And yet comparisons with reading-level matched control groups are better able to avoid the confound of the skills gained through reading experience. Only findings of poorer performance than RL-matched control groups can be interpreted as demonstrating that morphological processing is a possible *cause* of reading difficulties. Such findings are remarkably difficult to locate (though we will consider the cases in which they did emerge in due course).

One key possibility is that dyslexics' and poor readers' difficulties with morphological processing (at least in comparison to chronological age matches) may originate in their more fundamental phonological difficulties. Support for this proposal comes from findings of equivalence on morphological processing tasks once phonological awareness is controlled (e.g., Joanisse et al., 2000), and from findings of particular difficulties on morphological tasks involving phonological change items (e.g., Fowler and Liberman, 1995). The approach of isolating subgroups of dyslexics with different general language skills (e.g., Joanisse et al., 2000; Casalis et al., 2004) offers a way of determining whether phonology and/or more broad language deficits, including those in morphology, could be the source of difficulties for some, but not all dyslexics. Such approach needs to be extended to larger samples.

And yet phonological difficulties are unlikely to be the sole explanation of difficulties with morphological and reading tasks. Dyslexics' and poor readers' performance was not always differentially impaired with words with phonological changes (e.g., Carlisle, 1987). Further, morphological awareness accounts for unique variance in reading outcomes, beyond phonological awareness, in both normal and poor reader groups (e.g., Nagy et al., 2003). We need to consider morphological awareness as independent, at least to some extent, from phonological abilities. In order to demarcate morphological tasks as potentially causally related to reading outcomes, we need to find poorer performance in dyslexics and poor readers when they are compared to reading-level matched controls. While not a common finding by any means, this pattern did emerge in several studies involving spelling of morphologically complex words. This result may emerge from a lack of consolidation of orthographic knowledge. The only study to include orthographically complex control words found similar difficulties in this domain (Shankweiler et al., 1996); thus, it is possible that dyslexics have generalized difficulties with orthographic representations. This possibility is bolstered by the findings that reading is predicted to a greater extent by items in morphological tasks that involve orthographic changes (Leong, 1989a; Deacon et al., 2006). And yet, we need to reserve judgment on this count given the recent demonstrations of equivalence to reading- (or spelling-) ability matches on morphological spelling and reading tasks (e.g., Bourassa et al., 2006); the comparison to spelling-ability matched individuals might be particularly important. This discrepancy calls for studying orthographic and morphological knowledge together in investigations of dyslexics to isolate the origins of reading difficulties.

A second domain in which dyslexics and poor readers performed below reading level matched controls were in tasks assessing the organization of the lexicon according to morphological principles in both more and less compensated dyslexics (Giraudo, 2001; Deacon et al., 2006). Notably, Leikin and Zur Hagit's (2006) data suggest a greater reliance on morphology in lexical access. Clearly, new research needs to target the organization of the lexicon, particularly in terms of the orthographic representations contained within it. Further, we need to consider the possibility that this pattern might emerge in dyslexics faced with learning to read in a morphosyllabic orthography (see Shu et al., 2006).

One the most promising approaches lies in the consideration of reciprocal relationships between reading-related variables advocated by several researchers. Poor phonological awareness is likely to lead to difficulties in accessing morphological information in oral language and orthographic representations (including those of morphemes), as well as causing difficulties in reading. Direct links between phonological awareness and individual skills are likely to be accentuated by reciprocal relationships, in which initially poor phonological awareness is likely to limit reading development, which, in turn, limits growth in morphological awareness (and orthographic knowledge). This could operate in tandem with an early relative strength in morphological awareness (as postulated by Bryant et al., 1998), such that initially strong morphological processing may impede the consolidation of already weak phonological awareness. Investigation of such possibilities requires the tracking of reading difficulties as they develop over time.

Further, it is possible that dyslexics and poor readers can achieve success in some aspects of morphological manipulation despite phonological impairments. Dyslexics and poor readers performed better than reading level matched controls in two studies on production of morphologically complex words in sentence contexts (e.g., Carlisle, 1987; Casalis et al., 2004). Casalis et al. suggested that phonological awareness and reading level limit the development of explicit segmentation of morphologically complex words, though they do permit the development of productive knowledge. This could further depend on the presence of sentence contexts (and associated syntactic information, and potential related reductions in memory demands), particularly given findings from Abu-Rabia et al. (2003) of poorer performance on productive tasks without sentences. Conclusions of reciprocal relationships among phonological, morphological and reading abilities, such as those offered by Casalis and colleagues, pose a real challenge to researchers, especially in that subtle aspects of tasks may allow a modest level of morphological skill to be apparent (and associated with earlier or later measures of the other factors). Alternatively, task differences could hide modest levels of ability, and, through lack of variability, conceal relationships with other factors. There is no simple solution to this problem, but it does call for carefully constructed measures with extensive testing of variations in task factors.

A final area of particular promise comes from Elbro and Arnbak's suggestion that older 'compensated' dyslexics have developed a relative strength in the use of morphological information in reading. This does not necessarily extend to a strength in morphological awareness (e.g., Elbro, 1990). Leikin and Zur Hagit (2006) articulated a similar idea, that 'dyslexic readers are forced to resort to morphological decomposition for lexical access since their decoding abilities are not developed and processing the word as a whole is slow and inefficient' (p. 486). Such differences can be viewed as an over-reliance on morphological information in lexical access; morphological processing may offer a *relative* strength in comparison to a phonological weakness (see also Bryant et al., 1998). Nevertheless, it is possible that older dyslexics (adolescents, adults) who have obtained extra print exposure through extensive reading practice may be able to overcome the orthographic knowledge disadvantage. They may also be able to overcome the phonetic decoding disadvantage with familiar words or with pseudowords that have common orthographic units as components. Orthographic, phonological, and semantic (morphological) units are extensively linked and mutually support each other's identification (see also Coltheart's 'cascaded' notion). Such possible routes to reading need to be investigated through confirmation of findings of greater performance than RL controls in designs that control for absolute verbal IQ for order to provide more concrete evidence of 'strengths.'

While we have attempted to clarify the status of research to date, we are nevertheless left with an unclear picture as to the underlying cause of difficulties with morphological tasks for individuals with reading difficulties (at least as uncovered in comparison to same age peers). New research needs to focus on these origins because they have a direct impact on the decision on how to help individuals with dyslexia. For example, the phonological deficit approach would nominate a continued emphasis on investigation of remediation of phonological difficulties because, according to this notion, morphological difficulties are simply a symptom of a phonologically based difficulty. Similar inferences could be drawn from Bryant's view of morphological abilities as early and transient strength, diverting attention away from the phonological foundations of script. It would seem that such an approach would advocate teaching about this phonological basis. An alternative implication of the phonological explanation is that if individuals do not respond to phonological training (as presumably is the case with many adult dyslexics), then literacy training at some point may need to rely more heavily upon other routes, such as the morphological pathway; this pathway may even be a means to build up word recognition skills. Finally, if it is indeed demonstrated that morphology is a useful strength upon which intervention programs can build, then such programs should be devised and tested (see e.g., Bowers and Kirby, 2006; Nunes and Bryant, 2006). Such studies should also test the possibility that early interventions should focus on phonology, whereas later interventions should target morphology (comparing the results of Bryant et al., 1998 and Elbro and Arnbak, 1996). Perhaps even more promising for dyslexics and poor readers is the possibility that teaching could integrate phonological and morphological instruction, particularly given the morpho-phonological nature of the English orthography (Chomsky and Halle, 1968).

NOTES

1 This difference is equivalent to finding a correlation between morphological awareness and reading, as has been uncovered in several predictive studies (e.g., Deacon and Kirby, 2004).

2 Note that this statistical approach can never entirely eliminate the effects of the pre-existing differences. These differences may have resulted from the use of teacher nomination for participant recruitment.

3 As could be expected, the RL group was both more accurate and faster (about twice as fast as the dyslexic group) in naming the target words, irrespective of their morphological structure. This latter result leaves open the possibility that the decrease in response time to semantically transparent compound words is associated more with slower word recognition than with dyslexia per se (perhaps building on Leikin and Zur Hagit's 2006 ideas).

4 The only exception to this pattern lies in the findings of similar size difference score for dyslexics and reading- and chronological-age match controls in Carlisle and Stone (2003), which may have been insensitive given the absence of developmental increase in difference scores.

REFERENCES

Abu-Rabia, S. (2006) 'The role of morphology and short vowelization in reading Arabic among normal and dyslexic readers in grades 3, 6, 9 and 12', *Journal of Psycholinguistic Research*, 36 (2); 89–106.

Abu-Rabia, S., Share, D., and Said, M. (2003) 'Word recognition and basic cognitive processes among reading–disabled and normal readers in Arabic', *Reading and Writing: An Interdisciplinary Journal*, 16 (15): 423–442.

American Psychiatric Association (1994) Diagnostic and statistical manual of mental disorders, 4th edition (DSM–IV). Available: http://www.behavenet.com/capsules/disorders/readingdis.htm

Avons, S. E. and Hanna, C. (1995) 'The memory-span deficit on children with specific reading disability: Is speech rate responsible?', *British Journal of Developmental Psychology*, 13 (3): 303–311.

Berko, J. (1958) 'The child's learning of English morphology', *Word*, 14: 150–177.

Berninger, V.W. (2001) 'Understanding the "lexia" in dyslexia: A multidisciplinary team approach to learning disabilities', *Annals of Dyslexia*, 51: 23–48.

Bishop, D.V. and Snowling, M.J. (2004) 'Developmental dyslexia and specific language impairment: Same or different?', *Psychological Bulletin*, 130 (6): 858–886.

Bishop, D.V.M. and Butterworth, G.E. (1980) 'Verbal-performance discrepancies: Relationship to birth risk and specific reading retardation', *Cortex*, 16 (3): 375–390.

Bishop, D.V. and Adams, C. (1990) 'A prospective study of the relationship between specific language impairment, phonological disorders and reading retardation', *Journal of Child Psychology and Psychiatry and Allied Disciplines*, 31 (7): 1027–1050.

Bourassa, D., Treiman, R. and Kessler, B. (2006) 'Use of morphology in spelling by children with dyslexia and typically developing children', *Memory and Cognition*, 34 (3): 703–714.

Bowers, P.N. and Kirby, J.R. (2006) 'Morpho-phonological word structure: Can instruction add transparency to opaque words?' Paper presented at the annual meeting of the Society for the Scientific Study of Reading, Vancouver, BC.

Bradley, L. and Bryant, P.E. (1983) 'Categorising sounds and learning to read—a causal connection', *Nature*, 301: 419–420.

Bruck, M. (1990) 'Word recognition skills of college students with a childhood diagnosis of dyslexia', *Developmental Psychology*, 26 (3): 874–886.

Bruck, M. (1993) 'Component spelling skills of college students with a childhood diagnosis of dyslexia', *Learning Disabilities Quarterly*, 16 (3): 171–184.

Bryant, P., Nunes, T. and Bindman, M. (1997) 'Backward readers' awareness of language: Strengths and weaknesses', *European Journal of Psychology of Education*, 12 (4): 357–372.

Bryant, P., Nunes, T. and Bindman, M. (1998) 'Awareness of language in children who have reading difficulties: Historical comparisons in a longitudinal study', *Journal of Child Psychology and Psychiatry*, 39 (4): 501–510.

Carlisle, J.F. (1987) 'The use of morphological knowledge in spelling derived forms by learning disabled and normal students', *Annals of Dyslexia*, 37: 90–108.

Carlisle, J.F. (1988) 'Knowledge of derivational morphology and spelling ability in fourth, sixth and eighth grades', *Applied Psycholinguistics*, 9 (3): 247–266.

Carlisle, J.F. (1995) 'Morphological awareness and early reading achievement', in L.B. Feldman, (ed.), *Morphological aspects of language processing*. Lawrence Erlbaum Associates, Publishers: Hillsdale, New Jersey. pp. 189–209.

Carlisle, J.F. and Stone, C.A. (2003) 'The effects of morphological structure on children's reading of derived words', in E. Assink and D. Santa (eds), *Reading complex words: Cross-language studies*. Dordrecht: Kluwer Academic Publishers. pp. 27–52.

Carlisle, J.F., Stone, C.A. and Katz, L.A. (2001) 'The effect of phonological transparency on reading derived words', *Annals of Dyslexia*, 51: 249–274.

Casalis, S., Colé, P. and Sopo, D. (2004) 'Morphological awareness in developmental dyslexia', *Annals of Dyslexia*, 54: 114–138.

Catts, H.W. (1989) 'Speech production deficits in developmental dyslexia', *Journal of Speech and Hearing Disorders*, 54 (3): 422–428.

Catts, H.W., Hu, C.-F., Larrivee, L. and Swank, L. (1994) 'Early identification of reading disabilities in children with speech-language impairments', in R. V. Watkins and M. L. Rice (eds), *Specific language impairments in children*. Baltimore, MD: Paul H Brookes Publishing. pp. 145–160.

Chialant, D. and Caramazza, A. (1995) 'Where is morphology and how is it processed? The case of written word recognition', in L.B. Feldman (ed), *Morphological aspects of language processing*. Hillsdale, NJ: Lawrence Erlbaum Associates. pp. 55–78.

Chomsky, N. and Halle, M. (1968) *The sound pattern of English*. New York: Harper and Row.

Coltheart, M., Rastle, K., Perry, C., Langdon, R. and Ziegler, J. (2001) 'DRC: A dual route cascaded model of visual word recognition and reading aloud', *Psychological Review*, 108 (1): 204–256.

Deacon, S.H. and Kirby, J.R. (2004) 'Morphological: Is it more than phonological? Evaluating the roles of morphological and phonological awareness in reading development', *Applied Psycholinguistics*, 25 (2): 223–238.

Deacon, S.H., Parrila, R. and Kirby, J.R. (2006) 'Processing of derived forms in high-functioning dyslexics', *Annals of Dyslexia*, 56: 103–128.

Egan, J. and Pring, L. (2004) 'The processing of inflectional morphology: A comparison between children with and without dyslexia', *Reading and Writing: An Interdisciplinary Journal*, 17 (6): 567–591.

Ehri, L. (2005) 'Learning to read words: Theory, findings, and issues', *Scientific Studies of Reading*, 9 (2): 167–188.

Elbro, C. (1990) *Differences in dyslexia. A study of reading strategies and deficits in a linguistic perspective*. Copenhagen: Munksgaard.

Elbro, C. and Arnbak, E. (1996) 'The role of morpheme recognition and morphological awareness in dyslexia', *Annals of Dyslexia*, 46: 209–240.

Fischer, F.W., Shankweiler, D. and Liberman, I.Y. (1985) 'Spelling proficiency and sensitivity to word structure', *Journal of Memory and Language*, 24 (4): 423–441.

Fowler, A. and Liberman, I. (1995) 'The role of phonology and orthography in morphological awareness', in L.B. Feldman (ed), *Morphological aspects of language processing*. Hillsdale, NJ: Lawrence Erlbaum Associates. pp. 157–188.

Giraudo, H. (2001) 'Rôle et représentation de l'information morphologique chez l'apprenti lecteur et l'enfant dyslexique' (The role and representation of morphological information in the beginning reader and in dyslexic children), *Annales Fyssen*, 16: 81–90.

Goswami, U. and Bryant, P. (1989) 'The interpretation of studies using the reading level design', *Journal of Reading Behavior*, 21 (4): 413–424.

Goswami, U. and Bryant, P. (1990) *Phonological skills and learning to read*. London: Lawrence Erlbaum Associates.

IDA (2006) International Dyslexia Association, Definition of Dyslexia (retrieved from www.interdys.org October 24, 2006).

Joanisse, M.F., Manis, F.R., Keating, P. and Seidenberg, M.S. (2000) 'Language deficits in dyslexic children: Speech perception, phonology and morphology', *Journal of Experimental Child Psychology*, 77 (1): 30–60.

Leikin, M. and Zur Hagit, E. (2006) 'Morphological processing in adult dyslexia', *Journal of Psycholinguistic Research*, 35 (6): 471–490.

Leonard, L., Eyer, J., Bedore, L. and Grela, B. (1997) 'Three accounts of the grammatical morpheme difficulties of English-speaking children with specific language impairment', *Journal of Speech, Language and Hearing Research*, 40 (4): 340–346.

Leong, C.K. (1989a) 'Productive knowledge of derivational rules in poor readers', *Annals of Dyslexia*, 39: 94–115.

Leong, C.K. (1989b) 'The effects of morphological structure on reading proficiency: A developmental study', *Reading and Writing: An Interdisciplinary Journal*, 1 (4): 357–379.

Leong, C.K. (1999) 'Phonological and morphological processing in adult students with learning/reading disabilities', *Journal of Learning Disabilities*, 32 (3): 224–238.

Leong, C.K. and Parkinson, M.E. (1995) 'Processing of English morphological structure by poor readers', in C.K. Leong and R.M. Joshi (eds), *Developmental and acquired dyslexia: Neuropsychological and neurolinguistic perspectives.* Dordrecht: Kluwer Academic Publishers. pp. 237–261.

Lyon, G., Shaywitz, S.E. and Shaywitz, B.A. (2003) 'A definition of dyslexia', *Annals of Dyslexia*, 53: 1–14.

Marslen-Wilson, W., Tyler, L., Waksler, R. and Older, L. (1994) 'Morphology and meaning in the mental lexicon', *Psychological Review*, 101 (1): 3–33.

Nagy, W., Berninger, V.W., Abbott, R.D., Vaughan, K. and Vermeulen, K. (2003) 'Relationship of morphology and other language skills in at-risk second-grade readers and at-risk fourth grade writers', *Journal of Educational Psychology*, 95 (4): 730–742.

National Reading Panel (2000) *Teaching children to read: An evidence–based assessment of the scientific literature on reading and its implications for reading instruction.* Bethesda MD: National Institute of Child Health and Human Development.

Nunes, T. and Bryant, P. (2006) *Improving literacy by teaching morphemes.* New York: Routledge.

Perfetti, C.A., Beck, I., Bell, L.C. and Hughes, C. (1987) 'Phonemic knowledge and learning to read are reciprocal: A longitudinal study of first grade children', *Merrill-Palmer Quarterly*, 33 (3): 283–319.

Plaut, D. C. (2005) 'Connectionist approaches to reading', in M. J. Snowling and C. Hulme (eds), *The science of reading: A handbook.* Oxford UK: Blackwell publishing. pp 24–38.

Seymour, P.H.K. (1999) 'Cognitive architecture of early reading', in I. Lundberg, F.E., Tønnessen, and I. Austad (eds), *Learning to spell.* Hillsdale, NJ: Erlbaum. pp. 319–337.

Shankweiler, D., Crain, S., Katz, L., Fowler, A.E., Liberman, A.E., Brady, S.A., Thornton, R., Lundquist, E., Breyer, L., Fletcher, J.M., Stuebing, K.K., Shaywitz, S.E. and Shaywitz, B.A. (1995) 'Cognitive profiles of reading-disabled children: Comparison of language skills in phonology, morphology and syntax', *Psychological Science*, 6 (3): 149–156.

Shankweiler, D., Lundquist, E., Dreyer, L.G. and Dickinson, C.C. (1996) 'Reading and spelling difficulties in high school students: Causes and consequences', *Reading and Writing: An Interdisciplinary Journal*, 8 (3): 267–294.

Share, D.L. and Leikin, M. (2004) 'Language impairment at school entry and later reading disability: Connections at lexical versus supralexical levels of reading', *Scientific Studies of Reading*, 8 (1): 87–110.

Share, D.L., McGee, R. and Silva, P.A. (1989) 'IQ and reading progress: A test of the capacity notion of IQ', *Journal of the American Academy of Child and Adolescent Psychiatry*, 28 (1): 97–100.

Share, D.L. and Silva, P.A. (2003) 'Gender bias in IQ-discrepancy and post-discrepancy definitions of readings disability', *Journal of Learning Disabilities*, 36 (1): 4–14.

Shu, H., McBride-Chang, C., Wu, H. and Liu, H. (2006) 'Understanding Chinese developmental dyslexia: Morphological awareness as a core cognitive construct', *Journal of Educational Psychology*, 98 (1): 122–133.

Snowling, M. (2000) *Dyslexia* (2nd ed.) Oxford, U.K.: Blackwell Publishers.

Taft, M. (1979) 'Recognition of affixed words and the frequency effect', *Memory and Cognition*, 7 (4): 263–272.

Tsesmeli, S.N. and Seymour, P.H.K. (2006) 'Derivational morphology and spelling in dyslexia', *Reading and Writing*, 19 (6): 587–625.

van der Leij, A. and van Daal, V. H. P. (1999) 'Automatization aspects of dyslexia: Speed limitations in word identification, sensitivity to increasing task demands, and orthographic compensation', *Journal of Learning Disabilities*, 32 (5): 417–428.

Vellutino, F.R. and Fletcher, J.M. (2005) 'Developmental dyslexia', in M.J. Snowling and C. Hulme (eds), *The science of reading: A handbook.* Malden, MA: Blackwell. pp. 362–378.

Vellutino, F.R. and Scanlon, D.M. (1989) 'Some prerequisites for interpreting results from reading level matched designs', *Journal of Reading Behavior*, 21 (4): 361–385.

World Health Organisation (2006) International Classification of Diseases -10 (ICD-10; retrieved May 24, 2007 from http://www.who.int/classifications/icd/en/).

Zoccolotti, P., De Luca, M., Di Pace, E., Gasperini, F., Judica, A. and Spinelli, D. (2005) 'Word length effect in early reading and in developmental dyslexia', *Brain and Language*, 93 (3): 369–373.

PART III

Educational Influences

Reading Intervention Research: An Integrative Framework

William E. Tunmer and Keith T. Greaney

This chapter

i) focuses on conceptual and methodological issues in reading intervention research;
ii) discusses the way in which contextual variables can also influence the effectiveness of reading interventions; and
iii) discusses the importance of recent studies of the neurobiological effects of successful reading interventions.

INTRODUCTION

Reading intervention research refers to research on instructional approaches designed to either *prevent* or *remediate* reading difficulties (Torgesen, 2004). Prevention programmes typically focus on at-risk children with limited amounts of crucial reading-related knowledge, skills and experiences at school entry who often, but not always, come from low-income family backgrounds. Remedial programmes target students who are failing to make adequate progress in learning to read. Designing, executing and replicating intervention studies is a complicated endeavour as noted by Lyon (1993, cited in Lyon and Moats, 1997), who suggested that the difficult challenges that reading intervention researchers face can be expressed in the form of a question.

Which instructional reading approach or method, or combination of approaches or methods, provided in which setting or combination of settings, under which student-teacher ratio conditions and teacher-student interactions, provided for what period of time and by which type of teachers, have the greatest impact on well-defined elements of reading behaviour and reading-related behaviours, for which children, for how long, and for what reasons? (p. 579)

CONCEPTUAL ISSUES

In addition to the complexity of the methodological issues involved in reading intervention research, there are conceptual issues as well. Researchers concerned with dyslexia (or reading disability) have concentrated their efforts on answering three key questions: What is it? What causes it? What can be done about it? Although the focus of this chapter is on the latter question, the answers to these questions are highly interrelated and cannot be pursued in isolation from one another. Our conceptualisation of what skilled reading is and how it is acquired will greatly influence how we define reading disability, what we think causes problems in learning to read, and what we believe are the most effective intervention strategies for helping students to overcome persistent literacy learning difficulties.

For example, until fairly recently reading instruction and intervention in New Zealand followed a predominantly constructivist, whole language approach in which it was argued that teaching alphabetic coding skills 'is a difficult, unnecessary and largely fruitless activity, creating distorted ideas about the nature and purpose of reading' and that 'to focus on decoding exercises, outside a meaningful context, is to run the risk of diverting the child's attention away from real reading and from developing other productive strategies' (Smith and Elley, 1994: 143, 145). In using the phrase 'other productive strategies' Smith and Elley were referring to a key theoretical assumption of whole language, which is that reading acquisition is primarily a process in which children learn to use multiple cues (syntactic, semantic, visual and graphophonic) in identifying unfamiliar words in text, with text-based cues generally being used to generate hypotheses about the text yet to be encountered and letter-sound cues being used mostly for confirmation and self-correction (Snow and Juel, 2005; Tracey and Morrow, 2006; Tunmer et al., in press). Clay (1998), the developer of the nationally implemented early intervention programme in New Zealand, Reading Recovery, stated that beginning readers

need to use their knowledge of how the world works; the possible meanings of the text; the sentence structure; the importance of order of ideas, or words, or of letters; the size of words or letters; special features of sound, shape and layout; and special knowledge from past literary experiences *before* they resort to left to right sounding out of chunks or letter clusters or, in the last resort, single letters (p. 9, italics added).

The major shortcoming of this instructional philosophy, however, is that it stresses the importance of using information from many sources in identifying unfamiliar words without recognising that skills and strategies involving phonological information are of *primary* importance in beginning literacy development (Perfetti, 1985; Pressley, 2006; Shankweiler and Fowler, 2004). Research has established that making use of letter-sound relationships to identify unknown words is the basic mechanism for acquiring sight word (i.e., word-specific) knowledge, including knowledge of irregularly spelled words (Adams, 1990; Ehri, 2005; Gough and Walsh, 1991; Perfetti, 1992; Share, 1995; Tunmer and Chapman, 1998; 2006). The formation of sublexical, visuophonological connections between printed words and their spoken counterparts in memory provides the basis for fast, efficient recognition of words, which in turn frees up cognitive resources for allocation to sentence comprehension and text integration processes (Perfetti, 1985; Pressley, 2006; Share, 1995). For children encountering difficulty in developing the ability to perceive redundant patterns and connections between speech and print, explicit instruction in phonemic awareness and alphabetic coding skills is likely to be critical. As Adams and Bruck (1993) argued, 'whenever children who cannot discover the alphabetic principle independently are denied explicit instruction on the regularities and conventions of letter strings, reading disability may well be the eventual consequence' (p. 90). In support of this claim is a large body of research indicating that the degree of explicitness and detail with which word-level skills and strategies are taught is important for most beginning readers and especially so for struggling readers (Adams, 1990; Ehri, 2004; Oakhill and Beard, 1999; Perfetti, 1991; Pressley, 2006; Shankweiler and Fowler, 2004; Snow and Juel, 2005).

Returning to the claim regarding the inseparability of the questions of what is reading disability, what causes it, and what can be done about it, a large-scale approach to preventing and remediating early reading difficulties called *response to intervention* (RTI) simultaneously addresses all three questions. The RTI model, which will be discussed in greater detail in a later section, includes procedures for identifying reading disability, for closely monitoring progress in acquiring the phonemically-based skills and strategies known to be causally related to early reading development, and for implementing research-based secondary and tertiary interventions for children with persistent literacy learning problems (Deschler et al., 2005; Fuchs and Fuchs, 2006).

METHODOLOGICAL ISSUES IN READING INTERVENTION RESEARCH

Several factors need to be considered in designing and evaluating reading intervention programmes (Lyon and Moats, 1997; Pressley et al., 2006; Tunmer et al., 2002). One factor relates to sample characteristics and sample heterogeneity. For example, poor readers with comorbid disorders such as attentional or behavioural problems may respond differently to particular interventions than children without these disorders. Motivational and attitudinal variables are also important.

Older poor readers with a history of failure in learning to read may not exert as much effort as other children because of their low expectations of success. For these children, particular emphasis may need to be placed on making them aware that successful attempts at identifying words or comprehending text are a direct consequence of the appropriate and effortful application of taught skills and strategies (Chapman and Tunmer, 2003).

The efficacy of different intervention programmes may also interact with the entry-level characteristics of participants, such as the stage of reading development at which the difficulty occurred, and the type and severity of the processing deficit responsible for the difficulty (Torgesen, 2004; 2005; Vellutino et al., 1996). As Vellutino et al. (1996) pointed out:

> Any given level of reading achievement is a by-product of a complex interaction between one's endowment and the quality of one's literacy experience and instruction, such that the child who is endowed with an adequate mix of the cognitive abilities underlying reading ability is better equipped to profit from experience and instruction in learning to read than is the child who is endowed with a less than adequate mix of these abilities. Indeed, the optimally endowed child may be able to profit from less than optimal experience and instruction, whereas the inadequately endowed child may have difficulty profiting from even optimal experience and instruction. (p. 602)

These considerations provide a likely explanation for the differential effectiveness of Reading Recovery (RR), a popular intervention programme used in several countries (Tunmer and Chapman, 2003). The programme appears to be beneficial for some struggling readers but not others, as indicated by the high percentage (up to 30 per cent) of RR students who do not complete the programme but, instead, are referred to by their RR tutor for further assessment and possible additional remedial assistance (Elbaum et al., 2000). Tunmer and Chapman (2004) argued that, as a consequence of developmentally limiting deficits in phonological awareness and knowledge of print at the outset of learning to read, many struggling readers take longer than usual to acquire the self-improving alphabetic coding skills necessary for achieving progress in reading. The process of phonologically decoding a specific printed word a few times ultimately cements the word's orthographic representation in lexical memory. Phonological decoding, therefore, functions as a self-teaching mechanism that enables beginning readers to develop sight-word knowledge (Share, 1995).

Delayed readers who have managed to acquire a working knowledge of the major grapheme-phoneme correspondences and possess a reasonable degree of phonemic awareness are able to execute phonological decoding operations, but only very slowly and laboriously. According to Ehri and McCormick (1998), these struggling readers have just entered the *full-alphabetic phase* of word learning and are described as 'gluing to print' because they painstakingly sound out and blend letter-sound associations when reading words. For these children, the heavy emphasis on text reading in RR lessons provides them with additional opportunities to apply their developing phonological decoding skills to identifying words. As their reading attempts become more successful, these delayed readers will begin making greater independent use of letter-sound information (possibly supplemented with text-based cues) to identify unfamiliar words from which additional spelling-sound relationships can be induced without explicit instruction. The extra practice in reading provided by RR is, therefore, likely to be beneficial in helping these struggling readers catch up with their peers.

A large proportion of struggling readers, however, operate at even lower phases of word learning, which Ehri and McCormick (1998) described as the *pre-alphabetic* and *partial-alphabetic phases*. Delayed readers who are still in these phases of development typically have limited or severely limited phonological awareness and alphabetic coding skills. Children who experience ongoing difficulties in detecting phonological sequences in words will not be able to fully grasp the alphabetic principle and discover spelling-to-sound relationships (Blachman, 2000; Ehri et al., 2001; Pressley, 2006). For these children, more intensive training in phonemically-based skills and strategies is likely to be required than what is provided in RR lessons.

Evidence in support of this claim comes from two studies. Chapman et al. (2001) found in a longitudinal study of RR that the students who failed to achieve significant progress in the programme and were referred on as a consequence, showed the most severe deficits on all phonological processing measures taken at the beginning of the programme, during the year preceding entry into the programme, and during the year following referral from the programme. In a second study, Iversen and Tunmer (1993) found that the effectiveness of RR could be improved considerably by incorporating into the programme more intensive and explicit instruction in phonological awareness and the use of letter-sound relationships (especially orthographic analogies), in combination with strategy training on how and when to use this knowledge to identify words while reading text and to spell words while writing messages.

A second major factor to consider in the design of reading interventions is the degree of *explicitness* and *intensity* with which specific reading-related knowledge, skills and strategies (phonological awareness, alphabetic coding, vocabulary, fluency, comprehension strategies) are taught. For word identification skills, research indicates that compared to normally achieving children, struggling readers are less able to discover letter-sound patterns as a by-product of more general reading, suggesting that these children require more explicit instruction in alphabetic coding (Calfee and Drum, 1986; Torgesen, 2004). In predominantly constructivist approaches to reading intervention like Reading Recovery, word analysis activities arise primarily as 'mini-lessons' given in response to children's oral reading errors during text reading. Although this intervention strategy may be suitable for children who are mildly at risk, children with more severe reading difficulties or higher degrees of risk appear to require a more highly structured, systematic approach that includes teaching word analysis skills *outside* the context of reading connected text (Foorman et al., 1998; Ryder et al., in press; Torgesen et al., 2001a; 1999; Tunmer et al., 2003). In a study of the effects of different methods of beginning reading instruction on the reading growth of at-risk first-grade students, Foorman et al. (1998) found that the degree of explicitness of instruction in the alphabetic code and related skills was positively associated with amount of improvement in reading, and that more explicit instruction in alphabetic coding resulted in less disparity between at-risk students in reading achievement at the end of the year than less explicit approaches to teaching spelling-sound patterns.

Relatedly, Morris et al. (2000) examined the effectiveness of *Early Steps*, a first-grade early intervention programme that is very similar to Reading Recovery, especially in the emphasis it places on contextual reading and writing. However, a fundamental difference is that Early Steps also includes direct, systematic study of orthographic patterns that is 'purposefully isolated from meaningful context so that the child can pay full attention to the patterns being studied' (p. 682). In discussing this important distinction between Early Steps and RR, Morris et al. argued that:

> We should not dismiss the possibility (as Clay seems to do) that some children might benefit from studying a single information source (e.g., spelling patterns) in isolation while simultaneously being offered the chance to integrate this knowledge in contextual reading and writing. However small this instructional distinction may seem, it is at the heart of a century-old debate concerning the role of isolated word study (phonics) in beginning reading instruction. (p. 251)

Providing struggling readers with explicit and systematic instruction in word analysis skills outside the context of reading text helps to ensure that these children see the importance of focusing on word-level cues as the most useful source of information in identifying words, as well as helping them to overcome their tendency to rely on sentence context cues to identify unfamiliar words in text rather than using context to supplement word-level information. One of the major distinguishing characteristics of struggling readers is their tendency to rely heavily on sentence context cues to compensate for their deficient alphabetic coding skills (Pressley, 2006).

Morris et al. (2000) found that Early Steps was highly effective, especially for those children who were most at risk. Similarly, Hatcher et al. (1994) reported that adding systematic training in phonological awareness combined with instruction in the alphabetic principle to a remedial reading programme modelled after RR was highly effective and produced greater gains in poor readers than either the remedial reading programme or phonological awareness training on its own. These findings are consistent with studies indicating that struggling readers who benefited least from RR, which does not include systematic instruction in either phonological awareness or alphabetic coding, were less advanced in phonological processing skills at the beginning of the programme than children who derived greater benefit from the programme (Center et al., 1995; Chapman et al., 2001; Iversen and Tunmer, 1993).

In addition to explicitness, the intensity of reading interventions needs to be considered. Because at-risk and struggling readers are already behind in the development of reading and reading-related skills, they must improve their reading skills at a faster rate than their typically achieving peers to close the gap in literacy achievement (Torgesen, 2004). To achieve this outcome, preventive and remedial instruction must be more intense than regular classroom instruction. Intensity can be increased by reducing group size and/or by increasing the duration of instruction (Vaughn and Linan-Thompson, 2003).

Regarding group size, students demonstrating unsatisfactory progress in regular classroom instruction (described as the *first tier* of multi-tiered models of reading intervention; Denton and Mathes, 2003) are often provided with one-to-one supplementary instruction such as Reading Recovery, which is a *second tier* intervention strategy. However, in a meta-analysis of one-to-one tutoring programmes for struggling readers, Elbaum et al. (2000) noted that:

> Despite the popular belief that one-to-one instruction is more effective than instruction delivered to larger numbers of students, there is actually little systematic evidence to support this belief. Each additional student that can be accommodated in an instructional group represents a substantial reduction in the per-student cost of the intervention, or alternatively, a substantial increase in the number of students that can be served. (p. 606)

To examine this issue further, Vaughn and Linan-Thompson (2003) carried out a study in which struggling readers in second grade were provided with the same treatment but in instructional groups that varied in size (1-to-1, 1-to-3, and 1-to-10). The treatment involved daily supplementary reading instruction of 58 sessions over a period of 12 weeks by 5 specially trained tutors. The intervention focused on increasing phonemic awareness, knowledge of letter-sound relationships, fluency, reading comprehension, and spelling. The results indicated that significant progress was made by the children in all three groups. However, there were no statistically significant differences in the outcome measures between the students in the 1-to-1 and 1-to-3 groups, although both groups outperformed the students in the 1-to-10 group. Similarly, in a study comparing the effectiveness of 1-to-1 RR instruction with RR instruction in pairs, Iversen et al. (2005) found that although RR instruction in pairs required somewhat longer lessons, there were no major differences between the groups on any measures at discontinuation and at the end of the year, nor was there a significant difference between the groups in mean number of lessons to discontinuation. These findings suggest that the same outcomes of (second tier) interventions can be achieved by teaching struggling readers in groups of two or three as by teaching them individually.

In a second study, Vaughn and Linan-Thompson (2003) examined variation in treatment duration for second grade struggling readers as a function of meeting a priori established criteria for treatment discontinuation. The struggling readers received the same research-based intervention that was used in the first study but all were taught in groups of three. The students were tested after each 10 weeks of instruction (approximately 50 sessions) for 3 10-week segments. Vaughn and Linan-Thompson (2003) reported that the students met the exit criteria at varying times (10-, 20-, 30-week exit or no exit). The results of the two studies provide useful guidelines about the efficacy of varying group size and the duration of instruction needed by struggling readers.

Another issue relating to the design of intervention programmes is the balance that needs to be achieved in the instructional components of each lesson, especially between learning new skills and actually using them. Focusing on explicit and systematic teaching of word analysis skills to struggling readers does not mean adopting a rigid skill-and-drill approach in which word identification skills are taught largely in isolation with little or no connection to actual reading. Although struggling readers should receive explicit instruction in letter-sound patterns outside the context of reading connected text (see above), they should also be taught how and when to use this information during text reading through demonstration, modelling, direct explanation and guided practice. It cannot be assumed that struggling readers who are successful in acquiring word analysis skills will automatically transfer them when attempting to read connected text (Lyon and Moats, 1997). Rather, struggling readers need to be encouraged to become *active* problem solvers with regard to graphic information in text. This includes adopting a 'set for diversity' (Gaskins et al., 1988) in which they learn to use irregular spelling patterns (which are common in English orthography), polyphonic spelling patterns (such as *ear* as in *bear* and *hear*, *own* as in *clown* and *flown*) and partial decoding attempts to generate alternative pronunciations of target words until one is produced that matches a word in their spoken vocabulary and is appropriate to the sentence context.

Supporting these claims are the results of two studies demonstrating that a balance in the *content* of reading intervention programmes between out of context training in word analysis skills and opportunities to use the newly acquired skills to identify unfamiliar words during text reading is more important than the particular approach to teaching reading adopted in the intervention programme (Hatcher et al., 2006; Mathes et al., 2005). Both studies reported similar positive outcomes when comparing the effects of intervention programmes based on more highly structured, direct transmission models of instruction with those based on less structured, cognitive strategy-oriented models, where the ultimate goal was teaching students to apply strategies independently. As Mathes et al. (2005) concluded on the basis of their results:

> Perhaps the most important finding of this research is that supplemental intervention approaches derived from different theoretical perspectives were both effective ... Both interventions provided for instruction in key reading skills, balanced with opportunities to apply reading and writing skills in connected text ... (p. 179)

In evaluating the effectiveness of reading interventions there are a number of issues that need to be considered. An essential one is obtaining an estimate of how struggling readers would have done without the intervention, which in single-subject designs means establishing a baseline, and in group designs means including a control group (established by randomly assigning students to conditions or by using appropriate procedures to match groups as closely as possible on all relevant variables). Regarding the latter, Hawthorne effects can be reduced by giving the children in the control group a treatment that should have little or no effect on reading and reading-related measures, preferably using the same materials and for the same amount of time as the children in the treatment group (e.g., Bradley and Bryant, 1983). Because many reading interventions involve multiple treatment components (phonological awareness training, word analysis activities, spelling, text reading, etc.), comparison groups can also be used to investigate the effectiveness of different components on relevant outcome measures by varying one component while holding the others constant (e.g., Iversen and Tunmer, 1993).

Other factors to consider in evaluating reading interventions include intervention duration, transfer effects and maintenance effects. Three questions need to be addressed regarding these factors. First, was the frequency of lessons, average instructional time of each lesson and overall duration of the intervention sufficient to produce positive effects in the skills that were the focus of the programme? Second, did the positive effects produced by the intervention generalise to other skills and materials? And third, were the positive effects of the programme maintained after the intervention was completed?

Teacher effects are another important consideration. Possible confounding effects due to differences in teacher characteristics can be reduced by examining the degree of teacher fidelity in the administration of the intervention and, if possible, by having each teacher provide treatment to students in both the experimental and comparison groups, in equal numbers. For example, Greaney et al. (1997) investigated whether one-to-one metacognitive training in the use of rime spelling units would be an effective intervention strategy for students with persistent reading problems. Disabled readers were randomly assigned to either a rime analogy training group or an item-specific training group involving the same instructional materials. Possible teacher effects were controlled by having each tutor use both intervention programmes, one with half the children they were working with, and the other intervention with the remaining half. The results showed that systematic training in the use of rime spelling units produced generalised achievement gains and transfer to uninstructed materials and was more effective than training that focused on item-specific learning and sentence-level strategies. One year follow-up results indicated that the superior post-intervention performance of the treatment group over the control group was maintained. These findings suggest that even students with persistent reading problems, most of whom had been referred on from Reading Recovery, were able to derive long-term benefits from explicit instruction in phonological processing skills (see Torgesen et al., 2003, for similar findings).

Contextual variables can also influence the effectiveness of reading interventions. If a reading intervention is in addition to the child's regular classroom reading programme, the effectiveness of the intervention may depend on the degree of compatibility between the instructional strategies used in the intervention and those used by the classroom teacher. Clay (1993), for example, claimed that Reading Recovery is compatible with all types of classroom literacy programmes, but offered no evidence in support of this claim. To test this claim,

Center et al. (2001) investigated whether the efficacy of RR varied as a function of classroom literacy program. They compared the effects of RR in 'meaning-oriented' (i.e., whole language) classrooms and 'code-oriented' classrooms (i.e., those that included explicit and systematic instruction in phonological awareness and alphabetic coding). Results indicated that at the end of the second year of schooling, students in the code-oriented classrooms (regular and RR students combined) significantly outperformed students in the meaning-oriented classrooms on measures of phonological decoding, reading connected text, and invented spelling, and on a standardised reading measure (see Christensen and Bowey, 2005, for similar findings).

The RR students in the code-oriented classrooms also significantly outper-formed the RR students in the meaning-oriented classrooms on all four literacy measures, with an average reading age advantage of 8 months on the standardised reading measure. However, the RR students in both classes failed to reach the average level of their peers on any of the literacy measures. Of particular interest were the findings that a much higher percentage of RR students from meaning-oriented classrooms (83 per cent) than from code-oriented classrooms (50 per cent) were considered to have been unsuccessfully recovered (which was defined as falling below the 30th percentile on at least three of the four literacy tests); that the mean number of weeks to discontinuation for RR students from meaning-oriented classrooms was significantly greater than for RR students from code-oriented classrooms (18 weeks vs. 14.5 weeks); and that a much higher percentage of RR students from meaning-oriented than code-oriented classrooms were either withdrawn or unsuccessfully discontinued from RR (25 per cent vs. 5 per cent). These findings contradict Clay's (1993) claim that the regular classroom context does not differentially affect the literacy performance of RR students. The results also provide further support for the argument that explicit training in phonemically based decoding strategies should be incorporated into reading intervention programmes.

ADVANCES IN ASSESSMENT AND DATA ANALYSIS TOOLS

The purposes of reading assessment include

1 *screening* at school entry or the beginning of the school year to identify weaknesses in reading or reading-related skills that are highly predictive of future reading achievement in order that the weaknesses can be addressed by teachers or remedial specialists before they develop into larger problems;
2 *diagnosis* of specific strengths and weaknesses as the basis for differential instruction, where classroom teachers and remedial specialists use assessment-driven instructional strategies to cater to the differing skill needs of students;
3 *progress monitoring* of the rate of improvement achieved by students in response to classroom or supplementary instruction to determine whether adequate progress is being

made or to compare the efficacy of different instructional strategies or intervention programmes; and

4   *outcome evaluation* conducted at the end of the school year or completion of an intervention programme to determine students' progress relative to grade level expectations or specified exit criteria (Kame'enui et al., 2005; Wagner et al., 2003).

Researchers have identified five broad areas of skills and knowledge that children must acquire as they learn to read: phonemic awareness, phonics, fluency, vocabulary and reading comprehension (Pressley et al., 2006). Torgesen (2004), for example, argued that:

> It is very important that young children (1) become aware of the phonemic elements in words (phonemic awareness), (2) learn to decode words they have not seen before in print by using knowledge about relationships between letters and sounds (phonics) and (3) learn to recognize large numbers of words by sight so that they can read fluently. At the same time, children must become able to (4) instantly retrieve the meanings of an increasingly large vocabulary of words and (5) think actively while they read in order to construct meaning (use comprehension strategies). (p. 362)

Comprehensive reading assessments must include developmentally appropriate measures of most or all of these skills, taking into consideration that children must first achieve a reasonable degree of fluency in reading text before the development of more advanced levels of reading comprehension can occur. Beginning readers who fail to develop fluency in recognising the words of text will encounter difficulty in comprehending and thinking about what they are reading because inefficient lexical access disrupts the temporary representation of text in working memory (Perfetti, 1985). Examples of evidence-based, early reading assessments are the Dynamic Indicators of Basic Early Literacy Skills (Good et al., 2001) and the Texas Primary Reading Inventory (Foorman et al., 2004).

In addition to assessing essential reading skills to determine the efficacy of interventions, Pressley et al. (2006) recommended using qualitative and naturalistic approaches, especially when evaluating complex interventions that include a number of components delivered over an extended period of time. The descriptive data obtained from such approaches can be used to assess treatment fidelity and gain greater understanding of the impact of reading interventions in different settings. As Pressley et al. (2006) argued, 'done well, such analyses can provide detailed portraits of how an intervention can be delivered, the challenges in doing so and the rich array of outcomes and relationships that might be influenced by the intervention' (p. 6).

New statistical tools such as hierarchical linear modelling and growth curve analysis are increasingly being used to examine the effects of various social, cultural, environmental and ecological factors on interventions (Lyon and Moats, 1997; Pressley et al., 2006). Nested models such as hierarchical linear modelling provide the basis for examining interactions between interventions and child, classroom and school variables. The models have also been used to examine contextual effects in risk determination, where individual risk for reading difficulties is nested within classroom and within school levels of risk (see Foorman et al., in press, for an example).

Until recently the evaluation of interventions has relied mostly on traditional pre-test/post-test designs. However, assessing the effects of interventions in this manner fails to provide estimates of intraindividual change. As Lyon and Moats (1997) pointed out, the advantage of growth curve analysis over traditional designs is that it enables the researcher to examine 'different forms and different patterns of growth at different stages of development and/or during treatment ... [and] ... provides the investigator with a new method for addressing the inevitable heterogeneity that will accompany any sample of children, no matter how carefully selected' (p. 584).

In addition to being useful in assessing the effects of interventions, the analysis of growth curves (which yields slopes and intercepts as variables) provides the basis for a recently developed approach for identifying students at risk for reading failure called *dual discrepancy*, where both the student's performance level and growth rate are below that of classroom peers (Fuchs et al., 2003). The approach involves two steps. A screening tool is first used to determine if students are performing below grade-level expectations. An analysis of individual growth curves is then used to measure rate of improvement in response to instruction (which may be supplemental instruction in a multi-tiered system). To illustrate the logic of this approach, Fuchs et al. (2003) gave the example of an endocrinologist considering the possibility of underlying pathology in a child's physical growth. Not only is the child's height measured at one point in time, but the child's growth trajectory is measured in response to an adequately nurturing environment. If both measures are below normal, the child is considered a likely candidate for special treatment.

Large-scale meta-analyses are also being used by researchers to evaluate the efficacy of reading interventions. Meta-analyses are sophisticated and systematic reviews of studies that involve the computation of effect size, which provides the basis for comparing the relative impact of different interventions, or for computing the average effect size of separate intervention studies that are grouped together on some basis. Although useful, meta-analysis has several limitations, such as differing criteria for including studies in the meta-analysis, inappropriate summing of all dependent variables in studies and the restriction of analyses of the effects of interventions to data generated in experimental and quasi-experimental designs (Pressley et al., 2006).

CONCEPTUAL ISSUES IN READING INTERVENTION RESEARCH

According to Torgesen (2004), children who enter school at risk for developing reading difficulties can be divided into two broad groups, those with adequate oral language ability but weaknesses in the phonological domain and those with weaknesses in both oral language ability and phonologically-related skills, typically children from low-income backgrounds. Torgesen (2004) further claimed that although there may be children who enter school weak in oral language but strong in the phonological skills required to learn to read words, such children are very rare.

Given that reading is a derived skill that builds on spoken language, reading can be defined as the ability to translate from print to a form of code from which the reader can already derive meaning; namely, the reader's spoken language. Although there are differences between spoken and printed language (such as in how language is represented in speech and in print), comprehending text requires the full set of linguistic skills needed to comprehend spoken language, including locating individual words in lexical memory, determining the intended meaning of individual words (most of which are polysemous), assigning appropriate syntactic structures to sentences, deriving meaning from individually structured sentences and building meaningful discourse on the basis of sentential meaning. If the child's fundamental task in learning to read is to discover how print maps onto their spoken language, then the process of learning to derive meaning from print can be adversely affected in one of two ways, or both: the child's spoken language system may be deficient in various ways, or the process by which print is connected to the child's spoken language system may be defective.

These basic ideas are represented in a model of the proximal causes of reading difficulties developed by Gough and Tunmer (1986). The model makes two claims; first, that reading may be decomposed into two components, decoding (or more generally, word recognition) and oral language comprehension; and second, that each of these components is necessary, neither being sufficient in itself. That is, $R = D \times C$, where R is reading comprehension, D is decoding skill, and C is oral language comprehension. Stated simply, students who have trouble recognizing the words of (age appropriate) text and/or have trouble understanding the language being read, will have trouble understanding the text.

An important feature of the model is that it provides a framework for conceptualizing three broad categories of reading difficulties, each of which may require a different intervention strategy. The model predicts that reading comprehension problems can result from weaknesses in recognizing printed words, weaknesses in comprehending spoken language or both. Students who can understand a text when it is read aloud to them but cannot decode the words even after receiving extensive (and appropriate) instruction are referred to as *dyslexics*; students who can read words accurately but have difficulty constructing the meaning of text are described as having *specific reading comprehension difficulties* (Nation, 2005); and students who have problems in both word recognition and oral language comprehension are described as having a *mixed* reading disability (Catts and Kamhi, 2005).

The language-based deficits that contribute to developmental reading problems vary across the three categories of reading difficulties. Dyslexia is generally associated with problems in the phonological domain, especially deficiencies in phonemic awareness and phonological decoding, both of which are crucial for developing word reading skills (Vellutino and Fletcher, 2005; Vellutino et al., 2004). As predicted by the model, the development of adequate facility in word identification is a necessary (though not sufficient) condition for the development of reading comprehension ability. Growth in the ability to construct meaning from text will therefore be impeded if children fail to develop the phonemically-based skills necessary for constructing adequate word-level representations (i.e., sight word knowledge). Stanovich (1996) succinctly described the canonical model of developmental dyslexia in a single sentence: 'Impaired language segmentation skills lead to difficulties in phonological coding which in turn impede the word recognition process which underpins reading comprehension' (p. 155). Systematic reading interventions involving dyslexic children have therefore targeted phonological awareness and decoding skills (Torgesen, 2004; 2005).

The majority of poor readers, however, have mixed reading disability. These children, who are also called 'garden variety' poor readers (Gough and Tunmer, 1986), have more widespread language impairments than are typically found among dyslexic children (Snowling et al., 2003; Tunmer and Chapman, 2007). In addition to phonological processing deficits, children with mixed reading disability have impairments in vocabulary, morphology, syntax and/or discourse-level processing. The resulting weakness in oral language comprehension places an upper limit on reading comprehension (Hoover and Gough, 1990; Hoover and Tunmer, 1993), which would account for recent research showing that in addition to phonological factors (e.g., phonological awareness), non-phonological oral language factors (e.g., expressive vocabulary, sentence or story recall) are predictive of long-term reading outcomes (Leach et al., 2003; Scarborough, 2005). It would also explain why prevention programmes for at-risk students with mixed deficits focusing mostly on teaching phonemic awareness and phonemically based decoding strategies initially show positive effects on reading achievement (typically word reading) but fail to maintain these positive effects in later grades when reading comprehension measures are used. Torgesen (2004) suggested that this pattern of results occurs 'for the simple reason that as reading material becomes more complex (with increasing vocabulary demands and more difficult concepts), the role of broad verbal ability in accounting for reading comprehension difficulties becomes larger ...' (p. 368). Consistent with this claim are results from a longitudinal study by Hoover and Gough (1990) revealing developmental changes in the relative contributions of decoding and oral language comprehension to the variance in reading comprehension performance in grades 1 through 4, with decoding accounting for more of the variance in the lower grades (see Vellutino et al., 2007, for similar findings). These results suggest that oral language comprehension becomes more important at later stages of learning to read after children have begun to master basic word identification skills, and when children's reading materials have become more advanced in components of language that are common to both oral language comprehension and reading comprehension (e.g., semantics, syntax and pragmatics).

The pattern of results that Torgesen (2004) described in prevention studies is even more pronounced in remedial intervention studies involving older poor readers. From an examination of 14 studies providing interventions to children with moderate to severe word-level reading difficulties, Torgesen (2005) found that reported gains for phonological decoding skills were consistently higher than those for reading comprehension skills (see his Table 27.2: 530). Relatedly, Blachman et al. (2004) reported positive effects of an intensive reading remediation programme for second and third grade children with poor word-level skills but in a one-year follow-up when the treatment children were no longer exposed to the experimental intervention, the modest positive post-test effects for reading comprehension were not maintained.

Two other essential reading skills that are difficult to remediate in older poor readers are vocabulary and fluency. Foorman et al. (2003) were concerned that the low vocabulary sizes of at-risk children in third and fourth grade would retard their reading comprehension as they began to confront more semantically complex reading materials across the curriculum, especially as the children moved into fourth grade, where they typically experience what is described as the 'fourth grade slump' (Chall, 1983). Foorman et al. (2003) therefore investigated the effects of a 20-week vocabulary enrichment programme for at-risk third and fourth graders and found that although the programme significantly improved knowledge of word meanings, the positive outcomes did not transfer to reading comprehension, a result that confirmed the findings of others.

Researchers have also found that although interventions for children with moderate or severe impairments in word reading ability can succeed in closing the gap in reading accuracy and, to some extent, reading comprehension, they generally fail to close the gap in reading fluency, even when the intervention allocated considerable instructional time to reading connected text or to modelling and practising fluent reading (Torgesen, 2004; 2005; Torgesen et al., 2001b). Torgesen (2005) compared outcomes for reading accuracy and reading fluency in remedial and preventive studies and found consistently large differences in outcomes favouring accuracy gains over fluency gains in remedial studies but little or no gap between accuracy and fluency gains in prevention studies. Torgesen suggested that the intractability of closing the gap in fluency in older poor readers is most likely attributable to the problems these children face in making up for the huge deficits in reading practice they have accumulated as a consequence of failing to learn to read during the first 3 or 4 years of school. Such lack of practice and restricted exposure to print would severely impair the development of their sight word knowledge (Ehri and McCormick, 1998).

In general, the difficulties that intervention researchers have experienced in attempting to help older poor readers close the gap in reading fluency, vocabulary knowledge and reading comprehension are most likely the result of negative (poor-get-poorer) Matthew effects in reading (Stanovich, 1986; Tunmer and Hoover, 1993). As a consequence of phonological processing deficits, the development of word recognition skill is impeded in both dyslexic poor readers and children with mixed reading disability (i.e., garden variety poor readers). Students with deficient word identification skills will not only receive less practice in reading but soon begin to confront materials that are too difficult for them, which (not surprisingly) results in avoidance of reading (Juel, 1988). These children are therefore prevented from taking full advantage of the reciprocally facilitating relationships (i.e., positive, or rich-get-richer, Matthew effects) between reading achievement and other aspects of development, including component skills of reading itself. These developmental spinoffs include vocabulary growth, ability to comprehend more syntactically complex sentences, development of richer and more elaborate knowledge bases, and greater reading practice opportunities for building fluency and facilitating implicit learning of letter-sound patterns, all of which facilitate further growth in reading and language by enabling children to cope with more difficult materials.

Although both dyslexic poor readers and children with mixed reading disability have weaknesses in the phonological domain, the more widespread oral language impairments of the mixed disabled readers further impede the development of their phonemic awareness and phonological decoding skills in at least three ways (Snowling et al., 2003; Tunmer and Chapman, 2007). First, vocabulary growth during the preschool years plays a major role in the development of preliterate phonological sensitivity by causing lexical representations to become more segmental (Carroll et al., 2003; Metsala, 1997; Walley, 1993). Because deficiencies in vocabulary growth are accompanied by more poorly specified phonological representations of spoken words, the development of phonemic awareness is likely to be more severely impaired in children with poorly developed vocabulary knowledge at school entry. Second, children with poorly developed vocabulary knowledge will have trouble identifying and assigning appropriate meanings to unknown printed words, especially partially decoded or irregularly spelled words, if the corresponding spoken words are not in their listening vocabulary. Third, deficiencies in syntactic knowledge (i.e., implicit knowledge of rules specifying structural relationships in sentences) will impair the development of word identification skills in children with mixed reading disability by limiting their ability to use sentence context as an aid to identifying partially decoded words, irregularly spelled words or words containing polyphonic spelling patterns. The use of sentence context to confirm hypotheses about what unfamiliar words might be, based on incomplete information from partial decoding attempts, results in correct word identifications which, in turn, facilitates the development of beginning readers' word-specific orthographic knowledge from which additional spelling-sound correspondences can be induced (Tunmer and Chapman, 1998; 2006).

Given these considerations, a prediction that follows from the classification scheme derived from the Gough and Tunmer (1986) model of reading disability is that mixed disabled readers should show greater phonological processing deficits than dyslexic poor readers at the beginning of school and during the early stages of learning to read. In support of this claim, Tunmer and Chapman (2007) found in a longitudinal study of language-related differences between mixed disabled readers and dyslexic poor readers that in addition to expected differences on oral language measures, the mixed disabled readers also showed consistently greater phonological processing deficits than the dyslexic poor readers across a range of phonological processing measures. These findings and those discussed earlier (Leach et al., 2003; Scarborough, 2005; Torgesen, 2005) suggest that for mixed disabled readers, which constitute by far the largest group of poor readers, early intervention programmes may need to focus on improving these children's oral language skills as well as their phonological skills (Gersten and Dimino, 2006).

In addition to dyslexic poor readers and mixed disabled readers, the third broad category of disabled readers specified by the Gough and Tunmer (1986) model comprises children with specific reading comprehension difficulties. These poor readers are generally free of phonological processing deficiencies and demonstrate satisfactory alphabetic coding skills, but (like the poor readers with mixed reading disability) show weaknesses in vocabulary, morphology, syntax, discourse-level processing and/or comprehension strategies which, in turn, negatively impact reading comprehension performance (see Nation, 2005, for a review of research). However, the developmental mechanism responsible for the oral language impairments in children with specific reading comprehension difficulties may be different from what causes such impairments in children with a mixed reading disability. For children with mixed reading disability, oral language impairments stem primarily from limited access to linguistic and environmental opportunities during the preschool years, whereas for children with specific reading comprehension difficulties, such impairments appear to be largely a consequence of having substantially less reading and reading-related experience than typically developing readers, which ultimately produces negative Matthew effects in reading (Nation, 2005). As Nation argued, 'Poor comprehenders may read less, and learn less from their reading experiences than their peers; therefore impacting on subsequent reading and learning opportunities over time and leading to the formation of weak "intellectual habits"...' (p. 264). Intervention programmes for children with specific reading comprehension difficulties may therefore need to focus particular attention on motivating these children to increase both the amount and range of their personal reading (see Guthrie and Humenick, 2004, for a review of research on motivational factors in learning to read).

One of the clear implications of the negative Matthew effects associated with each of the three broad categories of poor readers specified by the Gough and Tunmer (1986) model is the need for *early* intervention. Historically, the notion of 'unexpected underachievement' has been the central defining feature of the reading disability construct. Children are identified as reading disabled/dyslexic when factors that would be expected to cause problems in all areas of learning, not just reading, are excluded (e.g., mental retardation, emotional and social difficulties, attentional problems, limited access to linguistic and environmental opportunities, inadequate or inappropriate classroom instruction). In actual practice, however, reading disability is normally defined as a discrepancy between reading achievement and intellectual potential as measured by standardised intelligence tests. Most exclusionary factors are generally ignored, especially experiential and instructional deficits. As Vellutino and Denckla (1991) pointed out, 'virtually all of the research available has failed to evaluate or adequately control for the environmental and/or educational deficits that may cause a reading disorder' (p. 603).

An important consequence of the discrepancy-based assessment procedure is that children with reading disability are not normally identified until after they have been exposed to reading instruction for 2–3 years, and often longer. This 'wait-to-fail' approach to identification is antithetical to early intervention and the prevention of negative Matthew effects in reading (Fuchs and Fuchs, 2006). Even more damaging to the discrepancy-based approach is a considerable amount of research indicating that groups of poor readers formed on the basis of the presence or absence of IQ-achievement discrepancies do not reliably differ in long-term prognosis, response to intervention, or the cognitive subskills (e.g., phonemic awareness and phonological decoding) that underlie the development of word recognition (Fletcher et al., 1994; 2005; Francis et al., 2005; Fuchs and Young, 2006; Hatcher and Hulme, 1999; Stanovich, 1991; Stanovich and Siegel, 1994; Stuebing et al., 2002; Vellutino et al., 2000). These findings support the conclusion that IQ tests are largely irrelevant to the identification of reading disability.

An alternative strategy to identifying reading disability is to operationalise unexpected underachievement in terms of both low performance on reading and reading-related measures and poor response to high-quality instruction. This is the dual discrepancy approach described earlier. A major shortcoming of the definition-by-exclusion approach associated with discrepancy-based procedures for identifying reading disability is that poor achievement is typically assumed to reflect disability rather than poor teaching, when the latter is more often than not the primary contributing factor (Fuchs and Fuchs, 2006; Tunmer and Chapman, 1996; Vellutino et al., 1996; 2006). Vellutino et al. (2006) argued that because discrepancy-based approaches 'do not control for the child's preschool and educational history, they do not adequately distinguish between reading difficulties caused primarily by experiential and instructional deficits and reading difficulties caused primarily by biologically based deficits in reading-related cognitive abilities' (p. 157). As a consequence, the number of children classified as reading disabled is highly inflated.

Vellutino and colleagues (Vellutino et al., 1996; 2003) investigated the extent to which experiential/instructional deficits are primary causes of early and protracted reading difficulties, especially for children who have acquired such limited amounts of crucial reading-related knowledge, skills and experiences from home and preschool (collectively referred to as *literate cultural capital*; Tunmer et al., 2006) that they are unable to acquire basic literacy skills by means of regular classroom instruction without additional support. Vellutino and colleagues carried out a longitudinal study in which a large sample of children was tracked from the beginning of kindergarten to the end of third grade. The children who had significant reading problems by the middle of the first grade (approximately 9 per cent of their sample) were provided with one-to-one remedial instruction during the second semester of first grade. Vellutino et al. (1996) found that 67 per cent of these children (the 'readily remediated poor readers') were within the normal range of reading achievement following the remediation. In addition, these children performed significantly better than the 'difficult-to-remediate poor readers' (i.e., those who did not respond to the intervention) on measures of phonological processing administered prior to the intervention. Vellutino and colleagues concluded from these results that most children with early reading difficulties suffer from experiential and instructional deficits, and that the truly disabled readers (1.5 per cent of the sample) are those children with relatively severe phonological processing deficits who, as a consequence, do not respond to either regular classroom instruction or intensive, short-term intervention efforts.

Emerging from these findings and those of others is the response-to-intervention (RTI) approach to preventing and identifying reading disability (Deschler et al., 2005; Fuchs and Fuchs, 2006). In this approach, intervention serves as the 'test stimulus' and rate of growth (i.e., degree of responsiveness to intervention) serves as the 'test performance' in identifying reading disability (Fuchs and Fuchs, 2006: 95). RTI uses evidence-based instruction and continuous progress monitoring across multiple tiers (usually three) to provide early intervention for children at risk for reading failure and to develop a more reliable procedure for identifying students with reading disability.

The first tier of RTI models typically involves 'enhanced classroom instruction' (Denton and Mathes, 2003: 233) where literacy teaching in the earliest years of school addresses the individual needs of all of the children in the classroom, especially those experiencing early literacy difficulties. The second tier normally involves more explicit and extended (small group) instruction for children whose rates of progress in the first tier identify them as at risk for reading difficulties and in need of supplemental instruction (i.e., secondary intervention). Children who continue to progress at a very slow rate after the provision of second-tier supplementary instruction are placed in more intensive third-tier interventions (e.g., daily one-to-one tutoring) of longer duration (see Denton and Mathes, 2003, for a more detailed discussion of the three-tier model). Continuous monitoring of individual student progress is used in each of the three tiers to determine whether a child no longer needs supplemental instruction, needs continuing support at the existing level or is eligible for a higher level of support. A variety of multi-tiered, RTI models are currently being investigated (Al Otaiba and Fuchs, 2006; Denton et al., 2006; McMaster et al., 2005; O'Connor et al., 2005; Vaughn et al., 2003; Vellutino et al., 2006).

An important aim of the RTI model is to increase the accuracy of selecting children who are truly in need of secondary intervention (i.e., 'true positives') to ensure that the most vulnerable children receive supplemental instruction, thus preventing the development of more significant reading problems (Fuchs and Fuchs, 2006). Two types of errors can lower the degree of accuracy in identifying at-risk students, 'false positives' and 'false negatives'. Selecting students for intense services who are not in need of them results in false positives, which undermines the effectiveness of RTI models by inflating the number of at-risk children and stressing available resources for providing secondary interventions. False negatives occur when children score above the cut off scores on predictive measures but later develop reading difficulties. A high number of false negatives diminishes the preventive aspect of RTI models by depriving at-risk children of the additional support that they require. Research addressing these issues has demonstrated that RTI-based procedures are more effective in identifying genuine at-risk students (true positives) and not selecting those not in need (false positives) than standard psychometric screening procedures (Compton et al., 2006; Fuchs et al., in press; Vellutino et al., in press).

CONCLUDING REMARKS

We wish to conclude our chapter by drawing attention to recent studies of the neurobiological effects of successful reading interventions, especially evidence indicating plasticity in the neurophysiological processes involved in reading. The use of functional magnetic resonance imaging (fMRI) to describe the cerebral mechanisms that support reading has enabled cognitive neuroscientists to determine 'the exact temporal characteristics and anatomical distribution of neurophysiological activity that reflect inter-neuronal signalling within and between different brain areas' (Papanicolaou et al., 2003: 5). Three interrelated questions have been addressed in this research. First, what is the activation profile seen in skilled readers, and how did it change over time from unskilled to skilled reading? Second, what is the aberrant activation profile seen in older children with persistent reading difficulties, and what was the developmental course that led to the establishment of the aberrant activation profile? Third, and perhaps most important, to what extent can an evidence-based intervention programme focusing on phonemic awareness and phonemically-based decoding strategies alter the aberrant activation profiles seen in older students with persistent reading difficulties? As argued earlier, the primary cause of developmental reading problems in dyslexic and garden variety poor readers is poor context-free word recognition ability and associated phonological deficits.

The general picture that has emerged from this research is that typically developing readers initially rely primarily on a system in the parieto-temporal area of the left hemisphere to identify words in a slow, analytic manner by taking them apart and linking their letters to their sounds. However, as the student's reading skills develop, a system in the occipital-temporal area of the left hemisphere gradually takes over. Shaywitz (2003) described this system as the express pathway to reading, the 'word form' area of the brain where printed words come to be recognised very rapidly on sight. For very poor readers, however, the neural pathways in these two regions in the back of the brain are underactivated. Instead, poor readers activate compensatory reading systems near Broca's area in the left hemisphere and two regions in the right hemisphere. Sandak et al. (2004) hypothesised that 'the reason readers with RD tend to strongly engage inferior frontal sites is their increased reliance on covert pronunciation (articulatory recoding) in an attempt to cope with their deficient phonological analysis of the printed word' (p. 279). In neurophysiological terms, literacy learning problems in otherwise normally developing children are primarily due to the ongoing failure of the children to deploy the appropriate neurological systems in the brain when confronted with the task of learning to read and write in an alphabetic orthography. In behavioural terms, the literacy problems of struggling readers result from the continuing use of ineffective learning strategies, such as attempting to learn new words by relying on partial visual cues (such as the word's shape) and/or partial word-level cues (such as the initial letter of the word) in combination with contextual guessing.

This need not be a permanent state of affairs, however, as indicated by the results of studies of the neurophysiological processes involved in reading before and after remediation of reading impairments by means of interventions focusing on phonologically-based word-level skills and strategies (Aylward et al., 2003; Shaywitz et al., 2004; Simos et al., 2002; Simos et al., 2007). The most important finding emerging from these studies is that the activation profile of the successfully remediated poor readers becomes much more like the activation profile of normally developing readers and, with the passage of time, increasingly like that of skilled readers. In short, with the use of appropriate intervention strategies, many students with persistent reading difficulties can be taught to use their brains in a more effective manner.

REFERENCES

Adams, M.J. (1990) *Beginning to read: Thinking and learning about print.* Cambridge, MA: MIT Press.

Adams, M.J. and Bruck, M. (1993) 'Word recognition: The interface of educational policies and scientific research', *Reading and Writing,* 5: 113–139.

Al Otaiba, S. and Fuchs, D. (2006) 'Who are the young children for whom best practices in reading are ineffective? An experimental and longitudinal study', *Journal of Learning Disabilities,* 39: 414–431.

Aylward, E., Richards, T., Berninger, V., Nagy, W., Field, K., Grimme, A., et al. (2003) 'Instructional treatment associated with changes in brain activation in children with dyslexia', *Neurology,* 61: 212–219.

Blachman, B.A. (2000) 'Phonological awareness', in M.L. Kamil, P.B. Mosenthal, P.D. Pearson, and R. Barr (eds), *Handbook of reading research.* Mahwah, NJ: Erlbaum. Vol. 3: pp. 483–502.

Blachman, B.A., Schatschneider, C., Fletcher, J.M., Francis, D.J., Clonan, S.M., Shaywitz, B.A. and Shaywitz, S.E. (2004) 'Effects of intensive reading remediation for second and third graders and a 1-year follow-up', *Journal of Educational Psychology,* 96: 444–461.

Bradley, L. and Bryant, P.E. (1983) 'Categorising sounds and learning to read – a casual connection', *Nature,* 301: 419–421.

Calfee, R. and Drum, P. (1986) 'Research on teaching reading', in M.C. Whittock (ed.), *Handbook of research on teaching*. New York: MacMillan. pp. 804–849.

Carroll, J.M., Snowling, M.J., Hulme, C. and Stevenson, J. (2003) 'The development of phonological awareness in preschool children', *Developmental Psychology*, 39: 913–923.

Catts, H. and Kamhi, A. (2005) *Language and reading disabilities*. Boston, MA: Pearson.

Center, Y., Freeman, L. and Robertson, G. (2001) 'The relative effects of a code-oriented and a meaning-oriented early literacy program on regular and low progress Australian students in Year 1 classrooms which implement Reading Recovery', *International Journal of Disability, Development and Education*, 48: 207–232.

Center, Y., Wheldhall, K., Freeman, L., Outred, L. and McNaught, M. (1995) 'An evaluation of Reading Recovery', *Reading Research Quarterly*, 30: 240–263.

Chall, J.S. (1983) *Stages of reading development*. New York: McGraw-Hill.

Chapman, J.W. and Tunmer, W.E. (2003) 'Reading difficulties, reading-related self-perceptions, and strategies for overcoming negative self-beliefs', *Reading and Writing Quarterly*, 19: 5–24.

Chapman, J.W., Tunmer, W.E. and Prochnow, J.E. (2001) 'Does success in the Reading Recovery program depend on developing proficiency in phonological processing skills? A longitudinal study in a whole language instructional context', *Scientific Studies of Reading*, 5: 141–176.

Christensen, C.A. and Bowey, J.A. (2005) 'The efficacy of orthographic rime, grapheme-phoneme correspondence, and implicit phonics approaches to teaching decoding skills', *Scientific Studies of Reading*, 9: 327–349.

Clay, M.M. (1993) *Reading recovery*. Auckland, New Zealand: Heinemann.

Clay, M.M. (1998) *An observation survey of early literacy achievement*. Auckland, New Zealand: Heinemann.

Compton, D.L., Fuchs, D., Fuchs, L.S. and Bryant, J.D. (2006) 'Selecting at-risk readers in first grade for early intervention: A two-year longitudinal study of decision rules and procedures', *Journal of Educational Psychology*, 98 (2): 394–409.

Denton, C.A., Fletcher, J.M., Anthony, J.L. and Francis, D.J. (2006) 'An evaluation of intensive intervention for students with persistent reading difficulties', *Journal of Learning Disabilities*, 39: 447–466.

Denton, C.A. and Mathes, P.G. (2003) 'Intervention for struggling readers: Possibilities and challenges', in B.R. Foorman (ed.), *Preventing and remediating reading difficulties: Bringing science to scale*. Baltimore, MD: York Press. pp. 229–251.

Deschler, D.D., Mellard, D.F., Tollefson, J.M. and Byrd, S.E. (2005) 'Research topics in responsiveness to intervention: Introduction to the special series', *Journal of Learning Disabilities*, 38: 483–484.

Ehri, L.C. (2004) 'Teaching phonemic awareness and phonics: An explanation of the National Reading Panel meta-analyses', in P. McCardle and V. Chhabra (eds.), *The voice of evidence in reading research*. Baltimore, MD: Brookes. pp. 153–186.

Ehri, L.C. (2005) 'Development of sight word reading: Phases and findings', in M.J. Snowling and C. Hulme (eds.), *The science of reading: A Handbook*. Oxford: Blackwell. pp. 135–154.

Ehri, L. and McCormick, S. (1998) 'Phases of word learning: Implications for instruction with delayed and disabled readers', *Reading and Writing Quarterly*, 14: 135–163.

Ehri, L.C., Nunes, S.R., Willows, D.M., Schuster, B.V., Yaghoub-Zadeh, Z. and Shanahan, T. (2001) 'Phonemic awareness instruction helps children learn to read: Evidence from the National Reading Panel's meta-analysis', *Reading Research Quarterly*, 36: 250–287.

Elbaum, B., Vaughn, S. Hughes, M. and Moody, S. (2000) 'How effective are one-to-one tutoring programs in reading for elementary students at risk for reading failure? A meta-analysis of the intervention research', *Journal of Educational Psychology*, 92: 605–619.

Fletcher, J.M., Denton, C. and Francis, D. (2005) 'Validity of alternative approaches for the identification of learning disabilities: Operationalizing unexpected underachievement', *Journal of Learning Disabilities*, 38: 545–552.

Fletcher, J.M., Shaywitz, S.E., Shankweiler, D.P., Katz, L., Liberman, I.Y., Stuebing, K.K., et al. (1994) 'Cognitive profiles of reading disability: Comparisons of discrepancy and low achievement definitions', *Journal of Educational Psychology*, 85: 1–18.

Foorman, B.R., Fletcher, J.M. and Francis, D.J. (2004) 'Early reading assessment', in W.M. Evers and H.J. Walberg (eds.), *Testing student learning, evaluating teaching effectiveness*. Stanford, CA: The Hoover Institution. pp. 81–125.

Foorman, B.R., Francis, D.J., Fletcher, J.M., Schatschneider, C. and Mehta, P. (1998) 'The role of instruction in learning to read: Preventing reading failure in at-risk children', *Journal of Educational Psychology*, 90: 37–55.

Foorman, B.R., Seals, L.M., Anthony, J. and Pollard-Durodala, S. (2003) 'A vocabulary enrichment program for third and fourth grade African-American students: Description, implementation, and impact', in B.R. Foorman (ed.), *Preventing and remediating reading difficulties: Bringing science to scale*. Baltimore, MD: York Press. pp. 419–441.

Foorman, B.R., York, M., Santi, K.L. and Francis, D. (in press) 'Contextual effects on predicting risk for reading difficulties in first and second grade', *Reading and Writing*.

Francis, D.J., Fletcher, J.M., Steubing, K.K., Lyon, G.R., Shaywitz, B.A. and Shaywitz, S.E. (2005) 'Psychometric approaches to the identification of LD: IQ and achievement scores are not sufficient', *Journal of Learning Disabilities*, 38: 98–108.

Fuchs, D., Compton, D.L., Fuchs, L.S., Bryant, J. and Davis, G.N. (in press) 'Making "secondary intervention" work in a three-tier responsiveness-to-intervention model: Findings from the first-grade longitudinal reading study at the National Research Center of Learning Disabilities', *Reading and Writing*.

Fuchs, D. and Fuchs, L.S. (2006) 'Introduction to response to intervention: What, why, and how valid is it?', *Reading Research Quarterly*, 41: 93–99.

Fuchs, D., Fuchs, L.S., McMaster, K.N. and Al Otaiba, S. (2003) 'Identifying children at risk for reading failure: Curriculum-based measurement and the dual-discrepancy approach', in H.L. Swanson, H.R. Harris, and S. Graham (eds), *Handbook of learning disabilities*. New York: The Guilford Press. pp. 431–449.

Fuchs, D. and Young, C.L. (2006) 'On the irrelevance of intelligence in predicting responsiveness to reading instruction', *Exceptional Children*, 73: 8–30.

Gaskins, I.W., Downer, M.A., Anderson, R., Cunningham, P.M., Gaskins, R.M., Schommer, M., and the teachers of the Benchmark School (1988) 'A metacognitive approach to phonics: Using what you know to decode what you don't know', *Remedial and Special Education*, 9: 36–41.

Gersten, R. and Dimino, J.A. (2006) 'RTI (response to intervention): Rethinking special education for students with reading difficulties (yet again)', *Reading Research Quarterly*, 41: 99–108.

Good, R.H., Kaminski, R.A., Smith, S. and Laimon, D. (2001) *Dynamic indicators of basic early literacy skills (DIBELSs)*. Eugene, OR: Institute for the Development of Educational Achievement, University of Oregon.

Gough, P.B. and Tunmer, W.E. (1986) 'Decoding, reading, and reading disability', *Remedial and Special Education*, 7: 6–10.

Gough, P.B. and Walsh, M. (1991) 'Chinese, Phoenicians, and the orthographic cipher of English', in S. Brady and D. Shankweiler (eds), *Phonological processes in literacy*. Hillsdale, NJ: Erlbaum. pp. 199–209.

Greaney, K.T., Tunmer, W.E. and Chapman, J.W. (1997) 'Effects of rime-based orthographic analogy training on the word recognition skills of children with reading disability', *Journal of Educational Psychology*, 89: 645–651.

Guthrie, J.T. and Humenick, N.M. (2004) 'Motivating students to read: Evidence for classroom practices that increase reading motivation and achievement', in P. McCardle and V. Chhabra (eds), *The voice of evidence in reading research*. Baltimore, MD: Brookes. pp. 329–354.

Hatcher, P.J., Goetz, K., Snowling, M.J., Hulme, C., Gibbs, S. and Smith, G. (2006) 'Evidence for the effectiveness of the Early Literacy Support programme', *British Journal of Educational Psychology*, 76: 351–367.

Hatcher, P.J. and Hulme, C. (1999) 'Phonemes, rhymes, and intelligence as predictors of children's responsiveness to remedial reading instruction: Evidence from a longitudinal intervention study', *Journal of Experimental Child Psychology*, 72: 130–153.

Hatcher, P.J., Hulme, C. and Ellis, A.W. (1994) 'Ameliorating early reading failure by integrating the teaching of reading and phonological skill: The phonological linkage hypothesis', *Child Development*, 65: 41–57.

Hoover, W.A. and Gough, P.B. (1990) 'The simple view of reading', *Reading and Writing*, 2: 127–160.

Hoover, W.A. and Tunmer, W.E. (1993) 'The components of reading', in G.B. Thompson, W.E. Tunmer, and T, Nicholson (eds), *Reading acquisition processes*. Clevedon, UK: Multilingual Matters. pp. 1–19.

Iversen, S.A. and Tunmer, W.E. (1993) 'Phonological processing skill and the Reading Recovery program', *Journal of Educational Psychology*, 85: 112–125.

Iversen, S., Tunmer, W.E. and Chapman, J.W. (2005) 'The effects of varying group size on the Reading Recovery approach to preventive early intervention', *Journal of Learning Disabilities*, 38: 456–472.

Juel, C. (1988) 'Learning to read and write: A longitudinal study of 54 children from first through fourth grades', *Journal of Educational Psychology*, 80: 437–447.

Kame'enui, E., Fuchs, L., Francis, D. J., Good, R., O'Connor, R., Simmons, D.C., et al. (2006) 'The adequacy of tools for assessing reading competence: A framework and review', *Educational Researcher*, 35: 3–11.

Leach, J.M., Scarborough, H.S. and Rescorla, L. (2003) 'Late-emerging reading disabilities', *Journal of Educational Psychology*, 95: 211–224.

Lyon, G.R. (1993) *Treatment effectiveness for the learning disabled*. Bethesda, MD: National Institute of Child Health and Human Development.

Lyon, G.R. and Moats, L.C. (1997) 'Critical conceptual and methodological considerations in reading intervention research', *Journal of Learning Disabilities*, 30: 578–588.

Mathes, P.G., Denton, C.A., Fletcher, J.M., Anthony, J., Francis, D.J. and Schatschneider, C. (2005) 'The effects of theoretically different instruction and student characteristics on the skills of struggling readers', *Reading Research Quarterly*, 40: 148–182.

McMaster, K.L., Fuchs, D., Fuchs, L. and Compton, D. (2005) 'Responding to nonresponders: An experimental field trial of identification and intervention methods', *Exceptional Children*, 71: 445–463.

Metsala, J. (1997) 'Spoken word recognition in reading disabled children', *Journal of Educational Psychology*, 89: 159–173.

Morris, D., Tyner, B. and Perney, J. (2000) 'Early steps: Replicating the effects of a first-grade reading intervention program', *Journal of Educational Psychology*, 92: 681–693.

Nation, K. (2005) 'Children's reading comprehension difficulties', in M.J. Snowling and C. Hulme (eds), *The science of reading: A Handbook*. Oxford: Blackwell. pp. 248–265.

Oakhill, J. and Beard, R. (1999) *Reading development and the teaching of reading*. Oxford: Blackwell.

O'Connor, R.E., Fulmer, D., Harty, K.R. and Bell, K.M. (2005) 'Layers of reading intervention in kindergarten through third grade: Changes in teaching and student outcomes', *Journal of Learning Disabilities*, 38: 440–455.

Papanicolaou, A.C., Simos, P.G., Fletcher, J.M., Francis, D.J., Foorman, B., Castillo, E.M. and Sarkari, S. (2003) 'Development and plasticity of neurophysiological processes involved in reading', in B.R. Foorman (ed.), *Preventing and remediating reading difficulties: Bringing science to scale*. Baltimore, MD: York Press. pp. 3–21.

Perfetti, C.A. (1985) *Reading ability*. New York: Oxford University Press.

Perfetti, C.A. (1991) 'The psychology, pedagogy, and politics of reading', *Psychological Science*, 2, 70–76.

Perfetti, C.A. (1992) 'The representation problem in reading acquisition', in P. Gough, L. Enri, and R. Treiman (eds), *Reading acquisition*. Hillsdale, NJ: Erlbaum. pp. 107–143.

Pressley, M. (2006) *Reading instruction that works: The case for balanced teaching*. New York: The Guilford Press.

Pressley, M., Graham, S. and Harris, K. (2006) 'The state of educational intervention research as viewed through the lens of literacy instruction', *British Journal of Educational Psychology*, 76: 1–19.

Ryder, J.F., Tunmer, W.E. and Greaney, K.T. (in press) 'Explicit instruction in phonemic awareness and phonemically-based decoding skills as an intervention strategy for struggling readers in whole language classrooms', *Reading and Writing*.

Sandak, R., Mencl, W.E., Frost, S. J. and Pugh, K.R. (2004) 'The neurobiological basis of skilled and impaired reading: Recent findings and new directions', *Scientific Studies of Reading*, 8: 273–292.

Scarborough, H. (2005) 'Developmental relationships between language and reading: Reconciling a beautiful hypothesis with some ugly facts', in H.W. Catts and A.G. Kamhi (eds), *The connections between language and reading disabilities*. Mahwah, NJ: Erlbaum. pp. 3–24.

Shankweiler, D. and Fowler, A.E. (2004) 'Questions people ask about the role of phonological processes in learning to reading', *Reading and Writing*, 17: 483–515.

Share, D.L. (1995) 'Phonological recoding and self-teaching: *Sine qua non* of reading acquisition', *Cognition*, 55: 151–218.

Shaywitz, S. (2003) *Overcoming dyslexia*. New York: Alfred A. Knopf.

Shaywitz, B.A., Shaywitz, S.E., Blachman, B., Pugh, K.R., Fulbright, R.K., Skudlarski, P., et al. (2004) 'Development of left occipito-temporal systems for skilled reading in children after a phonologically-based intervention', *Biological Psychiatry*, 55: 926–933.

Simos, P.G., Fletcher, J.M., Bergman, E., Breier, J.I., Foorman, B.R., Castillo, E.M., et al. (2002) 'Dyslexia-specific brain activation profile becomes normal following successful remedial training', *Neurology*, 58: 1203–1213.

Simos, P.G., Fletcher, J.M., Sarkari, S., Billingsley-Marshall, R., Denton, C.A. and Papanicolaou, A.C. (2007) 'Intensive instruction affects brain magnetic activity associated with oral word reading in children with persistent reading disabilities', *Journal of Learning Disabilities*, 40: 37–48.

Smith, J.W.A. and Elley, W.B. (1994) *Learning to read in New Zealand*. Auckland, New Zealand: Longman Paul.

Snow, C.E. and Juel, C. (2005) 'Teaching children to read: What do we know about how to do it?', in M.J. Snowling and C. Hulme (eds), *The science of reading: A handbook*. Oxford: Blackwell. pp. 501–520.

Snowling, M.J., Gallagher, A. and Frith, U. (2003) 'Family risk of dyslexia is continuous: Individual differences in the precursors of reading skill', *Child Development*, 74: 358–373.

Stanovich, K.E. (1986) 'Matthew effects in reading: Some consequences of individual differences in the acquisition of literacy', *Reading Research Quarterly*, 21: 340–406.

Stanovich, K.E. (1991) 'Discrepancy definitions of reading disability: Has intelligence led us astray?', *Reading Research Quarterly*, 26: 7–29.

Stanovich, K.E. (1996) 'Toward a more inclusive definition of dyslexia', *Dyslexia*, 2: 154–166.

Stanovich, K.E. and Siegel, L. (1994) 'Phenotypic performance profile for children with reading disabilities: A regression-based test of the phonological-core variable-difference model', *Journal of Educational Psychology*, 86: 1–30.

Stuebing, K.K., Fletcher, J.M., LeDoux, J.M., Lyon, G.R., Shaywitz, S.E. and Shaywitz, B.A. (2002) 'Validity of IQ-discrepancy classification of reading disabilities: A meta-analysis', *American Educational Research Journal*, 39: 469–518.

Torgesen, J.K. (2004) 'Lessons learned from research on interventions for students who have difficulty learning to read', in P. McCardle and V. Chhabra (eds), *The voice of evidence in reading research*. Baltimore, MD: Brookes. pp. 355–382.

Torgesen, J.K. (2005) 'Recent discoveries on remedial interventions for children with dyslexia', in M.J. Snowling and C. Hulme (eds), *The science of reading: A handbook*. Oxford: Blackwell. pp. 521–537.

Torgesen, J.K., Alexander, A.W., Wagner, R.K., Rashotte, C.A., Voeller, K.K.S. and Conway, T. (2001a) 'Intensive remedial instruction for children with severe reading disabilities: Immediate and long-term outcomes from two instructional approaches', *Journal of Learning Disabilities*, 34: 33–58, 78.

Torgesen, J.K., Rashotte, C.A. and Alexander, A. (2001b) 'Principles of fluency instruction in reading: Relationships with established empirical outcomes', in M. Wolf (ed.), *Dyslexia, fluency, and the brain*. Timonium, MD: York Press. pp. 333–355.

Torgesen, J.K., Rashotte, C.A., Alexander, A., Alexander, J. and MacPhee, K. (2003) 'Progress towards understanding the instructional conditions necessary for remediating reading difficulties in older children', in B. Foorman (ed.), *Preventing and remediating reading difficulties: Bringing science to scale*. Baltimore, MD: York. pp. 275–289.

Torgesen, J.K., Wagner, R.K., Rashotte, C.A., Rose, E., Lindamood, P., Conway, T., et al. (1999) 'Preventing reading failure in young children with phonological processing disabilities: Group and individual responses to instruction', *Journal of Educational Psychology*, 91: 579–593.

Tracey, D.H. and Morrow, L.M. (2006) *Lenses on reading: An introduction to theories and models.* New York: Guilford Press.

Tunmer, W.E. and Chapman, J.W. (1996) 'A developmental model of dyslexia: Can the construct be saved?', *Dyslexia*, 2: 179–189.

Tunmer, W.E. and Chapman, J.W. (1998) 'Language prediction skill, phonological recoding ability and beginning reading', in C. Hulme and R.M. Joshi (eds), *Reading and spelling: Development and disorder.* Hillsdale, NJ: Lawrence Erlbaum Associates. pp. 33–37.

Tunmer, W.E. and Chapman, J.W. (2003) 'The Reading Recovery approach to preventive early intervention. As good as it gets?', *Reading Psychology*, 24: 337–360.

Tunmer, W.E. and Chapman, J.W. (2004) 'Reading Recovery: Distinguishing myth from reality', in R.M. Joshi (ed.), *Dyslexia: Myths, misconceptions, and some practical application.* Baltimore, MD: International Dyslexia Association. pp. 99–114.

Tunmer, W.E. and Chapman, J.W. (2006) 'Metalinguistic abilities, phonological recoding skills, and the use of sentence context in beginning reading development: A longitudinal study', in R.M. Joshi and P.G. Aaron (eds), *Handbook of orthography and literacy.* Mahwah, NJ: Erlbaum. pp. 617–635.

Tunmer, W.E. and Chapman, J.W. (2007) 'Language-related differences between discrepancy-defined and non-discrepancy-defined poor readers: A longitudinal study of dyslexia in New Zealand', *Dyslexia*, 13: 42–66.

Tunmer, W.E., Chapman, J.W., Greaney, K.T. and Prochnow, J.E. (2002) 'The contribution of educational psychology to intervention research and practice', *International Journal of Disability, Development and Education*, 49: 11–29.

Tunmer, W.E., Chapman, J.W. and Prochnow, J.E. (2003) 'Preventing negative Matthew effects in at-risk readers: A retrospective study', in B. Foorman (ed.), *Preventing and remediating reading difficulties: Bringing science to scale.* Timonium, MD: York Press. pp. 121–163.

Tunmer, W.E., Chapman, J.W. and Prochnow, J.E. (2006) 'Literate cultural capital at school entry predicts later reading achievement: A seven year longitudinal study', *New Zealand Journal of Educational Studies*, 41: 183–204.

Tunmer, W.E. and Hoover, W.A. (1993) 'Components of variance models of language-related factors in reading disability: A conceptual overview', in M. Joshi and C.K. Leong (eds), *Reading disabilities: Diagnosis and component processes.* Dordrecht, The Netherlands: Kluwer Academic Publishers. pp. 135–173.

Tunmer, W.E., Prochnow, J.E., Greaney, K.T. and Chapman, J.W. (2007) 'What's wrong with New Zealand's national literacy strategy?', in R. Openshaw and J. Soler (eds), *Reading across international boundaries: History, policy and politics.* Greenwich, CT: Information Age Publishing, pp. 19–42.

Vaughn, S., Linan-Thompson, S. (2003) 'Group size and time allocated to intervention: Effects for students with reading difficulties', in B. Foorman (ed.), *Preventing and remediating reading difficulties: Bringing science to scale.* Baltimore, MD: York Press. pp. 299–324.

Vaughn, S., Linan-Thompson, S. and Hickman, P. (2003) 'Response to instruction as a means of identifying students with reading/learning disabilities', *Exceptional Children*, 69: 391–409.

Vellutino, F.R. and Denckla, M. (1991) 'Cognitive and neuropsychological foundations of word identification in poor and normally developing readers', in R. Barr, M.L. Kamil, P.B. Mosenthal and P.D. Pearson (eds), *Handbook of Reading Research.* New York: Longman. Vol. 2: pp. 571–608.

Vellutino, F.R. and Fletcher, J.M. (2005) 'Developmental dyslexia', in M.J. Snowling and C. Hulme (eds), *The science of reading: A handbook.* Oxford: Blackwell. pp. 362–378.

Vellutino, F.R., Fletcher, J.M., Snowling, M.J. and Scanlon, D.M. (2004) 'Specific reading disability (dyslexia): What have we learned in the past four decades?', *Journal of Child Psychology and Psychiatry*, 45: 2–40.

Vellutino, F.R., Scanlon, D.M. and Jaccard, J. (2003) 'Toward distinguishing between cognitive and experiential deficits as primary sources of difficulty in learning to read: A two year follow-up of difficult-to-remediate and readily remediated poor readers', in B. Foorman (ed.), *Preventing and remediating reading difficulties: Bringing science to scale.* Baltimore, MD: York Press. pp. 73–120.

Vellutino, F.R., Scanlon, D.M. and Lyon, G.R. (2000) 'Differentiating between difficult-to-remediate and readily remediated poor readers: More evidence against the IQ-achievement discrepancy definition of reading disability', *Journal of Learning Disabilities*, 33: 223–238.

Vellutino, F.R., Scanlon, D.M., Sipay, E.R., Small, S.G., Pratt, A., Chen, R.S., et al. (1996) 'Cognitive profiles of difficult to remediate and readily remediated poor readers: Early intervention as a vehicle for distinguishing between cognitive and experimental deficits as basic causes of specific reading disability', *Journal of Educational Psychology*, 88: 601–638.

Vellutino, F.R., Scanlon, D.M., Small, S. and Fanuele, D.P. (2006) 'Response to intervention as a vehicle for distinguishing between children with and without reading disabilities: Evidence for the role of kindergarten and first-grade interventions', *Journal of Learning Disabilities*, 39: 157–169.

Vellutino, F.R., Scanlon, D.M., Zhang, H. and Shatschneider, C. (in press) 'Using response to kindergarten and first grade intervention to identify children at risk for long-term reading difficulties', *Reading and Writing*.

Vellutino, F.R., Tunmer, W.E., Jaccard, J.J. and Chen, R. (2007) 'Components of reading ability: Multivariate evidence for a convergent skills model of reading development', *Scientific Studies of Reading*, 11: 3–32.

Wagner, R.K., Muse, A.E., Stein, T.L., Cukrowicz, K.C., Harrell, E.R., Rashotte, C.A., et al. (2003) 'How to assess reading–related phonological abilities', in B. Foorman (ed.), *Preventing and remediating reading difficulties: Bringing science to scale*. Baltimore, MD: York Press. pp. 51–70.

Walley, A.C. (1993) 'The role of vocabulary development in children's spoken word recognition and segmentation ability', *Developmental Review*, 13: 286–350.

Assessment of Literacy Performance Based on the Componential Model of Reading

R. Malatesha Joshi and P.G. Aaron

This chapter

i) refers to the procedure based on the 'Discrepancy model' of diagnosis of reading disability;
ii) discusses the issues relating to discrepancy-based diagnostic procedures;
iii) proposes an alternate model, labeled the Componential Model of Reading, for diagnosing and treating reading disability, in the place of the IQ-reading score based discrepancy model.

INTRODUCTION

Reading disability, which is a major constituent of learning disability, has been traditionally diagnosed on the basis of a discrepancy between IQ scores and reading achievement scores. In this chapter, we will refer to this procedure as being based on the 'Discrepancy model'. When implemented, the discrepancy model-based–diagnosis of reading disability results in two categories of poor readers, one whose disability is expected because of their low cognitive ability, and the other unexpected. In spite of its long history, the discrepancy-based procedure has recently fallen into disfavor because of its many drawbacks.

Among the many problems of the Discrepancy model is that IQ is not a good predictor of reading scores because the correlation between IQ and reading achievement scores seldom exceeds 0.5. Furthermore, the relationship between IQ and reading performance is reciprocal rather than uni-directional. The most serious problem, however, is that the discrepancy-based diagnosis does not lead to recommendations regarding remedial instruction.

In this chapter, we propose an alternate model for diagnosing and treating reading disability, in the place of the IQ-reading score–based Discrepancy model. The proposed model for diagnosing and instructing children with reading difficulties is based on the Componential Model of Reading, which focuses on the source of the reading difficulty and targets remedial instruction at the source of the reading problems.

BACKGROUND

The fact that some children find it extraordinarily difficult to learn to read was recognized more than one hundred years ago. It began to receive clinical attention when two British physicians, Hinshelwood and Morgan, independently reported, during the latter part of the 19th century, case histories of children who could not read and spell despite adequate intelligence and normal schooling. Hinshelwood called this condition 'congenital word-blindness'.

Between 1900 and 1920 several other reports were published, mainly by physicians, about children with average or higher intelligence who experienced a great deal of difficulty in learning to read. These reports were based on the implicit assumption that measured intelligence has an intimate relationship with reading skill and, therefore, children who are bright but could not read were an oddity. This condition was also referred to as 'unexpected reading failure'. On the other hand, children with below-average intelligence were not expected to read well, and therefore, their reading difficulty was not unexpected.

Today we have come to realize that the relationship between IQ and reading skill is neither strong nor straightforward. The nature of the association between the two has remained a controversial issue for a number of years. For instance, in 1921, Lucy Fieldes, a psychologist, published a study of 26 subjects diagnosed with congenital word blindness and noted that contrary to expectations no significant relationship between IQ score (based on the Binet-Simon scale, 1916) and reading performance could be found. The low correlation coefficient between IQ and reading scores can be explained this way. First, a majority of poor readers who have average or above-average intelligence find it difficult to learn to read because ability to decode printed language is very weak. Decoding, which is the ability to pronounce the written word, is a *skill* which is independent of general intelligence (Spearman's 'g' factor) which is what intelligence tests measure. Decoding is described as 'low-level processing skill', whereas comprehension as is described as 'higher level processing skill' by Carver (1998),

Catts and Kamhi (2005), and de Jong and van der Leij (2002; 2003). Understandably, the correlation between a skill and the general intelligence is low.

In spite of skepticism regarding the relationship between IQ and reading disability, the utilization of IQ-achievement difference in the diagnosis of reading problems has become deeply entrenched in the American educational system. This policy has also been officially endorsed by the American Psychiatric Association which, in its *Diagnostic and Statistical Manual of Mental Disorders* (DSM-IV; American Psychiatric Association, 1994: 74), defines reading disability as 'Reading achievement, as measured by individually administered standardized tests of reading accuracy or comprehension, is substantially below that is expected, given the person's chronological age, *measured intelligence*, and age-appropriate education.'

In the place of the IQ-achievement Discrepancy model, some investigators have proposed alternative approaches. One such approach is to use a measure of listening comprehension in the place of IQ scores for diagnosing reading disabilities (Aaron, 1991; Savage, 2001; Spring and French, 1990; Stanovich, 1991). As a diagnostic tool, listening comprehension does not have the many limitations of IQ. The advantages of using listening comprehension are that it is an integral component of the language process; a test of listening comprehension is easy to administer; and more importantly, the diagnostic findings based on listening comprehension can lead to recommendations regarding remedial instruction.

The idea of using listening comprehension to predict reading comprehension is not an entirely new one. Several decades ago, Ladd (1970) noted that listening comprehension is an important indicator of reading comprehension. More recently, Spring and French (1990) noted that identifying children with specific reading disability on the basis of discrepancy between their reading comprehension and listening comprehension is more appropriate than using the IQ-achievement discrepancy scores. Wood et al. (1988) obtained an impressive coefficient of correlation of 0.78 between reading and listening comprehension for groups of LD children. Townsend et al. (1987) concluded that apart from differences that arise from the modalities of input, reading comprehension and listening comprehension are mediated by the same cognitive mechanism. In a study of college students, Palmer et al. (1985) obtained a correlation coefficient of 0.82 between reading comprehension and listening comprehension, which led them to conclude that reading comprehension can be predicted almost perfectly by a listening comprehension measure. Joshi et al. (1998) found among a group of normal fourth graders, the coefficient of correlation between IQ and reading comprehension was 0.36, whereas the correlation coefficient between reading comprehension and listening comprehension of these children was 0.69. In addition, the use of a test of listening comprehension in identifying the source of reading difficulties has also been demonstrated (Aaron, 1991).

An added advantage in using listening comprehension to understand the nature of reading problem a child has is that the classroom teacher or the reading specialist can administer these tests and arrive at diagnostic conclusions.

In contrast, the administration of an individually administered IQ test requires specialized training.

Currently, three models of reading disability are in use. They are:

1 the Discrepancy model;
2 the Response to Intervention model; and
3 the Componential model.

For reasons stated above, the Discrepancy model has not yielded fruitful results. The Response to Intervention model is still in a state of evolution and is not well defined. The Componential model, on which the assessment procedures described in this chapter are based, is new to the field and has not been extensively implemented. A good model of reading disability should be easy to implement, lead to recommendations regarding instruction, and have empirical support. The Componential model-based diagnosis and remediation appear to satisfy these requirements. A description of the Componential model of reading is presented in the following paragraphs.

The Componential model is an elaboration of the 'Simple View of Reading' proposed by Gough and Tunmer (1986) and validated by Hoover and Gough (1990). The Componential model is designed to be comprehensive by adding psychological and ecological domains to the cognitive domain of the 'Simple view of Reading'. It is well established that the literacy performance of children in the classroom is affected by not only cognitive factors, but also by psychological factors as well as environmental factors (cf., Berninger et al., 2004; Dudley-Marling, 2004). In the following section, a brief outline of the Componential model and the assessment procedure based on the model are presented.

COMPONENTIAL MODEL OF READING

A component is defined as an elementary information-processing system that operates on internal representations of objects and symbols. To be considered a component, the process should be demonstrably *independent* of other cognitive processes (Sternberg, 1985). In the Componential model, components that have an influence on the acquisition of literacy skills are organized into three domains. The three domains of the Componential model are

1 cognitive domain;
2 psychological domain; and
3 ecological domain.

When applied to literacy acquisition, the Componential model envisages that a child can fail to acquire satisfactory levels of literacy skills because of deficiency in any component in any one of these three domains.

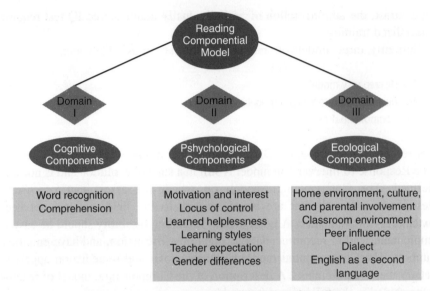

Figure 12.1   The Componential model of reading

The cognitive domain of the model, which is the focus of this chapter, has two components: word recognition and comprehension. The psychological domain includes components such as motivation and interest, locus of control, learned helplessness, learning styles, teacher expectation, and gender differences. The ecological domain includes the following components: home environment and culture, parental involvement, classroom environment, dialect, and English as a second language. It has to be added that the components of the cognitive domain can satisfy the condition of independence fairly well, whereas the components of the psychological and ecological domains do not satisfy this requirement nearly as well. Nevertheless, the component model provides a framework for teachers and psychologists for navigating their course through the various assessment formats and determining remedial strategies for use in the classroom. The three domains of the Componential model and their constituent components are shown in Figure 12.1.

In this chapter, we will address the assessment techniques based on the cognitive domain of the Componential model of reading.

THE COGNITIVE DOMAIN

Word recognition and comprehension

The conceptualization of the componential nature of reading comes from a proposal by Gough and Tunmer (1986), who expressed it in the form of a simple mathematical formula:

RC = D × LC, where, RC = reading comprehension, D = decoding of the printed word, and LC = linguistic comprehension. This means that decoding and comprehension are two factors of the cognitive module of reading. According to Gough and Tunmer (1986), if D = 0, then RC = 0; and if LC = 0, RC = 0. That is, if a child's decoding skill is zero, his reading comprehension skill is zero; when a child's listening comprehension is zero, then his reading comprehension skill will also be zero. In other words, a child who cannot decode the printed word cannot read and understand; similarly, a child who cannot listen and understand also cannot read and understand. The model as used in this chapter is slightly modified from the one shown above. The modified formula is RC = WR × LC where RC = reading comprehension; WR is word recognition; and LC = listening comprehension. It has to be noted that word recognition component has two processes, decoding and instant word recognition (sight word reading).

The independent nature of word recognition and comprehension is reported by Carver (1998), Catts and Kamhi (2005), and de Jong and van der Leij (2002; 2003). Other investigators have described word recognition skill and comprehension skill as lower level processing and higher level processing skills, respectively (Hannon and Daneman, 2001; Pressley, 2000). The 'verbal efficiency theory' (Perfetti, 1988) captures the essence of the bi-componential nature of reading by stressing the independent role of verbal efficiency and text comprehension.

After decoding skills reach a certain level, recognition of familiar words becomes fast and automatic, a skill also referred to as sight word reading. The word recognition component, therefore, is made up of two processes: decoding, and instant word reading. The term 'instant word reading' is preferred over 'sight word reading' since sight word reading creates a false impression that quick recognition of the printed word is entirely a visual process.

What is the relationship between decoding and instant word reading? Studies show that decoding skill is a precursor to instant word reading. In other words, whereas a few words can be read by using visual memory, building a large sight vocabulary depends on a well-developed decoding skill. Our visual memory has limited capacity, perhaps not exceeding a few thousand images, even though a mature reader can recognize more than eighty thousand words instantly.

Comprehension is a generic term which includes both listening comprehension and reading comprehension. Several studies have shown a high degree of coefficient of correlation, indicating they are mediated by the same cognitive mechanisms [Joshi, et al., (1998), r = 0.72; Palmer, et al., (1985), r = 0.85; Savage (2004), r = 0.81; Wood, et al., (1988), r = 0.78].

The validity of the formula for their simple view of reading was tested by Hoover and Gough (1990) by tracking and assessing 254 English-Spanish bilingual children from grades 1 through 4. The investigators found that a substantial proportion of the variance in reading comprehension was accounted for by the product of decoding and listening comprehension (grade 1, $r = 0.71$; grade 2, $r = 0.72$; grade 3, $r = 0.83$; grade 4, $r = 0.82$). Since then several studies have shown predictive nature of the Componential model for assessment and instruction (see Aaron and Joshi 1992; Aaron et al., 2008a; Adlof et al., 2006). Empirical evidence from experimental studies (Levy and Carr, 1990; Palmer et al., 1985);

developmental studies (Frith and Snowling, 1983; Leach et al., 2003; Oakhill et al., 2003; Shankweiler et al., 1995); neuropsychological studies (Marshall and Newcomb, 1973); and genetic studies (DeFries et al., 1987; Keenan et al., 2006; Olson, 2006) provide theoretical support for the view that word recognition and comprehension are independent of each other. The variance contributed by decoding and comprehension, however, can vary from 40 to 60 per cent, depending on the type of measures used and grade levels of the students.

The Componential model is applicable to languages other than English as well. In one of our studies (Joshi and Aaron, 2007) of Spanish speaking subjects, approximately 60 per cent of the variance in reading comprehension was explained by decoding and linguistic comprehension in grade levels 2 and 3. Interestingly, third grade Spanish speaking subjects performed as well as fourth grade English speaking subjects on decoding tasks, which may be due to the transparency of Spanish language.

In the following section, assessment procedures that can be used for identifying the components are described along with certain pitfalls that are to be avoided in literacy assessment.

Component 1: Word recognition

Phonological and phonemic awareness

The first component in the cognitive domain of the Componential model is word recognition. This component is also referred to by several related terms such as lexical processing, phonological decoding, and grapheme-phoneme conversion. Studies that have probed the word recognition skill further suggest that phonemic awareness, which is described as an awareness that spoken language is made up of separate speech sounds, compliments word recognition. Before we go further, we want to draw a distinction between two frequently encountered phrases: *phonemic awareness* and *phonological awareness*. Phonemic awareness is the knowledge, usually implicit, that speech is made up of discrete sounds called the phonemes (Ball and Blachman, 1991; Blachman et al., 1999). Phonological awareness includes phonemic awareness, as well as the ability to segment words into syllables and the ability to produce rhyming words. Thus, phonological awareness is a comprehensive term that includes phonemic awareness. Rhyming skill can be readily assessed by providing a word orally and then requiring the student to produce similar-sounding words. Segmenting skill can be assessed by providing a word orally and asking the child to indicate, by knocking on the desk or by clapping, how many syllables the word contains.

Because phonemic awareness is a strong correlate of reading skill (Ball and Blachman, 1991; Bradley and Bryant, 1985; Muter, 1998; Stahl and Murray, 1994) and a good predictor of reading skills of kindergarten children, it is assessed often, particularly in early elementary grades and kindergarten. Among the standardized tests of phonemic awareness are the Test of Phonological Awareness (TOPA, Torgesen and Bryant, 1995), and Comprehensive Test of

Phonological Processing (CTOPP, Wagner et al., 1999). Tests of phonemic awareness include tasks of phoneme identification and phoneme manipulation. Phoneme identification task requires the child to indicate the number of phonemes in a spoken word by tapping on the desk or by clapping hands. Phoneme manipulation is the ability to identify and deal with individual phonemes in a word. For instance, the examiner says the word 'cat' and asks the child to take the first sound out and put another sound in its place. Some researchers (Cisero and Royer; 1995; Durgunoglu et al., 1993; Quiroga et al., 2002) have developed foreign language tests of phonological measures which are also referred to as Auditory Analysis Test (AAT). Test of Phonological Processing in Spanish (TOPPS; August, et al., 2001) is the Spanish equivalent of CTOPP.

A word of caution is in order here. When preschool children are administered a test of phoneme awareness, it is important to make sure that these young children understand the nature of the task that is required of them. Tasks such as phoneme manipulation can be difficult for some children, not because they are not sensitive to phonemes, but because they fail to understand what they are supposed to do which can lead to erroneous responses.

Many studies report that training in phonemic awareness in young children increases their reading skills when they enter the early elementary grades not only in English (Ball and Blachman, 1991; Blachman et al., 1999) but in other languages such as Danish (Lundberg et al., 1988), French (Leybaert and Content, 1995), Spanish (Sebastian-Gallés and Vacchiano, 1995), Portuguese (Pinheiro, 1995), and Italian (Cossu et al., 1995). But critics have argued that many preschool children come with a prior knowledge of written letters and that no study has provided unequivocal evidence that there is a causal connection between phonological awareness and success in reading and spelling (Castles and Coltheart, 2004). On the basis of his meta-analysis studies, Hammill (2004) concluded that the best predictors of reading are abilities involving print – such as print awareness, phoneme-letter correspondences, word recognition, alphabet knowledge, and comprehension. Hammill also notes that the current attention to non print abilities such as phonological awareness, rapid naming, and memory might be overemphasized. It has also been reported that some children who demonstrate good phonemic awareness skills in grades 1 and 2 turn out to be poor readers when they reach grades 3 and 4 mainly because at these higher grades, comprehension becomes more important than word recognition. In other words, in grades 1 and 2 children learn to read but beyond these grades children read to learn.

Letter knowledge of children when they are in kindergarten is another good predictor of reading skill when they will reach the first grade. There is evidence to show that children who do not have alphabetic knowledge by the end of first grade experience problems in reading as they progress through the grades (Adams, 1990; Juel, 1994). It is obvious that letter knowledge is one step beyond phonemic awareness. That is, letter knowledge requires the ability not only to be aware of the phonemes of the language but also the ability to relate these sounds to the letters of the alphabet.

Decoding

Decoding skill can be assessed with the aid of a test of nonword reading and a test of spelling. Nonwords are also referred to as pseudowords; *daik* and *brane* are examples of nonwords. Nonword reading (or pseudoword reading) is a recognition task whereas spelling is a recall task. This makes spelling a more sensitive test of decoding skill than nonword reading. There is a misconception that all nonwords are alike. This is not true because some words can be read by analogy. For example, the nonword 'dake' can be read more easily if the child is familiar with rhyming words such as 'cake', 'bake', and 'take'. Thus, 'dake' has many neighbors which makes it a 'friendly' nonword. In contrast, a nonword such as 'daik' has few neighbors, and is therefore, 'unfriendly', Unfriendly nonwords cannot be decoded by using the analogy strategy. For this reason, it is essential that nonword lists designed to test decoding skill use as many unfriendly nonwords as possible. Word attack subtests can be found in many standardized tests such as Woodcock Johnson tests of Achievement and Cognitive abilities (Woodcock et al., 2001a; 2001b) as well as Woodcock Language Proficiency Battery (Woodcock, 2001). Many of these standardized tests have not taken care to include many 'unfriendly' nonwords in their lists.

Instant word recognition

Beyond third grade, the speed with which written words are recognized becomes an important factor. Being able to recognize the words in the text instantly and effortlessly releases the attention of the reader to focus on comprehension. Slow reading of words is indicative of the reader's poor decoding skills. A fluent reader must posses, good decoding skills, adequate comprehension skills, and the ability to process information at an optimal rate. In a review of 17 studies, Compton and Carlisle (1994) found that students with weak word recognition skills are slower in naming words and nonwords which led them to conclude that word reading speed is an important factor in differentiating individuals with reading disability from readers with normal ability. In fact, in languages such as German and Italian which have almost one-to-one correspondence between spelling and pronunciation, dyslexia is diagnosed not by children's nonword reading performance, but mainly on the basis of the speed with which children read words and sentences.

Some children who are given ample training in decoding and phonics may be able to pronounce pseudowords accurately, but they do so slowly and laboriously. Under such circumstances, unless the time it takes to finish the task is not taken into account, test scores alone will give an incorrect impression that the child has adequate word recognition skills. In one study (Joshi and Aaron, 2002), 37 fifth graders were administered the word-attack subtest from the Woodcock Language Proficiency Battery–Revised (Woodcock, 2001). This is not a timed test.

When word recognition skill was evaluated by using a composite index of accuracy and time, it was found that many children who obtained average decoding scores in fact had composite scores in the lowest quartile. These children, who were slow but accurate decoders, could escape diagnosis as poor decoders and, therefore, represent instances of false negatives. For this reason, when measuring decoding through the use of nonwords, both speed and accuracy have to be taken into consideration.

A simple way to control for the speed factor is to administer a timed standardized word-naming test. The Test of Word Reading Efficiency (TOWRE; Torgesen et al., 1998) is a good example of such a test. The TOWRE has two subtests. One subtest is sight word efficiency which assesses the number of printed words that can be accurately read aloud within a period of 45 seconds; the second subtest measures the number of nonwords that can be read within 45 seconds.

Reading speed can be assessed in more than one way. The Rapid Automatized Naming (RAN) test, developed by Denckla and Rudel (1976a; 1976b) requires the reader to name a series of colors, pictures of objects, and letters. This test reliably distinguishes between poor and normal readers across a broad range (Bowers and Wolf, 1993; Vellutino et al., 1996; Wolf and Bowers, 1999). In a recent study (Aaron et al., 1999), we demonstrated that children from grade 2 took longer to name a common word than the time it took to name a letter of the alphabet, the difference being statistically significant. However, children from grade 3 and up, including college students, named both letters and words at about the same rate. This indicates that by about the third grade most children have mastered decoding skills and have become instant word readers. The time it takes to name a letter of the alphabet and a common content word, therefore, could be used by the classroom teacher to assess instant word-reading skill. When a list of 20 common monosyllabic content words (nouns, verbs, and adjectives) is named as rapidly as a list of 20 letters, then it can be concluded that these words are read as sight words. Of course, the word list would vary from grade to grade.

Spelling

Spache, as early as 1940, noted that children who are poor spellers also are deficient in decoding skills. In a study which specifically examined the question of whether children use similar processes to read and spell words, Waters et al. (1985) found that third grade children, regardless of their ability level, used spelling–sound correspondences for both reading and spelling. Excessive spelling errors, therefore, often indicate a weakness in phonological skill and should not be interpreted, without strong evidence, as an indication of poor visual memory (Joshi and Aaron, 1991). In spite of it being a good diagnostic tool, spelling is seldom utilized as a test of decoding skill.

Traditionally, spelling ability is assessed by dictating a list of words to children and then scoring their output as right or wrong. This kind of quantitative assessment has two drawbacks. First, it is quite possible that students tend to spell unfamiliar words phonetically which often will lead to spelling errors. Under such a condition, these spelling errors do not reflect a deficit in spelling skill *per se* but rather limited vocabulary knowledge. Familiarity with words, as indicated by the ability to pronounce the written words, has to be taken into account when spelling lists are constructed. Spelling scores derived from standardized spelling tests are particularly susceptible for this type of misinterpretation. A mistake of this nature can be avoided if teachers use in their spelling tests, only those words already introduced in the classroom.

The second problem with quantitative assessment in which spelled words are dichotomized as 'right' or 'wrong' arises from the fact that the ability to spell falls on a continuum. Exclusive reliance on quantitative assessment of spelling can yield an incomplete and distorted picture of the child's ability to spell. For instance, a child who spells 'KAT' for 'cat' has better knowledge of letter–sound correspondence than a child who spells 'cat' as 'TCA' even though both are incorrect when scored right or wrong. Further, dichotomizing spelling performance as 'right' or 'wrong' may not provide clues as to the source of children's spelling difficulties. Quantitative assessment also does not inform the teacher how to design spelling instruction to the children in the classroom. In contrast, a close examination of the misspelled words is assessment of spelling performance from a qualitative perspective, which can provide useful insights about spelling instruction.

A quasi-qualitative assessment procedure of spelling is provided by Tangel and Blachman (1995). Under this procedure, a score of 0 is assigned to random symbols with little or no alphabetic representation and a score of 6 is given to correct spelling. Scores 1 through 5 are assigned depending upon the degree of proximity to real spelling.

Several studies indicate that the acquisition of grapheme-phoneme conversion (GPC) skill follows a developmental trend moving from a mastery of simple to complex spelling–sound relationship (Calfee et al., 1969; Ehri, 1991; 1997; Moats, 1995; Treiman,1993; 1998; 2006; Venezky, 1976; 2000). For instance, hard 'c' as in 'cat' is mastered earlier than soft 'c' as in 'city' and hard 'g' as in 'girl' is learned before soft 'g' as in 'gem.' The spelling of words that are described as 'irregular words' whose constituent letters do not have a systematic relationship with the pronunciation of the word take much longer to learn. Examples are 'sew', 'though', 'knife', etc. A list of words designed to test the decoding skill should, therefore, contain words that assess a wide range of words representing different degrees of GPC relationship. Based on this observation, Shearer and Homer (1994) suggest that a child's stage of spelling development could be judged by examining the spelling errors. A child could be in the phonemic, letter-name spelling, early phonetic, phonetic, and correct spelling stage. Of course, the misspellings of children usually place them in more than one stage.

As noted earlier, qualitative analyses of spelling errors could also be helpful in designing corrective instruction. A detailed phonological analysis of spelling errors such as substitution of consonant phonemes, omission of consonants in blends, omission of unaccented vowels (schwa), or syllable omission can be useful in identifying the source of spelling (and decoding) errors of the child whose attention could be drawn to those errors (Joshi, 2003).

In sum, spelling, being a recall task, is a more rigorous test of decoding skill than nonword reading. The validity of spelling tests could be improved by administering only those words the child could read aloud correctly. Spelling instruction could be made effective by utilizing the results of qualitative or quasi-qualitative analyses of spelling errors.

Component 2: Comprehension

Comprehension is a generic term that includes both reading and listening comprehension.

Listening comprehension

A number of studies have shown that except for modality differences, reading comprehension and listening comprehension are mediated by the same cognitive processes. As noted earlier, the correlation between reading and listening comprehension is reasonably high. In a recent study, Savage (2001) found the correlation coefficient between listening and reading comprehension to be 0.81. Listening comprehension, therefore, can be used to assess comprehension without being confounded by decoding skill. The discrepancy between reading comprehension and listening comprehension can tell us whether decoding or comprehension *per se* is the source of the reading problem.

Listening comprehension can be assessed by more than one test and, consequently, results can vary somewhat depending on the test used (Joshi et al., 1998). One test that has both listening and reading comprehension subtests is Woodcock Language Proficiency Battery in which both comprehension subtests were normed on the same population and are in the same cloze format. This makes reading and listening comprehension comparable. The Diagnostic Achievement Battery (Newcomer, 1999) and the Wechsler Individual Achievement Test-II (WIAT-II, Wechsler, 2001) also have subtests of listening comprehension.

Reading comprehension

A common misconception is that all standardized tests of reading comprehension are alike. Tests differ from each other in the strategy they use for assessing comprehension. For example, the Stanford Diagnostic Reading Test (Karlsen and Gardner, 1995) and Gates-MacGinitie Reading Tests (MacGinitie et al., 2000) require the student to read passages and answer questions that are in multiple choice format. Under such a format, the ability not only to comprehend but also to remember the passage read play a role in answering the comprehension questions. Memory ability, therefore, can become a confounding factor.

Another strategy used for assessing reading comprehension is the cloze procedure. In the cloze procedure, the reader is required to furnish words which are systematically deleted from sentences. The assumption is that the reader cannot supply the correct word unless he or she has understood the meaning of the sentence. Tests that follow this format do not usually impose time restriction. A weakness of this form of assessment is that tests in a cloze format are somewhat removed from the reading of a paragraph or story and comprehending text. Thus, scores obtained using sentences in cloze format may not be ecologically valid measures of comprehension. The Woodcock Reading Mastery Test—Revised (Woodcock, 1998), the Woodcock Language Proficiency Battery—Revised (Woodcock, 2001), and the Woodcock Diagnostic Battery (Woodcock, 1997) have subtests that assess reading comprehension by relying on the cloze format.

The Peabody Individual Achievement Test—Revised (Markwardt, 1998) follows a different technique to assess reading comprehension. In this test, the individual reads a sentence and chooses one picture from among four that fits the sentence. Even though this form of testing reduces the memory load, correct understanding of the pictures requires a good deal of reasoning ability. This is particularly true at higher grades. One advantage of this form of testing is that it can be used for individuals with hearing impairments.

Many of the tests of comprehension take 45 minutes or more to complete and are meant to be given in a single session. Blanchard et al. (2001) found that when the test was split into two halves and administered in two separate sessions, the reading comprehension scores improved. This strategy can be useful for assessing reading comprehension skills of students who are slow readers because of weak decoding skills.

Hence, it is recommended that the reading comprehension be measured by using two separate types of tests such as one in cloze format and another in the text format. Additionally, researchers and diagnosticians should use caution while selecting the tests. Some comprehension tests may include too many passage independent questions (those questions that can be answered without reading the passage such as why did Pat go to Macdonald's?). A recent study by Keenan and Betjemann (2006) showed that many questions on Gray Oral Reading Test (GORT; Wiederholt and Bryant, 1992; 2001) can be answered without reading the passage and that on some of the passages, normal readers and children with reading disability obtained similar scores.

Vocabulary

Even though in the Componential model, 'vocabulary' is not accorded the status of a separate component, because it is not totally independent of comprehension. Developing a larger vocabulary is often a critical factor in improving reading comprehension (see Joshi, 2005). Nevertheless, vocabulary knowledge is a prerequisite of comprehension skill. The coefficients of correlation between vocabulary and reading comprehension range from 0.66 to 0.75 (Just and Carpenter, 1987). A meta-analysis of vocabulary studies by Stahl and Fairbanks (1986) suggested that vocabulary knowledge very likely plays a causal role in comprehension even though the role of vocabulary as a causal factor of reading comprehension is uncertain. That is, merely knowing the words in a text will not guarantee adequate comprehension of that passage. Furthermore, reading experience is an important source of vocabulary development, particularly in upper grades, and poor readers tend to avoid reading and acquire fewer words compared to their reading peers. However, the poor reading vocabulary score of a child with reading disability could be the result of decoding problems rather than the consequence of impoverished vocabulary. In fact, some children with reading disability can have excellent oral vocabulary.

Even though it would appear to be an uncomplicated undertaking, valid vocabulary assessment is a difficult task. This is so because standardized tests can assess only a sampling of a child's vocabulary. The child may know many words, but may not know the words in the vocabulary test because many words in standardized tests are taken from textbooks used in the classrooms. In order to obtain a reliable estimate of the students' vocabulary knowledge, it is desirable to administer tests of both reading and listening vocabulary. The Woodcock Language Proficiency Battery—Revised (WLPB-R, Woodcock, 1994) has subtests of both listening and reading vocabularies.

Many of these tests are also available in Spanish version. For instance, Batería III Woodcock-Muñoz (Woodcock et al., 2006) is a comprehensive set of tests that assesses both cognitive abilities and achievement levels of Spanish-speaking individuals between the ages of 2 years and 90+ years. And Tejas Lee is the Spanish version of Texas Primary Reading Inventory. Center for Applied Linguistics has developed a website 'Development of Literacy in Spanish Speakers (DeLSS)' (http://www.cal.org/delss/products/delss-tests.html) that provides information for the different types of literacy tests available for speakers of the Spanish language. Most of the tests are developed with the funding by National Institute of Child Health and Human Development and the Institute of Education Sciences of the Department of Education. Additional information about the different types of tests such as achievement tests, diagnostic tests, informal measures, curriculum-based measures, and portfolios can be found in Aaron et al. (2008b).

INTERPRETING THE ASSESSMENT OUTCOME USING THE COMPONENTIAL MODEL

Assessing reading problems using Componential model has various advantages. Since it does not involve administering intelligence tests, teachers or teachers' aids either in the regular classroom or in special education classes can administer the tests. Further, Componential model is helpful in identifying the source of reading problems (decoding or comprehension), and thus recommend appropriate remedial procedures (see Aaron et al, 1999; 2008b). The hypothetical profiles of normal students and those with reading disability are shown in Table 12.1.

Table 12.1   Reading test performances

Reader type	1	2	3	4	5
Test					
Listening comprehension	100	100	80	80	80
Reading comprehension	100	80	80	80	90
Decoding	100	80	100	80	90

Notes on reader types

1 *Normal reader.* All scores are within average range.
2 *Poor reader with word recognition deficit.* The profile of a reader with dyslexia. As shown by the listening comprehension score, comprehension is within the average range. However, reading comprehension score is low because of poor decoding skill.
3 *Poor reader with comprehension deficit.* The profile of student with comprehension deficit. Decoding score is within average range but since comprehension is poor as reflected in both reading and listening tasks.
4 *Poor reader with both word recognition and comprehension deficits.* The profile of a 'slow learner' or 'garden variety poor-reader'. Both decoding and comprehension scores are low.
5 *Poor reading due to inconsistent attention.* This can be the profile of a reader with attentional problems. Tests of listening comprehension require close attention, whereas tests of reading comprehension are not that sensitive to attention. Thus, individuals with a higher reading comprehension score than listening comprehension score can be suspected of having inconsistent attention. (See Aaron et al. 2002; 2004).

By identifying the weak component, appropriate instructional procedures can be applied. The validity of the Componential model was examined recently (see Aaron, et al., in press). Based on the nature of the reading component they were deficient in (word recognition or comprehension), 125 children in the treatment group received word recognition training; 46 children received reading comprehension strategy training. A comparison group did not receive such differentiated instruction but received undifferentiated instruction in the resource rooms. After 16 weeks of instruction, the treatment groups performed better on different tests of reading while the comparison group did not show such significant gains.

Applications

The three components of reading—decoding, comprehension, and fluency—can be assessed either by educational diagnostician, reading specialist, or the classroom teacher. Once the weak component is identified, remedial techniques to improve the weak component can be used. For instance, children with weak decoding skills can be provided phonological awareness training (cf., Adams et al., 1998; Ball and Blachman, 1988; 1991; Foorman et al., 1997; Torgesen et al., 1997) and then followed by a structured, sequential, explicit instruction in decoding skills which can be delivered through multisensory training (Carekker, 2005a, 2005b; Lindamood and Lindamood, 2005), the Orton Gillingham approach, or the Spalding Method (Spalding and Spalding, 2005). All these methods are based on the sound–syllable structure of English language and have proved to be successful in improving decoding skills of children at risk (Joshi et al., 2002; Henry, 2003).

Children with poor comprehension skills can be trained to apply comprehension strategies when they read. These strategies include activating relevant schemata, utilizing visual imagery, generating questions, predicting outcomes, and summarizing. Comprehension instruction can be delivered using the Reciprocal Teaching strategy. There is evidence to show that comprehension strategy instruction can be effective in improving comprehension skills (Anderson et al., 1995; Boulware-Gooden et al., 2007; Cain and Oakhill, 1998; Oakhill et al., 1998; Palinscar and Brown, 1984; Rosenshine and Meister, 1994). Studies by Lovett et al. (1988), and Tunmer (1998) suggest that fluency can be improved by repeated practice in reading. It can also be accelerated by improving decoding skills.

SUMMARY

It is estimated that approximately 25 per cent of school children have some form of reading problem. At the present time, these children are diagnosed on the basis of the discrepancy between their IQ and achievement scores. However, diagnosis based on IQ scores does not lead to recommendations regarding remediation, instruction, and management of reading problems. In the place of discrepancy formula, we offer an alternate model called 'The Componential Model of Reading' (Joshi and Aaron, 2000). According to this model, fluent reading consists of word recognition and comprehension. Fluency is not treated as a component because it is uncertain if it is independent of word recognition skills. In this paper, we have outlined the various tests that could be used in assessing these components. Some pitfalls to be avoided in testing different aspects of reading and spelling are presented. The Componential model, in addition to providing a reasonably accurate picture of the poor reader's strengths and weaknesses, has the advantage of leading to directions for remediation.

NOTE

Part of this chapter appeared as R.M. Joshi (2003) 'Misconceptions about the assessment and diagnosis of reading disability', *Reading Psychology*, 24: 247–266. Reproduced by permission of Taylor and Francis, Inc., http://www.routledge-ny.com.

REFERENCES

Aaron, P. G. (1991) 'Can reading disabilities be diagnosed without using intelligence tests?', *Journal of Learning Disabilities*, 245: 178–186.

Aaron, P. G. (1997) 'The impeding demise of the discrepancy formula', *Review of Educational Research*, 67: 461–502.

Aaron, P. G. and Joshi, R. M. (1992) *Reading problems: Consultation and remediation.* New York: Guildford.

Aaron, P. G., Joshi, R. M., Ayotollah, M., Ellsberry, A., Henderson, J. and Lindsey, K. (1999) 'Decoding and sight-word naming: Are they two independent components of word-recognition skill?', *Reading and Writing: An Interdisciplinary Journal*, 14: 89–127.

Aaron, P.G., Joshi, R.M., Boulware-Gooden, R., and Bentum, K. (2008a) Diagnosis and treatment of reading disabilities based on the component model of reading: An alternative to the discrepancy model of learning disabilities, *Journal of Learning Disabilities*, *41*, 67–84.

Aaron, P.G., Joshi, R.M., Palmer, H., Smith, N. and Kirby, E. (2002) 'Separating genuine cases of reading disability from reading deficits caused by inattentive behavior', *Journal of Learning Disabilities*, 35: 425–435.

Aaron, P.G., Joshi, R.M. and Phipps, J. (2004) 'A cognitive tool to diagnose predominantly inattentive ADHD behavior', *Journal of Attention Disorders*, 7: 125–135.

Aaron, P.G., Joshi, R.M. and Quotrochi, J. (2008b). *The professional reading teacher*. Baltimore, MD: Paul H. Brookes Publishing Company.

Aaron, P. G., Joshi, R. M. and Williams, K. A. (1999) 'Not all reading disabilities are alike', *Journal of Learning Disabilities*, 32: 120–137.

Adams, M. (1990) *Beginning to read: Thinking and learning about print*. Cambridge, MA: MIT Press.

Adams, M. J., Foorman, B. R., Lundberg, I. and Beeler, T (1998) *Phonemic awareness in young children: A classroom curriculum*. Baltimore: Paul H. Brookes.

Adlof, S.M., Catts, H.W. and Little, T.D. (2006) 'Should the simple view of reading include a fluency component?', *Reading and Writing: An Interdisciplinary Journal*, 19: 933–958.

American Psychiatric Association (1994) *Diagnostic and statistical manual of mental disorders* (4th ed.). Washington, DC: Author.

Anderson, V., Chen, C. K. and Henne, R. (1995) The effects of strategy instruction on the literacy models and performance by reading and writing-delayed middle school students. In K. A. Hinchman, D. J. Leu, & C. K. Kinzer (eds.), *Forty-fourth yearbook of the National Reading Conference* (pp. 180–189). Rochester, NY: National Reading Conference.

August, D., Kenyon, D., Malabonga, V., Caglarcan, S., Louguit, M., Francis, D. and Carlo, M. (2001). *Test of phonological processing in Spanish (TOPPS)*. Washington, DC: Center for Applied Linguistics.

Ball, E. W., & Blachman, B. A. (1988) Phoneme segmentation training: Effect on reading readiness. *Annals of Dyslexia, 38*, 208–225.

Ball, E. and Blachman, B. (1991) 'Does phoneme awareness training in kindergarten make a difference in early word recognition and developmental spelling?', *Reading Research Quarterly*, 26: 49–66.

Berninger, V.W., Dunn, A., Lin, S.C. and Shimada, S. (2004) 'School evolution: Scientist-practitioner educators creating optimal learning environments for all students', *Journal of Learning Disabilities*, 37: 500–508.

Binet, A. and Simon, T. (1916) *The development of intelligence in children* (The Binet-Simon Scale). Paris: Flammarion.

Blachman, B. A., Tangel, D. M., Ball, E. W., Black, R. and McGraw, C. K. (1999) 'Developing phonological awareness and word recognition skills: A two-year intervention with low-income, inner-city children', *Reading and Writing: An Interdisciplinary Journal*, 11: 239–273.

Blanchard, J.S., Di Cerbo, K.E., Oliver, J. and Albers, C.A. (2001, July) *Can divided time administration raise test scores? The relation between attention and standardized reading comprehension tests*. Paper presented at the annual meeting of the Society for the Scientific Studies of Reading, Boulder, CO.

Boulware-Gooden, R., Carreker, S., and Joshi, R.M. (2007) 'Instruction of metacognitive strategies to enhance reading comprehension and vocabulary achievement of third grade students', *The Reading Teacher*, 61: 70–77.

Bowers P. and Wolf, M. (1993) 'Theoretical links among naming speed, precise timing mechanisms, and orthographic skill in dyslexia', *Reading and Writing: An Interdisciplinary Journal*, 5: 60–85.

Bradley, L. and Bryant, P.E. (1985) *Rhyme and reason in reading and spelling*. Ann Arbor, MI: University of Michigan Press.

Cain K. & Oakhill, J. (1998) Comprehension skill and inference-making ability: Issues of causality. In C. Hulme and R. M. Joshi (eds.), *Reading and spelling: Development and disorders.* Mahwah, NJ: Lawrence Erlbaum, pp. 329–342.

Calfee, R.C., Venezky, R.L. and Chapman, R.S. (1969) 'Pronunciation of synthetic words with predictable and nonpredictable letter-sound correspondence', (Technical Report No. 111) Research and Development Center, University of Wisconsin, Madison.

Carreker, S. (2005a) 'Teaching reading: Accurate decoding and fluency', in J.R. Birsh, (ed.), *Multisensory teaching of basic language skills.* Baltimore, MD: Paul H. Brookes Publishing Co. pp. 213–255.

Carreker, S. (2005b) 'Teaching spelling', in J.R. Birsh, (ed.), *Multisensory teaching of basic language skills.* Baltimore, MD: Paul H. Brookes Publishing Co. pp. 257–295.

Carver, R.P (1998) 'Predicting reading level in Grades 1 to 6 from listening level and decoding level: Testing theory relevant to simple view of reading', *Reading and Writing: An Interdisciplinary Journal,* 10: 121–154.

Castles, A. and Coltheart, M. (2004) 'Is there a causal link from phonological awareness to success in learning to read?', *Cognition,* 91: 77–111.

Catts, H. W. and Kamhi, A. G. (2005) 'Causes of reading disabilities', in H. W. Catts and A. G. Kamhi (eds), *Language and reading disabilities.* Boston, MA: Allyn and Bacon. pp. 94–126.

Cisero, C.A. and Royer, J.M. (1995) 'The development and cross-language transfer of phonological awareness', *Contemporary Educational Psychology,* 20: 275–303.

Cossu, G., Gugliotta, M. and Marshall, J.C. (1995) 'Acquisition of reading and written spelling in a transparent orthography: Two non parallel processes?', *Reading and Writing: An Interdisciplinary Journal,* 7: 9–22.

Compton, D. L., and Carlisle, J. F. (1994) Speed of word recognition as a distinguishing characteristic of reading disabilities. *Educational Psychology Review, 6,* 115–140.

DeFries, J., Fulker, D. and LaBuda, C. (1987) 'Evidence for a genetic etiology in reading disability in twins', *Nature,* 329: 537–539.

de Jong, P.F. and Van der Leij, A. (2002) 'Effects of phonological abilities and linguistic comprehension on the development of reading', *Scientific Studies of Reading,* 6: 51–77.

de Jong, P. F. and van der Leij, A. (2003) 'Developmental changes in the manifestation of a phonological deficit in dyslexic children learning to read a regular orthography', *Journal of Educational Psychology,* 95: 22–40.

Denckla, M.B. and Rudel, R.G. (1976a) 'Naming of object-drawings by dyslexic and other learning disabled children', *Brain and Language,* 3: 1–15.

Denckla, M.B. and Rudel, R.G. (1976b) 'Rapid automatized naming (R. A. N.): Dyslexia differentiated from other learning disabilities', *Neuropsychologia,* 14: 471–479.

Dudley-Marling, C. (2004) 'The social construction of learning disabilities', *Journal of Learning Disabilities,* 37: 482–489.

Durgunoglu, A.Y., Nagy, W.E. and Hancin-Bhatt, B.J. (1993) 'Cross-language transfer of phonological awareness', *Journal of Educational Psychology,* 85: 453–465.

Ehri, L.C. (1991) 'Development of the ability to read words', in R. Barr, M.L. Kamil, P. Mosenthal, and P.D. Pearson (eds), *Handbook of reading research.* New York, Longman. Vol. 2: pp. 383–417.

Ehri, L.C. (1997) 'Learning to read and learning to spell are one and the same, almost', in C.A. Perfetti, L. Reiben, and M. Fayol (eds), *Learning to spell: Research, theory, and practice across languages.* Mahwah, NJ: Lawrence Erlbaum Associates. pp. 237–269.

Foorman, B., Francis, D., Winikates, D., Mehta, P., Schatschneider, C. and Fletcher, J. (1997) 'Early interventions for children with reading disabilities', *Scientific Studies of Reading,* 1: 255–276.

Frith, U. and Snowling, M. (1983) 'Reading for meaning and reading for sound in autistic and dyslexic children', *British Journal of Developmental Psychology,* 1: 320–342.

Gillham, B. (ed.) (1978) *Reconstructing educational psychology.* London: CroomHelm.

Gough, P. B. and Tunmer, W. E. (1986) 'Decoding, reading, and reading disability', *Remedial and Special Education,* 7: 6–10.

Hammill, D. D. (2004) 'What we know about correlates of reading', *Exceptional Children,* 70: 453–468.

Hannon, B. and Daneman, M. (2001) 'A new tool for measuring and understanding individual differences in reading comprehension', *Journal of Educational Psychology*, 93: 103–128.

Henry, M.K. (2003) *Unlocking literacy: Effective decoding and spelling instruction*. Baltimore, MD: Paul H. Brookes Publishing Co.

Hinshelwood, J. (1917) *Congenital word blindness*. London: Lewis.

Hoover, W. and Gough, P. B. (1990) 'The simple view of reading', *Reading and Writing: An Interdisciplinary Journal*, 2: 127–160.

Joshi, R.M. & Aaron, P.G. (2000). The component model of reading: Simple view of reading made a little more complex, *Reading Psychology*, 21, 85-97.

Joshi, R.M. (2003) 'Misconceptions about the assessment and diagnosis of reading disability', *Reading Psychology*, 24: 247–266.

Joshi, R.M. (2005) 'Vocabulary: A critical component of comprehension', *Reading and Writing Quarterly*, 21: 209–219.

Joshi, R.M. and Aaron, P.G. (1991) 'Developmental reading and spelling disabilities: Are these dissociable?', in R.M.Joshi (ed.), *Written language disorders*. Boston: Kluwer Academic Publishers. pp. 1–24.

Joshi, R.M. and Aaron, P.G. (2002) 'Naming speed and word familiarity as confounding factors in decoding', *Journal of Research in Reading*, 25: 160–171.

Joshi, R.M. and Aaron, P.G. (2007, July) *Can Componential Model be applied to Spanish Orthography?* Paper presented at the annual meeting of the Society for the Scientific Studies of Reading, Prague, Czech Republic.

Joshi, R. M., Dahlgren, M. and Boulware-Gooden, R. (2002) 'Teaching reading through multi-sensory approach in an inner city school', *Annals of Dyslexia*, 53: 235–251

Joshi, R. M., Williams, K. A. and Wood, J. (1998) 'Predicting reading comprehension from listening comprehension: Is this the answer to the IQ debate?', in C. Hulme and R. M. Joshi (eds.), *Reading and spelling: Development and disorders*. Mahwah, NJ: Erlbaum. pp. 319–327.

Juel, C. (1994) *Learning to read and write in one elementary school*. New York: Springer-Verlag.

Just, M.A. and Carpenter, P.A. (1987) *The psychology of reading and language comprehension*. Boston, MA: Allyn and Bacon.

Karlsen, B. and Gardner, E.F. (1995) *Stanford diagnostic reading test*. San Antonio, TX: Harcourt Brace.

Keenan, J.M. and Betjemann, R.S. (2006) 'Comprehending the Gray oral reading test without reading it: Why comprehension tests should not include passage-independent items', *Scientific Studies of Reading*, 10: 363–380.

Keenan, J. M., Betjemann, R. S.,Wadsworth, S. J., DeFries, J. C. and Olson, R. K. (2006) 'Genetic and environmental influences on reading and listening comprehension', *Journal of Research in Reading*, 29: 75–91.

Ladd, E. M. (1970) 'More than scores from tests', *The Reading Teacher*, 24: 305–311.

Leach, J.S., Scarborough, H. and Rescorla, L. (2003) 'Late-emerging reading disabilities', *Journal of Educational Psychology*, 95: 211–224

Levy, B.A. and Carr, T.H. (1990) 'Component process analysis: Conclusions and challenges', in T.H. Carr and B.A. Levy (eds.), *Reading and its development: Component skills analysis*. New York: Academic Press. pp.423–438.

Leybaert, J. and Content, A. (1995) 'Reading and spelling acquisition in two different teaching methods: A test of the independence hypothesis', *Reading and Writing: An Interdisciplinary Journal*, 7: 65–88.

Lindamood, P. and Lindamood, P. (2005) *The Lindamood phoneme sequencing program for reading, spelling, and speech – Third Edition*. Bloomington, MN: Pearson.

Lovett, M. W., Ramsey, M. J., & Barron, R. W. (1988) Treatment, subtype, and word type effects on dyslexic children's response to remediation. *Brain and Language, 34*, 328–349.

Lundberg, I., Frost, J. and Petersen, P. (1988) 'Effects of an extensive program for stimulating phonological awareness in preschool children', *Reading Research Quarterly*, 23: 263–284.

MacGinitie, W.H., MacGinitie, R.K., Maria, K. and Dreyer, L.G. (2000) *Gates-MacGinitie reading tests*. Chicago, IL: Riverside Publising Co.

Markwardt, F.C. (1998) *The Peabody individual achievement test—Revised*. Circle Pines, MN: American Guidance Services.

Marshall, J.C. and Newcombe, F. (1973) 'Patterns of paralexia', *Journal of Psycholinguistic Research*, 2: 179–199.

Moats, L.C. (1995) *Spelling, development, disabilities, and instruction*. Baltimore, MD.: York Press.

Muter, V. (1998) 'Phonological awareness: Its nature and its influence over early literacy development', in C. Hulme and R.M. Joshi (eds.), *Reading and spelling: Development and disorders*. Mahwah, NJ: Lawrence Erlbaum Associates. pp. 343–367.

Newcomer, P. (1999) *Diagnostic achievement battery-3*. Austin, TK: Pro-ED.

Oakhill, J.V., Cain, K. and Bryant, P.E. (2003) 'The dissociation of word reading and text comprehension: Evidence from component skills', *Language and Cognitive processes*, 18: 443–468.

Oakhill, J., Cain, K., & Yuill, N. (1998). Individual differences in children's comprehension skill: Toward an integrated model. In C. Hulme & R. M. Joshi (eds.), *Reading and spelling: Development and disorders* (pp. 343–367). Mahwah, NJ: Erlbaum.

Olson, R. K. (2006) 'Genetic and environmental influences on the development of reading and related cognitive skills', in R.M. Joshi and P.G. Aaron (eds), *Handbook of orthography and literacy*. Mahwah, NJ: Lawrence Erlbaum Associates. pp. 693–707.

Palinscar, A. S., & Brown, A. L. (1984). Reciprocal teaching of comprehension fostering and monitoring activities. *Cognition and Instruction, 1*, 117–175.

Palmer, J., McCleod, C., Hunt, E. and Davidson, J. (1985) 'Information processing correlates of reading', *Journal of Memory and Language*, 24: 59–88.

Perfetti, C.A. (1988) 'Verbal efficiency theory in reading ability', in M. Daneman, G.E. MacKinnnon, and T.G. Waller (eds), *Reading research: Advances in theory and practice*. New York: Academic Press. pp. 109–143.

Pinheiro, Â. M. V. (1995) 'Reading and spelling development in Brazilian Portuguese', *Reading and Writing: An Interdisciplinary Journal*, 7: 111–138.

Pressley, M. (2000). What should comprehension instruction be the instruction of? In M.L. Kamil, P.B. Mosenthal,, D. Pearson and R. Barr (eds). Handbook of reading research., vol. 3, (pp. 545–561). Mahwah, NJ. Lawrence Erlbaum.

Quiroga, T., Lemos-Britton, Z., Mostafapour, E., Abbott, R.D. and Berninger, V.W. (2002) 'Phonological awareness and beginning reading in Spanish-speaking ESL first graders: Research into practice', *Journal of School Psychology*, 40: 85–111.

Rosenshine, B. and Meiser, C. (1994) Reciprocal teaching: A review of the research. *Review of Educational Research, 64*, 479–530.

Savage, R. (2001) 'The "simple view" of reading: Some evidence and possible implications', *Educational Psychology in Practice*, 17: 17–33.

Savage, R. S. (2004) 'Motor skills, automaticity and developmental dyslexia: A review of the research literature', *Reading and Writing: An Interdisciplinary Journal*, 17 (3): 301–324.

Sebastian-Gallés, N. and Vacchiano, A. P. (1995) 'The development of analogical reading in Spanish', *Reading and Writing: An Interdisciplinary Journal*, 7: 23–38.

Shankweiler, D., Crain, S., Katz., L., Fowler, A.E., Liberman, A., Brady, S., Thornton, R., Lundquist, D., Dreyer, L., Fletcher, J., Steubing, K., Shaywitz, S. and Shaywitz, B. (1995) 'Cognitive profiles of reading-disabled children: Comparison of language skills in phonology, morphology, and syntax', *Psychological Science*, 6: 149–156.

Shearer, A.P. and Homer, S.P. (1994) *Linking reading assessment to instruction*. New York: St. Martin Press.

Siegel, L. (1989) 'IQ is irrelevant to the definition of leaning disabilities', *Journal of Learning Disabilities*, 22: 469–479.

Spache, G.D. (1940) 'Characteristic errors of good and poor readers', *Journal of Educational Research*, 34: 182–189.

Spalding, R. B. and Spalding, W. T. (2005) *The writing road to* reading – Fifth Revised Edition. Phoenix, AZ: Spalding Education International.

Spring, C. and French, L. (1990) 'Identifying children with specific reading disabilities from listening and reading discrepancy scores', *Journal of Learning Disabilities*, 23: 53–58.

Stahl, S., & Fairbanks, M. (1986) The effects of vocabulary instruction: A model based meta-analysis. *Review of Educational Research, 56*, 72–110.

Stahl, S. and Murray, B. (1994) 'Defining phonological awareness and its relationship to early reading', *Journal of Educational Psychology*, 86: 221–234.

Stanovich, K. E. (1991) 'Discrepancy definitions of reading disability: Has intelligence led us astray?' *Reading Research Quarterly*, 26: 7–29.

Stanovich, K. E. (1993) 'Problems in the differential diagnosis of reading disabilities', in R. M Joshi and C. K. Leong (eds), *Reading disabilities: Diagnosis and component processes.* Dordrecht, Holland: Kluwer Academic Publishers. pp. 3–31.

Stanovich, K. E., Cunningham, A. E. and Freeman. (1986) 'Intelligence, cognitive skills, and early reading process', *Reading Research Quarterly*, 23: 360–407.

Sternberg, R.J. (1985). *Beyond IQ: A triarchic theory of human intelligence.* New York: Cambridge University Press.

Tangel, D. M. and Blachman, B. A. (1995) 'Effect of phoneme awareness instruction on Kindergarten children's invented spelling', *Journal of Reading Behavior*, 24: 133–161.

Torgesen, J. K. and Bryant, B. R. (1995) *Test of phonological awareness.* Austin, TX: Pro-Ed.

Torgesen, J. K., Wagner, R. K. and Rashotte, C. A. (1997) 'Prevention and remediation of severe reading disabilities: Keeping the end in mind', *Scientific Studies of Reading*, 1: 217–234.

Torgesen, J. K., Wagner, R. K. and Rashotte, C. A. (1999) *Test of word reading efficiency.* Austin, TX: Pro-Ed.

Townsend, D. J., Carrithers, A. and Bever, T. G. (1987) 'Listening and reading processes in college- and middle- school age readers', in R. Horowitz and S. J. Samuels (eds) *Comprehending oral and written language.* New York: Academic Press. pp. 217–242.

Treiman, R. (1993) *Beginning to spell.* New York: Cambridge University Press.

Treiman, R. (1998) 'Beginning to spell in English', in C. Hulme and R. M. Joshi (eds), *Reading and spelling: Development and disorders.* Mahwah, NJ: Lawrence Erlbaum Associates. pp. 371–393.

Treiman, R. (2006) 'Knowledge about letters as a foundation for reading and spelling', in R.M. Joshi and P.G. Aaron (eds), *Handbook of orthography and literacy.* Mahwah, NJ: Lawrence Erlbaum Associates. pp. 581–599.

Tunmer, W. E. (1998) Language prediction skill, phonological recoding ability, and beginning reading. In C. Hulme and R. M. Joshi (eds.) *Reading and spelling: Development and disorders.* Mahwah, NJ: Erlbaum. pp. 33–67.

Vellutino, F. R., Scanlon, D. M., Sipay, E., Pratt, A, Chen, R. and Denckla, M. B.(1996). Cognitive profiles of difficult-to-remediate and readily remediated poor readers: Early intervention as a vehicle for distinguishing between cognitive and experiential deficits as basic causes of specific reading disability. *Journal of Educational Psychology, 88*, 601–638.

Vellutino, F., et al., (1996) 'Cognitive profiles of difficult-to-remediate and readily remediated poor readers: Early intervention as a vehicle for distinguishing between cognitive and experienced deficits as basic causes of specific reading disability', *Journal of Educational Psychology*, 88: 601–638.

Venezky, R. (1976) *Theoretical and experimental base for teaching reading.* The Hague: Mouton.

Venezky, R. (2000) *The American way of spelling.* New York: Guilford.

Wagner, R. K., Torgesen, J. K. and Rashotte, C. A. (1999) *Comprehensive test of phonological proficiency.* Austin, TX: Pro-ed.

Waters, G., Bruck, M. and Seidenberg, M. (1985) 'Do children use similar processes to read and spell words?', *Journal of Experimental Child Psychology*, 39: 511–530.

Wechsler, D. (2001) *Wechsler individual achievement test-II.* San Antonio, TX: Harcourt.

Wiederholt, J. L. and Bryant, B. R. (1992) *Gray oral reading test, Third Edition.* Austin, TX: PRO–ED.

Wiederholt, J. L. and Bryant, B. R. (2001) *GORT 4: Gray oral reading tests examiner's manual.* Austin, TX: PRO-ED.

Wood, T. A., Buckhalt, J. A. and Tomlin, J. G. (1988) 'A comparison of listening and reading performance with children in three educational placements', *Journal of Learning Disabilities*, 8: 493–496.

Woodcock, R. W. (1997). *Woodcock Diagnostic Reading Battery*. Itasca, IL: Riverside Publishing Company.

Woodcock, R. W. (1998). *Woodcock reading mastery test—revised*. Circle Pines, MN: American Guidance Services.

Woodcock, R.W. (2001) *Woodcock language proficiency battery-revised*. Chicago, IL: Riverside.

Woodcock, R. W., McGrew, K.S. and Mather, N. (2001a) *Woodcock-Johnson® III NU tests of achievement*. Rolling Meadows, IL: Riverside Publishing Co.

Woodcock, R. W., McGrew, K.S. and Mather, N. (2001b) *Woodcock-Johnson® III NU tests of cognitive aboilities*. Rolling Meadows, IL: Riverside Publishing Co.

Woodcock, R.W., Muñoz-Sandoval, A.F., McGrew, K.S. and Mather, N. (2006) Batería III Woodcock-Muñoz. Chicago, IL: Riverside Publishing Company.

Wolf, M. and Bowers, P. (1999) 'The double-deficit hypothesis for the developmental dyslexia', *Journal of Educational Psychology*, 91: 415–438.

The Definition of Learning Disabilities: Who is the Individual with Learning Disabilities?

Linda S. Siegel and Orly Lipka

This chapter

i) reviews 111 articles on learning disabilities from the *Journal of Learning Disabilities* spanning the period from the journal's beginning in 1968 until September 2007;
ii) discusses how investigators have translated the conceptual definition of learning disabilities (LD) to operational definitions;
iii) identifies four common components in the conceptual definition of LD; and
iv) provides a suggested definition for LD.

INTRODUCTION

This chapter reviews 111 articles on learning disabilities from the *Journal of Learning Disabilities* spanning the period from the journal's beginning in 1968 until September 2007. The purpose of the review was to determine how investigators translated the conceptual definition of learning disabilities (LD) to operational definitions. Four common components in the conceptual definition of LD can be identified. These are:

- achievement;
- discrepancy;

- IQ; and
- exclusion.

These components were identified and analyzed in the articles that were reviewed. The chapter also includes comment on 39 years of study in the LD field in relation to recent research. As a result of this investigation the chapter will also provide a suggested definition for LD.

The purpose therefore of this chapter is to review the operational definition of LD from the initial publication of the *Journal of Learning Disabilities* to the present. Over the past 39 years, the *Journal of Learning Disabilities* has been a mirror reflecting the different conceptions of LD in vogue at a particular point in time. The journal has been, and is, a platform for the ongoing discussion in the field of LD as researchers attempt to discuss theoretical, empirical, and practical issues in the field.

In North America, learning disabilities refers to difficulties in some academic area (reading, spelling, and/or arithmetic) in spite of normal intelligence. The term includes dyslexia, also known as a reading disability. The equivalent of learning disabilities in the UK is learning difficulties.

When the *Journal of Learning Disabilities* was first published in 1968, its purpose was to 'erve as a vehicle for the exchange of clinical information and interdisciplinary dialogue emphasizing very practical approaches in an effort to make its pages of optimum use to all concerned' (Barnes, 1968: 55). In the first article of the first volume of the *Journal of Learning Disabilities*, published in January 1968, Barsch raised a basic question, which even now continues to challenge investigators: 'who is the individual with learning disabilities?' (p. 7) This chapter will review how this question has been answered in the *Journal of Learning Disabilities* over the past 39 years.

COMMON COMPONENTS OF THE DEFINITION OF LEARNING DISABILITY

The term 'learning disability' was found occasionally, prior to 1963, as a term in the educational literature, and served as a foundation for future LD concept (Kavale and Forness, 1995). Samuel Kirk (1966), an educator, provided one of the first formal definitions, 'A learning disability refers to a specific retardation or disorder in one or more of the processes of speech, language, perception, behavior, reading, spelling, or arithmetic' (pp. 1–2). Kirk additionally described who is omitted from the learning disability definition:

> Not all children who show retardation in school can be considered children with learning disabilities. A deaf child, for example, has a language disability and speech disability; yet, he cannot be classified as having a learning disability since his retardation in language and speech is the result of his inability to hear. (p.1)

Since Kirk's attempt to define LD, at least 11 definitions have been accepted as the 'official' definition of LD (Hammil, 1990). As well as these 11, various committees and other professionals in the field have suggested many other definitions. Kirk's definition provided a description of disabilities and he also mentioned what/who should be excluded. It is important to note that the basic components of Kirk's original ideas have been incorporated into most of the other definitions of LD in the decades following his research.

Since Kirk's attempt to define LD, the definition has been used as a label to describe many individuals. In 1975, in the US the Congress passed Public Law 94-142 (Education of All Handicapped Children Act), now codified as IDEA (Individuals with Disabilities Education Act). In order to receive federal funds, states must develop and implement policies that assure a free, appropriate public education to all children with disabilities. In 1985, it was reported that within the entire population of disabled individuals, students classified as learning disabled represent the largest group of exceptionalities being served under the provisions and funding authorization of P.L. 94-142 (U.S. Department of Education, 1985).

There are several common conceptual definitions that are accepted in the LD field. However, problems are revealed when investigators translate these conceptual definitions into operational definitions in order to diagnose or deter- mine who is actually suffering from a LD. Different definitions include a variety of components, which are an integral part of determining if an individual has a LD. Four components of the conceptual definitions that are frequently used are exclusion of other conditions and/or factors, discrepancy, IQ, and achievement difficulty (Durrant, 1994; Kavale and Nye, 1981). Each one of these components has a historic, well-established background as one of the basic criteria in the definition of LD.

Exclusion component

The exclusion component was initiated to eliminate groups that should not be considered as LD. Kirk was the first one to suggest the exclusion component in his LD definition. According to his definition, and the others that followed it, a clear effort should be made to distinguish LD from other general handicapping conditions, such as mental retardation and visual and hearing impairments. These conditions, such as low IQ, limited visual ability or limited hearing ability, may influence individual academic performance; however, these condi- tions may require different interventions, so these groups are excluded. Typically, second language and lack of conventional instructional opportunity are also exclusionary factors.

Most definitions suggest that LD must not be primarily the result of another handicapping condition. The exclusion component was necessary to establish LD as a separate and discrete category of special education. LD required an identity of its own in order to provide funding and legislation for program implementation (Kavale and Forness, 2000). This component was essential during the early days of the field in order to recognize the existence of the LD group and to provide special and appropriate support to students falling within the LD category.

Formula component

The second component of the conceptual definition is an effort of integrating the conceptual definition of LD into an operational one. One common formula that is used to define LD is the discrepancy between actual achievement and the measured 'intelligence' or measured 'potential'. This difference is then used to distinguish LD from mental retardation or other nonspecific learning problems.

The definition offered by Bateman (1965) is an example of this discrepancy concept:

> Children who have learning disorders are those who manifest an educationally significant discrepancy between their estimated intellectual potential and actual level of performance related to basic disorders in the learning process, which may or may not be accomplished by demonstrable central nervous system dysfunction, and which are not secondary to generalized mental retardation, educational or cultural deprivation, severe emotional disturbance, or sensory loss. (p. 220)

It should be noted that since Bateman's attempt to solidify the idea of discrepancy within a definition of LD, other investigators in the field have suggested various formulae to calculate the discrepancy. Other common formula that is used to define LD is the discrepancy between achievement and grade or chronological age. The idea of this formula is that if there is significant discrepancy between a student's reading, spelling, and/or arithmetic skills and his or her age, the student will be considered as having learning disability. Another formula that has been used to determine learning disability is a discrepancy between verbal and performance IQ.

IQ Component

The third component is the concept of intelligence as measured by IQ. Some definitions require at least an average IQ to distinguish the LD group from the group with mental retardation. Others use the IQ component as part of the LD definition to prove discrepancies between so-called *potential* measured by IQ test and actual performance.

Achievement

The fourth component of the LD conceptual definition is achievement. In this context, achievement refers to the basic skills taught in school, including reading, writing, spelling, and arithmetic. School curricula are designed in such a way as to gradually build on the complexity of these skills during the school years.

In each grade, there are certain skills that a student needs to master. These skills can be measured by achievement tests that compare the performance of the individual with norms from a population of the same age or grade.

OPERATIONAL VS. CONCEPTUAL DEFINITIONS

Although the conceptual definition of LD is more or less accepted in the field, great confusion exists about a common operational definition. An operational definition indicates how a particular concept is measured. It is essential to understand the nature of operational definitions; if different researchers use different ways of measuring the same variable, then it is not clear that they are measuring the same concept.

The lack of correspondence between the conceptual and operational definition of LD means that conflicting independent views of LD are often presented. Specifically, most investigators agree about conceptual definitions that use words and concepts to describe the variable. Problems arise when dealing with the operational definition of LD. The lack of an operational definition of LD reveals some very unclear issues in the field and that no precise operational definition of LD has received universal agreement. There is a need for an operational definition of LD for practical purposes such as the accurate diagnosis and classification of students (Kavale and Forness, 2000).

In order to assess whether or not a student has LD, accepted common criteria must be established. Following that, a set of measuring tools must also be used to demonstrate some consistency among students. For academic and methodological purposes, one needs to define the criteria for a diagnosis of LD when collecting samples for research. If different investigators use different criteria, then the findings of research have limited generalizability and practical utility.

Kavale and Nye (1981) reviewed the criteria in 307 LD research studies published between 1968 and 1980. They found five different ways to identify LD in those studies. One-half of the participants were selected on the basis of previous classification or diagnosis, however; the investigator did not report on those criteria or the extent to which the chosen participant met established criteria. In 24 per cent of the studies, the participants were identified on the basis of psychometric tests. One in five studies were selected on the basis of intact or established criteria based upon federal or state guidelines. Idiosyncratic identification criteria were used in 6 per cent of the studies and very few studies (1 per cent) provided no discernible identification criteria. In the latter, the title of the studies was the indication that LD participants were included in the sample. Another study also reported on similar results. Torgesen and Dice (1980) surveyed 105 studies. They found that LD populations were selected on the basis of previous classification or diagnosis in 16 per cent of the studies, but that no evidence was presented for the diagnosis.

The goal of operationalizing the term 'learning disability' is to enhance the ability to replicate and generalize research findings to other samples with similar characteristics (Swanson, 1991). Therefore, for both practical reasons within educational settings and for academic/methodological reasons, there is a real need to establish operational criteria that will provide a clear framework for investigators as well as teachers, students and examiners.

Therefore, this chapter will review the operational definitions of LD, as published in the last 39 years in the *Journal of Learning Disabilities*, with specific focus on four main components: exclusion, discrepancy, IQ, and achievement.

METHOD

All the articles that were included in this research were published in the *Journal of Learning Disabilities* from the first year that the journal was published (1968) up to September 2007.

In the selection process, all the articles that were published between 1968 and 2007, and whose title or abstract indicated a focus on children with LD were eligible for inclusion in the analysis of this study. In most of the cases, three articles per year of publication were selected on a random basis for a total of 111 articles. When the title or the abstract did not indicate a study about LD, the paper was not included in the current study. In most of the years, three articles that matched these criteria are included in this review; however, in several years, only two articles were included, because there was no third article that matched the review's selection criteria.

The participants in the articles were either in elementary or high school (ages 6–18 years) and the articles reported on empirical data. In this review, studies that focused on children with hyperactive and/or attention disorder characteristics were excluded. Overall, 111 articles representing the last 39 years of publication were reviewed.

RESULTS

In order to examine how the components were represented in the LD definition over the years, the four components were analyzed in three ways. First, an examination for general trends relating to each component was conducted. Second, the four components were analyzed in each decade in which they were originally reported: 1968–1979, 1980–1989, 1990–1999, 2000–2007. This analysis allowed the investigation of trends in each decade.

Across the 39 years of articles, the four components were incorporated in more than 61 per cent of the articles. The exclusion was used in 61.26 per cent of the articles, a formula was found in 81.98 per cent of the studies, IQ was noted in 81.98 per cent of the studies, and achievement was used in 76.57 per cent of the studies.

EXCLUSION COMPONENT

Table 13.1 summarizes the number of cases and percentage of studies using the exclusion component from 1968 to 2007. Over 39 years, exclusion was used in 68 out of the 111 studies (61.26 per cent) to describe the sample population. Investigators provided different interpretations of the exclusion component. The different interpretations can be categorized into three types. The first category is general description of the exclusion component, but there was no specification regarding exclusion criteria nor were the assessment tools used to identify excluded children were specified. In 3.6 per cent of the articles, the general use of the exclusion component was provided. For example, articles included statements such as: 'the subjects did not qualify for placement in any other category' or 'their learning problems were primarily a result of their learning disability'.

The second category provided information and criteria about the excluded groups, but did not identify the assessment tools that were used to evaluate these groups. In 45.94 per cent of the articles there was information about excluded groups, for example, articles included statements such as 'the LD is not primarily the result of sensory, lack of opportunity or emotional disabilities'.

The third category, provided a complete description of exclusion groups, including the assessment tools that were used and specific values of these assessments. In only 11.71 per cent of the articles, a definition that included a complete description of the exclusion criteria was used. For instance, articles included statements such as: 'The learning problem was not primarily due to vision, as indicated by 20/30 or better corrected vision on the Snellen Eye Chart ...'. In 37.5 per cent of the articles, the exclusion component was not mentioned at all.

Overall, the research that identified participants as LD used mostly the 'specific exclusion criteria' category more than the two other categories, providing criteria about the excluded groups, but with no specification about the assessment tools.

Table 13.1   Number of cases and percentage of the exclusion component analyzed across the years and by decade

Category	1968–1979 (n=31)		1980–1989 (n=30)		1990–1999 (n=30)		2000–2007 (n=20)		Total (n=111)	
	n	%	n	%	n	%	n	%	n	%
Exclusion was in the definition	18	58.06	19	63.33	21	70.0	10	50.0	68	61.26
General mention of exclusion	0	0	1	3.33	3	10.0	0	0	4	3.60
Specific exclusion criteria	15	48.38	14	46.66	14	46.66	8	40.0	51	45.94
Complete description of exclusded groups	3	9.67	4	13.33	4	13.33	2	10.0	13	11.71
No mention of exclusion	13	41.93	11	36.66	9	30.0	10	50.0	43	38.73

In order to understand the trends in the use of the exclusion component during the years, analysis of the component was conducted by decades. In the 1970s, about 60 per cent of the articles incorporated the exclusion criteria in the LD definition. In many of the studies provided, 48.38 per cent described specific exclusion criteria but did not indicate assessment tools, 9.67 per cent provided complete descriptions of the excluded groups, and none of the sampled studies used general description.

In the 1980s, similar proportion (63.3 per cent) of studies incorporated the exclusion component into their LD definition. Again, most of the studies, about 46.55 per cent, provided specific exclusion criteria but with no assessment tools, 13.3 per cent of the articles provided complete descriptions of the excluded groups, and 3.33 per cent of the studies mentioned the exclusion component.

In the 1990s, most of the studies, 70 per cent, identified exclusion criteria in their operational LD definition. The highest category, 46.66 per cent, provided the specific exclusion criteria but with no assessment tools. Between the years 2000 and 2007, in 50 per cent of the LD definitions, exclusion criteria were noted, mostly indicating, as in previous years, the exclusion criteria with no specific assessment tools.

Overall, there was an increase in the use of the exclusion component as part of the LD definition from the 1970s and the 1980s to the 1990s, and a small decrease from the 1990s to the 2000 years.

DISCREPANCY/FORMULA COMPONENT

The next section will review results pertaining to the discrepancy formula. The number of cases and percentage of this component from 1968 to 2007 is summarized in Table 13.2. The formula component was used in 91 out of the 111 studies (81.98 per cent) to describe the sample population. Some of the studies did not provide a clear formula or operational definition for LD and therefore, were not considered as studies that used a formula in this analysis. Sixteen studies (14.41 per cent) mentioned school designation or participating

Table 13.2 Number of cases and percentage of the formula component analyzed across the years and by decade

Category	1968–1979 (n=31)		1980–1989 (n=30)		1990–1999 (n=30)		2000–2007 (n=20)		Total (n=111)	
	n	%	n	%	n	%	n	%	n	%
Formula was in the definition	19	61.29	24	80	28	93.33	20	100	91	81.98
IQ vs. achievement	1	3.22	8	26.66	18	60.0	9	45.0	36	32.43
Grade/age vs. achievement	15	48.38	14	46.66	7	23.33	8	40.0	44	39.63
Combined definitions	2	6.45	2	6.66	3	10	2	10.0	9	8.10
Verbal-performance IQ	1	3.22	0	0	1	3.33	0	0	2	1.80
No mention of formula	11	35.48	6	20	2	6.66	1	5.0	20	18.01
Unclear cases	2	6.45	1	3.33	0	0	1	5.0	4	3.60
School designation	9	39.03	5	16.66	2	6.66	0	0	16	14.41

in a program of LD as the only criteria to identify LD. These studies also were not considered as cases that provided formula, and were categorized in 'school designation' category. For example, articles included statements such as: 'children were selected by the school as having learning disorder'. Also, four studies (3.60 per cent) did not provide clear formula and, thus we could not categorize them under any formula. These studies were categorized under 'unclear cases'. For example, articles included statements such as: '... their diagnosis of a learning disability was based on an overall evaluation from series of consultations by school psychologist, classroom teachers and appropriate other specialist were indicated. The diagnostic evaluation included the administration of standardized achievement and intelligence tests'. The rest of the studies used a formula to identify LD and were divided into four categories.

The first, and most popular formula, was the grade/age vs. achievement and it was incorporated into the definitions over the years in 39.63 per cent of the cases. Articles included statements such as: 'achievement levels for all were at least two years below expected grade level' or 'severe academic deficit, usually of two or more years in one or more areas'. Since this formula relies on discrepancy between the age/grade and achievement, it would be expected that the studies report on the discrepancy value, that is, what is the required standard deviation, in order to define a LD. Indeed, 23 articles from the 44 articles that used grade/age vs. achievement formula reported on a discrepancy value. For instance: 'the disabled readers were defined as children who had ... and reading age of two or more years behind chronological age' or 'those standards required that student's academic achievement fall at least 1.5 SD below educational expectancy'. As can be seen, there is no standard discrepancy that is used in all studies.

The IQ vs. achievement discrepancy formula was used in 32.43 per cent of the sampled papers. Articles included statements such as: '... an academic discrepancy of at least 1 SD between the child's achievement and estimate potential as measured by the intelligence test' or 'all subjects with learning disability had been certified as LD by the school district, based on a state-adopted discrepancy between potential and performance'. Since also this formula relies on discrepancy, it would be expected that the studies report on discrepancy value that was used in order to define a LD, but often they did not do so. Indeed, 26 articles of the 36 articles that used the discrepancy formula reported a specific standard deviation. Interestingly, when the value of the standard deviation was included, it varied from study to study from 1 SD to more than 2 SD.

For both, the IQ achievement discrepancy formula and grade/age achievement formula, studies reported on many different types of tests to assess achievement skills, for instance, reading comprehension, word recognition, spelling, and/or arithmetic skills.

Very few cases in our study used more than one formula to select their LD sample. In fact, in nine studies (8.10 per cent), the investigators used more than one formula to select their LD sample.

In order to understand the trends in the use of the different formulas during the years, analysis of the component was conducted by decades. In the 1970s, the most frequently used formula in approximately 50 per cent of the sampled articles was the 'grade/age vs. achievement' formula. There were 6.45 per cent of the articles that used the combined definitions and one article used the 'IQ vs. achievement' discrepancy formula. There were 6.45 per cent studies that did not provide a clear formula, and 39.03 per cent of the studies that used school designation to describe the way their sample was collected.

In the 1980s, the most frequently used formula was again the 'grade/age vs. achievement' formula, in 46.66 per cent of the cases, followed by 26.66 per cent of the case that used the IQ achievement formula. However, there were 20 per cent of unclear cases.

In the 1990s, there is a dramatic change and the most frequently used formula was the 'IQ vs. achievement' formula in 60 per cent of the sampled articles. There were 23.33 per cent of the articles that used the 'grade/age vs. achievement' formula. There was a decrease in the cases that did not clearly report clearly an operational definition and only two studies used the school designation as the way to define their LD sample.

Between the years 2000 and 2007, the IQ achievement formula continued to be the most dominant one (45 per cent) followed by grade vs. age achievement formula (40 per cent).

In conclusion, while in the 1970s and 1980s, the grade/age vs. achievement formula was the most used formula to identify LD children, from the 1990s until 2007, the use of the IQ–achievement discrepancy formula increased, and became the most frequent one. The number of the LD sample that was identified by school designation decreased over the decades.

INTELLIGENCE TEST SCORES

Table 3 shows the number of cases and the percentage of the IQ component from 1968 to 2007. Over 39 years, IQ was used in 91 out of the 111 studies (81.98 per cent) to describe the sample population. The first, and most general, use was related to an average IQ range, but the range was not specified nor was the IQ assessment tool identified. Articles included statements such as: 'subjects were at the average range on standard intelligence test'; 'subjects were in the normal IQ range.' In 25 of the articles, the IQ test that related to an average IQ was named, with no value of specific IQ.

In the second group, the IQ range was not specified but the IQ assessment tool was provided. For example, articles included statements such as: 'average intellectual ability or the potential for average ability was measured by the WISC–R and ...', 'their intelligence score was within the normal range as measured on the WISCIII'. In 29 of the articles, the IQ range was not specified but the assessment tools were indicated.

The third group provided information about the IQ range and provided a value, but did not identify the specific IQ test that was used. For example, articles included statements such as: 'all the subjects had IQ scores higher than 80'. In 15 of the articles, there was a definition that included an IQ range with specific value.

The fourth group provided a complete description of IQ scores, including the assessments tools that were used and the IQ subtests. For instance, articles included statements such as: 'intelligence test scores on the WISC were available for the 15 children, whose verbal IQ ranged from 84 to 113 (mean 93), and performance IQ from 71 to 139 (mean 90)'. In 22 of the articles, there was a definition that includes a complete description of the IQ.

In order to understand the trends of the use of the IQ component during the years, analysis of this component was conducted by decades, as presented in Table 13.3. In the 1970s, 41.93 per cent of the studies provided most complete category, 'complete IQ description,' was used more frequently than the other three categories. The other three categories were used at approximately the same level throughout the period of this review. In the 1980s, 26.6 per cent of the studies used IQ scores but did not specify a value. In the 1990s, the dominant category was the one that provided information about the assessment tools, but no numerical range of the IQ scores. This trend continued between 2000 and 2007, and the same category was the most dominant one (26.12 per cent), followed by a general description category of the IQ, in which there is description of normal range, but with no specific value or assessment tool (22.52 per cent).

Overall, there was a trend of decrease in the use of IQ as part of the LD definition over the four decades: in the 1970s, 83.87 per cent of the studies incorporate IQ as part of the LD definition; in the 1980s, 80 per cent incorporated the IQ in the LD definition; and in the 1990s, 89.99 per cent of the studies used the IQ as part of the definition; and finally between 2000–2007, a large decrease in the use of the IQ in the definition (75 per cent).

Table 13.3   Number of cases and percentage of the IQ component analyzed across the years and by decade

Category	1968–1979 (n=31)		1980–1989 (n=30)		1990–1999 (n=30)		2000–2007 (n=20)		Total (n=111)	
	n	%	n	%	n	%	n	%	n	%
Using IQ in definition	26	83.87	24	80.0	26	89.99	15	75.0	91	81.98
Average/Normal IQ range no value specified	3	9.67	8	26.66	10	33.33	4	20.0	25	22.52
Normal IQ range, assessment tool specified	4	12.90	6	20.0	14	46.66	5	25.0	29	26.12
Numerical IQ range value specified	6	19.35	4	13.3	2	6.66	3	15.0	15	13.51
Complete IQ description	13	41.93	6	20.0	0	0	3	15.0	21	18.91
No mention of IQ	5	16.12	6	20.0	4	13.3	5	25.0	20	18.01

ACHIEVEMENT COMPONENT

The fourth component in this study of the LD definitions was the achievement component. Table 13.4 presents the number of cases and the percentage of the studies using achievement component from 1968 to 2007. The achievement component was used in 85 out of the 111 studies (76.57 per cent) to describe the sample population and can be categorized into four types. The first, and most general, was related to the achievement component, but did not specify the achievement skills nor were the assessment tools used to identify achievement provided. For example, articles included statements such as: 'children whose educational achievement was very poor despite apparent normality of other adaptive behavior.' In 17.11 per cent of the articles, the general use of the achievement component was used.

The second type provided information about the skills that need to be measured under the achievement component, but did not identify the assessment tools that were used to assess the achievement skills. For example, articles included statements such as: 'the child exhibits an impediment in one or more of the basic learning processes involved in the understanding or in the reception, organization, or expression of written or spoken language'. In 22.52 per cent of the articles, a description of the achievement skill was provided. The third type provided information about the assessment tools, but not on the skills. In 7.20 per cent of the articles, a definition that includes assessment tools of achievement was provided.

The fourth category provided a complete description of the achievement component, including the assessment tools that were used. For instance, articles included statements such as: 'deficit in oral expression was assessed by the Northwestern Syntax Screening Test. Listening comprehension was assessed by the Carrow Test for Auditory ...'. In 29.72 per cent of the articles, a definition that included a complete description of the achievement assessment tools was provided.

In order to understand the trends in the use of the achievement component over the years, analysis of the component was conducted by decades, as presented in

Table 13.4 Number of cases and percentage of the achievement component analyzed across the years and by decade

Category	1968–1979 (n=31)		1980–1989 (n=30)		1990–1999 (n=30)		2000–2007 (n=20)		Total (n=111)	
	n	%	n	%	n	%	n	%	n	%
Including achievement	20	64.51	21	70.0	26	86.66	18	90.0	85	76.57
Minimal description	5	19.35	7	23.33	6	20.0	1	5.0	19	17.11
Specific skill	6	16.12	6	20.0	5	16.66	8	40.0	25	22.52
Specific assessment	2	6.45	1	3.33	5	16.66	0	0	8	7.20
Complete achievement description	7	22.58	7	23.33	10	33.33	9	45.0	33	29.72
No mention achievement	11	35.48	9	30.0	4	13.33	2	10.0	26	23.42

Table 4. In the 1970s, most of the studies that included the achievement component in the definition (64.5 per cent) used a complete description of achievement (22.58 per cent). In the 1980s, there were 23.33 per cent of articles that used information about minimal description of achievement skills, and 23.33 per cent of the articles that used complete descriptions of the achievement component, including the assessment tools.

In the 1990s, many of the studies used complete description of the assessment tools to evaluate achievement skills (33 per cent). Between 2000 and 2007, the highest category was the one that provided a complete description of achievement skills (45 per cent), followed by a specific description of the skills, but with no description of assessment tools (40 per cent).

There was an increase in the use of the achievement component over the years. In the 1970s, 64.51 per cent of the articles used the achievement skills in the LD definition; in the 1980s the number increased to 70 per cent. In the 1990s, 86.66 per cent of the articles used the achievement component in the LD definition and between 2000 and 2007, 90 per cent of the studies incorporate the achievement in their LD definition. Also, there is a trend toward a more detailed description of the achievement skills, with more specification of the assessment tools.

Overall, each one of the four components that were reviewed in this paper was interpreted differently by various researchers. In other words, the conceptual definition of LD was operationalized in many different ways.

IMPLICATIONS

Learning disabilities have had numerous operational definitions. Although there is some agreement on the basic components that should be included in conceptual definition, the operational definition is a different reality. This review has concentrated on the four components of the LD definition: exclusion, discrepancy formula, IQ, and achievement, in order to determine how the field transforms the conceptual definition into an operational one.

Overall, investigators have interpreted the four basic components of the conceptual definition in various ways and each component has received a variety of interpretations. Some aspect of the exclusion component was incorporated in 61.26 per cent of the sampled articles. However, most studies were not specific about how the exclusionary criteria were applied. In addition, different factors ranging from sensory impairment to neurological conditions to emotional disorders were used in different studies. Overall, there was an increasing use over the last four decades by investigators of exclusion component in the LD definition. Additionally, investigators that who included the exclusion component in the LD definition specified the exact exclusion criteria, but in most of the cases did not specify the assessment tools that were used in order to eliminate groups of students who were not qualified to be identified as LD.

In most of the cases, the exclusion component incorporated disabilities such as emotional disturbances, sensory handicapped, and neurological deficit. These conditions can be difficult to assess objectively. Sometimes emotional problems lead to low motivation, which lead to a learning disability. However, the reverse may be true. How can one distinguish between cause and effect? Is it really necessary to do so?

Another unresolved issue is how to determine what is the specific 'level' of an emotional problem that will determine whether a student is excluded from the LD definition and is instead be labeled as 'emotionally disabled'.

In summary, examination of the exclusion component has raised some problematic issues. First, what are exclusion criteria and what assessment tools should be used in order to assess these disabilities? Secondly, is it really necessary to do so? Another issue that complicates the diagnosis relates specifically to how to assess problems that are cannot be measured objectively, but rather are more subjectively and less clearly, such as emotional and sometimes social disabilities.

The discrepancy formula is another controversial component in the LD definition. Our review of research from the last 39 years revealed studies that used different formulas to define LD. Some of the studies used the discrepancy formula between IQ and achievement, some used the grade/age vs. achievement formula, and many of the studies relied on school designation or did not provide the readers with the specific formula that was used in order to identify the children with LD. There was a growing trend of the use of the IQ and achievement discrepancy formula throughout the years.

Interestingly, even when investigators have used the same formula there was still an inconsistent use of cutoff levels, the achievement tests that were used, and the IQ subtest. Different investigators used different cutoff levels for this discrepancy formula: one, one and a half, or even two standard deviations. These findings are consistent with previous research. Perlmutter and Parus (1983) found that some schools required a discrepancy of one standard deviation between ability and performance to classify a student as LD/RD, while other schools required two standard deviations or relied on a clinical judgment.

Another issue about the cutoff is that no study with IQ-achievement discrepancy required that the achievement scores be below average. The implication of this is that 'gifted students' with above-average IQ scores and also above-average achievement test results can demonstrate a significant discrepancy between the IQ score and achievement score. According to the definition of RD, this student will be included as RD, even though his/her reading ability is above average. These students do not have the same deficit as these with low reading scores (e.g., O'Malley et al., 2002). It is illogical to include students who are good readers in the dyslexic category.

Furthermore, there was inconsistency in the type of achievement tests that were used to assess achievement in both the IQ-achievement discrepancy formula and achievement and grade formulas. Different schools and studies use a variety of achievement tests to assess discrepancy in students with LD. This situation was identified in a study conducted by Perlmutter and Parus (1983). Their study examined the use of different diagnostic criteria and tests to assess LD using a discrepancy between IQ and performance as the definition. They found that schools used a different number and types of tests in the assessment process. The types of those tests varied from 2 in one district to 13 in another school. The problem is that different tests of the same skill may yield different scores (e.g., Siegel, 1999).

Although there is a growing trend of using the discrepancy formula between IQ and achievement, the use of the IQ test as part of the formula to define LD is problematic (for a review of the issues, see Siegel, 1989). Many studies have provided evidence that standard IQ tests are not valid for measuring potential learning ability for reading disabled (RD) individuals (e.g., Fletcher et al., 1989; 1992; Siegel, 1988; 1989; 1992).

The IQ component is also relevant to the LD definition as a way to determine individuals who are in the 'normal' range of intelligence. This is important since mentally retardation is different category of disability that clearly required different intervention than LD. In our review there were studies that used IQ tests and the subtests in different ways. First, investigators used different IQ subtests to calculate the IQ score. Some studies interpreted the use of IQ testing as the use of either the verbal or the performance scale, some used the full scale IQ, and many of the studies did not even report the way in which the IQ test was used. This, in all probability, did influence the reliability of the assessment technique. Second, there were different interpretations of the cutoff to define normal IQ. Different studies used different cutoff scores. Again, the use of different cutoff scores means that different children will be classified as LD in each study.

Our review also revealed that 81.98 per cent of the studies incorporate information about the IQ in the LD definition. Additionally; over the years investigators have presented more information about the scale and the subtests that were used to assess LD. It is still uncertain exactly which IQ tests/subtests were administered or how they were being used. For example, Siegel (1988) conducted a study to determine whether reading disabled and non-reading disabled children with different IQ scores would show distinctive patterns of performance on cognitive tasks. The surprising result was that IQ scores do not appear to be predictors of the cognitive processes involved in reading, spelling, language skills, and memory tasks. Therefore, we should abandon the IQ test in the analysis of children with learning disabilities.

Furthermore, in term of intervention program, recent studies have demonstrated that IQ scores did not predict ability to benefit from remediation program. The IQ scores did not differentiate between poor readers who were found to be readily remediated and poor readers who were difficult to remediate (Vellutino et al., 2000).

Overall, standardized IQ tests measure, among other abilities, expressive language skills, short-term memory, speed of processing information, speed of responding, and knowledge of specific facts (Siegel, 1990). Studies indicate that these functions are deficient in many individuals with learning disabilities (e.g., Siegel, 1985; Siegel and Feldman, 1983; Siegel and Linder, 1984; Siegel and Ryan, 1984; 1988; Swanson, 1993; 1994; Vellutino, 1978; 1979). Therefore, the IQ test cannot be a valid measure of the intelligence of individuals with RD.

Another variable that might influence the validity of the IQ measure as part of the LD formula is the 'Matthew Effect' (Stanovich, 1986). Stanovich described this effect associated with reading when he wrote, '... Reading itself develops other related cognitive abilities' (Stanovich, 1993). In other words, the cognitive skills in individuals who read less, such as students with RD, will be influenced and underdeveloped, thus resulting in lowered performance on IQ tests.

There is also a general claim that IQ tests are not valid as measures of individual ability. Researchers have suggested alternate ways to conceptualize ability (e.g., Gardner, 1983; Goleman, 1995; Lazear, 1994). Gardner (1983) suggested the concept of multiple intelligences. He claimed that there is not just one type of intelligence that correlates with success in life but several kinds of intelligences. He defined intelligence as a multidimensional phenomenon that is present at multiple levels of our brain. He noted that IQ tests are based on a very limited idea of intelligence.

Overall, from previous, as well as current research, it seems clear that IQ is irrelevant to the definition of LD, except possibly to define the border between LD and retardation. This is especially due to the fact that during the past, 40, different studies have used this component inconsistently to assess LD. In addition, recent studies have demonstrated the limitation of this tool in assessing LD students. In conclusion, the continued use of IQ is based on a tradition of IQ testing, rather than support from research showing its relevance to LD. The IQ test has been used because it was believed that this assessment tool could accurately assess actual or potential intelligence despite evidence to the contrary from recent research. The available evidence suggests that IQ is irrelevant as part of the definition of LD.

In a manner similar to IQ, the achievement component has not been clearly defined. The achievement component was used in some of the studies as part of the discrepancy formula and in the other cases as part of the grade and achievement formula. Also, the achievement tests were used in some cases to determine the participant's specific disability. There is growing use of the achievement component throughout the years. Also, in the 1990s, there was a trend toward more detailed descriptions of achievement assessment tools than in the 1970s.

There are several problems with the achievement component. First, investigators did not report on achievement tests that were used to assess achievement skills. Second, investigators assessed different skills under the title 'achievement', and finally, informal as well as standardized achievement tests were used.

In some of the cases, investigators used achievement in their formula to diagnose LD, but in one study reading skills were administered while on the other it was reading and spelling and some times even mathematics tests. As a consequence, including different types of LD may influence the results of these studies. Reading and arithmetic disabilities are very different types of learning disabilities, and therefore investigators need to distinguish between the subtypes of LD.

A portion of the studies that were reviewed also did not describe how specific skills were assessed. This information is important because there are different ways to assess achievement skills and each way can involve the student using different skills. Therefore, if one student is being assessed for reading comprehension using a close reading task and the same student is assessed by multiple-choice test, these tests could show different performance even though the same skill was apparently being assessed.

A portion of the studies reviewed used standardized achievement tests, while some used informal assessment tools. Standardized achievement tests use norms that offer the opportunity to compare the performance of the student being assessed with the level of achievement of their age or grade peers from the normal population. Informal achievement tests are subjectively interpreted so there are no norms to which to compare a student's performance. This means that there is no way to consistently evaluate or describe the performance of individual students. Therefore, different teachers/investigators/examiners are working with subjective diagnoses according to the 'informal' results. Detailed reporting about achievement assessment tools can only help future research to replicate studies and to produce more valid and consistent results.

Our review indicated that different investigators used different achievement tests as part of their achievement component in the formula. The field should aim for some standardization in the achievement skills that are used. Reading ability should be assessed by word recognition task, pseudoword reading, and reading comprehension tasks (Siegel, 1999). Since there are also writing and arithmetic disabilities, spelling and computational mathematics skills should be assessed. Writing is complicated to assess, but the Woodcock-Johnson has some subtests that may be useful (Woodcock and Johnson, 1989).

This foregoing discussion about the four components has revealed that each contributes to problems in identifying the LD child. In fact, an examination at the last 40 years of LD research reveals a variety of interpretations of each one of the four components by researchers and schools. This trend demonstrates that there is much ambiguity about definitional variables and inconsistent criteria in an area where specificity is a necessity. A more specific examination at each decade of the last 40 years reveals a growing trend in the use of the four components when defining a sample with LD. There is a trend to be more specific in reporting about assessment tools than there was in the 1960s and the 1970s, yet the investigators in this review used many different techniques to assess LD in their interpretation of the conceptual definition.

CONCLUSION

In conclusion, the review of the four components in LD research highlights some important issues that need to be taken into consideration in future research as well as in educational and diagnostic setting. Furthermore, there are two main implications of our study. First, this review has shown that studies have used widely different operational definitions to define LD. Also, researchers in many studies did not report the measures that were used in order to diagnose the sample as LD. This situation can result in critical consequence to the research as well to practice. For research, it is essential to be able to replicate a study. Since research in some of the cases used different operational definitions and in other cases did not report on the assessment tools, it is not possible to replicate the study. For educational settings, part of our studies examined students who were in special programs for LD in schools. In some schools, students will be defined as LD under one definition, while in another school, they might not be defined as LD because of different operational definitions. The consequences are that students who were fortunate enough to be categorized as LD received the support they required. Other students, perhaps in different school districts, states, provinces, or even in neighboring schools, were not fortunate enough to be recognized as LD, and therefore did not receive the additional educational support they required. Unfortunately, misdiagnosis of LD has academic and social consequences for an individual. We know from research that reading disabilities have serious social implications, as studies on homeless and runaway adolescents who have committed suicide have revealed a high prevalence of reading disabilities (Barwick and Siegel, 1996; McBride and Siegel, 1997). Therefore, it seems crucial to agree upon an operational definition in order to move research on LD forward in a constructive manner.

Another implication of our study is that the definition of LD needs to be considered in terms of subtypes. The term LD is too general and vague. Subtypes would provide researchers and diagnosticians with more precise results and diagnoses. Learning disabilities should be defined in terms of the domain of the deficit; reading disability and arithmetic disability are the two most common but others may be possible also. In order to replicate studies and to obtain consistent results, the sample of a study should consist of a valid representation of the population. Investigators must pay attention to their samples so their results will be valid. Each one of the subtypes (as described above) has unique characteristics and processes. More careful on research of each subgroup will lead to more practical and consistent results and conclusions. The general term 'LD' should be abandoned for more specific and productive sub-groupings.

So far, we discussed the role of the four vital components to the LD definition and reflect, through our review, the problematic use of each of these components. Each of these components has an essential role.

In relation to the exclusion component, there are disabilities such as autism, mental retardation, and language disorders that need to be considered in relation to LD. It is reasonable to distinguish autism from LD. Some features of autistic disorders are the presence of markedly abnormal or impaired development in social interactions and communication and markedly restricted repertoires of activity and interest. The impairment in reciprocal social interaction is significant and sustained. Also the impairment in communication is marked and sustained and affects both verbal and nonverbal skills. This disorder is clearly different from other disorders. Therefore, there is no doubt that the category of autism is different in terms of its diagnosis and the remediation that should be provided. Two other categories that should be differentiated from LD are hearing impairments and blindness. These categories have special remediation practices that differ from LD and should therefore be excluded.

However, not like autism, hearing impairments and blindness, language disorders are in a borderline category of LD. Some researchers argue that this category differs from LD (Aram and Hall, 1989) while others see it as subcategory of LD (e.g., Catts, 1989; Denckla, 1977). In either case, remediation and assistance is quite often the same for students with LD or language disorders and can, therefore, be considered as a form of LD.

The use of IQ in the definition has become increasingly common in spite of the evidence to suggest that it is not necessary. There is no justification for the use of the IQ-achievement discrepancy formula. The current research has shown that discrepant children with RD did not differ from non-discrepant children with RD. The IQ component was noted in most of our reviewed studies to eliminate children who were below average in IQ scores. An essential feature of mental retardation is significantly below average general intellectual functioning (IQ level below 70) which is accompanied by significant limitations in adaptive functioning in at least two of the following skills areas: communication, self-care, home, living, social/interpersonal skills, use of community resources, self-direction, functional academic skills, work, leisure, health, and safety (American Psychiatric Association, 1994). Therefore, the IQ test should be considered for administration only in those cases in where the main cause for low achievement is suspected to be mental retardation.

A diagnosis for LD should be established on the basis of achievement tests; achievement tests show if the individual has deficits in skills compared to his or her age group. Therefore, the formula that should be used to diagnose LD in an accurate way is the grade/age vs. achievement formula. In this formula, the scores of the achievement tests should be significantly below the age or the grade level scores.

In summary, an IQ above 70 with significantly low performance on reading, spelling, and/or arithmetic achievement test (measured by a low percentile or standard score) are the necessary basic components that should be part of the LD definition.

In 1963, when Kirk established the basic components of LD definition, a group of individuals, previously ignored, was suddenly acknowledged. This was when support and remediation for these individuals began to be provided. A growing trend in the field has been to further subdivide the LD category, identifying individuals as reading disabled, math disabled, spelling disabled, etc. Recognizing individuals and their specific disabilities will help to include all individuals who struggle, help schools assess their students more efficiently, and bring more consistent results to the field of LD research.

In his very first article in 1968, Barsch attempted to "set forth past, present and possibilities for 'the future of the field'.

It is now time to establish clear and consistent operational definitions of learning disabilities.

NOTE

The research used in this chapter was supported by a grant from the Natural Science and Engineering Research Council of Canada and the Canadian Language and Literacy Research Network to L. S. Siegel.

REFERENCES

American Psychiatric Association (1994) *Diagnostic and Statistical Manual of Mental Disorders,* *4th* edition (DSM–IV) Washington, DC: American Psychiatric Association.

Aram, D. and Hall, N. (1989). Longitudinal follow-up of children with preschool communication disorders: Treatment implications. School Psychology Review, 18(4): 487–501.

Barnes, B. (1968) 'Statement of purpose', *Journal of Learning Disabilities,* 1(1): 53–57.

Barsch, R. H. (1968) 'Perspectives on learning disabilities: The vectors of a new convergence', *Journal of Learning Disabilities,* 19(1): 4–20.

Barwick, M. and Siegel, L. S. (1996) 'Learning difficulties in adolescent client of a shelter for runaway and homeless street youth', *Journal of Research on Adolescence,* 6(4): 649–670.

Bateman, B. D. (1965) 'An educational view of a diagnostic approach to learning disorders', in J. Hellmuth (ed.), *Learning Disorders.* Seattle, WA: Special Child. pp. 219–239.

Catts, H. W. (1989) 'Phonological processing deficit and reading disabilities', in A. Kamhi and H. Catts (eds), *Reading Disabilities: A Developmental Language Perspective.* Austin, TX: PRO-ED.

Denckla, M. B. (1977) 'Minimal brain dysfunction and dyslexia: Beyond diagnosis by exclusion', in M. Blaw, I. Rapin and M. Kinsborne (eds), *Topics in Child Neurology.* New York: Spectrum Publication. pp. 79–86.

Durrant. J. E. (1994) 'A decade of research on learning disabilities: A report card on the state of the literature', *Journal of Learning Disabilities,* 27(1): 25–33.

Fletcher, J. M., Epsy, K. A., Francis, D. J., Davidson, K. C., Rourke, B. P. and Shaywitz, S. E. (1989) 'Comparison of cutoff score and regression-based definitions of reading disabilities', *Journal of Learning Disabilities,* 22(6): 334–338.

Fletcher, J. M., Francies, D. J., Rourke, B. P., Shaywitz, S. E. and Shaywitz, B. A. (1992) 'The validity of discrepancy-based definitions of reading disabilities', *Journal of Learning Disabilities,* 25: 555–61.

Gardner, H. (1983) *Frames of Mind: The Theory of Multiple Intelligences.* New York: Basic Books.

Goleman, D. (1995) *Emotional Intelligence.* New York: Bantam Books.

Hall, J. W., Wilson, K. P., Humphreus, M. S., Tinzmann, M. B. and Boyer, P. M. (1983) 'Phonemic similarity effects in good vs. poor readers', *Memory and Cognitive*, 11(5): 520–527.

Hammil, D. D. (1990) 'On defining learning disabilities: An emerging consensus', *Journal of Learning Disabilities*, 23(2): 74–84.

Kavale, K. and Nye, C. (1981) 'Identification criteria for learning disabilities: A survey of the research literature', *Learning Disability Quarterly*, 4(4): 383–388.

Kavale, K. A. and Forness, S. R. (1995) *The Nature of Learning Disabilities*. Mahwah, NJ: Lawrence Erlbaum.

Kavale, K. A. and Forness, S. R. (2000) 'What definition of learning disability say and don't say', *Journal of Learning Disabilities*, 33(3): 239–256.

Kirk, S. A. (1966) *The Diagnosis and Remediation of Psycholinguistic Disabilities*. University of Illinois.

Lazear, D. (1994) *Multiple intelligence approaches to assessment*. Tucson, AZ: Zephyr Press.

McBride, H. and Siegel, L. S. (1997) 'Learning disabilities and adolescent suicide', *Journal of Learning Disabilities*, 30(6): 652–659.

O'Malley, K. J., Francis, D. J., Foorman, B. R., Fletcher, J. M. and Swank, P. R. (2002) 'Growth in precursor and reading-related skills: Do low-achieving and IQ-discrepant readers develop differently?', *Learning Disabilities Research and Practice*, 17(1): 19–34.

Perlmutter, B. F. and Parus, M. V. (1983) 'Identifying children with learning disabilities: A comparison of diagnostic procedures across school district', *Learning Disability Quarterly*, 6(3): 321–328.

Siegel, L. S. (1985) 'Psycholinguistic aspects of reading disabilities', in L. S. Siegel and F. J. Morrison (eds), *Cognitive Development in Atypical Children*. New York: Springer-Verlag. pp. 45–66.

Siegel, L. S. (1988) 'Definitional and theoretical issues and research on learning disabilities', *Journal of Learning Disabilities*, 21(5): 264–270.

Siegel, L. S. (1989) 'IQ is irrelevant to the definition of learning disability', *Journal of Learning Disabilities*, 22(8): 469–486.

Siegel, L. S. (1990) 'IQ and learning disabilities: R. I. P.', in H. L. Swanson and B. Keogh (eds), *Learning Disabilities: Theoretical and Research Issues*. Hillsdale, NJ: Erlbaum. pp. 111–128.

Siegel, L. S. (1992) 'An evaluation of the discrepancy definition of dyslexia', *Journal of Learning Disabilities*, 25(10): 618–629.

Siege, L. S. (1993) 'The development of reading', in H. W Reese (ed.), *Advances in Child Development and Behavior*. San Diego, CA: Academic Press. pp. 63–97.

Siegel, L. S. (1999) 'Issues in the definition and diagnosis of learning disabilities: A perspective on Guckenberger v. Boston University', *Journal of Learning Disabilities*, 32(4): 304–319.

Siegel, L. S. and Feldman, W. (1983) 'Non-dyslexic children with combined writing and arithmetic difficulties', *Clinical Pediatrics*, 22(4): 241–244.

Siegel, L. S. and Linder, B. A. (1984) 'Short-term memory process in children with reading and arithmetic learning disabilities', *Developmental Psychology*, 20(2): 200–207.

Siegel, L. S. and Ryan, E. B. (1984) 'Reading disability as a language disorder', *Remedial and Special Education*, 5(3): 28–33.

Siegel. L. S. and Ryan, E. B. (1988) 'Development of grammatical-sensitivity, phonological, and short-term memory skills in normally achieving and learning disabled children', *Developmental Psychology*, 24(1): 28–37.

Stanovich, K. E. (1986) 'Matthew effects in reading: Some consequences of individual differences in the acquisition of literacy', *Reading Research Quarterly*, 21(4): 360–407.

Stanovich, K. E. (1993) 'The construct validity of discrepancy definitions of reading disability', in G. R. Lyon., D. B. Gray., J. F. Kavanagh and N. A. Krasemgor (eds), *Better Understanding Learning Disabilities*. Baltimore, Maryland: Paul Brookes Publisher.

Swanson, H. L. (1991) 'Operational definitions and learning disabilities: An overview', *Learning Disability Quarterly*, 14(4): 242–254.

Swanson, H. L. (1993) 'Individual differences in working memory: A model testing and subgroup analysis of learning-disabled and skilled readers', *Intelligence*, 17(3): 285–332.

Swanson, H. L. (1994) 'Short-term memory and working memory: Do both contribute to our understanding of academic achievement in children and adults with learning disabilities?', *Journal of Learning Disabilities*, 27(1): 34–50.

Torgesen, J. K. and Dice, C. (1980) 'Characteristics of research on learning disabilities', *Journal of Learning Disabilities*, 13(10): 531–535.

U. S. Department of Education (1985) *Seventh Annual Report to Congress on the Implementation of Public Law 94–142: The Educational for All Handicapped Children Act.* Washington, DC: U.S. Office of Special Education.

Vellutino, F. R., Scanlon, D.M. and Lyon, G.R. (2000). Differentiating between difficult-to-remediate and readily remediated poor readers: More evidence against the IQ-achievement discrepancy definition of reading disability. *Journal of Learning Disabilities*, 33(3): 223–238.

Vellutino, F. R. (1978) 'Toward an understanding of dyslexia: Psychological factors in specific reading disability', in A. L. Benton and D. Pearl (eds), *Dyslexia: An Appraisal of Current Knowledge.* New York: Oxford University Press. pp. 61–112.

Vellutino, F. R. (1979) *Dyslexia Theory and Research.* Cambridge, MA: MIT Press.

Woodcock, R. W. and Johnson, M. B. (1989) *Woodcock-Johnson – Revised Test of Achievement.* Itasca: IL; Riverside Publishing.

14

Students with Phonological Dyslexia in School-Based Programs: Insights from Tennessee Schools

Diane J. Sawyer and Stuart Bernstein

This chapter

i) reports on a retrospective study of 100 children who were assessed in the Tennessee Center for the Study and Treatment of Dyslexia;
ii) reports on the monitoring of school-based instructional intervention; and
iii) discusses the long-term effects of intervention on components of achievement specific to literacy attainment.

This chapter reports on a retrospective study of 100 children who were assessed in the Tennessee Center for the Study and Treatment of Dyslexia. It was determined that the profile of strengths and weaknesses each exhibited was consistent with the form of dyslexia that is characterized by a core deficit in phonological processing. Following assessment, students' progress in school-based instructional intervention was monitored twice each year for 2–3 years. The long-term effects of this intervention on components of achievement specific to literacy attainment are the focus of this chapter.

BACKGROUND

Collaboration among the state government, a private donor, and Middle Tennessee State University (MTSU) led to the establishment of the Chair of Excellence in

Dyslexic Studies in 1988. The syndrome of dyslexia was not well understood at that time. Students with dyslexia were not provided the kind of special education services needed to support school success. Katherine Davis Murfree believed that something could be done to change that. Funding for a Chair of Excellence was the vehicle she chose to address her goal.

This Chair of Excellence is intended to serve the following purposes:

1 inform the public about dyslexia;
2 engage in activities that will yield enhanced services to students with dyslexia throughout the state;
3 engage in research that will add to the knowledge base regarding dyslexia.

The first and current holder of this endowed chair was installed in the fall of 1989.

THE TENNESSEE CENTER FOR THE STUDY AND TREATMENT OF DYSLEXIA

In response to a proposal crafted by the Murfree Chair and submitted by MTSU, the Tennessee General Assembly voted, in May 1993, to provide financial support for establishment of the Tennessee Center for the Study and Treatment of Dyslexia. That support continues today. The Center operates as a unit attached to the College of Education and Behavioral Science. Oversight responsibility rests with the Murfree Chair of Excellence.

The Center is the service arm of the Murfree Chair. It provides an integrated model to address three specific goals.

* to offer assessment and recommendations for targeted interventions for students with dyslexia
* to offer consultation and inservice education to aid school personnel in identification and instruction of students with dyslexia
* to make resources available and to inform preservice teachers about the special needs of students with dyslexia.

For a detailed description of the establishment of this Center, see Sawyer and Knight (1997).

DEFINING DYSLEXIA

In 1993, there was no generally accepted definition of dyslexia. During the previous 25 years, research around the world had consistently identified the ability to analyze and manipulate component sounds in spoken words as critical for the acquisition of reading (Elkonin, 1973; Foorman and Francis, 1994;

Liberman, 1973; Lundberg et al., 1988; among others). Another large body of research had suggested that this inability may be the root dysfunction among individuals with dyslexia (see but not exclusively, Bradley and Bryant, 1983; Stanovich and West, 1989; Torgesen et al., 1994; Vellutino et al., 1994; Wagner and Torgesen, 1987). On the strength of this research, and in the absence of a generally accepted definition of dyslexia, the following definition was crafted to guide the work of the Center.

> Dyslexia is a language-based learning disorder that is biological in origin and primarily interferes with the acquisition of print literacy (reading, writing, and spelling). Dyslexia is characterized by poor decoding and spelling abilities as well as deficits in phonological awareness and/or phonological manipulation. These primary characteristics may co-occur with spoken language difficulties and deficits in short-term memory. Secondary characteristics may include poor reading comprehension (due to the decoding and memory difficulties) and poor written expression as well as difficulty organizing information for study and retrieval.
>
> (Operational definition of dyslexia prepared for the Tennessee Center for the Study and Treatment of Dyslexia, Sawyer, D.J., August 1993.)

IDENTIFYING STUDENTS WITH DYSLEXIA

With an operational definition in place, center staff tackled the practical issue of developing a diagnostic battery that would effectively differentiate dyslexia from other types of reading problems and other learning disabilities. The Simple View of Reading (Gough and Tunmer, 1986) was an appealing theoretical framework on which to build this battery. The simple view frames reading comprehension as the product of word recognition and linguistic comprehension. Linguistic comprehension is often indexed through a measure of listening comprehension. Word recognition and listening comprehension are reasonably independent of each other but were found to be highly correlated with reading comprehension (Hoover and Gough, 1990).

To develop a profile of phonological dyslexia that rested on the Simple View of Reading but could effectively distinguish a student with dyslexia from other types of reading problems, we drew on procedures for a differential diagnosis as outlined by Pennington (1991) and Aaron and Joshi (1992). With reading comprehension as the preferred outcome variable, Pennington (1991) had proposed the Specific Dyslexia Algorithm. To fit this algorithm, several conditions must be met: a standard score of 93 for at least one non-reading or writing measure is required; all scores for reading and spelling must be lower than the non-reading measure with at least one measure being 15 or more points lower; at least one reading or spelling score must represent a delay when compared to either age or academic potential. Pseudoword reading was considered as supportive evidence but is not included in the algorithm. Aaron and Joshi (1992) proposed that the diagnosis of dyslexia must also include a measure of listening comprehension as a measure of linguistic comprehension. They proposed that dyslexia may be assumed if the listening comprehension score is in the average range and is significantly higher than the reading comprehension score.

Table 14.1   Diagnostic profile of dyslexia

- Intelligence and Listening Comprehension ≥ 90
- Reading Comprehension < Listening Comprehension (R.C. typically 8 or more standard score points less)
- Word Recognition ≤ Reading Comprehension and 15 or more points < Listening Comprehension and I.Q.
- Spelling ≤ Word Recognition and 15 or more points < Listening Comprehension and I.Q.
- Word Attack ≤ Word Recognition
- Phonological Awareness and Phonological Sequencing are well below age level expectations
- Naming Speed *may* also be well below age level expectations

Elements of a differential diagnosis of dyslexia as proposed by Pennington (1991) and Aaron and Joshi (1992) did not specifically address the essential symptom of dyslexia—difficulty reading and spelling single words. Neither did they address the pattern of relative strengths and weaknesses in specific skill areas often identified when students with dyslexia were compared to normally progressing readers (Bruck, 1988; Goldsmith-Phillips, 1994; Connors and Olson, 1990; Manis et al., 1993; Rack et al., 1992; Spring and French, 1990; among others).

Among those studies that compared dyslexic readers to typical readers matched for age or reading achievement, a particular pattern of achievement among the several components of reading was revealed. This pattern served to distinguish dyslexics from normally developing readers: listening comprehension > reading comprehension ≥ word recognition > spelling ≥ word analysis ≥ phonological awareness. Center staff blended this characteristic pattern of skill strengths and weaknesses with the theoretical work of Pennington and Aaron and Joshi to arrive at the diagnostic profile of dyslexia that continues to guide Center assessments (please refer to Padget et al., 1996 for a detailed discussion of the development of the diagnostic profile). The profile is summarized in Table 14.1.

The skills within the profile are presented in a sequence that highlights the pattern of relative strengths and weaknesses observed among dyslexic readers. Tests used to evaluate each of these skills at the time the profile was established are presented in Table 14.2.

Norm-referenced and criterion-referenced measures were selected to support the differential diagnosis of phonological dyslexia. Norm-referenced measures permit comparisons of standard scores and grade equivalents. Criterion-referenced measures provide a more extensive sample of behavior to verify the pattern of strengths and weaknesses to guide intervention planning. As new tools and new editions of norm-referenced measures have become available, they have been added to the battery or have replaced previous measures.

A FRAMEWORK FOR TARGETING INTERVENTION

The differential diagnosis offered by the Tennessee Center serves two principal purposes: 1) evaluation of the pattern of skill strengths and weaknesses observed to determine if the profile of dyslexia may be inferred and 2) identify specific

Table 14.2   Tests for differential diagnosis of dyslexia

Component skill	Norm-referenced test	Criterion-referenced measure
Listening comprehension	Wechsler Individual Achievement Test (WIAT: Wechsler, 1992)	
Reading comprehension	WIAT	Oral reading fluency in graded passages (Spargo, 1989)
Word recognition	WIAT	ADEPT graded word lists (Sawyer, 1998)
Spelling	WIAT	ADEPT graded word lists, ADEPT developmental phase lists, Developmental Spelling Analysis (Ganske, 1994)
Word analysis	Word Attack Subtest, Woodcock Reading Mastery Test-Revised (Woodcock, 1987)	ADEPT developmental phase lists pseudoword reading, Phonic Pattern Subtest of the Decoding Skills Test (Richardson and DiBenedetto, 1985)
Phonological awareness	Comprehensive Test of Phonological Processing (CTOPP: Wagner et al., 1999)	Test of awareness of language segments (Sawyer, 1987) ADEPT segmenting and manipulating tasks Lindamood Auditory Conceptualization Test (Lindamood and Lindamood, 1979)

skill deficits on a continuum of development to provide schools with recommended entry points for targeted intervention.

Previous study (Sawyer, 1992) had suggested the potential utility of the hierarchical model of skill development, proposed by Uta Frith (1985; 1986), around which to organize assessment and intervention. Frith theorized that failure to become a skilled reader may be explained in terms of arrested development at some point along a continuum of hierarchical steps. Each step requires that the novice reader take on a new strategy which differs significantly from previous strategies applied. Each new strategy supports/facilitates greater speed and accuracy in decoding. To illustrate her theory, Frith proposed a three-phase model of reading acquisition—the logographic phase, the alphabetic phase, and the orthographic phase. In the logographic phase, beginning readers use a variety of environmental or context cues to recognize whole words (e.g., 'coke' based on script and color cues). In the alphabetic phase, children learn to apply the strategy of grapheme-phoneme correspondences to decode words. The orthographic phase involves the application of letter clusters and morphemic units to facilitate rapid word analysis and recognition.

Ehri (1987; 1994) elaborated on the basic phases proposed by Frith and advocated for the division of the alphabetic phase into an early phase and a later phase. She described the shift from the logographic to the alphabetic phase as initially involving the use of only the initial or final letter names or sounds in conjunction with surrounding context cues to recognize words (e.g., 'Coke' not 'Pepsi'; 'Burger King' not 'McDonalds'). It is during the mature alphabetic phase that readers learn to apply a sequential, left to right application of grapheme-phoneme correspondences to decode words. Both Frith and Ehri characterize the orthographic phase as involving a shift from attention to single letters for decoding to the analysis of larger units including rhymes, syllables, or morphemes, as well as an increasing familiarity with spelling patterns. Ehri (2000) explains the development of increasingly sophisticated grapheme-phoneme associations within the framework of connectionist theory and the process of *amalgamation or consolidation*. According to Ehri, seeing and pronouncing words strengthens the connections between sounds contained in words and the letters that code those sounds. Repeated exposure binds spelling to pronunciation and consolidates the association between the phonemic and graphemic units at various levels. It is reasonable to assume that it is this process of consolidation of skills at one phase of development that supports the transition to the next phase.

Drawing on the theoretical framework provided by Frith (1985; 1986) and the substantial elaborations of the type and nature of skill development within and between the phases as provided by Ehri (1987; 1994), Center staff created a checklist of hierarchically ordered skills. This Developmental Phase Checklist (detailed in Padget et al., 1996) serves to:

1 identify the specific outcomes of instruction that may be documented through aspects of the Center's assessment battery;
2 reveal the point of entry for future instruction;
3 identify those skills that will likely result in the greatest benefit in the shortest time.

MONITORING PROGRESS OF STUDENTS IN SCHOOL-BASED PROGRAMS

Assessments in the Center culminate with a projected plan for intervention including annual goals and intermediate benchmarks for achievement. Goals and benchmarks are tied to the mastery of skills in the Center's Developmental Phase Checklist. To offer recommendations for instructional interventions at this level of specificity, the development of criterion-referenced measures was necessary. To this end, a battery of tests—the Assessment of Encoding and Decoding Progress Test (ADEPT: Sawyer, 1998; 2001)—was developed.

Construction and utilization of ADEPT

This assessment tool was developed, within the phase model of skill development, to document initial skill levels (at the time of Center assessment) and to monitor progress in skill areas necessary for decoding and spelling. The tasks include measures of phonemic awareness, word feature lists, grade level lists, and passages to assess oral reading fluency. Phonemic awareness tasks and the word feature lists (words selected to match the orthographic features associated with all but the logographic phase) require analysis of both real and pseudowords.

The specific features assessed within each phase were identified following a detailed analysis of several published programs that were designed to instruct very poor readers through the presentation of carefully sequenced code elements. These programs include the *Wilson Language Program* (Wilson Language System, 1988), *Language!* (Greene, 1995; 2000); The A. D. D. program (Lindamood and Lindamood, 1975), and Process Phonics (Pollack and Minner, 1995). Those elements which appeared initially, across these programs, are assessed within the alphabetic features tasks. More complex elements identified across these programs were hierarchically ordered for assessment across five levels of orthographic features (see Table 14.3 for an illustration of tasks across all feature lists).

Six parallel forms were created for each subtest and level of development in ADEPT to allow for repeated testing. The *Baseline Assessment* is used to determine students' initial skill levels. Results of this assessment form the basis for the specific recommendations included in the intervention plan that is forwarded to the child's school. Five additional forms of the battery permit repeated measures of growth in the same, as well as more advanced, skill areas over a period of 2–3 years. ADEPT measures are independent of the specific instructional resources used in school or tutorial settings.

Components of ADEPT
ADEPT tasks align with the divisions of the Developmental Phase Checklist. The student is asked to demonstrate mastery of phoneme-level skills and to demonstrate the ability to read and spell hierarchically ordered lists of real and pseudowords. Pseudowords were formed by changing one letter of a word in the companion list of real words. Spelling lists are identical to the reading lists. Students read the word lists first and then go on to spell the same words as pronounced by the examiner. In addition, grade level lists are included for reading and spelling and grade level passages are included to assess oral reading fluency.

Phonemic awareness tasks
These address the skills linked to the logographic and alphabetic phases of development. These include phoneme segmenting and manipulation applied to both words and pseudowords.

Phase level feature lists
Examples of tasks and items for each phase feature list appear in Table 14.3.

Two studies examined the validity of the sequence of features included in the alphabetic lists (Young, 1997) and across the five orthographic phases lists (Jones, 2001). A sequential progression toward mastery over decoding the elements within and across the lists was observed among normally progressing students in grades 1 through 8.

Grade level lists
Words for these lists were randomly selected from word lists for reading, compiled by Harris and Jacobson (1982), and word lists for spelling, compiled by Henderson and Templeton (1994).

Table 14.3 Levels in ADEPT Phase Lists

Developmental phase	Features	Examples
1 Alphabetic	short vowel CVC	*fit, chin, crust* *rit, chom, drant*
2 Relational orthographic I	2 syllable, ing, ed, long vowels	*rabbit, hitting, walked, kite* *sabbit, motting, falked, lipe*
3 Relational orthographic II	er, ful, ly, un, re, dis, soft c, soft g, soft ch, open/closed	*smaller, careful, badly, cell* *cranner, smatful, huply, cipe*
4 Hierarchical orthographic I	ai, oa, ea, -able, -ible, -ary, mis, pre, ex, inter, in	*stain, customary, explain,* *traig, huckomary, extrobe*
5 Hierarchical orthographic II	er, ar, oy, or, ind, eigh/eigh, -ture	*fern, dark, oyster, pastor, grind, reign* *serm, flarm, hoypest, flaptor, pind, fleigh*
6 Hierarchical orthographic III	cious, au, ue, trans, non, age, tion, ance, sion, aw, ew, ou (as ow), oo	*gracious, fault, flue, fransform, nonsense* *slacious, zault, plue, translot, nonselp*

Oral reading passages

Passages for grades pre primer—grade 3—were drawn from those provided on the University of Oregon website and are in the public domain. Passages for grades 4–12 were selected from grade level books in the *Timed Readings* series (Spargo, 1989). The Fry readability formula (1977) was applied to each passage selected for use with ADEPT assessments to provide additional documentation of the grade level of difficulty assigned by the publisher.

Accuracy of assignment to phases

To assess the validity and reliability of staff assignments of students to different developmental phases, based solely on test performance, a study utilizing discriminant analysis was designed (Sawyer and Kim, 2000). Results indicated 81 per cent agreement with the original classifications and this was highly significant ($p = .0001$). The clustering of scores for 95 of 117 students in this study—74 Center cases (44 at the alphabetic level – AP; 30 at the orthographic level – OP) and 43 average readers from an area school—agreed with the designations assigned by Center staff. The scores for only 2 AP students clustered with those classified as OP; scores for 4 OP students clustered with those classified as AP. Scores for 3 students in each group failed to cluster with any of the three classifications

STUDENTS' PROGRESS IN SCHOOL-BASED PROGRAMS

Although parents and school personnel are provided detailed statements of goals and benchmarks to target future skill development, the responsibility for providing that intervention, and for selecting the specific approach to intervention, rests with the schools. The study herein reported was undertaken to 1) document the effect of school-based instruction among a large sample of students with phonological dyslexia; 2) to assess the long-term effects of improvement in phonemic awareness on the acquisition of skills at subsequent levels of the developmental phases, on decoding, word reading, reading comprehension, and oral reading fluency.

The sample

One hundred case files were drawn from Center archives. All had met center criteria for dyslexia with the core phonological deficit. None had documented or suspected histories of language impairments, hearing or vision impairments, or untreated attention deficits. All attended an initial assessment visit followed by semi-annual monitoring visits. The sample included 68 males and 32 females ranging in age from 6–5 to 15–9. They were in grades 1 through 10 when initially assessed. These students were being educated in 36 different school systems (28 per cent of all systems) across Tennessee. Participant characteristics are summarized in Table 14.4.

Assessing progress over time

Norm-referenced measures of progress

Children's progress as measured by norm referenced tests, specifically the word reading, spelling, and comprehension subtests of the Wechsler Individual Achievement Test (WIAT: Wechsler, 1992) is presented in Table 14.5. These tests were administered during the initial and final visits only.

In word reading, children's grade equivalent scores showed a significant gain of 1.9 grades over 2.7 years (0.7 grades of progress per year) but progress toward closing the gap between themselves and peers of the same grade was not evident. Standard scores did not differ between initial and final testing. In spelling, children's grade equivalent scores showed a significant gain of 1.3 grades over 2.7 years (0.5 grades of progress per year). However, standardized scores show that children lost significant ground relative to their peers. Only in the area of reading comprehension did these children show significant gains relative to their same age peers—about 6 standard score points—and a significant improvement of 2.5 grade levels over 2.7 years (0.9 grades of progress per year).

Table 14.4   Participant characteristics

	Early ID (K-3)	Late ID (4-10)	Overall
N	44	56	100
Age	8.6 (0.8)	11.1 (1.4)	10.0 (1.7)
Grade	2.5 (0.7)	5.1 (1.3)	3.9 (1.7)
Gender	M = 29, F =15	M = 39, F = 17	M = 68, F = 32
WISC-III verbal	102.1 (12.4)	101.5 (11.9)	101.7 (12.1)
WISC-III performance	103.8 (13.0)	102.4 (13.9)	103.0 (13.4)
WISC-III full scale	102.8 (11.9)	102.3 (11.5)	102.5 (11.6)
WIAT listening comp SS	106.0 (12.7)	100.1 (9.1)	102.7 (11.2)
WIAT listening comp grade	3.9 (1.9)	5.8 (2.7)	5.0 (2.6)

Table 14.5   Standardized achievement test scores Pre/Post

	Initial	Final	t (p)
Word reading			
Standard	81.0 (8.9)	81.9 (11.6)	1.118 (.267)
Grade equiv.	2.3 (1.6)	4.2 (1.8)	*** 15.519 (.001)
Pseudoword reading			
Standard	74.3 (14.0)	—	
Grade equiv.	2.0 (2.0)	—	
Spelling			
Standard	79.9 (9.0)	76.9 (10.8)	*** −3.852 (.001)
Grade equiv.	2.4 (1.1)	3.7 (1.5)	*** 4.621 (.001)
Reading comprehension			
Standard	84.8 (12.8)	90.7 (15.4)	*** 4.621 (.001)
Grade equiv.	3.2 (2.5)	5.7 (3.2)	*** 10.315 (.001)

* $p < .05$, ** $p < .01$, *** $p < .001$

Criterion-referenced measures of progress

Progress in *phonemic awareness* (PA), as reflected on the tasks in the ADEPT battery, is presented in Table 14.6. Table 14.6 summarizes children's initial and final scores on the various tasks, the number of children who achieved mastery on each task (scores of 9 or 10 correct twice in a row), and how long it took, on average, to achieve mastery on these tasks.

When children began the study, the average participant was able to segment and manipulate the phonemes in monosyllabic words with open and closed syllables (e.g., *bet, at, cot, me*) and monosyllabic pseudowords (e.g., *rem, op, pob, bo*), but experienced difficulty with consonant blends in words (e.g., *bend, slid, grand*) and pseudowords (e.g., *flin, pront, stend*). Children made significant progress in all six tasks over the course of monitoring. However, one-fourth of children never achieved mastery in the most difficult tasks; their final scores in segmenting pseudowords ($M = 6.8$, $SD = 1.2$) and manipulating phonemes in pseudowords using with blocks ($M = 7.0$, $SD = 0.9$) were less than 90 per cent. A multivariate analysis of variance was conducted to evaluate any differences associated with age of diagnosis. No differences due to age were identified. The early (grades 1–3) and late (grades 4–10) diagnosis groups made equivalent progress in the six tests of phonemic awareness, $F(6, 87) = 1.150$, $p = .341$.

Table 14.6   Phonemic awareness: Initial scores and progress in ADEPT

	Mean (SD) 10 max		Mastery information	
	Initial	Final	# Child mastered	Years to mastery
Segmenting words	6.5 (1.7)	9.5 (1.1)	81	1.5 (1.1)
Manipulating word letters	8.6 (1.4)	9.9 (0.6)	95	0.7 (1.1)
Manipulating word blocks	7.1 (2.2)	9.4 (1.5)	82	1.2 (1.0)
Segmenting Pwords	5.9 (2.1)	9.2 (1.4)	73	1.7 (1.0)
Manipulating Pword letters	7.8 (2.0)	9.7 (0.8)	89	0.9 (1.1)
Manipulating Pword blocks	6.6 (2.4)	9.0 (1.8)	74	1.4 (1.1)

Children's ability to *read and spell words sampled from grade level appropriate materials* was assessed and monitored with sets of 20 item lists. The grade levels for the reading lists ranged from preprimer to grade 12. Spelling lists were similar but did not include a preprimer level. The frequencies for initial and final mastery are presented in Figure 14.1.

When children were first tested, many were at readiness level and could not complete any list of words, most had not achieved mastery (accuracy of 90 per cent or better) in reading lists of pre-primer words (e.g., *all, by, box, eat, put, stop*) or spelling any lists of words. At final testing, children's average level of mastery in word reading approached the third grade level (e.g., *cottage, floppy, scissors, pitcher, million, recognize*) and their average level of mastery in spelling was at the second grade level (e.g., *king, same, moon, teeth, people, telling*).

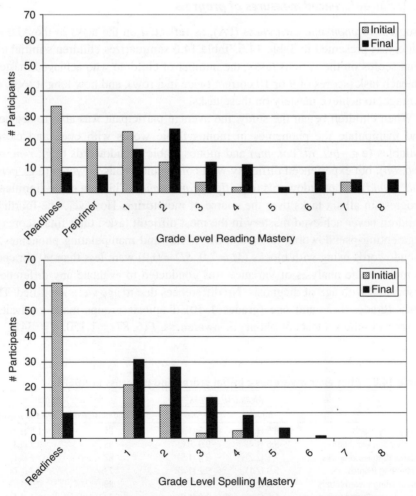

Figure 14.1　Grade level reading and spelling progress in ADEPT

Children's initial and final mastery in *reading and spelling items from the developmental phase lists* is presented in Figure 14.2. When children were first tested, they had not yet mastered reading or spelling lists of items that represent the alphabetic phase of development: words with closed syllables, short vowels, consonant digraphs, and consonant blends (e.g., *fit, tan, mud, chin, camp, crust*) and matched lists of pseudowords (e.g., *rit, vad, lut, chom, gomp, drant*). At final testing, most children had mastered lists from the alphabetic phase and some had also mastered lists from the first orthographic phase. These lists include words with two closed syllables (e.g., *rabbit, nutmeg*), regular plurals (e.g., *foxes, places*), regular past tense (e.g., *called, walked*), long vowels spelled with final *e*, (e.g., *kite, note*), and participles (e.g., *kating, running*). Very few children mastered lists at the second orthographic phase and beyond. Lists at the first level of orthographic features include words with open and closed syllables (e.g., *tiger, secret*), a mix of prefixes and suffixes (e.g., *smaller, careful, return, disarm*), soft *c* (e.g., *cell, city*), and adverbs (e.g., *finally, badly*).

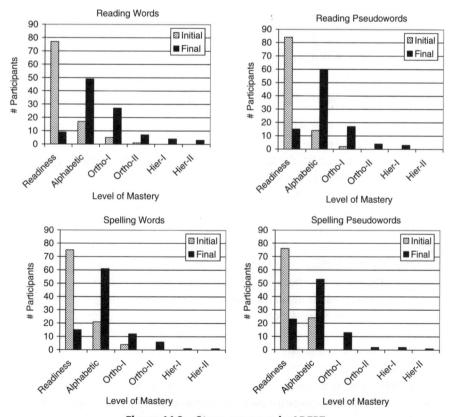

Figure 14.2 Stage progress in ADEPT

ACCOUNTING FOR DIFFERENCES IN OUTCOMES

Children's achievements in decoding, word recognition, spelling, oral reading fluency, and reading comprehension varied greatly at both initial and final testing. The next set of analyses addressed relationships among these four outcomes along with age, language ability, and phonemic awareness to shed light on the possible sources of differences in achievement. The analyses began with selection of measures. The next step was to transform scores in decoding, word recognition, and spelling from discrete levels of mastery into continuous variables reflecting the total number of items correct. Calculation of Pearson correlations and a series of regression analyses followed.

Selected measurement for language abilities

Language abilities were inferred from verbal IQ scores attained on the WISC-III (Weschler, 1991). The verbal IQ score is derived from performance on several subtests—information, similarities, arithmetic, vocabulary, and comprehension. These scores were chosen in the current study in place of listening comprehension because verbal IQ scores were normally distributed and equivalent in both the early and late identification groups. In contrast, listening comprehension scores on the WIAT were positively skewed and the average standard score was significantly higher for the early ID than for the late ID children, $t(98) = 2.732$, $p < .01$. The same was true for grade level scores, $t(97) = 3.820$, $p < .001$.

Selected measurement of phonemic awareness

Phonemic awareness in ADEPT is measured with three tasks: segmentation, phoneme manipulation with blocks, and phoneme manipulation with letters. Scores for each subtest are the number correct out of 10. Participants' phonemic awareness scores selected for the inferential analyses that follow is an average of the scores obtained in all three subtests for pseudowords only. The pseudoword scores were used in order to provide measurements of phonemic awareness that are free of word knowledge.

Phonemic awareness scores at the final assessment showed a ceiling effect in that 75 per cent of children had mastered the tasks and showed no variation. Consequently, for the purpose of the inferential analyses, phonemic awareness scores were sampled from all of children's semi-annual progress monitoring visits and outcomes were scored as the time in years to mastery (accuracy of 90 per cent or better, twice in a row). Participants not reaching mastery were assigned the maximum possible value for years to mastery, 2.7 years, which was the average time interval between their initial tests and final monitoring visits. Although this decision places an artificial limit on the scores of the participants who did not master phonemic awareness, the limit does not appear to yield a significant consequence. An analysis conducted to assess the possible impact of this limitation indicated that eliminating these participants does not change the outcomes of the regressions presented in Tables 14.8 and 14.9.

Selected decoding measures

Initial and final decoding skill levels were measured using the pseudoword lists that are part of the developmental phase lists in ADEPT. Scores reflect the total number of items correctly pronounced. There are 25 items on each of the developmental phase lists—alphabetic; orthographic I-V. If participants were advanced enough to start with a more advanced list (e.g., orthographic I), their scores were calculated to include a perfect 25 for each list before their beginning level.

Selected word reading and spelling measures

Initial and final word reading and spelling were measured using the grade level lists that are part of ADEPT. Scores reflect the total number of items correctly pronounced. There are 20 items on each of the grade level lists. As with decoding, if participants were advanced enough to start with a later grade level list, their scores include a perfect 20 for each list before their beginning level. Because spelling does not have a preprimer list, a constant of 20 was added to scores to make the final values comparable to the grade level reading scores.

Oral reading fluency

Passage reading fluency scores reflect the total number of words read correctly in one minute from a grade level appropriate passage taken from sources noted earlier (p. 319). Participants read for three minutes. The examiner marks the last word read at the end of each minute. The two segments containing the fewest and the most words read correctly are eliminated. The number of words read correctly during the remaining one-minute segment is the score that is recorded. The grade level of the initial passage given to a child was determined by their grade level equivalent score on the word reading subtest of the WIAT. If performance on the first passage provided is at the level of instructional competence, they are tested with a passage from the next higher grade level during the same session. The grade level for passages provided in subsequent monitoring sessions and the final visit was based upon the highest grade level passage for which the instructional level of competence was achieved during the previous visit.

Selected comprehension measure

Reading comprehension scores for each child are the grade level equivalent scores from the reading comprehension subtest on the WIAT (Wechsler, 1991). These scores were chosen because they relate performance to that of students at specific grade levels within the norming sample and permit approximately equivalent comparisons to performance on grade leveled word lists.

DESCRIPTIVE ANALYSES

Means and correlations

Means and correlations among the measures at initial and final testing appear in Table 14.7. These correlations reflect relationships among the measurements at initial and final testing.

Table 14.7 shows that the variables in the diagnostic profile share significant variance. For instance, variations in initial word reading are found to be significantly related to decoding, phonemic awareness, and verbal IQ. Given the strength of these associations, the correlations also indicate that no one score may be viewed as a pure measurement of that ability. Thus, performance in one ability cannot be viewed as the principal source of variance accounted for in

Table 14.7 Correlations among measurements at initial and final testing

Initial testing	Age	Grade	Verbal	PA[1]	Decode[2]	Word[3]	Spell[4]	Fluency[5]	Comp[6]
Age (years)		***.933	.015	.089	*.229	**.549	**.469	**.483	**.655
Grade			.063	.134	*.221	**.564	**.504	**.497	**.667
Verbal IQ (std)				.148	*.249	**.317	**.263	**.305	**.375
Phonemic awareness					**.555	**.414	**.299	**.285	**.298
Decoding						**.580	**.474	**.411	**.521
Word reading							**.769	**.772	**.805
Spelling								**.684	**.642
Fluency (wcpm)									**.703
Mean	10.0	3.9	101.7	7.7	13.9	45.4	41.4	63.7	3.1
Stdev	1.7	1.7	12.1	1.6	11.0	37.9	22.3	34.8	2.5
Final testing	Age	Grade	Verbal	PA-YM[7]	Decode[2]	Word[3]	Spell[4]	Fluency[5]	Comp[6]
Age (years)		**.936	.006	.035	*.218	**.347	**.377	**.313	**.379
Grade			.046	.046	*.256	**.310	**.367	**.326	**.386
Verbal IQ (std – initial)				-.155	**.424	**.429	**.371	**.394	**.499
Phonemic awareness YTM					**-.329	**-.310	**-.268	-.090	**-.309
Decoding						*.532	**.491	**.395	**.562
Word reading							**.766	**.668	**.761
Spelling								**.611	**.669
Fluency (wcpm)									**.571
Mean	12.7	6.4	101.7	1.2 ytm	41.4	82.2	71.5	83.6	5.7
Stdev	1.7	1.7	12.1	0.8	20.8	48.9	25.9	29.5	3.2

$*p < .05, **p < .01, ***p < .001$
1 Total number of pseudowords pronounced correctly on the ADEPT stage lists
2 Total number of words pronounced correctly on the ADEPT grade lists
3 Total number of words spelled correctly on the ADEPT grade lists
4 Total number of words spelled correctly on the ADEPT grade lists
5 Max correct words per minute reading grade level text
6 WIAT reading comprehension grade level score
7 Average time to mastery, 90% correct or better, for the 3 pseudoword tasks in ADEPT

another ability. To tease out the relative contributions of predictor to outcome variables, regression analyses were conducted to assess the unique variance in outcomes associated with each independent variable. Regressions were conducted separately for initial and final testing.

WHAT ARE THE GREATEST CONTRIBUTORS TO PROGRESS AMONG THESE STUDENTS?

Initial testing

The first set of five regressions, reported in Table 14.8, examine the relationships among variables at initial testing. The analyses are designed to measure the extent to which variation in word level skills, including decoding or word reading, is related to variation in more complex skills, including fluency and comprehension.

The series of regression analyses began with the assessment of the unique contributions of differences in age, verbal IQ, and phonemic awareness to measures of initial decoding. Decoding was then entered into the equation to become an additional factor in the regression for word reading accuracy as the dependent variable. Word reading accuracy was next added to the equation as an additional factor in the regression to address fluency. Finally, fluency became an additional factor in the regression analysis for reading comprehension. All factors were entered simultaneously. Standardized regression coefficients, beta weights, appear in Table 14.8 along with the total r^2 at the bottom of each column.

The beta weights in Table 14.8 show that age and language ability (verbal IQ) bear significant relationships to the outcome measurements. Differences in age at initial testing accounted for significant variance in all outcomes except fluency. Differences in oral language, represented by verbal IQ, were also significantly related to variation in all outcomes except fluency.

The beta weights in Table 14.8 show a progression that one would expect in reading: Variation in phonemic awareness accounts for the largest amount of variance in decoding. Variation in decoding, in turn, accounts for the largest amount of variance in word reading and spelling. Variation in word reading then accounts for the largest amount of variance in fluency and comprehension.

The beta weights in Table 14.8 also show that, when initially tested, children with dyslexia fail to show some associations one would normally expect in reading. Variations in phonemic awareness did not account for significant variance in word reading or spelling. Variations in decoding did not account for significant variance in comprehension or fluency.

A commonality analysis (Amado, 1999) was conducted to explore the relatively weak relationship between phonemic awareness and word reading at initial diagnosis. This analysis is conducted with r^2, which is the unique variance associated with each factor, rather than with beta weights, which are standardized regression coefficients. The unique variance associated with phonemic awareness

Table 14.8   Unique contributions (standardized β weights and *r²*) of diagnostic scores to initial and final outcomes

	Decoding	Word reading	Spelling	Fluency	Comp
Initial testing	*n* = 100	*n* = 100	*n* = 100	*n* = 100	*n* = 98
Age	*.181	***.454	***.391	.097	***.326
Verbal IQ	*.178	**.205	*.172	.087	*.152
Phonemic awareness[4]	***.515	*.160	.075	−.008	−.029
Decoding[5]	—	***.336	**.300	−.048	.123
Word reading[6]	—	—	—	***.722	***.414
Fluency[7]	—	—	—	—	.129
total r²	***.371	***.575	***.394	***.610	***.749
Final testing (gains over initial)	*n* = 99	*n* = 99	*n* = 98	*n* = 98	*n* = 93
Initial score	.095	***.589	***.498	***.538	***.349
Age at final testing	*.202	−.030	.094	−.052	−.016
Verbal IQ (initial testing)	**.338	.141	.110	.093	.136
Phon. awareness YTM[8]	**−.252	−.049	−.099	.101	−.061
Decoding at final testing[1]	—	**.218	***.250	.059	.161
Word reading[2]	—	—	—	**.286	***.405
Fluency[3]	—	—	—	—	−.014
r² over initial score	***.201	***.086	***.121	**.074	***.226
total r²	***.301	***.605	***.553	***.620	***.715

* *p* < .05, ** *p* < .01, *** *p* < .001

1 Total number of pseudowords pronounced correctly on the ADEPT stage lists
2 Total number of words pronounced correctly on the ADEPT grade lists
3 Total number of words spelled correctly on the ADEPT grade lists
4 Average score out of 10 for the 3 pseudoword tasks in ADEPT
5 Total number of pseudowords pronounced correctly on the ADEPT stage lists
6 Total number of words pronounced correctly on the ADEPT grade lists
7 Max correct words per minute reading grade level text
8 Average time to mastery, 90% correct or better, for the 3 pseudoword tasks in ADEPT

is 1.8 per cent of the variation in word reading achievement. However, the shared variance between phonemic awareness and other factors is 15.3 per cent. Together, the analysis shows that phonemic awareness accounts for 17.1 per cent of the variance in word reading achievement, but most of this variance (12 per cent) is shared with decoding.

FINAL OUTCOME

The five regressions in the lower half of Table 14.8 explore the relationships among the components of the diagnostic profile for dyslexia and growth in outcomes observed by the time of final testing. Growth was modeled by conducting step-wise regressions in which initial scores were entered first as autoregressors and the remaining model components were entered in a second step. The numbers listed next to each factor are standardized beta weights. The next to last line contains the variance accounted for by the regression components after initial score is factored out. The last line contains the total amount of variance accounted for by the regression analyses, including variance attributed to competence at initial assessment.

- *Phonemic awareness.* This measurement reflects years to mastery—90 per cent or better over two consecutive monitoring sessions on the ADEPT pseudoword tasks. It appears that those who mastered the phonemic awareness tasks on ADEPT over shorter time periods made significantly larger gains in decoding.
- *Decoding.* Participants with higher initial decoding scores made greater gains in word reading and spelling; faster mastery of phonemic awareness did not contribute substantially to gains in these skills.
- *Word reading.* Gains in word reading, which themselves were partially attributable to gains in decoding, were the only factor accounting for significant gains in fluency and comprehension.

Final outcomes by initial grade

To study the possible effects of age and prior educational experience at the time of diagnosis, final outcome regressions were repeated separately for children in an early identification group, those receiving assessment for dyslexia during grades 1 through 3, and children in a late identification group, those assessed for dyslexia in grades 4 and beyond. These results are presented in Table 14.9.

Table 14.9   Unique contributions (standardized β weights and r^2) of scores at diagnosis to final outcomes by initial grade

	Decoding	Word reading	Spelling	Fluency	Comp
Initial grade 1–3	n = 44	n = 44	n = 44	n = 43	n = 41
Initial score	**.377	***.483	**.406	.174	.084
Age at final testing	−.125	.175	.112	−.039	−.031
Verbal IQ (initial testing)	.207	.078	−.117	.166	*.227
Phon. awareness YTM	−.243	.014	−.139	.172	−.191
Decoding at final testing	—	***.404	**.438	−.088	**.377
Word reading	—	—	—	*.489	.197
Fluency	—	—	—	—	.169
r^2 over initial score	.135	**.164	**.232	.172	***.488
total r^2	**.341	***.630	***.446	***.380	***.718
Initial grade 4 +	n = 55	n = 55	n = 55	n = 55	n = 52
Initial score	−.127	***.533	***.531	***.693	***.451
Age at final testing	*.258	.095	.158	.049	−.125
Verbal IQ (initial testing)	***.459	*.236	***.287	.137	.043
Phon. awareness YTM	*−.316	−.086	−.038	.032	.023
Decoding at final testing	—	.108	.117	.070	.125
Word reading	—	—	—	.097	***.561
Fluency	—	—	—	—	−.114
r^2 over initial score	*.071	*.081	**.142	.043	***.211
total r^2	***.367	***.655	***.665	***.771	***.737

* $p < .05$, ** $p < .01$, *** $p < .001$

Early identification group

For children who were initially diagnosed in grades 1 through 3, variations in word reading and spelling at final diagnosis were strongly related to differences in decoding. As with the overall analysis of final outcome data, children demonstrating mastery over phonemic awareness in shorter time periods did achieve greater gains in decoding (the effect approached significance, $p = .082$) but they did not achieve more than their peers in word reading and spelling. Unlike the overall analysis of final outcome data, differences in decoding ability among the early ID children accounted for significant variation in comprehension.

Late identification group

These children made equally large gains in decoding ($M = 30$, $SD = 24$ items more than initial testing) compared to the early ID group ($M = 24$, $SD = 15$ items more than initial testing), $t(98) = 1.434$, $p = .155$, but variation in decoding ability did not contribute meaningfully to gains in any of the outcome variables of interest. Instead, variations in word reading and spelling were significantly influenced by verbal IQ at initial assessment. Among students in this late ID group, variation in fluency was unrelated to any factor other than initial score. Finally, word reading ability was the only factor, other than initial score, that contributed significantly to variation in comprehension among children in this group.

Implications

The effects of two or more years of school-based interventions among 100 students with phonological dyslexia appear mixed. Although norm-referenced measures (Table 14.5) indicate that all children made significant grade level gains in word reading, spelling, and reading comprehension, standard scores reveal a different pattern. When compared to peers of the same age, the gap in achievement is essentially unchanged for word reading and actually increased for spelling. Only reading comprehension shows a substantial gain of about 6 standard score points, on average.

The practical significance of observed gains in grade level performance on norm-referenced measurements must be considered. These students were generally reading more words and comprehending more difficult passages but the potential for genuine success in the curriculum of the grades in which they were enrolled was only marginally improved. That is, these students had not closed the achievement gap with their peers but neither had they fallen further behind. They did benefit from the interventions they had been provided, whatever that might have been. However, the extent of benefit must be viewed as marginal.

Teachers, students, and parents expect that focused intervention will, over time, enable students to gain increased independence in their involvement with the grade level curriculum. To examine students' growth in mastery over reading words that sample grade level curriculum, we examined their status on ADEPT graded word lists following three years of school-based intervention. As can be seen in Figure 14.1, nearly three years following initial assessment only about half of the students were successful in reading words from grade level lists at third grade and beyond; only about 10 per cent were able to demonstrate mastery on lists sampling words at the fifth grade to eighth grade levels. Progress in spelling was even more restricted. About 70 per cent were still unable to spell words at grade 3 and beyond; about 10 per cent were still at readiness level— unable to spell high-frequency beginning level words (*at, can, to, the*).

When performance on measures of decoding, designed to assess attainment of hierarchically ordered orthographic features (ADEPT word lists), is considered (Figure 14.2) it is clear that most had not yet mastered reading and spelling words at the first orthographic level—sampling words containing the final *e* pattern, common inflectional ends (*s, es, ed, ing*) or two-syllable short vowel words (cvccvc). These features are typically mastered by the end of grade 1 (Young, 1997). We must conclude that school-based instruction for these 100 students did not adequately support the acquisition of a basic scaffold of decoding knowledge on which to build higher order decoding and word reading competencies. Some evidence for this may be inferred from the pattern of contributions to variance accounted for in word reading and comprehension reported in Table 14.9. Among students in the younger group, decoding competence at final testing contributed significantly to word reading, spelling, and reading comprehension. Among students in the older group, however, decoding competence at final testing made no substantial contribution to these dependent variables. Only word reading competence at final testing contributed significantly ($p < .001$) to reading comprehension over and above initial comprehension scores. Until a basic scaffold of decoding knowledge is so well mastered that responses to these elements are automatic, the reader is left with only two strategies for word reading— slowly sounding out each letter or learning and remembering words as whole units. Dependence on these strategies will seriously limit fluency and children who are not fluent readers, of even words that follow highly decodable patterns, are not likely to engage in reading.

At the time of initial assessment, phonological awareness (PA) was identified as the core deficit among the students in this study. Recommendations for intervention focused on this area as the entry point for intervention and the necessity for mastery of skills at all levels—segmenting, manipulating, and blending— was stressed in the intervention plans provided. At final monitoring, all children demonstrated improvement in their ability to segment and manipulate phonemes in pseudowords, even in the most stringent measure of these skills (Table 14.6). Most had mastered these tasks in one to two years, many in less than one year.

We had assumed that among students with a core deficit in phonological skills, growth in decoding, word reading, and spelling would be enhanced as a result of increased abilities to segment and manipulate phonemes. This retrospective study of students receiving school-based interventions does support the assumption that PA skills, assessed through application to pseudowords, contribute significantly to growth in decoding ability. However, there was little direct impact on any of the other outcome measures of interest (Table 14.8) despite the fact that correlations for PA with all outcome measures of interest indicate strong associations across the board. Analyses of commonality suggest that PA does make the greatest contribution to decoding and that this influence extends through decoding to the other dependent measures of literacy competence we studied. It may be reasonable to consider this observed pattern to be an illustration of the process of consolidation as described by Ehri (2000).

The assumption that more rapid mastery of PA skills would offer an advantage to those with the core deficit was also examined. When considering the group as a whole, it appeared that those who had mastered PA skills earlier also demonstrated greater gains in decoding overall (Table 14.8). However, when we consider decoding gains among younger (grades 1–3) compared to older (grades 4–10) students at initial assessment (Table 14.9), the significance of time to mastery over PA appears to be relevant only among those in the older group.

Several possible explanations for this finding may be considered. It is possible that PA skills were routinely included in the instruction for students in grades 1–3 yielding a more compressed period for mastery. A trend toward a significant advantage for those who mastered PA skills earlier was noted ($p = .08$). Conversely, it is not likely that PA skills are routinely addressed in the curriculum for grades 4–12. Those older students, for whom tutorials incorporated PA skills, might have mastered the skills earlier and most effectively linked them to decoding. Other explanations are also possible. It may be that the proportion of students with severe deficits in phonological processing was greater among the older students. This would serve to both extend the group time to mastery and limit gains in decoding overall. Such a disproportionate representation in the older group would yield an apparent benefit for those able to master PA in relatively less time. A combination of severity of deficit and access to intervention for PA skills is also possible. Although patterns observed in this retrospective study do substantiate the supportive role of PA in the acquisition and development of literacy skills among students with the core deficit, they cannot offer assurance of a relative advantage for those who master these skills sooner rather than later.

Spelling achievement in light of growth in PA skills was also of interest to the authors. Abilities associated with phoneme segmenting, blending, and manipulation logically support the process of spelling words. Although years to mastery (YTM) of PA was highly correlated with WIAT spelling scores at final monitoring, regression analyses did not identify its unique contribution to variance in spelling achievement for the whole group or for either of the age-related sub-groups. Beyond the level of initial competence in spelling, decoding competence at final monitoring made the only significant contribution to the variance in spelling achievement at the same time point (Table 14.8). However, when divided into groups by grade at initial assessment, an interesting pattern emerged (Table 14.9). The significance of decoding competence at final monitoring held for the younger group but not for the older group. When this finding is considered in combination with the contribution of PA to decoding, it seems to suggest a supportive relationship flowing from PA to decoding to spelling at least among students in the younger group.

Among the group of older students at initial assessment, only verbal IQ contributed significantly more than initial spelling competence to the variance accounted for in spelling achievement at final monitoring. Decoding made no appreciable contribution to any of the outcome variables of interest—word reading, spelling, oral reading fluency, and reading comprehension. This observed pattern of contributions, or lack thereof, to components of literacy competence among students in the older group lends support to the speculation that students in this group may have relied heavily on a whole-word approach to reading and spelling. As noted earlier, only competence in word reading at final monitoring added significantly to variance accounted for in reading comprehension over and above the contribution of initial competence. This pattern seems to suggest that older students who are struggling to survive in the school setting seek expediency over efficiency—use their native abilities and life experiences to acquire a store of word units to support reading and spelling words and comprehending text. Students in both age/grade groups came to learning with essentially the same levels of intellectual abilities. Differences in the application of these abilities to acquiring literacy skills are suggested. These differences may be the consequence of both the instructional interventions provided and the demands for performance in the school setting.

CONCLUSIONS

Results of this retrospective study of 100 students exhibiting the characteristics of the phonological core deficit type of dyslexia suggests the need to redirect school-based interventions from a focus on raw indicators of grade level achievement to that which develops the skills necessary to reduce if not close the achievement gap that separates them from their non-affected peers. The accomplishment of this goal will require a reassessment and restructuring of teacher preparation as well as in-school practices.

Currently, schools depend on the 'pull-out' approach to intervention—offering a few minutes of direct instruction several times a week in settings outside the regular classroom. Increasingly, published materials are available to guide the sequential development of essential skills in ways that ensure mastery of basic elements before focusing on those that are more advanced. However, there are two principal barriers to effective utilization of these resources—intensive teacher training and an integration of concepts addressed in the intervention setting with the routine demands of the classroom

Several of the most carefully developed programs require extensive training before teachers may be expected to use them effectively. These include the Wilson Language System, Language!, and LETRS (Moats, 2003–2005). Even when school systems make the commitment to train one or two teachers in the use of these programs, the fact of teacher turn over seriously erodes the potential impact of that training. In Tennessee, about 44 per cent of all teachers leave the profession in the first 5 years; 16 per cent leave after the first year

(Southern Regional Education Board, 2003). It was not uncommon to learn that students in our sample had a different teacher responsible for intervention each year and a few experienced multiple teachers in a given year.

'Pull-out' programs cannot offer sufficient in-school time to learn, apply, and master the complex of skills that are essential for continuous and appropriate progress toward competent literacy performance. When we consider time dedicated to supportive interventions it is important to note that, typically, these interventions were independent of the day-to-day reading or language arts, or English curriculum demands. Time spent in the intervention classes ranged from daily sessions to twice per week and typically were scheduled for about 30 minutes. Among those in grades 6–12, these intervention sessions often were committed to the completion of assignments for the regular classroom. Even when opportunities to acquire the basic skills necessary to support growth in component skills were available, instruction was disconnected from the performance demands of the classroom. Modifications and accommodations were often provided in the regular classrooms to assist in meeting the demands of the grade level curriculum. This might serve to further explain the significant role apparently played by word recognition in reading comprehension performance among the older group of students in this study.

Although the infusion of well-crafted instructional programs into our schools is essential, the ways in which they are utilized with students such as those in our sample do not offer an efficient response to the problem we face. In the US, dyslexia is the most common learning disability, accounting for 80 per cent of all learning disabilities (Katusic et al., 2001). It is imperative that all teachers be educated to understand the nature of dyslexia, its degree of incidence in the general population (5–15 per cent),[1] the specific difficulties these students encounter in their progress toward literacy, and how to best support their learning in the classroom. To achieve an integrated approach to the support of literacy instruction for students with dyslexia, a new view of pre-service and in-service teacher education will be necessary—a view that assigns to all teachers the responsibility for the effective development of literacy skills among all students, including students with dyslexia.

NOTE

1 U.S. Department of Health & Human Services, National Institutes of Health, 1988; Shaywitz et al., 1990; Katusic et al., 2001.

REFERENCES

Aaron, P. G. and Joshi, R. M. (1992) *Reading Problems: Consultation and Remediation.* New York: Guilford Press.

Amado, A. J. (1999) *Partitioning predicted variance into constituent parts: A primer on regression commonality analysis.* Paper presented at the Annual Meeting of the Southwest Educational Research Association, San Antonio, TX.

Bradley, L. and Bryant, P. E. (1983) 'Categorizing sounds and learning to read — a causal connection', *Nature*, 301: 419–421.

Bruck, M. (1988) 'The word recognition and spelling of dyslexic children', *Reading Research Quarterly*, 23: 51–69.

Conners, F. and Olson, R. K. (1990) 'Reading comprehension in dyslexic and normal readers: A component skills analysis', in D. A. Balota, G. B. Flores d'Areais and K. Rayner (eds), *Comprehension Processes in Reading*. Hillsdale, NJ: Lawrence Erlbaum Associates.

Ehri, L. C. (1987) 'Learning to read and spell words', *Journal of Reading Behavior*, 19: 5–31.

Ehri, L. C. (1994) 'Development of the ability to read words: Update', in R. B. Ruddell, M. R. Ruddell and H. Singer (eds), *Theoretical Models and Processes of Reading* (Fourth ed.). Newark, DE: International Reading Association, pp. 323–358.

Ehri, L. C. (2000) 'Learning to read and learning to spell: Two sides of a coin', *Topics on Language Disorders*, 20 (3): 19–36.

Elkonin, D. B. (1973) 'U.S.S.R.', in J. Downing (ed.), *Comparative Reading*. New York: MacMillan, pp. 551–580.

Foorman, B. R., and Francis, D. J. (1994) 'Exploring connections among reading, spelling, and phonemic segmentation during the first grade', *Reading and Writing*, 6: 65–91.

Frith, U. (1985) 'Beneath the surface of developmental dyslexia', in K. Patterson, M. Coltheart and J. Marshall (eds), *Surface Dyslexia*. Mahwah, NJ: Lawrence Erlbaum Associates, pp. 301–330.

Frith, U. (1986) 'A developmental framework for developmental dyslexia', *Annals of Dyslexia*, 36: 69–81.

Fry, E. (1977). Fry's readability graph: clarification, validity and extension to level 17. *Journal of Reading*, 20: 242–252.

Ganske, K. (1993) *Developmental Spelling Analysis*. Barboursville, VA: Author.

Goldsmith-Phillips, J. (1994) 'Toward a research-based dyslexia assessment', in N. C. Jordan and J. Goldsmith-Phillips (eds), *Learning Disabilities: New Directions for Assessment and Intervention*. Boston, MA: Allyn and Bacon, pp. 85–100.

Gough, P. B. and Tunmer, W. E. (1986) 'Decoding, reading, and reading disability', *Remedial and Special Education*, 7 (1): 6–10.

Greene, J. F. (1995) *LANGUAGE! A Reading, Writing, and Spelling Curriculum for At-risk and ESL Students (Grades 4–12)* Longmont, CO: Sopris West.

Greene, J. F. (2000) *Language! A Literacy Intervention Curriculum.* (Second ed.). Longmont, CO: Sopris-West.

Harris, A. J. and Jacobson, M. D. (1982) *Basic Reading Vocabularies*. New York: MacMillan.

Henderson, E. H. and Templeton, S. (1994) *Spelling and Vocabulary*. Boston, MA: Houghton-Mifflin.

Hoover, W. A. and Gough, P. B. (1990) 'The simple view of reading', *Reading and Writing: An Interdisciplinary Journal*, 2: 127–160.

Jones, K. M. (2001) *Investigation of normal readers' progress through the development stages of reading words that do not follow strict letter/sound correspondences.* Murfreesboro, TN: Middle Tennessee State University.

Katusic, S. K., Colligan, R. C., Barbaresi, W. J., Schaid, D. J. and Jacobsen, S. J. (2001) *Incidence of Reading Disability in a Population-based Birth Cohort, 1976–1982*, Rochester, MN.

Liberman, I. Y. (1973) 'Segmentation of the spoken word and reading acquisition', *Bulletin of the Orton Society*, 23: 65–77.

Lindamood, C. H. and Lindamood, P.C. (1975) *The A.D.D. Program, Auditory Discrimination in-depth: Books 1 and 2.* Allen, TX: DLM Teaching Resources.

Lindamood, C. H. and Lindamood, P. C. (1979) *Lindamood Auditory Conceptualization Test*. Chicago, IL: Riverside Publishing.

Lundberg, I., Frost, J. and Petersen, O.-P. (1988) 'Effects of an extensive program for stimulating phonological awareness in preschool children', *Reading Research Quarterly*, 23: 263–284.

Manis, F. R., Custodio, R. and Szeszulski, P. A. (1993) 'Developental of phonological and orthographic skill: A 2-year longitudinal study of dyslexic children', *Journal of Experimental Child Psychology*, 56: 64–86.

Moats, L. C. (2003–2005) *LETRS: Language Essentials for Teachers of Reading and Spelling (Books 1–6)* Longmont, CO: Sopris West.

Padget, S. Y., Knight, D. F. and Sawyer, D. J. (1996) 'Tennessee meets the challenge of dyslexia', *Annals of Dyslexia*, 46: 51–72.

Pennington, B. F. (1991) *Diagnosing Learning Disorders: A Neuropsychological Framework*. New York: Guilford Press.

Pollack, C. and Minner, D. (1995) *Process Phonics*. Rochester, NY: Bennett.

Rack, J. P., Snowling, M. J. and Olson, R. K. (1992) 'The nonword reading deficit in developmental dyslexia: A review', *Reading Research Quarterly*, 27: 29–53.

Richardson, E. and DiBenedetto, B. (1985) *Decoding Skills Test*. Los Angeles, CA: Western Psychological Services.

Sawyer, D. J. (1992) 'Language abilities, reading acquisition, and developmental dyslexia: A discussion of hypothetical and observed relationships', *Journal of Learning Disabilities*, 25: 82–95.

Sawyer, D. J. (1998, 2001) *Assessment of Decoding and Encoding Progress Test*. Murfreesboro, TN: Middle Tennessee State University, Center for the Study and Treatment of Dyslexia.

Sawyer, D. J. and Kim, J. K. (2000) 'Variation in the development of decoding and encoding skills among students with phonological dyslexia', *Thalamus*, 18 (2): 1–16.

Sawyer, D. J. and Knight, D. F. (1997) 'Tennessee meets the challenge of dyslexia', *Perspectives: The Orton Dyslexia Society*, 23 (2): 8–10.

Shaywitz, S. E., Shaywitz, B. A., Fletcher, J. M. and Escobar, M. D. (1990) 'Prevalence of reading disability in boys and girls. Results of the Connecticut Longitudinal Study', *Journal of the American Medical Association*, 264: 996–1002.

Southern Regional Education Board (2003) 2003 Study of teacher supply and demand in Tennessee. Available www.sreb.org/main/HigherEd/Leadership/TN_Teacher_Supply_Demand.pdf

Spargo, E. (1989) *Timed Readings: Fifty 400-word Passages with Questions for Building Reading Speed* (Third ed.). Providence, RI: Jamestown Publishers.

Spring, C. and French, L. (1990) 'Identifying children with specific reading disabilities from listening and reading discrepancy scores', *Journal of Learning Disabilities*, 23: 53–58.

Stanovich, K. E. and West, R. F. (1989) 'Exposure to print and orthographic processing', *Reading Research Quarterly*, 24: 402–433.

Torgesen, J. K., Wagner, R. K. and Rashotte, C. A. (1994) 'Longitudinal studies of phonological processing and reading', *Journal of Learning Disabilities*, 27: 276–286.

U.S. Department of Health and Human Services. (1988) *Developmental Dyslexia and Reading Related Disorders*. Bethesda, MD: National Institutes of Health.

Vellutino, F. R., Scanlon, D. M. and Tanzman, M. S. (1994) 'Components of reading ability: Issues and problems in operationalizing word identification, phonological coding, and orthographic coding', in G. R. Lyon (ed.), *Frames of Reference for the Assessment of Learning Disabilities*. Baltimore, MD: Paul Brookes, pp. 279–329.

Wagner, R. K. and Torgesen, J. J. (1987) 'The nature of phonological processing, and its causal role in the acquisition of reading skills', *Psychological Bulletin*, 101: 192–212.

Wagner, R., Torgesen, J. and Rashotte, C. (1999) *Comprehensive Test of Phonological Processing*. Austin, TX: Pro-Ed.

Wechsler, D. (1991) *Wechsler Intelligence Scale for Children* (3rd ed.). San Antonio, TX: Psychological Corporation.

Wechsler, D. (1992) *Wechsler Individual Achievement Test*. San Antonio, TX: Psychological Corporation.

Wilson, B. A. (1988) *Wilson Reading System Program Overview*. Millbury, MA: Wilson Language Training.

Woodcock, R. W. (1987) *Woodcock Reading Mastery Tests–Revised*. Circle Pines, MN: American Guidance Service.

Young, C. (1997) *Monitoring Progress in Reading and Spelling among Average First-Grade Students*. Murfreesboro, TN: Middle Tennessee State University.

15

Individual Tutoring for Struggling Readers: Moving Research to Scale with Interventions Implemented by Paraeducators

Patricia F. Vadasy and Elizabeth A. Sanders

This chapter

i) summarizes findings from a series of studies of supplemental tutoring provided by trained paraeducators for at-risk kindergarten and first-grade students;

ii) discusses the implications of these findings for taking effective reading interventions to scale in schools serving children at risk; and

iii) discusses the influences that place students from disadvantaged backgrounds at high risk for reading problems.

INTRODUCTION

Children from less advantaged backgrounds are significantly at risk for reading difficulties which can often be prevented with scientifically based reading instruction. Yet sufficient well-trained teachers are not available to help the large numbers of at-risk students who are most often enrolled in the lowest quality schools. This chapter summarizes findings from a series of studies of supplemental tutoring provided by trained paraeducators for at-risk kindergarten and first-grade students. The results indicated that when provided with training and research-based instruction, paraeducators are able to help many at-risk students attain grade-level reading skills. The implications of these findings for taking effective reading interventions to scale in schools serving children at risk will be discussed in this chapter.

Early reading skill is influenced strongly by the child's home language and literacy environment. These influences place students from disadvantaged backgrounds at high risk for reading problems. Hart and Risley (2003) documented differences between early language environments of children from different socioeconomic backgrounds, and the widening gap between the vocabularies of these children. As Hart and Risley (2003) observed, 'estimating the hours of intervention needed to equalize children's early experience makes clear the enormity of the effort that would be required to change children's lives'. Children from low-income families often arrive at school less prepared to learn to read than their middle-class peers (Lee and Burkam, 2002; Snow et al., 1998). They may have less experience with print and books (Nicholson, 1997), and less developed phonological awareness skills which are most predictive of early reading achievement (Bowey, 1995; Share et al., 1984; Snow et al., 1998; Tunmer et al., 1988).

This widening gap between good and poor readers, often described by the 'Matthew effect' (Stanovich, 1986) suggests that schools intervene as soon as a student is identified as a struggling reader. The nature of reading development also calls for early intervention, because word identification underpins higher level reading skills. The underlying problem that characterizes most students with serious reading disabilities is their struggle learning the code, which for English readers means learning the not always obvious or regular relationships between letters and sounds in words. For children who are least advantaged and most likely to struggle with learning to read, effective instruction in word reading skill is essential.

The timing is critical because as Shaywitz and Shaywitz (2004) remind us, children are only seven or eight years old once in their lifetime. Children who start out as poor readers rarely catch up with their peers (Baydar et al., 1993; Stevenson and Newman, 1986; Torgesen et al., 1997; Tramontana et al., 1988).

Early reading intervention that is explicit and intensive can bring the word-level reading skills of many students at risk for reading problems into the average range (Torgesen, 2002; Vellutino, et al., 1996). These interventions include early, explicit, intensive, and often extended instruction in phonemic decoding and comprehension skills (Foorman and Torgesen, 2001; Vellutino, et al., 1996).

Yet there is an often overlooked disconnect between research and school practice: many students who most need explicit and intense early reading instruction are found in schools with the most limited resources for providing effective early reading instruction (Lee and Burkam, 2002). In 2000, the funding gap between the highest and lowest poverty districts was $996 per pupil (Carey, 2003). Additional funding disparities exist within districts as high poverty and low performing schools pay the lowest teacher salaries, further reducing teacher talent for the most needy students (Roza and Hill, 2003).

Kindergarten students from lower income backgrounds are enrolled in schools with larger class size; students from minority and non-English speaking backgrounds attend schools with less experienced teachers (Lee and Burkam, 2002). Further, teachers are often ill-prepared for the demands of effectively teaching critical early language and reading skills (Moats, 1995; 1999), in particular for at-risk readers (Bursuck et al., 2002).

Supplemental reading interventions are one means of addressing the instructional needs of students most at risk for reading problems. Individual or small-group tutoring is a means of adding instruction in the basic word reading skills that most often challenge at-risk students. Because supplemental reading instruction is often provided by nonteacher tutors, including paraprofessional and parent tutors, it is cost effective and feasible for schools that cannot allocate significant or teacher or specialist time for individual or small group tutoring. Finally, there need not be large trade offs in the benefits of using nonteacher- vs. teacher-implemented supplemental intervention. In a review of one-to-one tutoring programs in reading for elementary students at risk for reading failure, Elbaum et al. (2000) reported positive findings for tutoring provided by trained tutors; interventions for younger students were more effective than interventions serving older students.

Features of effective tutoring programs have been discussed by Wasik (1998) and Juel (1996). In her review of 17 volunteer tutoring programs, Wasik described four features that characterized successful programs:

- a designated coordinator with a reading background to provide tutor guidance;
- structured tutoring activities that include reading new material and rereading familiar books and texts;
- word analysis and letter-sound relationship instruction; and
- writing that emphasized composing.

In her review of tutoring programs, Juel (1996) also identified four features of effective programs:

- word-level instruction, including reading texts with a high level of word overlap and repetition;
- direct instruction in letter-sound relationships;
- scaffolded instruction in word reading and spelling; and
- tutor modeling and explanations.

These are many of the same features that characterize the effective expert tutoring interventions delivered by teachers (Torgesen et al., 1997; Vellutino et al., 1996), and are features that can be incorporated into the instruction provided by trained paraeducators.

A COST-EFFECTIVE ALTERNATIVE

If tutoring is the 'gold standard' for reading intervention (Institute of Education Sciences, 2003), then extended individual or small group tutoring by a trained reading specialist would be desirable. As Allington (2004) has illustrated, however, this is an elusive goal given the limited school funding available. Education funding seems unlikely to rise soon to meet that gold standard. Further, many schools continue to use older and untested reading programs provided by teachers who may not be prepared to address the needs of large numbers of diverse learners (Nolen et al., 1990). Many of these are the schools that serve large numbers of students from low-income backgrounds most at risk for reading problems.

An alternative that has not been sufficiently examined is to increase the use of trained paraeducators to supplement classroom instruction in critical areas of reading development. The most appropriate areas in which these non-teacher staff might be utilized include early reading instruction in phonological awareness, alphabetics, phonics, and fluency practice. These are often skill roadblocks for struggling readers. Further, these are skills which often require reinforcement and practice, rather than teaching new concepts, areas in which, as Shaywitz (2003) has pointed out, parents and non-teachers can be highly effective. Students who struggle to acquire the reading basics often need far more practice to learn fluency or word identification skills than classroom teachers or even reading specialists can provide (again, assuming our current situation of limited education resources). Students who require overlearning might receive supervised and scaffolded extended practice with trained paraprofessional tutors.

Most early reading interventions have been designed and evaluated for use by teachers (Bus and van IJzendoorn, 1999; Elbaum et al., 2000; Santi et al., 2004). A few programs, however, have been developed and/or evaluated for use by paraeducators. These include the *Phono-Graphix* (www.readamerica.net, Fill et al., 1998; McGuinness et al., 1996), *Spell Read P.A.T.* (www.spellread.com, Rashotte et al., 2001), and research-based code emphasis instruction (Simmons et al., 2003) in early reading skills; the *Read Naturally* (Hasbrouck et al., 1999) and *Great Leaps* (Mercer et al., 2000) fluency building programs; and, the *REWARDS* word attack and rate development program (Archer et al., 2000; Archer, 1981; Vachon, 1998).

INTERVENTION COMPONENTS AND DESIGN

Over the past 15 years, we have conducted a series of studies on early reading interventions provided by trained paraeducators for at-risk kindergarten and first grade students. We initially developed a first-grade, and later a kindergarten, version of an intervention (Vadasy et al., 2004) which specifically targets four areas of instruction recommended by the National Reading Panel: phonemic awareness, phonics, fluency, and motivation. The interventions target beginning readers, when tutoring interventions are found to be most effective; use one-on-one tutoring, a highly effective means of helping students who struggle with reading (Cohen et al., 1982; Juel, 1996; Wasik, 1998; Wasik and Slavin, 1993); and, finally, reflect principles of effective instructional design (Rosenshine and Stevens, 1984), with guided learning and practice for students encountering challenges and problems in learning to read:

1 Mediated scaffolding – Tutors are trained to provide mediated scaffolding to adjust instructional support for individual student needs (Gunn et al., 1998).
2 Strategic integration – Instructional components are linked to help students make connections between areas of literacy knowledge. For example, letter-sound correspondence is integrated with phonemic decoding and encoding; letter-sound correspondence is linked with storybook reading (Dixon et al., 1992).
3 Judicious review – The lessons have been field-tested and designed to provide adequate review for students with a range of reading needs. Each lesson component provides repeated opportunities to practice discrete skills students are learning (e.g., letter-sound correspondences, phonemic segmentation, phonemic decoding) (Dixon, et al., 1992; Kameenui and Carnine, 1998).

The individual lesson components offer ample opportunities for word identification in context-free as well as connected text conditions (Juel, 1988; Stanovich, 1980); carefully selected storybooks with a low rate of introduction of novel words (Barr, 1984; Gambrell et al., 1981) to increase motivation and minimize error rates which influence reading progress; varied contexts for word recognition practice, to avoid drill and to promote transfer of writing/spelling skills in various situations (Walker and Buckley, 1972); task variation and pacing through short skill sessions within lessons and changes in tasks over the course of the intervention, to decrease boredom and promote motivation (Friedman and Medway, 1987; Samuels, 1988); explicit correction procedures for tutors to follow; and, ongoing systems for student progress feedback, as well as metacognitive reminders to increase student awareness of task purpose and applications (Cunningham, 1990). The first-grade intervention components are fully described elsewhere (Jenkins et al., 2004).

The interventions provide students with explicit and systematic instruction in letter-sound relationships, decoding strategies, and carefully coordinated spelling instruction. Students have daily opportunities to practice accurate and fluent reading in decodable stories that feature the letters and sounds they are learning. Letter-sound relationships are introduced at a reasonable pace, with extensive practice opportunities and cumulative review of previously taught relationships. Decoding instruction is explicit, with guided practice, scaffolding, and modeling.

Tutors are provided with mastery tests to monitor student progress, and to identify areas for additional review and practice. Training prepares tutors to adjust their pace of instruction and provide additional review, scaffolding, and modeling, based on each student's needs.

Progress reports are used to help tutors communicate with classroom teachers and parents. The interventions have been tested in conjunction with varied classroom reading programs, and complement a range of classroom reading instruction.

FIRST-GRADE STUDIES

We will first summarize the remedial outcomes for the first-grade intervention, which we field-tested initially in a series of three experimental (randomized design) and five quasi-experimental (nonequivalent groups design) studies comparing tutored students to untutored controls receiving classroom instruction only (Jenkins et al., 2004; Vadasy et al., 1997a;b; 2000; 2005; 2002). Students averaged in the lowest quartile in reading skills at the beginning of the studies. Across the eight cohorts, students were tested on standardized reading measures including: The Woodcock Reading Mastery Test-Revised (Woodcock, 1987, 1998) word attack and word identification subtests, the Wide Range Achievement Test-Revised (Jastak and Wilkinson, 1984) reading and spelling subtests, as well as measures of discrete reading skills. Convergent evidence shows overall posttest means for tutored students averaged at grade level (standard score of 100). When average effect sizes across the eight studies were examined, they ranged from .41 to .99, and average overall .70. Effect sizes for decoding/word attack averaged .66, and those for word identification averaged .74. Spelling effect sizes averaged .67. In a follow-up study (Vadasy and Sanders, 2008) we examined the long-term growth of reading skills following one year of the supplemental first-grade intervention. A group of 79 first graders with reading skills averaging in the lowest quartile were assessed post-intervention and at one-year intervals through the end of third grade. Growth model results indicated that students continued to benefit from first-grade intervention through the end of third grade, with average performance near 50th percentile on decoding and reading fluency, near 40th percentile on word reading and comprehension, and near 30th percentile on spelling.

KINDERGARTEN INTERVENTION I

The kindergarten intervention was subsequently evaluated in three studies, two randomized and one quasi-randomized. In the first randomized study (Vadasy et al., 2006), paraeducator tutors provided 18 weeks of individual instruction in phonemic and alphabetic skills to kindergarten students who averaged in the

10–25th percentile at pretest in receptive vocabulary, phonological awareness, and reading accuracy. Instructional components were:

1   Letter-sound correspondence – Letter names and sounds were introduced at a rate of about one new letter name/sound every two lessons. Students practiced pointing to the letters, saying the sound, and writing the letters that matched the sounds provided by the instructor. Instruction design featured cumulative review of all letters, and added review on vowel sounds. If a student required additional practice in learning letter names, and particularly letter sounds, the paraeducator and the student practiced with a letter-sound card for a few extra minutes each lesson. For this practice, students were required to point and match the letter name/sound to the printed letter and pictured key word on the card, in a procedure described by Berninger (1998).

2   Phoneme segmenting – Students practiced segmenting consonant-vowel-consonant (cvc) words into three phonemes. Paraeducators modeled one word, and then orally presented four words for the student to segment using 3-part Elkonin boxes (squares drawn on a piece of paper with one square for each phoneme). Students were instructed to repeat the word, point to each box as they spoke a phoneme, and then sweep their finger under the boxes and say the word fast.

3   Word reading and spelling – Paraeducators first modeled phoneme blending by pointing to an example word in each lesson, stretching out the sounds without stopping between phonemes, and then saying the word fast. Students then practiced blending orally 6–9 words per lesson, with scaffolding and assistance. If needed, paraeducators added practice on weak letter sounds by having the student identify the sound in the initial, final, and middle position in a spoken word. Finally, the paraeducator dictated three words for the student to spell (words including the new sound, a difficult sound, and ending with an easy word). This activity provided explicit instruction in how to map letters to phonemes. Students repeated each word before they attempted to spell it, learned to segment each word into phonemes, and reread all the words they spelled. Each tutor used a handwriting chart with numbered arrows to guide letter strokes to help students form the letters efficiently. Students also fingerpoint-read short sentences constructed with previously taught words.

4   Irregular word instruction – The lessons featured high-frequency irregular words that appeared in the decodable texts. The paraeducator supplied the word, and the student pointed to the word, spelled it aloud, and read the word again.

5   Phoneme blending – To add practice in recognizing orally blended words, the paraeducator asked the student to guess the word (say it fast) that the tutor said in a slow, stretched out way (without stopping between phonemes, just as the student was learning to do in the word reading activity).

6   Alphabet naming practice – Depending upon the student's progress in alphabetic skills, the paraeducator implemented one of these activities: (a) say the alphabet (letter names) while pointing to the letters on the letter sound card, (b) say the alphabet (letter names) without looking at the letters/chart, (c) point to the letters that the tutor names, or, (d) name the letters that the tutor points to.

7   Assisted oral reading practice – Students practiced reading aloud in decodable storybooks for the last 10 minutes of each instructional session. Students read each book twice

the first time it was introduced, and reread books as there was available lesson time. Paraeducators were trained to choose a book reading method best suited for the individual student. Most students read the book independently, with tutor assistance, and some read the story with the paraeducator (partner reading), or reread a line of text after the instructor read the same line (echo reading).

At posttest, tutored students scored significantly higher than classroom controls in word reading accuracy and efficiency, oral reading fluency, and developmental spelling. Effect sizes were large for reading accuracy ($d = 1.02$) and oral reading fluency rate ($d = 0.81$), and moderate for reading efficiency ($d = 0.61$) and developmental spelling ($d = 0.57$). We also observed positive treatment effects on growth on the Dynamic Indicators of Basic Early Literacy Skills (DIBELS: Good and Kaminski, 2002) Phonemic Segmentation Fluency and Nonsense Word Fluency subtests. Tutored students at posttest averaged in the 45th and 32nd percentiles in reading accuracy and efficiency, respectively, compared to controls who averaged at the 25th percentile. Tutored students maintained higher levels of performance across reading outcomes through the end of first grade.

KINDERGARTEN INTERVENTION II

In designing the study that follows, we set out to replicate the Vadasy et al. (2006) findings with a second cohort of kindergarten students. Because many schools remain hesitant to explicitly teach beginning reading skills to kindergarten students, including students in high-risk groups for reading failure, we regarded a replication warranted to add confidence to the earlier findings.

Sample

The research sites were 13 schools in two urban school districts serving large numbers of students from minority and low-income backgrounds. In December, teachers referred 166 students for study screening, 154 of whom were screened for reading difficulties. Eighty-two non-retained students were considered eligible for study participation with performance of less than 7 letter sounds correct on a measure of letter sound fluency, and less than 15 letter names correct on DIBELS Letter Name Fluency subtest. Eligible students were randomly assigned within school to treatment (tutoring) or control (no tutoring) groups. Attrition during the intervention year included 14 students: 13 moved (7 treatment and 6 control), and 1 treatment student was removed because her tutor resigned and we were unable to find a replacement. The final sample size was $N = 68$ ($n = 33$ treatment, $n = 35$ control).

For each participating student, demographic data were collected and are summarized in Table 15.1 on the following page (there were no statistically significant differences between groups on any demographic variable).

Table 15.1 Year 2 sample characteristics

	Treatment n = 33		Control n = 35		
	f	(%)	f	(%)	$\chi^2(1)$
Male	15	45	20	57	0.929
Minority	23	70	29	83	0.962
Title I	16	48	18	51	0.059
ESL	8	24	8	23	0.018
SPED	1	3	1	3	0.002

All $ps > .05$.

Intervention

Tutoring began in the first week of January. Paraeducators provided tutoring for 30 minutes per day, 4 days per week, for 18 weeks. The lesson activities were similar to those described above. Treatment students completed $M = 49$ lessons ($SD = 10.8$, Range $= 25$–62 lessons), and attended $M = 51$ tutoring sessions ($SD = 8.9$, Range $= 32$–64 sessions), corresponding to approximately 26 hours of instruction, on average.

Fidelity

Throughout the school year research staff visited paraeducators approximately once per week to observe tutoring instruction. Treatment fidelity was rated using a protocol that describes the components of tutoring instruction as well as paraeducators' behaviors during tutoring. Lesson components were rated on a 5-point scale for each criterion ($0 =$ not at all; $5 =$ always). Paraeducators' tutoring behaviors (e.g., 'organized materials' and 'has quick pace') were also rated on a 5-point scale, ranging from 0 (very poor) to 5 (very good). Reliability among 6 pairs of raters was established at $r = .78$ or higher on components, and .73 or higher for behaviors. After 209 observations of the 17 paraeducators (for an average of 12 observations per tutor), component fidelity was $M = 3.7$ ($SD = 0.38$) and behavior fidelity was $M = 3.6$ ($SD = 0.44$).

Assessments

Students were pretested, midtested, and posttested in December, February/March, and May/June, respectively. All tests were individually administered by testers unaware of group assignment. The following measures were used:

1   Receptive language was measured at pretest with the standardized *Peabody Picture Vocabulary Test-IIIA* (PPVT-IIIA; Dunn et al., 1997).
2   Rapid automatized naming was measured at pretest with the standardized *Comprehensive Test of Phonological Processing (CTOPP)* Rapid Color Naming subtest (Wagner et al., 1999).
3   Alphabetic knowledge was measured using the *Dynamic Indicators of Basic Early Literacy Skills* (DIBELS; Good and Kaminski, 2002) Letter Name Fluency subtest.

4   Phonological awareness was assessed using six measures. The three phonological awareness subtests of the *Comprehensive Test of Phonological Processing* (CTOPP; Wagner et al., 1999) include: Blending Words, Elision, and Sound Matching. The two DIBELS measures of phonological awareness include the Initial Sound Fluency and Phoneme Segmentation Fluency subtests. Finally, Rapid Letter Sounds, one of our screening criteria, required the student to say the sounds of as many letters as he/she can in one minute.

5   Decoding was assessed using three measures: The *DIBELS* Nonsense Word Fluency subtest; The *Test of Word Reading Efficiency (TOWRE)* Phonemic Decoding subtest (Torgesen et al., 1999); and, the *Woodcock Reading Mastery Test-Revised/ Normative Update* (WRMT-R/NU; Woodcock, 1987, 1998) Word Attack subtest.

6   Word reading was assessed using two measures: The TOWRE Sight Word subtest (Torgesen et al., 1999), and the WRMT-R/NU Word Identification subtest.

7   Passage reading fluency was assessed using the DIBELS Oral Reading Fluency subtest.

8   Reading Comprehension was assessed using the WRMT-R/NU Passage Comprehension subtest (Woodcock, 1987, 1998).

9   Spelling was assessed using developmental scoring of the *Wide Range Achievement Test-Revised* (WRAT-R; Jastak and Wilkinson, 1984) Spelling subtest. Similar to Fuchs et al. (2001), we applied the Tangel and Blachman (1992) developmental scoring rubric to all words attempted (within normal test administration guidelines). This rubric allows us to credit students for partial and less phonemically sophisticated responses. Items are scored from 0 (random string of letters) to 6 (entire word correctly spelled).

Results

A series of one-way analyses of variance (ANOVAs) showed no significant differences between groups on any pretest measure. A series of analyses of covariance (ANCOVAs) were conducted for posttests in which a pretest was available (e.g., alphabetics) (otherwise one-way analyses of variance were used). Results, shown in Table 15.2 for pretests and posttests, revealed large treatment effects for measures of alphabetics, phonological awareness, decoding, word reading, and passage reading. Posttest scores for tutored students were at or near grade level across reading outcomes. Moderate effects were detected for developmental spelling but not standardized spelling. These results are highly similar to the findings from the previous kindergarten study, although this second cohort of students also show improved treatment effects for phonological awareness measures.

KINDERGARTEN INTERVENTION III

In this study (Vadasy and Sanders, in press), we considered the influence of the student:tutor ratio on reading outcomes. A group of kindergarten students from 30 classrooms, the majority from minority backgrounds and Title I eligible, were quasi-randomly assigned to one of three conditions: 1:1 ($n = 22$) or 1:2 ($n = 32$) code-oriented instruction by paraeducator tutors, or to no-tutoring ($n = 22$) (classroom-only instruction). Twenty-one paraeducators provided 18 weeks of explicit instruction in phonemic and alphabetic skills to students during the latter half of kindergarten.

Table 15.2 Descriptive statistics on pretest and posttest outcomes

	SPK Tutoring (n = 33)							Classroom Instruction Only (n = 35)							Posttest	
	Pretest			Posttest				Pretest			Posttest					
	M	(SD)	Rank	M	(SD)	Adj M	Rank	M	(SD)	Rank	M	(SD)	Adj M	Rank	F	d
Receptive Language																
PPVT-IIIA (standard)	89	(18.0)	24%	—	—	—	—	88	(17.1)	21%	—	—	—	—	—	
Rapid Automatized Naming																
CTOPP Rapid Color Naming (standard)	91	(18.7)	27%	—	—	—	—	93	(17.4)	30%	—	—	—	—	—	
Alphabetics																
DIBELS Initial Sounds (per min)	4	(5.5)	deficit	24	(9.8)	25	estab	6	(6.6)	deficit	17	(10.9)	16	emerg	17.95*** (1,65)	1.04
DIBELS Letter Naming (per min)	5	(4.5)	deficit	25	(13.9)	25	deficit	5	(3.6)	deficit	23	(10.6)	22	deficit	0.85 (1,65)	.22
DIBELS Nonsense Words (per min)	1	(1.8)	deficit	23	(12.3)	23	emerg	1	(2.6)	deficit	11	(11.3)	11	deficit	25.24*** (1,65)	1.22
Phonological Awareness																
DIBELS Phon Segmenting (per min)	5	(7.9)	deficit	27	(15.6)	27	emerg	4	(5.9)	deficit	14	(13.5)	14	emerg	15.72*** (1,65)	.96
Rapid Letter Sounds (per min)	2	(2.0)	—	32	(15.0)	33	—	3	(2.2)	—	15	(11.9)	15	—	37.87*** (1,65)	1.50
CTOPP Blending (standard)	95	(5.8)	37%	102	(11.9)	103	58%	95	(5.5)	37%	94	(10.3)	94	34%	14.29*** (1,65)	.92
CTOPP Elision (standard)	92	(5.8)	30%	93	(13.5)	93	32%	93	(5.4)	32%	88	(10.9)	88	21%	7.70** (1,65)	.67
CTOPP Sound Matching (standard)	92	(6.3)	30%	98	(9.9)	98	46%	92	(4.7)	30%	92	(9.9)	92	30%	6.27* (1,65)	.61
Decoding																
WRMT-R/NU Word Attack (standard)	94	(0.0)	34%	105	(8.7)	—	62%	94	(0.0)	34%	96	(7.2)	—	38%	20.27*** (1,66)	1.09
Word Reading																
WRMT-R/NU Word ID (standard)	86	(3.2)	18%	101	(10.5)	102	54%	87	(3.1)	18%	90	(15.8)	90	25%	13.32*** (1,65)	.89
Passage Comprehension																
WRMT-R/NU Psg Comp (standard)	—	—	—	95	(8.6)	—	37%	92	—	—	92	(9.3)	—	30%	1.85 (1,66)	.33

(Continued)

Table 15.2 Descriptive statistics on pretest and posttest outcomes—Cont'd

| | SPK Tutoring (n = 33) | | | | | | | Classroom Instruction Only (n = 35) | | | | | | | | |
| | Pretest | | | Posttest | | | | Pretest | | | Posttest | | | | | |
	M	(SD)	Rank	M	(SD)	Adj M	Rank	M	(SD)	Rank	M	(SD)	Adj M	Rank	F	d
Passage Fluency																
Rate (words correct per min)	—	—	—	9	(9.4)	—	—	—	—	—	3	(4.0)	—	—	(1,66) 13.75***	.90
Accuracy (% correct per min)	—	—	—	47%	(31%)	—	—	—	—	—	16%	(22%)	—	—	(1,66) 24.00***	1.19
Spelling																
Development Spelling (total points)	—	—	—	38	(30.0)	—	48%	—	—	—	18	(25.5)	—	38%	(1,66) 8.26**	.70
WRAT-R Spelling (standard)	—	—	—	99	(10.4)	—	—	—	—	—	96	(10.3)	—	—	(1,66) 1.06	.25

Note. PPVT-IIIA = Peabody Picture Vocabulary Test IIIA; CTOPP = Comprehensive Test of Phonological Awareness; DIBELS = Dynamic Indicators of Basic Early Literacy Skills; Rapid Letter Sounds = isolated letter sounds (one minute timed); WRMT-R/NU = Woodcock Reading Mastery Test Revised/Normative Update; Rate/Accuracy = words correct/percent correct on one minute timed passage "Mac Gets Well"; Developmental Spelling = Tangel-Blachman scoring for words attempted on the Wide Range Achievement Test-Revised (WRAT-R) Spelling subtest. One-way analyses of variance (ANOVAs) used for pretest comparisons; one-way analyses of variance or covariance (ANCOVAs) used for posttests. Group comparisons showed no pretest differences. Treatment effect size used is Cohen's *d* based on adjusted mean differences. * *p* < .05; ** *p* < .01; *** *p* < .001.

Multilevel model results (taking into account between-classroom variability) showed that tutored students outperformed non-tutored controls on posttest measures of phonological awareness, word reading accuracy, oral reading fluency, spelling, and comprehension. No reliable differences, however, were found between the two tutored groups on any measure, suggesting that code-oriented tutoring for pairs of students is a viable alternative to the gold standard of individual instruction. Specifically, tutored students averaged in the 63rd percentile in word reading accuracy and 40th percentile in comprehension at posttest. Comparatively, non-tutored students performed in the 48th and 30th percentiles, respectively. This pattern was highly similar to results from our earlier two cohorts and by Al Otaiba et al. (2005) for a one-to-one tutor-assisted kindergarten intervention for at-risk children.

This study also explored the question of why dyad tutoring appeared as effective as individual tutoring. Analyses showed that dyads more discrepant in levels of phonological awareness had higher comprehension posttest scores compared with less discrepant dyads. However, this finding must be regarded as tentative since between- and within-dyad differences could reflect school-level disparities (i.e., less discrepant dyads may exist in schools with students who perform at similarly low levels). Further, the National Reading Panel (2000) speculated that reasons for the advantage that small group phonological awareness instruction had over individual instruction included enhanced attention, social motivation, and learning opportunities. Tutors in the present study mentioned developing dyad dynamics that seemed to add student motivation and enjoyment of the paired tutoring sessions. The influence of dyad characteristics warrants further study, including the influence of skill discrepancies.

Paraeducator tutors provided explicit skill-focussed instruction with clear and appropriate supports, as indicated by high levels of treatment fidelity. Tutors closely followed scripts that allowed them to provide the type of intentional teaching (Pianta, 2006) considered appropriate to engage young children in learning abstract early literacy skills. For kindergarten children at risk for poor reading outcomes, there are two pedagogical implications of these findings. First, intensive and explicit instruction in alphabetics and code skills was effective for children identified as at risk in December of kindergarten. At pretest, students averaged in the 'at risk' range on alphabetic knowledge (letter naming fluency), and in approximately the 20th percentile on phonological awareness. At posttest, tutored students attained mean standardized scores at grade level in word reading accuracy and near grade level in comprehension. Second, findings suggest that schools might utilize paraeducators more effectively to supplement early reading instruction for children most needing more intensive instruction.

INTERVENTION OUTCOMES FOR ENGLISH LANGUAGE LEARNER (ELL) STUDENTS

In light of the growing numbers of English language learner (ELL) students in our schools, we have examined how well this group of students responds to the interventions. Below we summarize our limited data on ELL students who were included across all three kindergarten cohorts, as well as earlier first grade cohorts. After selecting only ELL students, we collapsed each set of cohorts (grades K and 1) into two sub-samples and compared groups using a series of one-way analyses of variance. At pretest we found no reliable differences between groups (importantly, we did not investigate all possible variables such as demographics—only pretests—and therefore the results presented here are tentative). At posttest, ELL treatment students in both grades appear to outperform their non-tutored peers on measures of decoding and word reading (Table 15.3). Small sample sizes and mixed cohort analyses yield suggestive findings only, and a study with a large sample of ELL students is currently underway.

Findings in Table 15.3 show that kindergarten effect sizes for our ELL sub-groups average .67; whereas first-grade ELL subgroup effect sizes average .65. For decoding outcomes in particular, effect sizes of .92 (both grades) imply that treatment students' posttests were nearly 1 standard deviation higher than controls'; treatment students averaged at grade level after five months of intervention (above 50th percentile) whereas non-tutored students averaged in the 30th percentile.

SUMMARY

The federal government, states, and businesses have set clear standards that schools must meet for adequate yearly progress in reading. These reading goals

Table 15.3 Findings for ELL subgroups in kindergarten and first-grade cohorts

	Treatment n = 31		Control n = 25		Treatment vs. Control	
Grade K	M	(SD)	M	(SD)	F (1, 53)	d
Alphabetics	31	(15.0)	16	(13.7)	13.703***	1.00
Phonological Awareness	22	(15.6)	12	(14.1)	6.096*	.66
Decoding	102	(10.7)	93	(9.5)	11.748***	.92
Word Reading	98	(10.4)	92	(10.5)	4.572*	.57
Reading Fluency	10	(8.6)	5	(6.2)	5.299*	.62
Comprehension	92	(9.6)	90	(9.6)	0.750	.23
Spelling	36	(31.0)	18	(18.7)	6.768*	.70
	Treatment n = 43		Control n = 20		Treatment vs. Control	
Grade 1	M	(SD)	M	(SD)	F (1, 61)	d
Alphabetics	55	(16.0)	41	(16.8)	8.804**	.80
Decoding	104	(12.0)	92	(14.0)	11.542***	.92
Word Reading	99	(11.8)	92	(13.8)	4.347*	.56
Reading Fluency	31	(21.2)	25	(29.8)	0.583	.26
Comprehension	96	(8.1)	91	(9.5)	2.379	.57
Spelling	88	(14.2)	78	(9.4)	8.323**	.78

Note. Measures same as Table 15.2. Sample derived from subgroup of ELL students in cohorts as follows: kindergarten ELL sub-sample comprises 03-04, 04-05, 05-06 cohorts; first-grade sub-sample comprises 99-00, 00-01, 01-02 cohorts. One-way analyses of variance of pretests (not shown) showed no reliable differences between groups ($ps > .05$). Results from one-way analyses of variance of posttests shown (all effects favor treatment). For spelling, homogeneity of variance violations exist; actual F-tests shown since results from analyses of log-transformed data showed similar results. * $p < .05$, ** $p < .01$, *** $p < .001$.

become increasingly important to prepare students for their roles as citizens of a democracy in an increasingly complex world. The research on how to effectively teach students, including those at risk, how to read is clear and widely accessible. The evidence on the effectiveness of intensive, explicit early reading interventions shows that we can reduce the numbers of students with reading disabilities. The challenge is how to take these effective interventions to scale (Denton and Fletcher, 2003).

The studies presented here describe just one means of using paraprofessionals to effectively supplement early reading instruction for at-risk students. The phonics-based interventions described include features associated with the sustained use of reading interventions: high student acceptance; practical, concrete, and accessible materials; high degree of specificity; professional development that includes modeling of strategies and ongoing problem solving; attention to implementation in typical schools; and perceived benefits for students (Gersten et al., 2000; Klingner et al., 1999). Getting research-based reading programs and trained reading teachers into all schools is the first priority for translating research on early reading interventions into practice. Yet currently, many schools serving the most at-risk students overlook the instructional potential of paraprofessional staff. In particular, these staff can help make primary prevention instruction (Foorman and Torgesen, 2001; Simmons et al., 2003) available for the large numbers of students at risk for reading disability—up to one in five students according to one estimate (Shaywitz, 2003). Students who fail to respond to this first line of instruction can then be evaluated in a timely manner for more intense and more skilled intervention. With training in effective research-based instruction and well-designed curricula, paraprofessional tutors can help accelerate early reading skills for struggling readers. Paraprofessionals can be particularly effective in supplementing carefully chosen reading skills that often require extended practice opportunities, repetition, and overlearning. More careful consideration of the role that paraprofessionals can play in providing research-based tutoring may allow us to leave fewer at-risk children behind at the starting gate of learning to read.

REFERENCES

Al Otaiba, S., Schatschneider, C. and Silverman, E. (2005) 'Tutor-assisted intensive learning strategies in kindergarten: How much is enough', *Exceptionality*, 13: 195–208.

Allington, R. (2004) 'Setting the record straight', *Educational Leadership*, 61: 22–25.

Archer, A. (1981) *Decoding of multisyllable words by skill deficient fourth and fifth grade students*. Unpublished doctoral dissertation, University of Washington, Seattle.

Archer, A., Gleason, M. and Vachon, V. (2000) *REWARDS: Reading Excellence: Word Attack and Rate Development Strategies*. Longmont, CO: Sopris West.

Barr, R. (1984) 'Beginning reading instruction: From debate to reformation', in P.D. Pearson (ed.), *Handbook of Reading Research*. New York, NY: Longman. pp. 545–581.

Baydar, N., Brooks-Gunn, J. and Furstenberg, F. F. (1993) 'Early warning signs of functional illiteracy: Predictors in childhood and adolescence', *Child Development*, 64: 815–829.

Berninger, V. W. (1998) *Process Assessment of the Learner (PAL): Guides for Intervention and PAL Intervention Kit.* San Antonio, TX: The Psychological Corporation.

Bowey, J.A. (1995) 'Socioeconomic status differences in preschool phonological sensitivity and first-grade reading achievement', *Journal of Educational Psychology*, 87: 476–487.

Bursuck, W.D., Munk, D.D., Nelson, C. and Curran, M. (2002) 'Research on the prevention of reading problems: Are kindergarten and first grade teachers listening?', *Preventing School Failure*, 47: 4–9.

Bus, A.G. and van IJzendoorn, M.H. (1999) 'Phonological awareness and early reading: A meta-analysis of experimental training studies', *Journal of Educational Psychology*, 91: 403–414.

Carey, K. (2003) *The Funding Gap: Low-Income and Minority Students Receive Fewer Dollars in Many States.* Washington, DC: The Education Trust.

Cohen, P., Kulik, J. and Kulik, C. (1982) 'Educational outcomes of tutoring: A meta-analysis of findings', *American Educational Research Journal*, 19: 237–248.

Cunningham, A. (1990) 'Explicit vs. implicit instruction in phonemic awareness', *Journal of Experimental Child Psychology*, 50: 429–444.

Denton, C.A. and Fletcher, J.M. (2003) 'Scaling reading interventions', in B.R. Foorman (ed.), *Preventing and Remediating Reading Difficulties: Bringing Science to Scale.* Timonium, MD: York Press. pp. 445–463.

Dixon, R., Carnine, D. and Kame'enui, E.J. (1992) 'Math curriculum guidelines for diverse learners', *Curriculum/Technology Quarterly*, 3: 1–3.

Dunn, L. M., Dunn, L. M. and Dunn, D. M. (1997) *Peabody Picture Vocabulary Test-IIIA* (Third Edition) Circle Pines, MN: American Guidance Service.

Elbaum, B., Vaughn, S., Hughes, M. and Moody, S. (2000) 'How effective are one-to-one tutoring programs in reading for elementary students at risk for reading failure? A meta-analysis of the intervention research', *Journal of Educational Psychology*, 92: 605–619.

Fill, M., Gips, M. and Hosty, K. (1998) 'The Phono-Graphix method for teaching reading and spelling', *The Clinical Connection*, 11: 4.

Foorman, B. R. and Torgesen, J. (2001) 'Critical elements of classroom and small-group instruction promote reading success in all children', *Learning Disabilities Research and Practice*, 16: 203–212.

Friedman, D.E. and Medway, F.J. (1987) 'Effects of varying performance sets and outcome on the expectations, attributions, and persistence of boys with learning disabilities', *Journal of Learning Disabilities*, 20: 312–316.

Fuchs, D., Fuchs, L.S., Thompson, A., Al Otaiba, S., Yen, L., Yang, N.J., Braun, M. and O'Connor, R.E. (2001) 'Is reading important in reading-readiness programs? A randomized field trial with teachers as program implementers', *Journal of Educational Psychology*, 93: 251–267.

Gambrell, L.B., Wilson, R.M. and Gantt, W.N. (1981) 'Classroom observations of task-attending behaviors of good and poor readers', *Journal of Educational Research*, 24: 400–404.

Gersten, R., Chard, D. and Baker, S. (2000) 'Factors enhancing sustained use of research-based instructional practices', *Journal of Learning Disabilities*, 33: 445–457.

Good, R.H. and Kaminski, R.A. (2002) *Dynamic Indicators of Basic Early Literacy Skills* (DIBELS: Sixth Edition) Eugene, OR: Institute for the Development of Educational Achievement.

Gunn, B.K., Simmons, D.C. and Kameenui, E.J. (1998) 'Emergent literacy: Research bases', in D.C. Simmons and E. J. Kameenui (eds), *What Reading Research Tells us about Children with Diverse Learning Needs: Bases and Basics.* Mahwah, NJ: Erlbaum. pp. 2–50.

Hart, B. and Risley, T.F. (2003) 'The early catastrophe: The 30 million word gap', *American Educator*, 27: 4–9.

Hasbrouck, J.E., Ihnot, C. and Rogers, G.H. (1999) '"Read Naturally": A strategy to increase oral reading fluency', *Reading Research and Instruction*, 39: 27–38.

Institute of Education Sciences (2003) *Identifying and implementing educational practices supported by rigorous evidence.* Washington, DC: U.S. Department of Education. Available: www.ed.gov/rschstat/research/pubs/rigorousevid/index.html.

Jastak, S. and Wilkinson, G. S. (1984) *The Wide Range Achievement Test-Revised.* Wilmington, DE: Jastak Associates.

Jenkins, J., Peyton, J., Sanders, E. and Vadasy, P. (2004) 'Effects of decodable texts in supplemental first grade tutoring', *Scientific Studies of Reading*, 8: 53–85.

Juel, C. (1996) 'What makes literacy tutoring effective?', *Reading Research Quarterly*, 31: 268–289.

Juel, C. (1988) 'Learning to read and write: A longitudinal study of 54 children from first through fourth grades', *Journal of Education Psychology*, 80: 437–447.

Kameenui, E.J. and Carnine, D. (eds) (1998) *Effective Teaching Strategies that Accommodate Diverse Learners*. Columbus, OH: Merrill-Prentice Hall.

Klingner, J., Vaughn, S., Hughes, M. and Arguelles, M. (1999) 'Sustaining research-based practices in reading: A 3-year follow-up', *Remedial and Special Education*, 20: 263–74, 263–274.

Lee, V.E. and Burkam, D.T. (2002) *Inequality at the Starting Gate: Social Background Differences in Achievement as Children Begin School*. Washington, DC: Economic Policy Institute.

McGuinness, C., McGuinness, D. and McGuinness, G. (1996) 'Phono-Graphix: A new method for remediation of reading difficulties', *Annals of Dyslexia*, 46: 73–96.

Mercer, C.D., Campbell, K.U., Miller, M.D., Mercer, K.D. and Lane, H.B. (2000) 'Effects of a reading fluency intervention for middle schoolers with specific learning disabilities', *Learning Disabilities Research and Practice*, 15: 179–189.

Moats, L. (1999) *Teaching Reading is Rocket Science*. Washington, DC: American Federation of Teachers.

Moats, L. (1995) 'The missing foundation in teacher preparation', *American Educator*, 19: 43–51.

National Reading Panel. (2000) *Teaching Children to Read: An Evidence-based Assessment of the Scientific Research Literature on Reading and its Implications for Reading Instruction*. Washington, DC: National Institute of Child Health and Human Development.

Nicholson, T. (1997) 'Closing the gap on reading failure: Social background, phonemic awareness and learning to read', in B.A. Blachman (ed.), *Foundations of Reading Acquisition and Dyslexia: Implications for Early Intervention*. Mahwah, NJ: Lawrence Erlbaum. pp. 381–408.

Nolen, P., McCutchen, D. and Berninger, V. (1990) 'Ensuring tomorrow's literacy: A shared responsibility', *Journal of Teacher Education*, 41: 63–72.

Pianta, R. (2006) 'Teacher-child relationships and early literacy', in D. Dickinson and S. Neuman (eds), *Handbook of Early Literacy, Volume 2*. New York: Guilford Press. pp. 149–162.

Rashotte, C.A., MacPhee, K. and Torgesen, J.K. (2001) 'The effectiveness of a group reading instruction program with poor readers in multiple grades', *Learning Disability Quarterly*, 24: 119–134.

Rosenshine, B. and Stevens, R. (1984) 'Classroom instruction in reading', in D. Pearson (ed.), *Handbook of Research on Reading*. New York: Longman. pp. 745–798.

Roza, M. and Hill, P. (2003) *How Within-District Spending Inequities Help some Schools Fail*. Seattle, WA: Center on Reinventing Public Education, University of Washington.

Samuels, S.J. (1988) 'Decoding and automaticity: Helping poor readers become automatic at word recognition', *The Reading Teacher*, 41: 756–760.

Santi, K., Menchetti, B. and Edwards, B. (2004) 'A comparison of eight kindergarten phonemic awareness programs based on empirically validated instructional principles', *Remedial and Special Education*, 25: 189–196.

Share, D.L., Jorm, A.F., MacLean, R. and Matthews, R. (1984) 'Sources of individual differences in reading acquisition', *Journal of Educational Psychology*, 76: 1309–24.

Shaywitz, S. (2003) *Overcoming Dyslexia: A New and Complete Science-based Program for Reading Problems at any Level*. New York: Alfred A. Knopf.

Shaywitz, S. and Shaywitz, B. (2004) 'Reading disability and the brain', *Educational Leadership*, 61: 6–11.

Simmons, D., Kameenui, E., Stoolmiller, M., Coyne, M. and Harn, B. (2003) 'Accelerating growth and maintaining proficiency: A two-year intervention study of kindergarten and first-grade children at risk for reading difficulties', in B. Foorman (ed.), *Preventing and Remediating Reading Difficulties: Bringing Science to Scale*. Baltimore, MD: York Press. pp. 197–228.

Snow, C.E., Burns, M.S. and Griffin, P. (eds) (1998) *Preventing Reading Difficulties in Young Children*. Washington, DC: National Academy Press.

Stanovich, K.E. (1986) 'Matthew effects in reading: Some consequences of individual differences in the acquisition of literacy', *Reading Research Quarterly*, 21: 360–407.

Stanovich, K.E. (1980) 'Toward an interactive-compensatory model of individual differences in the development of reading fluency', *Reading Research Quarterly*, 16: 32–71.

Stedman, L.C. and Kaestle, C.E. (1987) 'Literacy and reading performance in the United States from 1880 to the present', *Reading Research Quarterly*, 22: 8–46.

Stevenson, H.W. and Newman, R.S. (1986) 'Long-term prediction of achievement and attitudes in mathematics and reading', *Child Development*, 57: 646–659.

Tangel, D. M. and Blachman, B. A. (1992) 'Effect of phoneme awareness instruction on kindergarten children's invented spelling', *Journal of Reading Behavior*, 24: 233–261.

Torgesen, J.K. (2002) 'Lessons learned from intervention research in reading: A way to go before we rest', *British Journal of Educational Psychology: Learning and Teaching in Reading*, 1, 89–104.

Torgesen, J. K., Wagner, R. K. and Rashotte, C. A. (1999) *Test of Word Reading Efficiency*. Austin, TX: PRO–ED.

Torgesen, J., Wagner, R., Rashotte, C., Alexander, A. and Conway, T. (1997) 'Preventive and remedial interventions for children with severe reading disabilities', *Learning Disabilities: An Interdisciplinary Journal*, 8: 51–62.

Tramontana, M.G., Hooper, S. and Seltzer, S.C. (1988) 'Research on preschool predication of later academic achievement: A review', *Developmental Review*, 8: 89–146.

Tunmer, W.E., Herriman, M.L. and Nesdale, A.R.(1988) 'Metalinguistic abilities and beginning reading', *Reading Research Quarterly*, 23: 134–158.

Vachon, V. (1998) *Effects of mastery of multisllabic word reading component skills and of varying practice contexts on word and text reading skills of middle school students with reading deficiencies*. Unpublished doctoral dissertation, University of Oregon, Eugene.

Vadasy, P. F., Jenkins, J. R., Antil, L. R., Wayne, S. K. and O'Connor, R. E. (1997a) 'Community-based early reading intervention for at-risk first graders', *Learning Disabilities Research and Practice*, 12: 29–39.

Vadasy, P. F., Jenkins, J. R., Antil, L. R., Wayne, S. K. and O'Connor, R. E. (1997b) 'The effectiveness of one-to-one tutoring by community tutors for at-risk beginning readers', *Learning Disability Quarterly*, 20: 126–139.

Vadasy, P. F., Jenkins, J. R. and Pool, K. (2000) 'Effects of tutoring in phonological and early reading skills on students at risk for reading disabilities', *Journal of Learning Disabilities*, 33: 579–590.

Vadasy, P.F., Sanders, E.A. and Abbott, R.D. (2008) 'Effects of supplemental early reading interventions at 2-year follow up: Reading skill growth patterns and predictors', *Scientific Studies of Reading*, 12: 51–89.

Vadasy, P.F. and Sanders, E.A. (in press) 'Code-oriented instruction for kindergarten students at risk for reading difficulties: A replication and comparison of instructional groupings', *Reading and Writing: An International Journal*.

Vadasy, P.F., Sanders, E.A. and Peyton, J.A. (2006) 'Code-oriented instruction for kindergarten students at risk for reading difficulties: A randomized field trial with paraeducator implementers', *Journal of Educational Psychology*, 98: 508–528.

Vadasy, P. F., Sanders, E. A. and Peyton, J. A. (2005) 'Relative effectiveness of reading practice or word-level instruction in supplemental tutoring: How text matters', *Journal of Learning Disabilities*, 38: 364–380.

Vadasy, P. F., Sanders, E. A., Peyton, J. A. and Jenkins, J. R. (2002) 'Timing and intensity of tutoring: A closer look at the conditions for effective early literacy tutoring', *Learning Disabilities Research and Practice*, 17: 227–241.

Vadasy, P. F., Wayne, S. K., O'Connor, R. E., Jenkins, J. R., Pool, K., Firebaugh, M. and Peyton, J. A. (2004) *Sound Partners: A Supplementary, One-to-One Tutoring Program in Phonics-based Early Reading Skills*. Longmont, CO: Sopris West.

Vellutino, F.R., Scanlon, D.M., Sipay, E.D., Small, S.G., Pratt, A., Chen, R. and Denckla, M.B. (1996) 'Cognitive profiles of difficult-to-remediate and readily remediated poor readers: Early intervention as a vehicle for distinguishing between cognitive and experiential deficits as basic causes of specific reading disability', *Journal of Educational Psychology*, 88: 601–638.

Wagner, R., Torgesen, J. K. and Rashotte, C. A. (1999) *Comprehensive Test of Phonological Processing.* Austin, TX: Pro–Ed.

Walker, H.M. and Buckley, N.K. (1972) 'Programming generalization and maintenance of treatment effects across time and across settings', *Journal of Applied Behavior Analysis*, 5: 209–224.

Wasik, B. A. (1998) 'Volunteer tutoring programs in reading: A review', *Reading Research Quarterly*, 33: 266–292.

Wasik, B. and Slavin, R. (1993) 'Preventing early reading failure with one-to-one tutoring: A review of five programs', *Reading Research Quarterly*, 28: 179–200.

Woodcock, R. (1987, 1998) *Woodcock Reading Mastery Test-Revised/Normative Update.* Circle Pines, MN: American Guidance Service.

Dyslexia Friendly Primary Schools: What can We Learn From Asking the Pupils?

Mary Coffield, Barbara Riddick,
Patrick Barmby, and Jenny O'Neill

This chapter

i) draws together the views of primary school pupils on the 'dyslexia friendliness' of their classroom teachers;

ii) discusses the implications of the pupils' responses in relation to the development of school policy and practice; and

iii) discusses the usefulness of using a questionnaire as a means of consulting pupils.

INTRODUCTION

An important part of developing and evaluating dyslexia friendly practice is listening to the pupils these practices are designed to support. This study draws together the views of a sample of primary pupils from one Local Authority on the 'dyslexia friendliness' of their classroom teachers. The schools concerned had all taken part in the county's project on dyslexia friendly schools and pupils' views were collected by means of a questionnaire, developed in consultation between local authority staff and a member of the school of education at a neighbouring university. The implications of the pupils' responses in relation to the development of school policy and practice are discussed along with the usefulness of using a questionnaire as a means of consulting pupils.

BACKGROUND

The project to help schools develop 'dyslexia friendly' practices began in 2003. It drew on the earlier experiences of Swansea LEA in the late 1990s, reported in the British Dyslexia Association's Dyslexia Friendly Schools resource pack which has since been updated several times (BDA, 2005). The project was run jointly by the County's Learning Support and Education Psychology Services (LSS and EPS), and involved approximately 17 per cent of the mainstream schools. 37 primary (16 per cent) and 9 secondary (25 per cent) schools took part over a two-year period. Since the project started, the British Dyslexia Association (BDA) has launched a national quality mark procedure and, more recently, the DfES (2005) in collaboration with SureStart has provided advice to schools on 'learning and teaching for dyslexic children'.

Key staff from the project schools identified many positive benefits from taking part in the project, including their raised awareness of the range of difficulties pupils might encounter in their classrooms and their increased confidence in finding ways to help pupils to overcome, or at least reduce, the impact of these difficulties. However, there was no information from the pupils themselves about the impact of the project on them. A questionnaire was therefore designed, the main aim of which was to find out if pupils were aware of 'dyslexia friendly' practices, resources and strategies being used in their classrooms and if they found these helpful. Questions were also asked that related to pupil confidence and self-esteem. The questionnaire was developed by the project leaders in consultation with university staff and was piloted and amended before being used in the project schools.

All 17 of the primary schools involved in the second year of the project were invited to identify a group of approximately 6 pupils to complete the questionnaires. 10 schools agreed to do this. In addition a further 8 out of the 20 schools that had been part of the first year of the project were invited to take part. They were selected because they had attended course sessions regularly, and had contributed resources and materials for use in county conferences. Overall just under half of the primaries that had taken part in the project (49 per cent) agreed to select pupils for the questionnaire. A small number of secondary schools also selected groups to complete the questionnaires but as they constituted such a small proportion of the secondary schools in the county (3 schools, 8 per cent of the total secondary schools), their responses have not been included in this report.

As dyslexia friendly strategies are said to be effective for a much wider range of pupils than those just with dyslexia (see for example Riddick et al., 2002), school staff were asked to identify two higher, two middle and two lower achieving pupils, ideally from the same class within Key Stage 2, to complete the questionnaires. They were asked to include pupils who had been identified (either formally or informally in school) as having indicators of dyslexia but in practice the groups also included pupils with different types of special educational needs and some with no special needs. In all, 93 KS2 pupils and 11 KS1 pupils completed questionnaires as indicated in Table 16.1.

Table 16.1   Breakdown of questionnaires completed

Year Group	Number of questionnaires completed			
	Total	Dyslexia	SEN	No SEN or Dyslexia
Year 2	11	4	0	7
Year 3	14	10	0	4
Year 4	28	9	2	17
Year 5	37	13	4	20
Year 6	14	7	2	5
Total	**104**	**43**	**8**	**53**

The questionnaire itself was based on a schools' audit document contained in existing county guidance. For the majority of questions and statements pupils were given the option of choosing between four different levels of agreement – usually, sometimes, occasionally and never. There were also some questions that were left open for pupils to write or dictate their own views. The questionnaires were administered to each of the groups of pupils by project workers who were members of the LSS or EPS as it was not considered appropriate for class teachers or SENCOs to collect potentially sensitive information about their own practices from pupils. Pupils were assured that their responses would remain confidential. In order to accommodate reading difficulties the questions were read to all the respondents and where appropriate, written answers were scribed for the pupils.

In addition to asking the pupils about specific classroom practices, the questionnaire also included statements about pupils' enjoyment of school and how they felt in class (e.g. I enjoy school; I like reading; I get enough time to copy things down; My teacher often praises me). Pupils were asked whether they agreed, disagreed or were neutral about these statements. Their responses were coded numerically (agree = 2, neutral = 1 and disagree = 0). The data from nine different statements were combined together to give an overall measure for the attitude of pupils towards their classroom learning.

The unidimensionality of the measure was checked using factor analysis to confirm that it provided a coherent measure of attitude. The statistical reliability of the measure was also checked, a Cronbach alpha value of 0.73 being above the recommended value of 0.7. In this study, this measure of attitude was used in order to try to identify classroom practices that improved pupils' attitude towards classroom learning. This was done by examining the extent to which the attitude measure correlated with pupils' responses with regards to classroom practices. More positive correlations between attitude measure and classroom practice statements were used to identify more important classroom practices regarding dyslexia.

PUPILS' VIEWS

The data were also analysed in accordance with the teachers' categorisation of the pupils as having indicators of dyslexia, some other special educational need or no special educational needs. According to the pupils with dyslexia, the most common ways that teachers provided support for them were:

- reading important information out to the whole class rather than expecting all pupils to be able to read it independently (65 per cent);
- providing support materials such as word mats, alphabet strips, special dictionaries, and table squares (57 per cent);
- being prepared to repeat instructions (53 per cent);
- making work sheets easy to follow by highlighting important information (45 per cent).

These strategies were also identified by pupils without dyslexia in similar proportions. However, this still leaves 35–55 per cent of pupils in classes where these basic strategies do not appear to be being employed on a regular basis. Therefore, while it is encouraging to find that 65 per cent of pupils with dyslexia felt confident that they would not have to read out loud in class unless they wanted to, this still leaves 35 per cent of pupils with dyslexia potentially facing the daily humiliation of having their poor or faltering reading skills exposed to their peers. This state of affairs does not appear to be unique to this study. Humiliation in front of the class was also one of the key features of poor teaching identified by Johnson (2004).

Just over half the pupils with dyslexia (54 per cent) agreed with the statement 'I get lots of red marks in my exercise books', which suggests that there is still some way to go towards establishing sympathetic marking systems for pupils whose spelling difficulties should perhaps be accommodated in a more positive way. A further 21 per cent of the dyslexic pupils said they did not have time to write their homework down and they were nearly twice as likely as their non-dyslexic peers to perceive teachers as being more likely to get cross if they brought the wrong equipment to lessons. Overall this suggests a continued lack of understanding of common difficulties associated with dyslexia (even among staff that had received training on this) and a degree of failure to establish systems to respond to pupils' difficulties in a sympathetic and supportive way.

Those teachers who were using 'dyslexia friendly approaches' in their classrooms tended to focus more on making sure that tasks were introduced and explained clearly and on providing support materials to help pupils write their own answers rather than looking at ways to assist pupils with the writing process itself. This is illustrated by the fact that one of the least common activities for children with and without dyslexia was 'working with a partner who writes down my ideas for me'. It is perhaps not surprising therefore, that 32 per cent of pupils with dyslexia said they did not have time to finish their written work in class.

When it came to tests, however, 68 per cent of pupils with dyslexia and 60 per cent of those without said that they did have someone to read questions and/or write their answers. While one wonders how well they could adapt to working with a scribe in tests if they had little experience of this in their normal class work, it is interesting to note that having someone to help with reading or writing in tests seemed to be strongly correlated with positive pupil feelings. The more positive the pupils felt, the less likely they were to avoid using difficult words in their own writing.

In addition to responding to specific statements, pupils were asked to identify 'One thing that really helps me…' in class. Overall 106 comments were made. There were some individual responses from pupils with dyslexia that were not replicated in the overall group. For example, one pupil said that he preferred to sit by himself; another said spelling tests were helpful. One pupil identified a particular structured reading programme and another named a computer spelling programme. Two pupils identified using their coloured overlays.

The three highest scoring responses from the combined groups of pupils to this sentence starter were:

- asking the teacher or getting help from the teacher (43 responses);
- access to supportive resources in the classroom (such as word books, special dictionaries, alphabet strips and number fans (24 responses);
- working with a friend or partner (21 responses).

This pattern was mirrored to a certain extent by the pupils with dyslexia. Of the 36 responses received from this group of pupils, 13 identified teacher help and 11 identified access to supportive resources in the classroom. However, only 4 mentioned working with a friend while 3 identified working on computers.

It is worth looking at these responses in a little more detail as getting help from the teacher was identified by many pupils, both with and without dyslexia. The biggest group of pupils to complete the questionnaires was from Y5 so it is perhaps not surprising that the majority of pupils who identified teacher help were from this age group. Although slightly more middle and low achieving pupils within this group identified teacher help (17 and 16 respectively), a significant number of high achieving pupils without dyslexia or any form of SEN also felt they benefited from teacher help (10 pupils in all).

At face value, these responses could be interpreted as confirming the positive impact of teachers' willingness to help individual pupils. To an extent this mirrors the responses from pupils in Johnson's (2004) study where key characteristic of good teachers included being kind and helpful, patient and approachable. In some cases in the current study further information was provided by the pupils detailing the exact nature of their teachers' positive roles. For example, one middle achieving pupil wrote 'the teacher because she always reads out things. She's kind and she's helpful'. Similarly a low achieving pupil valued the fact that 'The teacher reads to me'.

Johnson (2004) summarised what pupils with dyslexia needed as, 'teachers who are clear and concise, pleasant with their classes and prepared to recognise that not everyone understands the first time' (2004: 248). However, there is a less favourable interpretation of the reliance of some of the pupils in the current study on teacher help. Where all pupils in a class identified the teacher as their major source of help, this could signify over-reliance on teacher help because lessons were insufficiently differentiated to enable pupils to work independently.

By contrast, one could form the hypothesis that schools where pupils identified other forms of help, such as availability of a range of supportive classroom resources, might well be more dyslexia friendly because they provided the support structure to help pupils to work independently. Indeed in one school that has since gone on to work towards a county standard for Dyslexia Friendly Schools, all of the pupils identified specific resources that helped them such as a handwriting pen, a special dictionary, a spelling programme or special computer programme. All these pupils responded positively to statements such as 'I am doing the best school work that I can', 'I am happy at school most of the time' and 'I am proud of my work'. None of these pupils worried about school.

In addition to being asked to identify one thing they really liked, pupils were also asked to write down one thing they 'really hated'. The biggest number of responses from the whole group to this sentence came from 10 pupils who identified forms of bullying (hitting, being picked on etc.). Five pupils commented negatively about teachers shouting and a further 5 commented on teachers getting cross or bossy. Johnston (2004) similarly found that a third of the pupils he interviewed complained about teachers' shouting.

A number of pupils identified specific subjects that they disliked. Interestingly there was considerable variation in their choices. Maths was the subject that was singled out the most (6 votes). Predictably literacy and spelling received 3 and 4 votes respectively but surprisingly science received 5 votes with geography and history both getting 2 votes.

Again this pattern was mirrored to some extent by the 25 comments from the pupils with dyslexia. Four pupils identified bullying and 6 pupils singled out teachers either shouting or getting cross. However the biggest response (14 in all) from the pupils with dyslexia related to difficulties with individual subjects. Again these were dominated by spelling, numeracy and writing. However other subjects such as science were again highlighted and it would have been interesting to know whether it was the subject itself or the prospect of writing up the results of experiments that was causing the difficulty.

FINAL COMMENTS

It is difficult to draw general conclusions about the dyslexia friendliness or otherwise of schools based on the views of a very small sample of pupils (approximately 20 per cent of one class or year group within a school) on one or two teachers within the school. Therefore, there is no guarantee that examples of beneficial or less helpful practice identified by the pupils are a true representation of practice within their own schools as a whole. Investigation into other aspects of 'dyslexia-friendliness' such as the development of reliable systems for the early identification of pupils and the provision of high quality literacy interventions for targeted groups or individuals is beyond the scope of this study.

However, putting these limitations to one side for the moment, there were some very positive outcomes from asking the pupils for their views. The majority of pupils were able to identify some aspects of classroom practice that they found beneficial. These included teachers reading out information to the whole class, the provision of cue cards and other support materials, the use of readers and scribes in examinations and, in some cases, the possibility of working with a partner. Pupils clearly valued the help they generally received from their teachers and other adults in their classrooms. However, this should not be at the expense of differentiated lessons to enable pupils to work independently.

On the other hand, the number of pupils that still perceive their teachers as being unhelpful, and at times insensitive, is a matter of concern, as is the number of pupils that brought up the negative effects of teachers shouting. If nearly one-third of the pupils in this study did not feel confident that they would not be asked to read out loud in class unless they wanted to, what would the response be from pupils in classes where teachers had not attended courses on dyslexia friendly approaches? In particular, teachers need to make sure that pupils are not put off subjects that they traditionally do well in (such as science) because their teaching styles does not take account of the pupils' difficulties in reading, writing and spelling. It would seem that lack of understanding of dyslexia leading to an unsympathetic approach to pupils and an unsupportive classroom environment is still a common occurrence in our classrooms. Too many pupils are still having to face potentially stressful situations such as being asked to read aloud in class, being given insufficient time to write down their homework and having their written work covered in corrections and negative comments.

The number of new proposals thrust on schools by national and local governments is frightening and can result in schools become bogged down by an 'alphabet soup of initiatives' (Johnson, 2004: 254). Given this situation, one might be forgiven for asking why schools should be volunteering to take on another initiative in the form of the dyslexia friendly schools movement. One very good reason would be a causal link between dyslexia friendly approaches and raised pupil attainment. Several authors have made such a claim (e.g. Mackay, 2003) but in practice direct links between teaching approaches and pupil outcomes are extremely difficult to establish.

The recent debate over the role of learning styles serves as a salutary warning against making claims that cannot be easily verified (Coffield, 2005). The study reminds us that that there are no simple solutions to the complex problems of teaching and learning. There could be any number of influential factors contributing to a pupil's improved scores, say, in SATs tests or later in GCSE exam results. While dyslexia friendly approaches may form part of the equation, other influential factors include ability of pupil, motivation, amount of time spent revising, ability to sit exams, attitude and subject knowledge of teacher, appropriate pedagogy, resources etc.

A number of authors have pointed out that as a group, pupils with dyslexia often have low academic self-esteem (see for example, Riddick et al., 2002; Humphrey, 2002; Burton, 2004). Therefore, one might argue that a more pressing reason for introducing dyslexia friendly practice would be to enhance self-esteem and confidence and to prevent pupils from becoming damaged learners.

However, it is again rather difficult to establish a direct causal link between events in the classroom and pupils' high or low self-esteem. The responses of the 43 pupils with dyslexia in this small study suggest that their self-esteem was neither consistently high nor low. Many dyslexic pupils responded positively to statements such as 'I am happy at school most of the time' (39 pupils), 'I am doing the best school work that I can' (41 pupils) and 'I am proud of my work' (34 pupils). Nevertheless, while 29 pupils agreed that they were as important as everybody else in the class, less than half of the pupils agreed with the statement 'My ideas are as good as everybody else's in the class' (37 per cent) and an even smaller number of 12 pupils agreed with the statement 'I think my work is as good as everybody else's in class' (28 per cent).

Perhaps a more encouraging reason for schools to develop dyslexia friendly practice is the hope that it might benefit a much wider group of pupils than just those with dyslexia. In this study, there were certainly more similarities than differences between the comments of the pupils with and without dyslexia, with many overlaps in their likes and dislikes. Does this mean that that good dyslexia friendly practice is largely indistinguishable from good professional practice?

If this is the case, can we conclude that it is the process of working towards a state of 'dyslexia friendliness' that is more important that the end result? Is it necessary or even appropriate to establish lengthy and perhaps costly bureaucratic procedures for formal accreditation of practice that is considered to be good for one group of pupils, when the national and local thrust is towards inclusion of pupils with a much wider range of special educational needs? How does the dyslexia-friendly schools movement fit with the DfES's Circles of Inclusion (DfES, 2005)? Here the setting of suitable learning challenges, responding to pupils' diverse needs and overcoming potential barriers to learning are all considered to be essential aspects of the provision of effective learning opportunities for *all* pupils, not just those with dyslexia.

The phrase 'dyslexia friendly' has a high appeal for policy makers, schools and parents alike. One advantage of working towards a formal accreditation such as a kite mark could be that it is likely to raise the status of that particular initiative, in this case giving dyslexia friendly classroom practice a central role rather than an optional bolt-on extra. However, for the accreditation to mean something more than the acquisition of another certificate for the staffroom wall, there needs to be a clear understanding of what standards of policy and practice are required to justify the term 'dyslexia-friendly' along with a clear plan for how such policy and practice will be maintained and developed. As Riddick (2006: 146) asks, 'Put quite simply, how friendly is friendly enough to adequately meet the needs of students with dyslexia?'

Even if dyslexia-friendly practice can be sufficiently defined, how many staff (teachers, support assistants, and classroom assistants) have to use such approaches for a school to be considered as dyslexia friendly? Will anything less than 100 per cent of staff be credible? What management conditions need to be in place to maintain this commitment? If a smaller percentage of staff is acceptable, say 75 per cent or even 90 per cent, what happens to pupils being taught by the 25 per cent or 10 per cent that are not dyslexia friendly. As Mackay (2003: 230) warns, 'a school that is accredited as dyslexia friendly but that does not deliver is likely to find itself and the LEA answering some very hard questions, perhaps in tribunal and possibly even in the courts.'

As Riddick points out, it remains to be seen if the dyslexia friendly schools movement is sustainable and able to make a major contribution to education policy and practice. Perhaps it will be a rallying and focusing call that co-ordinates and propels appropriate action', but the danger remains that it will merely be 'a pleasant and vague 'feel good term' that promises much and delivers little'? (2006: 151). Strong leadership from school governors, the head teacher, and senior management team, supported by local authority services, may help to promote the former position and would seem to be essential in ensuring that dyslexia friendly policy is fully understood and is translated into practice that can be established and maintained.

The development of 'dyslexia friendly standards' for all schools within a local authority (see Appendix 1 for an example) can provide a useful tool for school staff wishing to see where they stand in terms of dyslexia friendliness, by helping them to identify areas of strength and areas where further training is required. Completing this process at regular intervals can also play a part in helping staff and senior managers to monitor and evaluate their own perform-ance along with that of their pupils. Staff may wish to go on to look at approaches and support strategies recommended for pupils with other types of difficulties such as autism spectrum disorders or attention disorders in order to put together a menu of strategies and approaches that could, for example, contribute to the mapping of provision within individual schools that is currently recommended by the DfES.

However, care still needs to be taken to ensure that the needs of *individual* pupils are not overlooked. The difficulties a pupil with dyslexia experiences are not all the same. Teachers cannot assume that putting one or two strategies into place that are generally considered suitable for pupils with dyslexia will suffice when it comes to meeting the range of educational and emotional needs that these pupils might have. One size does not necessarily fit all.

It is clear from this study that what worked well for some pupils was much less effective for others. For example, one pupil was particularly upset because 'When Mr. X. walks past me he doesn't say that's good work' but two other pupils in the same class singled out getting attention (i.e., help) from the teacher as the thing they most disliked. There is a great deal to be learned from consulting individual pupils as part of a wider process of formative assessment with high-quality feedback.

A shortened version of the pupil questionnaire used in this study (Appendix 2) would be a useful tool for teachers to gain some insight from their pupils into what seems to be working well in the classroom and what needs further attention.

Above all we must strive to prevent significant groups of pupils becoming disaffected or disengaged before the end of primary education. Some pupils with dyslexia are in danger of falling into this category. In order to reduce the number of pupils affected in this way, Hargreaves suggests that:

'all young people should:

- View themselves as someone able to learn successfully,
- Understand learning and themselves as a learner,
- Leave school with a positive attitude to continued learning.' (2004: 82)

These three aims are as relevant for pupils with dyslexia as for everyone else. Teachers seeking to create learning environments that will help all pupils to develop the kind of positive concepts of themselves as learners that are outlined above are likely to be well on the way to establishing schools that are 'friendly' towards pupils with all manner of special educational needs including dyslexia. It is hoped that the pupil questionnaire developed for this study, will be used more widely in schools to contribute to this process of consultation.

REFERENCES

British Dyslexia Association (2005) *Achieving Dyslexia Friendly Schools*, 5th ed., Oxford: Information Press.

Burton, S. (2004) 'Self-esteem groups for secondary pupils with dyslexia', *Educational Psychology in Practice*, 20 (1): 55–73.

Coffield, F. J. (2005) *Learning Styles: Help or Hindrance?* London: Institute of Education, NSIN Research Matters, p. 26.

Department for Education and Science (2005) *Learning and Teaching for Dyslexic Children*, 1184-2005 CD, London: HMSO.

Hargreaves, D.H. (2004) *Learning for Life: The Foundations for Lifelong Learning.* Bristol: The Policy Press.

Humphrey, N. (2002) 'Teacher and pupil ratings of self-esteem in developmental dyslexia', *British Journal of Special Education*, 29 (1): 29–36.

Johnson, M. (2004) 'Dyslexia-friendly schools – policy and practice', in Reid, G. and Fawcett, A. (eds) *Dyslexia in Context: Research, Policy and Practice.* London: Wiley.

Mackay, N. (2003) *Achieving the Dyslexia Friendly School – The Hawarden* Approach, 5th BDA International Conference, BDA website.

Mackay, N. (2004) 'The case for dyslexia friendly schools', in Reid, G. and Fawcett, A. (eds) *Dyslexia in Context: Research, Policy and Practice*, London: Wiley.

Riddick, B. (2006) 'Dyslexia friendly schools in the UK', *Topics in Language Disorders*, 26 (1): 142–154.

Riddick, B., Wolfe, J. and Lumsdon, D. (2002) *Dyslexia: A Practical Guide for Teachers and Parents*, London: David Fulton.

APPENDIX 1
Curriculim access and resources

Curriculum access and resources		Evidence
Pupils have access to a comprehensive range of resources (such as personal word books, organisers, vocabulary lists, different types of dictionaries, electronic spell checkers, coloured overlays, cue cards, pencil grips, etc.) in order to develop their independent learning strategies.	Pupils have a wide range of resources in the classroom and are taught how to use these effectively.	4
	Pupils have access to some resources in the classroom.	3
	Teaching staff are aware that some pupils require classroom resources to aid independent working in the classroom and are beginning to make these available in the classroom. Pupils are rarely provided with resources to support independent learning strategies.	2
		1
Staff take measures to ensure that pupils with dyslexia have access to written material by taking account of readability of key texts and using a variety of ways to adapt reading materials such as taped books, encouraging use of word processors with speech feedback.	All staff actively make arrangements to ensure that class texts and other written materials are accessible for pupils.	4
	The majority of staff make arrangements to ensure that class texts and other written materials are accessible for pupils.	3
	A few staff make arrangements to ensure that some class texts and other written materials are accessible for pupils.	2
	Staff expect all pupils in their classes to read the same written material.	1
Pupils are offered alternatives to writing (such as drama, role play, mind mapping, creating posters and wall charts, use of a computer, highlighting,classifying and creating tables) to show their knowledge and understand of different subjects.	The majority of staff are aware that some pupils need access to a wide range of alternatives to written recording. Pupils are taught how to use these alternatives effectively.	4
	Some staff are aware that there are pupils who need access to a range of alternatives to written recording. Pupils are taught how to use these alternatives effectively.	3
	A few teaching staff are aware of alternatives to written recording and are beginning to try some of these with pupils.	2
	Pupils are rarely offered alternatives to written recording.	1
Where appropriate, pupils with dyslexia have regular access to technology to support learning such as word processing, software with a speech facility, tape recorders, calculators, spreadsheets, digital cameras etc.	Pupils have access to technology during lessons and at other times during the school day to support their learning.	4
	Pupils sometimes have access to technology during lessons and at other times during the school day.	3
	Pupils have limited access to technology at other times during the school day.	2
	Pupils have little access to technology except in designated technology teaching sessions.	1
Staff are sensitive to particular difficulties associated with dyslexia (such as lengthy copying, writing from dictation or reading aloud in class) and make adjustments so that, where possible, pupils with dyslexia are not required to do these things.	All staff ensure that copying and dictation are kept to a minimum. Pupils are not asked to read aloud in class unless they want to.	4
	The majority of staff ensure that copying and dictation are reduced. Pupils are not usually asked to read aloud unless they want to.	3
	Some staff are aware of the need to reduce the volume of copying and dictation and are beginning to do this in their lessons. Pupils are rarely asked to read aloud in class unless they want to.	2
	Staff expect pupils to do the same amount of copying and writing from dictation as the rest of the class. Pupils may be asked to read out loud in class.	1

The school has appropriate homework and marking policies ensuring that pupils have an accurate record of the homework set. The amount of homework may be adjusted for individual pupils and content is marked as well as presentation (handwriting, spelling, etc).	School homework and marking policies as described are in place.	4
	School homework and marking policies are in place but do not include reference to the amount of home-work set or marking for content as well as presentation.	3
	The Governing Body and senior managers are considering the need to incorporate the features described into their homework and marking policies.	2
	There are no plans to revise homework and marking policies to include the features descsribed.	1
There is an expectation that all staff will follow the homework and marking policies as described above.	All staff ensure that the school's homework and marking policies are applied and take steps to ensure that pupil has an accurate record of homework set. There is differentiation in the way that homework is set and marked.	4
	The majority of staff take account of the school's homework and marking policies and take steps to ensure that every pupil has an accurate record of homework set. There is some differentiation in the way that homework is set and marked.	3
	A few staff take account of the school's homework and marking policies. There is some differentiation in the way homework is set and marked.	2
	There is no differentiation in the way that homework is set and marked.	1
Pupils have the opportunity to access peer support (e.g., buddy systems) to help them work more independently.	Staff make regular use of peer support.	4
	Staff make some use of peer support.	3
	Staff are aware of peer systems and are beginning to introduce these in the classroom.	2
	Peer support is not used.	1

APPENDIX 2

Questionnaire for Pupils

We would like to know what you think about how your teachers help you to do your work in school. Please listen to each statement and put a tick in the box that shows how you feel about the following statements.

You will be asked to write your name and school at the end of the questionnaire. This is because we may want to ask some pupils if they can tell us a bit more about what they have written. You do not have to tell us any more if you don't want to. Everything that you write on these sheets is confidential. This means that your teachers and parents will not know what you have written unless you give your permission and want to tell them.

How do you feel?	Agree	Sometimes	Disagree
1 I enjoy school.	☺	☺	☹
2 I get enough time to copy things down.	☺	☺	☹
3 My teacher often praises me.	☺	☺	☹
4 I get help with my spelling.	☺	☺	☹
5 My teacher thinks I am good at things.	☺	☺	☹
6 I am as important as everybody else in the class.	☺	☺	☹
7 My ideas are as good as everybody else's in the class.	☺	☺	☹
8 I get told off for bad spelling.	☹	☺	☺
9 I get told off for bad handwriting.	☹	☺	☺
10 I often avoid words I can't spell when I am writing.	☹	☺	☺
11 My work is often put on show where everyone can see it.	☺	☺	☹
12 I have time to finish my written work in class.	☺	☺	☹
13 I have time to write homework down.	☺	☺	☹
14 I have the right equipment for lessons.	☺	☺	☹
15 I think I spend twice as long on my homework as other people in my class.	☹	☺	☺

Accessing the curriculum	Usually	Sometimes	Never
16 I work with a partner who writes down my ideas for me.			
17 Teachers repeat instructions if I have forgotten.			
18 Teachers read important information out to the whole class so that I don't have to try to read it by myself.			
19 Teachers take marks off if I make spelling mistakes.			
20 There are helpful things for me to use in class, like words on bookmarks, word mats, a special dictionary, alphabet strips or tables squares.			
21 Teachers give me writing frames to help me with my writing.			
22 I use special software on the school computers to help me with my writing and spelling			
23 I know that I don't have to read out loud in class unless I want to.			
24 I am doing the best school work that I can.			
25 I am happy at school most of the time.			
26 I worry a lot about school.			
27 I am proud of my work.			
28 One thing that really helps me is			

29 One thing I really hate is ....

My name is _____

I go to _____ school.

Thank you for taking the time to complete this questionnaire.

Dyslexia and Learning Styles: Overcoming the Barriers to Learning

Gavin Reid and Iva Strnadova

This chapter

i) explores how the use of learning styles in the classroom can assist in overcoming the barriers to learning that can be experienced by students with dyslexia;

ii) indicates how learning styles can provide guidance on planning lessons and classroom teaching; and

iii) provides insights into how children learn.

Children with dyslexia can be particularly vulnerable throughout the different stages of the learning process. It is important therefore to recognise that learning styles are not limited to how materials are presented, but incorporates the complete learning experience. The learning environments, as well as cognitive processes, need to be considered in addition to planning for learning and developing curriculum objectives. Knowledge of learning styles and children's particular learning preferences are important.

It is appreciated that the research in learning styles is controversial and inconclusive. Studies critical of learning styles (Coffield, 2005) cite flawed research designs, the use of ambiguous self-report instruments and the lack of evidence that matching learning styles to intervention has the impact on learning that is claimed by many of the supporters of learning styles. While there is some substance to these claims, the important issue which is often overlooked is that learning styles can promote self awareness of learning and in particular the learning process. Moreover it encourages teachers to think in terms of the quality of the learning experience they are providing for the learner. Arguably it may also lead to more innovative and more appropriate teaching (Reid and Strnadova, 2006). It is important therefore to view learning styles and dyslexia within this perspective.

Learning styles relate to the learning experience. This involves the task and how it is presented, the outcome – that is how performance is assessed and the nature and structure of the learning environment. These all relate to learning styles and the learning experience.

LEARNING THEORY

There are a number of different theoretical perspectives on how children learn and there are many competing views on learning strategies and particularly how these strategies should be applied in practice. There are however some points of general consensus and importance. These include the following:

- leaning is a process;
- learning requires a period of consolidation;
- learning is more effective when the content is familiar;
- over learning in different contexts and over time enhances the chances of retention and understanding;
- intrinsic (within child) as well as extrinsic (environmental) factors can influence learning and
- learning is a life-long process.

Yet despite these general points there are points of controversy. These include for example the view that:

- specific styles of learning should be used for certain types of information;
- each person has their own style – their own learning fingerprint and
- learning occurs in age-related stages.

These points above can be seen as controversial and each has been the subject of various comments and investigations by researchers and practitioners and will be discussed in this chapter.

LEARNING NEEDS

It is important to place learning styles within the context of learning needs. This implies that before effective learning can take place, it is necessary to ascertain the learner's specific needs. One of the strengths of using learning styles is that it is possible to individualise the programme of work using learning styles for a student. This is particularly important for students with dyslexia.

When engaging in learning, there are a number of criteria the student needs to consider. These include the need to:

- *understand* the task/information being presented;
- *recognise* what the task, or the information is suggesting;
- *identify* the key points in the task/information;
- *implement* the task /use the information;
- *become 'autonomous'* in accessing the information and carrying out the task;
- *be able to transfer* the new learning to other learning tasks.

These points are crucially important for learners with dyslexia as there is evidence that learners with dyslexia may have weaknesses in metacognitive awareness (Tunmer and Chapman, 1995). It is important, therefore, the role of learning and the learning process is given a high priority when planning interventions for students with dyslexia.

AUTONOMOUS LEARNING

The autonomous stage of learning is extremely important in the development of learning skills. Being an autonomous learner can be seen as a measure of how successfully the individual has understood the information being learnt and been able to apply his/her own strategies to the task. If the learning experience is successful then it is likely that the learner will be able to re-apply those strategies to other learning tasks. Fitts and Posner (1967) suggest that the 'autonomous' stage of learning occurs only after extensive practice. This practice involves the learner using the information and through this 'automaticity' in carrying out the task is achieved. At this autonomous stage, the learner often loses conscious awareness of how the task is done and it is carried out without too much conscious thought. Automaticity leads to the learner being able to transfer learnt skills to new learning situations. A crucial index of learning achievement is in fact the extent of the individual's ability to transfer learnt skills to new situations.

Nicolson and Fawcett (2004) suggest that this highlights the difference between 'controlled processing' that requires attentional control and uses up working memory capacity, and 'automatic processing that, once learned in long-term memory, operates independently of the individual's control and uses no working memory resources. Because the learner has control over the process, the learner can be coached and trained to use this process more effectively. Almost everyone has the potential to be trained to become an efficient learner. The learning process therefore needs to be personalised for each learner. This is important for learners with dyslexia as often they have a specific and unique style of learning and they may need to be coached in using and utilising their own style in their own way. Study skills can be helpful, but it is important that any strategy selected is personalised by the learner.

LEARNING AND SELF-ESTEEM

A positive self-esteem is crucial for learning as a positive self-esteem can provide the learner with confidence and motivation, enabling the learner to utilise metacognitive approaches to re-inforce learning (Reid, 2007). A learner with a low self-concept will very likely have a cautious approach to learning and will have an over reliance in the structure provided by the teacher. It is unlikely that such learners will develop a high metacognitive awareness as they will not have the confidence to become responsible for their own learning. It is important that students assume responsibility for their own learning and in time develop their own structures and eventually have the skills to assess their own competencies in tasks.

It is important that tasks, indeed all learning and learning experiences are directed to developing the student's self-esteem. In order to develop self-esteem, the learner must have some perception of success. It is obvious that if a learner is continually in a failure situation this will in turn have some influence on the learner's self-esteem. It is crucial therefore that tasks are developed to ensure that the learner will succeed. This may require tasks to be broken down into manageable units for the learner. This would ensure that the learner will achieve some early success when undertaking a task and this will provide motivation for subsequent learning. Lannen (2002) suggests that the principal priority in a school offering specialist provision for students with dyslexia is to boost self-esteem. Without this principal focus on self-esteem, effective learning will not progress irrespective of the programmes that are in use at the school.

IDENTIFYING LEARNING STYLES

Given and Reid (1999) suggest there are at least 100 instruments designed to identify individual learning styles. A recent study by Coffield et al. (2004) identified 70 learning styles instruments. Attempts have been made to categorise these instruments so that the background influences and psychological and cognitive perspectives can be made clearer. Given and Reid (1999) suggested these instruments usually focus on factors that are seen to be influential in the learning process. These factors include:

- modality preference: the preference for visual, auditory, tactual or kinesthetic input;
- personality types: such as intuitive, risk taking, cautious and reflective;
- social variables: including the need to work alone or with others;
- cognitive processes: such as memory, comprehension and methods of information processing; and
- movement and laterality; such as active learning and left and right hemispheric activities.

Coffield et al. (2004) attempted to group seventy learning styles instruments into some form of classification to make sense of the range of instruments and views that contribute to these models. They developed a continuum of models based on the extent the developers of these models believed that learning styles represented a fixed trait. At one end of the continuum Coffield et al. placed theorists who believed that learning styles were fixed by inherited traits, and at the other end they placed those theorists who focused more on personal factors such as motivation and environmental factors and also those who incorporated the influences of curriculum design and institutional and course culture.

At various points throughout the continuum Coffield et al. placed models that acknowledge external factors, particularly the immediate environment and models that are based on the idea of dynamic interplay between self and experience.

Following a scrutiny of the literature on learning styles (Strnadova and Reid, 2006) believe that the following categories can be used:

- personality styles;
- environmental factors;
- cognitive styles;
- metacognitive styles; and
- social styles.

Over and above those factors, all styles of learning are mediated by:

i) the learners culture;
ii) the classroom and school climate;
iii) teaching style;
iv) classroom dynamics and environment and
v) curriculum expectations.

LEARNING STYLES CRITIQUE

It needs to be stated that the research in learning styles in peer-reviewed journals is in the main highly critical of the concept of learning styles. The criticism rests on a number of key issues. These include:

- the lack of reliability in many of the learning styles instruments;
- the competing perspectives on what constitutes learning styles, even among supporters of the concept;
- the notion that it is impractical to adhere to the individual learning styles of all children in a class;
- the controversy whether matching individual learning styles to teaching style and teaching materials does actually produce more effective learning and
- the commercial element that often accompanies a particular leaning style's perspective. Usually, to implement a specific approach teachers need to attend a training workshop and purchase expensive materials.

As a result, learning styles do not have a sound image in the educational psychology literature. However, it is argued here that this is mainly due to a misunderstanding of the purposes and in particular the underlying conceptual understanding of learning styles, certainly as it is applied in the classroom situation. Many see learning styles as a fixed, perhaps genetically determined, trait like size and hair colour. Using this type of criteria it is not surprising that instruments do not stand up to scientific scrutiny. It is well known that environmental influences are very powerful in determining a young person's characteristics, both in terms of learning and behavioural factors. Learning styles is therefore no exception to those influences. Additionally, it needs to be recognised that many, indeed most, of the instruments measuring learning styles are based on self-report and the accuracy of the data relies on the respondents awareness and accuracy in identifying his/her own preferences. Some learners may not be able to identify their own preferences in this way. It is important therefore that identification of learning styles is supplemented through the use of interactional and observational data as well as through self-report responses.

IDENTIFYING LEARNING STYLES – SOME FACTORS

There are a number of factors that need to be considered in relation to the learning environment. These include the following:

- design;
- colour;
- wall displays;
- light;
- sound;
- visual and auditory distractions;
- space; and
- other learners in the same environment.

Reid and Strnadova (2004) translated the above observational framework into two instruments – one a self-report instrument aimed at students to help them identify their own learning preferences, the other focusing on the teachers, observation of the students learning preferences.

Reid and Strnadova 2004 have piloted these instruments with both primary and secondary students, and the responses from the teachers who implemented the piloting were promising indicating that the instruments provided information that could be used to implement teaching and learning materials to cater for the range of styles in most classrooms. The instrument has been refined three times following the piloting process and is in the form of a rating scale.

Examples of both instruments are shown in the appendix to this chapter. The information received from these two instruments will provide pointers for the identification of the learning preferences of the student and for the development of teaching approaches and can also help with classroom organisation and group work, particularly in deciding the composition of groups.

POINTERS FOR PRACTICE

Teachers who used the above instruments reported that they were able to accumulate information that proved to be relevant in planning and implementing interventions.

Some of the comments included:

- 'Seems to like other children around him';
- 'Lacks self-confidence';
- 'Likes to change different methods when learning';
- 'Problems in becoming part of group';
- 'Needs strong leadership';
- 'Places high demands on herself';
- 'Accepts failure with great difficulty';
- 'Does not promote himself'.

The teachers who used the instruments reported that it would help them in the following way. The learning styles instruments:

- 'Helped me to choose group leaders and to decide on the composition of groups';
- 'I had to ensure the environment was clam for the child';
- 'I had to change the group activities more frequently than I thought I might have to';
- 'Helped me to rearrange the layout of the classroom'.

LINKING ASSESSMENT WITH PRACTICE

The responses from a learning styles instrument should have practical implications for the teacher as well as for the learner. If there are thirty learners in a class then the teacher will have difficulty in catering for thirty different styles. It is almost certain, however, that there will not be thirty different styles and there will be some types of styles that the teacher can combine. For example, learners who are visual are often kinaesthetic and may also be global – meaning that they prefer to see the whole before the individual pieces of information - and prefer working in groups. This would mean that learners in this category will be able to access similar materials and respond effectively to similar teaching and learning approaches.

It can be suggested that students can become more independent in their learning as a result of knowing their strengths and weaknesses. Students therefore can develop more effective learning strategies which they can use outside the classroom.

Coffield et al. cite the views of Alexander (2000) who distinguishes between 'teaching' and 'pedagogy'; and they argue that the learning styles literature is principally concerned with teaching rather than pedagogy. They take this as evidence that teachers need to be cautious about using the learning styles literature as a guide to classroom practice and argue that there is a need to be highly selective as some approaches are more relevant than others.

One of the key questions that needs to be considered by the teacher when planning on using learning styles is 'what is it being used for'? In other words learning styles should not be identified in isolation but in relation to the learning environment, the task and the curriculum. Using a learning context for learning styles can be more meaningful if one ensures that the approaches used and the materials developed are not developed only for the student but in relation to the task the student is to embark on. This means it is important that every subject, teacher has knowledge of learning styles as well as the student's individual profile. Although all learners' styles should be accommodated in every subject, there may be some variability and restriction depending on the subject. The important point is that the identification of learning styles needs to be linked to teaching plans, teaching methods, and teaching strategies. It is for this reason that the framework described earlier in this chapter (Given and Reid 1999) was developed. This framework allows for flexibility and can be used to accommodate to the learning and teaching needs of all students in all subjects of the curriculum.

The learning process is integral to, and affected by, the interaction between teaching and learning style. It is important that this should be seen as a high priority even although the research to support this may not be abundant. Coffield (2005) argues that one needs to be careful about attempting to match teaching and learning style because of the conflicting research evidence. It is important, as Coffield also claims, that students and staff in schools and colleges reflect on their own learning and that of others. This should lead to learners being taught to set explicit, challenging goals and to identify strategies to reach these goals. This is one of the reasons why the identification of learning styles is important as it can help students become more aware of their own learning and be able to reflect more effectively on the actual learning strategies and the learning environment.

CONCLUDING COMMENTS

It is important to integrate the identification and the use of learning styles with the other relevant data that is collected prior to planning interventions. It is a crucial part of the assessment information that can assist in developing programmes of work, lesson plans and in deciding the method and the means of evaluating student progress.

It should not bee seen as a separate task but included in the battery of prerequisite and necessary information for planning for learning. It is also important to use learning styles to enhance the learner's self-knowledge. Used in this way it can be empowering for the student and provide the type of information that can assist towards the goal of learner self-awareness and learner autonomy. It is also important that learning styles should not be acknowledged only in the presentation of lessons but should be incorporated in the processes involving assessment and planning and curriculum development.

REFERENCES

Alexander R (2000). Culture and pedagogy: International comparisons in primary education. Oxford: Blackwell.

Burden, B. (2002) 'A cognitive approach to dyslexia: Learning styles and thinking skills', in G. Reid and J. Wearmouth (eds) *Dyslexia and literacy, theory and practice.* Wiley.

Coffield, F., Moseley, D., Hall, E. and Ecclestone, K. (2004) *Should we be using learning styles? What research has to say to practice.* London: DfES.

Coffield, F. (2005) 'Kineshetic nonense', *Times Educational Supplement* 14.1.05 pg. 28.

Dockrell, J. and McShane, J. (1993) *Childrens' learning difficulties – A cognitive approach.* Oxford: Blackwell.

Fitts, P.M. and Posner, M.I. (1967) *Human Performance.* Belmont, CA: Brooks Cole.

Gadwa, K. and Griggs, S. A. (1985) The school dropout: Implications for conusellors. *School Counsellor.* 33, 9–17.

Given, B.K. and Reid, G. (1999) *Learning styles: A guide for teachers and parents.* Lancashire: Red Rose Publications.

Grainger, J. (1999) 'Attention deficit hyperactivity disorder and reading disorders: How are they related?', in A.J. Watson and L.R. Giorcelli (eds) *Accepting the literacy challenge.* Australia: Scholastic Publications.

Knivsberg, A-M, Reichelt, K.-L. and Nodland, M. (1999) 'Comorbidity or coexistence, between dyslexia and attention deficit hyperactivity disorder', *British Journal of Special Education,* 26 (1): 42–47.

Lannen (2002) 'The Red Rose School' E801 Course DVD Open University, Milton Keynes, UK.

Montague, M. and Castro, M. (2004) 'Attention deficit hyperactivity disorder: Concerns and issues', in P. Clough, P. Garner, J.T. Pardeck and F. Yuen (eds) *Handbook of emotional and behavioural difficulties.* Sage Publications.

Reid, G. (2006) *Learning styles and inclusion.* Sage Publications.

Reid, G. and Strnadova, I. (2006) The development of a learning styles instrument for teachers. Pilot report 1. University of Edinburgh, Charles University, Prague.

Reid, G. and Strnadova, I. (2006) The development of a learning styles instrument for teachers. Pilot report 2. University of Edinburgh, Charles University, Prague.

Reid. G. (2007) *Motivating learners in the classroom: Ideas and strategies.* Sage Publications.

Tunmer, W. E. and Chapman, J. (1996) A developmental model of dyslexia. Can the construct be saved? *Dyslexia.* 2(3), 179–89.

APPENDIX

Pupil's Assessment of Learning Styles (PALS)© (Pilot version)
Reid and Strnadova 2004

Social

1. After school would you prefer to go home in a group rather than alone?
2. Do you like playing computer games with others?
3. Do you enjoy working in groups in class?
4. Have you got a lot of friends?
5. Do you like team games?
6. Do you enjoy being with a lot of people?
7. Do you like discussing topics in groups?
8. Do you like doing your school work with friends/others?
9. Do you enjoy spending your weekend with other people?
10. Do you see yourself as a leader?
11. Are you happy to share your desk with others?

Environmental

1. Is your desk/work place to be neat and tidy?
2. Do you like quiet surroundings?
3. Does sound annoy you when you are studying?
4. Do you like having lots of space around you when you work?
5. Do you prefer to read when sitting at a desk instead of sitting on the floor?
6. Do you prefer light colours (white, yellow) in the room to darker ones (red, dark blue)?
7. Do you prefer learning indoors to outdoors?

Emotional

1. Do you change your mind about things a lot?
2. Do you often feel sad?
3. Do you find it difficult to make decisions?
4. Do you feel confident?
5. Do you worry a lot?
6. Do you consider yourself to be reliable?
7. Do you have often headaches?
8. When you start completing your task, do you finish it?
9. Do you consider yourself as having good concentration?

Cognitive

1. Do you enjoy doing crosswords puzzles?
2. Do you remember lists?
3. Do you like to learn through reading?
4. Do you enjoy picture puzzles?
5. Does drawing help you to learn?
6. Do you like to use coloured pencils a lot?
7. Do you learn best by watching a video or television?
8. Do you enjoy experiments?
9. Do you learn best by building things?
10. Do you learn best through experiences?
11. Do you learn best by visiting places?

Metacognitive

1. Do you like to make a plan before doing anything?
2. Do you usually think how you might improve your performance in any activity or task you have done?
3. Do you usually avoid making very quick decisions?
4. Do you usually ask a lot of people before making a judgement on something?
5. Do you find it easy to organise your ideas?

TEACHER'S OBSERVATION OF LEARNING STYLES (TOLS) © (REID AND STRNADOVA, 2004)

Social

Interaction
1. Is the child's best work accomplished when working in a group?

Communication
2. Does the child communicate easily with teachers?
3. Does the child like to tell stories with considerable detail?
4. Can the child summarize events well?

Environmental

Mobility
5. Does the child fidget a lot and move around the class frequently?

Time of Day
6. Is the child most alert in the morning?
7. Is the child most alert in the afternoon?

Emotional

Persistence
8. Does the child stick with a task until completion without breaks?
9. Does the pupil require only a little teacher direction in doing the task?

Responsibility
10. Does the child take responsibility for his own learning?
11. Does the child attribute his successes and failures to self?
12. Does the child work independently?

Emotions
13. Does the child appear happy and relaxed in class?

Cognitive

Modality Preference
14. Does the child readily understand written type of instructions?
15. Does the child readily understand oral type of instructions?
16. Does the child readily understand visual type of instructions?
17. When giving instructions, the child (mark 1-4):
     *   asks for a lot more information
     *   draw maps (for example mind maps)
     *   take notes

Sequential or Simultaneous Learning
18. Does the child begin with step one and proceed in an orderly fashion rather than randomly jump from one step to another?
19. Are the child's responses delayed and reflective rather than rapid and spontaneous?

Tasks
20. Is there a relationship between the child's 'misbehavior' and difficult tasks?

Metacognitive

Prediction
21. Does the child make plans and work toward goals rather than let things happen as they will?
22. Does the child demonstrate enthusiasm about gaining new knowledge and skills rather than hesitate?

Feedback
23. How does the child respond to different types of feedback (1 = low/negative response, 4 = high/positive response):
  • non-verbal (smile)
  • check mark
  • oral praise
  • a detailed explanation

Structure
24. Are the child's personal effects (desk, clothing, materials) well organized?
25. Does the child respond negatively to someone imposing organizational structure on him/her with resistance?
26. When provided specific, detailed guidelines for task completion, does the child faithfully follow them?
27. Does the child seem to consider past events before taking action?

18

Dyslexia and Inclusion in the Secondary School – Cross Curricular Perspectives

Moira Thomson

This chapter

  i) discusses the identification of dyslexia at secondary school;
 ii) looks at the impact of dyslexia within the subject curriculum;
iii) discusses students learning/teaching preferences;
 iv) makes reference to classroom management issues and
  v) arrangements for examinations.

In inclusive secondary schools, it is the responsibility of every subject teacher to provide a suitably differentiated curriculum, accessible to all students, that provides each with the opportunity to develop and apply individual strengths while meeting the additional needs of all learners, including those with dyslexia (SEED 2004). Most secondary teachers' training and expertise is specific to their subjects – and all will know about learning disabilities and special educational needs, and the use of teaching and learning strategies that are sensitive to the diversity of students' abilities, learning preferences and styles. But this may not be enough to help them recognise learning 'differences' related to dyslexia that may cause difficulties in the subject curriculum. Teachers need to be aware that, while dyslexia is not linked to ability, able dyslexic learners may persistently underachieve and that many dyslexic students use strategies such as misbehaviour for coping with difficulties they do not necessarily understand themselves (Thomson, 2007a: 7).

Many secondary subject teachers assume that their students arrive from the primary school with the ability to read, write and compute at a certain level, and that those whose skills do not reach that level will be supported in the subject curriculum through the provision of additional resources and specialist help. While some dyslexic students who experience severe difficulties in accessing the secondary curriculum due to failure to master the early stages of literacy are provided with additional support, most learners with dyslexia spend their entire time at secondary school in subject classes supported only by subject teachers who may struggle to relate students' dyslexic difficulties to their delivery of the curriculum.

IDENTIFICATION OF DYSLEXIA AT SECONDARY SCHOOL

It is often assumed that any dyslexia is identified and assessed at primary school, but this is not necessarily the case. Some dyslexic students who coped with the early stages of literacy acquisition may experience difficulties with higher order skills, which do not appear until secondary school and some aspects of dyslexia do not become apparent until students encounter problems within the secondary curriculum (The National Assembly for Wales, 2006: 61). This may be due to differences between the primary classroom and the busy secondary school timetable, causing dyslexic problems to emerge for students accustomed to having all the time they need to complete set tasks. The move to secondary school may have eliminated many of the support strategies that 'hidden' dyslexic students developed at primary level to mask that they were experiencing difficulties – difficulties that do not become apparent until the demands of the secondary subject curriculum outweigh these coping strategies. A mismatch between a student's apparent ability and the quality (and quantity) of written work in some subjects may be the first indication that dyslexia is present, but this may appear to be unrelated to the curriculum, often being interpreted by subject teachers as the result of students' lack of interest, effort or concentration (Thomson, 2007b: 8).

It is important that subject teachers are aware that they will be the first to recognise that students are experiencing difficulties in the curriculum, and they must not assume that these are already known to support staff and parents (Thomson 2007a: 7). Some students' difficulties may first appear at home – perhaps changes in attitude and behaviour, especially where homework is involved – and parents often assume that these are known in school. Both parents and teachers could be wrong and it is very important that a school's specialist teacher is consulted at the earliest opportunity – if the student's dyslexia is already known, this consultation may become part of on-going monitoring of progress, and if there is no previous record of dyslexic difficulties, an investigation can be started.

INDICATIONS OF DYSLEXIA IN THE SECONDARY CURRICULUM

Secondary teachers want to know how dyslexia will affect individual students' learning in their subjects, but there is no single simple definition that will predict its impact on learning – and definitions of dyslexia that are remote from what is happening in the classroom are not of much practical use. While there are many lists of known characteristics of dyslexia available to teachers (BDA, 2006a; Dyslexia Scotland, 2005), there is no set of symptoms that are always present and no predictable circumstances that will always result from dyslexia (Peer and Reid, 2001: 10–11).

It may be difficult for teachers to detect dyslexia in the context of the subject curriculum. Many dyslexic students become discouraged by constantly meeting barriers to learning, perhaps resulting in an assumption that they are inattentive or lazy, when they are actually making much more effort than their classmates. In addition to struggling with literacy issues, dyslexic students may appear to avoid set work, and are often restless and unable to concentrate or easily tired, inattentive and uncooperative (Thomson, 2007b: 10). It is common for learning differences related to dyslexia that cause unexpected difficulties within the subject curriculum to be mistaken for behavioural problems – students appear disaffected; they may persistently underachieve, concealing difficulties – leading teachers to attribute poor progress to lack of interest or effort, misbehaviour or illness (Thomson, 2006: 17). Dyslexic students often lack stamina and have low self-esteem – which may have a powerful impact on their ability to cope with the demands of the subject curriculum (Peer and Reid, 2001: 232–233).

Students whose dyslexia has not been recognised or fully understood will probably not be successful learners and so they are unlikely to be motivated to learn (Peer and Reid, 2000: 5), but dyslexia is not the result of poor motivation – or emotional disturbance, sensory impairment or lack of opportunities – although it may occur alongside any of these, and is all too frequently mistaken for one or more of them.

MULTILINGUALISM AND DYSLEXIA

Bi-lingual students who continue to exhibit an auditory-verbal processing delay are often considered simply to be taking longer to develop fluency or perhaps struggling with cultural differences and unfamiliar subject vocabulary, when they are actually demonstrating dyslexic difficulties. The underlying language processing problems experienced by many dyslexic students can make learning any new language difficult (Schnieder and Crombie, 2003: 4–5). Differences between the developing aural/oral abilities of students who are learning a new language and their written work in that language is to be expected, but dyslexic reading deficiencies may be more difficult to detect, since all students will experience some problems with pronunciation, impeding fluent reading.

When multilingual learners fail to make progress in the curriculum as they begin to develop fluency in the new language, subject teachers should not assume that their language status is the only reason. Specialist teachers and psychologists have tended to misdiagnose or ignore dyslexia indicators in multilingual students because of the multiplicity of possible causes for failure to make progress and the risk of a 'false positive' result (Peer and Reid, 2000: 5). Schools should look carefully at all aspects of multilingual students' performance in different subjects to establish whether any problems in the classroom arise from special educational needs, including dyslexia (DfES, 2001a: 67).

HIDDEN DYSLEXIA

Dyslexia is often hidden, masked by a student's high ability or by distracting behaviour patterns, even deliberately concealed by teenagers who are desperate not to be 'different' from their peers.

Dyslexic students can achieve well in some subjects, so their additional needs may not be observed for some time (Dodds and Thomson, 1999) leading teachers to assume that weaker performance in other areas is due to a lack of interest or effort. Subject ability may be masked by dyslexia, when students perform at the expected level but are actually limited by underpinning dyslexic difficulties resulting in unidentified underachievement (Montgomery, 2003: 8). Dyslexic students may be talented in performance-related activities or gifted academically – they may be superb athletes, have good problem-solving skills or strongly developed spatial awareness, but they often fail to achieve at a level commensurate with their ability because of their dyslexia, perhaps even appearing to lose interest, becoming frustrated or bored and disruptive (Thomson, 2006: 21, 30).

Sometimes, students may have overcome their dyslexic difficulties to such an extent that the reading demands of certain subjects do not appear to pose particular problems and inconsistent spelling and slowness in completing assignments may be the only indications of dyslexia in their written work. As a result, subject teachers may assume that the dyslexia is in some way 'cured' and that a student's dyslexic profile no longer applies. But there is no 'cure' for dyslexia although some people develop very efficient strategies for compensating for their difficulties. . Subject teachers should remain aware that dyslexic difficulties may re-appear at any time as a student progresses through the secondary curriculum, particularly in stressful situations such as a change of teacher, beginning a new course and sitting exams (Thomson, 2007a: 7).

Specialist dyslexia teachers can provide subject colleagues with details of individual dyslexic students' strengths and weaknesses that may be used to predict likely barriers to learning and inform the development of support strategies as each student begins to engage with the subject curriculum (Peer and Reid, 2003: 60–62) enabling teachers to anticipate the needs of dyslexic students and adjust their delivery of the curriculum appropriately (McKay, 2005: 52–59). Subject teachers' use of effective support strategies that anticipate barriers to learning and attainment in the subject curriculum can result in dyslexic students' first taste of success.

DYSLEXIA IN THE SUBJECT CURRICULUM

Many dyslexic students lack confidence in their ability to learn and have an expectation of failure – not only because of prior experience of struggling with literacy but also because they may not have developed the underpinning study skills of independent learners. The acquisition of subject-specific study skills in the secondary curriculum is often largely incidental; during normal delivery of their subjects, teachers model responses and advise students on revision techniques. Few dyslexic students can access this type of input – they may lack the energy or time to absorb incidental comments or to reproduce techniques explained by teachers 'in passing'.

Subject teachers should consider dyslexia in the context of their own subject and anticipate the possible learning needs of dyslexic students when preparing lesson materials, avoiding approaches that require unnecessary dependence on text, providing support to guide the flow of work, allowing extra time for dyslexic students to organise thoughts and develop new skills (McKay, 2005: 58–59). Homework tasks should be planned as part of the lesson – dyslexic students often have problems with time management and prioritising, resulting in incomplete and poorly presented work, so teachers should anticipate problems with this (Reid and Green, 2007: 68). Teachers should take care when developing differentiated materials that the tasks set for students with dyslexia are appropriate to their ability level. Differentiation should lead to the curriculum being presented in a more accessible format, but teaching and learning resources and activities must not be over-simplified in the process (Peer and Reid, 2001: 270).

Most teachers expect dyslexic students to have difficulties with reading and writing – but not all will experience the same problems – and many may have already developed strategies to compensate for weaknesses.

Reading in the subject curriculum has a number of different functions, and dyslexic students may cope well with some of these but struggle with others (Cogan and Flecker, 2004: 2–3). Those who experience visual processing difficulties may complain of visual distortions/words moving around when reading, headaches, dizziness or nausea; they may rub their eyes, blink rapidly when concentrating; complain of scratchy or itchy eyes when using a computer. They may also complain they can't see the board, that the page or room is too bright and hurts their eyes. While conditions related to visual deficits can be helped by introducing tinted overlays or lenses (Jordan, 2000: 20–22), teachers can help by adjusting classroom lighting and adopting teaching styles that support weak visual processing (Irlen, 1991: 176–178).

Dyslexic students often process information and read differently from classmates, but subject teachers can support them by making curricular materials more easily accessible with simple changes to the way texts are presented (BDA, 2006b). For example, using italics or underlining can make words appear to run together creating additional problems for dyslexic readers, so key information might be highlighted and separated from the rest of the text – for example, in a box – and continuous prose broken up using bullets or numbers. Those who have a history of slow, inaccurate reading may have a single strategy for study – reading one word at a time, slowing reading so much that meaning is lost altogether, so different strategies will be needed for different types of reading tasks (Ostler, 2000: 35; Turner and Pughe, 2003: 7).

In many subjects, understanding is tested or reinforced by reading activities and dyslexic students may struggle to locate key information in text passages, have to re-read frequently to understand content and may be unable to relate the questions to the text – so a students' reading ability may determine success rather than knowledge or understanding of the subject. Dyslexic students may have additional difficulties with multiple-choice questions due the similarity of the choices offered and they may be unable to recognise key words out of context. Some dyslexic students who have difficulty processing new subject vocabulary often experience barriers to accessing text materials or to the production of written work linked to this. Pre-teaching new vocabulary – perhaps as homework – can minimise such difficulties.

Subject teachers should bear in mind that it takes dyslexic students longer to read the questions, compose answers in their heads, then get them down on paper, and that their entitlement to support extends to assessments. Providing alternative arrangements for tests requiring fluent reading skills, such as student/teacher discussion, practical tasks, and interpretation of diagrams or illustrations of subject content might raise the attainment of all students (Reid and Fawcett, 2004: 253).

Dyslexic students often avoid writing, finding it stressful and exhausting; written work may take a long time and be illegible, full of spelling errors, with little punctuation and poor organisation. Many students with dyslexia have poor fine motor skills and handwriting is slow, laboured and non-automatic, lacking fluency. They may be unable to write continuously without frequent rests. There may be unusual spatial organisation of the page with words widely spaced or tightly squashed together with margins ignored and writing off the line. Diagrams may be incorrectly labelled, wrongly proportioned or reversed and columns misaligned (McKay, 2005: 198–202). Messy written work may result in a reader assuming carelessness and content that matches presentation – which is not necessarily the case for many dyslexic students who have done the best they can.

When marking dyslexic students' work teachers should not penalise for poor presentation of work or bizarre spelling (Reid and Green, 2007: 97). Subject teachers are not expected to teach dyslexic students handwriting, but, where graphic skills are part of the subject curriculum, they should offer strategies for improving these.

Dyslexic students are acutely aware of their difficulties, often feeling frustrated by their inability to express their understanding through writing, making it difficult for them to demonstrate their grasp of a subject to the same extent as other students. There may be a huge difference between their ability to tell you something and their ability to write it down (Cogan and Flecker, 2004: 180–181). It may be difficult for dyslexic students to plan written work and follow an ordered sequence in the development of ideas. In some subjects, like English, teachers actually teach how to write essays of different types and give students a framework, structured prompt or template to support writing in different formats, for example giving an opening phrase for each paragraph and suggested vocabulary (Reid and Green, 2007: 65–66), but there may be an assumption that in other areas students already know how to produce structured written responses, and some subject teachers do not see it as their responsibility to teach this.

No matter what the experience and skills of the rest of the class, dyslexic students need specific instruction in how to structure written work, as they may be unable to transfer skills acquired in one subject to a different context. Subject teachers should issue writing guidelines and paragraph headings to support the structure of extended writing and introduce alternatives to extended writing, for example, charts/diagrams, mind-maps, using bullet points or recording voice files to be transcribed later. The writing difficulties of many dyslexic students are often resolved by the introduction of ICT (Reid and Fawcett, 2004: 312) – and subject teachers should make an effort to ensure that this is readily accessible in the classroom.

Many dyslexic students are unable to take accurate notes or to copy from a board, screen or book so teachers could provide templates or copies of class notes in an accessible format – for example, large print versions, or they might provide skeleton notes – giving the headings of content to be covered in a lesson – to support note-taking. For those with visual processing and short-term memory difficulties – copying may be impossible. The results will certainly be unreliable and inaccurate (Reid and Green, 2007: 94). When copying, a dyslexic student looks up, visually 'grabs' a little information, writes it down then repeats the process over and over, rarely demonstrating any comprehension of the material (Fawcett, 2001: 287). When notes are dictated, phonological processing difficulties often cause dyslexic students to lag behind and rushing to catch up invariably results in missing sections and illegible writing that even they cannot read or understand after even a very short interval. Many will remember nothing of lesson if they have to concentrate on completing notes – being unable to process what the teacher is saying quickly enough to make sense or to listen and write at the same time (Cogan and Flecker, 2004: 117). To ensure that dyslexic students have accurate subject notes, teachers could identify a 'partner' whose notes can be photocopied as soon as possible after a lesson or issue prompt cards summarising key points or full lesson notes, and encourage students to highlight key points on these while listening instead of copying or completing skeleton notes.

Dyslexic students may make good progress in the subject curriculum and cope well with most set tasks but they may take 3 to 4 times longer to complete the same assignment as classmates, so teachers should structure class activities to provide this additional time – for example, in maths, teachers should ensure that dyslexic students have enough time to complete a set task before giving results to the class. Drawing or completing diagrams with labels can be particularly challenging for some dyslexic students and it might be appropriate for copies of these to be issued – a useful way of 'creating' extra time for dyslexic students to complete other set work.

LEARNING/TEACHING PREFERENCES

All students have preferred learning styles and these affect the efficiency with which they learn. Pupils with dyslexia are less able than their classmates to cope when the teaching input is delivered in a style that is different from their individual preference (Given and Reid, 1999: 15–16). When there is a mismatch between a teacher's preferred style and a student's learning preference, learning is likely to be incomplete and concentration may be difficult in that class (Ostler, 2000: 3). Subject teachers must remain aware of the need to vary their style of curriculum delivery and to develop ways of working with learners drawing from a number of different approaches. Many teachers deliver the curriculum by talking – not always effective for dyslexic students, whose slower processing of auditory input causes them to lose the thread and become confused when trying to make sense of lesson content. Those teachers who have a visual preference should remember that it is unlikely that dyslexic students will be able to create their own versions of mind maps or diagrams unless these are specifically taught. McKay (2005: 114–118) refers to 'comfort zones' of learning preferences, identifying many dyslexic students' preference for visual and kinaesthetic styles and the need for them to become more comfortable with text and language. Problems with literacy may lead to some dyslexic students developing unconventional coping strategies and ways of thinking, and they should be encouraged to explore their own learning styles to identify strengths.

Having a strong preference for one learning style does not mean that students are unable to use features of other styles (Peer and Reid, 2001: 117–118). Dyslexic students may find themselves adopting different approaches to learning different subjects, depending on teachers' preferred styles of lesson delivery, resulting in unexpected attainment or lack thereof in different subjects for example, they may make excellent progress in a subject where a teacher chooses to teach using mind maps and encourages students to develop these, but may be unable to progress beyond the basics in a subject where they are expected to take personal notes and generate extended written pieces.

In any subject classroom there will be a wide variety of learning styles, barriers to learning and support needs for which provision must be made, so it is important for subject teachers to recognise and respond effectively to the learning needs of all students, providing additional support when necessary (Given and Reid, 1999: 81–83). Many teaching and learning strategies appropriate for dyslexic students that take account of a range of strengths and learning differences are effective for all students (Reid and Fawcett, 2004: 231–233).

CLASSROOM MANAGEMENT ISSUES

Dyslexic students encounter barriers to learning across the whole curriculum so it is important for subject teachers to remain aware that dyslexia may prevent them from producing work that matches their level of understanding of the subject curriculum. The impact of dyslexia varies from one student to another and may apply only to some aspects of performance – for example, poor written work may lead to false assumptions about attitude and effort – some dyslexic students complete written assignments to the best of their ability, only to find their work returned with negative comments about presentation or lack of effort because of the discrepancy between their comprehension of subject material and their ability to write legibly or spell consistently (Reid and Fawcett, 2004: 224).

The structure of the secondary curriculum offers additional challenges that may put considerable pressure on dyslexic students who have problems with their short-term memory. Some cannot hold as much information in working memory as other students (Kay and Yeo, 2003: 14), finding it hard to remember instructions just after they were given or carry out all the steps in problem solving. Some dyslexic students are unable to hold numbers in short term memory while doing calculations or forget what they were going to say in the middle of a sentence or while waiting for a pause in the conversation. Difficulties accessing long-term memory reduce working memory capacity and slow the ability to recall familiar sequences or to select and apply previously learned procedures to current activities.

Dyslexic students may be slow to respond to a teacher's spoken instructions and find that the rest of the class is getting on with a piece of work while they have no idea where to begin, often asking for a page number immediately after the teacher has given it. This inability to remember spoken instructions or process written directions may be interpreted as lack of attention or indiscipline when they ask classmates what to do next. Teachers might anticipate such problems – for example, always write page and question numbers on the board – and should evaluate the likely impact on dyslexic students of class activities set, providing alternatives that ensure their inclusion – such as checking that instructions are fully understood by asking students to repeat them aloud or encourage all students to discuss the nature of tasks before starting.

Some dyslexic students misuse familiar words and have difficulty remembering new or unfamiliar words – resulting in reluctance to talk in class. They often struggle to respond appropriately to questions due to the need to process the language first before being able to process the question. If a teacher speaks quickly, or gives too much information at once, dyslexic students will probably catch only parts of this (Reid and Green, 2007: 4) and may be reluctant to admit that they missed information, preferring the teacher and classmates to believe that they were not paying attention. They may misunderstand complicated questions, confuse sequences of instructions or fail to respond to questions even when they know the answer.

In discussion, dyslexic students may be unable to remember questions/instructions or be slow to respond to others' comments in good time resulting in them making apparently irrelevant remarks or contributions. Short-term memory difficulties can add to problems with turn-taking and dyslexic students may interrupt others to comment, afraid they will forget what they wanted to say if they don't speak at once. This may make them unable to participate in group work – they may appear to make little or no attempt to begin, concentrating on personal concerns instead of setting down to work – often considered by teachers to be indications of laziness or disaffection. All students are more willing to consult the person next to them than ask the teacher when they are unsure of something (Thomson, 2007b: 10–11). Pupils being asked for help by dyslexic classmates often benefit from the opportunity to talk about the work, and their own understanding may be clarified and their attention focused by having the chance to explain something to another student.

Dyslexia is not only a series of difficulties – it includes a range of specific abilities. A dyslexic student may be original, creative, artistic or orally very able and knowledgeable and the disparity between difficulties and abilities of is often noted in a student's profile (Montgomery, 2003: 7–9; McKay, 2005: 15). Some dyslexic students may have problems identifying simple shapes, but the three-dimensional visualisation skills of other dyslexics help them to 'see' relationships and concepts more quickly and clearly than others.

Many dyslexic students appear to do everything the long way – concentration is easily lost and they are unable to pick up from where they left off, often having to start all over again, sometimes leading them to become restless or disruptive to draw attention away from their difficulties. They may start a task well but there is often a rapid deterioration of the quality of work, especially when writing. The level of concentration and effort needed for 'normal' class activities may cause fatigue in dyslexic students, so teachers might vary activities so that they become less fatigued or build-in mini-breaks to allow them to rest briefly. Setting short, well-defined tasks and setting time limits for the duration of activities may help prevent some dyslexic students spending so much time on initial tasks that they fail to participate in the rest of the lesson. If clearly defined targets are set, showing the intermediate steps to be completed in an activity, dyslexic students may learn how to monitor their progress and pace themselves appropriately.

Many dyslexic students are disorganised or forgetful of equipment and homework – even turning up in class at the wrong time. Poor organisational skills are often exacerbated by an inability to remember sequences of events, tasks, instructions and a tendency to forget books and work to be handed in and fail to meet deadlines for assignments or to complete tasks on time. When planning lessons, subject teachers might structure tasks for dyslexic students and help them to prioritise – especially when problems are associated with homework. Teachers should monitor the correct use of the homework diary and involve parents for example, accepting homework scribed by parents or in an alternative format to writing (Peer and Reid, 2001: 270–271). Dyslexic students tend to lose themselves (and their possessions) regularly and they may be unable to retrace their steps because they have no memory of how they arrived at a place. The use of equipment checklists and personal timetables with deadlines clearly marked will support dyslexic students' development of personal strategies for coping with the complexities of the secondary curriculum.

In the secondary subject classroom, students with dyslexia face not only problems caused by dyslexia, but also experience feelings linked to self-esteem that may contribute to lack of progress (Peer and Reid, 2003: 41). They are acutely aware of their problems and may overreact to casual comments and general remarks made by teachers and take everything personally (Thomson, 2007b: 13). Subject teachers should remain alert for difficult situations for dyslexic students and be ready to defuse any potentially embarrassing circumstances.

Organising life around a timetable (Peer and Reid, 2001: 270) and remembering which books to take to school on any given day can be very difficult for dyslexic students whose coping strategies vary from taking no books at all to carrying all books all the time. They may forget essential books, equipment and homework or which day of the week it is, and follow the wrong timetable or get lost, being unable to find the way around when corridors all look the same. They are often late to arrive at school and at subject classrooms, hand in homework late and take a very long time settling to tasks. Many dyslexic students spend a disproportionate amount of time searching for books and equipment, often forgetting what they are looking for.

Persistent fine and gross motor difficulties have been linked to dyslexia for many years (Peer and Reid, 2003: 10–11) and dyslexic students often appear clumsy and uncoordinated, due to deficits in perceptual skills and speed of visual and auditory information processing. They may have problems in corridors/stairs being unable to anticipate others' actions and are unable to judge distance/speed or play team and ball games. Strategies to help dyslexic students determine their own position in relation to others and to anticipate common hazards – like doors opening towards them, passing people on stairs – must be specifically taught, as they lack the 'automatic' ability to identify and predict common hazards in the environment.

Practical tasks such as measuring, cutting out or reading scales could be a source of difficulty for dyslexic students in subject classes (Peer and Reid, 2003: 10–11). Some may have motor-planning problems affecting the ability to predict or follow a series of steps in the right order; other have fine/gross motor problems affecting ability to manipulate objects and write, affecting the completion of practical tasks – they may have a strange/awkward way of holding tools and equipment, lack the fine motor skills required to draw/measure accurately and be unable to use a ruler to draw straight lines. They often have little or no understanding of scale, experience confusion about appropriate measures for different tasks and are unable to complete practical activities involving direction. Dyslexic students' inability to record results of experiments clearly and logically and to construct suitable tables for recording data may be easily resolved by teachers issuing skeleton notes for completion.

Dyslexic difficulties linked to orientation and direction may affect the understanding of patterns and sequences as well as making it difficult for students to cope with aspects of some subjects, for example, geography, chemistry. Pupils may have little or no sense of direction confusing left and right and may also have problems reading figures in the correct direction/order or have difficulty with the vocabulary of directionality and position – above/below, forward/back. Dyslexic students may have difficulty extracting information from tables, charts and graphs or be unable to tell the time on an analogue clock (DfES, 2001b: 9). When asked what time it is, may say something ridiculous like 'It's half past quarter to' and have difficulty estimating the passage of time, being unable to work out when 'in 15 minutes' would be.

Teachers should bear in mind that many dyslexic students are inconsistent workers, managing to do something correctly one day, but unable to repeat it the next.

ARRANGEMENTS FOR EXAMINATIONS

Any alternative arrangements for examinations should be based on the needs of individuals and on the demands of an assessment, not on disability – if a dyslexic student is able to achieve the required outcomes of a course of study, but is unable to demonstrate this in the usual way – then alternatives may be put in place (Thomson, 2004: 1–2). If there is a marked discrepancy between a dyslexic student's subject ability and writing skills, a written exam may prevent accurate assessment, so an alternative arrangement – such as a scribe – may be requested (JCQ, 2008: 12).

For dyslexic candidates, the examination itself is often a barrier to the demonstration of attainment. Dyslexic profiles may include difficulties related to reading and writing, problems with memory and organisation or difficulties created by placing time limits on examinations. If a dyslexic candidate is unable to read the examination paper within the time allowed, then the opportunity to demonstrate attainment is not being provided. Introducing additional time or a reader – electronic or human – to compensate for slow text processing may be requested to minimise this barrier. Schools should identify candidate's needs at an early stage, put support arrangements into the subject curriculum and reflect these in the arrangements made for examinations.

The combination of low self-esteem and stress linked to the examination system is likely to result in impaired performance by dyslexic students. Matching exam arrangements to familiar support strategies that are regularly used in the curriculum, together with opportunities to rehearse in 'mock' exams will go a long way to minimise these (Thomson, 2007b: 11).

With the provision of appropriate support, dyslexic students will be able to access the secondary mainstream curriculum and experience success at an appropriate level.

REFERENCES

British Dyslexia Association (2006a) *Indications of dyslexia.* Available http://www.bdadyslexia.org.uk/indications.html

British Dyslexia Association (2006b) *Dyslexia style guide.* Available http://www.bdadyslexia.org.uk/extra352

Cogan, J. and Flecker, M. (2004) *Dyslexia in secondary school – A practical handbook for teachers, parents and students.* London: Whurr.

Department for Education and Skills (2001a) *SEN code of practice.* London: DfES. Available http://www.teachernet.gov.uk/_doc/3724/SENCodeOfPractice.pdf

Department for Education and Skills (2001b) *Guidance to support pupils with dyslexia and dyscalculia.* Available http://publications.teachernet.gov.uk/eOrderingDownload/DfES-0512-2001.pdf

Dodds, D. and Thomson, M. (1999) *Dyslexia: An in-service training pack and handbook for teachers.* Edinburgh City of Edinburgh Council: Education.

Dyslexia Scotland (2005) *Teachers' guide.* Available http://www.dyslexiascotland.org.uk/documents/Guide%20for%20Teachers%20A4.pdf

Fawcett, A. (ed.) (2001) *Dyslexia: Theory and good practice.* London: Whurr.

Given, G.K. and Reid, G. (1999) *Learning styles: A guide for teachers and parents.* St Annes-on-Sea: Red Rose Publications.

Irlen, H. (1991) *Reading by the colors.* New York: Pedigree.

Joint Council for Qualifications (JCQ) (2008) *Access arrangements and special consideration regulations and guidance relating to candidates who are eligible for adjustments in examinations 2007–8.* Available http://www.jcq.org.uk/attachments/published/428/Final%20%20RAG%2007–08.pdf

Jordan, I. (2000) *Visual dyslexia – A guide for parents and teachers.* Barnetby-Le-Wold: Desktop Publications.

Kay, J. and Yeo, D. (2003) *Dyslexia and maths.* London: David Fulton.

McKay, N. (2005) *Removing dyslexia as a barrier to achievement.* Wakefield: SEN Marketing.

Montgomery, D. (ed.) (2003) *Gifted and talented children with special educational needs: Double exceptionality.* London: NACE/Fulton.

Ostler, C. (2000) *Study skills a pupil's survival guide.* Godalming: Ammonite Books.

Peer, L. and Reid, G. (eds) (2000) *Multilingualism, literacy and dyslexia – A challenge for educators.* London: David Fulton.

Peer, L. and Reid, G. (eds) (2001) *Dyslexia – Successful; inclusion in the secondary school.* London: David Fulton.

Peer, L. and Reid, G. (2003) *Introduction to dyslexia.* London: BDA.

Reid, G. and Fawcett, A. (eds) (2004) *Dyslexia in context – Research, policy and practice.* London: Whurr.

Reid, G. and Green, S. (2007) *100 ideas for supporting pupils with dyslexia.* London: Continuum International.

Schneider, E. and Crombie, M. (2003) *Dyslexia and foreign language learning*. Abingdon Oxon: David Fulton Publishers.

Scottish Executive Education Department (SEED) (2004) *Supporting children's learning code of practice*. Available http://www.scotland.gov.uk/Publications/2005/08/15105817/58187

The National Assembly for Wales (2006) *Inclusion and pupil support*. Available www.wales.gov.uk/inclusionandpupilsupport

Thomson, M. (2004) *Alternative assessment arrangements for dyslexic students*. Available http://www.thedyslexiashop.co.uk/pdfdocuments/MoiraThomsonAtDyslexiaScotland-20040911

Thomson, M. (2006) *Supporting gifted and talented pupils in the secondary school*. London: Sage.

Thomson, M. (2007a) *Supporting dyslexic pupils in the secondary curriculum 1.1 identification and assessment of dyslexia at the secondary school*. Edinburgh: Dyslexia Scotland.

Thomson, M. (2007b) *Supporting dyslexic pupils in the secondary curriculum 1.3 classroom management of dyslexia at secondary school*. Edinburgh: Dyslexia Scotland.

Turner, E. and Pughe, J. (2003) *Dyslexia and english*. London: David Fulton.

19

Dyslexia and Self-Concept: A Review of Past Research with Implications for Future Action

Robert Burden

This chapter

i) reviews previous research findings on the nature of the relationship between aspects of self-concept and learning disabilities/dyslexia;
ii) considers some of the main problems relating to terminological confusion in this area;
iii) identifies key issues that need to be addressed but are often overlooked;
iv) provides a more focused examination of recent research linking learning disabilities/dyslexia to aspects of self-concept, self-esteem and identity formation; and
v) offers some tentative conclusions and suggestions for future research.

It has long been recognised that how people think and feel about themselves and their attributes in various fields of endeavour is likely to be closely related to their perceived levels of achievement in those endeavours. More than a century ago, early educational psychologists such as William James emphasised the importance of their self-concept in people's lives. What has never been satisfactorily established, however, is whether a positive self-concept is the cause or the effect of successful achievement, but it does seem likely that it plays a significant mediating role in contributing to an individual's effort in specific domains. Nowhere is this more true than in the area of dyslexia. Because literacy is a highly valued achievement in all developed societies, it stands to reason that perceived failure or extreme difficulty in that domain is likely to have a negative effect on an individual's view of themselves. Consequent negative self-appraisal in turn may well affect that individual's subsequent efforts to achieve. How pervasive and long-lasting these effects may be has been a topic of much heated debate.

BACKGROUND

A meta-analytic review by Chapman of studies carried out between 1974 and 1986 of the relationship between learning disabilities and self-concept came to the conclusion that children with learning disabilities were significantly more likely to view themselves negatively than their normally achieving peers (Chapman, 1988). In a follow-up review, Zeleke (2004) highlights both the narrowness of this earlier work, as well as some unresolved theoretical issues in self-concept research with learning disabled children, before reaching conclusions somewhat at variance with those of Chapman. What these and other meta-analytic studies do is highlight the difficulties of comparing the results of one research study with another in an area as complex as this. Apart from the fact that in comparing North American findings with those from the rest of the world we are forced to assume a general sense of equivalence between what is understood by such terms as dyslexia, learning disabilities and specific learning difficulties, the whole area of self-concept research is fraught with terminological confusion.

I shall begin this chapter, therefore by establishing my own terms of reference, whilst nevertheless conscious of the fact that this may at times produce at least as many problems as it solves. In order to make possible any kind of international comparisons and overarching summaries of indicators or trends, it will be necessary to treat the terms dyslexia, specific learning difficulties and learning disabilities as if they are being used to refer to similar populations, even though there can be no guarantee that this is the case. Definitions and descriptors of dyslexic populations are in a continuous process of change (compare for example previous and present definitions by ICD-10, DSM-IV, Dyslexia Action, the British Dyslexia Association and the British Psychological Society). At the same time, Specific Learning Difficulties and Learning Disabilities are generic terms which may well cover a wide range of specific difficulties at variance with a person's general cognitive abilities or other educational attainments.

In the realm of the self-concept the terminological and methodological issues are just as complex. Hansford and Hattie (1982), for example, discovered in their meta-analytic review of studies relating self-concept to achievement that such terms as self-concept and self-esteem were often used interchangeably and rarely ever defined. (See also Byrne, 1996). It will be necessary before going any further, therefore, to differentiate between the meaning and application of a range of terms used in the literature under the general umbrella of self-concept research and theory.

MODELS AND TERMS USED IN SELF-CONCEPT RESEARCH

One of the major problems bedevilling self-concept research has been the enormously wide range of approaches to assessment employed by investigators and the often dubious foundations upon which many of these are built. The current consensus amongst academics is that self-concept is a multidimensional construct (see Harter et al., 1996; Marsh and Hattie, 1996). What this means is that a person's general self-concept (GSC) is considered to be constructed from an amalgamation of their perceptions of how they are functioning in various academic spheres (Academic Self-Concept/ASC), in a range of social situations (Social Self-Concept/SSC), in their physical endeavours (Physical Self-Concept/PSC) and so on. Most self-concept scales attempt to cover a wide range of these aspects, but this can mean that only a few of the questionnaire items are devoted to one specific aspect in order to make the whole questionnaire manageable. This lack of specificity may well account for the weak associations sometimes found in studies seeking to discover the existence of an association between self-concept and achievement. It was precisely for this reason that the Myself-As-A-Learner Scale was developed (Burden, 1995), in order to make possible more in-depth investigation of learners' academic self-concepts. With respect to dyslexia, for example, there is a need to differentiate between how dyslexics see themselves in general and, more specifically, as learners. As Durrant et al. (1990) point out, 'It is important that research in this area acknowledges the heterogeneity of the LD population and the multidimensionality of the self-concept in order to gain a fuller understanding of the self-perceptions of these children'(p. 662).

Self-esteem, by contrast, is most appropriately used to refer to how a person feels about themselves in general but also with regard to specific aspects of their self-concept. General self-esteem (GSE) is often used synonymously with global self-worth (GSW). Specific aspects of a person's self esteem will undoubtedly be related to the significance that that person attributes to the particular domain. If a child does not see learning to read and write as important, then their academic self-esteem is unlikely to be negatively affected by failure in these areas. In a society which values an oral tradition of storytelling above the written word, this could well be the case. Alternatively, in order to protect their sense of self-worth, a person may well build up a series of defences against recognising as important the particular domain in which they are failing (see Covington, 1992).

Whilst self-esteem is often assessed by means of a general scale such as that devised by Rosenberg (1979), it is more likely to be helpful to focus upon specific ways in which individuals feel about their personal attributes. It is partly for this reason that applying Bandura's notion of self efficacy has come to be seen by many researchers as a potentially more productive avenue for examining aspects of a person's self esteem than such general measures (Bandura, 1997; Bandura et al., 1999; Pajares, 1999; Schunk, 1991). Self efficacy was termed by

Bandura as a way of representing an individual's feelings of competence and confidence of success when faced with specific learning and/or assessment tasks. At a more general level, it has also come to represent a person's sense of their general ability to cope and perform well academically. It is seen as a mediating factor in regulating human feelings of well-being and attainment, such that our behaviour is considered to be very much under the control of what we believe we are capable of achieving.

At the other end of the scale, is the possibility that an individual with learning difficulties might sink into a sense of learned helplessness (Abramson et al., 1978), which can even lead to chronic depression (Seligman et al., 1979; Seligman, 1991).

Finally, what needs to be taken into account is that terms such as self-concept, self-esteem and so on, are all constructs which contribute to our efforts to understand individuals' developing sense of identity. This will not be accomplished by the mere application of standardised measures, but is likely to require personal interviews, observations made by significant others, and possibly even behavioural observations.

Sorting through this complex set of issues leaves us with some fundamental questions of the following nature.

1   How do people of both sexes, manifesting specific learning difficulties of a dyslexic nature of differing degrees, coming from different ethnic and cultural backgrounds make sense of their learning difficulties at different ages and stages of their lives?
2   How do these reflections affect the self perceptions of dyslexics in both an academically specific and a general sense (i.e. their learning and general self-concepts)?
3   How does this make them feel about themselves in general (i.e. their general level of self-esteem) and their sense of identity as members of a community?
4   In what significant ways are these thoughts and feelings shaped by their interactions with significant others in their lives (parents, siblings, friends, same aged peers, teachers) and cultural expectations and stereotypes?

Unfortunately we are nowhere near ready as yet to answer such questions with any degree of specificity. Most reported studies confabulate all or most of these variables, which leaves the critical reader in the position of having to make best guesses as to what can reasonably be concluded from the evidence provided. It is rare for precise details to be given of the nature and selection of the sample population and of the specific purpose and underlying rationale of the techniques employed.

The review which follows will attempt as far as possible to take these factors into account where the necessary information is forthcoming, but it has to be acknowledged that this is often not possible. Where this is the case, general findings will be cited with caveats about their specificity and consequent generalisability.

ACADEMIC SELF-CONCEPT

A meta-analysis by Zeleke (2004) of 28 studies investigating the academic self-concept of children with learning disabilities found that the large majority (89 per cent) produced results demonstrating that LD children had more negative ASC than their normally achieving peers. These studies varied in sample size from 8 to 106, covered age ranges from 7 to 16+ (Grades one through twelve), and employed a wide range of measurement instruments. No information is given about possible gender differences or about the severity of the learning disabilities. Most involved some form of comparison grouping, but within the studies themselves the sizes of comparison groups differed considerably. Of the two studies producing markedly different findings, that by Durrant et al., (1990),comparing the academic self concept of children with diagnosed learning disabilities (LD) with their high, average and low achieving peers, as well as those with and without behaviour difficulties, found that academic self-concept was at least as strongly related to behavioural factors as it was to achievement levels, but also that when this was taken into account, the ASC of children with LD did not differ significantly from that of their normally achieving peers.

These findings should not give any cause for surprise or concern. If it is accepted that a person's academic self-concept is a reflection of the accuracy with which they perceive their academic skills and attributes, then it is surely to be expected that those with learning difficulties of whatever nature should see themselves as less successful than their normally achieving peers. In fact, it would be evidence of a mismatch between achievement and reasonably accurate perception of this that should raise further questions. As a result of their study of the relationship between academic-self concept and achievement in 600 Norwegian primary school children, Skaalvik and Hagvet (1990) concluded that ASC acts as a mediating variable between academic performance and global self-esteem as well as having a causal influence on academic achievement.

It would seem from some studies that the academic self-concepts of LD children is likely to remain stable over time (Bear et al., 1993; Chapman, 1998; Cosden, 1999; Kistner and Osborne, 1987, Vaughn et al., 1992), or even decrease as children move through the school system (Leonardi, 1993; Renick and Harter, 1989).However, as Burden (2005) discovered in his in depth study of the learning careers of 50 dyslexic boys attending a specialist independent school, academic self-concept is not only open to change, but that evidence of such change may be an important index of educational progress. Whilst the overall ASC of the dyslexics was found to be some 9 points below that of the standardisation sample of secondary school pupils on the Myself-as-a-Learner Scale, more fine grained analysis of the responses revealed a steady and significant growth in MALS scores from well below average in Year 8 to slightly below average in Year 10. Moreover, this increase in ASC was due to specific improvement on such items as 'When I get stuck with my work, I can usually work out what to do next,' and 'I like having difficult work to do.'

SOCIAL SELF-CONCEPT

Despite the concern that has sometimes been expressed about the possible effects of dyslexic difficulties on social interactions and a consequent sense of social isolation, the research evidence in this area is, at best, equivocal. Zeleke's (2004) review of 30 studies comparing the social self-concept of children with LD with that of their normally achieving peers revealed that 70 per cent found no significant differences between the groups, 20 per cent showing significant differences in favour of the NA groups, and 7 per cent showing differences in favour of those with LD. Further light is thrown on this confusing state of affairs by the study of Durrant et al. (1990), which attempted to break down the LD category into more homogeneous groups and found as a result that their sample of LD children with comorbid behaviour disorders showed signs of comparatively poor social self-concepts, whilst those without such associated difficulties did not. This effect has been found to remain constant over different ages and school grades. The fact of the matter is that a person's social self-concept is likely to have been influenced by a wide range of contributing factors, most of which are unrelated to their specific learning difficulties. This is confirmed by a number of studies involving one-to-one interviews with both adolescent and adult dyslexics (Bear et al., 1991; Burden, 2005; Ingessson,2007; Kistner and Osborne,1987; Vaughn et al., 1998).

Maughan (1995) takes a somewhat different perspective by focussing upon the potential long term outcomes of developmental reading problems with particular reference to social adjustment and psychological well-being. Beginning with the Isle of Wight epidemiological studies of Rutter et al. (1970), which indicated strong links between specific reading retardation and conduct disorders in middle childhood and adolescence, Maughan concludes that the bulk of the research evidence favours a 'shared risk' model of causation over one which sees either reading retardation or behavioural disorders as the main cause. She points out also that a number of longitudinal studies have found that reading problems played little if any role in the persistence of psychiatric disorder after middle childhood. Spreen (1987), on the other hand, found that learning disabled groups were more likely than others to have been seen by psychiatrists whilst in their teens, but not in the early twenties. This is in sharp contrast to a slightly earlier study by Bruck (1985), where no significant problems of general adjustment were found in her sample of young adults with learning disabilities, most of whom reported a marked drop in their social adjustment difficulties on reaching adulthood.

Longitudinal studies of British national cohorts have included investigations of depressed mood and other psycho-social difficulties in adulthood and have attempted to relate these to childhood developmental factors (ALBSU, 1987; Ekinsmyth and Bynner, 1994). Evidence was produced in both studies to show that developmental difficulties with literacy and numeracy were likely to be prognostic indicators of later feelings of depression, particularly in women, and employment difficulties in men. Such findings are complicated by the fact that they were mainly based on self reports of feelings at particular moments in time and linked to other factors in the respondents' lives. Taken as a whole, Maughan concludes that the available evidence is that many of the problems evident in the school years may be avoidable in adult environments that are supportive, or present a known range of challenges, and where reading skills are of more limited salience (Maughan, 1995: 366).

GENERAL SELF-CONCEPT

A multitude of studies, from Chapman's (1988) early work onwards have tended to reveal few significant differences between the general self-concepts of children with LD or dyslexia. Zeleke's (2004) meta-analysis of 28 studies in this area found that just under 70 per cent showed no significant difference in GSC between LD children and their normally achieving peers. Again, these effects were found to remain constant across different ages and school grades. As indicated above, this should come as no surprise to those who recognise the GSC as multi-faceted, with academic success as just one of a number of contributory factors. However, Zeleke (2004: 148) argues, somewhat surprisingly, that general self-concept, global self-esteem, global self-worth and general self-esteem are terms which can and have been used synonymously to denote one's personal perception of overall self worth. What this viewpoint fails to take into account is the difference between the accuracy of a person's self perceptions, how that person feels about those perceptions and the effects that this has upon their behaviour. As indicated above, this is a highly complex area which is unlikely to be illuminated by the mere application of a simple scale. It is for this reason that issues relating to the assessment of self-esteem and the nature of the possible effects of dyslexia/learning disabilities on the developing person's general feelings of self-worth and self-efficacy in specific domains will be considered separately in the next section.

SELF-ESTEEM

Global studies of the self-esteem of adolescents and adults with longstanding reading difficulties, whether carried out by surveys or individual interview, have tended to find, in contrast to most studies on the self-concept of similar groups, lower levels of self-esteem than that of their normally achieving peers (Fairhurst and Pumfrey, 1992; Gerber et al, 1990; Gjessing and Karlsen, 1989). In the USA, studies by Saracoglu et al. (1989) and Lewandowski and Arcangelo (1994) both reported low self-esteem in adults with learning disabilities and accompanying difficulties with emotional adjustment in later life. An interview study by Hughes and Dawson (1995) of 47 adults attending a Dyslexia Institute for help with their ongoing difficulties revealed a typical pattern of failure at school leading to long lasting negative feelings of self-worth, together with personal perceptions of low intelligence. A large proportion of this group, however, appeared to indicate that one of the root causes of their continuing difficulties was lack of early diagnosis and support. Humphrey and Mullins (2002) concluded from the results of their study that the experience of dyslexia has clear and demonstrable negative effects on the self-concept and self-esteem of children, adding that 'the parallels between learned helplessness and children with reading difficulties are striking' (p.197).Similarly, when Riddick and her co-workers compared the educational histories of a small number (n=16) of dyslexic university students with matched controls, they found that the dyslexics displayed significantly lower self-esteem than the controls and reported themselves as more anxious and less competent in their written work than their contemporaries. Moreover, data from the British birth cohort longitudinal study revealed a vulnerability to depression amongst those with perceived continuing literacy difficulties (ALBSU, 1987).

The question of whether this represents a developmental trend amongst dyslexics was examined by Ingesson (2007), who interviewed 75 Swedish dyslexic teenagers and young adults (27 female; 48 male) to investigate their school experiences with regard to their feelings of well-being, their educational achievements, their self esteem, their peer relationships and their future expectations. In this study a discrepancy definition of dyslexia was used, whereby reading and spelling attainment two years or more below that anticipated from a Full Scale IQ score was considered indicative of dyslexia. Most of the participants in the study, aged between 12 and 19, were interviewed in person (but 10 by telephone) at least 3 years after their original diagnosis. All had received some form of special support in school, but none had attended a special class or school for dyslexics.

The responses of the young people in this study revealed a developmental trend whereby general feelings of low well-being at elementary school (ages 7–10) tended to become worse at middle school, but then began to improve, until by the time they reached upper secondary school over 70 per cent rated their satisfaction levels as 'good' or 'very good'. This contrasts with the findings of a survey carried out by Bender and Wall (1994) in the United States, which suggested that the social and emotional development of those with learning disabilities showed an increased risk of deterioration with increasing age. However, of the 39 in Ingesson's study who had completed upper secondary school, only 5 (13 per cent) had chosen to go to college, which is well below the average of 43 per cent in Sweden. Typical comments about early school years were in the nature of, 'I knew that something was wrong with me, but I didn't know what it was then,' and 'I felt I was the most stupid child in the class.' This is very much in line with the findings of earlier studies by Palombo (2001) and McNulty (2003), which found that dyslexics, by early to middle school, encountered unexplained difficulties or failures that called into question their sense of intelligence and motivation.

When it came to school achievements, the great majority of the respondents felt that being dyslexic had had a significant negative influence; no-one considered that they had done well at elementary or middle school, but about half felt they had succeeded much better as they moved up through the education system. This may have been related to the ever widening range of options open to students in Swedish upper secondary schools. These personal perceptions were found to be strongly associated with the respondents' actual school reports and examination successes.

The participants in this study were asked the simple question of whether and to what extent their reading and writing difficulties had affected their self esteem. A significant minority (40 per cent) considered that their self esteem had been affected 'quite a lot' or 'very much,' with those affected in this way also holding much more negative views about their future prospects. Interestingly, those who had left school, particularly if they were in regular employment, tended to hold more positive views about the future than those remaining within the education system. This finding would appear to be in line with Zeleke's (2004) similarly negative conclusion from his meta-analysis of over 40 studies on academic self esteem in students with learning disabilities. What should be borne in mind, however is that this data is open to re-interpretation as the *majority* of the respondents in Ingesson's study did not feel that their self esteem had been negatively affected.

Most of the dyslexic students did not feel that their learning difficulties had had any negative effect on their relationships with their peers. In fact, friendships appeared to be one of the most positive aspects of school for them. However, almost a third claimed to have been teased or bullied because of their literacy difficulties, which is higher than the general expectation of about 10 per cent. Moreover, there was a close relationship between experiences of being bullied and feelings that dyslexia had had a very negative impact on self esteem. This raises the issue of the importance of support from friends and family members in helping overcome the potentially negative emotional consequences of finding oneself struggling with literacy difficulties in the early school years. McNulty (2003) suggests that although negative emotions are never completely avoidable, parental and professional support can reduce the frequency and intensity of these feelings. The significant role played by parents in this respect has been highlighted also by the research carried out for the Buttle Foundation on behalf of the British Dyslexia Association by Griffiths et al. (2004).

One other factor identified as important by Ingesson in the developing sense of identity in dyslexic children is the timing and nature of diagnosis, and the children's reactions to this. In this study the mean age of diagnosis was twelve years, and appears to have provoked a variety of reactions at the time (see also Zetterquist-Nelson, 2003). Although just under half of the respondents claimed not to remember the time at which they were informed that they were dyslexic, those who did were fairly evenly split between those who had not reacted in any particular way, those who felt devastated and those who felt relieved to find that they were not really stupid. A similar set of reactions was forthcoming in an

English study of 50 dyslexic boys (Burden, 2005), which serves to emphasise that this process may well serve as a significant life event in the developing self concept and self esteem of dyslexic children. A positive acceptance of the diagnosis and its implications appears to be a key feature in the future emotional and educational development of the dyslexic child (Davenport, 1991) and to later adult adjustment and success in life (Maughan,1995).

One of the major problems relating to studies of self-esteem is that they do not always have a solid grounding in psychological theories of learning and development. As Butler and Gasson point out in their 2005 review of self esteem/self-concept scales for children and adolescents, the literature on self continues to be beset with confusing terminology, with the result that there remains noticeably little agreement on nomenclature, despite the fact that over one thousand articles are published each year making reference to self esteem alone. The solution proposed by these authors is to make a comprehensive analysis of the most widely used self-esteem scales, concluding that most scales could be improved in terms of their validity, reliability and general psychometric properties (Butler and Gasson, 2005: 199). The approach to be taken here, however, differs markedly from such a reliance on single measures of self-esteem. Instead, the approach suggested by Humphrey and Mullins (2002) will be adopted, whereby the attributions of those with specific learning difficulties of a dyslexic nature in seeking to make sense of their difficulties will be examined, particularly with regard to the nature and locus of their reasons for success and failure in learning and whether they view these as fixed or changeable. Consideration will also be given to evidence of feelings of self-efficacy or learned helplessness amongst dyslexic populations.

ATTRIBUTION THEORY

In brief, Attribution theory suggests that one of the most important motivating factors in peoples lives is the sense they make of their perceived successes and failures (Weiner, 1974). Specifically, it is suggested that there is a limited set of reasons that people draw upon, that these reasons may be seen as internal to the individual or due to external forces or influences, as changeable or fixed, and controllable or uncontrollable. Thus someone with learning difficulties of a dyslexic nature may come to see their difficulties as being due to limited intelligence (internal locus) or to poor teaching (external locus). They may see themselves as capable of developing their literacy skills by hard work (controllable), or they may see themselves as simply unable to learn to read, however hard they try (uncontrollable, learned helplessness). Thus, in one of the few studies attempting to apply an attributional approach to learning disability, Butkowsky and Willows (1980) claim to have found that good and poor readers display different attributional styles, with poor readers being more likely to blame themselves for failure and to attribute success to luck. Poor readers also appeared to have lower expectations of success (negative self-efficacy) and to respond more negatively to failure.

In their comparison study of the academic self-perceptions and attributions for success and failure of 20 children with dyslexia with 20 normally achieving matched controls, Frederickson and Jacobs (2001) found that the dyslexic children displayed significantly lower academic self-concepts than the controls, but their feelings of global self-worth were not significantly lower. However, they also found that children with a strong internal locus of control tended to have higher academic self-concepts than those who saw success and failure as outside their control, even when actual levels of reading attainment were taken into account. Although this contrasts with an earlier study by Jacobson et al. (1986), who found that children with learning disabilities tended to see both success and failure as outside their control, it mirrors the results of a two year longitudinal study by Kistner et al. (1988), who found that that the academic progress of children with specific learning difficulties was greatest in those with an internal locus of control.

In their conclusion to their interview study, Riddick et al. (1999) suggest an important way forward for future research into the possible longstanding effects of dyslexia on the developing young person's self-esteem, when they state (p. 244),

> We need to identify those dyslexic students who are low in self-esteem and/or high in anxiety and evaluate what forms of environmental changes and support will be most effective in raising their self-esteem and lowering their anxiety . . . (therefore) . . . consideration should be given to using measures such as these as part of students' overall assessment.

This reflects to some extent the findings of Thomson (1990), who found that the academic self-esteem of pupils attending a residential specialist school for dyslexics increased considerably in accordance with the time the pupils spent at the school. Herrington and Hunter-Carsch (2001) also point to the need for a research/assessment/teaching framework in which the multi-faceted, dynamic nature of dyslexia is recognised and explored, including more than literacy difficulties and the characteristic cognitive profile, and focusing on whole-person factors and the developing dynamics of the cognitive-affective constellation with personality aspects (p. 115).

Burden's in depth study (2005) of the changing sense of identity of 50 adolescent boys attending an independent specialist school for dyslexics attempted to explore many of the issues raised above. Voluntary interviews of about one hour with each boy were carried out, during which they were asked about their personal definitions of dyslexia and its causes, the time when and manner in which they were first diagnosed, their initial reactions and understanding of what was meant by the term, and the subsequent reactions of significant others (parents, teachers, peers). They were asked also who had helped them most to understand and deal with their difficulties, and to speculate upon their future prospects. Each interviewee completed the Myself-as-a-Learner Scale together with questionnaires about their feelings of self-efficacy, locus of control, learned helplessness and possible feelings of depression. Additionally, the boys were asked to construct a metaphor to summarise their feelings about dyslexia.

The results showed that the general level of academic self-concept of this group was below that of the standardisation sample of mainstream pupils of a similar age, but that this approached more nearly to the norm the longer they remained at the specialist school and their academic attainments improved. A clear sense of internal locus of control was revealed, together with strong feelings of self-efficacy and very few indications of learned helplessness or depression. However, the kinds of metaphors that were produced appeared to provide further helpful insights into the nature and strength of the barriers that each individual perceived his dyslexic condition as presenting (Burden and Burdett, 2007). An analysis of the boys' learning careers indicated further that by the onset of adolescence those manifesting dyslexic difficulties are likely to have established a set of core constructs about themselves as learners which will be related to their attributions for success and failure, their feelings of self-efficacy or learned helplessness, their sense of internal locus of control and degree of optimism about their future prospects. These constructs are most likely to have been shaped by the time and manner in which their difficulties were initially recognised and the action taken by significant others as a result of this diagnosis. In particular, the ongoing support of parents and appropriate remedial action by key figures within the educational system are likely to make an essential contribution to the child's continuing motivation to succeed.

SOME TENTATIVE CONCLUSIONS

The overwhelming body of evidence from a considerable range of studies indicates that children faced with specific learning difficulties of a dyslexic nature are most likely to develop low academic self-concepts as a result of these difficulties. If the theory and measurement of academic self-concept is to carry any real meaning, this is not at all unexpected. What we are not as yet in a position to state with anything like the same level of certainty is the exact nature of the relationship between the degree of a child's literacy difficulties and their academic self-concept, nor the best age at which a diagnosis of dyslexia should be made. However, once such a diagnosis has been made and appropriate action follows, then there appears to be good reason to expect that the academic self-concept can and should improve in accordance with the child's educational progress.

On the other hand, there is little evidence to support the notion that children with dyslexic difficulties are likely to suffer from poor social self-concepts solely as a result of their learning difficulties. On the contrary, not only are dyslexic children likely to see themselves as popular as other children, but may well cite the support and understanding of friends as being a key factor in their adjustment to school.

The fact that the construction of the self-concept is generally considered to be related to a number of separate developmental factors makes it highly unlikely that any consistent relationship will be found between GSC and dyslexia, as many studies have shown, except in circumstances where the attainment of literacy may be seen to be of overriding significance in a person's life. This may well prove to be the case for individuals with severe dyslexic difficulties in societies where literacy is seen to be of paramount importance. As yet, however, no evidence on this score appears to be forthcoming. It is nevertheless important to recognise the distinction between general self-concept (GSC) and global self-esteem (GSE), despite the apparent belief of some researchers that the two terms can be used interchangeably.

Although studies of GSE have tended to show that children and adults with learning disabilities, including dyslexia, have lower self-esteem than their normally attaining peers, the present author is in agreement with critics such as Humphrey (2004) who question the value of seeking to establish such simplistic associations. The approach taken here has been to examine the research evidence from studies of a more attributional nature in which the contribution of feelings of self-efficacy, learned helplessness, internal locus of control and depth of understanding of the reasons for their difficulties can make a difference to those individuals' lives. Although the evidence remains as yet somewhat limited, it does appear that such an approach may well provide a missing piece to the jigsaw of how best to help those suffering from dyslexia.

As has been indicated above, there remains a great deal of as yet uncompleted research in the study of dyslexic individuals' developing sense of identity. Few studies differentiate between the thoughts and feelings of dyslexic males and females, for example, or even between dyslexics of different age groups. We do not yet know, as indicated previously, how important the degree of a person's literacy difficulties may be in affecting their feelings about themselves, or whether the discrepancy between their attainments in literacy and other cognitive or life skills is a significant contributing factor. Nor do we know whether the apparently highly promising approach of attribution re-training can provide an important value-added factor to more conventional intervention techniques, or whether helping dyslexics to reconstruct the metaphors they draw upon to visualise their difficulties could help them overcome some barriers to learning. What is clear, however, is that further in-depth research into factors relating to the developing sense of identity of specific subgroups of children and adults suffering from learning disabilities of a dyslexic nature is both warranted and necessary, if we are ever to be able to fully understand this complex and perplexing condition.

REFERENCES

Abramson, L.Y., Seligman, M.E.P. and Teasdale, J.D. (1978) 'Learned helplessness in humans: critique and reformulation', *Journal of Abnormal Psychology*, 87: 49–74.

Adult Literacy and Basic Skills Unit (ALBSU) (1988) *After the Act; Developing basic skills work in the 1990s.* London : ALBSU.

Bandura, A.(1997) *Self-efficacy: the exercise of control.* New York: W.H.Freeman

Bandura, A., Pastorelli, C. and Caprara, G.V.(1999) 'Self-efficacy pathways to childhood depression', *Journal of Personality and Social Psychology,* 76: 258–269.

Bear, G.G., Juvonen, J. and McInery, F. (1993) Self-perceptions and peer relations of boys with and boys without learning disabilities in an integrated setting: a longitudinal study, *Learning Disabilities Quarterly,* 19(1), 23–32.

Bender, W. and Wall, M.E. (1994) 'Social-emotional development of students with learning disabilities'. *Learning Disability Quarterly,* 17: 323–341.

Boetsh, E.A., Green, P.A. and Pennington, B.F. (1996) 'Psychological correlates of dyslexia across the life span', *Development and Psychopathology,* 8: 539–562.

Bracken, B.A. (ed.) (1996) *Handbook of self-concept: developmental, social and clinical considerations.* New York: Wiley.

Bruck, M. (1985) 'The adult functioning of children with specific learning disability', in I.Siegel (ed), *Advances in Applied Developmental Psychology.* Norwood,NJ: Ablex.

Burden, R.L.(2000) *The Myself-As-Learner Scale (MALS).* Windsor: NFER-Nelson.

Burden, R.L. (2005) *Dyslexia and Self Concept: Seeking a dyslexic identity.* London: Whurr.

Burden, R.L. and Burdett, J. (2007) What's in a name? Students with dyslexia: their use of metaphor in making sense of their disability, *British Journal of Special Education,* 34(2), 77–81.

Butkowski, T.S. and Willows, D.M. (1980) 'Cognitive motivation and characteristics of children varying in reading ability: evidence of learned helplessness in poor readers', *Journal of Educational Psychology,* 72: 408–422.

Butler, R.J. and Gasson, S.L. (2005) 'Self-esteem/elf-concept scales for children and adolescents: A review', *Child and Adolescent Mental Health,* 10 (4):190–201.

Byrne, B.M. (1996) Academic self-concept: its structure, measurement and relation to academic achievement, In B.A. Bracken (ed) *Handbook of Self-Concept; Developmental, social and clinical considerations.* New York; Wiley. 287–316.

Chapman, J.W. (1988) 'Learning disabled children's self-concepts', *Review of Educational Research,* 58 (3): 347–371.

Cosden, M., Elliott, K., Noble, S. and Kelemen, E. (1999) Self-understanding and self-esteem in children with learning disabilities, *Learning Disabilities Quarterly,* 22(4), 279–290.

Covington, M.V. (1992) *Making the Grade.* Cambridge: Cambridge University Press.

Davenport, L. (1991) 'Adaptation to dyslexia: acceptance of the diagnosis in relation to coping efforts and educational plans', *Dissertation Abstracts International,* 52(3–B), ISSN 0419–4217.

Durrant, J.E.,Cunningham, C.E.and Voelker, S. (1990) 'Academic, social and general concepts of behavioural subgroups of learning disabled children', *Journal of Educational Psychology,* 82 (4): 657–663.

Elkinsmyth, C. and Bynner, J. (1994) *Young Adults' Literacy and Numeracy Problems: Some evidence from the British Cohort Study.* London : ALBSU.

Fairhurst, P and Pumfrey, P.D. (1992) 'Secondary school organisation and the self-concepts of pupils with relative reading difficulties', *Research in Education,* 47: 17–27.

Frederickson, N. and Jacobs, S. (2001) 'Controllability attributions for academic performance and the perceived scholastic competence, global self-worth and achievement of children with dyslexia', *School Psychology International,* 22 (4): 401–416.

Gerber, P.J., Schneiders, C.A. and Paradise, L.V. (1990) 'Persisting problems of adults with learning disabilities: self-reported comparisons from their school age and adult years', *Journal of Learning Disabilities,* 23: 570–573.

Gjessing, H.J. and Karlsen, B. (1989) *A Longitudinal Study of Dyslexia.* New York: Springer.

Griffiths, C. Norwich, B. and Burden,R.L. (2004) '"I'm glad that I don't take no for an answer": Parent-professional relationships and dyslexia', Research Report on behalf of the Buttle Trust and the British Dyslexia Association: Exeter University School of Education and Lifelong Learning.

Hansford, B.L. and Hattie, J.A. (1982) The relationship between self and achievement/performance measures, *Review of Educational Research*, 52, 123–142.

Harter, Keith and Bracken (1996) in *Handbook of self-concept: developmental, social and clinical considerations.* New York: Wiley.

Harter, S. Historical roots of contemporary issues involving self-concept. In B.A. Bracken (ed) 1–37.

Herrington, M. and Hunter-Carsch, M. (2001) 'A social interactive model of specific learning difficulties', in M.Hunter-Carsh (ed.) *Dyslexia: A Psycho-Social Perspective.* London: Whurr.

Hughes, W. and Dawson, R. (1995) 'Memories of school: Adult dyslexics recall their school days', *Support for Learning*, 10 (4): 181–184.

Humphrey, N. (2002) 'Teacher and pupil ratings of self-esteem in developmental dyslexia', *British Journal of Special Education*, 29 (1): 29–36.

Humphrey, N. (2004) 'The death of the feel good factor? Self-esteem in the educational context', *School Psychology International*, 25 (3): 347–360.

Humphrey, N. and Mullins, P.M. (2002) 'Personal constructs and attribution for academic success and failure in dyslexia', *British Journal of Special Education*, 29 (4): 196–203.

Ingesson, G. (2007) 'Growing up with dyslexia: Cognitive and psychosocial impact and salutogenic factors', Doctoral thesis, Psychology Department, Lund University, Sweden.

Jacobson, B., Lowery, P. and Du Cette, J. (1986) 'Attributions of learning disabled children', *Journal of Educational Psychology*, 78: 59–64.

Keith, L.K. and Bracken, B.A. Self-concept instrumentation: a historical review. In B.A.Bracken (ed) 91–170.

Kistner, J. and Osborne, M. (1987) 'A longitudinal study of LD children's self-evaluations', *Learning Disability Quarterly*, 10 (4): 258–266.

Kistner, J.A., Osbourne, M. and Le Verrier, L. (1988) 'Causal attributions of learning disabled progress', *Journal of Educational Psychology*, 80: 82–89.

Leonardi, A. (1993) comparability of self-concept among normal achievers, low achievers, and children with learning difficulties, *Educational Studies*, 19(3), 357–371.

Lewandowski, L. and Arcangelo, K. (1994) 'The social adjustment and self-concept of adults with learning disabilities', *Journal of Learning Disabilities*, 27: 598–605.

McNulty, M.A. (2003) 'Dyslexia and the life-course', *Journal of Learning Disabilities*, 36: 363–381.

Marsh and Hattie (1996) in *Handbook of self-concept: developmental, social and clinical considerations.* New York: Wiley.

Marsh, H.W. and Hattie, J.A. Theoretical perspectives on the structure of self-concept. In B.A. Bracken (ed) 35–90.

Maughan, B. (1995) 'Annotation: Long-term outcomes of developmental reading problems', *Journal of Child Psychology and Psychiatry*, 36: 357–371.

Palombo, J. (2001) *Learning Disorders and Disorders of the Self in Children and Adolescents.* New York: Norton.

Pajares, F. (1999) Current directions in self-efficacy research. www.emory.edu/EDUCATION/mpf/effchapter.htm

Resnick, M.J. and Harter, S. (1989) 'Impact of social comparisons on the developing self-perceptions of learning disabled students', *Journal of Educational Psychology*, 81: 631–638.

Riddick, B., Sterling, C., Farmer, M. and Morgan, S. (1999) *Dyslexia*, 5: 227–248.

Rosenberg, M. (1979) *Conceiving the Self.* Princeton, NJ; Princeton University Press.

Rutter, M., Tizard, J.and Whitmore, K.(eds) (1970) *Education, health and behaviour.* London: Longman.

Saracoglu, B., Minden, H.and Wilchesky, M. (1989) 'The adjustment of students with learning disabilities to university and its relationship to self-esteem and self-efficacy', *Journal of Learning Disabilities*, 22: 590–592.

Schunk, D.H.(1991) 'Self-efficacy and academic motivation', *Educational Psychologist*, 26: 207–231.

Seligman, M.E.P. (1991) *Learned Optimism.*New York: Knopf.

Seligman, M.E.P., Abramson, L.Y., Semmel, A.and Baeyer, C.V. (1979) 'Depressive attributional style', *Journal of Abnormal Psychology*, 88: 242–247.

Skaalvik, E.M. and Hagvet, K.A. (1990) 'Academic achievement and self-concept: an analysis of causal predominance in a developmental perspective', *Journal of Personality and Social Psychology*, 58: 292–307.

Spreen, O.(1987) *Learning disabled children growing up: a follow-up into adulthood.* Lisse, Netherlands: Swets and Zeitlinger.

Thomson, M. (1990) *Developmental Dyslexia.* London: Whurr.

Vaughn, S. Elbaum, B.E., Schumm, J.S.and Hughes, M.T. (1998) 'Social outcomes for students with and without learning disabilities in inclusive classrooms', *Journal of Learning Disabilities*, 31 (5): 428–436.

Weiner, B. (1974*) Achievement motivation and attribution theory.* Morristown, NJ: General Learning Press.

Zeleke, S. (2004) 'Self concepts of students with learning disabilities and their normally achiving peers: A review', *European Journal of Special Needs Education*, 19: 145–170.

Zetterquist-Nelson, K. (2003) Dyslexi – en diagnos pa gott och ont. Barn, foraldrar och larare berattar (Dyslexia – diagnosis for good and bad. Children, parents and teachers tell). Lund, Sweden: Studentlitteratur.

The Role of Parents

Gavin Reid, Shannon Green
and Corey Zylstra

This chapter

i) discusses school supports that can assist parents;
ii) makes reference to the nature of effective home/school links;
iii) describes strategies that can be used by parents at home;
iv) discusses the tensions parents can experience; and
v) refers to national and international trends in legislation and practice on the rights and needs of parents within the education system.

INTRODUCTION

This chapter will discuss the key issues from research and practice on the role that parents can play in the assessment process, intervention and in effective communication with schools. Examples from North America, New Zealand and Europe will be referred to and comments will be made on the legislation and its impact on practice.

This chapter will also highlight some of the experiences and views of parents of children with dyslexia. The data for this chapter was obtained from questionnaires and interviews with parents (and children) in different countries of the world. It was interesting to note how parent's experiences differed – even among those parents living in the same geographical areas.

One of the points to emerge from the research evidence gathered for this chapter is that, however careful and sensitive the education authority/system might be in developing procedures for identifying and dealing with dyslexia, there will still be a number of parents whose needs are simply not met. This situation can arise for a number of reasons including misunderstandings and communication difficulties between the school and parents. Often it was noted that the agendas and perhaps the priorities of parents and schools differ. They may also differ in the usage of labels following any diagnosis. This has the potential to cause confusion and conflict. For that reason it is important that schools address, as a matter of priority, the range of supports they can offer to parents.

SCHOOL SUPPORTS

School climate and ethos

Parents need to feel welcome in the school and they can be sensitive to the school climate and overall school ethos. Parent's needs should be considered in the development of the school ethos. It is therefore important to ensure that communication with parents is positive and effective.

Communication

Effective communication is the key to unlocking any confusions and contradictions that may arise between the needs of parents and those of the school. It is important that parents and school link effectively and have shared and agreed views on how to approach the child's learning difficulty.

Basic level communication can be achieved through a regular opportunity to connect during the child's drop off at school or pick up after school. However, this can prove unreliable and inconsistent when factoring in busy schedules and the lack of discretion this may offer. Many schools provide young learners an opportunity to use an agenda to aid in the learning of time management. Since this is already intended to be a daily tool that travels between home and school, it can be easily used for notes between the family and educators. Comments about upcoming assignments, accommodations for existing projects, homework successes and struggles, and timelines for current work can all be noted into an agenda, keeping all parties apprised of the child's academic load. It is important, however, that using the child's agenda as a communication tool remain a positive experience for the child. In cases where agendas are not used, a communication book can be set up using a simple ring-bound notebook.

Another effective form of communication to support the child is through email. With technology being so readily available, teachers and other special educators involved with the child may be willing to share email addresses so that channels of communication are enhanced between all parties. Among the many advantages to using email are the opportunities to share information through copies emailed to all professionals involved with the child, the dated documentation of requests along with the written replies to those requests, and the ability to easily save and store communication occurring over a long period of time.

An additional suggestion to families using email is to follow up face-to-face conversations regarding a child's progress or accommodation with an email to all professionals involved, summarizing the conversation and notes of action that were agreed upon.

If a child has been identified as having a learning disability, team meetings including all members involved in the child's academic success should be organised. Those involved may include parents, teachers, specialty teachers, tutors and other professionals such as speech language pathologists, counsellors, psychologists, if appropriate. These meetings can occur a few times each school year and should strive to accomplish smooth transitions between one school year and the next, set goals for success in the school year including updating the child's individualized education plan, and monitor success of supports during the year. Written documentation of these meetings should be taken and shared with everyone involved.

Ultimately, the vehicles of communication need to be successfully implemented and used by those involved in order to benefit the child, as it is communication itself, rather than its form, that is of utmost importance.

STRATEGIES THAT CAN BE USED BY PARENTS AT HOME

Parents are usually keen to help their child with reading. It is important that they link with the school over this to ensure that the approaches are consistent and that the reading materials are appropriate. It is also important to recognise the value of using strategies such as pre-reading discussion.

Pre-reading discussion

It is important to engage in pre-reading discussion with children before they start reading the text. There is a body of research that suggests that pre-reading discussion is one of the best predictors of a successful outcome in a reading activity.

Some questions that can provide a framework for pre-reading discussion are shown below.

Pointers for pre-reading discussion

- Where does the story take place?
- What is the time period?
- Main characters/anything unusual about the main characters.
- How the story starts?
- What to look out for in the story.
- How does the book/story relate to the learner's previous knowledge/experience?

It might be more effective if the parent reads the passage first to the child, or perhaps use paired reading (see appendix to this chapter, and then present some of the questions shown above to the child).

It is also a good idea to monitor comprehension and to ensure the reader has understood the key points of the book. This could be carried out at regular intervals and for some children it will be necessary to do this at short intervals, such as after every paragraph, page or part of a chapter depending on the child's level of reading. It is important that parents are aware of this; otherwise the child may spend quite a bit of time and effort reading but get very little from the book.

Monitoring comprehension comes naturally and effortlessly for many readers. There are many strategies they may use to monitor their comprehension without recognizing that is what they are doing. They may slow down when reading text that they don't understand, they may reread, look up a word in the dictionary, look for context clues, relate the text to their own experience or background knowledge and all because they realize they have stopped comprehending and need to do something to get back on track. Many students are so busy decoding and reading for accuracy that they don't actually realize they are not comprehending. They don't have the ability to monitor their own comprehension. Parents can help by reading with their child and stopping regularly to check and make sure the child still comprehends. Then they can encourage the child to use the same strategies when they are reading alone so that eventually the child learns to monitor their comprehension independently. The creation of a reading strategy by Palinscar and Brown (1984) called Reciprocal Teaching is a powerful tool in helping children with comprehension monitoring. It looks at a structured approach to reading with your child while enabling the child to monitor their comprehension through a four-step process: summarizing, questioning, clarifying and predicting.

This approach is often used by teachers in the classroom but can also be used successfully when reading one-on-one with a parent. To begin the process of reciprocal teaching, the parent reads a few paragraphs from the reading then summarizes for the child what he/she has read. The parent then clarifies any concepts that may be confusing or words that may not be understood, asks a few questions about the passage and then makes a prediction about what will happen next. The child then takes a turn reading and goes through the same four steps of summarizing, questioning, clarifying and predicting. The exact order of the steps is not important but it may be useful to make up cue cards with visuals for each of the four steps. It is also important to recognize the different levels of comprehension and be sure to ask questions that go beyond the literal meaning. Many children can answer literal questions which reflect specific pieces of information written in the text; however, they struggle with levels that go beyond a literal level. Questions which are creative may ask the child to change the ending to a story, or ask what they would have done if they were in the same situation as one of the characters. They require the child to use their creativity to think of an answer. A critical question will ask the child to make judgements about the author, the characters or the way the story is written. One of the most difficult types of questions will be at an inferential level. These questions require the child to infer meaning from information in the story that is not directly stated. This is a very important level of comprehension that should not be overlooked.

Reciprocal teaching is a useful strategy for parents to use when they are concerned about comprehension. Ideally, children will become independent with this approach and will eventually learn to monitor their comprehension. Until they are able to do that, however, it is important to put strategies in place that will get them to the point where they will automatically recognize what they do not comprehend and know what to do about it. Reciprocal reading forces them to recognize whether or not they understand what they are reading.

LITERACY

It is important for parents to understand that literacy involves more than reading accuracy. The experience of language is vital for a critical appreciation of literacy. For example the social, cultural and cognitive impact of literacy could be achieved through some other medium, apart from reading such as, discussion, film or through listening. This can help to provide the child with an enriched language experience and promote the development of conceptual understanding of language and a deeper level of processing. These higher order thinking skills are crucial if children are to reach their potential. If access to print is to be a significant barrier to obtaining this language experience, then other means need to be sought. Discussion and different forms of media are therefore important to help the child access enriched language experiences and deep thinking skills that they may not be able to obtain from print. It is important for parents to appreciate this and this is why effective communication with the schools is so important.

MEMORY SKILLS

Children with dyslexia usually have difficulties in remembering, retaining and recalling information. This may be due to short-term, or working memory, difficulties. It may also be due to a naming difficulty, that is, difficulty in recalling the name of an object or place. It is important therefore to encourage parents to at least be aware of strategies that may facilitate remembering and recall. Such strategies can include:

- repetition and over-learning;
- mnemonics;
- mind mapping and other visual strategies that the learner may develop him/herself.

Memory strategies can be made into a game and the fun element can help to enhance memory without too much pressure being put on the child. One parent in our research suggested the following.

'Kitchen cupboards' is a favourite, you have to identify all the products in the kitchen, play around with the products using part of the name, adding it on to part of another products name. For example we may take flour, marmalade, milk, washing powder and work our way through the different combinations of sounds from each of the products. From this we make up silly products like 'marwashder'. My son remembers the sounds and combinations much more easily when I relate it to some fun activity'.

PARENT'S EXPERIENCES – TENSIONS AND SUCCESSES

It is important to listen to parents and take their concerns seriously. Bigger and Barr (1996) indicated, following research with parents, schools and children on self-esteem, that the child can be sensitive to any discord between schools and home.

Some of the challenges from which tensions can arise according to the parents interviewed for this chapter include the need to:

* maintain the child's self-esteem;
* help the child start new work when he/she had not consolidated previous work;
* protect the dignity of the child when dealing with professionals/therapists;
* help the child with their personal organisation;
* consider the anxieties that can arise from peer insensitivity;
* be aware of the misconceptions and misunderstanding of dyslexia that might be shared by teachers, other parents and children.

These responses are quite interesting because they touch on some of the key areas particularly the emotional aspect of dyslexia. They also touch on the misunderstandings and misconceptions that many people can have of dyslexia.

SELF-ESTEEM

It is crucial that parents do not focus exclusively on the achievement aspect by focusing solely on their child's progress in reading and spelling. The emotional well-being of the child is a critical factor if he/she is to make any real progress. This can be gauged by the child's attitude to learning and their level of self-esteem. Boosting self-esteem is therefore important. There are a number of ways of helping to maintain and to boost the self-esteem of children with dyslexia. One obvious and perhaps effective way of boosting self-esteem is to ensure that they achieve some success and receive genuine praise. In order for praise to be effective, the child has to be convinced that the praise is worthy of their achievements. When children feel a failure, it is difficult to reverse these feelings and often they need to change their perceptions of themselves. This can be a lengthy process and ongoing support, praise and sensitive handling is necessary.

A summary of the comments of parents who participated in our research is shown below. The parents found the following useful for developing self-esteem and helping their child achieve some success:

- paired reading;
- reciprocal reading;
- training in positive thinking;
- mind mapping, including software mapping;
- memory games;
- using learning styles;
- opportunity for the child to use to use verbal ability by encouraging discussion;
- focusing on areas of success.

PARENTS' VOICES

As indicated above, it is important to listen to parents – they have a great deal of knowledge and experience in relation to their child's needs. This is highlighted in the extracts below.

'Self-esteem is a huge issue and one that is not helped by dyslexia being seen as a deficit! The continued emphasis on academic achievement and the issues of labelling are problematic for me. A major difficulty with the teaching profession is attitudinal - a lack of knowledge on dyslexia is apparent, although I have found there are also some exceptional teachers, but it is always difficult for a parent to know what advice to take. By the time they are in a position to decide it can be too late, or less effective than it could have been.'

'The balance between home and school is a key issue and although I have had little advice on this I have still had to argue a case for the need for school to understand the fatigue element in a long day. I feel like my child is a square peg in a round hole.'

'We lived with the effects of our son's dyslexia ... there was a failure to recognise that he had a learning difficulty at school and this had a very negative effect as the school labelled him as 'behavioural' but also said he was polite and not the typical 'thug'. No teacher ever mentioned he had learning problems at school – when he was tested at almost 16 years of age his auditory memory was at a six-year-old level.'

'Having fun as a family is important. Home is a safe place, no criticism, try not to push, push, push. Encourage your child to pursue the things he/she is good at. Keep self-esteem high. Set up a good working relationship with the school teacher. Keep trying, there is help available, just keep chipping away.'

'We feel frustrated by the education system – we know there is no quick fix but constantly feel we are just being pacified by the school management. We know as soon as our son moves to the high school he will no longer be a problem for the primary schools' statistics.'

'I am very aware that I have been very fortunate that the education services in our education authority have provided teachers with up to date training in dyslexia and this has greatly benefited me and my dyslexic children. Having a teacher who is very aware of dyslexia and understanding is incredibly supportive'.

One parent living in the United States who decided to home-school her dyslexic son listed the struggles that had to be endured. These include being 'accused of not understanding him, accused of showing favouritism between him and his other siblings, teaching him to read, keeping his attention and making him want to learn, finding the right resource and finding people who are supportive to me.'

The key factors to emerge from these extracts are:

- The issues of self-esteem and the need for parents and the school to collaborate to help the child develop a positive self-esteem.
- The need to ensure that communication takes place as early as possible to prevent the negative effects of failure being experienced by the child.
- The issue of homework and the need to ensure a balance exists between home and school. As one parent above indicated, the child can experience fatigue very easily and it is important to consider this factor when planning homework and to take into account the fact that the child will likely take longer to complete the same piece of work as other children.
- The potential for a learning difficulty to be transformed into a behavioural difficulty – often if this happens the presenting difficulty will be acknowledged as a behaviour one and the actual learning difficulty might be given less attention. It is important to focus on the cause and not only the symptom.
- The need to have faith that your child will succeed and to enjoy family life –fun activities will help the child maintain a relaxed attitude and help to minimise the anxieties that can be caused by reading difficulties.
- It is important that schools value each individual and express this to the parents. It is interesting that one parent quoted above indicated that she felt the school did not want to deal with children with learning disabilities. This is unfortunate, as it undermines the learning and potential for success of children with dyslexia.
- A positive teacher and a positive school can make the world of difference to parents.
- It is important that parents are aware of the potential of some dyslexic children to be overshadowed by siblings. This underlines the need to highlight the child's strengths and not to highlight their difficulties all the time.
- It is important for parents to establish support groups. For many parents this is crucial as it can prevent the feeling of being alone. Additionally it can be a valuable source of information.

TENSIONS – IDENTIFICATION

Some of the tensions that exist around parents and schools relate to identification and assessment. The research in dyslexia and early intervention (Crombie et al., 2004) clearly indicates the advantages of early identification and indicates that early intervention will be more successful if a clear profile of the child's difficulties and strengths are available.

Reid Lyon (1998) in discussing the situation in the United States made the following comment. 'We have learned that for 90–95 per cent of poor readers, prevention and early intervention programs that combine instruction in phoneme awareness, phonics, fluency development and reading comprehension strategies, provided by well-trained teachers, can increase reading skills to average reading levels. However, we have also learned that if we delay intervention until nine-years-of-age, (the time that most children with reading difficulties receive services), approximately 75 per cent of the children will continue to have difficulties learning to read throughout high school.'

This emphasises the importance of early identification and the recognition of appropriate early intervention. Many schools do have well developed policies for the early years, but children with dyslexia will usually require additional considerations and perhaps more intensive input such as that is briefly described above by Reid Lyon (Reid Lyon, 1998, Reid Lyon et al., 2004). It is important therefore that schools link with parents as early as possible to ensure that early identification can take place.

FRUSTRATION

Schools however have to meet the needs of individuals as well as the needs of all learners. Teachers have also to meet the demands placed on them by the management and the education system. These demands are usually set by politicians and are often based on principles relating to accountability and results. It is important to appreciate that the progress made by children with dyslexia may not always be easily measured, and certainly not by conventional means. For example, for some children with dyslexia merely attending school can be a measure of success, but schools may not record this as progress and would rather focus on progress on attainments such as reading, spelling and writing. This is perfectly reasonable but children with dyslexia may not make significant progress in this area, at least in the short term. This can lead to some frustration on the part of parents and highlight very clearly the different agendas that can be seen between home and school. This underlines the importance of effective and shared communication.

LACK OF UNDERSTANDING

Many parents in our research indicated that schools, or some teachers in schools, did not have much knowledge of dyslexia or learning disabilities. This varies from country to country and indeed within countries from area to area. Additionally the level of knowledge of dyslexia within a school will be different. This can be frustrating for parents and underlines the need for extensive staff development in schools in the area of learning disabilities.

NATIONAL AND INTERNATIONAL TRENDS IN LEGISLATION AND PRACTICE – THE RIGHTS AND NEEDS OF PARENTS WITHIN THE EDUCATION SYSTEM

The United States

One of the most influential pieces of legislation on dyslexia that has a potential impact on parents is the No Child Left Behind Act (2001). It is seen as a landmark in education reform in the United States and is designed to improve student achievement and change the culture of America's schools. President George W. Bush described this law as the cornerstone of his administration. It focuses on four main areas: accountability for results; an emphasis on doing what works based on scientific research; expanded parental options and expanded local control and flexibility.

No Child Left Behind targets resources for early childhood education so that all young children get the right start. Each state must measure every public school student's progress in reading and math in each of grades 3 through 8 and at least once during grades 10 through 12. This educational reform also requires that all states and school districts give parents easy-to-read, detailed reports on schools and districts, telling them which ones are succeeding and why. Under *No Child Left Behind*, such schools must use their federal funds to make needed improvements. In the event of a school's continued poor performance, parents have options to ensure that their children receive the high-quality education to which they are entitled. That might mean that children can be transferred to higher-performing schools in the area or receive supplemental educational services in the community, such as tutoring, after-school programs or remedial classes. *No Child Left Behind* gives states and local education agencies more flexibility in the use of their federal education funding. There is also an emphasis on implementing educational programs and practices that have been clearly demonstrated to be effective through rigorous scientific research.

Some of the key points of *No Child Left Behind* that may help parents and children with dyslexia include the following:

- schools can receive more money;
- schools can be more accountable for results;
- it provides states and cities with more control and more flexibility to use resources where they are needed most;
- it focuses on teaching methods that have been proven to work; and can allow parents to transfer their child to a better public school if the state says the school your child attends needs to improve.

The United States is also the main hub of the International Dyslexia Association that has branches in every State as well as affiliate branches in some other countries such as Brazil, Canada, Czech Republic, Israel and the Philippines. The IDA is a very influential group and is consulted in legislative reform and provides comprehensive advice and sources of support for parents.

Canada

In Canada, while there have been tremendous gains in the past decade to publicly acknowledge and accommodate students with language-based learning disabilities/dyslexia, many families are unaware of how to ensure that their child can access the kinds of accommodations or supports they require.

The Canadian Charter of Rights and Freedoms is an important document that ensures education rights of Canadian students. Section 15 of the Charter states: 'every individual is equal before the law and has the right to equal protection and equal benefit of the law without discrimination and, in particular, without discrimination based on race, national or ethnic origin, colour, religion, sex, age or mental or physical disability.' The Supreme Court of Canada has interpreted this to include learning disabilities. However, each province and territory and the federal government have their own separate human rights statute.

Parents who feel that their child has been discriminated against due to their learning disability, are able to launch a complaint with the Human Rights Commissions in their respective province. Since 1993, there have been only a few cases that involve broad education issues, and only seven cases involving a learning disability or dyslexia.

United Kingdom

In the United Kingdom the Special Educational Needs and Disability Act (2001) (SENDA), which includes the code of practice, is the main legislative instrument to help meet the needs of parents. This Act is an amended form of the Disability Discrimination Act (1995) (DDA) that was revised to cover education. The Act provides greater powers to the Special Educational Needs Tribunal and places a duty on Local Education Authorities to provide and advertise both a parent partnership scheme and conciliation arrangements.

The words 'disability' and 'discrimination' are key words in the Act. The Act states that schools cannot discriminate against disabled pupils (the definition of dis- ability is very broad and dyslexia can be seen in terms of the Act as a disability) in all aspects of school life, including extra curricular activities and school excursions.

Parents can claim unlawful discrimination by putting a case to a Special Educational Needs and Disability Tribunal. Under the Act it is unlawful for schools to discriminate in admissions and exclusions and a school cannot deliberately refuse an application from a disabled person for admission to the school. Discrimination is evident when a pupil is treated less favorably and may be at a disadvantage because the school has not made 'reasonable adjustments'. What is meant by 'reasonable' is not explicitly defined in the Act as this depends on individual cases and can be a matter for the Tribunal or an appeal panel to decide.

Essentially the Act aims to incorporate parents as partners in the education of their child. This of course is very important in relation to children with special educational needs and parents need to be informed when a special educational needs provision is made for their child.

PARENT PARTNERSHIP SCHEMES

In England and Wales Local Education Authorities are required to set up Parent Partnership Schemes on a statutory basis, although there are no national standards set. The aim of PPS is to provide a range of services for parents whose children have special education needs (SEN) so that parents can play an active and informed role in their child's education. This implies that if parents are consulted and their views valued then the education experience for the child, the parents and the school would be more harmonious and meaningful.

Many of the points in this chapter can be generalised to parents in all countries and not only those countries specifically mentioned in the chapter. Recognition of dyslexia and introduction of new policies are taking place in many countries that previously had none or did not have a specific and explicit policy. Parents have had a key role to play in this. A good example of this took place in New Zealand when in April 2007 the main national newspapers were emblazoned with the headline – 'New Zealand Government to recognise dyslexia'. Interestingly enough, the article that accompanied the headline featured the endeavours of a parent to achieve this. It is not the first time that parents have been instrumental in successfully lobbying for change.

SUMMARY

This chapter has outlined some of the concerns and anxieties of parents directly from parents themselves. One of the striking points is that parents often have to take the initiative to seek the best for their child and many have done this very successfully. It is also apparent that parents value good communication with the school and dialogue with teachers who are knowledgeable on dyslexia. Parents nevertheless can have a number of anxieties relating to the extent to which their children can reach their potential. It is now well known that there is a positive side to dyslexia (Galaburda, 1993, West, 1997) and it is important that this is recognised and harnessed in policy and practice and in assessment and intervention and parents can have an important role to play in all of these aspects.

REFERENCES

Biggar, S. and Barr, J. (1996) The emotional world of specific learning difficulties. In Reid, G. (Ed.), *Specific Learning Difficulties (Dyslexia) Perspectives on Practice*. Edinburgh, Moray House Publications.

Crombie, M., Knight, D. and Reid, G. (2004) 'Dyslexia: Early identification and early intervention', in G. Reid and A. Fawcett (eds) *Dyslexia in context, research, policy and practice*. London: Whurr, pp. 203–216.

Dept. for Education and Skills (1994, revised 2001) Special Education Needs Code of practice. London: DfES.

Galaburda, A. (ed.), (1993) *Dyslexia and development: Neurobiological aspects of extraordinary brains*. Cambridge, MA: Harvard University Press.

Government of Ireland (2001) Republic of Ireland was the Report of the Task Force on Dyslexia (July 2001).

HMG (2001) Special Educational Needs and Disability Act (2001) SENDA, London: HMSO

HMG (1995) Disability Discrimination Act (1995) London: HMSO.

Lyon, Reid, G., Shaywitz, S.E., Chhabra, V., and Sweet, R. (2004) 'Evidence-based reading policy in the U.S.', in G. Reid and A. Fawcett (eds) *Dyslexia in context, research, policy and practice*. London: Whurr.

Lyon, Reid, G. (1998) Statement of Dr. G. Reid Lyon, Chief Child Development and Behavior Branch, National Institute of Child Health and Human Development, National Institutes of Health to the Committee on Labor and Human Resources Room 430 Senate Dirkson Building Washington, DC April 28, 1998. http://www.readbygrade3.com/readbygrade3co/lyon.htm.

Palincsar, A. and Brown, A. (1984) 'Reciprocal teaching of comprehension fostering and comprehension monitoring activities', *Cognition and Instruction*, 1 (2): 117–175.

Northern Ireland Education Dept (2002) Task Group Report on Dyslexia. Belfast.

SEED (2004) Education (Additional Support for Learning) (Scotland) Bill. Edinburgh: HMSO.

Task Force on Dyslexia. (2001). Report. Dublin: Governemnt Publications. Available *http://www.irlgov.ie/educ/pub.htm* US Government (2001) Reauthorization of the Elementary and Secondary Education Act.

US Government (2001) No Child Left Behind Act (2001). Washington DC.

Reid, G. (2004) *Dyslexia: A complete guide for parents*. Wiley.

Reid, G., Green, S. and Zylstra, C., (2005) *Dyslexia and Parents*. Paper presented at International Dyslexia Association – Denver, USA.

Topping, K. (1995) Paired reading, writing and spelling: The handbook for parents and teachers. Cassell Education, Continuum International Publishing Group, London.

West, T. G. (1991, second edition 1997) *In the mind's eye. Visual thinkers, gifted people with learning difficulties, computer images and the ironies of creativity*. Buffalo, NY: Prometheus Books.

APPENDIX

Paired reading

Studies indicate an increase in reading accuracy, fluency and expression through the use of paired reading (Topping, 1995). In addition, research indicates that children find the method easy to use, and feel they are more competent readers as a result of paired reading. The procedure is as follows:

At the first reading session
1. student and tutor agree on reading times
2. they also agree on a starting signal
3. tutor reviews how technique works

Before reading
4. student chooses reading materials and can change them at any time
5. find a quiet spot away from distractions

Reading in duet
6. Always begin by reading together
7. Non-critical correction of errors works best: if an error is made, the tutor says the word and the student repeats it

Reading solo
8. Student and tutor agree on a solo reading signal
9. Tutor praises the student when the signal is used
10. Tutor continues to offer support and praise during solo reading

Return to duet reading
11. Tutor corrects student's mistake (gives word/student repeats it).
    Return to duet reading until the student signals to go solo again
    'Talk'
12. Remember to relax and talk about what you have read

Dyslexia and Different Languages

PART IV

Dyslexia and Different
Languages

Dyslexia in Different Orthographies: Variability in Transparency

John Everatt and Gad Elbeheri

This chapter

 i) discusses the relationship between orthography and literacy difficulties;
 ii) discusses the transparency between language sounds and written symbols;
 iii) analyses the processing deficits related to dyslexia;
 iv) draws comparisons between English and Arabic; and
 v) discusses the implications for theory and practice across different languages.

Although dyslexia has been identified amongst individuals learning to read and write in a wide variety of languages and, therefore, is not determined specifically by the language spoken (Smythe et al., 2004), the manifestation of dyslexia may vary across different languages and, as such, is not language independent. The important contribution of language and its critical influence on both the nature and incidence of dyslexia has been captured in the framework model of Morton and Frith (see Frith, 1997) which considered language, along with other environmental elements such as teaching, to be in constant interaction with the biological, cognitive and behavioural levels of analysis that best explain dyslexia. Indeed, on the cognitive level of analysis, if the current dominant causal model is correct, that dyslexia is caused by phonological processing deficits which lead to problems associating the written form with its verbal counterpart (e.g., Snowling, 2000; Stanovich, 1988), then it may be hardly surprising that the manifestation of dyslexia varies across languages, since languages vary in the way their orthography represents phonology. Therefore, one of the main features that may determine the manifestation of dyslexia across languages is variability in orthography. Despite commonalities in literacy learning across languages, there is evidence that the factors which predict literacy learning, and that distinguish the dyslexic from the non-dyslexic, may vary across languages (see discussions in: Aaron and Joshi, 1989; Geva and Seigel, 2000; Goswami, 2000; Harris and Hatano, 1999; Katz and Frost, 1992; Leong and Joshi, 1997; Smythe et al., 2004). The aim of this chapter is to explore the current research literature which attempted to consider dyslexia in different orthographies and to discuss some of the evidence for similarities and differences across orthographies. Such work holds the promise of increasing our understanding of the processes involved in normal literacy acquisition and, hence, the problems faced by children with literacy learning difficulties. Identification of causes of deficits in literacy learning that may be common across languages should inform procedures for identifying the individual with dyslexia, as well as theories of dyslexia that are based on the characteristic features of the learning difficulty.

The chapter starts with a general discussion of the main feature of orthographies that has been considered important in this area of research; that is, the relationship between an orthography and the language it represents. The chapter will then go on to discuss research specifically related to Arabic and contrast findings from this language with those associated with work on the English language, the main language on which much of our understanding of and procedures related to dyslexia has been formed. This will be presented as a way of discussing some of the factors that vary across orthographies and how these may affect identification procedures and theoretical models.

ORTHOGRAPHIC TRANSPARENCY

The degree of correspondence between written symbols and the language sounds that they represent has been considered by dyslexia research studies to be one of the primary features which leads to variations across languages when attempting to investigate literacy acquisition. In some orthographies, this relationship is relatively simple: there is close to a one-to-one correspondence between the written symbol (grapheme) and the basic sound (or phoneme) that it represents. In other orthographies, this correspondence is less transparent. A letter may represent several sounds, and a particular sound may be represented by different letters, depending on the context within which the letter or sound is presented. The English orthography is the best example of this less than transparent relationship between letters and sounds; there are many English words that may be considered irregular or exceptions based on the typically taught correspondence between graphemes and phonemes (e.g., HAVE, SAID, YACHT, MONK). However, this level of divergence from what may be called the alphabetic principle (see Adams, 1990; Gillon, 2004) is not universal. Although most languages have some peculiarities, or complexities, in the relationship between graphemes and phonemes, most have rules that connect letters with pronunciation that are more consistent and, potentially, simpler to learn than is the case for English. For example, Greek (see discussions in Harris and Giannouli, 1999) is relatively regular in letter-sound correspondences for reading, though it is less so for spelling. The written form of Greek has changed relatively little over time in contrast to the spoken form (see Mazi et al., 2004). The spelling of a Greek word, therefore, reflects its historical background rather than its modern spoken form, meaning that a child learning Greek may need to assimilate some key morphological rules in order to spell words correctly. However, in reading, a letter or group of letters is/are relatively consistent in the sound they represent.

German, in contrast, is relatively transparent for both reading and spelling (see discussions in Wimmer, 1993; Zeigler and Goswami, 2005). Although there are some exceptions (e.g., the length of vowel representations may require some more complex rule learning), once the relationships between basic written symbols and sounds have been learnt, German written words should be pronounced with a good degree of accuracy. Similarly, Hungarian has a highly transparent orthography (see Smythe et al., 2004), meaning that the Hungarian child should be able to pronounce written words relatively accurately simply from sounding-out the individual letters or letter combinations within a word. For the Hungarian child, a new word can be sounded-out with relative ease, leading to good word decoding accuracy levels and potentially increasing written-word learning.

The potential importance of orthographic transparency can be seen in studies which suggest that word recognition and non-word decoding processes develop faster in more transparent orthographies (see Everatt et al., 2002; Geva and Seigel, 2000; Seymour et al., 2003; Veii and Everatt, 2005). This relationship between the rate of literacy improvements and orthographic transparency suggests that there may be fewer problems with learning a more transparent orthography than a less transparent one, which might mean that dyslexia as a word-level literacy learning difficulty may be less evident in languages that use a relatively simple relationship between letters and sounds – or, to put it another way, the behavioural manifestation of dyslexia (such as literacy deficits) may vary across languages (see discussions in Goswami, 2000; Symthe and Everatt, 2004; Zeigler and Goswami, 2005). From a practical perspective, assessment measures used to identify dyslexia may have to vary across languages. For example, Everatt et al. (2004) found that although alliteration and rhyme phonological awareness tasks could distinguish groups of grade 3 children with and without literacy deficits in English, they were less reliable at distinguishing similar groups of Hungarian children. The same reduction in the ability to identify poor literacy learners from their peers has been found for decoding skills amongst German learners (see Wimmer, 1993), a measure that has often been used in English language dyslexia assessment procedures. These findings suggest the potential need to consider different tests measures in dyslexia assessments across languages, particularly those that vary on the orthographic transparency dimension.

At present, the dominant causal viewpoint about dyslexia is the phonological deficit hypothesis. This perspective has been derived from the substantial evidence that difficulties in phonological processing, particularly when related to phonological decoding, have been a major distinguishing factor between dyslexics and non-dyslexics from early literacy learning to adulthood (see Beaton et al., 1997; Bruck, 1993; Elbro et al., 1994; Rack et al., 1992; Snowling, 2000) and that early phonological training (together with suitable linkage to orthography and literacy experience) improves word literacy and reduces the likelihood of literacy difficulties (see Bryant and Bradley, 1985; Cunningham, 1990; Elbro et al., 1996; Olofsson and Lundberg, 1985; Schneider et al., 1997). As such, the main measures common to most English dyslexia assessment procedures have been those which focus on phonological processing skills, particularly those which assess phonological awareness – that is, the ability to recognise sounds within words (see, e.g., the Dyslexia Screening Test, Fawcett and Nicolson, 1996; the Phonological Assessment Battery, Frederickson et al., 1997). Children who find it difficult to distinguish sounds within verbally presented words would be predicted to have problems learning the alphabetic principle and, hence, should be those children who are most likely to be dyslexic based on the phonological deficit position. However, these phonological awareness measures are the very tasks that have been found to vary in their ability to distinguish good and poor readers across orthographies of different transparency (Everatt et al., 2004). Therefore, when it comes to distinguishing children with and without literacy learning problems in a relatively transparent orthography, other measures apart from those specifically used to assess phonological awareness may be better identifiers. From the phonological perspective, these alternative measures may be measures of rapid naming or short-term/working memory (see Everatt et al., 2004; Wimmer, 1993), since these areas of processing may also rely on phonological skills. However, these cross-transparency differences pose a potential threat to the universality of the phonological deficit viewpoint. At the very least, in order to account for such findings, and retain phonological deficits as the main characteristic of dyslexia across languages, the phonological deficit hypothesis may have to incorporate more than phonological awareness weaknesses as a characteristic feature of the deficit. Also, as yet, the theory has not provided an explanation that incorporates these disparate tasks within the same phonological processing system, nor has it accounted for their variability in prediction of literacy ability across languages (though Zeigler and Goswami, 2005, provide one example of this cross-language level of explanation). Cross-orthographic studies, therefore, may not only inform assessment practice but also theoretical viewpoints about the potential cause or causes of dyslexia.

The developmental model of Goswami and colleagues (see Goswami, 1999; 2000; Ziegler and Goswami, 2005) has suggested that phonological processing skills develop along with literacy learning. For example, Goswami (1999) presented evidence suggesting that the phonological units that correspond to the vowel and subsequent consonants of a word or non-word (e.g., /ink/ in 'think' or 'nink') were most salient to young English readers in comparison to young French readers, but were not salient to young Spanish and Greek readers who seemed to show more evidence of a sensitivity to phonemes. Based on these findings, Goswami (1999) concluded that children learning a relatively transparent orthography develop an awareness of phonemic units at a very early stage of learning to read, and much earlier than expected based on data from studies of less transparent scripts (see also Ziegler and Goswami, 2005). If this is the case, a poor reader with a weakness in phonological awareness (a dyslexic child under the phonological deficit viewpoint) may not be as disadvantaged when learning a relatively transparent orthography compared to their counterparts having to decode a less transparent orthography with a much more complex relationship between letters and sounds. A dyslexic child might be able to rely on relatively simple grapheme–phoneme association rules to support decoding and use these from an earlier age than their counterparts learning a less transparent orthography. This simplicity of association may not task the weak phonological system as much as when they are expected to learn an orthography with a more complex and irregular correspondence between graphemes and phonemes. Indeed, given the reciprocal relationship between literacy learning and phonological skills (Lukatela et al., 1995; Morais et al., 1979), learning a more transparent language may lead to improvements in the phonological processing skills of the dyslexic (Everatt et al., 2002). Hence, decoding skills may be better developed in the dyslexic learning to read a more transparent language, leading to reading accuracy been relative good compared to that presented by dyslexics learning a less transparent orthography. Consistent with this, evidence suggests that word reading accuracy may be less of an identifier of dyslexia in more transparent orthographies. For example, Landerl et al. (1997) compared the reading abilities of English and German dyslexics and found that English dyslexics made comparatively more word reading errors than their German counterparts. It may be that the relatively transparent German orthography may serve as a protective factor against the severe reading deficits associated with dyslexia because German children are able to rely on the high rate of consistency between graphemes and phonemes enabling them to decipher infrequent words and non-words more easily than their English counterparts. However, although the reading accuracy of poor readers from more transparent orthographies are usually found to be higher than those of poor readers from less transparent orthographies, Landerl et al. (1997) found that the German dyslexics presented evidence of slow reading speeds (see also Cossu, 1999; Wimmer, 1993). This finding suggests that phonological decoding deficits can be overcome to some extent by a slow process of translating letters into sound. However, if reading is slow, due to weak phonological decoding, then general reading efficiency may suffer, potentially leading to poor understanding of text (reading comprehension deficits), less experience of new words (lower vocabulary levels) and a lack of enjoyment of reading that may lead to de-motivation to improve reading and spelling skills (Everatt et al., 2002; Snowling, 2000; Stanovich, 1986). Hence, although accuracy levels may be better amongst children with dyslexia learning a more transparent orthography, and even phonological awareness may improve faster when learning a transparent orthography, weak efficiency may still lead to the same general problems with literacy outcome as found amongst children learning a less transparent orthography. This fluency (speed) deficit may help explain why measures of speed have been implicated in assessment procedures for transparent orthographies. For example, research has suggested that rapid naming measures may be a good identifier of literacy deficits/dyslexia, particularly when relatively transparent scripts are considered (di Filippo et al., 2005; de Jong and van der Leij, 1999; Landerl, 2001; Wolf et al., 1994). Wimmer (1993) found that amongst German speaking children, rapid naming of numbers was the largest predictor of variance in speed of reading text and non-word reading. Relatively slow rapid naming speeds were characteristic of German dyslexic children, even though they generally do well on reading accuracy. Similarly, Landerl (2001) suggested that rapid naming tasks presented much stronger relationships with measures of reading speed, whereas phoneme-based tasks were mainly related to reading accuracy. In terms of Arabic, Saiegh-Hadded (2005) found that the strongest predictor of reading fluency in vowelized Arabic was letter recoding speed, which was itself predicted by measures of rapid naming, in addition to tasks requiring phoneme isolation. Overall, then, more regular orthographies may require assessments of literacy skills that test speed of reading rather than accuracy, and measures of speed of reading may be better predicted by measures of speed of processing, such as rapid naming tasks, rather than measures of phonological awareness. Hence, the improved performance in word decoding and the change in main predictors found in previous studies contrasting less and more transparent scripts may be explained under this framework, although further work is necessary to confirm these predictions.

THE ARABIC ORTHOGRAPHY

Our own work in this area has focussed on the Arabic orthography. Arabic is an interesting exception to the above transparency discussion. Consistent with most Semetic languages (such as Hebrew), it has a highly regular/transparent orthography (the marked or vowelized form of the writing system), but it is based on a highly derivational morphological system, the emphasis on which leads to a reduction in the importance of the relationship between letter and sound except as a means of initial learning. Once learning of the basic association between written and verbal form has taken place, the emphasis of the written form is on meaning, which is primarily conveyed by morphological components. Hence, despite languages such as Arabic and Hebrew having a highly regular orthography when fully marked (or fully vowelized), this form of the orthography is rarely used in literature read by the more experienced reader. Once beyond initial schooling grades, the Arabic child experiences mainly non-vowelized text in which short vowel markers are removed leading to an orthography that is highly opaque in its relationship between letters and sounds, and to texts that contain a large number of homographic words (i.e., words that look alike but which represent different concepts and are often pronounced very differently). Such non-vowelized text needs to be read 'in context'. This means that an adult or child experiencing such writings needs to recognise the context within which a word is written, such as the meaning of words around the homograph or the general theme of the passage, to be able to understand the meaning of the word and even pronounce that word correctly. Hence Arabic goes from a relatively transparent form in early learning (consistent with languages such as German) to a relatively non-transparent form, more akin to English, once initial learning has occurred. An understanding of learning to read and write in Arabic, therefore, may require an understanding of learning to read and write across the orthographic transparency dimension.

Consistent with the English language work, research in Arabic has indicated that phonological processes are predictive of reading levels amongst Arabic children and that poor Arabic readers show weak phonological decoding and low levels of phonological awareness in comparison to matched normal readers (see Abu-Rabia et al., 2003; Al-Mannai and Everatt, 2005; Elbeheri and Everatt, 2007). However, the cross-orthographic data discussed above would predict that the difference between Arabic and English in the simplicity of the relationship between graphemes and phonemes, at least at the beginning reading stage, should lead to differences between the languages in terms of the prediction provided by phonological awareness measures. At least in the early years of learning, phonological awareness measures should not be as predictive of literacy difficulties in Arabic as they are in English. There is some evidence consistent with this prediction. Studies of Arabic literacy have found that the level of prediction provided by phonological processing skills seems less than expected from previous research in English (Elbeheri et al., 2006). Although far from conclusive, these findings again suggest that variability in orthographic transparency may affect the relationship between phonological processing skills and literacy ability levels. Such data also suggest that, although phonological measures can provide the basis on which to identify and predict literacy learning difficulties in Arabic, additional measures may provide more precise levels of prediction that may be more specific to Arabic literacy learning. Tests of phonological processing may need to be supplemented by additional tasks that focus more on the specific features of the writing system. One possibility is that an awareness of the morphological roots and patterns that are embedded within the Arabic writing system may provide a unique contribution to Arabic literacy acquisition that explains the reduced level of prediction found for phonological processing measures. Recent data suggest that morphological awareness can predict unique variability in initial literacy levels over and above that explained by phonological awareness measures (Elbeheri et al., in preparation). The importance of morphological awareness in Semitic languages has been discussed previously. For example, Bentin and Frost (1995) argued that morphological analysis was necessary for readers of the Hebrew language, particularly for morphologically complex Hebrew words, and Abu Rabia (2002) concluded that morphological analysis was necessary for Arabic reading comprehension. Frost et al. (1997) have provided data suggesting that lexical access to a Hebrew word was facilitated by other words that shared the same root compared to words that were based on similar orthographic patterns, but which did not share the same morphemic root, and similar evidence has been presented for Arabic speakers by Boudelaa and Marslen-Wilson (2005). Abu Rabia and Taha (2004) found a significant increase in the number of morphological errors produced in reading and spelling tasks by Arabic-speaking dyslexics compared to their peers. As such, morphological awareness may play a useful role in future dyslexia assessment procedures in Arabic.

Furthermore, as discussed above, the use of a more transparent orthography has also been found to lead to increased accuracy in literacy in the early years of acquisition. Assessments of literacy skills within such orthographies, therefore, have often focused on rate/speed of reading rather than reading accuracy (see discussions in Goswami, 2000; Smythe and Everatt, 2004). Therefore, the assessment of Arabic early literacy ability may have to consider measures of reading speed in addition to, or instead of, reading accuracy. However, again the Arabic data are not entirely consistent with the strong prediction derived from this argument. Current data suggest that measures of reading accuracy and phonological awareness can be useful in distinguishing ability differences amongst Arabic children, even in the initial grades of formal learning, and awareness measures may be more predictive of early literacy levels than measures of rapid naming (see Al-Mannai and Everatt, 2004). Arabic may be an exception in that a relatively transparent orthography is used in early learning, but this does not reduce the relationship between phonological processing and literacy ability to the levels found in other relatively transparent orthographies.

One reason why Arabic may vary from predictions based on transparent orthographies may be due to the feature that, after initial learning, the relationship between Arabic written symbols and verbal sounds becomes more complex due to the removal of the short vowel markers that provide clues to pronunciation. As the reader becomes more experienced, therefore, orthographic transparency becomes less reliable as a guide to pronunciation and the need to use the context within which a word is written becomes more important. Given that these more orthographically complex texts (i.e., those without short vowel markers) will be experienced as early as grade 3 in normal schooling, and potentially earlier outside of classroom teaching, then the advantage of a transparent orthography may not be as great for the Arabic learner as for children experiencing a consistently transparent form. In a recent study of the effects of vowelization on young Arabic readers (Elbeheri et al., in preparation), we gave children in grades 3 and 4 (the earliest grades when non-vowelized texts are used in formal learning in the educational context studied) passages with and without short vowel markers and assessed reading accuracy, rate and comprehension. Consistent with the view that a transparent orthography can be read more accurately, both grades scored higher on the reading accuracy measure with the vowelized text. However, reading rate was no different across the two types of text, and by grade 4, the non-vowelized text was associated with better reading comprehension scores than the vowelized text, potentially due to increasing experience of the less transparent orthography. Similarly, although both accuracy and rate were highly related across the two orthographic forms, comprehension levels were relatively independent by grade 4 and non-word reading and working memory measures were good predictors of non-vowelized but not vowelized text comprehension levels. These findings suggest that processes involved in reading comprehension are diverging somewhat across the two orthographic forms. By grade 4, non-vowelized text seems to be the more likely to be experienced and, therefore, may be more likely to show reliable ability differences for assessment procedures. Testing of the skills used when reading non-vowelized text also may be more appropriate for Arabic literacy theory development. Arabic, therefore, may quickly become more like English (i.e., a less transparent orthography) in its patterns of relationships and character- istics than its transparent orthography beginnings may at first suggest. Additionally, the data from these Arabic children suggested that phonological awareness was related to rate but not accuracy in both vowelized and non- vowelized forms, whereas rapid naming was related to both accuracy and rate measures. These latter findings diverge from those reported by Landerl (2001) with German-speaking dyslexic children – though they are more consistent with an association between fluency and phoneme isolation in vowelized Arabic words, as suggested in the data of Saiegh-Hadded (2005). Again, the variation in transparency seems to lead to a divergence from findings with more transparent orthographies than English. As such, Arabic does not seem to produce results entirely consistent with either less transparent orthographies (i.e., English) or more transparent orthographies (e.g., German).

CONCLUSIONS

Overall, then, the current work on the Arabic orthography suggests that literacy learning difficulties may be best predicted on the basis of assessment procedures that include measures of phonological processing, including phonological awareness. Despite variations in orthographic transparency, these measures seem to present the best tools for predicting literacy weaknesses and identifying the underlying problems associated with dyslexia. However, further work is needed to determine whether assessment procedures would be better supplemented by additional measures that focus more on the specific features of the writing system, such as an awareness of morphemic roots and patterns. Similarly, in terms of assessing literacy levels themselves, the current data suggest that, at least for older children (grade 3 or 4 and above), reading words in context (i.e., reading text), as well as measuring the rate of reading, may be a better determinants of the level of Arabic literacy skills than measures that focus on the accuracy of reading individual isolated words. Additionally, taking experience into account, text that is non-vowelized may better represent ability differences across older Arabic children than measures of fully vowelized word reading, which may be more appropriate for younger cohorts (grades 1 and 2). In terms of theory, these data are consistent with the phonological deficit viewpoint – that is, a child with a phonological deficit is likely to show problems with learning the Arabic orthography. However, they point to a need to further investigate hypotheses derived from such causal viewpoints across languages, given that the specific features of the language can lead to variations in the relationship between phonological skills and literacy levels, as well as how literacy deficits will manifest in the language. The findings reported here suggest that Arabic shows more comparability with less transparent orthographies, specifically English, despite the use of a relatively transparent orthography with beginning literacy. They suggest that orthography transparency can be a useful predictor of variability across languages in literacy learning and literacy difficulties; however, such predictions need to be tempered by a consideration of additional factors related to learning, such as, in the case of Arabic, variability in the experience of the transparent orthography.

REFERENCES

Aaron, P.G. and Joshi, R.M. (eds) (1989) *Reading and writing disorders in different orthographic systems.* Holland: Kluwer Academic Press.

Abu-Rabia, S (2002) 'Reading in a root-based-morphology language: The case of the Arabic', *Journal of Research in Reading*, 25: 299–309.

Abu-Rabia, S., Share, D. and Mansour, M. (2003) 'Word recognition and basic cognitive processes among reading disabled and normal readers in the Arabic language', *Reading and Writing: An Interdisciplinary Journal*, 16: 423–440.

Abu-Rabia, S. and Taha, H. (2004) 'Reading and spelling error analysis of native Arabic dyslexic readers', *Reading and Writing: An Interdisciplinary Journal*, 17: 651–689.

Adams, M.J. (1990) *Beginning to read.* Massachusetts: M.I.T. Press.

Al-Mannai, H.A. and Everatt, J. (2005) 'Phonological processing skills as predictors of literacy amongst Arabic speaking Bahraini school children', *Dyslexia*, 11: 269–291.

Beaton, A., McDougall S. and Singleton, C. (eds) (1997) 'Dyslexia in literate adults', *Journal of Research in Reading*, 20 (1).

Bentin, S. and Frost, R. (1995) 'Morphological factors in visual word identification in Hebrew', in LB Feldman (ed.), *Morphological aspects of language processing.* Hillsdale, NJ: Lawrence Erlbaum Associates.

Boudelaa, S. and Marslen-Wilson, W.D. (2005) 'Discontinuous morphology in time: Incremental masked priming in Arabic', *Language and Cognitive Processes*, 20: 207–260.

Bruck, M. (1993) 'Word recognition and component phonological processing skills of adults with childhood diagnosis of dyslexia', *Developmental Review*, 13: 258–268.

Bryant, P. and Bradley, L. (1985) *Children's reading problems.* Oxford: Blackwell.

Cossu, G. (1999) 'Biological constraints on literacy acquisition', *Reading and Writing*, 11: 213–137.

Cunningham, A.E. (1990) 'Explicit versus implicit instruction in phonemic awareness', *Journal of Experimental and Child Psychology*, 50: 429–444.

de Jong, P. and van der Leij, A. (1999) 'Specific contributions of phonological abilities to early reading acquisition: Results from a Dutch latent variable longitudinal study', *Journal of Educational Psychology*, 91: 450–476.

di Filippo, G., Brizzolara, D., Chilosi, A., De Luca, M., Judica, A., Pecini, C., Spinelli, D., and Zoccolotti, P. (2005) 'Rapid naming not cancellation speed or articulation rate, predicts reading in an orthographically regular language (Italian)', *Child Neuropsychology*, 11: 349–361.

Elbeheri, G., AlMenaye, N. and Everatt, J. (in preparation) 'Reading vowelized and non-vowelized Arabic'.

Elbeheri, G. and Everatt, J. (2007) 'Literacy ability and phonological processing skills amongst dyslexic and non-dyslexic speakers of Arabic', *Reading and Writing*, 20: 273–294.

Elbeheri, G., Everatt, J., Reid, G. and Al Mannai, H. (2006) 'Dyslexia assessment in Arabic', *Journal of Research in Special Educational Needs*, 6: 143–152.

Elbeheri, G., Mahfoudhi, A. and Everatt, J. (in preparation) 'The contribution of morphological sensitivity to literacy development among dyslexic and normal speakers of Arabic'.

Elbro, C., Nielsen, I. and Petersen, D.K. (1994) 'Dyslexia in adults: Evidence for deficits in non-word reading and in the phonological representation of lexical items', *Annals of Dyslexia*, 44: 205–226.

Elbro, C., Rasmussen, I. and Spelling, B. (1996) 'Teaching reading to disabled readers with language disorders: A controlled evaluation of synthetic speech feedback', *Scandinavian Journal of Psychology*, 37: 140–155.

Everatt, J., Smythe, I., Ocampo, D. and Veii, K. (2002) 'Dyslexia assessment of the bi-scriptal reader', *Topics in Language Disorders*, 22: 32–45.

Everatt J., Smythe I., Ocampo D. and Gyarmathy, E. (2004) 'Issues in the assessment of literacy-related difficulties across language backgrounds: A cross-linguistic comparison', *Journal of Research in Reading*, 27: 141–151.

Fawcett, A.J. and Nicolson, R.I. (1996) *The dyslexia screening test manual.* London: The Psychological Corporation.

Frederickson, N., Frith, U. and Reason, R. (1997) *Phonological assessment battery.* Windsor: NFER-Nelson.

Frith, U. (1997) 'Brain, mind and behaviour in dyslexia', in C. Hulme and M. Snowling (eds) *Dyslexia: biology, cognition and intervention.* London: Whurr.

Frost, R., Foster, K.I. and Deutsch, A. (1997) 'What can be learned from the morphology of Hebrew? A masked-priming investigation of morphological representation', *Journal of Experimental Psychology: Learning, Memory, and Cognition*, 23: 829–856.

Geva, E. and Siegel, L. (2000) 'Orthographic factors in the concurrent development of basic reading skills in two languages', *Reading and Writing: An Interdisciplinary Journal*, 12: 1–30.

Gillon, G.T. (2004) *Phonological awareness: From research to practice.* New York: Guilford Press.

Goswami, U. (1999) 'The relationship between phonological awareness and orthographic representation in different orthographies', in M. Harris and G. Hatano (eds), *Learning to read and write: A cross-linguistic perspective.* New York: Cambridge University Press.

Goswami, U. (2000) 'Phonological representations, reading development and dyslexia: Towards a cross-linguistic theoretical framework', *Dyslexia*, 6: 133–151.

Harris, M. and Hatano, G. (eds), (1999) *Learning to read and write: A cross-linguistic perspective.* New York: Cambridge University Press.

Harris, M. and Giannouli, V. (1999) 'Learning to read and spell in Greek: The importance of letter knowledge and morphological awareness', in M. Harris and G. Hatano (eds), *Learning to read and write: A cross-linguistic perspective.* New York: Cambridge University Press.

Katz, L. and Frost, R. (1992) 'The reading process is different for different orthographies: The orthographic depth hypothesis', in R. Frost and L. Katz (eds), *Orthography, phonology, morphology and meaning.* Amsterdam: North–Holland.

Landerl, K. (2001) 'Word recognition deficits in German: More evidence from a representative sample', *Dyslexia*, 7: 183–196.

Landerl, K., Wimmer, H. and Frith, U. (1997) 'The impact of orthographic consistency on dyslexia: A German-English comparison', *Cognition*, 63: 315–34.

Leong, C.K. and Joshi, R.M. (eds) (1997) *Cross-language studies of learning to read and spell: Phonologic and orthographic processing.* Dordrecht: Kluwer Academic Press.

Lukatela, K., Carello, C., Shankweiler, D. and Liberman, I.Y. (1995) 'Phonological awareness in illiterates: Observations from Serbo-Croatian', *Applied Psycholinguistics*, 16: 463–487.

Mazi, M., Nenopoulou, S. and Everatt, J. (2004) 'Dyslexia in Greece', in I. Smythe, J. Everatt and R. Salter (eds), *The international book of dyslexia, Part 2*. London: Wiley.

Morais, J., Cary, J., Alegria, J. and Bertelson, P. (1979) 'Does awareness of speech as a consequence of phones arise spontaneously?', *Cognition*, 7: 323–331.

Olofsson, A. and Lundberg, I. (1985) 'Evaluation of long-term effects of phonemic awareness training in kindergarten: Illustrations of some methodological problems in evaluation research', *Scandinavian Journal of Psychology*, 16: 21–34.

Rack, J.P., Snowling, M.J. and Olson, R.K. (1992) 'The nonword reading deficit in developmental dyslexia: A review', *Reading Research Quarterly*, 27: 29–53.

Saiegh-Hadded, E. (2005) 'Correlates of reading fluency in Arabic: Diglossic and orthographic factors', *Reading and Writing*, 18: 559–582.

Schneider, W., Küspert, P., Roth, E., Visé, M. and Marx, H. (1997) 'Short- and long-term effects of training phonological awareness in kindergarten: Evidence from two German studies', *Journal of Experimental Child Psychology*, 66: 311–40.

Seymour, P.H.K., Aro, M. and Erskine, J.M. (2003) 'Foundation literacy acquisition in European orthographies', *British Journal of Psychology*, 94: 143–174.

Smythe, I. and Everatt, J. (2004) 'Dyslexia – a cross linguistic framework', in I. Smythe, J. Everatt and R. Salter (eds), *The international book of dyslexia, Part 1*. London: Wiley.

Smythe, I., Everatt, J. and Salter, R. (eds), (2004) *The international book of dyslexia*. London: Wiley.

Snowling, M.J. (2000) *Dyslexia* (second edition). Oxford: Blackwell.

Stanovich, K.E. (1986) 'Matthew effects in reading: Some consequences of individual differences in the acquisition of reading', *Reading Research Quarterly*, 21: 360–407.

Stanovich, K.E. (1988) 'Explaining the difference between the dyslexic and the garden-variety poor reader: The phonological-core variable-difference model', *Journal of Learning Disabilities*, 21: 590–612.

Veii, K. and Everatt, J. (2005) 'Predictors of reading among Herero-English bilingual Namibian school children', *Bilingualism: Language and Cognition*, 8: 239–254.

Wimmer, H. (1993) 'Characteristics of developmental dyslexia in a regular writing system', *Applied Psycholinguistics*, 14: 1–33.

Wolf, M., Pfeil, C., Lotz, R. and Biddle, K. (1994) 'Towards a more universal understanding of the developmental dyslexias: The contribution of orthographic factors', in V.W. Berninger (ed.), *The varieties of orthographic knowledge*. Dordrecht: Kluwer Academic.

Zeigler, J.C. and Goswami, U. (2005) 'Reading acquisition, developmental dyslexia, and skilled reading across languages: A psycholinguistic grain size theory', *Psychological Bulletin*, 131: 3–29.

Dyslexia and Foreign Language Learning

Michael Dal

This chapter

i) identifies a number of verbal and written language problems students with dyslexia experience in learning a foreign language;
ii) discusses the complex process required involving the interaction and application of several skills when learning a foreign language;
iii) discusses the role of the orthographic mapping system;
iv) highlights the characteristics of dyslexic friendly language instruction; and
v) discusses the role of new technology in assisting with language learning.

INTRODUCTION

The enormous progress in information technology and the globalisation of trade and commerce have increased the need for children and adults to be able to understand and communicate in foreign languages. Learning a foreign language is therefore presently regarded as important in primary as well as in secondary school. Learning at least one foreign language can be an extra load on dyslexic students who are striving to acquire basic oral and written language skills in their mother tongue (Peer and Reid, 2000; Simon, 2000; Lundberg, 2002; Siegel and Smythe, 2004).

In the late 1970s and 1980s, research in foreign language learning examined the relation of cognitive factors (i.e., IQ) and psychological factors (i.e., student anxiety and motivation) to foreign language learning problems. In the beginning of the nineties, Richard Sparks and Leonore Ganschow took a somewhat different approach to understanding foreign language learning problems. In a number of studies, they documented the relation between students' native oral and written language skills and their foreign language acquisition and today a large body of research has found a strong support for this hypothesis, the so called Linguistic Coding deficit Hypothesis (Sparks et al., 1989; Sparks and Ganschow, 1993; Ganschow and Javorsky, 1998). Problems learning a foreign language are closely related to the students' verbal and written language skills in the native language (Downey and Snyder, 2000). Furthermore, lack of motivation in learning a foreign language and feelings of anxiety in having to communicate in a foreign language also are regarded as consequences of the students' foreign language learning problems.

Depending on the severity of the native language problems, dyslexic students exhibit a number of verbal and written language problems in a foreign language. Dyslexic students may exhibit problems in acquiring both basic and more advanced language skills. As in dyslexics' native language profiles, a large variation is seen in the severity of the foreign language learning problems and in the various verbal and written language skills affected in the foreign language. Thus, dyslexic students may have problems distinguishing between words in the foreign language, storing new words and retrieving words from long-term memory (vocabulary). They might have problems learning the pronunciation of foreign words, becoming aware of the sound structure of foreign words (phonological awareness), learning the phoneme-to-grapheme-correspondences, the syntactic structures, the word formation patterns, and the grammar of the foreign language. Furthermore, dyslexic students often suffer from a slow reading rate, poor comprehension of written materials and problems writing in the foreign language (Sparks et al., 1989; Sparks, 1993; Sparks and Ganschow, 1993).

FOREIGN LANGUAGE LEARNING

Learning a foreign language is a complex process requiring the interaction and application of several skills. The foreign language learners need to be able to use their

1 analytic skills in order to understand the formal linguistic structures of the foreign language learning;
2 meta-cognitive skills to enable self-correction and error analysis; and
3 memory, for example, in storing and subsequently accessing new vocabulary.

A fourth aspect, which is linked to all the points above, is having the confidence to use the foreign language both productively (speaking and writing) and receptively (listening and reading).

THE INTERLANGUAGE

One of the most distinguished goals for learning a foreign language is to get the learner to understand, produce and develop knowledge of the foreign language.

Exactly how this is done is still more or less an unsolved riddle that linguistics is looking for the final answer to. Since the late 1960s linguists have collected different kind of knowledge about the complex processes of learning a foreign language. One of the major breakthroughs in this field was undoubtedly the discovery of the necessity to relate and analyze the language the learner themselves develop and use during the process of learning. This language is identified as the interlanguage. The idea of interlanguage is founded upon the assumption that a foreign language learner, at any particular moment in his learning sequence, is using a language system which is neither his or her first language, nor the foreign language. It is a third language, with its own grammar, its own lexicon and so on. The rules used by the learner are to be found in neither his own mother tongue, nor in the target language. One can define the interlanguage as an emerging linguistic system that has been developed by a learner of a foreign language who has not yet become fully proficient but is only approximating the target language: preserving some features of their mother tongue in speaking or writing the target language and creating innovations. An interlanguage is idiosyncratically based on the learners' experiences with the foreign language he or she is in the process of learning (Selinker, 1994).

Before the recognition of the importance of the interlanguage, language learning was solely seen and understood as an issue which implied a direct connection between the mother tongue and the foreign language. This resulted among other things in focusing on the language learner's ability to translate from one language to another. In order to oblige these demands language teachers focused on teaching their language students grammar and translation in the classroom. By recognising the interlanguage, both the research and the teaching of foreign language needed to focus more on the learner's needs and ability to communicate a message on the target language.

Interlanguage is based on the theory that there is a 'psychological structure latent in the brain' which is activated when one attempts to learn a second language. The theory of the interlanguage was proposed by mainly three persons, S. Pit Corder, William Nemser and Larry Selinker. Corder was the first to argue that language errors should not be looked upon as a negative impact on language learning (Corder, 1982). Nemser is the first to understand the interlanguage as an independent language system. However, the theory first really became generally accepted when Larry Selinker published his article 'Interlanguage' (1972). In this article Selinker noted that in a given situation the utterances produced by the learner are different from those native speakers would produce though they attempted to convey the same meaning. This comparison reveals a separate linguistic system and the system can be observed when studying the utterances of the learners who attempt to produce a target language norm.

Taking the interlanguage into account, linguists have tried to clarify to what extent the process of foreign language learning can be compared to learning the mother tongue or the first language. Longitudinal and extensive studies on the matter have been made and the conclusion is that there are many similarities but also many differences. Some of the differences are thought provoking. It has been proved that learners never fail to learn their mother tongue. However, some learners fail to learn a foreign language. Also it is verified that children do not need classroom teaching to learn their mother tongue, while learners learning a foreign language definitely benefit from being taught the foreign language. Also, the studies provide evidence for that a native language learners never ossify in any of the stages of learning the mother tongue. This means among other things that language errors are not permanent and lasting. The native language learner corrects his own errors along the way. Many foreign language learners, however, ossify while learning a second language. That means that they get stuck on a certain linguistic level and are not able to develop their linguistic abilities on the target language. The learner's linguistic abilities on the foreign language can even worsen. This indicates that learning a foreign language is not at all a simple and linear process, where the learner automatic gets closer and closer to the target language (Selinker, 1994; Tornberg, 2001).

FLUENCY AND ACCURACY

When it comes to writing and speaking a foreign language there is also the relation between fluency and accuracy be taken into consideration. Fluency refers among other things to the fact that a conversation or writing process should not stop or break down because the foreign language learner is not able to remember a certain word or phrase. Instead, language learners are encouraged to find other ways to explain or express what he or she means. Instead of using the exact and accurate term the language learner is encouraged to use the word he or she already is familiar with. In some cases this can slow down the development of the learner's active vocabulary and in its extreme this learning strategy can result in that fluency is given priority at the expense of accuracy (Ebsworth, 1998).

Conclusively one can state that over the last few decades modern language teaching has undergone a series of stages characterized by changing theories, learning strategies and methods. By going from a rigid grammatical to a more dynamic communicative approach in foreign language teaching, the language learner today uses and activates communicative strategies. Spoken language in the classroom is far more visible today than it was twenty years ago (Krashen, 1981; 1982; Scarcella et al., 1990).

MODERN FOREIGN LANGUAGE ACQUISITION AND THE DYSLEXIC STUDENTS

The challenge for the teachers of modern languages is to make the language as motivating as possible. The students need a reason to learn, and that needs to be more than passing an exam or a test. One of the most important things is perhaps to make the language seem 'doable' by providing the supports necessary. Certainly, it is very important for dyslexic students to be given every encouragement and to be reassured that success, however limited, is possible.

Foreign language learning also makes intensive use of memorization. In order for words and phrases to be memorized, they first have to enter short-term working memory, so they can be transferred to long term memory. At a later stage they must then be recalled into working memory to be assembled into coherent messages, an important cognitive ability which is seen as a necessity for developing the language learner's interlanguage. However, dyslexic students are likely to have difficulty at all stages, so each stage will require consolidation.

At this point it is important to point out that 'difficult' does not mean 'impossible'. Dyslexic students, like others, will vary in the degree of difficulty they experience with different activities. What is important for all learners is to identify the specific strategies and techniques that can make learning easier.

The general development in language teaching has in some ways contributed to making it easier to include dyslexic students naturally in foreign language classes. Audio-visual media and language programmes for computers are today natural components in modern language teaching and also of great help for the dyslexic student to decipher language codes and therefore help dyslexic students establish and develop an interlanguage. In this context it is worth noting that dyslexic students do not only have problems learning grammar and writing a foreign language but often experience severe difficulties with phonological coding – that is, converting symbols to sounds and sounds to symbol and forming a representation in memory. This is likely to have far-reaching effects on their foreign language learning and their ability to develop an active interlanguage. Studies show that students who struggle to discriminate between different sounds may fail to appreciate how the sounds produced by letters and groups of letters blend together (Schneider and Crombie, 2003).

THE ORTHOGRAPHIC MAPPING SYSTEM

The process of learning to read is facilitated by the ability to associate phonemes with alphabetic letters, for which phonemic segmentation is crucial. In some languages, such as Italian, this mapping is fairly straightforward, that is it associates a particular letter or cluster of letters to one particular phoneme. The spelling system of, for example, English is more arbitrary and unpredictable. Consequently, there is an extra layer of difficulty for dyslexic student using a less transparent language. This can be exemplified by considering English, which uses an alphabet comprising 26 letters, compared to its phonemic inventory of over 40, but for historical reasons, it has not developed a regular phonemic/orthographic mapping system. For example, the single letter 'i' can represent three distinct phonemes in English (unlike, say Italian, where there is a one-to-one mapping), whose differences can be captured by using the

International Phonetic Alphabet, a system of representation devised by linguists to distinguish phonemes (rather than letters)

(1) Bid /bId/

Bird /bɜ:d/

Bide /baId/

A further example of a lack of a direct sound-to-letter association in English can be provided with the common cluster of letters – tough covering different possibilities of pronunciation:

(2) Bough /bau/

Cough /kDf/

Rough /rʌf/

Thorough /θʌrə/

Though /ðəu/

Through /θru:/

These examples illustrate some of the irregularities of English spelling, and if the sounds are not in your head to start with, it can be very difficult to learn to read the words and integrate them in the learner's interlanguage. Learning to read relies heavily on phonemic awareness and impairment puts dyslexics at an immediate disadvantage.

IMPORTANT FOCUS POINTS

Also the dyslexic students may be unable to remember sounds for long enough or clearly enough to repeat them accurately and may have difficulty understanding the relationships between letters or groups of letters and the sounds they make. All this makes it difficult to sustain concentration on spoken language and to pronounce written words correctly. Listening, speaking, reading and writing will all, directly or indirectly be affected. It is therefore incorrect to assume that dyslexic students have difficulty with reading and writing only and that the solution to the problem lies in avoiding these language areas. On the contrary, to develop the learner's interlanguage, all four language skills should be allowed to interact and failure becomes much less likely (Holmberg, 2001).

To help dyslexic students overcome their problems and to develop their inter-language, it seems important to focus especially on questions concerning:

1 phonological processing (poor grasp of sound, lack of awareness of individual sounds within words);

2 memory (working memory might be limited, there may be inaccurate representations in long-term memory);

3 auditory discrimination (uncertainty of the sound which has been heard, difficulty in discrimination between similar sounds, difficulty in knowing where a spoken word ends and a new word begins);

4 sequencing (getting things in order, e.g., letter order in words);

5 speed of processing information (tendency to be slower in responding to incoming information);
6 visual discrimination/recognition (poor ability to differentiate between similar-looking words).

Although many language teachers focus on the communicative method, much of the work done in the modern language classroom is based on texts which often highlight a weakness of which the dyslexic student is all too well aware. To counteract this one should take every opportunity to enrich the language-learning experience by offering additional channels of input and output which will exploit students' strengths. One of the ways to help dyslexic students learn the core skills of reading and writing in a foreign language is finding a variety of ways of making use of direct multisensory structured approaches in language teaching that is, the approach suggested by Orton and Gillingham (2004). A study made in Poland even suggests that using a direct multisensory approach improves the dyslexic student's ability to relate phonemes to their graphic representations and thus the students improve their reading ability (Nijakowska, 2004).

DYSLEXIC STUDENTS IN THE FOREIGN LANGUAGE CLASSROOM

In a multinational survey conducted in primary schools in Austria, Denmark and Iceland the aim was, among other things, to find out what the schools do to help dyslexic students participate in language classes, what language teachers do to help dyslexic students in language classes, what specific tools are used to help dyslexic students and what the language teachers see as the main problems of the dyslexic students learning a foreign language (Dal et al., 2005).

One part of the survey examines how the school policy is concerning dyslexic students and language learning. There was a particular interest in finding out whether schools from the teacher's viewpoint acknowledge that dyslexic students might have difficulties learning a foreign language and what schools do for dyslexic students experiencing difficulties learning a foreign language. Even though the results of the survey indicates that in most of the participating schools dyslexic students are integrated in normal language classes, almost a fifth of the respondents claim that their school does not acknowledge that dyslexic students have problems learning a foreign language. Furthermore, the survey concludes that most schools offer none or only very little remedial training to students experiencing difficulties learning English as a foreign language.

Only very few of the respondents claim that it is included in their school's policy to offer language teachers courses or further education in identifying learning problems for dyslexic students. Conclusively, inclusion is practiced widely in all three participating countries but this is done without offering the necessary means of support to both teachers and students.

In another section of the study the participants were asked which areas of language learning would be especially difficult for dyslexic students to master. The participants were specifically asked to consider whether it is difficult or easy for the dyslexic students to master knowledge of the letter/sound system, the grammar and syntax (morphology), vocabulary acquisition, pronunciation, reading comprehension and spelling and writing. The respondents stated that they are aware of the symptoms they actually are confronted with in a classroom context. However, the teachers seemed less able to recognize dyslexia in foreign language learning when dealing with more basic language processing.

Most of the respondents agree about the importance of dyslexic students attending foreign language classes. However, in general, teachers seem indecisive and uncertain about ways of implementing specific methods supporting the dyslexic students in foreign language classes. The most common way to help dyslexic students today seems to be to make sure that the dyslexic student gets the required reading material in a taped audio version when it is available.

All together the results of the survey indicate that in general, the schools' policy is to include dyslexic students in foreign language, but at the same time most of the schools do not have any policy on how they can offer remedial training for the same group of students. It is though noteworthy that there seems to exist a huge variation within schools in each country, which can be interpreted as if there is not a completely clear school policy in the matter of offering dyslexic students compensatory tools in foreign language classes. Also, there seems to be a discrepancy between the represented countries. In Iceland it seems as if more schools have a policy of offering dyslexic students compensatory tools in language classes. In most of the represented schools the problem of helping dyslexic students in foreign language classes seems not to be a matter dealt within the common school policy but is a matter only dealt with by the individual teacher or a group of teachers. The data on what kind of remedial tools are used in language classes also tells us that the language teachers generally have limited access to usable remedial tools for dyslexic students in language classes.

The results also suggest a need of making the problems of the dyslexic students in foreign language classes much more transparent in the official policy of the schools. A great majority of teachers agree upon that dyslexic students should be offered remedial training in foreign language, that is, by having special study books and computer programs and be offered compensatory tools even though that only a few of the participating teachers say that they make sure that the dyslexic student has the necessary remedial tools when making their homework. Also an overwhelming majority of teachers agree upon that dyslexic students should learn all four skills in a foreign language and not only for example oral skills. However, the results of the survey indicate that the teachers do not have the necessary tools or time to deal with the problems of having dyslexic students in language classes. And in those cases when teachers do have some remedial tools, they do not always know how to use them. In other words: if language teachers use some kind of a remedial tool it is not guaranteed that they produce the expected results for the dyslexic student because the teacher is not properly trained to use the specific tool. In that aspect it seems as if there is a great need to define and describe some guidelines to a learning model on how the language teacher can better and more efficiently include the dyslexic student population in foreign language classes.

DYSLEXIC FRIENDLY LANGUAGE INSTRUCTION

As mentioned above the development of the learner's interlanguage is crucial for learning a foreign language. Dyslexic students often experience problems in developing their interlanguage sufficiently because of problems linked to among other things phonological processing, inaccurate representation in long term memory, sequencing, poor ability to differentiate between similar looking words and difficulty to discriminate between similar sounds. A dyslexic friendly language instruction therefore needs to take these obstacles into consideration.

SUPPORT TO DEVELOP PHONOLOGICAL AWARENESS

Research in the acquisition of written language skills has thoroughly documented the importance of a student's awareness of the sound system of his mother tongue for the development of effective reading and writing skills, both in his native language and in any foreign language he is to learn. Not surprisingly, phonological awareness training has turned out to be one of the most powerful components of successful intervention programmes for students at risk of dyslexia. Thus, an important goal of teaching a foreign language to dyslexic student is to help dyslexic students become aware of the sound system of the target language (i.e., English). A well-developed phonological awareness will enhance the dyslexic students' word reading and spelling skills in the foreign language as well as their pronunciation of new vocabulary.

Phonological awareness is mostly integrated in the foreign language curriculum at beginner's level of foreign language learning. It is typically exercised through games of rhyming, subtracting and changing the first and last part of spoken words. However, because of their phonological processing problems, dyslexic students often need more time and training to reach an acceptable level of skill. Thus, it might be necessary to prepare special exercises in phonological awareness for dyslexic students. As most traditional foreign language learning materials do not include phonological awareness training at the phoneme level, the foreign language teacher is faced with the problem of designing and preparing a systematic programme for phonological awareness (Arnbak, 2001).

If the target language is English, one option could be to use phonological awareness training programs composed for learners who have English as a mother tongue. These phonological awareness programs normally make use of an every-day vocabulary. When using these instruction programs at a beginner's level one should though be aware that foreign language learners do not know that many words in English and therefore these programmes can be difficult to use in foreign language teaching. Visual prompts (i.e., pictures representation of words) are commonly used in programmes like this, and a typical task would be to order a row of pictures according to which words rimed or to order the words according to the first sound of the words. Such easy tasks would properly be very difficult for dyslexic students simply because they would not know the names of these everyday things in English. A variation of this kind of exercise would be to produce and use own flash cards with picture representation of a known vocabulary and use these to drill phonological awareness.

For many dyslexic students, it can be extremely hard to develop a sufficient phonological awareness but studies indicate that most language learners on a beginner's level can easily manipulate larger sound segments. That is why it can be recommended to work with syllable segments in words (i.e., what is left if you take away *car* in *carpet*?). Becoming aware of syllables in words is fairly easy for most students, and the dyslexic students most likely will experience success with this kind of tasks. The exercise will be easier for the student if the syllable is also a meaningful unit, that is a word or a morpheme as it eases the load on the student's working memory. Then one can gradually move on to syllables that are nonsense segments (i.e., what's left if you take away /tic/ from the word tic-ket = ket). Later on in the learning process it can be advised to work with onsets and rimes in one-syllable words (i.e., what is left if you take away /m/ in the word *mice*? Can you get another word if you change the first sound of *mice* for example shift it with a /d/ = *dice*). And later on move on to awareness of phonemes in words (i.e., what is the first sound in the word *mice* = /m/).

It is fairly easy for students to identify the rhyming segment of a word (i.e., what is left of the word plan if you take away /pl/; /an/). Start out by having the student focus on the rime part (i.e., do these word pairs rime: sway/lay, lay/low, hat/cat?). Then move on to awareness of the onset of one, syllable words (i.e., what is left if you take away /k/ from the word cat or what word do you get if you replace /k/ in cat with /s/? = sat). Becoming aware of the second consonant in onsets made up of consonant clusters is by far the most difficult task (i.e., what word do you get if you take away /l/ from the word flat (fat).

It is especially difficult for dyslexic students to manipulate the individual sounds of words. However, awareness of the individual phonemes of words is the most important prerequisite of word identification (decoding) and spelling. The phonological awareness teaching should include a large number of exercises at the phoneme level (i.e., what is the first sound of the word 'cat' or 'say the sounds in the word cat' (/k-a-t/, what word do you get if you take away the last sound in the word bus*t* = bus). As it is easier to hold meaningful units in working memory than nonsense segments, the task is much easier if the remaining part of the word is also a meaningful unit (i.e., as in the example with the word bus*t* = bus).

Today one of the major theories concerning the cause of the phonological processing difficulties of dyslexics is concerned with the quality of the phonological identities (i.e., how the sound of a word or word segment is stored) in lexicon (Elbro, 1999). The theory argues that the phonological identities of dyslexics are more indistinct than those of normally reading peers, and results from a number of studies seem to confirm this theory. Indistinct phonological identities would result in poor ability to discriminate between words or sounds that share many common traits (i.e., /p/ and /b/) and consequently poor word learning and listening comprehension. Thus, one can conclude that helping the dyslexic student to get a higher degree of phonological awareness also will make it easier for the same person to develop a useable interlanguage.

SUPPORT TO LISTENING COMPREHENSION

Phonological awareness is especially important in developing reading and written skills in a foreign language but also in connection with listening comprehension. To support listening comprehension it can be of a big help if the foreign language teacher 'sets the stage' before each listening comprehension exercise. It can be done by showing pictures that relate to the topic which the exercise deals with. Also, the foreign language teacher can provide information about the main characters or events in the text before the students listen to the text. Dyslexic students might need to listen to the information several times before recounting the information or answering questions about it. Listening comprehension is often done in the classroom by presenting the text by playing the CD or tape for the whole class. Today it is very inexpensive and easy to duplicate CD-materials and if the foreign language teacher has access to more than one CD-player (i.e., laptops), he or she has the chance to let students work with listening assignments in groups. In this way the groups can work more differentiated with the listening assignment. The groups do not even have to listen to the same text and they can listen to the text as often as they find it necessary. At least it is almost certainly a great help for the dyslexic student if he or she get the opportunity to listen to exercises like that in smaller groups. Under certain circumstances the dyslexic students might also hear a 'slowed down' version of the text so that they have longer time to comprehend the information. However, it is important that the speech sounds are not distorted in the process.

SUPPORT TO WORD LEARNING

Word learning is seen as a precondition to develop the learner's interlanguage, and language acquisition is normally expected to take place when an individual is exposed to language and is engaged in various communicative language acts. However, the dyslexic student's phonological processing problems impede the inductive word learning practice which is normally practised through exercises of the communicative language classes. Thus, it is suggested that dyslexic students need extra time to learn new vocabulary and that they participate in special word learning tasks to help them improve their vocabulary.

Dyslexic students' vocabulary acquisition and memory is enhanced if they learn all the lexical identities of a new word: the pronunciation, the meaning, the grammatical status, and the spelling. The more strongly the lexical identities of a word are related, the higher the chance that the student will be able to retrieve the orthographic as well as the semantic, and phonological identity from memory. It is therefore suggested that dyslexic students must learn the pronunciation of the word and use it in spoken language exercises to cement both the meaning and sound of the word, and they must also learn the spelling and use the word in their own writing as well as be able to read it.

Quite a large number of games and language methods are available to support dyslexic student's word learning and to develop vocabulary. *The Concept of Definition Map* is a popular method. The purpose of the concept of definition map is to support vocabulary and concept learning by giving students a strategy for defining and clarifying the meaning of unknown words. Also *Mind Mapping* is an effective method when it comes to develop dyslexic students' vocabulary. A mind map is a graphic organizer. Mind maps are also effective tools in word learning because they present a visual overview over important properties of the word.

As indicated above, multi-sensory language teaching programs can also help dyslexic students develop their vocabulary. Multi-sensory means simultaneously teaching the visual, auditory and kinesthetic-tactile elements to enhance memory and learning. Most language teaching in schools is done using either sight or hearing (auditory sensations). The child's sight is used in reading information, looking at diagrams or pictures, or reading what is on the teacher's board. The sense of hearing is used in listening to what the teacher says. A dyslexic child may experience difficulties with either or both of these senses. The child's vision may be affected by difficulties with tracking, visual processing or seeing the words become fuzzy or move around. The child's hearing may be satisfactory on a hearing test, but auditory memory or auditory processing may be weak. The answer is to involve the use of more of the child's senses, especially the use of touch and movement. This will give the child's brain tactile and kinetic memories to hang on to, as well as the visual and auditory ones. If English is the target language there are several programs available for this purpose (Sparks and Ganshow, 1991).

SUPPORT FROM NEW TECHNOLOGY

The dyslexic students can today greatly benefit from using new computer techniques in the process of learning a foreign language. Especially when reading a text in a digital format. Today it is possible to get a broad range of screen readers which analyze texts on screen and output it as synthetic speech. There are very sophisticated packages available which give a high level of control over what is read out, from individual characters to continuous reading of long documents. A wide range of modern language options is also available, but the main limitation is that text can only be read out if the computer recognizes it as text. If it is displayed as a picture of the text, as in some PDF-files and web pages, it cannot be read. Synthetic speech has also made significant advances during the recent years. The goal of generating natural-sounding human speech is an elusive one, requiring the understanding of speech components as well as other factors such as the speaker's volume, pitch, mood and emphasis. However, research clearly shows that synthetic speech helps dyslexic students better to understand written language.

Also it is today very easy to get a screen reader installed for free or if one prefers a little more sophisticated program it is possible to download pretty affordable and advanced software applications. Some of the available screen reader programs offer the user more sophisticated solutions such as a read and record mode (i.e., The Soliloquy Reading Assistant if English is the target language). In such a setting the students are urged to read aloud the text they have called forward while it is recorded. The words to be read aloud are highlighted in black during the reading process and then turn grey as each word is read aloud. The software program has included some kind of automated 'tutor' that will supply the pronunciation of a word if the student hesitates for a predetermined number of seconds and allow time for the student to repeat the word. After having read and recorded the story the student has the opportunity to listen to his or hers own reading of the text in which errors have been edited.

Even though the internet and other digitalized texts nowadays is very much used in language teaching, pupils in primary and upper primary still mostly read texts from paper. Also in this situation computer aided teaching can to some extent help the dyslexic student. Another technical and efficient tool is the 'talking pen'. Shortly described a 'talking pen' is a handheld scanner which can scan texts from books to the inner memory of the pen and displays it on a build in display. Also the 'talking pen' is able to transfer the scanned paper text to a computer so that one can display parts of texts or whole texts digitally in, for example, a Word file. More advanced examples of the 'talking pen' can read the scanned text line aloud with a synthetic voice if the student connects a headset to the pen. One can say that the the 'talking pen' is somewhat a forerunner for the screen readers that have been developed for computers today, besides being a mini-scanner.

Computer programs such as *Hot Potatoes* (Arneil and Holmes, 2003–2007) can successfully be used for making interactive drill exercises for certain language problems. A lot of spelling programmes are on the market today, and even though experts have debated long and hard over the most effective way to use spelling programs there is little question that they mostly are very effective. Also, one can find many different programs focusing on word learning and developing vocabulary. If English is the target language, the language teacher might find very helpful advice and teaching tools in English multi-sensory programs for reading-disabled students that is, 'Go Phonics' (Foundation for Learning LLC, 2007).

At present there has been developed a vast number of computer programs that in one or the other way can help dyslexic student in learning a foreign language – and just as many programs will probably be developed in a near future. Which programs one chooses all depends on individual purpose, taste and needs. Today most homes and students have access to a computer and the internet and in the cases where dyslexic students have access to these technical facilities, it seems as an absolute demand that the foreign language teacher secure that the dyslexic student has access to tools such as a screen reader (or 'talking pen') and the necessary language programs both in school and at home.

CONCLUDING REMARKS

The global challenge of today demands that both children and adults learn at least one foreign language. In most of those European countries that don't have English as a native language, English is today taught as an obligatory foreign language. Learning a foreign language can be an extra load for dyslexic students, because of problems in acquiring both basic and more advanced language skills. Dyslexic students may have problems distinguishing between words in the foreign language, storing new words and retrieving words from long-term memory (vocabulary). They might also have problems learning the pronunciation of foreign words, becoming aware of the sound structure of foreign words (phonological awareness), learning the phoneme-to-grapheme-correspondences, the syntactic structures, the word format patterns, and the grammar of the foreign language. These problems might make it difficult for the dyslexic students to develop a satisfactory interlanguage.

Research calls attention to the fact that the problems dyslexic students might experience learning a foreign language are closely related to written and oral skills in their mother tongue. Research also shows us that most language teachers and schools acknowledge that dyslexic students might have difficulties learning a foreign language, and a majority of schools seem to work out from a policy of inclusion and include dyslexic students in normal foreign language learning classes. A majority of language teachers also strive to make dyslexic students learn all four basic receptive and productive skills in a foreign language. However, many language teachers at the same time seem to be uncertain how this should be done and how they should use remedial tools in and out of the classroom. Also, it seems that the most schools leave it to the individual or a minor group of language teachers to deal with problems arising from dyslexic students learning a foreign language.

It is suggested that dyslexic students get especial help and support to develop a phonological awareness when learning a foreign language. The reason for this is that theories concerning the cause of the phonological processing difficulties of dyslexic student are concerned with the quality of the phonological identities in lexicon. This can be seen as a new challenge for the language teacher and demands new types of exercises and tasks for the dyslexic student population. Also it is suggested that dyslexic students get special instructions in how they can learn new words and integrate them in their vocabulary. Methods based on the concepts of definitions maps and map minding can be especially useful in that respect and multi-sensory teaching is also advisable.

In the last decade or so new technology and the internet has come in as an important and useful tool for dyslexic students learning a foreign language. As mentioned earlier, phonological awareness training is not normally a part of the foreign language learning curriculum after the introductory years. Many foreign language teachers might want to use computer-based phonological awareness programs that allow the dyslexic student to work with exercises at his or her level of skills. The computer is a very systematic and patient 'teacher' and the dyslexic student will be able to repeat the exercises until he or she has mastered the skill involved. Various useful computer programs are available, that is LIPS: The Lindamood® Phoneme Sequencing Program for Reading, Spelling, and Speech (Lindamood and Lindamood, 2006). It is though important to stress that new technology cannot substitute more traditional language learning methods and always will be an additional tool to the process of learning. After all, language learning will always be a question of communication between people.

REFERENCES

Arnbak, E. (2001) 'Hvordan kan vi gøre fremmedsprog mindre fremmed for ordblinde elever', *Nyt om ordblindhed*, 28: 2–8.

Arneil, S. and Holmes, M. (2003–2007) Hot potatoes, half-baked Software Inc., Victoria, Canada. Available http://www.halfbakedsoftware.com/index.php.

Corder, S. P. (1982) *Error analysis and interlanguage*. Oxford: Oxford University Press.

Dal, M., Arnbak, E. and Brandstätter, H. (2005) *Dyslexic students and foreign language learning*. Reykjavik: Iceland University of Education.

Downey, D. M. and Snyder, L. (2000) 'College students with LLD: the phonological core as risk for failure in foreign language classes', *Top Lang Disord*, 21: 82–92.

Ebsworth, M. E. (1998) 'Accuracy vs. fluency: which comes first in ESL instruction?', *ESL Magazine*, 1: 24–26.

Elbro, C. (1999) 'Dyslexia: core difficulties, variability and causes', in J. Oakhill, R. Beard and D. Vincent (eds) *Reading development and the teaching of reading*. Cambridge: Blackwell. pp. 131–156.

Foundation for Learning LLC (2007) Go Phonics.com, Foundation for Learning LLC, Chelan, Available http://www.gophonics.com/

Ganschow, L., Sparks, R. and Javorsky, J. (1998) 'Foreign language learning difficulties: A historical perspective', *Journal of Learning Difficulties*, 31: 248–258.

Holmberg, M. (2001) Hur kan personer med dyslexi lära sig läsa och skriva på engelska?, Språk Loss, Stockholm. Available http://www.sprakaloss.se/engelskamalin.htm.

Krashen, S. D. (1981) *Second language acquisition and second language learning*. Oxford: Pergamon Press.

Krashen, S. D. (1982) *Principles and practice in second language acquisition*. Oxford: Pergamon.

Lindamood, P. and Lindamood, P. (2006) LIPS: Teh Lindamood® Phoneme Sequencing Program for Reading, Spelling, and Speech, Pearson, Bloomington, Minneapolis. Available http://ags. pearsonassessments.com/group.asp?nGroupInfoID=a11420.

Lundberg, I. (2002) 'Second Language Learning and reading with the additional load of dyslexia', *Annals of Dyslexia*, 502: 165–187.

Nijakowska, J. (2004) Teaching English as a foreign language to Polish dyslexic students, British Dyslexic Association. Available http://www.bdainternationalconference.org/2004/presentations/sun_p1_c_22.shtml.

Orton-Gillingham Academy (2004) What is the Orton-Gillingham Approach?, Academy of Orton-Gillingham Practioneers. Available http://www.ortonacademy.org/.

Peer, L. and Reid, G. (2000) *Multilingualism, literacy and dyslexia: A challenge for educators*. London: David Fulton Publishers.

Scarcella, R. C., Andersen, E. and Krashen, S. D. (1990) *Developing communicative competence in a second language*. New York: Newbury House.

Schneider, E. and Crombie, M. (2003) *Dyslexia and foreign language learning*. London: David Fulton.

Selinker, L. (1972) 'Interlanguage', *International Reveiw of Applied Lingustics*, 10: 101–125.

Selinker, L. (1994) *Rediscovering Interlanguage*. London: Longman.

Siegel, L. and Smythe, I. (2004) 'Dyslexia and English as an additional language (EAL): Towards a greater understanding', in G. Reid and A. Fawcett (eds) *Dyslexia in context – Research, policy and practice*. London: Whurr Publishers.

Simon, C. S. (2000) 'Dyslexia and learning a foreign language: A personal experience', *Annals of Dyslexia*, 50: 155–187.

Sparks, R. (1993) 'Perceptions of low and high risk students with LDS about HS FL courses', *Foreign Language Annals*, 26: 93.

Sparks, R., Ganschow, E. and Pohlman, J. (1989) 'Linguistic codin deficits in foreign language learners', *Annals of Dyslexia*, 39: 179–195.

Sparks, R. and Ganschow, L. (1993) 'The impact of native language learning problems on foreign language learning: Case study illustrations the Linguistic Codin Deficit Hypothesis', *The Moderne Language Journal*, 77: 58–74.

Sparks, R. and Ganshow, L. (1991) 'Use of an Orton-Gillingham Approach to teach a foreign language to dyslexic', *Annals of Dyslexia*, 41: 456–467.

Tornberg, U. (2001) *Sprogdidaktik*. Copenhagen, LR Uddannelse.

PART V

Beyond School

Adults with Learning Disabilities and Self-Disclosure in Higher Education and Beyond

Lynda A. Price and Paul J. Gerber

Price, L.A. Gerber, P.J. (2008) in The Dyslexia Handbook eds...

This chapter

 i) provides insights into the perceptions of adults with dyslexia;
 ii) discusses how dyslexia can impact on all aspects of life;
iii) highlights the importance of listening to, and acknowledging the needs of adults with dyslexia;
iv) discusses the importance of self-disclosure as a means of achieving self-advocacy for young people with dyslexia.

Much of the literature on learning disabilities and dyslexia has focused on facts and figures to illustrate important concepts about this often confusing, invisible disability. Nevertheless, there is much more to the picture than that – the stories of real people in real-life situations. This is especially important when discussing adults with learning disabilities. Little current empirical information is available describing what actually happens to children with learning disabilities/dyslexia when they grow up and strive to become successful adults (Blackorby and Wagner, 1996; McLouglin et al., 2002; Reid and Kirk, 2005; Smith et al., 1997).[1]

Thomas' story illustrates this well. When he was interviewed in the United States as part of the 'To Be or Not to Be LD' study, he had a wealth of life experience at 58 years of age to share with the researchers.

> Thomas began his story in elementary school where he 'always had trouble with book learning'. Raised in a large family in the rural American South, he quit school in the '5th or 6th grade' to help support his brothers and sisters. He remembers having some academic problems, but 'it was because I got in trouble and didn't pay attention.' His parents had no formal education and were unable to help him with schoolwork. Thomas grew up to have a big family of his own. He supported them for many years as a construction worker. As he said, 'I was better at jobs where [I] used my hands'. He always avoided any jobs that involved reading or writing.
>
> When Thomas was interviewed for the study, he was on state aid due to a construction accident. (He was also diagnosed by that agency.) At that time, Thomas seemed happy and content with his life. He had a loving extended family of children, grandchildren and assorted relatives. He had many devoted friends in his neighborhood, especially at his church. (He really enjoyed the music, although he often had problems reading the words to the hymns.) Overall, Thomas saw himself as a success and felt that he had achieved a very satisfying quality of life at his age.
>
> However, similar to most adults, Thomas also had his share of negative experiences in life -- some specifically connected to his learning disability. For instance, when he was younger, Thomas would never talk about his learning problems to anyone, especially in the workplace because he was ashamed. If he needed help filling out forms, he would try to do more 'hard labor' tasks in exchange for the help from one of his co-workers. Having grandchildren with 'learning problems' gave Thomas a totally new attitude about self-disclosing his secret disorder: '[I am] famous for lecturing the kids on the importance of education. [I] spend a lot of time talking [with them] about their school and their lives . . . 'Talking about his learning disabilities became easier as he got older: '[I] just don't care as much about what people think of [me], but I can see how younger people would be worried. . . . [I] used my own experiences to talk about [succeeding through] trial and error . . .'

While Thomas clearly has a rich and fulfilling life, unfortunately many American adults with learning disabilities do not share his fate. For instance, approximately 75 per cent of Americans with disabilities are either unemployed or significantly underemployed, with the largest group being people with learning disabilities (Boles and Brown, 2001). Studies have shown that over half of all American adolescents with learning disabilities will drop out of high school before graduation. Many will be incarcerated (National Adult Literacy and Learning Disabilities Center, 1996). An increasing number will go on to college, but numerous adults often have problems completing their degree program (Valeri-Gold et al., 2001). Employment can be equally frustrating. Often adults with learning disabilities will work in entry-level jobs with minimum wage and few benefits (Blackorby and Wagner, 1996). Countless adults with learning disabilities may still be illiterate, so they will be unemployed or significantly underemployed (Boles and Brown, 2001; Gerber and Brown, 1997; Greenbaum et al., 1996; Vogel and Adelman, 2000).

Given these problems, why did Thomas' life turn out so differently? His story underscores an important, but little understood component of learning disabilities – the phenomena of self-disclosure. Consequently, the focus of the To Be or Not To Be LD study was to explore the dynamics of self-disclosure further, especially in terms of its impact on the daily lives of Americans with learning disabilities.

LITERATURE REVIEW

Self-disclosure has yet to be a process that is well understood in the field of learning disabilities. As seen with Thomas' story, it becomes particularly important during the adult years when the invisibility of learning disabilities presents the option of disclosing or not disclosing.

Self-disclosure is also a very important element of self-determination (Wehmeyer, 1995; Field and Hoffman, 1994) and the foundation for 'normalization' of persons with disabilities (Wolfensberger, 1972). It literally means taking control of one's destiny, a critical factor reported on the research of highly successful adults with learning disabilities (Gerber et al., 1992; Reiff et al., 1997). It is also the basis for effective self-advocacy and transition training as mandated by the Individuals for Disabilities Education Improvement Act (2006), which requires planning specifically in independent living, competitive employment, participation in community and family roles and pursuit of leisure activities (Field and Hoffman, 1994; Roffman et al., 1990). Therefore, self-disclosure can best be understood by making it context-specific, consistent with the realities of adult functioning and current literature on adult outcomes for persons with learning disabilities (Gerber and Brown, 1997; Price and Gerber, 2001; Price et al., 2003).

A few studies have addressed self-disclosure specifically for adults with learning disabilities. For example, Roffman et al. (1994) assessed the effectiveness of a college course for greater disability awareness. They found that greater self-understanding leads to willingness to disclose in social and employment settings. On the other hand, Lynch and Gussell (1996) explored disclosure and self-advocacy in postsecondary students with learning disabilities and found they feared stereotyping and attribution of unfounded characteristics associated with learning disabilities. Vogel and Adelman (2000) investigated former college students 8–15 years past graduation. They discovered that 41 per cent chose not to disclose on the job, and if they did it was for the purpose of obtaining job accommodations. Witte et al. (1998) determined that the majority of college students with learning disabilities in their sample 'indicated that they did not to disclose their learning disabilities in the workplace.' Greenbaum et al. (1996) investigated the post-college occupational and social status of adults with learning disabilities and discovered that a majority of the respondents were socially involved and happy while at work, but they seldom disclosed their learning disabilities either during the application/interview process or as part of their regular employment duties. Moreover, they noted fear of discrimination was a pivotal reason behind an 80 per cent non-disclosure rate for the adults in their study. Finally, Price et al. (2002) and Price et al. (2005) in a pair of comparative qualitative studies pertaining to employment found reluctance to disclose in samples on American and Canadian adults with learning disabilities. These selected studies cause one to wonder the degree of penetration of the Americans with Disabilities Act (the ADA), which for individuals with learning disabilities in the United States is predicated on the process of disclosure in order to access reasonable accommodations. Consequently, the work of the To Be or Not To Be LD study was centered on exploring self disclosure for adults with learning disabilities within a framework of adult-oriented issues, contexts and relevant legislation.

AN OVERVIEW OF THE TO BE OR NOT TO BE LD STUDY

The focal point for this study was an in-depth investigation of three interrelated research questions.

1   How do adults with learning disabilities view their disabilities in terms of self-disclosure, especially in different adult-oriented contexts (i.e., employment, family/home, postsecondary education/training, recreation/leisure, community and partnerships/friendships?
2   What factors are critical to understand the complex process of self-disclosure of adults with learning disabilities? and
3   What impact has the ADA had on adults with learning disabilities, especially in terms of transition planning?

A qualitative research design was chosen to address these questions to use inductive strategies and examine original phenomena with an analysis of the interviewees' comments about their local environment (Maxwell, 1996; Merriam, 1998; Miles and Huberman, 1994; Strauss and Corbin, 1997).

The researchers used purposive sampling techniques to enlist the participation of 70 adults with demonstrable learning disabilities from eight geographic regions throughout the United States (i.e., California, Florida, Kansas, Maryland, Massachusetts, Minnesota, Texas and Washington). A site coordinator from each region visited different locations (i.e., colleges, vocational training sites, adult basic education programs, etc.) to initially recruit approximately 150 adults with learning disabilities. Seventy adults completed confidentiality forms and discussed compensation for study participation. Each adult met two primary criteria: 1) a formal learning disabilities diagnosis; and 2) past or current work experience. Materials documenting specific learning disabilities were provided by each participant of the study.

The study took approximately one and one half years to complete. An initial pilot was conducted with 18 adults with learning disabilities, who met the sample criteria. They were interviewed with the *Gerber and Price Self-Disclosure Interview Protocol*. The data were analyzed using a constant comparative method (Gerber and Price, 2005). After the pilot, the protocol was revised as necessary.

Site coordinators conducted face-to-face interviews in various locations (e.g., researcher's office, participant's home or various public locations of the adult's choice) using the interview protocol. All interviews varied in length from 45 to 120 minutes. Completed field notes were mailed to Temple University where a review of each interview was conducted. Every protocol was retyped, if necessary, rechecked for accuracy and assigned a confidential code so that it could be tracked throughout the entire study.

All 70 protocols were divided equally at random by site and given to the four researchers at Temple University for a first round of analysis as described by Miles and Huberman (1994) and Lincoln and Guba (1985). Each interview was coded by a researcher using constant comparative analysis to reduce the raw data into a set of preliminary patterns. After the preliminary patterns were organized, the data were analyzed again to reflect the theoretical framework and extant literature base. The themes were sorted again by the Temple University researchers in an exhaustive, face-to-face examination. A variety of qualitative methods of verification were used to assure appropriate reliability and validity such as: a) member checks; b) use of one site coordinator to assure consistency for each geographic area; and c) an extensive audit trail (Lincoln and Guba, 1985; Miles and Huberman, 1995). External validity was facilitated through both reader generalizibilty/reader applicability and analytical or theoretical generalizibilty (Merriam, 1998; Yin, 1994).

RESULTS OF THE STUDY

The participants in the study had much to say about their self-disclosure experiences. More importantly, they often had similar comments about critical issues and themes inherent in adulthood and learning disabilities. As a result, their experiences have been organized under five interrelated themes:

1   the process of self-disclosure;
2   the context of self-disclosure;
3   transition planning and self-disclosure;
4   the ADA and self-disclosure; and
5   the dichotomy of acceptable loss/potential gain inherent in self-disclosure.

All are described in greater detail below and illustrated with case studies.

THE SELF-DISCLOSURE PROCESS

The consequences of learning disabilities in adulthood, especially in terms of self-disclosure, are multifaceted. As a result, four sub-themes emerged within this category. They are described, along with quotes from the interviewees to further illustrate each sub-theme.

Trust and rapport in the self-disclosure process

Young children often feel free to blurt out innocently to strangers or acquaintances the first thoughts that come to their minds. However, through the trials and errors of adolescence and adulthood, one learns to distinguish loyal friends from casual friends or untrustworthy individuals. The interviewees in the study went through the same trial and error process with one unique element – who could or could not be trusted with such personal information as learning disabilities.

For example, one adult saw he was successful at work due to a special supervisor: 'My disability has always caused me to work harder [and] I cannot spell very well. I have been working with "Rose" my whole time . . . she has been great. I have extended time on tests, but that is all the help I need.' Because of this relationship, he self-disclosed to others as well: 'It does not matter to me anymore, but it used to . . . I will talk about it to anyone. My friends make fun [of me] sometimes, but it's all fun and games.' Trust and rapport were seen as the foundations in the self-disclosure process. As another adult explained: 'If I'm not comfortable, then it wouldn't come up'.

STIGMA AND THE SOCIAL IMPLICATIONS OF SELF-DISCLOSURE

While trustworthiness was fundamental to self-disclosure, shame and embarrassment were also viewed as components of the process. Many of the interviewees emphasized the dangers of self-disclosure to the wrong people at the wrong time: '[I] never talked about it with anyone. You know how cruel people can be. It's a gamble talking about it and I don't gamble'. Another participant emphasized: 'I'm embarrassed to say I have a LD because they'll fire me [at work] and say I won't learn'.

Moreover, shame was a powerful social deterrent that fed loneliness and isolation. As one adult explained: 'I don't really join any groups. I don't because of that [LD]. I'd like to, but I don't. I tend not to understand what's going on at all and it's too embarrassing. . .'. These social messages were so strong that one interviewee felt that it was more socially acceptable to have a serious drug addiction than a learning disability: 'I'm not going to tell anyone. . . . I'd rather tell someone that I'm a crack-head then LD, because at least then I'd be seen as able to fix it'.

SELF-DISCLOSURE AS A FUNCTION OF AGE AND MATURITY

For some individuals, becoming adults radically changed the way they saw their learning disabilities. For instance, one adult found that his perception of his learning disability radically changed when he moved from a white-collar to a blue-collar job. After struggling to become certified as an optician, he quickly became frustrated in his new position: 'It wasn't a good fit. I hated that job.

My boss never understood I will be slower at first when I'm learning, but I'll do what it takes to get it done'. He gambled by quitting and working in a small machine shop where he was happily employed for last ten years. When he traded in his suit and tie for overalls, his viewpoint about his learning disabilities changed as well: 'I feel that I have become a success after coming out of failure. I was always good with my hands, but I had to find the right environment'. While this adult's environment changed, other interviewees' perceptions evolved though adult experiences. As a study participant said, 'I feel alright talking about it but [I] didn't when I was younger. As I got older and more mature, I feel comfortable [with self-disclosure].' A second said simply, '[I] understand it [learning disabilities] more now.'

DENIAL OF ONE'S LEARNING DISABILITIES ALTOGETHER

Sometimes age clarified the puzzle of learning disabilities for the adults in the study. But a few found that the older they got, the less they believed they had a disability at all. The researchers found this to be particularly striking as these same individuals were recruited for the study exactly because they had documented learning disabilities. However, they still refused to believe the diagnosis. It soon became apparent in their interviews that these adults had nothing to self-disclose because they truly did not consider themselves to be learning disabled in any way. As one individual told the researchers, 'I honestly think I don't have LD'. His comments were echoed by a second adult who said, 'I really don't feel that like I have one [a specific learning disability]'. As these quotes illustrate, self-disclosure is clearly a complex, very personal process. One example was Joe who came to terms with his learning disability after years of trial and error.

Joe was a 25 year old Caucasian male who graduated from high school and a two-year community college. He reported having over 25 jobs in the last five years (i.e., auto repair, graphic designer, lawn care, computer instructor, waiter, retail clothing sales). He described himself as having a 'math disability' which he said, 'was really hard on me [because] my parents didn't have the time, energy, [or] patience to teach math [to me]. I had to have a tutor teach [me] the basics'. When interviewed, he was successfully employed both as a salesman for up-scale men's clothing as well as running his own graphic design business.

Joe felt very proud that he was able to overcome the pessimistic messages that he received from his family: 'My parents [and grandparents] are very negative people. I don't let them get me down anymore'. Joe never discussed his learning disability at any of his jobs. As he explained, 'No, it's a past thing, just a phase probably. I barely remember much of it, like old childhood. . . I still have a math disability in certain areas [and] I get very frustrated and confused'. Joe purposefully chose to keep his disability a secret. As he explained, he re-took algebra in college several times and worked unsuccessfully with a tutor: 'I feel helpless like when I was young, very difficult, frustrated, sad, very depressing, [it] can really get you down [like you are] not going anywhere'. Joe was also reluctant to share any personal information with friends or neighbors in his local community: 'I tell only true friends. A lot of people do not know. It's none of their business'. Despite his secrecy about his disability, Joe felt that he had found a satisfying quality of life as an adult: 'My career path is positive! I'm happy [now] not depressed'.

THE CONTEXT OF SELF-DISCLOSURE: ADULT-ORIENTED ENVIRONMENTS

Joe's story underscores an important theme found in the study. Where someone talks about learning disabilities is often just as important as how one talks about it. As a result, the interviewees described self-disclosure in settings familiar to all adults—postsecondary settings, community, home and the workplace.

Employment

Many of the adults had strong feelings about not disclosing at work. As one said, 'In my job, [we] don't really talk about personal stuff. [I] don't want to talk about anything that could be used against me'. His caution was justified, as reflected by the comments of a second adult: 'I had a bad experience when my boss found out [about my learning disability]. He made up some excuse and let me go . . . It destroyed me there'. However, some adults in the study described more positive experiences in the workplace: Yes, I absolutely discuss my LD very openly with a supervisor or co-worker . . . My manager doesn't understand. . . . So I go to the person under him who knows my disability. [He] asks me to do the parts I can do well and gets others to do the rest'.

Community

Another familiar environment where adults find themselves everyday was one's local community. However, informal socializing in a neighborhood or community often seemed to discourage self-disclosure, while also feeding isolation and loneliness. As one interviewee confessed, 'I don't really join any groups or stuff like that . . . because of that [learning disabilities]. I'd like to, but I don't'. He later elaborated'. I tend not to understand what's going on at all and it's too embarrassing so I don't do it now . . . [I] quit a lot of sports teams when I was younger because [I] just didn't understand the coach's directions'. One exception for a few adults was their local church or synagogue: 'I have spoken about it in church youth group because I know I can talk about it with them. [I] feel safe. [I] don't really talk about it any other place'.

Home and family

While work and community were viewed by many as unsafe for self-disclosure, most of the adults found their home to be the exact opposite. For instance, an interesting trend was the relationship between self-disclosure and marriage:

> [My] husband is very supportive and knows [all about] my LD. He has advocated [for me] before with [instructors] and [bosses] . . . Helping [me] when I need it is like 'second nature to him. He is the one who reads the directions to put things together around the house . . . He does the cooking and reads the recipes and [I am] the one who does the cleaning.

[We] each have [our] strengths and we know each other so well that [we just do] our jobs around the house accordingly.

Other interviewees cherished the comfort provided by a few close friends: 'My family is in denial, but my friends accept me and they help me. I talk to my friends and ask them how they do things. IT REALLY HELPS'.

Postsecondary education

Such ambiguity about self-disclosure was also discovered in post-secondary education. As a college student in the study explained: 'There have been people who say to me "people just get diagnosed with ADHD and LD and it's a cop-out" . . . I find it frustrating [they] think it's made up and not real'. Other adults, like Kathy, had a different experience. Her success in college is described in the case study below.

> Kathy was a 35-year-old Caucasian female who was diagnosed as learning disabled in adulthood in the areas of spelling, writing and organization. Academics as a child were very challenging for her: 'My K-12 experience was confusing. I had difficulty understanding course work and was accused of being unmotivated.' As an adult college student, Kathy used a great deal of technology, self-advocacy and self organization to finish an undergraduate and a graduate degree. When interviewed, she was successfully employed for two years in Education and Human Services and 'working on my self-concept and self-esteem'. Nevertheless, when asked about self-disclosure in her adult life, she was very guarded. Employment was clearly a setting where Kathy was very cautious about her learning disability: 'I'm not comfortable talking about my LD in the workplace. My supervisor knows, but we don't talk about it. . . . I do not request accommodations at work'. Despite her success in postsecondary education, she still felt ambivalent about self-disclosure there: 'I've talked with fellow students and some instructors; however I did not request accommodations for my LD'. Kathy was also careful self-disclosing in her community: 'It [my LD] rarely comes up because my hobbies are physical. Learning styles rarely come up. When I have conversations with friends or acquaintances that have no role in my professional development, I am more candid'. She found reinforcement from her family: 'Sure, my family is very supportive. I haven't had any negative reactions'. Her guidance to others with learning disabilities reflects her varied experiences in different settings: 'Be careful. It's important to take a stand especially if you need accommodations. However, people have biases . . . and it may work better not to say anything. I know that's the opposite advice you would receive from [a disability counselor], but I'm just being honest'.

TRANSITION PLANNING AND SELF-DISCLOSURE

The transition of students with disabilities from secondary education into successful adulthood has long been a concern in the United States. As Gajar et al. (1993) explain:

> Transition from school to adult life for individuals with disabilities has become a national priority. School dropout rates, underachievement, lack of appropriate career/vocational counseling, assessment, programs, limited parental involvement and work experiences and the lack of cooperative programming and support systems have resulted in

serious unemployment and other problems that hinder an efficient and satisfying adult experience. (p. 7)

American special education has addressed these serious concerns through the Individuals with Disabilities Education Improvement Act (IDEA), which mandated transition education for adult life in employment, independent living, community and postsecondary education. While transition planning has been available for over 25 years in American public schools, the results from the To Be or Not To Be LD study revealed a new finding in this area.

The majority of the interviewees never received any transition assistance at all. This is a special concern, as many of them were in secondary school when transition planning was mandated. One spoke for most when asked about transition planning, 'No. I haven't gotten information anywhere'. Another elaborated, '[I] really hadn't thought about it as something that [I] should or should not do until this interview'. Of the 70 adults interviewed, only three even mentioned the term 'transition' during the discussion with the researchers. As one adult said, [I know about] self-disclosure from the transition coordinator, but not much. The relationship between self-disclosure and transition planning was exemplified by Freddy's story.

Freddy was a 46-year-old Hispanic male who attended high school only through the 10th grade. He was employed in a warehouse for a number of years and was currently working to complete his high school diploma. While Freddy was diagnosed with his learning disability late in life, he recalls: '[I] struggled the entire time that [I] was in school. [I] got extra help from tutors, but everyone made fun [of me] for that. . . . [I] was one of 14 children, so [I just wanted] to stay out of fights, the neighborhood was very rough . . .'. Freddy believed that his learning disability directly influenced his employment, especially with one job: 'I was required to meet a certain quota in a certain about of time. I had difficulty counting everything and getting it all lined out in the time frame. I told my boss right away. He was [aware] of [my LD], but it didn't matter'. Freddy discussed his learning disability at the Adult Educational Center, where he found support and tutoring. He talked to his sister, when he saw that his two nephews were wrestling with the same problems that he had at their age: 'I see a lot of myself [in them]. If those boys don't understand something or they need more explaining, I tell them to get that extra help. Not to be ashamed of needing that extra help . . . so they don't end up like me'. When asked about transition, self-disclosure and his learning disability, Freddy taught himself what he needed to know – primarily through the local library and the Internet: 'I did research on my own. I know it runs in my family. I see that now'. It was his own self-initiative that encouraged him become a self-advocate for himself and his nephews.

SELF-DISCLOSURE AND KNOWLEDGE OF THE ADA

While self-disclosure is not specifically legislated when doing transition planning, it is the key criteria to receive support under the ADA and other federal legislation. (It should be noted that the ADA is the primary legislative safety-net for American adults with disabilities.) However, a clear trend emerged from the comments of the 70 adults about the crucial connections between self-disclosure and the ADA. The majority of the participants interviewed had little or no knowledge of ADA. The adults were also questioned specifically to see if the ADA had any influence on their decision to self-disclose, or not, in adult settings. Again, the majority answered negatively to the influence of ADA on their self-disclosure. Their responses also fell naturally into two groups: (1) those that had no knowledge of ADA; and (2) those that had rudimentary familiarity with the law, but clearly did not understand how the ADA applied to learning disabilities.

Almost the entire sample (64 out of 70) reported no previous knowledge of ADA. For example, most of the adults said, 'No' when asked specifically if they knew about the ADA. A related question was if they had ever used it to access support for their learning disabilities in the workplace. Again, the vast majority said no. While three of the study participants had heard of ADA, but they too had no clue about how the law could be applicable to them. As one adult said, 'The ADA doesn't apply to me'. One however added: 'Knowing that you have those protections are helpful'.

This theme is best illustrated by Sam.

> Sam was a 21-year-old Caucasian male who was diagnosed in the first grade with learning disabilities in spelling, reading and writing. He described his learning disability as: 'Problems concentrating and learning things. [I] need extra repetition to learn something. Learning was hard [but] math was [my] strongest area. I don't remember being aware of having LD at the time.' Sam received his high school diploma but has never attended college or vocational training. He was employed in five different jobs in the last three years (e.g., supermarket bagger, cashier, customer service manager, bottler in a bottling factory and automobile salesman). Sam has never talked about his learning disability at work, home or in the community. As he commented, '[I'm] not exactly thrilled to be LD. I kind of kept it hush-hush. It's a stigma'. Again, despite this being mandated by legislation, Sam never received any knowledge about transition, self disclosure or the ADA during his public school education. When asked specifically about the ADA, he replied, 'No, I've never heard of it, but [I] figured it was for people with physical or mental problems'.
>
> When the researcher explained the ADA to him for the first time, he immediately became interested and asked if he should self-disclose to his current employer. He seemed to think that he would not get fired for not meeting his quota if he was protected under the law. (It is unclear if Sam ever followed through with this or not.)

ACCEPTABLE LOSS/POTENTIAL GAIN

One theme that emerged from the data analysis was acceptable loss versus potential gain in the disclosure process. Throughout the interviews, adults stressed that the core of the self-disclosure process for persons with learning disabilities was personal risk assessment. Typically, this kind of assessment emanates from a business model (evolving from cost/benefit analysis), but it can also be extended to personal issues such as religion, medical status and sexual orientation in social contexts. It can also be connected to an earlier phenomena observed in the adults with learning disabilities research described as 'goodness of fit' which refers to a suitable match between one's environment and the expectations and requirements of that setting (Gerber et al., 1992).

Evaluating the personal acceptable loss versus potential gain is a complex, little understood process for adults with learning disabilities. For instance, when assessing the risk of each new social, academic or vocational encounter, an adult is at a crossroads with two possibilities – not to disclose, leading one to the dynamic of acceptable loss or to disclose because of the potential gain emanating from the disclosure process.

Potential gain, however, denotes an expectation that something positive (generally greater understanding and in some cases accommodation) will ensue from self-disclosure and increase the quality of the context in which learning disabilities is disclosed. (Two good examples of potential gain stem from the benefits of disclosure using Section 504 and the ADA.) For example, repeatedly interviewees stated that the workplace was central to their lives as adults, but also a key battleground for self-disclosure. As one adult explained:

> . . . it's important to lay low, and honestly an uncomfortable feeling. I like to be honest and open, but what is the right answer [to] get what I need to do my job well versus making myself vulnerable. I'm going to have to think about it. It's a trade-off and delicate balance . . . .

On the other hand, a few others in the study found potential gain in the workplace by talking openly about their learning disabilities. As one commented, 'I'm really not bothered by my LD. I use it as a weapon [to get accommodations] or get what I want when I am in a negative situation'.

While employment was clearly a lightning rod for self-disclosure issues for the interviewees, the contradictions of acceptable loss/potential gain also came up for many adults in postsecondary educational settings as well. This is an ironic twist, as in the United States, there is an established legal history to assure all people with disabilities that they will receive full, personalized support as needed, due to both Section 504 and the ADA. Some of the adults' comments reflected this confidence and only saw the potential gain to self-disclose to faculty or postsecondary staff: '[I have] never had a bad experience with a college professor, but I do not want to risk it'. Others, such as Mary described below, found that her 'loss' less acceptable.

> Mary, a 28-year-old Caucasian female, had a high school diploma, an undergraduate and graduate degree in Education and was completing a third graduate degree in Counseling. In addition, Mary had three jobs in the last five years – all involving teaching at-risk youth. When interviewed, she was the director of a program for students with special behavior problems. Mary was diagnosed in elementary school with specific learning disabilities in the areas of reading, math, memory and understanding oral or written directions. As she recalls, 'In spite of my reading and spelling deficits, I discovered a love and talent for writing'. While Mary was comfortable self-disclosing to family and friends about her invisible disability, she found mixed reactions at work: 'I'm generally pretty open about my LD at my current job [although] I did not talk about it with one past employer because I felt it would do more harm than good. She also become aware of this uncertainty in college: 'My experience at college was positive . . . [but] I had a professor who did not believe in learning disabilities

and was very resistant to letting me take my tests un-timed. The grades that she gave me were consistently lower than the grades from other professors in the department'. Mary's advice to other adults with learning disabilities underscored her qualms about risk management and self-disclosure: 'Never disclose by saying "I have this LD and this is what you need to do for me". This puts them on the defense, tells them that you are using your LD as an excuse. Always disclose by saying, "I have this LD, these are my strengths". . . Always highlight the positive.'

DISCUSSION

This chapter has attempted to integrate the research-driven issues of self-disclosure with the voices of adults with learning disabilities. Indeed, one complements the other. This work has portrayed a concept that is typically simplified into one that has complexities that are beyond what is currently described in the learning disabilities-specific literature. The following practical ideas should be considered in the self-disclosure process.

Self-disclosure is driven by context and situation

Because there are numerous contexts in adulthood (i.e., employment, education, family, community and leisure/recreation) disclosure is advantageous only at the right time and in the right place.

Self-disclosure is the management of personal information

All information pertaining to disability is private and confidential. Whether all or part of that information is shared, and how it is shared, is at the discretion of the person with the (learning) disability. Indeed, there are many options and subsequent decisions attached to effective disclosure.

Self-disclosure is nestled in the larger concept of self-determination

Disclosure is just one part of self-determination that empowers persons with learning disabilities to have control over the choice of disclosure. The choice is particularly relevant because of the invisibility of the learning disability itself.

Invisibility is an important factor

Because learning disabilities are a set of cognitive phenomena with no apparent physical characteristics, invisibility provides the opportunity of disclosing or not disclosing. Disclosure can have a variety of benefits apropos to a specific setting.

There is risk in self-disclosure

There are no guarantees in disclosure. Without question it can be a plus (particularly when legal protections are operational), and it can be a negative when disclosure foments misunderstanding, stigma or bias. Trust and the capacity of understanding to the person(s) who is the recipient of the disclosure information is crucial.

Disclosure 'protections' in some adult contexts

Laws in the United States, Canada and Great Britain need to be connected to the adult contexts where they pertain (i.e., employment and the Americans with Disabilities Act for persons with learning disabilities). They can help structure the disclosure process and frame ensuing interactions pursuant to legal provisions.

Disclosure must include information and not just the label

The term learning disabilities lacks specificity and even has different meanings in different countries such as the United States and England. Because of its imprecision, self-disclosure needs to include in concrete terms what functional limitations are associated with the label. It is most helpful if disclosure is elaborated upon with the reality of challenges specific to the adult context and needed accommodations.

Disclosure is just the beginning

When the decision to disclose is made, it is important to consider that it is the beginning of a dynamic process that will necessitate self-advocacy skills. Thus the overall goal is to use advocacy to enrich understanding, provide *in vivo* commentary and work for effective accommodations in order to be more adaptive in various adult settings.

Adults seem to be more understanding

Understanding and acceptance of persons with learning disabilities seems to be more likely in the adult years. Typically, non-disabled adults tend to view learning disabilities as a profile of strengths and weaknesses very much like their own experience of what they can do well and what they tend to stay away from.

CONCLUSION

An important realization that emerges from the research is that self-disclosure is the beginning of a very important conversation. It is the 'opening gambit' of a process housed under the umbrella of self-determination, but driven by very skillful self-advocacy skills. Those who wish to isolate disclosure without thinking through its broad implications and requisite self-advocacy skills are doing an injustice to persons with learning disabilities in preparation for life beyond school and throughout the numerous years of adulthood.

Much is embedded in the concept of self-disclosure that is central to the stage of adulthood. The key adjective is SELF which is characterized by the developmental demands of being truly adult characterized by – autonomy, independence and actualization. Thus, the cluster of 'SELF challenges' in adulthood are predicated on self-awareness, self-knowledge, self-understanding, self-determination and self-actualization as they connect to learning disabilities. The ultimate standard, however, is how those decisions foster a good quality of life in the many contexts that adults with learning disabilities experience each day of their lives.

ACKNOWLEDGEMENTS

The authors gratefully acknowledge the ACLD Foundation for funding this study. Thanks are also extended to the individuals who were research site coordinators for this work: Dr. Eleanor Higgins, formally of the Frostig Center, Pasadena, CA; Ms. Noelle Kurth, Kansas University, Lawrence, KS; Dr. Steve Nourse, Pacific Lutheran University, Tacoma, WA; Dr. James Patton, Pro-ED, Austin, TX; Dr. Henry Reiff, McDaniel College, Westminster, MD; Dr. Arlyn Roffman, Lesley University, Cambridge, MA; Dr. Ann Ryan, the University of St. Thomas, Minneapolis, MN and Dr. Mary Sarver, the University of South Florida, Tampa, FL. Additionally, thanks to Patty Williams of Temple University for her assistance in the data analysis.

NOTES

1 The term 'learning disabilities' (LD) is used in this chapter and refers in this instance to dyslexia.

REFERENCES

Americans with Disabilities Act (1990) P.L. 101–336. 42 U.S.C.

Blackorby, J. and Wagner, M. (1996) 'Longitudinal post-school outcomes of youth with disabilities: findings from the National Longitudinal Transition Study', *Exceptional Children*, 62: 105–123.

Boles, R. N. and Brown, D. S. (2001) *Job-Hunting for the so-called handicapped*. Berkeley, CA: Ten Speed Press.

Field, S. and Hoffman, A. (1994) 'Development of a model for self-determination', *Career Development for Exceptional Individuals*, 17: 159–169.

Gajar, A., Goodman, L. and McAfee, J. (1993) *Secondary schools and beyond: Transition of individuals with mild disabilities*. New York: Merrill.

Gerber, P.J. (1993) 'Researching adults with learning disabilities from an adult development perspective', *Journal of Learning Disabilities*, 27: 62–64.

Gerber, P. J. and Brown, D. S. (1997) *Learning disabilities and employment*. Austin, TX: Pro-ED Publishers.

Gerber, P. J., Ginsberg, R. and Reiff, H. B. (1992) 'Identifying alterable patterns in employment success for highly successful adults with learning disabilities', *Journal of Learning Disabilities*, 25: 475–487.

Gerber, P.J. and Price, L.A. (2005) *The gerber and price self-disclosure interview protocol*.

Gerber, P. J. and Price, L. A. (in press) 'Self-disclosure and adults with learning disabilities: Practical ideas about a complex process', *Learning Disabilities: A Multi-Disciplinary Journal*.

Gerber, P. J., Price, L. A. and Shessel, Isabel (2002) 'Adults with learning disabilities and employment: A Canadian perspective', *Thalamus*, 24: 21–32.

Gerber, P.J., Price, L.A., Mulligan, R. and Williams, P. (2005) 'To be or not to be learning disabled: A preliminary report on self-disclosure and adults with learning disabilities', *Thalamus*, 23: 18–29.

Gerber, P. J. and Reiff, H. B. (1991) *Speaking for themselves: Ethnographic interviews of adults with learning disabilities*. Ann Arbor, MI: The University of Michigan Press.

Goffman, E. (1961) *Stigma: Notes on the management of a spoiled identity*. Englewood Cliffs, NJ: Prentice-Hall Publishers.

Greenbaum, B., Graham, S., and Scales, W. (1996) 'Adults with learning disabilities: Occupational and social status after college', *Journal of Learning Disabilities*, 29: 167–175.

Lincoln, Y. S. and Guba, E. G. (1985) *Naturalistic inquiry*. Newbury Park, CA: Sage Publications.

Lynch, R. T. and Gussel, L. (1996) 'Disclosure and self-advocacy regarding disability-related needs: Strategies to maximize integration in postsecondary education', *Journal of Counseling and Development*, 74: 352–358.

McLoughlin, D., Leather, C. and Stringer, P. (2002) *The adult dyslexic*. London: Whurr Publishers.

Merriam, S. B. (1998) *Qualitative research and case study applications in education*. San Francisco: Josey-Bass Publishers.

Maxwell, J. A. (1996) *Qualitative research design: An interactive approach*. Thousand Oaks, CA: Sage Publications.

Miles, M. B. and Huberman, A. M. (1994) *Qualitative data analysis: An expanded sourcebook* (2nd ed.). Thousand Oaks, CA: Sage Publications.

National Adult Literacy and Learning Disabilities Center (1996) *Correctional educational programs for adults with learning disabilities*. Washington, DC: National Institution for Literacy. (ERIC Document Reproduction Service No. ED 406 517).

Price, L.A. and Gerber, P. J. (2001) 'At second glance: How adults with learning disabilities are faring in the Americans with disabilities act era', *Journal of Learning Disabilities*, 34: 202–210, 248.

Price, L. A., Gerber, P. J. and Shessel, I. (2002) 'Adults with learning disabilities and employment: A Canadian perspective', *Thalamus*, 4: 1–32.

Price, L. A., Gerber, P. J. and Mulligan, R. K. (2003) 'The Americans with Disabilities Act and adults with learning disabilities: The realities of the workplace', *Remedial and Special Education*, 24: 350–359.

Price, L.A., Gerber, P. J. and Mulligan, R. (2005) 'To be or not to be learning disabled: A preliminary report on self-disclosure in adults with learning disabilities', *Thalamus*, 23: 18–27.

Reid, G. and Kirk, J. (2005) *Dyslexia in adults: Education and employment*. West Sussex, England: Wiley and Sons.

Reiff, H. B., Gerber, P. J. and Ginsberg, R. (1997) *Exceeding expectations: Successful adults with learning disabilities*. Austin, TX: Pro-ED Publishers.

Roffman, A. J., Herzog, J. E. and Wershba-Gershon, P. M. (1990) 'Helping young adults understand their learning disabilities', *Journal of Learning Disabilities*, 27: 413–419.

Roffman, A. J. (2000). *Meeting the challenges of learning disabilities in adulthood*. Baltimore: Paul H. Brookes Publishing Company.

Rehabilitation Act (1973) P. L. 93–112. Title V, Section 504.

Smith, T. E. C., Dowdy, C. A., Polloway, E. A. and Blalock, G. (1997) *Children and adults with learning disabilities*. Boston, MA: Allyn and Bacon.

Strauss, A. and Corbin, J. (1997) *Grounded theory in practice*. Thousand Oaks, CA: Sage Publications.

Valeri-Gold, M., Kearse, W., Deming, M. P., Errico, M. and Callahan, C. (2001) 'Examining college developmental learners' reasons for persisting in college: A longitudinal retention study', *Research and Teaching in Developmental Education*, 17: 27–40.

Vogel, S. A. and Adelman, P. B. (2000) 'Adults with learning disabilities 8–15 years after college', *Learning Disabilities: A Multi-Disciplinary Journal*, 10 (3): 165–182.

Wehmeyer, M. (1995) 'A career education approach: Self-determination for youth with mild cognitive disabilities', *Intervention in School and Clinic*, 30: 157–163.

Witte, R. H., Philips, M. and Kakela, M. (1998) 'Job satisfaction of college graduates with learning disabilities', *Journal of Learning Disabilities*, 31 (3): 259–265.

Wolfensburger, W. (1972) *Normalization: The principles of normalization in human services*. Toronto: National Institute of Mental Retardation.

Yin, R. K. (1994) *Case study research: Design and methods*. Thousand Oaks, CA: Sage Publications.

Dyslexia: Workplace Issues

Gavin Reid, Fil Came and Lynda A. Price

This chapter

i) highlights some of the current and potential issues that adults with dyslexia and employers have to deal with in the workplace;
ii) discusses the principles of an effective and dyslexia-friendly work environment;
iii) discusses issues from employers and employees perspectives;
iv) looks at the importance of emerging practices from colleges and universities; and
v) refers to the legislation in different countries and the influence this can have on the workplace.

BACKGROUND

Dyslexia in the workplace is an area where highly developed practices have yet to fully emerge, although the recent supports developed in many colleges and universities in a number of countries will eventually pave the way for more enlightened workplace practices. At the same time initiatives such as the Employers Guide to Dyslexia (BDA, 2005) will also help to establish a firm basis for developing awareness and effective workplace support for adults with dyslexia.

The lack of employer awareness of dyslexia can have a profound effect on the worker. This chapter will provide perspectives from government, employees and employers. The legislation in different countries will be referred to and how this might influence practice.

THE NEED FOR UNDERSTANDING

Young and Browning (2004) suggested that there are no comprehensive studies of employment outcomes for those with dyslexia seeking employment.

They also suggest that the studies that have been carried out are mainly anecdotal or suffer from selection bias and that one aspect that has been missing from previous research is an evaluation of the issues from the adults perspective. Most studies about adults with Learning Disabilities/Dyslexia have focused on reading skills and how to address and remediate these. There is however significant evidence (Fawcett and Nicolson, 2004) that dyslexia is more than a reading difficulty, but it can have a significant effect on life skills. There is a need to ensure that employers are aware of the nature of dyslexia and that they understand how these factors can affect the employee in carrying out their daily work. There is also a need to understand the strengths that can be shown with people with dyslexia. It is important to dispel the notion that dyslexia equals disability as this can influence employers to unfairly, and perhaps unwittingly, discriminate against employees or potential employees with dyslexia.

IDENTIFYING THE BARRIERS

Reid and Kirk (2001) interviewed a number of adults with dyslexia to help identify the nature of the workplace barriers they had experienced and how these were dealt with by the individual and by employers. Some of these are shown below:

> 'I struggled at university and in the end I just wanted to pass and get a job. In my job as a speech therapist I sometimes have time management difficulties, planning my diary and writing up my case notes can be difficult. I usually need a lot of time to write reports and filling out forms at work can be a nightmare. Usually I miss out something in a form and often I am pulled up by my boss for such omissions. I get very involved with the client and spend a lot of time discussing different aspects but then when it comes to putting it into words- that is when it becomes very difficult'.

This extract above highlights some of the difficulties often experienced by people with dyslexia. These include report writing, accurately completing forms and essentially following the conventions of the workplace. This extract highlights the individuality of dyslexia and the fact that they need scope to develop their own practices and work habits. This makes it difficult for them to accommodate to existing routines, particularly if these are quite rigid. It also emphasises the need for an understanding employer.

The strengths of adults with dyslexia however can be noted in the next extract.

> 'Although I have difficulties with reading and writing I find at meetings and in informal discussions with colleagues I always seem to be able to see things or think of things which other people miss. Some of my colleagues are quite rigid in the way they process information. I feel I can see things as a whole and I can often add points at meetings. I feel the main thing is knowing your strengths and use these as far as possible'.

This highlights the potential creativity of people with dyslexia and the potential for thinking 'outside the box'.

DISCLOSURE

Reluctance to self - disclose (handwritten note)

It is important to emphasise to adults with dyslexia that they must disclose they are dyslexic in application forms and at interviews. Many however are reluctant to do this because of the risk of employers discriminating against them – despite the anti-discrimination legislation that is in force in many countries. This is the reality of the situation and it is difficult to persuade dyslexic people looking for employment to put their trust in the system. Yet they must, if they are going to get the support they will need once employed. It can be difficult to cover up for their dyslexia, but many attempt to do this as the extract below shows:

> 'No one at work knows I am dyslexic and I try to spot my mistakes before they do. When I am learning a new skill or task at work I need a base frame work, that is usually quite difficult at it takes time, but once I get that basic framework it is easier to learn and remember'.

There are several important points here – firstly that a basic framework provides security for individuals with dyslexia – this also means that routine can be important and they need to establish a basic format for the tasks they have to undertake. The second point is that this particular individual has been successful, but many are not and need support to establish a basic framework or routine. If the employer does not know the employee is dyslexic then it becomes difficult to provide the understanding and the support needed. Often a crisis point is reached when the employer seeks to discipline the employee due to incompetence because they have no knowledge of the person's dyslexia (Reid, 2006 personal correspondence, see also TUC report below).

ADVANCEMENT

Many people with dyslexia can excel in their careers and are often encouraged to seek promotion and increased responsibility. This can be beneficial for self-esteem but many dyslexic adults are reluctant to seek promotion because it is usually accompanied by new and sometimes unknown job demands, perhaps further study and examinations. It is important that employers are aware of this and encourage and support dyslexic employees to advance in their careers. The extract below provides an encouraging example of this.

> 'I have been a youth worker for 25 years then 3 years ago I was told I had to obtain a formal qualification. I immediately panicked but was confident and sensible enough to tell my employers that I was dyslexic and would likely have difficulty obtaining the qualification. I then did the extended training which I successfully completed – luckily I had a sympathetic manager'.

In the same vein career challenges can occur when the nature of a workers employment changes due to the introduction of new methods or new technology. This can provide a degree of stress for the employee and may put the individual's job at risk (Reid, 2007 personal correspondence).

TECHNOLOGY

It is fortunate that technology is now abundant and becoming highly sophisticated in the type of support it can provide to the employee with dyslexia. The BDA Employers Guide (2005) highlighted this. The guide lists spellcheckers, thesaurus, personal organisers, reading pens, voice recorders, predictive text, voice recognition, read back scanners and software as well as the increased portability of computers as all being of benefit to the dyslexic individual in the workplace. The important issue is that employers have to realise that with these type of supports the barriers caused by dyslexia can be significantly minimised.

DIVERSITY IN OCCUPATIONS

It is quite common for a young adult with dyslexia to be hesitant over career choice. They are often confused and uncertain. Additionally, going for a career can be risky and they may feel reluctant to take risks. At this stage it is important that they receive appropriate advice and counselling. The focus of this should not be 'I am dyslexia what can I do?' But rather looking at the individual's skills, interests and ambitions and working out how accommodations and support can be put in place to make any ambitions and decisions possible.

Some questions and concerns they may ask include.

- What type of work would I be able to do?
- Are there any professions /occupations I should avoid?
- Will I be supported in a college or university course?
- How can I develop strategies to deal with dyslexia?

It is important that these questions are answered in a positive way. A young person with dyslexia who has an interest in journalism, medicine, law or accountancy can, with support, achieve that ambition. Certain occupations can be more challenging because of, and indeed depending on, the nature of the dyslexic difficulties, but no occupation should necessarily be ruled out.

Reid (2005) produced the table below to highlight the point that all professions, with support, are within the reach of individuals with dyslexia.

Table 24.1 shows that no profession should be outwith the scope of the individual with dyslexia. The extract below highlights one such example of this. It is commonly believed that people with dyslexia can have difficulty with literacy and with writing. The extract below shows how these barriers can be overcome.

'Becoming a writer was a real challenge for me, but my friends were helpful with proof reading, but now my word processor does so much of that for me, it has been a great help. I like a challenge which is probably why I became a writer and I am also creative. The plot for the novel I have written came to me in a dream. This started me off in my career as a writer. I am now also a freelance travel writer'.

Table 24.1 An A-Z of professions, challenges and accommodations for dyslexic people (Gavin Reid[c])

Profession	Challenges	Accommodations
Armed Forces	Entry qualifications, organisation, report writing, reading fluently, remembering instructions	Lot of support available in the UK. Recognises the importance of supporting dyslexic people.
Accountancy	Close and accurate number work, tables and statistics, memory work, examinations, detailed and accurate knowledge of tax legislation	Use of technology – working in teams – using dictaphone for reports
Art careers	Usually very well suited for dyslexic adults but can experience difficulty in examinations, order and sequence of practical work	Use visual strategies, mind mapping to remember information
Building trades	Examinations, remembering quantities, ordering materials, figures, time management	Work in pairs, use calculator
Computer work	Usually very popular choice for dyslexic adults. Passing examinations, may include some maths, writing reports and letters, filing software and general administration work	Spend time to organise data and get some assistance with this if possible
Dentistry	Examinations, organisation, memory, record keeping	Study skills support, memory strategies
Engineering	Usually a popular profession for dyslexic adults, mathematics, accuracy in figures and measurements, report writing	Have formula prepared, work in teams
Fire services	Memory, report writing, concise instructions	Usually team work is important
Garage work	Report writing, memory, visual skills, maybe maths and formulae	Customer relations important
Hairdressing	Ordering stock, remembering different lotions for different purposes, examinations	Develop customer relations and social skills
Insurance work	Maths, statistics may be necessary, accuracy with figures, report writing	Use technology, calculators, software programmes –dictaphone for letters
Journalism	Reading and writing at speed, summarising information, grammar and accuracy.	Use dictaphone for interviews, use good word processing package with advanced spellcheck such as Texthelp©
Law	Entry qualifications may be high, a lot of reading, need to remember facts, need to be able to summarise information	Use secretarial support, use dictaphone, some good word processing packages available for helping with summaries
Librarian	Accuracy in cataloguing, reading, ordering books sequencing, organisation	Take time to check and re-check. Ensure that you are familiar with the recording, shelving and filing system at the outset
Mechanic	Technical language, memory, maths and remembering diagrams	Mind mapping and other study techniques, Take formulae into exams
Nurse	Exams, medical terminology, time keeping, reading medicines, prescriptions	Working in teams, more time to check medicines, extra time for exams.
Optician	Examinations, accuracy with figures, practical work, length of course	Take extra time to check figures
Police force	Entry qualifications, accuracy in reading, responding quickly	Use dictaphone to record notes

Continued

Table 24.1 An A-Z of professions, challenges and accommodations for dyslexic people (Gavin Reid[c])—Cont'd

Profession	Challenges	Accommodations
Restaurant work	Counting accurately, remembering orders, ordering materials	Write down everything including table number –try not to get flustered and develop good polite customer relations
Sales person	Remembering orders and product information	Use lightweight laptop computer to record information, use mind maps to remember product inforamtion
Teaching	Popular choice, need to be aware of your weaknesses e.g. spelling and try to compensate for these, planning lessons, organisation	Use strategies to ensure that you use your strengths. Plan well ahead so that you are not unawares by any situation.
Vet	Long course, examinations, practical work, accuracy, memory	Use visual diagrams, work in teams, use the support assistance that is available
Youth worker	This is also a popular choice for adults with dyslexia, there will be examinations, memory work and punctuality will be important.	Work in teams, make sure that any legal and statutory implications of your work are explained to you rather than you having to read regulations
Zoo worker	Remembering routine, ordering materials	Make a mind map of any duties such as time of feeding animals and type of food – ensure that the safety requirements are explained to you.

The following extract also highlights how confronting the issues might be embarrassing at first but soon eventually they can be accepted by others.

'I have just finished working in a nursery school. I enjoyed that enormously but I found reading aloud to the children very difficult and very embarrassing! But after the initial embarrassment it was fine – the children thought I was joking with them'.

It is important therefore not to restrict the individual with dyslexia but to offer them the choice and diversity that would be available to all others.

DISCRIMINATORY PRACTICES?

Despite the positive experiences described above the system is still open to discriminatory practices and these are reported widely and are frequently featured in legal cases.

Young and Browning, in the US (Young and Browning, 2004), highlight this and show that some groups of young dyslexic adults may still be disadvantaged. They suggest that studies show that (identified) persons with Learning Disabilities/Dyslexia tend to do show only marginal differences in success compared to those with other disabilities in employment and education. Furthermore, they argue that these employment studies and other studies of persons with Learning Disabilities/Dyslexia tend to focus mainly on white males who had been identified and had received special educational services, and had graduated high school. The NICHD research, according to Young and Browning however strongly indicates that of the two-thirds of those with Learning Disabilities/Dyslexia who have not been identified by the school systems within the US and the UK tend to be poor, if not very poor, disproportionately female and minority, and had not been identified, had not received services and, more often than not, had not graduated high school.

The New York Post (17th August 2001) reported on how a dyslexic woman finally won her eight-year fight to take the state bar exam, to qualify as a barrister, with a computer and other aids to help overcome her disability. The judge ruled that the state board's failure to accommodate to her reading impairment was a substantial factor in her failure to pass the bar.

The Forensic Echo (2000) also reported on a similar type of case. In this situation an employee required additional training to develop skills in new computer operations. The employee requested extra training and practice time. But she also was informed during this period that she would not be promoted to a supervisory position because she was not deemed to have the appropriate skills.

There is evidence of a number of issues here in relation to the application of the Americans with Disabilities Act (ADA) to individuals with dyslexia. By not providing additional training, the employee was effectively prevented from developing her skills sufficiently to enable her to qualify for promotion. It is crucial if the dyslexic individual is to progress in the workplace that the employer has an understanding of the information processing differences experienced by the dyslexia person. Additional training and time could have made a significant difference in the above case and with more employer understanding of dyslexia, a stressful and traumatic episode could have been prevented.

EMPOWERMENT AND THE SOCIAL MODEL OF DISABILITY

There is a role for increased awareness of dyslexia in society and in the workplace. This can be achieved through educating employers, which was the purpose of the British Dyslexia Association Employers Guide, but it can also be achieved through more widespread and more accurate detection of dyslexia. This is particularly the case in the adult workforce where there are a great number of undiagnosed dyslexic people. This is due to the detection of dyslexia at school only gaining a strong foothold over the last ten years and even now such detection is still not uniform with many countries and states still lagging behind in this area (Reid, 2005). But it is only through detection that acceptance can become a reality and acceptance can pave the way for empowerment. The current situation is quite a bit from the individual with dyslexia feeling empowered as often they have to fight and struggle to achieve their rights. Yet empowerment is necessary for full inclusion in society. This is illustrated in the examples from the court cases above.

McLaughlin (2004) from the Adult Dyslexia and Skills Development Centre in London suggests that if dyslexic people are to be fully included in society, the emphasis should be on empowerment or enablement rather than a model of disability that perceives the 'dyslexic as a victim'.

He suggests that empowerment comes from

- Self-understanding – dyslexia is often referred to as a 'hidden disability'. Dyslexic people therefore have to advocate for themselves, and can only do so if they have a good understanding of the nature of their difficulty, how it affects them and what they need to do about to improve their performance.
- Understanding by others, particularly employers – if dyslexic people have to deal with managers and colleagues whose understanding of the nature of dyslexia is limited it is likely the dyslexic person will be excluded, rather than included.

If employers are enlightened and informed, discriminatory practices should be minimized. This paves the way for re-thinking the concept of disability along the lines of the social model of disability.

The social model of disability opposes the medical model commonly used in the health professions. The Social model of disability makes an important distinction between the terms impairment and accommodation. This can be seen in the example below from Southampton Council in the UK (http://www.southamptoncil.co.uk/social_model.htm).

Essentially this distinction emerges from Social Constructivism and determines that disability is a social construct and that any limitations experienced by the individual are imposed on him/her by the conventions of society. This means that individuals with impairments are not disabled by their impairments, but by the barriers that exist in society which do not take into account their needs. See Table 24.2.

The implications of this for dyslexic people is that society needs to recognize the diversity and the differences in methods of information processing displayed by dyslexic individuals. This has implications for education and for training, in particular for assessment and recognition of achievement. This also has implications for ensuring the learning environment at college and in the workplace is suited to the needs of the individual with dyslexia.

Table 24.2 Examples of how society could change to allow disabled people to participate equally

Medical model problem	Social model solution
Painful hands, unable to open jars, doors	Better designed lids, automatic doors
Difficulties in standing for long periods	More seats in public places
Unable to climb steps into buildings	Ramps and lifts in all buildings
Other people won't give you a job because they think you couldn't do it	Educate people to look at disabled people's abilities rather than looking for problems

This means there needs to be a focus on support. At college and in the workplace this can involve support with the following:

- organization of work area and of work load;
- reading strategies – and particularly reading fluency;
- note-taking – and be able to organise and make sense of notes;
- listening to instructions – and not feel embarrassed to ask them to be repeated or to write them down;
- writing reports – and being offered support to proof read and additional time to write the reports;
- making presentations – identifying the key points can be problematic;
- preparing for exams and generally trying to memorize information.

In the UK and the US, support at college and university is gaining momentum and many have institutional policies for dyslexia and disabilities. At the same time there appears to be quite a distance to go before there is adequate support for all students with learning disabilities. Price and Gerber (2008) suggest that only 16–20 per cent of the high school graduates with learning disabilities (vs. 50 per cent of all graduates without learning disabilities) will go on to college, with less than half of that group completing their degree program. This and as the debate described below indicates that despite legislation the reality of the situation is that many dyslexics who need support for whatever reason will not receive it.

SUPPORTS

Trade Unions

The Trade Union Congress (TUC) report (December 2004, UK) urged employers to take notice of the need to make accommodations for dyslexia in the workplace. The report suggested that more could be done to tackle the discriminatory practices experienced by some people with dyslexia. They cited the instance when one Company initially treated an employee's clerical, spelling and filing errors, as a disciplinary/capacity issue, and even when the employee was identified as dyslexic, the company chose to ignore the advice and dismiss the person for incapacity. The report warned that managers who do not appreciate the link between dyslexia and common performance problems can often judge dyslexic employees unfairly. The report also revealed that many people with dyslexia were unaware of their condition and are likely to be anxious, frustrated and suffer from low self-esteem at work. This has implications for identification of dyslexia at an earlier age. Despite the increase in awareness of dyslexia at school, there are still a vast amount of people who have undiagnosed dyslexia and entering the workforce or tertiary education. For example, Singleton (1999) found that almost one-third of all first year dyslexic students at university were diagnosed for the first time when entering university.

The TUC report highlighted the most common problems that dyslexics suffer at work which include the following:

- following written or spoken instructions;
- dealing with maps, charts and tables;
- writing memos, letters and reports;
- giving presentations;
- scheduling work and meetings and keeping track of appointments.

The report recognized that while dyslexic people may have problems with certain aspects of their work, they are likely to have strengths in other areas and amending working practices can ensure that both the employee and the company benefit. This is the message that is given out to employers – that is to utilize the strengths of adults with dyslexia.

THE WAY FORWARD

Career advice

Reid and Kirk (2001) show how many people with dyslexia have succeeded in a variety of occupations. McLaughlin (2004) indicates that being dyslexic is not necessarily a barrier to occupational success and supports this view. He says

> there are too many dyslexic people in all occupations to refute this, but some occupations are more dyslexia-friendly than others, tapping the dyslexic person's strengths rather than their weaknesses. There are undoubtedly dyslexic people who are in the wrong job, that is, they are in a situation where the demands on tasks they find difficult outweigh those on their competencies and strengths. Career guidance/counselling geared towards the needs of dyslexic people is arguably one of the most important, but under-resourced professional activities. (p. 180).

Without doubt, ongoing career advice is important. This will allow the young person to have several choices and if one does not work out will be able to discuss this with the careers person. Key points for career advice would be before subject choice in secondary school, before applying to college or university, when applying for a job and after having been in employment for a period of time to discuss how the dyslexic person may advance in that career or an alternative one.

SELF-ADVOCACY

Self-advocacy is a crucial area. It is important in order to establish 'rights' which may not be easy to achieve without some form of struggle or lobbying. The TUC study and report indicates that it may be challenging for some individuals to assert their needs and to advocate for their rights.

A shift towards greater personal responsibility, self-direction and self-advocacy is crucial to the attainment of employment success (McLoughlin et al., 1994; Brown, 1997). Employment success may be dependent upon whether a disabled individual knows the dimensions of his or her disability well and to know how, and when, to compensate for them within their job contexts because there may not be available advice. This could be because the employer is unwilling or indeed because they have not a clear view of what kind of support would be beneficial.

Reid and Kirk (2001) suggest that one of the reasons self-advocacy is difficult to achieve for adults is because there are few opportunities to practice self-advocacy skills at school, or in further and higher education.

This point has been recognised by a group of special educators in Rochester, New York (Weimer et al., 1994) who developed a working proposal on self-advocacy for adolescents with special needs. Their proposal suggests that self-advocacy should begin at least by the middle school because that is when students are given more curriculum choice and encouraged to think independently. Weimer et al. recognised that even in high school and post high school many students still lacked skills to evaluate their strengths and weaknesses. Three of the goals in their self-advocacy programme include:

- developing an understanding of self-advocacy and how it can apply to the student;
- the importance of the knowledge gained on self-advocacy and self-awareness and how that can be transformed into life skills and techniques; and
- allowing the student to understand that success in life can depend greatly on ones ability to self-advocate.

Weimer et al. suggest that this type of structured programme introduced early in the school years can help students with all types of special needs overcome the barriers they will very likely meet in education, employment and sometimes in interpersonal skills.

THE LAW – IS IT SUFFICIENT?

Although there are quite well-established discrimination legislation in place in a number of countries, this may not always have the desired results. The DDA (1996, 2004) in the UK and The Americans with Disabilities Act (1990) attempts to ensure that employers provide reasonable accommodations to protect the rights of individuals with disabilities. Yet this is still not a reality. The act makes suggestions such as re-structuring job descriptions to ensure a dyslexic employee can be employed if he/she is finding the existing job too demanding, altering the layout of offices and factories and adapting and purchasing equipment. It is also illegal not to employ an individual on account of their dyslexia.

But the crucial issue is the implementation of the act and the persuasion of employers to adhere to the spirit as well as the letter of the legislation.

CONCLUSION

This chapter has highlighted the needs of adults with dyslexia in a changing and in some ways a more competitive and accountable employment situation. Yet it is important that the needs of adults with dyslexia are not placed secondary to the acute needs of business and job performance. In order for that to become a reality, the social model of disability needs to be acknowledged as well as the skills and potential of people with dyslexia. Legislation can go so far but ultimately it is the responsibility of society including employers and educational institutions. It will only be when the notion of disability is re-framed in a positive and constructive fashion that people with dyslexia will feel secure to assert their rights in society and in the workplace.

REFERENCES

British Dyslexia Association (2005) The employers guide to dyslexia, BDA, Sundial Events, Key 4 Learning, UK.

Brown, D. S. (1997) The New Economy in the 21st Century: Implications for individuals with learning disabilities. In Gerber, P. J. and Brown, D. S. (eds.) *Learning Disabilities and Employment*. Texas, US: PRO-ED, pp. 19-38.

Fawcett, A. and Nicolson, R. (2004) Learning from the science of learning: implications for the classroom, in G. Reid and A. Fawcett (eds.) *Dyslexia in Context: Theory and Practice*, Wiley, Chichester.

The Forensic Echo – Behavioural and Forensic Sciences in the Courts (2000) Dyslexia a disability, but training enough hi-tech employee's discrimination case sputters, Volume 4, Issue 6 Published: Sunday, Apr 30, 2000 http://echo.forensicpanel.com/2000/4/30/dyslexiaa.html.

HMG (1995) Disability discrimination act (1995, 2004) London: HMSO.

McLoughlin, D., Fitzgibbon, G. and Young, V. (1994) *Adult dyslexia, assessment, counselling and training*. London: Whurr.

McLoughlin, D., Leather, C. and Stringer, P. (2002) The adult dyslexic. London: Whurr Publishers.

McLoughlin, D., Leather, C. and Stringer, P. (2002) *The adult dyslexic interventions and outcomes*. London: Whurr Publishers.

New York Post (2001) 'Dyslexic woman wins fight to take bar exam'. New York Post 17th August 2001. New York.

Price, L. and Gerber, P. (2008) 'Students with dyslexia in further and higher education: Perspectives and perceptions', in G. Reid, A. Fawcett, F. Manis and L. Siegel (eds) *The dyslexia handbook*. London: Sage Publications.

Reid, G. and Kirk, J. (2001) *Dyslexia in adults: Education and employment*. Wiley.

Reid, G. (2005) *Dyslexia: A complete guide for parents*. Wiley, Chichester.

Reid, (2006) Pre-assessment discussions with adult and employer. Personal correspondence Reid 2006.

Reid, (2007) Pre-assessment discussions with adult and employer. Personal correspondence Reid 2007.

Report on working practices on Dyslexia. Trade Union Congress report December 2004. London, TUC.

Singleton, C.H. (Chair) (1999) *Dyslexia in higher education: policy, provision and practice*. Report of the National Working Party on Dyslexia in Higher Education. Hull: University of Hull.

US Department of Education, Office of Vocational and Adult Education, Division of Adult Education and Literacy (2000). Learning disabilities and Spanish-speaking adult populations: The beginning of a process. USA government, Washington DC.

US Government (2001) Full funding of the individuals with disabilities education Act, 2001.

Young, G. and Browning, J. (2004) 'Learning disability/dyslexia and employment', in G. Reid and A. Fawcett (eds) *Dyslexia in context, research, policy and practice*. London: Whurr.

Index

Page references followed by f indicate an illustrative figure; t indicates a table

Aaron, P.G. (1991), 270
Aaron and Joshi (1992), 273, 314, 315
Aaron et al. (1999), 277, 281
Aaron et al. (in press), 273, 281, 282
Abarbanel et al. (1996), 16
Abramson et al. (1978), 398
Abu-Rabia, S. (2002), 434
Abu-Rabia and Taha (2004), 434
Abu-Rabia et al. (2003), 214, 225, 227, 231,
    233, 433
academic self-concept, 397, 399
Ackermann et al. (2007), 87
Adams, M.J. (1990), 11, 243, 275, 428
Adams and Bruck (1993), 243
Adams et al. (1998), 282
A.D.D. program (Lindamood), 318
ADEPT (Assessment of Encoding and
    Decoding Progress Test), 317-9, 319t,
    322f, 323f, 324-5, 326t, 328t, 329, 330-1
ADHD (attention deficit hyperactivity
    disorder), 33, 34, 35, 37, 44, 83, 88, 102,
    126, 206, 465
Adlof et al. (2006), 273
adolescents, morphology study, 218, 220, 223,
    226, 227, 229, 231, 233
adolescents and balance, 195-6
adolescents and self-concept see self-concept
    study
Adult Dyslexia and Skills Development
    Centre, London, 480-1
adults
    morphology study, 213, 218, 223, 225,
        227, 231
    visual and auditory experiments among,
        19-20f, 24t
    see also employment; self-concept study;
        self-disclosure study
Al-Mannai and Everatt (2004), 433, 434
Al Otaiba and Fuchs (2002), 185
Al Otaiba and Fuchs (2006), 259
Al Otaiba et al. (2005), 349
ALBSU (1987), 400, 402
Albus, J.S., 80

Alexander, R. (2000), 376
Allington, R. (2004), 340
Allum et al. (1998), 88
alphabetic processing, 14-5, 57, 244-6, 134-5,
    138, 139, 275-6, 316, 318, 325, 343,
    345, 347t
    eye function and letter order, 61
    International Phonetic Alphabet, 444
    see also spelling
alternative treatments for reading disability, 90
Amado, A.J. (1999), 327
American Psychiatric Association (1994), 216,
    270, 308
Americans with Disabilities Act (ADA), 459-60,
    461, 466-7, 468, 480, 484
Anderson, J.R. (1982), 202
Anderson et al. (1995), 283
Andreou and Kuntsi, 39
Andrews Espy et al. (2004), 105
Angold et al., 33, 34, 35
ANOVA (analysis of variance), 111, 112f,
    159, 346
Arabic, 225, 432-6
Aram and Hall ((1998), 308
Archer, A. (1981), 340
Archer et al. (2000), 340
arithmetic, 306, 307, 308
Arnback, E. (2001), 447
Arneil and Holmes (2003-2007), 451
asynchrony phenomenon, 11-29
    alphabetic processing, 14-5
    basis of, 11-2
    between left and right hemispheres 22-4
    between posterior and anterior brain sites,
        21-2
    biological systems, 12, 13
    cognitive processes, 12, 13-4
    preconditions for, 12
    speed of processing (SOP)
        differences between different brain
            entities, 15-7
        gap between different brain entities 12,
            14, 20, 24-5, 24t, 26

asynchrony phenomenon *(Continued)*
    speed of transfer from posterior to
        anterior brain sites, 22
    visual and auditory, 17-21, 17f, 18f,
        19f, 20f
Atkinson and Shiffrin, 12
attention and m- system, 62-3
attribution theory, 404-6
auditory factors, 64-8, 70, 71-2, 73, 113t, 114f,
    115, 116, 199, 201, 301, 308, 388
    cross-modal transfer, 194
    discussion of phonological deficit and motor
        skills problems, 82, 84, 86, 90-1
    listening comprehension method of
        assessment, 270, 279, 314
    listening skills, learning a foreign language,
        383-4, 444, 449
    morphological processing and oral
        presentation, 219-20
    speed of processing (SOP), 17-21, 17f, 18f,
        19f, 20f
    see also phonological processing
Augur, J. (1985), 83
Austria, 445
autism, 206, 308, 364
automatisation deficit, 84, 193, 194-6, 202,
    203, 204, 391
autonomous learning, 371-2
Avons and Hanna (1995), 220
Aylward et al. (2003), 261

Badian, N.A. (1985), 83
Bailey et al. (2004), 171
Baizer et al. (1999), 204
balance, 87-8, 196
Ball and Blachman (1988), 282
Ball and Blachman (1991), 274, 275, 282
Ballan, E. (in preparation), 25
Bandura, A. (1997), 397-8
Bandura et al. (1999), 397
Banich, M.T. (2004), 22, 23
Barnea and Breznitz, 16
Barr, R. (1984), 341
Barsch, R.H. (1968), 309
Bartley et al. (1997), 34, 36
Barwick and Siegel (1996), 307
Batería III Woodcock-Muñoz, 281
Bateman, B.D. (1965), 293
Bates and Dick (2002), 85
Baum and Owen (1988), 42
Baydar et al. (1993), 338
Bayesian statistics, 136
Bear et al. (1991), 400
Bear et al. (1993), 399
Beaton et al. (1997), 430
Beauducel and Debener (2003), 111
behaviour, pupil's difficult, 390, 418

Ben-Yehudah et al. (2007), 87
Benasich et al. (2002), 105
Benbow, C.P. (1988), 43
Bender and Wall (1994), 402
Bentin, S. (1989), 16
Bentin and Frost (1995), 433-4
Benton, A. (1978), 83
Bergman and Magnussen (1997), 34
Berninger, V.W. (1998), 343
Berninger et al. (2004), 271
Berko, J. (1958), 220
Berninger, V.W. (2001), 216
Binet-Simon scale, 269
Birch and Belmont (1964), 194
Bishop and Adams (1990), 217
Bishop and Butterworth (1980), 218
Bishop and Snowling (2004), 218
Blachman, B.A. (2000), 245
Blachman et al. (1999), 274, 275
Blachman et al. (2004), 255
Blaiklock, K. (2004), 134
Blackorby and Wagner (1996), 457, 458
Blanchard et al. (2001), 280
blindness, 308
blinking, 88, 204, 208, 385
Boles and Brown (2001), 458
Bonte and Blomert (2004), 107
Boudelaa and Marslen-Wilson (2005), 434
Boulware-Gooden et al. (in press), 283
Bourassa et al. (2006), 228, 232
Bowers and Kirby (2006), 220, 234
Bowers and Wolf, (1993), 277
Bowey, J.A. (1995), 338
Bowey and Rutherford (2007), 152-3, 159,
    160, 167, 170
Bowey et al. (2007), 159
boys, study of self-concept, 399, 404, 405-6
Bradley and Bryant (1983), 129, 194, 214,
    249, 314
Bradley and Bryant (1985), 274
Bradley and Corwyn (2002), 109
Brady et al. (1983), 82
Brandeis and Lehmann (1994), 16
Brazil, 420
Breznitz, Z. (2002), 11, 12, 16, 25
Breznitz, Z., (2003), 16
Breznitz, Z., (2005), 16
Breznitz, Z. (2006), 11, 12, 16-7, 20, 21, 25, 26
Breznitz and Berman (2003), 21
Breznitz and Horowitz (under review), 26
Breznitz and Itzchak (2005), 26
Breznitz and Meyler (2003), 16
Breznitz and Misra (2003) 11, 12, 16, 25
Breznitz and Navat (2004), 26
Brindley, G. S. (1964), 80
British Dyslexia Association (BDA), 357, 383,
    386, 396, 403, 474, 480

British Psychological Society 11, 396
Broca's speech production area, 68, 69, 70, 80, 86, 102, 206, 261
Brodal, A. (1981), 79
Brody and Mills (1997), 34, 40
Brookes and Sterling (2005), 87
Brookes et al. (2007), 88, 204
Brown (1997), 484
Bruck, M. (1985), 400
Bruck, M. (1990), 218
Bruck, M. (1993), 430
Brunswick et al. (1999), 22
Bryant et al. (1998), 215, 229, 233, 234
Bryden et al. (1994), 33
bullying, 403
Burden, R.L. (1995), 397
Burden, R.L. (2005), 399, 400, 405-6
Burden and Burdett (2007), 406
Burgess and Lonigan (1998), 116, 177
Bursuck et al. (2002), 339
Burton, S. (2004), 363
Bus and van IJzendoorn (1999), 134, 340
Bush, G.W., 420
Butcher et al. (2006), 34, 35, 36, 44
Butkowsky and Willows (1980), 404
Butler and Gasson (2005), 404
Buttle Foundation, 403
Byrne, B.M. (1996), 396

Cain and Oakhill (1998), 283
Calfee and Drum (1986), 245
Calfee et al. (1969), 278
Campos et al. (2000), 132
Canada, 420, 421, 459, 470
Carekker, S. (2005), 282
Carey, K. (2003), 339
Carlisle, J.F. (1987), 225-6, 227, 232, 233
Carlisle, J.F. (1988), 222, 228
Carlisle, J.F. (1995), 219
Carlisle and Stone (2003), 228
Carlisle et al. (2001), 223
Carroll et al. (1971), 155
Carroll et al. (2003), 256
Carrow Test, 301
Carter, R. (1998), 22
Carver, R.P. (1998), 269, 273
Casalis et al. (2004), 221, 230, 231, 232, 233
Case et al. (2003), 181
Cassanova et al. (2002), 43
Castles and Coltheart (1993), 150-1, 152, 153, 159
Castles and Coltheart (1996), 170, 171
Castles and Coltheart (2004), 275
Castles et al. (1999), 132, 152, 153, 159, 167, 168, 170
Castro-Caldas et al. (1998), 57
CAT 301, 58, 60, 65, 67

Cattell, R.B. (1966), 111
Catts, H.W. (1989), 82, 220, 308
Catts and Kamhi (2005), 269, 273
Catts et al. (1994), 218
Center et al. (1995), 246
Center et al. (2001), 250
Center for Applied Linguistics, 281
cerebellum, 66-7, 77-98, 204, 206
    role in cognition, 80-2, 81f, 86-7, 92
    role in motor skills, 82-3
    structure, 79-80, 89
cerebellar deficit hypothesis, 83-92, 84f
    as causal explanation, 91-2
    criticisms of, 89-91
    evidence, 84-5
    further findings, 86-8
    status of 92-3
Chall, J.S. (1983), 255
Chapman, J.W. (1974-86), 396
Chapman, J.W. (1988), 396, 401
Chapman, J.W. (1996), 399
Chapman and McCrary (1995), 111
Chapman and Tunmer (2003), 244
Chapman et al. (2001), 245, 246
Changeaux, J.-P. (1985), 39, 44
chemistry, 392
Cheng et al. (2004), 62
Cheour et al. (2000), 127
Cherny et al. (2004), 39
Chialant and Caramazza (1995), 223
Chinese language, 224
choice reaction (CRT), 197f
Chomsky, N., 64
Chomsky, N. (1965), 198
Chomsky, N. (1995), 198
Chomsky and Halle (1968), 234
Christensen and Bowey (2005), 250
Christian and Thompson (2003), 204
chromosome 3, 44
chromosome 6, 44, 71
Chung and Martin (2002), 40
Circles of Inclusion (DfES), 363
classification of developmental dyslexia, 150-3, 174-91
    hybrid model, 187-8
    response to intervention (RTI) approaches, 176, 181-7
    traditional approaches, 176-81
    see also learning disabilities, defining
classroom management issues, secondary schools, 389-92
Clay, M.M. (1987), 100
Clay, M.M (1993), 249, 250
Clements and Peters (1962), 31
Cloninger, C.R. (2002), 34
cloze procedure, 280
Coffield, F.J. (2005), 362, 376

Coffield et al. (2004), 369, 372, 373, 376
Coffin et al. (2005), 88, 204
Cogan and Flecker (2004), 385, 387
'Cognitive Mosaic Model', 125
Cohen, J, (1988), 129
Cohen et al. (1982), 341
Coltheart, M. (1978), 150
Coltheart, M. (1983), 150
Coltheart et al. (2001), 169, 215, 216
commonality analysis, 327-8
componental model of reading, 268-89
   background, 269-71
   cognitive domain, 272-81, 272f
      word comprehension, 272-4, 279-81
         listening comprehension, 270, 279
         reading comprehension, 270, 279-80
         vocabulary, 280-1
      word recognition, 272-4, 274-9
         decoding, 276, 277, 279
         instant, 276-7
         spelling, 277-9
   definition of, 271-2, 272f
   interpreting the assessment outcome, 281-3,
      282t
Comprehensive Test of Phonological Processing
   (CTOPP), 188, 274-5, 346, 347t
Compton and Carlisle (1994), 276
Compton et al. (2006), 187, 260
Conn, M.T. (1992), 44
Connecticut Longitudinal Study, 178
Connors and Olson (1990), 315
coordination 77-8, 204
Corballis, M. (2002), 85
Corder, S.P. (1982), 441
Cornelissen et al. (1995), 62
Cornelissen et al. (1997), 61
corpus callosum, 103, 104
Corriveau et al. (1988), 58, 72
Cosden, M. (1999), 399
Cossu et al. (1995), 275
Covington, M.V. (1992), 397
Craggs et al. (2006), 43, 44
Crombie et al. (2004), 418
Cronbach alpha values, 358
cross curricular perspectives see secondary
   schools, cross curricular perspectives study
cross-modal transfer, 194
Cossu, G. (1999), 431
Crawford and Higham (2001), 60
Crowder and Wagner (1992), 175, 176
Cunningham, A. (1990), 341
Cunningham and Stanovich (1990), 156
Curran, T. (1999), 111
Czech Republic, 420

Daal et al. (2005), 445
data analysis tools, advances in, 250-2
Davenport, L. (1991), 404

Davis and MacNeilage (2000), 85
DCD (developmental coordination disorder),
   33, 34
DCDC2 gene, 44
de Jong and van der Leij (1999), 101, 432
de Jong and van der Leij (2002), 140, 270, 273
de Jong and van der Leij (2003), 101, 270
De Smet et al. (2007), 86
Deacon and Kirby (2004), 225
Deacon et al. (2006), 218, 226-7, 232
Dean, P. (early 1990s), 83
definition map, concept of, 450
Defries et al. (1979), 34, 36
Defries et al. (1987), 274
Demb et al. (1997), 62
Démonet et al. (2004), 44, 127
denial of learning disabilities, 463
Denckla, M.B. (1977), 308
Denckla, M.B. (1985), 83
Denckla and Rudel (1976), 86, 135, 277
Denckla et al. (1985), 83
Denmark, 445
   Danish language, 101, 228, 275
Denton and Fletcher (2003), 351
Denton and Mathes (2003), 247, 258
Denton et al. (2006), 186, 259
Department for Education and Science (DfES),
   UK (2003), 357
Department for Education and Science (DfES),
   UK (2005), 363
Department of Health and Human Services,
   USA (2001, 2003), 109
depression, 398, 400
Deschler et al. (2005), 243, 259
Desmond and Fiez (1998), 81f
Development of Literacy in Spanish Speakers
   (DeLSS) website, 281
Developmental Coordination Disorder
   (DCD), 204
Developmental Phase Checklist (Padget et al.),
   317
di Filippo et al. (2005), 432
Diagnostic Achievement Battery, 279
diagnostic profile, Tennessee Center, 315t
diagnostic tests for differential diagnosis,
   Tennessee Center, 316t
Diamond, A. (2000), 85
Dick et al. (2007), 44
Differential Ability Scales (DAS), 109, 110
Disability Discrimination Act (DDA) (1995),
   421, 484
Dixon et al. (1992), 341
Dodds and Thomson (1999), 384
Dore exercise-based 'cerebellar' stimulation, 90
Doris, J.L. (1998), 31
Doya, K. (1999), 201f
Doyon and Benali (2005), 202
Doyon and Ungerleider (2002), 202, 203

Doyon et al. (2003), 203
Downey and Snyder (2000), 440
Down's syndrome, 55
drawing skills, secondary school, 388, 392
DSM-IV, 216, 217, 270, 396
dual discrepancy reading failure, 252
Dudley-Marling, C. (2004), 271
Duncan Multiple Range Test, 159
Dunn and Dunn (1981), 154, 167
Dunn and Dunn (1997), 109, 345
Dunn et al. (1998), 17
Durrant, J.E. (1994), 292
Durrant et al. (1990), 397, 399, 400
Dutch language, 101, 136
Dynamic Indicators of Basic Early Literacy
    Skills (DIBELS), 251, 344, 345, 346, 347t
Dyslexia Action, 396
Dyslexia Scotland (2001), 383
Dyslexia Screening Test (Fawcett and
    Nicolson), 430
Dyspraxia, 88

Early Phonological and Language Processing
    (EPLP), 129-31
early intervention, need for, 257-8, 338
    see individual tutoring for struggling readers
        by paraeducators study *for wider
        discussion*
Early Steps, 246
Ebsworth, M.E. (1998), 442
Eccles et al. (1967), 78, 80
echo reading, 344
Eden et al. (1996), 62
Edinburgh Handedness Inventory, 109
EEG, 16, 110
Egan and Pring (2004), 215, 230
EGIS, 110
Ehri, L.C. (1987), 316, 317
Ehri, L.C. (1991), 278
Ehri, L.C. (1992), 169, 170
Ehri, L.C. (1994), 316, 317
Ehri, L.C. (1997), 278
Ehri, L.C. (2000), 317, 332
Ehri, L.C. (2004), 243
Ehri, L.C. (2005), 213, 243
Ehri and McCormick (1998), 244, 245, 255
Ehri et al. (2001), 134, 135, 245
Eide and Eide (2006), 34
Ekinsmyth and Bynner (1994), 400
Elbaum et al. (2000), 244, 247, 340
Elbeheri and Everatt (2007), 433
Elbeheri et al. (2006), 433
Elberehi et al. (in preparation), 433, 434
Elbro, C. (1990), 229
Elbro, C. (1999), 449
Elbro and Arnbak (1996), 215, 228-9, 231,
    233, 234
Elbro et al. (1996), 430

Elbro et al. (1998), 101, 137
Elkonin, D.B. (1973), 313
Elliott, C. (1990), 109
Elliott, J. (2006), 56
Ellis (1993), 443
email, communication between parents and
    school, 412-3
EMG, 110
emotional factors, 303
    depression, 398, 400
    stress, 386
    see also self-concept; self-esteem
Employers Guide to Guide to Dyslexia (BDA,
    2005), 474, 480
employment, 401, 458, 459, 464, 468, 469,
    474-85
    A-Z of professions, challenges and
        accommodations (Reid, G.), 478-9t
    advancement, 476
    career advice, 478-9t, 483
    disclosure, 464, 469, 476
    discrimination, 476, 479-80
    diversity in occupations, 477
    empowerment and social model of
        disability, 480-2, 485
    examples of enabling equal
        participation, 481t
    legislation, sufficiency of, 484-5
    need for understanding, 474-5, 481
    self-advocacy, 483-4
    technology, 477
    trade unions, 482-3, 484
empowerment, 480-2, 481t
English language, 77, 101, 135, 136, 137, 155,
    175, 220, 224-5, 234, 248, 275, 282, 334,
    338, 387, 443-4, 447
    as a second language, 228, 272, 339, 445,
        447-8, 450, 451, 452
    bilingual English-Spanish, 273
    English Language Learner (ELL)
        students, individual tutoring study,
        349-50, 350t
    inflections, 220
    lack of transparency between letter and
        sounds, 428-9, 431
    comparison with Arabic, 433, 435, 436
environmental factors, 31, 33, 36-8, 37f, 38f,
    43, 54, 22, 123f, 132-4, 199, 201, 257,
    258, 272f, 316
    self-disclosure, 460, 464-5
    see also social disadvantage; social
        implications
ERPs (event-related potentials), 16, 17f, 18f,
    19f, 20, 22, 23, 24t
    identifying familial risk, 100, 104-17, 112f,
        113t, 114f, 115f, 127, 128
Erskine and Seymour (2005), 125
ethnicity, 398

Everatt et al. (2002), 429, 431
Everatt et al. (2004), 430
examinations, arrangements for, 392-3
Exception Word Reading, 155, 157, 158f,
    158t, 159, 160, 162, 164, 165, 167, 168,
    169, 170
exclusion, 291, 292-3, 296-7, 296t, 308
eye blink conditioning, 88, 204, 208
eye fixation, 60, 175, 202
eye movement abnormalities, 82, 92
    rebuttal of myth concerning, 175-6

Facoetti et al. (2001), 62
Fairhurst and Pumfrey (1992), 401
Falconer and Mackay (1996), 37, 38
familial dyslexia risk, early identification and
    prevention of dyslexia *see* Jyväskylä
    (JLD) study
familial predictors of dyslexia study, 99-120
    ERPs and identifying risk, 100, 104-17
    identifying cognitive skills, 100, 101
    newborn infants, studies of risk, 105-7
    parental reports and preschoolers, 108-17
        measures, 109
        methods, 108-9
        procedures, 110
        results, 110-5, 112f, 113t, 114f, 115f
    pediatric studies, 101-17
    school-age children, 107, 115
    see also genetics; Jyväskylä (JLD) study
Fawcett, A. (2001), 387
Fawcett and Nicolson (1990), 84, 87
Fawcett and Nicolson (1992), 87, 196
Fawcett and Nicolson (1994), 196
Fawcett and Nicolson (1995), 196
Fawcett and Nicolson (1996), 430
Fawcett and Nicolson (2002), 88
Fawcett and Nicolson (2004), 475
Fawcett and Nicolson (2007), 93, 132
Fawcett et al. (1996), 84
Field and Hoffman (1994), 459, 459
Fieldes, L. (1921), 269
Fill et al. (1998), 340
Finch et al. (2002), 85
Finnish longitudinal project *see* Jyväskylä
    (JLD) study
first-grade, 342
    see individual tutoring for struggling readers
        by paraeducators study *for wider
        discussion*
Fischer et al. (1985), 223
Fischer et al. (1998), 82
Fischer et al. (2000), 60, 82
Fisher and DeFries (2002), 127
Fisher and Francks (2006), 208
Fitts and Posner (1967), 202, 371
Fitzgerald and Picton (1983), 17

Fletcher et al. (1989), 304
Fletcher et al. (1992), 177, 180, 304
Fletcher et al. (1994), 258
Fletcher et al. (1999), 33
Fletcher et al. (2003), 177, 180
Fletcher et al. (2005), 258
Fletcher et al. (2006), 177, 178, 179, 180,
    183, 185
Fletcher et al. (2007), 31, 32, 33, 149, 162, 171
FMRI (functional magnetic resonance), 62,
    68-9, 70, 104, 117, 260
foetal alcohol syndrome, 88
foetal brain development, 72, 85
Foorman and Francis (1994), 313
Foorman and Torgesen (2001), 338, 351
Foorman et al. (1997), 282
Foorman et al. (1998), 245, 246
Foorman et al. (2003), 255
Foorman et al. (2004), 251
Foorman et al. (in press), 252
Forensic Echo, 480
Foundation for Learning (2007), 451
foveal splitting, 57-8
Fowler, A. (1991), 85
Fowler, M.S. (1991), 60
Fowler and Liberman (1995), 224, 226, 231
Fowler et al. (1990), 61
Fowler et al. (1992), 64
Francis et al. (1996), 177, 180
Francis et al. (2005), 178, 258
Francks et al (2004), 71
Frank and Levinson (1973), 78
Frederickson and Jacobs (2001), 405
Frederickson et al.(1997), 430
French language, 230, 275, 431
Friedman and Medway (1987), 341
Frith, U. (1985), 316, 317
Frith, U. (1986), 316, 317
Frith, U. (1997), 427
Frith, U. (2001), 39
Frith and Snowling (1983), 274
Frost et al. (1997), 434
Fuchs and Deshler (2006), 183-4
Fuchs and Fuchs (1988), 181
Fuchs and Fuchs (1998), 181, 184
Fuchs and Fuchs (2002), 34
Fuchs and Fuchs (2006), 243, 258, 259, 260
Fuchs and Young (2006), 185, 258
Fuchs et al. (2003), 181, 252
Fuchs et al. (2004), 181, 184
Fuchs et al. (in press), 184, 260
funding, 338-9, 340
fusiform gyrus, 68-70, 69f

'g' factor, Spearman's, 269
Gajar et al. (1993), 465-6
Galaburda, A. (1993), 422

Galaburda et al. (1985), 68
Galaburda et al. (1994), 66
Gallagher et al. (2000), 129
Gambrell et al. (1981), 341
Ganschow and Javorsky (1998), 440
Gardner, H. (1983), 305
Gaskins et al. (1988), 248
Gates-MacGinitie Reading Tests, 279
Gayán and Olson (2003), 39
Gayán et al. (1999), 39
Gayán et al. (2005), 34, 36, 39
GCSE, 362
genetics, 30-52, 45f, 54, 55, 77, 122, 123f, 274
    causes of m- cell defect, 71, 72
    comorbidity and related conditions, 33-4
    correlated traits, and multivariate
        phenotypes, 34-7, 36f, 37f
        four components of phenotypic
            variance/covariance, 35
    immune control, 71-2
    importance of genetic correlation r_G, 37-9, 38f
    MHC (major histocompatibility) genes, 58,
        71-2
    multivariate problem as a problem of
        discriminate validity, 39-40, 41-2t
    other end of continuum of ability, 40, 42-3
    overview of knowledge of, 31-3
        list of essential problems, 33
        list of well accepted conclusions, 32
    see also familial predictors of dyslexia
        study; Jyväskylä (JLD) study
geography, 361, 392
Gerber and Brown (1997), 458
Gerber and Price (2005), 460
Gerber and Price Self-Disclosure Interview
    Protocol, 460-1
Gerber et al. (1990), 401
Gerber et al. (1992), 459
Gerlai, R. (1996), 44
German language, 101, 136, 276, 429, 431,
    432, 433
Gersten and Dimino (2006), 257
Gersten et al. (2000), 351
Gerwig et al. (2007), 88
Geschwind, N. (1982), 31, 40, 42, 82
Geschwind and Galaburda (1987), 31, 40, 42, 43
Geva and Seigel (2000), 429
giftedness, 42
Gilger and Kaplan (2001), 34, 39, 44
Gilger and Wilkins (in press), 34, 39, 44
Gilger and Wise (2004), 44
Gilger et al. (1996), 31
Gillon, G.T. (2004), 428
Gillingham and Stillman (1956), 194
Gilmore Oral Reading Test, 187
Giraudo, H. (2001), 224-5, 227, 232
Given and Reid (1999), 372, 376, 388, 389

Gjessing and Karlsen (1989), 401
Gladstone and Best (1985), 23
Gladstone et al. (1989), 23
'Go Phonics', 451
Goldsmith-Phillips, J. (1994), 315
Goleman, D. (1995), 305
Good and Kaminski (2002), 344, 345
Good et al. (2001), 184, 251
Goswami, U. (1995), 135
Goswami, U. (1999), 430
Goswami, U. (2000), 430, 434
Goswami, U. (2005), 93
Goswami and Bryant (1989), 217, 224
Goswami and Bryant (1990), 129, 215
Gough and Tunmer (1986), 253, 254, 256,
    271, 272-3, 314
Gough and Walsh (1991), 243
Goulandris and Snowling (1991), 170, 171
grapheme/phoneme relationship, 278, 316,
    317, 428-9, 431, 440
Gray Oral Reading Test (GORT), 280
Greaney et al. (1997), 249
Great Leaps (Mercer et al.), 340
Greek language, 77, 429, 431
Green et al. (2000), 85
Greenbaum et al. (1996), 458, 459
Greene, J. F. (1995), 318
Greene, J.F. (2000), 318
Greenhouse-Geisser correction, 111
Greenough et al. (2002), 44
Griffiths and Snowling (2002), 160, 171
Griffiths et al. (2004), 403
Grigorenko, E. (2001), 100, 104, 107, 149
Grigorenko, E. (2005), 208
Gross-Glenn and Rothenberg, 23
group size in reading intervention, 247, 339
    see individual tutoring for struggling readers
        by paraeducators study *for full
        discussion*
growth curve analysis, 251, 252
Gunn et al. (1998), 341
Guthrie and Humenick (2004), 257
Guttorm et al. (2001), 105, 106, 116, 127
Guttorm et al. (2005), 100, 105, 106, 107,
    116, 128

h^2, 32, 54
Hackley et al. (1990), 17
Hagoort et al. (1999), 21
Hahn et al. (1978), 39, 44
Hallahan and Mock (2003), 175
Hallgren, B. (1950), 31
Hämäläinen et al. (2007), 128
Hammill, D.D. (1990), 292
Hammill, D.D. (2004), 275
Hanley et al. (1992), 164, 170, 171
Hannon and Daneman (2001), 273

Hannula-Jouppi et al. (2005), 44
Hansford and Hattie (1982), 396
Hargreaves, D.H. (2004), 365
Harlaar et al, (2005), 132
Harm and Seidenberg (1999), 151-2, 160,
　　169-70
Harm and Seidenberg (2004), 14
Harris and Giannouli (1999), 429
Harris and Jacobson (1972), 318
Harris and MacRow-Hill (1999), 63
Hart and Risley (2003), 338
Harter et al. (1996), 397
Hasbrouck et al. (1999), 340
Haslum, M. (1989), 83
Hatcher and Hulme (1999), 258
Hatcher et al. (1994), 246
Hatcher et al. (2005), 134
Hatcher et al. (2006), 248
Hawthorne effects, 248
Hebrew, 432, 433-4
Heil et al. (1999), 15
helplessness, sense of learned, 398, 402, 404,
　　406, 407
Henderson and Templeton (1994), 318
Henry, M.K. (2003), 282
heredity see genetics
Herrington and Hunter-Carsch (2001), 405
Heschl's gyrus, left, 103
heterogeneity, 124-6, 125f, 149-73, 397
　　review of literature on subtypes of dyslexia,
　　　150-3
　　study of subtypes, 154-71
　　　results, 156-69, 158f, 158t, 160t, 163t,
　　　　166t
　　　tests, 154-6, 155t
Hewitt, J.K. (1993), 35, 36f, 37f
Hickey, K. (1992), 209
hierarchical linear modelling, 251-2
higher education, 482, 483
　　see also self-disclosure study
Hinshelwood, J. (1917), 31
Hinshelwood and Morgan (19th C), 269
Hintikka et al. (under review), 140
Hintikka et al. (2005), 136, 137
history, 361
Hockfield and Sur (1990), 58, 60, 67, 71
Holmes, G. (1917), 78, 80
Holmes, G., (1922), 79
Holmes, G. (1939), 78, 80
Holopainen et al. (2000), 101
Holopainen et al. (2001), 101
homework, 391, 412, 418
Hoover and Gough (1990), 254, 271, 314
Hoover and Tunmer (1993), 254
Hoskyn and Swanson (2000), 185
Hot Potatoes, 451
Huey, E.B. (1908), 192

Hugdahl et al. (1998), 102
Hughes and Dawson (1995), 401-2
Humphrey, N. (2002), 363
Humphrey, N. (2004), 407
Humphrey and Kramer (1994), 17
Humphrey and Mullins (2002), 402, 404
Hungarian language, 429
Huttenlocher, P.R. (2002), 44
Hynd et al. (1990), 102

ICD-10, 216, 217, 396
Iceland, 445
ICT, 135, 136-7, 281, 387, 412-3, 450-2, 453,
　　477, 481
IHTT (inter-hemisphere time transfer), 23
Iles et al. (2000), 62
Imamizu et al. (2003), 87
immune control, 71-2
individual personalised learning, need for,
　　371-2
individual tutoring for struggling readers
　　by paraeducators study, 337-55
　　a cost-effective alternative, 340
　　first-grade studies, 342, 350t
　　intervention components and design, 340-2
　　intervention outcomes for English Language
　　　Learner (ELL) students, 349-50, 350t
　　Juel's four features of effective programmes,
　　　339
　　kindergarten interventions, 342-9, 350t
　　　descriptive statistics on pretest and
　　　　posttest outcomes, 347-8t
　　　sample characteristics, year 2, 345t
　　　treatment fidelity, 345-6
　　summary, 350-1, 350t
　　Wasik's four features of a successful
　　　programme, 339
Individuals with Disabilities Education
　　Improvement Act (IDEA), USA, 182,
　　292, 459, 466
inferior frontal gyrus (IFG), 70-1
Ingesson, G. (2007), 400, 402
International Dyslexia Association (IDA), 213,
　　216, 420-1
Institute of Education Sciences, 281
Institute of Education and Science (2003), 340
Ioffe et al. (2007), 88
IQ, 33, 41-2t, 44, 54, 55, 56, 218, 219, 234,
　　269-70, 402
　　definition of learning disabilities study,
　　　299-300, 300t, 308
　　Tennessee schools study, 324, 326, 327,
　　　330, 333
IQ-achievement discrepancy approach, 176-7,
　　222-4, 230, 268-9, 270, 271, 283
　　definition of learning disabilities study, 293,
　　　297-9, 297t, 308

IQ-achievement discrepancy approach
(Continued)
  hybrid model with RTI, 187-8
  reliability issue, 178-9, 184
  validity issue, 179-81, 185-6
  'wait to fail' model, 177, 182, 258
Irlen, H. (1991), 63, 385
Israel, 420
Israel et al. (1980), 17
Italian language, 275, 276, 443
Ito, M. (1984), 78, 80
Iversen and Tunmer (1993), 245, 246, 249
Iversen et al. (2005), 87, 247

Jacobson et al. (1986), 405
James, W. (19th -early 20th C.), 395
Japanese language, 57, 228
Jastak and Wilkinson (1984), 342
Jeffries and Everatt (2004), 34
Jenkins et al. (2004), 341, 342
Joanisse et al. (2000), 214, 229, 231-2
Johansson et al. (1995), 132
Johnson, M. (2004), 359, 360, 361, 362
Johnson, R. (1995), 16
Johnson et al. (2002), 39, 44
Johnston et al. (1996), 118, 134
Johnston and Watson (1997), 135
Johnstone et al. (1996), 17
Jones, K.M. (2001), 318
Jones and Murray (1991), 39, 44
Jordon, I. (2000), 385
Joshi, R.M. (2003), 279
Joshi, R.M. (2005), 280
Joshi et al. (1998), 279
Joshi and Aaron (1991), 277
Joshi and Aaron (2000), 283
Joshi and Aaron (2002), 276
Joshi and Aaron (2007), 274
Joshi et al. (1998), 270, 273
Joshi et al. (2002), 282
Journal of Learning Disabilities, definition of
    learning disabilities study, 290, 291, 295
Juel, C. (1988), 256, 341
Juel, C. (1994), 275
Juel, C. (1996), 339, 341
Just and Carpenter (1987), 280
Justus and Ivry (2001), 86
Jyväskylä (JLD) study, 85, 101, 121-46
  conclusions drawn from JLD study,
      134-41
  early language development, 128-32,
      130t, 131f
  environmental factors, 132-4
  heterogeneity/homogeneity in
      developmental pathways, 124-6, 125f
  neurobiological factors, 127-8
  role of motor skills, 132

Kame'enui and Carnine (1998), 341
Kame'enui et al. (2005), 251
Kana, 57
Kanji script, 57
Kaplan et al. (1998), 132
Kaplan et al. (2001), 34
Karlsen and Gardner (1995), 279
Karni et al. (1998), 204-5
Karolyi and Winner (2004), 40
Katusic et al. (2001), 334
Kavale and Forness (1995), 291
Kavale and Forness (2000), 292, 294
Kavale and Mattson (1983), 176
Kavale and Nye (1981), 292, 294
Kay and Yeo (2003), 389
Keating and Manis (1998), 155
Keenan and Betjemann (2006), 280
Keenan et al. (2006), 274
Kelly and Strick (2003), 86
Key et al. (2006), 111
Key Stage 1& 2, questionnaires, pupils point
    of view study, 357-8, 358t
KIAA 0319, 71, 72
Kibby et al. (in press), 44
kindergarten, 339, 342-9
  see individual tutoring for struggling readers
      by paraeducators study *for wider
      discussion*
  see also preschool children
Kirk, S. (1963), 309
Kirk, S. (1966), 291-2
Kirk and Elkins (1995), 31
Kistner and Osborne (1987), 399, 400
Kistner et al. (1988), 405
Klicpera and Schabmann (1993), 140
Klingner et al. (1999), 351
Korman et al. (2003), 204-5
Kramer et al. (1991), 17
Krashen, S.D. (1981), 442
Krashen, S.D. (1990), 442
Kuhl, P.K. (2000), 199
Kuhl, P.K. (2004), 199f
Kujala et al. (in press), 136

Laakso et al. (1999), 133, 138
Laakso et al. (2004), 133
LaBuda et al. (1987), 34, 36
Ladd, E.M. (1970), 270
Landerl, K. (2001), 432
Landerl and Wimmer (in press), 140
Landerl et al. (1997), 431
Lannen (2002), 372
Lannen (2007), 372
Language! (Greene), 318, 333
language, learning a foreign, 439-54
  classroom, international perspectives, 445-7
  fluency and accuracy, 442

language, learning a foreign *(Continued)*
  focus points to support dyslexics, 444-5
  friendly instruction, 447
  interlanguage, 440-2, 447, 449
  listening comprehension, 449
  modern languages, 442-3
  new technology, 450-2, 453
  orthographic mapping, 443-4
  phonological awareness, support to develop,
    447-9
  requirements for learning, 440
  word learning, 449-50
language basis of dyslexia, Vellutino's view,
    78, 194
language delays, 214, 229
language development, 219, 222, 226, 229,
    231-2, 308, 314, 324
  acquisition of, 198-200, 199f
  declarative and procedural language system
    205-6, 207
  motor skills and, 132, 205-6, 207
  parents language skills, effect of, 132-3,
    138, 338
  pre-cursive and predictive aspects of early,
    128-32
  SLI (specific language impairment), 33, 65,
    103, 206, 218
  see also individual countries; language,
    learning a foreign languages, study of
    dyslexia and different; morphological
    processing; multilingualism;
    phonological processing; speech,
    spelling
languages, study of dyslexia and different
    languages, 427-38
  Arabic, 432-6
  orthographic transparency, 428-32
Larsen et al. (1990), 102
Latent Growth Curve Analysis, 134
Lazear, D. (1994), 305
Leach et al. (2003), 254, 257, 274
learning, cognition and dyslexia study,192-211
  automatisation deficit hypothesis, 193,
    194-6, 202
  declarative and procedural, 193, 200-6,
    200f, 201f, 207f
  early studies, 194
  how best to help dyslexic children, 209
  identifying specific brain regions affected,
    207-8, 207f
  skill tests, 196-8, 197f
  studies on procedural learning, 203-5
'Learning and teaching for dyslexic children'
    (DfES 2005), 357
learning disabilities, defining, 290-311, 396
  achievement, 290-1, 293-4, 296, 301-2,
    301t, 305-6

learning disabilities, defining *(Continued)*
  exclusion, 291, 292-3, 296-7, 296t, 302-3,
    308
  IQ, 291, 293, 295-6, 299-300, 300t, 304-5,
    308
  IQ discrepancy/formula, 290-1, 292,
    297-9, 297t, 303-4, 308
  operational vs. conceptual definition, 294-5
    implications and conclusion, 302-9
    methodology, 295
    results, 295-6
  see also classification of developmental
    dyslexia
learning styles study, 369-80
  autonomous learning, 371-2
  critique of learning styles, 373-4
  identifying learning styles, 327-33, 374-5
  learning and self-esteem, 372 *see also*
    self-esteem
  learning needs, 370-1
  learning theory, 370
  linking assessment with practice, 375-6
  pointers for practice, 375
  pupils assessment of learning styles (PALS),
    378-9
  teacher's observation of learning styles
    (TOLS), 379-80
Lee and Burkam (200), 338, 339
legislation
  Canada, 421, 470
  New Zealand, 422
  UK, 421-2, 470, 484-5
  USA, 182, 292, 420, 459-60, 461, 466-7,
    468, 470, 480, 484-5
Leikin and Zur Hagit (2006), 214, 223, 225,
    231, 232, 233
Leinonen et al. (2001) et al., 122
Leonard et al. (1997), 214, 218
Leonard et al. (2001), 103
Leonard et al. (2002), 102-3, 104, 107
Leonardi, A. (1993), 399
Leong, C.K. (1989), 222, 224, 227, 232
Leong, C.K. (1999), 228
Leong and Parkinson (1995), 222
Leppänen et al. (1997), 127
Leppänen et al. (1999), 105, 106, 127
Leppänen et al. (2002), 105, 106, 127,128
Leppänen et al. (2003), 127
Leppänen et al. (2004), 127
LETRS (Moats), 333
Levinson, H.N. (1973), 78
Levinson, H.N. (1988), 78
Levinson's treatment, criticisms of, 90
Levy and Carr (1990), 273
Lewandowski and Arcangelo (1994), 401
Leybaert and Content (1995), 275
LGN (lateral geniculate nucleus), 59, 66, 72

Liberman, I.Y. (1973), 314
Lieberman, 64
Liepmann, 68
Light et al. (1998), 44
Lincoln and Guba (1985), 461
Lindamood and Lindamood (1975), 318
Lindamood and Lindamood (2005), 282
Lindamood and Lindamood (2006), 453
Linguistic Coding Deficit Hypothesis, 440
LIPS (Lindamood and Lindamood), 453
listening comprehension method of
    assessment, 270, 279, 314
Livingstone et al. (1991), 61
logographic phase, 316
Lonigan et al. (2007), 177
LORETA, use of, 16, 23f
Lovett et al. (1988), 283
Luck and Hillyard, (1994), 17
Lukatela et al. (2002), 431
Lundberg, I. (2002), 439
Lundberg et al. (1988), 275, 314
Luria, A.R. (1973), 44
Lynch and Gussell (1996), 459
Lyon, G.R. (1993), 241-2
Lyon, G.R. (1998), 419
Lyon, G.R. (2004), 419
Lyon and Moats (1997), 241, 243, 248, 251, 252
Lyon et al. (2001), 180
Lyon et al. (2003), 11, 176, 177, 180, 181, 216
Lyytinen and Lyytinen (2004), 128, 131
Lyytinen et al. (1995), 34, 127
Lyytinen et al. (1998), 122, 133
Lyytinen et al. (2001), 101, 129
Lyytinen et al. (2003), 101, 133, 138
Lyytinen et al. (2004), 85, 101, 105, 128, 135
Lyytinen et al. (2005), 127, 128, 129
Lyytinen et al. (2006), 105, 122, 125, 126,
    128, 135, 138
Lyytinen et al. (2007), 135, 136, 137, 139

m- system, 58-63, 66, 67-8, 73
    auditory m-, 65-6
    causes of m- cell defect, 71, 72
    magnocellular and parvocellular visual
        neurones (m-, p-), 58-9
    m- system, eye movements and reading, 60
    m- system and attention, 62-3
    m- system and dyslexia, 61-2
    sensitivity to light, 63-4
MacGinitie et al. (2000), 279
Mackay, N. (2003), 364
MacNeilage and Davis (2001), 85
Manis et al. (1993), 170, 315
Manis et al. (1996), 151, 152, 153, 170
Manis et al. (1999), 153
Manis et al. (2000), 187
Marcus, G. (2004), 44

Marien and Verhoeven (2007), 86
Marien et al. (2001), 86
Markee et al. (1966), 22, 23
marking student's work, 386-7, 389
Markwardt, F.C. (1998), 280
Marr, D. (1969), 80
Marsh and Hattie (1996), 397
Marshall and Newcombe (1973), 150, 274
Marslen-Wilson et al. (1994), 216
Maschke et al. (2003), 88, 204
Maslburg and von der Schneider (1986), 16
mathematics, 306, 361, 388
Mathes et al. (2005), 186, 248
Matthew Effect, 92, 255, 256, 257, 258,
    305, 338
Maughan, B. (1995), 400, 401, 404
Maxwell, J.A. (1996), 460
Mazi et al. (2004), 429
McBride and Siegel (1997), 307
McCathren et al. (1996), 133
McCoach et al. (2004), 42
McGuinness, D. (2004), 100
McGuiness et al. (1996), 340
McKay, N. (2005), 285, 286, 388
McLoughlin, D. (2004), 480
McLoughlin et al. (1994), 484
McLoughlin et al. (2002), 457
McMaster et al. (2005), 181, 186, 259
McNulty, M.A. (2003), 402, 403
Meares, O. (1980), 63
memory, 82, 86, 125f, 128, 185, 194, 220, 233,
    243, 244, 251, 253, 279, 371, 387, 389-90,
    391, 392
    declarative and procedural subsystems, 200,
        205, 206
    learning a foreign language, 440, 444, 450
    parents encouragement of child's memory
        skills, 415-6, 417
Mendeleev's theory, 92
Meng et al. (2005), 44
Menghini et al. (2006), 204
mental retardation, 308
Mercer et al. (2000), 340
Merigan and Maunsell (1990), 59
Merriman, S.B. (1998), 460, 461
meta-analysis, 252, 280-1, 396, 403
Metsala, J. (1997), 256
Metsala et al. (1998), 168
MHC (major histocompatibility) genes, 58, 71-2
Miall et al. (2000), 87
Middle Tennessee State University (MTSU),
    312-3
Middleton and Strick (2001), 86
Miles, E. (1989), 209
Miles, T.R. (1983), 83
Miles and Huberman (1994), 460, 461
Miles and Huberman (1995), 461

mind mapping, 450
mirror drawing, 204
Mismatch Negativity/Oddball paradigms, 127
mixed reading disability, 253, 254, 256,
        257, 260
Moats, L.C. (1995), 278, 339
Moats, L.C. (1999), 339
Moats, L.C. (2003-2005), 333
Mody, M. (2004), 31, 44
Moe-Nilssen et al. (2003), 87
Molfese, D.L. (2000), 100, 104, 105, 106, 116
Molfese and Molfese (1985), 105, 116
Molfese and Molfese (1997), 105, 116
Molfese et al. (2001), 104
Molfese et al. (2005), 105
Molfese et al. (2006), 111, 115, 116
Montgomery, D. (2003), 384
Morais et al. (1979), 57
Morgan, B.S. (1914), 31
Morgan, W.P. (1896), 31
morphological processing, 99, 102, 107, 131,
        206, 254, 257, 433-4, 446, 448
morphological processing study of dyslexics
        and poor readers, 212-37
    comparisons to younger normally reading
            participants, 224-7
    participants and design of study, 216-9
    strengths, 215-6, 227-31
    taxonomy of tasks, 219-21
        oral presentation, 219-20, 221
        task content, 220-1
        task or cognitive process, 221
        written presentation, 219, 220, 221
    weaknesses of, 214-5, 221-4
Morris et al. (1998), 149
Morris et al. (2000), 246
Morrison and Manis (1983), 92
Morton and Frith (1995), 124
Morton and Frith, framework model, 427
mother's reading skills, 133, 138
motor problems, developmental, 56, 67, 68,
        80, 82-3, 84, 85, 90, 126, 132, 204-5,
        208, 391-2
    declarative and procedural language system
            and 205-6, 207
    see cerebellum for wider discussion
    see also automatisation deficit hypothesis
MRI scans, 102, 103, 117
    see also FMRI
multilingualism, 384-4
    bilingual students, 273, 383
    second language issues 91, 228, 272, 339,
            445, 447-8, 450, 451, 452
    see also language, learning a foreign
Murfree, K. Davis, funding of Chair of
        Excellence, 313
Murphy and Pollatsek (1994), 151

Muter, V. (1998), 274
Muthén and Muthén (2004), 125, 131
Myself-As-A-Learner scale, 397, 399, 405

Näätänen, R. (1992), 127
Nagy et al. (2003), 214, 225, 232
Narhi and Ahonen (1995), 34
National Adult Literacy and Learning
        Disabilities Center, USA (1996), 458
National Assembly for Wales (2006)
National Institute of Child Health and Human
        Development, USA, 281, 479-80
National Reading Panel, USA, 180, 213, 214,
        341, 349
Neale and Cardon (1992), 37
Needle et al. (2006), 87
Needle et al. (under review), 204, 208, 209
Nelson et al. (2003), 186
Nemser, W., interlanguage, 441
neurobiological basis of dyslexia, 11, 30, 31, 32,
        33, 34, 43, 53-76, 127-8, 199, 260-1, 441
    arguments about existence of dyslexia, 56-7
    auditory/phonological processing, 64-8, 70,
            71-2, 73 see phonological
    processing for further discussion
    causes of m- cell defect, 71, 72
    immune control, 71-2
    learning and cognitive neuroscience, 200-3,
            201f, 204, 205-8, 207f, 209
    omega-3 fish oils, 72
    orthographic skills, 61, 67, 69-70, 73
        see spelling for further discussion
    reading network of brain, 68-71, 69f
    risk factors, 54-6
    visual input to reading, 57-63, 66-72, 261
    visual problems, remediation of, 63-4
neuropsychological studies, 274
newborn infants, risk factors, 105-7, 124
Newcomer, P. (1999), 279
Newell and Rosenbloom (1981), 198
New York Post (2001), 480
New Zealand, 242, 422
NICHD (2000), 90
Nicolson and Fawcett (1990), 78, 84, 193,
        195, 206
Nicolson and Fawcett (2000), 132, 204,
        208, 209
Nicolson and Fawcett (2001), 44
Nicolson and Fawcett (2004), 209, 371
Nicolson and Fawcett (2006), 89
Nicolson and Fawcett (2007), 89, 206,
        207f, 209
Nicolson and Fawcett (in press), 206
Nicolson et al. (1995), 84
Nicolson et al. (1999), 67, 84, 203, 208
Nicolson et al. (2001), 85
Nicolson et al. (2002), 88, 204

Nijakowska, J. (2004), 445
Njiokiktjien et al. (1994), 103
No Child Left Behind Act, USA (2001), 420
Northwestern Syntax Screening Test, 301
Norway, study of primary school children, 399
Nunes and Bryant (2006), 234

Oakhill and Beard (1999), 243
Oakhill et al. (1998), 283
Oakhill et al. (2003), 274
O'Connor et al. (2005), 259
Oldfield, R.C. (1971), 109
Olofsson and Lundberg (1985), 430
Olsen, R.K. (2002), 77
Olsen, R.K. (2006), 274
Olsen and Bryne (2005), 101
Olson et al. (1989), 54
Olson et al. (1994), 34, 36, 39
omega-3 fish oils, 72
one to one instruction, 247, 339
    see individual tutoring for struggling readers
        by paraeducators study *for wider
        discussion*
organisational skills, pupil's, 390-1
Orthographic Choice, subgroup study, 159,
    160, 164, 167, 168
Orton, J.K. (1966), 78, 209
Orton, S. (1928), 31
Orton and Gillingham (2004), 445
Orton-Gillingham multi-sensory teaching
    method, 194, 282, 445
Orton's theory of mixed cerebral dominance,
    rebuttal of, 175
Ostler, C. (2000), 386, 388
otitis media (glue ear), 91
Owen et al. (1971), 31

p-, 58, 65
P100-200, 17f, 19f, 20
P200, 23f, 24, 25, 26
P300, 17, 18f, 19f, 23, 25
Padget et al. (1996), 315, 317
Pajares, F. (1999), 397
Palinscar and Brown (1984), 283, 414-5
Palmer et al. (1985), 270, 273
Palmer et al. (1994), 17
Palombo, J. (2001), 402
Pammer and Wheatley, 61
Papanicolaou et al. (2003), 260
paraeducators *see* individual tutoring for
    struggling readers by paraeducators study
Parent Partnership Schemes, UK, 422
parents, 272f, 340, 411-24
    appendix on strategies to improve reading
        by paired reading, 423-4
    frustration, 419
    legislation

parents *(Continued)*
    Canada, 421
    New Zealand, 422
    UK, 421-2
    USA, 420-1
literacy, need for parents to understand, 415
memory skills, strategies to improve,
    415-6, 417
mother's reading skills, 133, 138
parents language skills, effect of, 132-3,
    138, 338
partnership schemes, 422
reading, shared between parents and
    children, 133-4, 413-5, 417, 423-4
    pre-reading discussion, 413
school supports, 412-3
    ethos of school, 412
    communication, 412-3
self-esteem, 416-7, 418
tensions and identification, 418-9
tensions and successes, 416
understanding, lack of, 419
voices of parents, 417-8
Pascual-Marqui, R.D. (1999), 16, 23
Pascual-Marqui et al. (1994), 16, 23
Passingham, R.E. (1975), 79
Paulesu et al. (2001), 22
Pavlidis, G.-T. (1985), 82
PCA (principal components analysis),
    111-5, 112f
PDP model 14
Peabody Individual Achievement
    Test-Revised, 280
Peabody Picture Vocabulary Test (PPVT), 110
    Revised (PPVT-R), 153, 154-5, 167
    Third Edition (PPVT-III), 109, 345, 347t
Peabody Word Recognition subtest, 152
Pearson correlations, 324
Peer and Reid (2000), 384, 439
Peer and Reid (2001), 383, 385, 388, 391
Peer and Reid (2003), 384, 391
Pennington, B.F. (1991), 314, 315
Pennington, B.F. (1999), 34
Pennington, B.F. (2002), 39
Pennington and Gilger (1996), 31
Pennington and Lefly (2001), 101, 126, 137
Pennington et al. (1999), 102
Perfetti, C. (1985), 12, 243, 251
Perfetti, C. (1988), 273
Perfetti, C. (1991), 243
Perfetti, C. (1992), 12, 243
Perfetti et al. (1987), 215
Perlmutter and Parus (1986), 304
PET (positron emission), 68, 87, 104, 117
Peterka, R.J. (2002), 88
Petersen et al. (1998), 21, 87
Petrill et al. (2005), 132

Philippines, 420
phoneme blending, 343
Phoneme Deletion, 155, 159, 160, 164, 165, 167
phoneme segmenting, 274, 343, 346
  phonemic Segmentation Fluency and
    Nonsense Word Fluency subtests,
    344, 346
phonemic awareness
  compared to phonological awareness,
    274, 431
  grapheme-phoneme conversion skill (GPC),
    278, 316, 317, 431, 440
  tests of, 275, 317, 318, 321t, 324-5, 326, 329
Phono-Graphix (web site), 340
Phonological Assessment Battery
    (Frederickson et al.), 430
phonological processing, 64-8, 70, 71-2, 73,
    116, 125f, 126, 185, 194, 206, 244-5,
    249, 252-4, 255, 256, 257, 259, 260,
    261, 343
  comparison with morphological processing,
    212-37
  component model, 274-9
  CTOPP, 188, 274-5, 346, 347t
  discussion of motor skills deficit and, 82,
    84, 86, 90-1
  distinction between surface and
    phonological dyslexia, 149-53 *see*
    149-73 *for details of study of*
    subgroups
  instability of SDs compared to PDs, 162
  learning a foreign language, 440, 444,
    447-9, 453
  phonological quality of Finnish language
    and general conclusions drawn, 128-
    32, 134-7, 138, 139, 140 *see* Jyväskylä
    (JLD) study *for greater detail*
  Piasta and Wagner (2007), 175
  Pihko et al. (1999), 105, 106, 127
  TOPA, 274
  see also languages, study of dyslexia and
    different languages
phonological processing, Tennessee Schools
    based study of phonological dyslexia,
    312-36
physical self-concept, 397
Pianta, R. (2006), 349
Pinheiro, Â.M.V. (1995), 275
planum temporale (PT), left, 102, 103, 104
Plaut, D.C. (2005), 216
Plaut et al. (1996), 151
play, 133, 135, 136-7, 139
Plomin R. (1994), 122, 123f
Plomin and McClearn, 35
Plomin et al. (2001), 35, 37, 38
Plomin et al., (1990), 38f
Poldrack et al. (1999), 70

Pollack and Milner (1995), 318
poor readers and morphological processing,
    212-37
Portuguese 275
preschool children, instructional deficit, 258-9
preschool children, reading experiences,
    257-8
preschool children, risk factors,108-17, 124,
    127-8
  early language development, 128-32,
    130t, 131f
  importance of letter knowledge, 275-6
  1-3 years, 138
  3-5 years, 134-5, 139
preschool children, tutoring by paraeducators
    see individual tutoring for struggling
    readers by paraeducators study
preschool children, vocabulary growth, 256
President's Commission on Excellence in
    Special Education (2002), 177, 181
Pressley, M. (2000), 273
Pressley, M. (2006), 243, 245, 246
Pressley et al. (2006), 243, 251, 251, 252
Price and Gerber (2007), 482
Price and Mechelli (2005), 208
Price et al. (2005), 459
Primary schools, pupils point of view *see*
    pupils point of view
prism adaptation, 88, 204, 208
procedural learning, 193, 200-6, 200f, 201f
Process Phonics (Pollack and Milner), 318
pseudowords, 155, 157, 158f, 158t, 159, 160,
    162, 164, 165, 167-70, 224, 228, 230,
    276, 277, 314, 317, 318
  ADEPT, 317, 318, 323f, 324, 328t, 329
PUFAs (polyunsaturated fatty acids), 72-3
Pugh et al (2000), 22
Pugh et al. (2005), 127
'pull-out' programs, 334
Puolakanaho et al. (2007), 128, 129, 140
pupil's asking questions of fellow pupils, 390
pupils assessment of learning styles (PALS),
    378-9
pupils point of view, primary schools study,
    356-68
  conclusions, 361-5
    three suggested aims, 365
  curriculum access and resources, 366-7t
  Key Stage 1& 2, questionnaires, 357-8
    breakdown of questionnaires
      completed, 358t
  pupil's views, 358-61
    three highest scores for response to 'one
      thing that really helps me', 360
    view of most common ways teachers
      provided support, list, 359
  questionnaire for pupils, 367-8

qualitative evaluation, 251, 278
quantitative evaluation, 277-8

Raberger and Wimmer (2003), 87
Rack et al. (1992), 315
Rack et al. (2007), 90
Rae et al. (1998), 67
Rae et al. (2002), 67
Ramnani, N. (2006), 86
Ramsey, D.S. (1984), 85
Ramus, F. (2001), 39
Ramus, F. (2004), 31, 34, 36
Ramus, F. (2006), 208
Ramus et al. (2003), 65, 87
RAP (reading acceleration training program), 26
rapid automatized naming (RAN), 135, 277
rapid color naming, 345, 347t
rapid naming, 185, 342
rapid naming-letters (RAN-L), 155-6, 159, 164, 188
Rashotte et al. (2001), 340
Ray et al. (2005), 64
Rayner, K. (1985), 176
Rayner, K. (1988), 175
Read Naturally (Hasbrouck et al.), 340
reading, examination of characteristics of writing, spelling and, 77-8, 84, 86
reading, paired, 414, 417, 423-4
reading, shared between parents and children, 133-4, 413-5, 417, 423-4
reading accuracy, 348t, 431-2
    compared to fluency, 255
    instructional components, early years, 343-4
    measuring accuracy of Arabic readers, 432, 434-5
reading aloud, 78, 192-3, 245, 277, 280, 319, 325, 333, 343-4
reading comprehension method of assessment, 270, 279-80
reading intervention study, integrative framework, 214-67
    conceptual issues, 242-3, 252-60
    data analysis tools, advances in, 250-2
    methodology, 243-50
        balanced intervention, 248
        code-oriented/meaning-oriented classrooms, 250
        content of intervention programme, 247
        duration, transfer and maintenance effects, 249
        early intervention, need for, 257-8
        evaluation of effectiveness, 248-50
        explicitness of intervention, 245-6
        group size, 247
        intensity of intervention, 246-7
        one to one instruction, 247
        teacher effects, 249

reading intervention study, paraeducators *see* individual tutoring for struggling readers by paraeducators study
reading network in the brain, 68-71, 69f
reading progress in ADEPT, 317-9, 319t, 322f, 323f, 325-6, 330-1
Reading Recovery programme (RR), 242-3, 244-5, 246, 247, 259
    accuracy of selection of children, 259-60
    compatibility of, 249-50
Reciprocal Teaching strategy, 283, 414
regression analysis, 327, 328-9
Reid, G. (2005), 477, 478-9t
Reid, G. (2006), 476
Reid, G. (2007), 372
Reid, G. (2007, personal correspondence), 476
Reid and Fawcett (2004), 386, 387, 389
Reid and Green (2007), 385, 387, 390
Reid and Kirk (2001), 475, 483, 484
Reid and Kirk (2005), 457
Reid and Strnadova (2004), 374, 378-80
reinforcement learning, 201f
Renick and Harter (1989), 399
response blending study, 204, 208, 209
response-to-intervention (RTI), 176, 181-7, 243
    hybrid model with traditional approach, 187-8
    problem of treatment resistors, 186-7
    reliability issue, 182-5
    validity issue, 185-6
    'wait to fail' model, 182
reversal errors, 175
REWARDS, 340
Reynolds and Nicolson (2007), 90
Rhee et al. (2005), 33, 34, 35
rhyme (rime), 249, 274, 276, 316, 429, 448
Rice and Brooks (2004), 34, 36
Richardson and Montgomery (2005), 72
Richardson and Puri (2002), 72
Richardson et al. (2003), 128
Riddick, B. (2006), 363
Riddick et al. (1999), 402, 405
Riddick et al. (2002), 357, 363, 364
Rippon and Brunswick (2000), 107
risk factors for dyslexia, 54-6 *see also* familial identification and prevention; familial predictors; genetics
Robinson, R.J. (1987), 132
Rockstroh et al. (1982), 111
Roffman et al. (1994), 459
Rondi-Reig et al. (1999), 44
Rosenberg, M. (1979), 397
Rosenshine and Meister (1994), 283
Rosenshine and Stevens (19840, 341
Roza and Hill (2003), 339
RT (reaction time), 17, 18f, 20f, 24t
Ruban and Reis (2005), 40, 42

Rudel, R.G. (1985), 83
Rumsey et al. (1997), 21
Rutter et al. (1970), 400
Rutter et al. (1997), 122
Rutter et al. (1999), 35
Ryder et al. (in press), 245

Saffran, E.M. (19850, 150
Saiegh-Hadded, E. (2005), 432
Salmelin et al. (1996), 21, 22
Samuels, S.J. (1988), 341
Santi et al. (2004), 340
Saracoglu et al. (1989), 401
SATs tests, 362
Satz et al. (1998), 33
Sawyer, D.J. (1992), 316
Sawyer, D.J. (1993), 314
Sawyer, D.J. (1998), 317
Sawyer, D.J. (2001), 317
Sawyer and Knight (1997), 313
Savage, P.G. (2001), 270, 279
Savage, P.G. (2004), 273
Scarborough, H. (1990), 101, 126, 129, 137
Scarborough, H. (2005), 254, 257
Scarborough and Dobrich (1994), 133
Scarborough et al. (1991), 133
Scarcella et al. (1990), 442
Scerif and Karmiloff-Smith (2005), 39, 44
Schatschneider, C. (2007), 183
Schmahmann, J.D. (2004), 66
Schmolesky et al. (1998), 15
Schnieder and Crombie (2003), 383, 443
Schneider et al. (1997), 430
Schulte-Körne, G. (2001), 39
Schulte-Körne et al. (1996), 137
Schultz et al. (1994), 102
Schumacher et al. (2007), 32, 34, 35, 39, 127
Schunk, D.H. (1991), 397
Scott et al. (2001), 66
Scree test, 111
Sebastien-Gallés and Vacchiano (1995), 275
secondary schools, cross curricular
    perspectives study, 381-94
  arrangements for examinations, 392-3
  classroom management issues, 389-92
  hidden dyslexia, 384-5
  identification of dyslexia, 382
  indications of dyslexia in secondary
      curriculum, 383
  learning/teaching preferences, 388-9
  multilingualism, 384-4
  subject curriculum, 385-8
SEED (2004), 381
Seidenberg, M.S. (1993), 92
self-advocacy, 459, 483-4
self-concept study, 395-410
  models and terms used, 397-406

self-concept study (Continued)
  academic self-concept, 397, 399
  attribution theory, 404-6
  general self-concept, 397, 401, 407
  self-esteem, 397,398, 401-4, 407
  social self-concept, 397, 400-1, 406
self-determination, 459, 469, 471
self-disclosure study, 457-73
  acceptable loss/potential gain, 467-70
  age and maturity factors, 462-3
  Americans with Disabilities Act (ADA),
      459-60, 461, 466-7, 468, 480
  context, adult oriented environments, 464-5
  denial of learning disabilities, 463
  literature review, 459-60
  self-disclosure process, trust and rapport,
      461-2
  stigma and social implications, 462
  'To Be or Not to Be' study, 458, 460-1
  transition planning and self-disclosure, 465-6
self-efficacy, 397-8, 404, 406, 407
self-esteem, 363, 365, 372, 383, 385, 393, 397,
    398, 401-4, 407, 416-7, 418, 476
self-worth, 397, 401, 402
Seligman, M.E.P. (1991), 398
Seligman et al. (1979), 398
Selinker, L. (1972), 441
Selinker, L. (1994), 441, 442
Semantic Categorization, 156, 168
sense of direction, pupil's, 392
sensitivity/specificity criteria, 184-5
sentence completion, 221, 230, 231, 233, 389
sentences, understanding complex, 254,
    256, 257
  Northwestern Syntax Screening Test, 301
  see also morphology
Seymour, P.H.K. (1999), 213
Seymour et al. (2003), 135, 429
Shankweiler and Fowler (2004), 243
Shankweiler et al. (1995), 214, 222, 225, 274
Shankweiler et al. (1996), 223, 232
Shapiro et al. (2002), 34
Share, D.L. (1995), 11, 160, 169, 170, 243, 244
Share and Leikin (2004), 217
Share and Silva (2003), 218
Share et al. (1984), 338
Share et al. (1989), 218
Shaul, S. (2006), 22
Shaul and Breznitz (under review), 22, 23, 25
Shaywitz, S. (2003), 260-1, 340, 351
Shaywitz and Shaywitz (2003), 180
Shaywitz and Shaywitz (2004), 338
Shaywitz and Shaywitz (2005), 208
Shaywitz et al. (1992), 180
Shaywitz et al. (2002), 162
Shaywitz et al. (2004), 261
Shillcock and Monaghan (2001), 58

Shu et al. (2006), 224, 232
Siegel, L.S. (1985), 305
Siegel, L.S. (1988), 304
Siegel, L.S. (1989), 304
Siegel, L.S. (1990), 305
Siegel, L.S. (1992), 177, 304
Siegel, L.S. (1999), 304, 306
Siegel, L.S. (2003), 180
Siegel and Feldman (1983), 305
Siegel and Linder (1984), 305
Siegel and Ryan (1984), 305
Siegel and Smythe (2004), 439
Silvén et al. (2007), 131
Silventoinen et al. (2007), 35
Silver, L.B. (1987), 90
Simmons et al. (2003), 181, 340, 351
Simon, C.S. (2000), 439
Simonton, D.K. (2005), 34
Simos et al. (2002), 70, 261
Simos et al. (2007), 261
Simple View of Reading, 271, 314
Singleton (1999), 482-3
Skaalvik and Hagvet (1990), 399
Skottun, B.C. (1997), 62
Skottun, B.C.(2001), 83
SLI (specific language impairment), 33, 65, 103, 206, 218
Smalley et al. (2004), 39
Smith, S.D. (2005), 44
Smith and Elley (1994), 242
Smith and Gilger (2007), 31, 33, 39
Smith et al. (1983), 31
Smith et al. (1997), 457
Smythe and Everatt (2004), 434
Smythe et al. (2004), 427, 429
Snellen Eye Chart, 296
Snider (1992), 369
Snow and Juel (2005), 243
Snow et al. (1998), 338
Snowling, M. (1980), 129
Snowling, M. (1981), 82, 88
Snowling, M. (1987), 194
Snowling, M. (2000), 213, 427, 431
Snowling, M. (2003), 101, 126
Snowling et al. (1996), 151
Snowling et al. (2003), 254, 256
social disadvantage, effect of, 337, 338
    limited resources at school, 337, 338-9
    see also environmental factors
social implications of reading disabilities, 307, 462
    see also employment; environmental factors
social interaction, 398
    see also self-disclosure study
social model of disability and empowerment, 480-2, 485
    examples of enabling equal participation, 481t

social self-concept, 397, 400-1, 406
Soliloquy Reading Assistant, 451
Sonuga-Barke (2003), E.J.S., 34, 36
Sousa, A.D. (2000), 12, 21, 26
Southampton Council social model website, 481
Spache, G.D. (1940), 277
Spalding and Spalding (2005), 282
Spalding Method, 282
Spanish language, 77, 274, 275, 281
    bilingual English-Spanish, 273
    TOPPS, 275
Sparks, R. (1993), 440
Sparks and Ganschow (early 1990s), 439-40
Sparks and Ganschow (1991), 450
Sparks and Ganschow (1993), 440
Sparks et al. (1989), 440
Spear-Swerling and Sternberg (1996), 177
Special Educational Needs and Disability Act (SENDA) (2001), UK, 421-2
Specific Dyslexia Algorithm, 314
Specific Learning Difficulties, use of term, 396
specific reading comprehension difficulties, 253, 257, 270-1
speech, 78, 85-6, 87, 90, 92, 113t, 114f, 115, 116, 125f, 126, 127-8, 139, 194, 199, 243, 252-3, 254, 256, 257, 301, 317
    Broca's speech production area, 68, 69, 70, 80, 86, 102, 206, 261
    developmental problems, 55-6
    pupil's asking questions of fellow pupils, 390
    sentence completion, 221, 230, 231, 233
    speed of articulation, 82, 88, 193, 276
    teacher's spoken instructions, 389-90
    Wernicke's area, 69, 70
    see also auditory factors; different countries; language, learning a foreign; languages, study of dyslexia and different languages
speed, relevance of, 22, 126, 196, 219, 228, 229, 276-7, 348t, 434, 445
    asynchrony phenomenon
    differences between different brain entities, 15-7
    gap between different brain entities 12, 14, 20, 24-5, 24t, 26
    speed of transfer from posterior to anterior brain sites, 22
    visual and auditory, 17-21, 17f, 18f, 19f, 20f
    RAN, 135, 277, 432
    RAN-L, 155-6, 159, 164, 188
    rapid color naming, 345, 347t
    rapid naming, 185, 432
speed of simple reaction (SRT), 197f
Spell Read P.A.T., 340

spelling, 61, 67, 69-70, 73, 126, 137, 140, 244,
        245, 248, 256, 261, 306, 308, 315,
        316-7, 332, 333, 342, 346, 348t, 361
    component model of reading, 277-9
    different languages and dyslexia, study of,
        427-38
    examination of characteristics of reading,
        writing and, 77-8, 84, 86
    morphological processing and, 215, 220-1,
        223-4, 225, 226, 227, 228, 230,
        232, 233
    orthographic awareness, RTI study, 185
    Orthographic Choice, subgroup study, 159,
        160, 164, 167, 168
    orthographic mapping and learning a
        foreign language, 443-5
    orthographic phase, 316
    progress in ADEPT, 317-9, 319t, 322f, 323f,
        325, 330-1
    skilled readers and lexical and sublexical
        procedures, 150
    see also alphabetic processing; individual
        countries; rhyme
Spreen, O. (1987), 400
Spring and French (1990), 270, 315
'square root rule', 209
Squire, L.R. (1987), 200
Squire et al. (1993), 200
SSD (speech sound disorder), 33, 35, 37
Stahl and Fairbanks (1986), 280-1
Stahl and Murray (1994), 274
Stanford-Binet verbal subset, 105
Stanford Diagnostic Reading Test, 279
Stanovich, K.E. (1980), 341
Stanovich, K.E. (1986), 92, 255, 305, 338, 431
Stanovich, K.E. (1988), 56, 82, 84, 90, 92,
        194, 427
Stanovich, K.E. (1991), 177, 180, 258
Stanovich, K.E. (1993), 305
Stanovich, K.E. (1996), 254
Stanovich and Siegel (1994), 152, 177, 180, 258
Stanovich and West (1989), 314
Stanovich et al. (1997), 152, 153, 159, 160,
        165, 167, 168, 170
statistical learning, 204
Stein, J. (1986), 66
Stein, J. (2001), 71, 82
Stein, J. (2003), 64
Stein and Fowler (1981), 63
Stein and Fowler (1982), 82
Stein and Fowler (1993), 82
Stein and Glickstein (1992), 80
Stein et al. (1985), 63
Stein et al. (2000), 63, 82
Steinlin, M. (2007), 80
Sternberg, R.L. (1985), 271
Stevenson and Newman (1986), 338
Stoerig and Cowey, 58

Stoodley et al. (2005), 67
Stoodley et al. (2006), 88
Strauss and Corbin (1997), 460
Strnadova and Reid (2006), 370, 373
Structural Equation Modelling, 129
Stuebing et al. (2000), 185
Stuebing et al. (2002), 177, 180, 258
subject curriculum, 385-8, 388-9, 392
supervised learning, 201-2, 201f, 204
Sure Start, 357
Swansea LEA, 357
Swanson, H.L. (1991), 295,
Swanson, H.L. (1993), 305
Sweden, study of self-concept, 402, 403

Taft, M. (1979), 222
Taipale et al. (2003), 127
Talcott et al. (2000), 55, 62, 64
Tallal and Piercy (1973), 65
Taylor and Stein (2002), 72
Taylor et al. (2000), 72
TE (twice exceptionality) 40, 42, 43
teacher's observation of learning styles
        (TOLS), 379-80
teacher's spoken instructions, 389-90
teaching, role of, 55, 124
    pupils view of, 356-68
    differences from pedagogy, 376
    theoretical rationale for good practice, 209
teaching, subject, 385-8
Tejas Lee, 281
Temple and Marshall (1983), 150
Temple University, 460-1
temporoparietal junction, 70
Tennessee Center for the Study and Treatment
        of dyslexia, 312, 313 see below for
        Center's study of dyslexia
Tennessee Schools based study of
        phonological dyslexia, 312-36
    defining dyslexia, 313-4
    framework for intervention, 315-7
        checklist, 317
        tests for differential diagnosis, 316t
    identifying students, 314-5
        diagnostic profile, 315t
    monitoring progress, 317-9
        levels in ADEPT Phase lists, 319t
    outcomes and implications, 324-34
        means and correlations, 326-7, 326t
        tables of unique contributions of
            diagnostic scores, 328t, 329t
        student's progress, 319-23
    participant's characteristics, 320t
    phonemic awareness scores, 321t,
        324-5, 328
    reading and spelling progress, 322f, 323f,
        325-6, 330-1
    standardized achievement test score, 321t

Test of Phonological Awareness (TOPA), 274
Test of Phonological Processing in Spanish
    (TOPPS), 275
Test of Word Reading Efficiency (TOWRE),
    277, 346
Texas Primary Reading Inventory, 251, 281
Thaler et al. (2004), 140
Thompson et al. (2001), 34, 36, 39
Thompson et al. (2002), 36, 39
Thomson, M. (1990), 405
Thomson, M. (2004), 392
Thomson, M. (2006), 384
Thomson, M. (2007), 381, 382, 383, 391
Title Recognition Test (TRT), 156, 167
'To Be or Not to Be' learning difficulties study,
    458, 460-1
Tonnessen et al. (1993), 71
Tonnquist-Uhlen, I. (1996), 17
Torgesen, J.K. (2000), 180, 186
Torgesen, J.K. (2002), 338
Torgesen, J.K. (2004), 241, 244, 245, 246,
    251, 252, 254, 255
Torgesen, J.K. (2005), 244, 254, 255, 257
Torgesen and Dice (1980), 294
Torgesen et al. (1994), 314
Torgesen et al. (1997), 282, 338, 339
Torgesen et al. (1999), 245
Torgesen et al. (2001), 140, 184, 245, 255
Tornberg, U. (2001), 441
Torppa et al. (2006), 135
Torppa et al. (2007), 134, 138, 140
Townsend et al. (1987), 270
Trade Union Congress (TUC), 482-3, 484
Tramontana et al. (1988), 338
Trauner et al. (2000), 132
Treffner and Peter (2004), 85
Treiman, R. (1993), 278
Treiman, R. (1998), 278
Treiman, R. (2006), 278
Trussell, L.O. (1997), 65
Tsesmeli and Seymour (2006), 214-5, 226, 227
Tukey test, 111
Tunmer, W.E. (1998), 283
Tunmer and Chapman (1995), 371
Tunmer and Chapman (1996), 258
Tunmer and Chapman (1998), 243, 256
Tunmer and Chapman (2003), 244
Tunmer and Chapman (2004), 244
Tunmer and Chapman (2006), 243, 256
Tunmer and Chapman (2007), 254, 256
Tunmer and Hoover (1993), 255
Tunmer et al. (1988), 338
Tunmer et al. (2002), 243
Tunmer et al. (2003), 245
Tunmer et al. (2006), 258
Turkeltaub et al. (2003), 208
Turner and Pughe (2003), 386
twins, 35, 54, 102, 152

Ullman, M. (2004), 205-6
Ullman and Gopnik (1999), 206
unsupervised learning, 201f

Vachon, V. (1998), 340
Vadasy and Sanders (in preparation), 346
Vadasy et al. (1997), 342
Vadasy et al. (2000), 342
Vadasy et al. (2002), 342
Vadasy et al. (2004), 341
Vadasy et al. (2005), 342
Vadasy et al. (2006), 342, 344
Vadasy et al. (in press), 342
Valeri-Gold et al. (2001), 458
van der Leij and van Daal (1999), 221
Van Orden, G.C. (1987), 156
Vaughn and Fuchs (2003), 181
Vaughn and Linan-Thompson, (2003), 247
Vaughn et al. (1992), 399
Vaughn et al. (1998), 400
Vaughn et al. (2003), 259
Veii and Everatt et al. (2002), 429
Velay et al. (2002), 23
Vellutino, F.R. (1978), 305
Vellutino, F.R. (1979), 78, 84, 194, 305
Vellutino and Denckla (1991), 258
Vellutino and Fletcher (2005), 213, 254
Vellutino and Scanlon (1982), 194
Vellutino and Scanlon (1989), 217
Vellutino et al. (1994), 314
Vellutino et al. (1996), 184, 244, 258, 338, 339
Vellutino et al. (2000), 149, 258, 304
Vellutino et al. (2003), 258
Vellutino et al. (2004), 129, 254
Vellutino et al. (2006), 258, 259
Vellutino et al. (in press), 260
Venezky, R. (1976), 278
'verbal efficiency theory', 273
vergence control, 61, 63
Vicari et al. (2000), 204
Vidyasagar, T.R. (2004), 60, 62
Viholainen et al. (2002), 85, 132
Viholainen et al. (2006), 132
Vilenius et al. (2007), 136
Vincent et al. (2002), 72
visual factors, 57-64, 66-72, 201, 204, 261,
    296, 385, 388, 445, 448
    cross-modal transfer, 194
    remediation of visual problems, 63-4
    speed of processing (SOP), 17-21, 17f, 18f,
        19f, 20f
    see also eye
visual motion area (V5/MT), 59, 62
visual what and where pathways, 59-60
visual word form area (VWFA), 60, 69-70
Voeller, K. (1999), 34, 36
vocabulary, component model for reading,
    280-1

vocabulary, support for foreign language
    teaching, 449-50
vocabulary enrichment programme, 255
vocabulary growth in preschool years, 256
Vogel and Adelman (2000), 458, 459
Vogler et al., 1985), 101

Wadsworth et al. (2006), 35, 36
Wagner and Torgesen (1987), 162, 314
Wagner et al. (1994), 116
Wagner et al. (1997), 101, 177
Wagner et al. (1999), 188, 275, 346
Wagner et al. (2003), 251
'wait to fail' model, 177, 182, 258
Walker and Buckley (1972), 341
Walley, A.C. (1993), 256
Wang and Zoghbi (2001), 80
Wasik, B.A. (1998), 339, 341
Wasik and Slavin (1993), 341
Waters et al. (1985), 277
Wechsler, D. (1991), 325
Wechsler, D. (1992), 320, 324
Wechsler, D. (2001), 279
Wechsler Individual Achievement Test
    (WIAT), 320, 324, 325, 332
Wechsler Individual Achievement Test-II
    (WIAT-II), 279
Wechsler Intelligence Scale for Children
    (WISC-III), 164, 299, 324
Wechsler Intelligence Scale for Children-
    Revised (WISC-R), 299
Wehmeyer, M. (1995), 459
Weimer et al. (1994), 484
Werker and Tees (1987), 129
Werker et al. (1989), 175
Wernicke's area, 21, 69, 70
West, T.G. (1997), 422
West, T.G. (1999), 42
White et al. (2006), 89
Wiederholt and Bryant (1992), 280
Wiederholt and Bryant (2001), 280
Wilkins and Nimmo Smith (1984), 63
Wilkinson, G.S. (1993), 109, 116
Willcut et al. (2002), 34, 36
Willows et al., (1993), 16
Wilson et al. (1998), 17
Wilson Language Program (Wilson Language
    System 1988), 318,333
Wimmer, H. (1993), 101, 429, 430, 432
Wimmer et al. (1999), 87
Witton et al. (2002), 65
Wolf and Bowers (1999), 84, 86, 277
Wolf et al. (1994), 432
Wolfensberger, W. (1972), 459

Wolff et al. (1990), 83
Wolff et al. (1995), 83
Wolff et al. (1996), 83
Wood and Flowers (1999), 34, 36
Wood et al. (1988), 270, 273
Woodcock, R.W. (1987), 154, 342, 346
Woodcock, R.W. (1994), 280, 281
Woodcock, R.W. (1997), 280
Woodcock, R.W. (1998), 280, 346
Woodcock, R.W. (2001), 276
Woodcock et al. (2001), 276
Woodcock et al. (2006), 281
Woodcock and Johnson (1989), 155, 306
Woodcock and Johnson (1998), 154
Woodcock Diagnostic Battery, 280
Woodcock-Johnson-Revised Cognitive
    Abilities test, 154
Woodcock-Johnson-Revised Cognitive
    Battery, 155
Woodcock-Johnson Test of Achievement-III
    Word Attack and Letter and Word
    Identification, 187, 276
Woodcock Language Proficiency Battery,
    276, 279
Woodcock Language Proficiency Battery-
    Revised, 280, 281
Woodcock Reading Mastery Tests-Revised,
    154, 280, 342, 346, 347t
Woodcock Word Identification grade
    equivalent, 159
Word Frequency Book, The, 155
workplace issues see employment
World Federation of Neurology, 77
World Health Organization (2006), 216
WRAT-R (wide range achievement test-
    revised, 342, 346, 248t
WRAT-Reading subscale (wide range
    achievement test), 109, 110, 113t, 116
writing, examination of characteristics of
    reading, spelling and, 77-8, 84, 86
writing skills in secondary school, 386-7,
    389, 392
    note taking, 387, 388

Yin, R.K. (1994), 461
Young, C. (1997), 318, 331
Young and Browning (2004), 474, 479-80

Zeffiro and Eden (2001), 89
Zeigler and Goswami (2005), 429, 430, 431
Zeleke, S. (2004), 396, 399, 400, 401, 403
Zetterquist-Nelson, K. (2003), 403
Zhou et al. (1989), 39
Zoccolotti et al. (2005), 221